THE CORRESPONDENCE OF *John Cotton*

To the Rev. Mr. John Dod

Grace & Peace be multiplyed to you in Jesus Christ.

Reverend & deare Sr

In ye latter end of ye last Sumer

The Elders of ye Churches in this Country Received [illegible] a lre from

sundry other of or Reverend & godly Brethren the Ministers of divers Churches in or native

Country, all of ym being knowen to divers of vs, & esteemed [illegible]

in ye lords vineyard [illegible] for this labor of love vnto or selves.

very highly in love both for your worke's sake, It seemeth you have

heard, yt or Practise here doth somewhat differ from yors there in ye Administration

of Gods Ordinances in ye Church: & doe there fore in yor lre require of vs ye Grounds

of or Difference from you, yt if they be found to beare weight in ye Ballance

of ye Sanctuary, you may give vs ye Right hand of Fellowship therein: but if

they be found too light, you may then endeavour in a brotherly way to

discover ye error of or course to vs. & as they doe thankfully Accept your brotherly love: so they

or brethren have taken yor motion into serious Consideration, as beholding ye face of Christ in it

holding forth & breathing a spirit of holy wisdome, Christian love, & faithfull & watchfull Care

of ye Establishment of ye Kingdome of ye Lord Jesus in Truth & Peace.

And they have desired me, to certefy vnto yor self, & doe desire you

to certefy ye rest of or reverend Brethren with you, that It is their

Purpose (by ye helpe of Christ) to Give you a plaine & just Account of

or Proceedings here according to all ye Demaunds, you Require of vs:

Wherein wee have been letted for a season, by some late

yeares wee have been Called vnto for ye Composing of some Contro-

versyes amongst or selves. Wch being now brought by ye hand of

ye Lord to some Issue, It is or next Care & endeavors

(by ye Lords Helpe) to Dispatch a speedy

Answer vnto you, by ye next trusty & convenient Passenger. Meanewhile let

vs still & ever enjoy ye Helpe & Comfort of yor brotherly love, & fervent

Prayers, & faithfull Advertisemts, as Occasion shall require.

Or Native Country, ye pure Ordinances of God therein, & or holy Brethren wee have left not in Affection, but in Place:

but or Native Corruptions & selves wee still carry about wth vs:

& Satan bestirreth himself as mightily, & as busily here, as amongst

you, if not more, as having great Wrath, agt ye simplicity of ye Name & Kingdome

& pouring Dishonor thereupon by ye infirmityes of his servants when he cannot prevail: but his Rage by ye wickednesse of enemyes. But ye Lord tread

downe Satan vnder yor & or feet shortly: strive wth vs in Prayer for yt

&c.

|| ye Synod began Aug. 30. 1637.

THE CORRESPONDENCE OF

John Cotton

Edited by Sargent Bush, Jr.

Published for the
Omohundro Institute of Early American
History and Culture, Williamsburg, Virginia,
by the University of North Carolina Press,
Chapel Hill and London

The Omohundro Institute of Early American History and Culture is sponsored jointly by the College of William and Mary and the Colonial Williamsburg Foundation. On November 15, 1996, the Institute adopted its present name in honor of a bequest from Malvern H. Omohundro, Jr.

Manufactured in the United States of America
Library of Congress Cataloging-in-Publication Data
Cotton, John, 1584–1652.
The correspondence of John Cotton / edited by Sargent Bush, Jr.
p. cm.
Includes bibliographical references (p.) and index.
ISBN 0-8078-2635-9 (cloth : alk. paper)
1. Cotton, John, 1584–1652—Correspondence. I. Bush, Sargent.
II. Omohundro Institute of Early American History & Culture.
III. Title.
BX7260.C79 A4 2001
285.8′092—dc21
[B] 00-051204

The paper in this book meets the guidelines for permanence and durability of the Committee on Production Guidelines for Book Longevity of the Council on Library Resources.

05 04 03 02 01 5 4 3 2 1

This book is

dedicated to the

memory of

Lawrance Thompson

and to

Everett Emerson

"In weaving these mystic utterances into a continuous scene, we undertake a task resembling, in its perplexity, that of gathering up and piecing together the fragments of a letter, which has been torn and scattered to the winds. Many words of deep significance—many entire sentences, and those possibly the most important ones—have flown too far, on the winged breeze, to be recovered. If we insert our own conjectural amendments, we perhaps give a purport utterly at variance with the true one. Yet, unless we attempt something in this way, there must remain an unsightly gap, and a lack of continuousness and dependence in our narrative. . . ."

—NATHANIEL HAWTHORNE, *The Marble Faun* (1860)

Acknowledgments

In the decade and more required to prepare this work, many people and institutions have contributed essential help. It is a pleasure to name them here.

The person whose work has been most essential in bringing this edition to completion is George Goebel, Review Editor of the *Dictionary of American Regional English,* whose translations of Latin and Greek and whose occasional suggestions for annotations on those passages are present throughout. Important contributions to the work also were provided by graduate research assistants at various points and for varying lengths of time, so, for their interest and investment of creative thought and energy in the project, I should like to express thanks to Dennis Perry, Katherine Leake, Ernest Suarez, Jonathan Little, Mark Hodin, Jean Marie Lutes, and Thomas Allen.

Key financial support has come in the form of a National Endowment for the Humanities Summer Stipend, a resident fellowship at the Massachusetts Historical Society, a Vilas Associates Fellowship from the University of Wisconsin–Madison, and support from the Graduate School and the College of Letters and Science at the University of Wisconsin, including a semester's leave at the beginning of the project and a sabbatical semester near the end of it. While serving for five and a half years as a part-time Associate Dean in Wisconsin's College of Letters and Science, I worked under three successive deans—a humanist, a social scientist, and a physical scientist. I take pleasure in noting that each of them tangibly supported the principle that administrative responsibility and research activity need not be mutually exclusive, granting my occasional modest but crucial requests for research assistance; I am happy to express thanks to Donald W. Crawford, M. Crawford Young, and Phillip R. Certain, all practitioners and friends of scholarship.

The primary documents in this edition are owned by a number of important libraries whose conservation efforts are the reason, above all others, that such an edition is now possible. So it is with thanks for their long-standing and ongoing work in preserving such written portions of our cultural heritage, as well as for particular courtesies, that I mention the following, all of whose librarians or governing bodies have given permission to publish items from their collections: the American Antiquarian Society; Yale University's Beinecke Library; the British Library; the Bodleian Library; the Boston Public Library; the Gemeente Archief of Leiden; the Massachusetts Historical Society; the Massachusetts State Archives; the New England Historic Genealogical Society; the Whitney Library of the New Haven Colony Historical Society; the New York Public Library; the Pilgrim Society and Pilgrim Hall, Plymouth, Massachusetts; and the Suffolk County, Massachusetts, Court House. To the approximately 140 other libraries in the United States, Great Britain, Ireland, the Netherlands, Germany, France, Belgium, and Switzerland who responded to inquiries about their holdings, I am also very grateful.

Certain particular debts incurred at some of these locations need to be mentioned. Most of all, the staff of the Rare Books and Manuscripts Department of the Boston Public Library, where I spent far more hours than at any other library, were unfailingly interested and helpful. I am especially grateful to Dr. Giuseppe Bisaccia, former Manuscripts Curator, Dr. William Faucon, current Manuscripts Curator, and Dr. Roberta Zonghi, Curator of Rare Books, for practical assistance but also for their predictably warm reception at any time of year. Dr. Laura V. Monti, former Keeper of Rare Books and Manuscripts at the same library, was also consistently supportive of the project. Another friend of this enterprise from the beginning has been Martha Clark, first Reference Supervisor and later Special Assistant to the Archivist at the Massachusetts State Archives, who introduced me to the Hutchinson Papers while the Archives still resided in the basement of the State House. More recently she assisted me on several occasions in the new, much more suitable home of the Archives on Columbia Point. Other librarians who have been particularly helpful are Peter Drummey, Librarian of the Massachusetts Historical Society, and members of his staff, including, especially, Virginia Smith, Brenda Lawson, Jennifer Smith, and Jennifer Tolpa; Nathaniel N. Shipton and Scott A. Bartley, former and present Manuscripts Curators, and Jerome Anderson, Reference Librarian, at the New England Historic Genealogical Society; Thomas Knoles, Manuscript Curator of the American Antiquarian Society; Dianne M. Gutscher, Curator of Special Collections, Bowdoin College Library; Ottilia Koel and James W. Campbell, former and present Librarians of the New Haven Colony Historical Society; Elizabeth C. Bouvier, Head of Archives at the Supreme Judicial Court, Boston; R. C. J. van Maanen, Deputy Keeper of the Records of the City of Leiden; A. Meerman, Municipal Archivist, Vlissingen, the Netherlands; W. H. Kelliher, Curator of Manuscripts, British Library; and Peter Allen, Archivist, Cranbrook School, Cranbrook, Kent. Closer to home, like all my colleagues who use the microfilms of the three installments of the *Short-Title Catalogue, 1641–1700* at the University of Wisconsin's Memorial Library, I owe many thanks to Ed Duesterheoft, Microforms Librarian. John Tedeschi, former Special Collections Librarian at Wisconsin's Memorial Library, gave helpful counsel, and Mary Jo Norton, formerly of the Wisconsin Historical Society's Microforms Department, offered valuable and timely assistance as well.

Jeremy Bangs, then Guest Curator at Pilgrim Hall, Plymouth, Massachusetts, generously shared with me his exciting news of finding a Cotton manuscript volume, a discovery that increased the inclusiveness of the present volume. Michael P. Winship, likewise, has pointed me to two more letters that I would otherwise have missed. I am also grateful to others who have shared relevant fruits of their own research with me: Mary Jane Lewis, Jesper Rosenmeier, Francis J. Bremer, Jon Butler, and Robert Scholz. Glenn LaFantasie, when about to publish his edition of Roger Williams's correspondence, generously shared copies of galleys of relevant items, together with his helpful comments. Other fellow scholars have been helpful in a variety of ways. At the beginning of my work on the project, I enjoyed the generous hospitality and valuable scholarly advice of Dr. Geoffrey Nuttall, whose early encouragement has continued to motivate my perseverance in this work. A fortuitous meeting during a visit to Cranbrook, Kent, resulted in my benefiting from the ongoing assistance of Gerald W. T. Cousins, whose intimate knowledge of local history and library resources in Kent has been extremely helpful through our long-distance correspondence. Also in England, I am grateful for the assistance of the Reverend B. R. White, Principal of Regents Park College in Oxford, and of the Reverend Canon Trevor Collins, contemporary incumbent in John Cotton's post at St. Botolph's Church, Boston. Ursula Brumm assisted my search for primary documents in Germany. And, once again, Frank Stubbings, former Librarian of Emmanuel College, Cambridge, has taken a lively and friendly interest.

In the New World, the interest of the late Alan Heimert was translated into very practical assistance at a key period in the project. At the outset of the task, I received valuable advice from A. Walton Litz, Mason I. Lowance, and Roy Winnick, as well as encouragement to proceed from Janet (Mrs. Lawrance) Thompson. Also providing help in various ways at particular moments were Norman Pettit, Wesley T. Mott, J. A. Leo Lemay, Constance Post, Robert Middlekauff, Daniel B. Shea, Philip F. Gura, and my late valued and always-supportive colleague, Merton M. Sealts, Jr. Other University of Wisconsin colleagues who have helped by sharing their own expertise are Rob Howell of the German Department, Johann Sommerville of History, and Jeffrey Wills of Classics. While they were on the Wisconsin campus, Kevin VanAnglen and James Lowe gave helpful counsel on Latin passages. At a critical moment Bruno Browning's computer skills were invaluable. The interdisciplinary Early American discussion group at Wisconsin provides a forum for the exchange of ideas and sharing of work. From that group, I am particularly grateful to Charles L. Cohen and Richard Leffler, both of the History Department, whose comments on this work in progress were especially useful. Various English Department colleagues and students have shown interest in the project, of whom I am especially thankful to Joseph Wiesenfarth, Thomas Schaub, and Donald Rowe, whose successive chairmanships of the department were supportive of my work, while the interest of Gordon Hutner, Jeffrey Steele, Dale Bauer, and E. N. Feltskog has provided an important local context for my work during the preparation of this book.

At the Omohundro Institute of Early American History and Culture, I have received encouragement and sound practical advice for the last several years of work on the project from Fredrika J. Teute, Editor of Publications, and at a late stage of editing from James Horn, Visiting Editor of Publications. Gil Kelly, managing editor at the Institute, and Susan Perdue also brought invaluable editorial experience to bear at the critical final stage. I have been fortunate, too, in having the benefit of the detailed reading of the entire manuscript by such distinguished historians as Michael McGiffert and Francis J. Bremer. All these people have made it better while bearing no responsibility whatever for its faults.

Beginnings are always critical, and this book could not exist without the catalytic effect of the two men to whom the volume is dedicated. Everett Emerson, the individual most responsible for the establishment and development of early American literature as a contemporary field of study, generously offered his friendship and encouragement early on in my career, and they have been of critical importance to me. More specifically, however, it was Everett who called my attention to the 1932 Columbia master's thesis of Lawrance Thompson, an edition of "The Letters of John Cotton," and who urged me to look into the possibility of carrying that work forward. Thompson's reputation rests upon his distinguished work on the likes of Henry Wadsworth Longfellow, Herman Melville, and Robert Frost, but to me he was primarily an inspiring teacher, especially in his famous undergraduate course on Melville, Twain, James, and Faulkner, where the deep appeal of literary study took firm hold upon me. The fact that it was he who had made the first attempt to bring together John Cotton's letters gave my own much later undertaking of the same task a very special appeal and satisfaction. In any scholar's career, the sine qua non is the "cloud of witnesses" who showed the way. Among the most important of mine are these two eminent teacher-scholars.

The other person without whom this book could not exist is my wife, Cynthia. She has been there for me and with me throughout, both literally and figuratively. A librarian with practical experience of the ways of Special Collections departments, she has often helped in the examination of manuscripts in libraries in the United States, England, and Holland while always cheerfully tolerating interruptions of vacations and occasional separations when manuscripts beckoned. Her appreciation of the importance of the task and her healthy sense that it needed to be brought to closure in this lifetime are among the key invisible ingredients here, and I am grateful to her for these manifestations of her love.

Contents

Illustrations

MAP

PLATES

Abbreviations and Short Titles

MANUSCRIPTS AND DOCUMENTS

AD Autograph Document
ADf Autograph Draft
ADfI Autograph Draft Initialed
AL Autograph Letter
ALI Autograph Letter Initialed
ALS Autograph Letter Signed
Copy Contemporary copy
DfL Draft Letter
LS Letter Signed
MS Manuscript
Tr Later Transcript, not by author

DEPOSITORIES

AAS
American Antiquarian Society, Worcester, Mass.
BL
British Library, London
Bodl
Bodleian Library, Oxford
BPL
Boston Public Library
LGA
Gemeente Archief, Leiden
MH
Houghton Library, Harvard University, Cambridge, Mass.
MHS
Massachusetts Historical Society Library, Boston
MSA
Massachusetts State Archives, Boston
NEHGS
New England Historic Genealogical Society Library, Boston
NHCHS
New Haven Colony Historical Society Library, New Haven, Conn.
NYPL
New York Public Library

PH

Pilgrim Society, Pilgrim Hall, Plymouth, Mass.

YBei

Beinecke Library, Yale University, New Haven, Conn.

SELECTED SOURCES

Alumni Oxonienses

Joseph Foster, ed., *Alumni Oxonienses: The Members of the University of Oxford, 1500–1714* . . . , 4 vols. (Oxford, 1891–1892).

ANB

American National Biography.

Anderson, *Great Migration*

Robert Charles Anderson, *The Great Migration Begins: Immigrants to New England, 1620–1633,* 3 vols. (Boston, 1995).

Battis, *Saints and Sectaries*

Emery Battis, *Saints and Sectaries: Anne Hutchinson and the Antinomian Controversy in the Massachusetts Bay Colony* (Chapel Hill, N.C., 1962).

Brook, *Lives of the Puritans*

Benjamin Brook, *The Lives of the Puritans* . . . , 3 vols. (London, 1813).

Calamy Revised

A. G. Matthews, *Calamy Revised: Being a Revision of Edmund Calamy's Account of the Ministers and Others Ejected and Silenced, 1660–2* (Oxford, 1934).

CSM, *Colls.*

Colonial Society of Massachusetts, *Collections.*

CSM, *Publs.*

Colonial Society of Massachusetts, *Publications.*

CSM, *Trans.*

Colonial Society of Massachusetts, *Transactions.*

DAB

Dictionary of American Biography.

Dexter, *Extracts*

Franklin Bowditch Dexter, ed., *Extracts from the Itineraries and Other Miscellanies of Ezra Stiles, D.D., LL.D., 1755–1794, with a Selection from His Correspondence* (New Haven, Conn., 1916).

DNB

Dictionary of National Biography.

Emerson, *Cotton*

Everett Emerson, *John Cotton,* rev. ed. (Boston, 1990).

Emerson, *Letters*

Everett Emerson, ed., *Letters from New England: The Massachusetts Bay Colony, 1629–1638* (Amherst, Mass., 1976).

Foster, *Long Argument*
Stephen Foster, *The Long Argument: English Puritanism and the Shaping of New England Culture, 1570–1700* (Chapel Hill, N.C., 1991).

Hall, *Antinomian Controversy*
David D. Hall, ed., *The Antinomian Controversy, 1636–1638: A Documentary History,* 2d ed. (Durham, N.C., 1990).

Hall, *Faithful Shepherd*
David D. Hall, *The Faithful Shepherd: A History of the New England Ministry in the Seventeenth Century* (Chapel Hill, N.C., 1972).

Hutchinson, *Collection*
[Thomas Hutchinson, ed.], *A Collection of Original Papers relative to the History of the Colony of Massachusets-Bay* (Boston, 1769).

Hutchinson, *History*
Thomas Hutchinson, *The History of the Colony of Massachusets-Bay* . . . , I (London, 1764).

Mather, *Johannes*
Cotton Mather, *Johannes in Eremo* . . . (Boston, 1695).

Mather, *Magnalia*
Cotton Mather, *Magnalia Christi Americana: or, The Ecclesiastical History of New England,* 2 vols. (Hartford, Conn., 1820).

I. Mather, *First Principles*
Increase Mather, *The First Principles of New-England* . . . (Cambridge, Mass., 1675).

MHS, *Colls.*
Massachusetts Historical Society, *Collections.*

MHS, *Procs.*
Massachusetts Historical Society, *Proceedings.*

NC, *Publs.*
Narragansett Club, *Publications,* 1st Ser. (Providence, R.I.).

NEHGR
New England Historical and Genealogical Register.

NEQ
New England Quarterly.

OED
Oxford English Dictionary.

Plymouth Church Records
Plymouth Church Records, 1620–1859, Colonial Society of Massachusetts, *Publications,* XXII, XXIII (Boston, 1920, 1923).

Records of the First Church
Richard D. Pierce, ed., *The Records of the First Church in Boston, 1630–*

1868, I, Colonial Society of Massachusetts, *Publications, Collections,* XXXIX (Boston, 1961).

Records of Massachusetts Bay
Nathaniel B. Shurtleff, ed., *Records of the Governor and Company of the Massachusetts Bay in New England,* 5 vols. (Boston, 1853–1854).

Rose-Troup, *John White*
Frances Rose-Troup, *John White, the Patriarch of Dorchester (Dorset) and the Founder of Massachusetts, 1575–1648, with an Account of the Early Settlements in Massachusetts, 1620–1630* (New York, 1930).

Rutman, *Winthrop's Boston*
Darrett B. Rutman, *Winthrop's Boston: Portrait of a Puritan Town, 1630–1649* (Chapel Hill, N.C., 1965).

Saltonstall Papers
Robert E. Moody, ed., *The Saltonstall Papers, 1607–1815,* I, Massachusetts Historical Society, *Collections,* LXXX (Boston, 1972).

Savage, *Genealogical Dictionary*
James Savage, *A Genealogical Dictionary of the First Settlers of New England . . .*, 4 vols. (Boston, 1860–1862).

Sprunger, *Dutch Puritanism*
Keith L. Sprunger, *Dutch Puritanism: A History of English and Scottish Churches of the Netherlands in the Sixteenth and Seventeenth Centuries* (Leiden, 1982).

Sprunger, *William Ames*
Keith L. Sprunger, *The Learned Doctor William Ames: Dutch Backgrounds of English and American Puritanism* (Urbana, Ill., 1972).

Stoever, *"A Faire and Easie Way to Heaven"*
William K. B. Stoever, *"A Faire and Easie Way to Heaven": Covenant Theology and Antinomianism in Early Massachusetts* (Middletown, Conn., 1978).

L. Thompson, "Letters of John Cotton."
Lawrance R. Thompson, "The Letters of John Cotton, Edited with Notes" (master's thesis, Columbia University, 1932).

P. Thompson, *History of Boston*
Pishey Thompson, *The History and Antiquities of Boston . . . in the County of Lincoln . . .* (Boston, Lincs., London, and Boston, Mass., 1856).

Venn, *Alumni Cantabrigienses*
John Venn and J. A. Venn, eds., *Alumni Cantabrigienses: A Biographical List of All Known Students, Graduates, and Holders of Office at the University of Cambridge, from the Earliest Times to 1900,* pt. 1, *From the Earliest Times to 1751,* 4 vols. (Cambridge, 1922–1927).

Williams, *Correspondence*
Glenn W. LaFantasie, ed., *The Correspondence of Roger Williams,* 2 vols. (Providence, R.I., 1987).

G. H. Williams et al., *Thomas Hooker*
George H. Williams, Norman Pettit, Winfried Herget, and Sargent Bush, Jr., *Thomas Hooker: Writings in England and Holland, 1626–1633,* Harvard Theological Studies, XXVIII (Cambridge, Mass., 1975).

Winthrop, *Journal*
Richard S. Dunn, James Savage, and Laetitia Yeandle, eds., *The Journal of John Winthrop, 1630–1649* (Cambridge, Mass., 1996).

Winthrop Papers
The Winthrop Papers (Boston, 1929–).

WMQ
William and Mary Quarterly.

Young, *Chronicles of the First Planters*
Alexander Young, ed., *Chronicles of the First Planters of the Colony of Massachusetts Bay, from 1623 to 1636* (Boston, 1846).

Ziff, *Career of John Cotton*
Larzer Ziff, *The Career of John Cotton: Puritanism and the American Experience* (Princeton, N.J., 1962).

Ziff, *Cotton on the Churches*
Larzer Ziff, ed., *John Cotton on the Churches of New England* (Cambridge, Mass., 1968).

Introduction

John Cotton now enjoys a well-established prominence in the history of the Puritan movement as a man who provided leadership through his preaching, his books, and his life as a Nonconformist minister. Because Cotton expressed himself in both formal and informal writings as well as in spoken discourse sometimes recorded in notes, he is readily available today as a spokesman for his Puritan contemporaries. His purpose, it must be said, was not to make himself or his colleagues well known. It was, rather, to use his words to carry God's message to his people—to be the tool of his Lord: "It little skilleth what the pen be, of a Goose or Swans quil, or Ravens, yet when God delighteth to use such an instrument . . . it challengeth from us the more due respect." Indeed, it was a basic principle for him that "in writing a Minister may and doth make use of spirituall gifts requisite in a Prophet or Preacher, to the exercise of his ministery."[1] He took it as a rule governing all of his writing and preaching always to put his writing "instrument" in command of his "spirituall gifts." He did so consistently. He was known for it among his contemporaries. And, in recent years, Cotton has become increasingly known to modern students of the Puritans. It is a rare study of Puritanism in the first half of the seventeenth century that does not include John Cotton.

This has not always been so. Nearly half a century ago Geoffrey Nuttall noted that Cotton had "hardly received from historians of English Nonconformity the attention which is his due."[2] Even then, however, historians of New England Puritanism had begun to focus more attention on Cotton than did the British historians of the seventeenth century that Nuttall had in mind.[3] With the burgeoning of scholarship about the Puritans on both sides of the Atlantic Ocean in the decades since then, Cotton has become a figure who is now often represented as "typical" of one or another strain of Puritan

1. John Cotton, *A Briefe Exposition with Practicall Observations upon the Whole Book of Ecclesiastes* (London, 1654), 5, 10.

2. Geoffrey Nuttall, *Visible Saints: The Congregational Way, 1640–1660* (Oxford, 1957), 15.

3. Cotton's importance in the development of colonial New England was recognized in various ways early in the revival of interest in the Puritans by Samuel Eliot Morison, *Builders of the Bay Colony* (Boston, 1930); Perry Miller, *Orthodoxy in Massachusetts, 1630–1650: A Genetic Study* (Cambridge, Mass., 1933) and *The New England Mind: The Seventeenth Century* (New York, 1939); Kenneth B. Murdock, *Literature and Theology in Colonial New England* (Cambridge, Mass., 1949).

Watertown
Newtown (Cambridge)
Charlestown
Boston
Boston Harbor
Roxbury
Dorchester
INSET
Saco R.
Casco Bay
Cape Elizabeth
Richmond Island
Saco
Wells
Piscataqua
Strawberry Bank (Portsmouth)
Exeter
Hampton
Merrimack R.
Salisbury
Ipswich
ATLANTIC OCEAN
Salem
Concord
Saugus (Lynn)
MASSACHUSETTS
Connecticut R.
Natick
Mt. Wollaston (Braintree)
Scituate
Springfield
Plymouth
Windsor
Hartford
Providence
PLYMOUTH
Sandwich
RHODE ISLAND AND PROVIDENCE PLANTATIONS
CONNECTICUT
Portsmouth
Newport
New Haven
Pequot (New London)
Aquidneck Island
N
0
40 miles

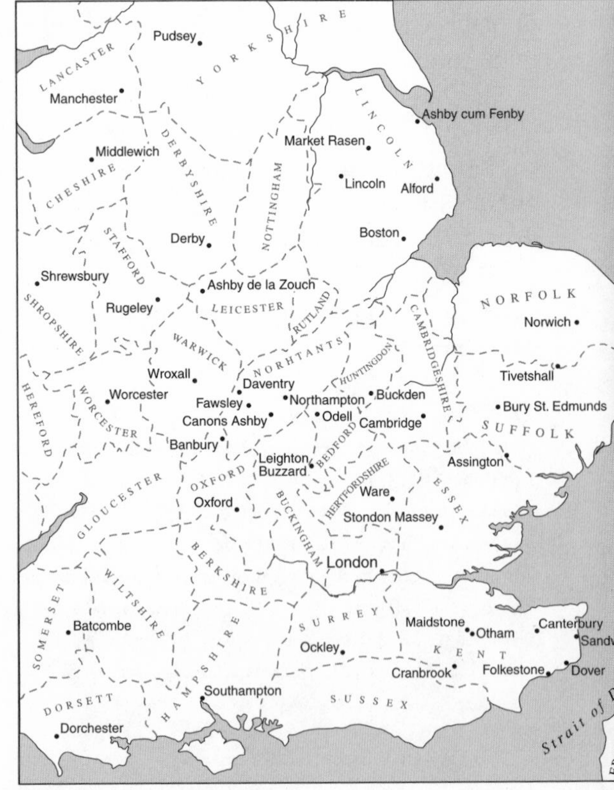
Pudsey
YORKSHIRE
LANCASTER
Manchester
LINCOLN
Ashby cum Fenby
Market Rasen
Middlewich
DERBYSHIRE
CHESHIRE
NOTTINGHAM
Lincoln
Alford
Boston
STAFFORD
Derby
Shrewsbury
Ashby de la Zouch
NORFOLK
Rugeley
LEICESTER
RUTLAND
CAMBRIDGESHIRE
Norwich
SHROPSHIRE
WARWICK
NORHTANTS
HUNTINGDON
Tivetshall
Wroxall
Daventry
HEREFORD
Worcester
Fawsley
Northampton
Buckden
Bury St. Edmunds
WORCESTER
Canons Ashby
Odell
Cambridge
SUFFOLK
Banbury
BEDFORD
Leighton Buzzard
Assington
GLOUCESTER
OXFORD
HERTFORDSHIRE
ESSEX
Oxford
BUCKINGHAM
Ware
Stondon Massey
BERKSHIRE
London
WILTSHIRE
SOMERSET
Batcombe
SURREY
Maidstone
Otham
Canterbury
HAMPSHIRE
Ockley
KENT
Cranbrook
Folkestone
Dover
Southampton
SUSSEX
DORSETT
Dorchester

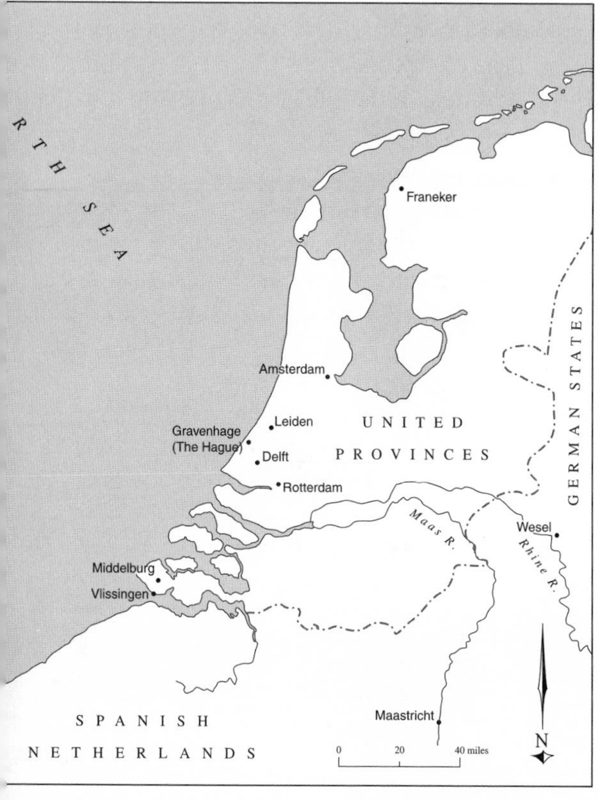
R T H S E A
Franeker
Amsterdam
Leiden
Gravenhage
(The Hague)
Delft
Rotterdam
U N I T E D
P R O V I N C E S
G E R M A N S T A T E S
Maas R.
Wesel
Rhine R.
Middelburg
Vlissingen
Maastricht
S P A N I S H
N E T H E R L A N D S
0
20
40 miles
N

thought or behavior. After several works centering on Cotton appeared in the 1960s, Richard Etulain saw the need to evaluate the changing interpretations of this one important Puritan.[4] The variety of emphases historians have given to Cotton's thought and career, however, bespeaks the complexity with which the entire Puritan movement is now understood. Just as we now recognize that there was, not one typical "Puritan" or "Puritanism," but various shadings of opinion and practice within the larger community made up of several generations of Puritans, so there are a variety of ways to see this one Puritan leader. Even though his centrality to the Puritan movement is not in doubt, he nevertheless eludes simple categorization. Thus thirty years after Nuttall noted Cotton's relative neglect, David D. Hall still observed that, for all of the many recent studies, "the career of John Cotton remains enigmatic."[5]

Certainly the ideas Cotton dealt with in his writings often involved fine and subtle distinctions, not always transparent to the modern reader. One of his major preoccupations was with church organization. Like most other emigrating Puritans, he came to oppose the English episcopacy on the grounds that it was not authorized by scriptural example. At the same time, he opposed formal separation from the English Church. He understood the Puritan movement as a reform movement aiming to improve and purify the church. Though he could not have foreseen it at the outset of his career, his strong beliefs made him a leader in New England's establishment of a church system valuing congregational autonomy—what became known as the New England Way. He is, in fact, credited with giving congregationalism its name and, in his several writings on the subject, with helping to define the new polity.[6]

Cotton also developed a theory of personal religious experience that stressed the relative passivity of the believer and the activity of the Holy Spirit in the experience of spiritual regeneration, an approach that encouraged a different psychological dynamic from that assumed by many of his peers. This has resulted in Cotton's often being presented in sharp contrast with "preparationist" preachers such as Thomas Hooker, Peter Bulkeley,

4. Richard Etulain, "The New Puritan: Recent Views of John Cotton," *Rendezvous,* VII (1972), 39–51. See also Etulain's earlier helpful compilation, "John Cotton: A Checklist of Relevant Materials," *Early American Literature,* IV (1969), 64–69.

5. David D. Hall, "On Common Ground: The Coherence of American Puritan Studies," *WMQ,* 3d Ser., XLIV (1987), 212.

6. See, for instance, Henry Martyn Dexter, *The Congregationalism of the Last Three Hundred Years as Seen in Its Literature* (1880; rpt. New York, 1970), I, 421–436; Larzer Ziff, "Introduction," in Ziff, *Cotton on the Churches,* esp. 2, 5; Hall, *Faithful Shepherd,* 93–120.

and Thomas Shepard, who urged the importance of the individual's spiritual activity in the early, "preparatory" stages of belief, whereas, in Cotton's schema, "for our first union [with Christ], there are no steps unto the Altar."[7] One modern remapping of Puritanism's subdivisions connects these tendencies to a larger network of like-minded Puritans, presenting him as the chief New England exemplar of a "Spiritual Brotherhood" stemming from the preaching and teaching of Richard Sibbes and John Preston, whose emphasis on God's benevolence and on the believer's passivity in the process of conversion, among other identifying traits of the group, Cotton carried forward.[8] Another study stresses contrasting qualities in Cotton's makeup, showing that, while he was "recognized as the leading intellectual in the colony," a "charismatic" preacher and church politician, "for all of his theoretical brilliance and personal charm, in the 1630s John Cotton was a decidedly dangerous man" for his ability and inclination to alter established religious practices.[9]

His role as representative Puritan has been imagined in other ways as well. He is typically cited as one of the leading preachers of his day, both in England and New England, even while his style is contrasted to that of such contemporaries as Hooker.[10] He has been put forth as a representative Puritan of the plain style of preaching and writing.[11] His use of the tradi-

7. John Cotton, *The New Covenant* . . . (London, 1654), 54. Charles Lloyd Cohen describes Cotton as "early New England's leading theologian of the Holy Spirit" in *God's Caress: The Psychology of Puritan Religious Experience* (New York, 1986), 126. See Norman Pettit, *The Heart Prepared: Grace and Conversion in Puritan Spiritual Life* (New Haven, Conn., 1966). On the tendency of Cotton and others to a spiritually charged, even mystical description of faith, see James Fulton Maclear, "'The Heart of New England Rent': The Mystical Element in Early Puritan History," *Mississippi Valley Historical Review,* XLII (1955–1956), 621–652.

8. Janice Knight, *Orthodoxies in Massachusetts: Rereading American Puritanism* (Cambridge, Mass., 1994). Knight contrasts this group with another subset of Puritans whose intellectual and spiritual genealogy she traces from William Ames through Hooker, Shepard, and others.

9. Darren Staloff, *The Making of an American Thinking Class: Intellectuals and Intelligentsia in Puritan Massachusetts* (New York, 1998), 27.

10. See Everett H. Emerson, "Introduction," in John Cotton, *God's Mercie Mixed with His Justice* . . . (1641; rpt. Gainesville, Fla., 1958), v–vi; Alfred Habegger, "Preparing the Soul for Christ: The Contrasting Sermon Forms of John Cotton and Thomas Hooker," *American Literature,* XLI (1969), 342–354; Eugenia DeLamotte, "John Cotton and the Rhetoric of Grace," *Early American Literature,* XXI (1986), 49–74; Teresa Toulouse, *The Art of Prophesying: New England Sermons and the Shaping of Belief* (Athens, Ga., 1987), 13–45; Emerson, *Cotton,* 13–17.

11. Perry Miller and Thomas H. Johnson, *The Puritans* (New York, 1938), 70–71, 79; Jesper Rosenmeier, "'Clearing the Medium': A Reevaluation of the Puritan Plain Style in Light of John Cotton's *A Practicall Commentary upon the First Epistle Generall of John,*" *WMQ,* 3d Ser., XXXVII (1980), 577–591. David Leverenz discusses the varying styles of Puritan preachers, including

tion of typology in his biblical exegesis has also given him prominence in the scholarly literature exploring that popular system for understanding the symmetry between the Old and New Testaments.[12] He is also the first minister known to have preached a millennial theme from a New England pulpit, and his millennialism has been much discussed.[13] His central entanglement in the Antinomian controversy in New England (1636–1638) is for some scholars the single defining event for Cotton and his fellow New England Puritans, sometimes revealing him as a supporter of a patriarchal power system, sometimes as a self-interested equivocator, sometimes as a diplomatic compromiser.[14] At least one study singles out the issue of the Puritans' vio-

---

Cotton, in *The Language of Puritan Feeling: An Exploration in Literature, Psychology, and Social History* (New Brunswick, N.J., 1980), esp. chap. 6. Michael W. Kaufmann also focuses on Cotton's language of conversion in *Institutional Individualism: Conversion, Exile, and Nostalgia in Puritan New England* (Hanover, N.H., 1998), 38–54.

12. The modern literature on seventeenth-century uses of typology in biblical interpretation is large. See Sacvan Bercovitch's "Annotated Bibliography," in Bercovitch, ed., *Typology and Early American Literature* (Amherst, Mass., 1972), 245–337. Among those who emphasize Cotton in their discussion of typology are Sacvan Bercovitch, "Typology in Puritan New England: The Williams-Cotton Controversy Reassessed," *American Quarterly,* XIX (1967), 166–191; Jesper Rosenmeier, "New England's Perfection: The Image of Adam and the Image of Christ in the Antinomian Crisis, 1634 to 1638," *WMQ,* 3d Ser., XXVII (1970), 435–459; Bercovitch, *The American Jeremiad* (Madison, Wis., 1978); Mason I. Lowance, Jr., chap. 3, "The Canticles Tradition," in Lowance, *The Language of Canaan: Metaphor and Symbol in New England from the Puritans to the Transcendentalists* (Cambridge, Mass., 1980).

13. See especially Theodore Dwight Bozeman, *To Live Ancient Lives: The Primitivist Dimension in Puritanism* (Chapel Hill, N.C., 1988), 229–262; but also John F. Wilson, *Pulpit in Parliament: Puritanism during the English Civil Wars, 1640–1648* (Princeton, N.J., 1969), 225–226; J. F. Maclear, "New England and the Fifth Monarchy: The Quest for the Millennium in Early American Puritanism," *WMQ,* 3d Ser., XXXII (1975), 223–260; Avihu Zakai, *Exile and Kingdom: History and Apocalypse in the Puritan Migration to America* (Cambridge, 1992), esp. 178–190; Andrew Delbanco, *The Puritan Ordeal* (Cambridge, Mass., 1989). This is not to suggest these scholars all tell the same story; in fact, while Maclear and Zakai, among others, present the view that millenarianism was a motivating factor in the emigration of Puritans to New England, Bozeman and Delbanco both provide strong arguments against that position. But Cotton is a central figure for all participants in this interpretive debate.

14. The vast literature on the Antinomian controversy frequently centers on Cotton as the key male figure in the episode, a centrality that Cotton himself felt very stressfully. See, for instance, Rosenmeier, "New England's Perfection," *WMQ,* 3d Ser., XXVII (1970). A full-scale examination of the controversy is Battis, *Saints and Sectaries.* The most indispensable resource for study of the controversy is Hall, *Antinomian Controversy.* Richard Etulain presents a balanced consideration of Cotton's ideas and actions in "John Cotton and the Anne Hutchinson Controversy," *Rendezvous,* II (1967), 9–18. The definitive work on the theological dimension of the controversy is Stoever, *"A Faire and Easie Way to Heaven."* Much modern scholarship focusing on

lence, both physical and rhetorical—not only against the Pequot Indians and white women but also against Roman Catholics—as a defining issue for his generation of Puritans. Again, Cotton is Exhibit A, especially in his late apocalyptic writings in which the anti-Catholic message is pronounced.[15]

His theology has been identified as focusing, like that of the apostle Paul, on the centrality of Christ in the individual's covenant relationship with God, distinguishing Cotton—in degree rather than in essence—from many of his contemporaries. In the view of one important reading, he is a more likely candidate for the title "the first consistent and authentic Calvinist" than Perry Miller's choice, Jonathan Edwards.[16] His affection for Calvin's thought is colorfully recorded in the memorable passage in Cotton Mather's biography of him:

> Such a *Calvinist* was our *Cotton!* Said he, *I have read the fathers and the schoolmen, and* Calvin *too; but I find, that he that has* Calvin *has them all.* And being asked, why in his latter days he indulged *nocturnal studies* more than formerly, he pleasantly replied, *Because I love to sweeten my mouth with a piece of* Calvin *before I go to sleep.*[17]

Not an original theologian, he was a careful and informed interpreter of a theological tradition that became a powerful factor in the thinking of his friends, neighbors, and descendants.

Cotton's notorious disagreements with Roger Williams, which began soon after Cotton's arrival in Boston, are central to the picture that some present of Cotton. He argued with Williams on two primary issues: Separatism and religious toleration. One-issue readings of Cotton sometimes stress his conservative thinking on the issue of religious freedom and on the ques-

---

women in early America makes Anne Hutchinson the central figure in the controversy and usually presents Cotton as foil to her. Cotton thus figures largely in such accounts of the episode as Amy Schrager Lang, *Prophetic Woman: Anne Hutchinson and the Problem of Dissent in the Literature of New England* (Berkeley, Calif., 1987), chaps. 2, 3; Mary Beth Norton, *Founding Mothers and Fathers: Gendered Power and the Forming of American Society* (New York, 1996), chap. 8; Jane Kamensky, *Governing the Tongue: The Politics of Speech in Early New England* (New York, 1997), 71–103; Staloff, *The Making of an American Thinking Class,* 40–72. See also Francis J. Bremer, ed., *Anne Hutchinson: Troubler of the Puritan Zion* (Huntington, N.Y., 1981).

15. Ann Kibbey, *The Interpretation of Material Shapes in Puritanism: A Study of Rhetoric, Prejudice, and Violence* (Cambridge, 1986).

16. John S. Coolidge, *The Pauline Renaissance in England: Puritanism and the Bible* (Oxford, 1970), 138. Miller made the claim for Edwards in his famous essay, "The Marrow of Puritan Divinity," originally published in CSM, *Publs.,* XXXII, *Trans.* (1933–1937), 247–300, but reprinted in *Errand into the Wilderness* (Cambridge, Mass., 1956), where he retracted the claim; see 49–50, 98.

17. Mather, *Magnalia,* I, 250.

tion of how much diversity of thought on religious matters is healthy for a society, usually contrasting him unfavorably to Williams.[18] This is a particularly interesting and complex matter, so that, while it is true that Cotton believed heretics did not belong in a godly society, he was not opposed to tolerating some variety of approaches to religion, as he explained in a letter to Sir Richard Saltonstall (Cotton to Saltonstall, [1652]). Likewise, while he is on record—and often quoted—as opposing democracy as a basis for civil government, his was also the voice that said no to the conditions for settlement in New England put forward by the prominent members of the English gentry Lord Brooke and Lord Saye and Sele, who would have attached a hereditary right to officeholding in the colonies by such gentlemen as themselves.[19] Intolerant of certain opinions while not against toleration, opposed to democracy while also against the establishment of an aristocracy in New England—such seemingly discordant ideas indicate the care and patience with which one needs to approach Cotton and his thought.

Two scholars in the twentieth century published studies focused entirely on Cotton's life and ideas.[20] Larzer Ziff's *Career of John Cotton: Puritanism and the American Experience* (1962) examines Cotton's professional life and remains the fullest scholarly account. He stresses the need to understand Cotton in

18. See, for instance, Harry Bamford Parkes, "John Cotton and Roger Williams Debate Toleration, 1644–1652," *NEQ*, IV (1931), 735–756. Helpful discussions of the issue include Irwin H. Polishook, ed., *Roger Williams, John Cotton, and Religious Freedom: A Controversy in Old and New England* (Englewood Cliffs, N.J., 1967); Jesper Rosenmeier, "The Teacher and the Witness: John Cotton and Roger Williams," *WMQ*, 3d Ser., XXV (1968), 408–431; Conrad Wright, "John Cotton Washed and Made White," in F. Forrester Church and Timothy George, eds., *Continuity and Discontinuity in Church History: Essays Presented to George Huntston Williams* . . . (Leiden, 1979), 338–350; Timothy L. Hall, *Separating Church and State: Roger Williams and Religious Liberty* (Urbana, Ill., 1998), 48–71.

19. See below, Cotton to William Fiennes, Lord Saye and Sele, [after March 1636], and Appendix.

20. Apart from the two published books, several doctoral dissertations have similarly focused on Cotton's life and thought. These include Donald Robert Come, "John Cotton, Guide of the Chosen People" (Ph.D. diss., Princeton University, 1949); Judith B. Welles, "John Cotton, 1584–1652, Churchman and Theologian" (Ph.D. diss., University of Edinburgh, 1948); Harry Alexander Poole, "The Unsettled Mr. Cotton" (Ph.D. diss., University of Illinois at Urbana-Champaign, 1956); Robert F. Scholz, "'The Reverend Elders': Faith, Fellowship, and Politics in the Ministerial Community of Massachusetts Bay, 1630–1710" (Ph.D. diss., University of Minnesota, 1966); Helle M. Alpert, "Robert Keayne: Notes of Sermons by John Cotton and Proceedings of the First Church of Boston from 23 November 1639 to 1 June 1640" (Ph.D. diss., Tufts University, 1974); Mary Jane Lewis, "A Sweet Sacrifice: Civil War in New England" (Ph.D. diss., State University of New York at Binghamton, 1986); Jean Elizabeth Cameron, "John Cotton's Role in the Trials of Anne Hutchinson" (Ph.D. diss., University of Minnesota, 1991).

his historical milieu, since his subject is otherwise more or less ungraspable to the modern sensibility, even rather "medieval." Much valuable work on the Puritans—some of it by Ziff himself—has been done since 1962, so the Puritans' apparent remoteness is not such a problem as it once seemed. But Ziff's point about the importance of seeing Cotton in his own context remains crucial. Ziff's picture of Cotton recounts his successful jousts with bishops and hostile local voices in Lincolnshire, where his Puritanism was contested, as well as his emigration to Massachusetts Bay and survival of a controversy there in which he was the object of immediate and harsh criticism by some of his peers and parishioners. He describes Cotton's later years as a time of continuing to distinguish between his own and his colleagues' views on grace, while asserting his authority in the area of civil law, to some extent controlling the outcome of the nervous struggle between democracy and autocracy in Massachusetts Bay. For Ziff, Cotton's ability not only to survive but to earn the lasting respect of his contemporaries in England and New England in the midst of these difficulties characterized the man. Cotton appears as an artful compromiser and a carefully diplomatic rhetorician. He was "a mild and scholarly man" whose "habit of mind was cautious observation and hesitancy before decision," a man of a "conservative frame of mind."[21] He was also, as Ziff recognizes, beset by troubles, so that his skills as a negotiator willing to take the time to untangle things in the interest of an outcome that might restore the community to the principles of love and communion, as urged by Governor John Winthrop in his famous sermon, "A Modell of Christian Charity," were invaluable to Cotton and to the Puritan movement. Yet he might also have been a bit too diffident, a little too ready to blow with the wind. Ziff's Cotton is a man able to negotiate the rocky shoals of both secular and ecclesiastical opinion—a politician, a survivor.

Everett Emerson's study, *John Cotton* (1965, revised in 1990), also emphasizes the importance of Cotton's "intellectual milieu, with such concerns as his interest in biblical prophecy, millennialism, and spirituality." While Emerson also affirms Cotton's "conservatism," he finds it linked dynamically with idealism, which in Cotton's best writings sounds a note of intellectual clarity and authority, even manifesting a "daring" quality.[22] This coexistence of conservatism and daring in his makeup again suggests the complexity in Cotton that makes him both fascinating and elusive.

In all of this, perhaps there is further corroboration of David Hall's sense that the disagreements about him in modern scholarship lead to the conclusion that Cotton remains an enigma. As his correspondence makes clear,

21. Ziff, *Career of John Cotton,* 46, 52, 104.

22. Emerson, *Cotton,* xi, 124–125.

he was, for all of his individuality, central to the movement that was driving him but that he was also helping to guide. His correspondence allows us to see him at the heart of a complex religious, social, and cultural reform movement in which he was a leader. He helped design, construct, and defend a radically new church as well as a civil order based on both English and divine law. The New England community was established on the Puritan principles of which Cotton was a primary spokesman. In England he was viewed as downright dangerous, whereas in New England he was consulted by magistrates and governors; his opinion, as John Davenport once said, was law.

The many ways in which scholars have seen Cotton are all supportable in at least some of the letters, which in their random survival tend to cut across the spectrum of his professional interests and opinions. He was an outstanding student and scholar, a preacher who could be powerfully eloquent, and a teacher whose rational objectivity could bring clarity to complex matters. But, when pressed on a sticky point, he could also be frustratingly opaque.[23] This is not the characteristic Cotton, but it is a trait that appears as both cause and effect of his troubles in the dispute that raged for two years in New England in 1636–1638. Yet opaqueness is not typical for Cotton. His letters confirm that he was, perhaps above all, a teacher—the title he was given in the colonial Boston church could not have been more appropriate.[24] In

23. Cotton was criticized for this at the time. Stoever comments on the problem: "Whether Cotton, in a given instance, was obscure because he was in an unsettled interval between convictions, because his position was insufficiently thought through, or because he wished to conceal something is difficult to say. Whatever the reason, the quality of Cotton's discourse in the spring of 1636 was such that people might readily hear things in it that were not explicitly there." Stoever, *"A Faire and Easie Way to Heaven,"* 39–40.

24. When Cotton arrived in the colony in September 1633, the Boston church already had a pastor in John Wilson. Cotton was quickly invited to become Wilson's colleague and was given the title "Teacher." This was the usual division of roles in early Puritan churches having more than one minister. Thomas Hooker gave a very clear description of the differing duties of the two officers, the pastor's being "to work upon the will and the affections," to "endeavour by heat of exhortation to quicken, . . . strengthen and incourage the soul in every holy word and work," and the teacher's being "to informe the judgement, and to help forward the work of illumination, in the minde and understanding, and thereby to make way for the truth, that it may be setled and fastned upon the heart" (*A Survey of the Summe of Church-Discipline* [London, 1648], pt. 2, 19–21). In theory, if not always in practice, the teacher educated and the pastor moved their congregation. The theory was surely more precise than the actual practice, since the distinction is in the end an artificial one, though it is faithful to the important distinction made by some ministers between the stages of grace, with the early stages working mainly on the mind and the later stages on the heart and affections; see Sargent Bush, Jr., *The Writings of Thomas Hooker: Spiritual Adventure in Two Worlds* (Madison, Wis., 1980), chap. 5, esp. 115. Norman S. Fier-

some degree these paradoxical qualities are themselves the result of the complicated times in which Cotton lived. Ziff, Emerson, and others are right to contend that he is not a figure who can be understood apart from those times. What we can now see more clearly is the extent to which epistolary communication served him and his correspondents as an important means for negotiating those times and for exercising his prophetic "instrument" in them.

JOHN COTTON'S WORLD

Cotton's world was a complicated setting, especially for one of his principled dedication to its reform. In early-seventeenth-century England, the state of religion was the central interest not just of average people but also of the government. "The Puritan turned to the theological aspects of a question as naturally as the modern man turns to the economic," wrote A. S. P. Woodhouse, on which Robert S. Paul elaborates that, for "men like Oliver Cromwell, Henry Vane, Thomas Fairfax, John Winthrop, and John Cotton," the theological dimension of a debate represented both idiom and essence. "If they put theology at the centre of their action, it cannot be ignored in the interpretation of that time."[25] There is no doubt that for Cotton the essential explanation of life lay in theology.

In England the church was a national church, with an officially sanctioned form of worship and an established ecclesiastic structure. From the late sixteenth century on, however, an outspoken minority within the church objected to certain of these forms of worship because they were not mentioned and thus not "authorized" in Scripture. An important strain of Puritan thought considered the church practice of its holy ordinances corrupt, so that it was necessary to seek to establish a purer, biblically ordered polity, to reestablish the practices of early Hebrew worship. It was necessary, as Cotton said, to "live antient lives."[26] Puritans—pejoratively named for their proclaimed interest in purifying the church's practice—were the target, in varying intensity from the 1570s through the 1630s, of ecclesiastical enforcers

---

ing provides important intellectual historical background on this issue in "Will and Intellect in the New England Mind," *WMQ,* 3d Ser., XXIX (1972), 537–541, and in *Moral Philosophy at Seventeenth-Century Harvard: A Discipline in Transition* (Chapel Hill, N.C., 1981), 110–137.

25. A. S. P. Woodhouse,ed., *Puritanism and Liberty* . . . (London, 1938), 39; Robert S. Paul, *The Assembly of the Lord: Politics and Religion in the Westminster Assembly and the "Grand Debate"* (Edinburgh, 1985), 7.

26. John Cotton, *A Practical Commentary . . . upon the First Epistle Generall of John* (London, 1656), 232. Bozeman, who borrowed Cotton's phrase in the title of his important study, *To Live Ancient Lives,* calls this element of Puritan thought "biblicist primitivism" (10).

of conformity to the prescribed rituals of the English Church.[27] Cotton's conversion to a Puritan way of thinking while he was at Cambridge was the turning point in his life: the strength of his commitment to nonconformity is what made life difficult and finally untenable for him in England, driving him to North America, where a new location and a new context for his faith and religious practice led to further challenges and changes in his own views. It was a time, therefore, in which the adoption of religious principles not in harmony with officially sanctioned ones could determine the direction of a person's life. Martyrs were created by such conditions, and—in much larger numbers—so were émigrés and expatriates.

Aiding this outward flow of principled individuals from England's shores was another of the key factors of the times, colonization. Companies were forming in England with the intention of establishing new communities of English people in North America. Their motives were varied, from economic gain to the conversion of the native population to Christianity. The ill-fated effort at Roanoke off the coast of what is now North Carolina in 1585–1587 was followed by renewed efforts to colonize America. Two settlements were attempted in 1607, for instance, one at Sagadahock in Maine and the other at Jamestown in Virginia. The former was abandoned after one winter, but the Jamestown Colony, despite terrible physical hardships, personnel clashes, drought, and other problems, survived for several decades. Plymouth Colony was settled in 1620 and the Massachusetts Bay Colony ten years after that, following an advance party's successful planting in Salem in 1628. The stories of these efforts to people a new continent are well known. But the fact that the effort was going forward at just the time that the Puritans were feeling forced out of their native land by ever-stricter enforcement of uniformity in worship practices in English churches served the purposes of both religious reform and colonization.

During the reign of James I (1603–1625), England stayed out of international conflicts. At home, James, despite his origins in Presbyterian Scotland, became a strong friend of the episcopacy and acted to strengthen the bishops and weaken the Puritans. Ministers were required to subscribe to the Thirty-nine Articles, which involved conforming in all details to episcopal authority and established worship practices—the very practices that Puritans found objectionable, even intolerable. He strengthened both the Star Chamber and the Court of High Commission, which took punitive action against

27. On the disagreement and downright animosity between Puritans and non-Puritans, see Peter Lake, "'A Charitable Christian Hatred': The Godly and Their Enemies in the 1630s," in Christopher Durston and Jacqueline Eales, eds., *The Culture of English Puritanism, 1560–1700* (London, 1996), 145–183.

many Puritan preachers over a number of years. In the first few years of his reign, 1604–1609, he removed about seventy-five Nonconformist ministers, and he tended to appoint bishops who were unfriendly to the Puritans.[28] He also issued in 1616 "The Kings Majesties Declaration to His Subjects concerning Lawful Sports to be Used," which became known as "The Book of Sports," and was a major bone of contention with the Puritans. The declaration supported the importance of church attendance on Sunday mornings but also allowed for the people's indulgence in various games and sports on the same day. This compromise, in the Puritans' view, encouraged the people to break the Sabbath and thus violate the fourth commandment.[29] Although during this period the church sought conformity from its ministers, the divisions, both religious and political, were sharpened still further under Charles I (1625–1649).[30] For many Puritans, things simply got worse after James's death. Movement of Nonconformists to the Netherlands, which had been occurring since the 1580s, again accelerated. In what became known as the Great Migration, 1620–1640, thousands emigrated to America, motivated by a complex mixture of reasons ranging from the entirely secular to the strongly religious.

Puritans felt that all was not well in England, and they began to say so. Nearby on the Continent the bloody war in the Palatinate, now known as the Thirty-Years' War, was raging. It was essentially a war between Catholics and Protestants, and it chased some survivors from Switzerland, Germany, and the Low Countries to England. That strife became a symbol for some English people of what could happen in a nation insufficiently godly. Thomas Hooker relied upon immediate acquaintance with the outrages committed against Protestants on the Continent in asking his English congregation to imagine a spreading of that war:

28. On James, the church, and the Puritans, see Kenneth Fincham, *Prelate as Pastor: The Episcopate of James I* (Oxford, 1990), esp. 35–67; William Hunt, *The Puritan Moment: The Coming of Revolution in an English County* (Cambridge, Mass., 1983), 87–112.

29. On the "Book of Sports," or the king's declaration for lawful sports, and its cultural context, see Nancy L. Struna, *People of Prowess: Sport, Leisure, and Labor in Early Anglo-America* (Urbana, Ill., 1996), 11–50; L. A. Govett, *The King's Book of Sports* . . . (London, 1890); Kenneth L. Parker, *The English Sabbath: A Study of Doctrine and Discipline from the Reformation to the Civil War* (Cambridge, 1988), 149–160; Julian Davies, *The Caroline Captivity of the Church: Charles I and the Remoulding of Anglicanism, 1625–1641* (Oxford, 1992), 172–204; Bruce C. Daniels, *Puritans at Play: Leisure and Recreation in Colonial New England* (New York, 1995), 163–167.

30. See David Underdown, *A Freeborn People: Politics and the Nation in Seventeenth-Century England* (Oxford, 1996), 1–44; Kevin Sharpe, *The Personal Rule of Charles I* (New Haven, Conn., 1992); Jacqueline Eales, "A Road to Revolution: The Continuity of Puritanism, 1559–1642," in Durston and Eales, eds., *The Culture of English Puritanism,* 184–209.

> Will you have England destroyed? Will you put the aged to trouble, and your young men to the sword? Will you have your young women widows, and your virgins defiled? Will you have your dear and tender little ones tossed upon the pikes and dashed upon the stones? Or will you have them brought up in Popery, in idolatry, under a necessity of perishing their souls forever, which is worst of all? Will you have these temples wherein we seem to worship God, will you have them and your houses burnt with fire? And will you see England laid waste without inhabitants?

These were the possible consequences of the tendency to "play mock holiday with God and with his Gospel." The signs were evident to many a prophet in England in the period of the Great Migration, and Hooker, the dramatic Boanerges, was blunt about the cause: England had lost its spiritual center.

> So glory is departed from England; for England hath seen her best days, and the reward of sin is coming on apace; for God is packing up of his gospel, because none will buy his wares. . . . God begins to ship away his Noahs, which prophesied and foretold that destruction was near; and God makes account that New England shall be a refuge for his Noahs and his Lots, a rock and a shelter for his righteous ones to run unto; and those that were vexed to see the ungodly lives of the people in this wicked land, shall there be safe.[31]

During the reign of Charles, and especially after his appointment of William Laud as archbishop of Canterbury in 1633, conformity was sought more strenuously than ever before. Those refusing to conform faced a difficult choice: resigning their calling as ministers of God or finding some place beyond the limits of England where they could practice that calling. For those who remained, the principles at issue continued to be a source of difficulty. Charles proved to be a relatively inflexible ruler, who did not see the value of compromise with his internal foes. The result was a clash with a Puritan-dominated Parliament and finally civil wars in the 1640s. The parliamentary party proved victorious, overthrowing the episcopacy, outlawing the hierarchy of bishops and archbishops, and ultimately executing both Laud and Charles. Change was dramatic—truly revolutionary—in the years 1640–1660, as England (temporarily, as it proved) became a sympathetic environment for members of the Puritan party. But after the reign of Oliver Cromwell as lord protector in the 1650s, with the emergence of a new English constitution, the nation would not return to the pre–civil war state of affairs. Though the monarchy was restored with the return of Charles II in 1660,

31. Hooker, "The Danger of Desertion," in G. H. Williams et al., *Thomas Hooker,* 244–246.

and some of the Puritans' efforts to change permanently certain customs in English life failed, the people had gained a measure of power through Parliament's successful assertion of its authority in opposition to the monarch. The course of English history had taken a sharp turn; a new era had begun.[32]

The story of this tumultuous period of English history is of course much too complicated for a brief narration, but the point here is that John Cotton's life was lived out through a period of tremendous change, with many attendant dangers, both physical and internal. His own life was irrevocably altered by the public conditions he encountered in England. Yet his talents were also encouraged by some of those conditions. He was molded by his education and by the use of that education in trying circumstances, both in Lincolnshire and in Massachusetts. Because of his strong education and his unique intellectual, spiritual, and psychological qualities, he became, not just another figure on the large canvas of contemporary history, but one who emerged from the background to figure prominently as a leader within a significant segment of the population. When he met the challenge most forcefully, early in his Lincolnshire ministry, he had already sorted out his principles, basing them on his complex understanding of the words of Scripture and of past Christian leaders, both from the early church, where the apostle Paul and the early bishop Cyprian were among his heroes, and from the Reformation period, where the likes of Calvin, Ursinus, Zanchius, Peter Martyr, and Bucer figured in his panoply of authorities. Later English churchmen also helped him establish the ground on which he took his own stand—men such as Paul Baynes, Thomas Cartwright, William Perkins, Laurence Chaderton, Arthur Hildersham, John Preston, and Richard Sibbes.

The thoughts of such men and many other influential voices were well represented in Cotton's working library, as his writings show. After the Bible itself, they provided the essential armor with which he repeatedly went into battle. His correspondence demonstrates that he was, above all, a thinking man, and these models of Protestant Christianity were crucial to his ability to negotiate the extremely challenging way that he had to go in a time of great turmoil and disruption. In a late letter to one Mr. Naylor, then ministering in Cotton's former parish in Lincolnshire, Cotton spoke of his own "love to the Trueth, w*hi*ch is to be searched after more then hidden Treasur," a quest that had guided him through his entire adult life. His means of con-

32. See Christopher Durston, "Puritan Rule and the Failure of Cultural Revolution, 1645–1660," in Durston and Eales, eds., *The Culture of English Puritanism,* 210–233. In the same volume, Patrick Collinson, taking a somewhat broader chronological perspective, shows how Puritan practice and values interacted with English culture with some more permanent effects; see "Elizabethan and Jacobean Puritanism as Forms of Popular Religious Culture," 32–57.

ducting this search was through meditation on and study of the word of God, and by steeping himself in the learning of his predecessors and his peers. In this effort, his skill in reading the ancient languages and his ability to think logically and to debate forcefully—all acquired in his early years in Derby and especially at Cambridge—were his chief tools. Many times he professed his desire to learn from others, but usually he ended up being the teacher (Cotton to [Edward?] Naylor, [1651–1652]).

The vast majority of Cotton's surviving words were public pronouncements—sermons, controversial literature, and responses to public inquiries. This fact makes the preservation and study of his more private papers especially important if we are to take his full measure. The present volume offers the first opportunity to understand this dimension of Cotton's life in a sustained, coherent way. Letters are, in most cases, direct communications from one individual to another. (There are occasional group communications in Cotton's correspondence, but they are a very small portion of the total.) Things are said and subjects addressed in private correspondence that would not always find their way into public discourse. Having all the extant letters to and from Cotton in a sequence covering more than thirty years offers an opportunity to grasp the complexity of his life and to witness the various kinds of individuals and situations to which he had to respond, thereby deepening our understanding of the man. The correspondence, moreover, dramatically reinforces the validity of the caution, previously noted, that we must always try to see him linked to the complex times in which he lived. His letters show a resilient man relishing his place in the midst of a movement that was attempting no less a task than bringing the external world and people's practices in it more in line with God's plan for it. If there is a single prominent theme in Cotton's letters, it is this. The world—the corrupt, depraved world—was in need of Christian purification. In his letters, just as in his more formal writings, he exercised his pen, whether goose or swan or raven's quill, as God's chosen instrument.

For Cotton, as for his fellow Puritans, the central issue in every person's life was the state of one's soul. Cotton's preaching focused on this issue. The church was the institutional means for the reform of a fallen world, and yet the church itself, they believed, was in critical need of purifying. To accomplish this, Cotton and others called for a strong, clear-sighted, principled cadre of ministerial leaders. Cotton's letters (many published here for the first time) show his lifelong dedication to working toward the achievement of a purer, more scripturally defined, Christ-centered church and a biblically oriented society. Whether he is writing to a bishop or a housewife, to a titled member of the House of Lords or a neophyte country clergyman, he is driven by the need to convey his spiritual understanding of life to his correspondents. His letters also show us a man sometimes conscious of his own limitations but always willing to venture a definitive opinion on a matter that is vexing his correspondent—what he and his contemporaries would have described as a "case of conscience." His grandson recalled that Cotton was known as a "most excellent *casuist.*" His letters show us why.[33]

Cotton's early life gave little indication that he was destined to play a major role in a key religious movement that would have profound significance for the nation's political future. He was born in Derby in 1584, the son of Mary Hurlbert, whom Cotton Mather called a "gracious" and "pious *mother,*" and Rowland Cotton, a lawyer who died while Cotton was still an undergraduate.[34] He matriculated at Trinity College, Cambridge, at the tender age of thirteen, apparently in 1598. He earned the bachelor of arts degree in 1602/3, received his master's in 1606, and then became fellow at Emmanuel College, where he remained until 1612.[35] It was doubtless during those final six years, while serving the college variously as head lecturer, dean, catechist, and tutor, that he cemented his reputation as a young scholar of linguistic skill, theological command, and intellectual probity, "much admired by the sparkling wits of the university."[36] As a member of Emmanuel's teaching staff, Cotton apparently discovered an ability and affection for teaching that endeared him to his students and that would remain a central quality of his ministerial career long after leaving the university setting.[37] His dramatic conversion to Puritanism by the preaching of Richard Sibbes—pub-

33. Mather, *Magnalia,* I, 251.

34. Mather, *Magnalia,* I, 232. There has been disagreement in various biographical summaries whether he was born in 1584 or 1585. The baptismal records of St. Alkmund's Church in Derby show, however, that he was born and baptized there in December 1584. Also, the name of his mother does not appear in any published biography of Cotton of which I am aware. I am grateful to Marshall K. Kirk, Assistant Reference Librarian at the New England Historic Genealogical Society in Boston, Mass., for allowing me to read his manuscript essay on Cotton genealogy, "Cottoniana," where he definitively identifies Mary Hurlbert as Cotton's mother.

35. These details on Cotton's Cambridge career are collected in Joan Schenck Ibish, "Emmanuel College: The Founding Generation, with a Biographical Register of Members . . . 1584–1604" (Ph.D. diss., Harvard University, 1985), 390–391.

36. Mather, *Magnalia,* I, 234.

37. "By his School-stratagems he won the hearts of his Pupils both to himself, and to a desire of Learning: they were to each other as the prophets, and the Sons of the Prophets: his Pupils were honourers, and lovers of him: and he was a Tutor, a Friend, and a Father to them." William Dillingham, *Laurence Chaderton, D.D. (First Master of Emmanuel), Translated from a Latin Memoir of Dr. Dillingham,* ed. Richard Farmer, with an essay by E. S. Shuckburgh (Cambridge, 1884), 5.

licly demonstrated in a plain sermon that Cotton preached in the university church, St. Mary's, in about 1608—attracted much notice.[38] His preaching was powerful enough to convert the learned and witty fellow of Queen's College, John Preston, who subsequently became influential at court while also succeeding the venerable Laurence Chaderton in the key Puritan post as master of Emmanuel College from 1622 until his early death in 1628. In 1612, the year in which he received his bachelor of divinity degree, Cotton made a gift to the Emmanuel College Library of Martin Chemnitz's *Examen Concilii Tridentini* (Frankfort, 1609) and then departed Cambridge to become the vicar of the beautiful St. Botolph's Church at Boston, Lincolnshire.[39] Preston kept track of Cotton after he left Cambridge, and, after moving from Queen's College to become master at Emmanuel, Preston developed the practice of sending promising students and graduates from Emmanuel to Cotton in Lincolnshire for final instruction and example in the ways of the Puritan ministry. Cotton's years at Cambridge were formative both intellectually and ecclesiastically, but no letters survive from that period.

JOHN COTTON AS LETTER-WRITER

After Cambridge, John Cotton extended his renown as a Puritan intellectual and scholar as well as a spiritual leader and pastor. In both England and New England he lived and worked in a climate of disagreement and debate over issues that were seen as critical to the church and society. For these very reasons, he was sought out by many who wished to know his opinion on some point or other, both in person and by letter. Although he is not particularly known today as a letter-writer, he had a reputation among his contemporaries as a generous correspondent. For some, this characteristic defined him. Matthew Swallowe, for instance, writing "from [his] Study in *London, May* 20, 1641," some eight years after Cotton had gone to New

38. Three early sources record Cotton's conversion, each highlighting different aspects of it. The earliest account was apparently Samuel Whiting's brief "Concerning the Life of the Famous Mr. Cotton . . . ," in Young, *Chronicles of the First Planters,* 421–422. Writing on March 1, 1654/5, Thomas Allen, who had spent twelve years as a neighboring minister of Cotton's in Massachusetts, wrote an "Epistle to the Reader" for Cotton's posthumous *Exposition upon the Thirteenth Chapter of the Revelation* (London, 1655), in which he reported the story of that sermon as he got it *"from the tongue of this our* Reverend Author *himselfe."* Soon thereafter, John Norton's biography of Cotton, *Abel Being Dead yet Speaketh; or, The Life and Death of That Deservedly Famous Man of God, Mr. John Cotton . . .* (London, 1658), 13–14, also recounted the story.

39. The book is still a part of the Emmanuel College Library's collection. See Sargent Bush, Jr., and Carl J. Rasmussen, *The Library of Emmanuel College, Cambridge, 1584–1637* (Cambridge, 1986), 43, 65–66.

England, cited Cotton's letter-writing as an important facet of his value to his English colleagues over "the whole Land almost, as also divers forraine parts, the Divines whereof some came to enjoy converse with him, others had intercourse with him by letter, have beene acquainted with, and doe retaine in memory his parts and graces; so that (as *Paul* said of *Titus*) his praise is in the Gospell, almost throughout all the Churches."[40] His friend, relative, neighbor, and correspondent, Samuel Whiting, also recalled in his biography that Cotton "answered many letters that were sent far and near; wherein were handled many difficult cases of conscience, and many doubts by him cleared to the greatest satisfaction."[41]

As his letters demonstrate, Cotton early acquired and maintained a popular reputation among his fellow Puritan ministers as a counselor, judge, and arbiter on vexing questions. His success in playing such a role was owing to his reputation for equanimity, candor, judgment, and deep learning. This admiration for his "parts and graces" is reflected in a comment written after the Restoration by Edward Reyner, a longtime English Puritan who was among Cotton's correspondents as early as 1627. More than a decade after Cotton's death, and thirty years after Reyner could last have seen him, he singled Cotton out from a list of "eminently Learned" New England ministers:

> [Cotton's] Name is as an ointment poured forth, a most deservedly famous man of God, of whom Mr. *Norton* . . . relates, that he was a General Scholar, studious to know all things, the want whereof might in one of his Profession be denominated Ignorance. The Greater part of the *Encyclopædia* he excelled in. Those *Arts,* which the University requires such a proficiency in from her Graduates, he both digested and refined by his more accurate knowledge of them. He was a good *Hebrician;* in *Greek* a Critic; and could with great facility both speak and write *Latine* in a pure elegant *Ciceronian* stile. He was a good *Historian;* no stranger to the *Fathers, Schoolmen, Councils;* abundantly exercised in Commentators of all sorts. His Library was great, his reading and Learning was answerable, himself a living and better Library. But though he was a constant Student, yet he had not all his Learning out of his books.[42]

40. Epistle "To the Christian Reader," in John Cotton, *Gods Mercie Mixed with His Ivstice* . . . (London, 1641), sig. A2v.

41. [Whiting], "Concerning the Life of the Famous Mr. Cotton," in Young, *Chronicles of the First Planters,* 425–426.

42. Edward Reyner, *A Treatise of the Necessity of Humane Learning for a Gospel-Preacher* (London, 1663), 232–233.

That a man with such a reputation should have received appeals for advice and counsel from many sources is not surprising. Another contemporary and correspondent, Thomas Allen, after remigrating to England recalled Cotton as "a man of peace, of a very sweet spirit, and had a special faculty of composing differences in the judgements of Brethren: and thus much I shall crave liberty to testifie of him, that, besides the multiplicity of occasions which was constantly upon him, he was not without care about the *Peace* and welfare of the Churches abroad; and notwithstanding his so vast a distance in body from the Churches and Saints in his Native Countrey, yet he had great thoughts of *heart* for the *Division* of his Brethren here, being seriously studious how to compose and heale their breaches."[43]

John Wilson, who was Cotton's Boston colleague during his nineteen years in New England, wrote a long letter to a member of Cromwell's circle after Cotton's death in which he abundantly bore out all these encomia. Wilson's vantage point was closer than that of Reyner or Allen or, indeed, any of Cotton's earliest biographers such as Samuel Whiting, John Norton, and John Davenport. Wilson's description of Cotton's method of dealing with cases that were put to him, therefore, is of particular interest. Cotton

> never had any question propounded, but took a pause to answere, consultinge first with heaven, desiringe first to heare what any other sayed (as his brethren) in any case of moment, and ever sure to acknowledg and attest that what soe ever was pertinent, gatheringe vp that was sayed by others, as to bring the matter to a satisfactorie conclusion vnto all, by what hee added of his owne. A most skilfull compounder of all differences in doctrine or practise according to God.

Not only was he deliberate and careful, according to Wilson, but also particularly in touch with the wisdom of God:

> I never knewe a man more moderate, and patient, and long suffering, and soe adheringe to the truth as not iustly to offend any gainesayer. He spoke generally nothing but the Oracles of God (a man would haue thought hee heard the prophet or Apostle himself speake, it was with such demonstration of *th*e spirit)[.] Hee had a better concordance in his head then is to bee found in any booke. His language was iust that [of] Canaan, whether hee spake or writt.[44]

43. Epistle "To the Reader," in John Cotton, *The Covenant of Grace Discovering the Great Work of a Sinners Reconciliation to God* (London, 1655). Cotton Mather later emphasized this quality in his grandfather: "Many cases were brought unto him far and near, in resolving whereof, as he took much time, so he did much good, being a most excellent *casuist*" (Mather, *Magnalia,* I, 251).

44. John Wilson to H. W., September 20, [1657?], in a manuscript volume, "Letters Ad-

Such unanimous confirmation by his remembrancers of his "special faculty of composing differences" led to the burden of an ever-broadening correspondence, both in the colonies and in his "Native Countrey." He was viewed by many of his fellow ministers as a kind of court of last appeal on difficult questions of conscience, especially as they related to polity and theology. (Wilson observed, with silent but pointed reference to New England's controversies during Cotton's lifetime: "His counsell in church matter and order was exact, and happie for vs if all had taken it at the first rise.") Ever willing to reply, Cotton eventually found the heavy demand a problem for him, one that he occasionally notes in his letters, apologizing for saying no more but excusing himself on the grounds of the amount of writing he was called upon to do. It was the price he paid for remaining, in the minds of his peers, at the heart of the Puritan movement.

Most of the letters Cotton wrote and received have now, three and a half centuries after they were written, long since disappeared. But, against great odds, a significant collection of 125 letters and letter fragments written by or to John Cotton has survived. All are published here, enabling us to bring into sharper focus John Cotton the letter-writer. In doing so, we gain a fuller understanding of Cotton the man. Those letters include some eighty-four correspondents, plus another thirty-nine signers of a single letter who were all members of Parliament or the Westminster Assembly.[45] A few of these correspondents are nameless to us now, though the great majority have been identified. There is also evidence that Cotton corresponded with still other known individuals whose letters have not survived. They include the earl of Lincoln, the earl of Dorset, bishop of Bangor Lewis Bayly, William Twisse, Hugh Peter, Edward Winslow, the poet Francis Quarles, New Haven's teacher William Hooke, Thomas Wilson of Otham, Kent, "Old Mr. Hall" (probably Bishop Joseph Hall), a Lincolnshire minister, Mr. Bell, and a young German minister, Egbert Grim. There must have been ex-

---

dressed to Oliver Cromwell," The Society of Antiquaries of London, MS 138 (1649–1658), no. 128. The letters in this collection that were specifically addressed to Cromwell were published by John Nickolls, the owner of the collection, in 1743. Wilson's letter—a copy, not in Wilson's hand, and presumably addressed to a member of Cromwell's circle—has not been published. The letter is quoted here with the kind permission of The Society of Antiquaries of London.

45. Several of the letters have more than one signer, but in almost every case it is clear that all the signers—in one case thirteen of them—were personally acquainted with Cotton. The one exception is the letter in 1642 from thirty-nine members of both houses of Parliament inviting Cotton to come as one of New England's representatives to the Westminster Assembly. Some of the signers knew Cotton personally, though clearly they are signing as members of a petitioning group rather than as personal acquaintances.

changes as well with such important friends as John Preston, Richard Sibbes, William Ames, John Angier, John Owen, and still others in the English Puritan community whom Cotton knew well. But his correspondents also include many who never rose to any particular eminence and are therefore forgotten today. Mary and Robert Burle, Nathaniel Norcross, Ralph Levett, and Lydia Gaunt, among others, were just such people whose letters, by chance, are preserved.

Letters were an important part of the postgraduate intellectual life for most in Cotton's generation of clerics. The Puritan network of correspondents was intricate, a critical component of their sense of community—of being connected even though they were increasingly dispersed during the Great Migration, having left their native shores for a distant wilderness. John Cotton played a central role in that network.[46]

The letters by and to Cotton that survive are seldom concerned with purely personal, domestic matters. Though there are fortunate exceptions—an earnest letter to his new wife, his "Sweet Hearte," Sarah, in 1632, a Latin letter in a youthful hand written to him by his eldest child, Seaborn, and a letter from Samuel Whiting sympathizing with him in the recent deaths of two of the Cotton children—the great majority of his letters deal with matters immediately related to his calling as a churchman and his adopted role as a teacher of his peers. They are almost never chatty and seldom reflect on the practical hardships and joys of daily life, though there are occasional glimpses of family illnesses or references to the day's journey, a borrowed saddle, a purchase of a barrel of meal for a friend, or simply admission of being overtired or of growing old. On several occasions, in fact, he replies to appeals for his counsel on the family concerns of his parishioners

46. Francis J. Bremer has mapped in detail the intricate connections within the Puritan community on both sides of the Atlantic Ocean. See Bremer, "Increase Mather's Friends: The Trans-Atlantic Congregational Network of the Seventeenth Century," American Antiquarian Society, *Proceedings,* XCIV (1984), 59–96. The role of letter-writing is central to Bremer's *Congregational Communion: Clerical Friendship in the Anglo-American Puritan Community, 1610–1692* (Boston, 1994). David Cressy devotes a chapter to the importance of correspondence to both those who emigrated and those who stayed behind in *Coming Over: Migration and Communication between England and New England in the Seventeenth Century* (Cambridge, 1987), chap. 9, "'A Constant Intercourse of Letters': The Transatlantic Flow of Information," 213–234. Larzer Ziff has maintained that "the Puritan party throughout the kingdom" became increasingly aware of Cotton's activities in Boston: "From conservative Archbishop Usher to zealous young Roger Williams, they sought correspondence or interviews with him, and Cotton's name was the most respected in a lengthening list of clergymen who were destined to serve in crucial public positions" (*Career of John Cotton,* 45).

or other acquaintances, dealing at such times with marriage proposals, an unwanted pregnancy, and the sexual profligacy of an unfaithful wife. The weather, though surely a major concern in seventeenth-century life, does not enter Cotton's correspondence. He is likewise silent about his diet, the birth of his children, and his finances. Perhaps this absence of reference to the particulars of daily experience in "the world" is a manifestation of the characteristic Puritan desire to subdue self; perhaps it is equally a function of the type of letters Cotton and others chose to save. But, as the correspondence now stands, what has been said of the letter-writing of Cotton's sometime adversary, Roger Williams, could equally describe Cotton: "He felt far more comfortable writing about public considerations or about the affairs of others than he did about himself."[47] Still, it would not be accurate to say the letters are impersonal. His love of scholarship and his deep immersion in it are frequently evident. His correspondence was an extension of his calling to the work of the Lord and to the specifically Puritan branch of Calvinist Protestantism that energized a religious and political movement in England and New England for a century and a half. His commitment to these values bespeaks the man; it is where he lived (Cotton to Sarah Cotton, Oct. 3, 1632; S[eaborn] C[otton] to Cotton, c. 1648–1651; Whiting to Cotton, [?1637–1652]).

Thus, if we are to take his full measure, we need to recognize that a considerable portion of his time was spent at his desk, in written dialogue with his contemporaries, both before and after his migration to New England. Indeed, some of the most immediately personal moments in his letters come when he occasionally recognizes the burden his correspondence and other professional commitments had become. An early English letter to Archbishop James Ussher mentions the shortage of time due to "continual Employments (too heavy for me)." In 1641, writing to Peter Bulkeley, he interrupts himself to say he cannot write any more that night because he is "knocked off," prevented by other demands on his time. In October 1651, "a busie season," with many letters to answer from abroad, he is again struggling to keep up, lamenting that he is a man "whose businesses are more than my dayes." The motif is recurrent; he pursued his work with what we would now call professional commitment. As Cotton Mather put it, "The work which lay upon him, could not have been performed without a *labour* more than ordinary" (Cotton to Ussher, May 31, 1626; Cotton to Bulkeley, Aug. 7, 1641; Cotton to John Elmeston, Oct. 18, 1651).[48]

47. Glenn W. LaFantasie, "Introduction," in Williams, *Correspondence,* I, xxx.

48. Mather, *Magnalia,* I, 251.

STAGES OF JOHN COTTON'S EPISTOLARY CAREER

Cotton's correspondence can be grouped in four successive phases of activity, each having a somewhat distinct focus of interest. The first phase comprises his entire twenty-one years as the vicar of St. Botolph's, Boston, in the diocese of Lincoln. Letters are extant only from the second half of that period, probably reflecting the increase of his letter-writing activity as his reputation broadened in both Puritan and non-Puritan circles throughout the nation, but perhaps also revealing an increased interest on his part in preserving his correspondence. These early letters are largely letters of counsel to other ministers, often younger than he, on how to be a good Puritan, though they are bracketed in 1621 and 1633 by letters to his bishop, John Williams.

The second phase of his career, overlapping with the end of the previous one, saw him focusing on the issue of emigration and the rationale behind it. His letters reveal his grappling with the question whether it would be better for him (and for others) to remain in England and face the possibility of punishment by the authorities or to flee overseas, where his ministry could continue.[49] The number of letters dealing with his confrontation of this issue is small, but they constitute an important group, given the profound significance of the dilemma for a whole generation of English Puritans. By the time he emigrated in the summer of 1633, he had established conversations with a wide circle of correspondents.[50]

No letters remain from the first fifteen months of Cotton's new life in America. Then there are just six before the spring of 1636, which saw the beginning of the controversy that would occupy his central energies for two years and more. Among those six are the beginnings of a long written exchange with Roger Williams regarding their fundamental disagreements on the two issues of Separatism and what Williams called "liberty of conscience." For better or worse, Cotton's contribution to this dialogue was important to the process through which the New England churches established their unique identity.

The third discernible period in Cotton's epistolary career, therefore, is devoted to controversy, chiefly the debate that became known as the Anti-

49. Janice Knight finds the tendency to accommodate certain compromises in order to stay at one's post and continue one's ministry a characteristic of the school of ministers with whom she associates Cotton. See *Orthodoxies in Massachusetts,* 44–49.

50. In his discussion of the various choices available to Puritan ministers faced with ecclesiastical challenges to their church practice, Tom Webster stresses the importance of consultation with other ministers in decision making (*Godly Clergy in Early Stuart England: The Caroline Puritan Movement c. 1620–1643* [Cambridge, 1997], 268–285).

nomian controversy, in which he was uncomfortably prominent. This episode would become a primary preoccupation in the intense period 1636–1638, during which his authority as spokesman for the Puritan way was severely challenged. The bitter argument ended in 1638, but troubling reminders persisted. Into the early 1640s, he continued to take up issues related to the matter. He had to defend himself repeatedly to his fellow colonists and to friends and critics in England and Scotland. His exchanges with Peter Bulkeley, who was writing a book on the Covenant of Grace, with John Wheelwright, living in forced exile in Exeter, and with William Coddington, grating under the penalty of disfranchisement while assuming a leadership role at Aquidneck, forced him again and again to return to key issues of the controversy.

His letters from the fourth period—the late 1640s until his death in 1652—are more miscellaneous than those of the earlier periods, though the single theme of baptism emerges from them, as it was beginning to do in the colony generally. Another topic that began to occupy the minds of laymen and clergy alike was authorship. Numerous letters show the increasing importance to Cotton and others of the writing and reception of books. The variety of issues he was asked to respond to was a consequence of his ever-widening circle of correspondents. The colony itself was growing and spinning off other colonies and communities outside its boundaries. Cotton corresponded with people in the colonies of Rhode Island, Connecticut, New Haven, and Plymouth as well as in outlying locations that are now in New Hampshire and Maine. Throughout his ministry, he continued to hear from and reply to English friends. His former congregation at St. Botolph's had often tried to lure him back. One letter, Pauline in its almost apostolic stance, was written to his friends there and published as the preface to a book Cotton said he wrote specifically for their benefit, *Of the Holinesse of Church-Members* (London, 1650) (Cotton to the Congregation and Church at Boston, Lincolnshire, 1650).

An exchange with Oliver Cromwell in 1651 indicates the care with which Cotton was following political developments in Britain and the respect with which he was still treated in English Puritan circles (a view registered nine years earlier in the letter from thirty-nine members of the houses of Parliament). His final letter, written to an ancient friend in Kent, takes up the subject of Cotton's interest in John Eliot's ministry to the Indians at Natick. In the last letters, from roughly 1649 to the end of his life, complaints of the symptoms of old age—physical infirmity, failing eyesight—become a leitmotif. Before contracting his final illness in the early autumn of 1652, he was well aware the end of his life and career was approaching (Cotton to John Elmeston, Oct. 12, 1652).

One of the most striking features of Cotton's correspondence throughout these three decades is the high level of confidence he had in his ability to give sound advice on church matters. This is reflected not only in the self-confidence expressed in his own letters but in the trust in his advice evident in the letters he received. One of his distinguished English Puritan correspondents, Dr. Thomas Goodwin, is said to have described Cotton as "that Apostle of this Age."[51] Goodwin's characterization of Cotton, implying his antitypical relationship to the apostles of the early Christian church, is apt. Cotton often seems to have been aware that he was playing such a role. This standing cannot be attributed simply to his being, like the early Christian apostles, a clerical leader in a land where new churches were frequently springing up, since he was already playing this role before emigration. From early in his career he studied the letters of the apostles and reflected on the meaning and efficacy of the art of epistolary composition. In an early sermon series on the First Epistle of John, Cotton listed six "benefits" from John's letter-writing: teaching, admonition, "practice" (stirring up to action), humiliation, strengthening the reader's faith, and increasing the reader's joy in faith. He purposely subordinated letter-writing to preaching, the latter being a converting ordinance, whereas (as in John's example) letters are written to those who are already believers.[52] So, while the potential results from writing are not as great as those from preaching, Cotton makes clear that in his own mind, and as Scripture proves, letter-writing is a valuable part of the acts of any apostle. His perseverance in this apostolic function continued throughout his life and was acknowledged by various voices on both sides of the ocean even long after his death.

Each period of his activity as a letter-writer has unique interest and sheds light on Cotton's nature and achievement. It must be acknowledged that any such construction of "stages" of his development as a letter-writer is artificial and even crude, given the fragmentary and partial survival of the primary evidence. But the four periods suggested here represent major phases of his active career, phases that, not surprisingly, are reflected in the content of the correspondence. Perhaps, therefore, focusing on some of the moments in each of the stages can bring us to fuller understanding of the man and his place and importance in the Puritan movement.

Cotton's premigration years are less frequently considered than his years in New England. But he is often cited as the example par excellence of the

51. Quoted in Increase Mather, *The Order of the Gospel, Professed and Practised by the Churches of Christ in New-England* (Boston, 1700), 74.

52. See John Cotton, *Christ the Fountaine of Life; or, Sundry Choyce Sermons on Part of the Fift Chapter of the First Epistle of St. John* (London, 1651), 178–181.

Puritan preacher who was able to stick to his post through repeated threats from the established church for nearly two decades, at a time when many others were succumbing to the church's demand for conformity. In the end, however, he was forced out at roughly the same time as most other prominent non-Separatist preachers. He avoided the sojourn in Holland that Thomas Hooker, John Davenport, Hugh Peter, Thomas Goodwin, Philip Nye, and others of their generation experienced, though he was in touch with colleagues there. Geoffrey Nuttall has observed that a Dutch contemporary, Johannis Hoornbeeck, claimed that the congregational church at Rotterdam was formed by Hugh Peter "on instructions from Cotton received by letter from New England." Since Hugh Peter was in Holland by 1628 and was already ordering the Rotterdam church by 1629 or 1630, Hoornbeeck was mistaken at least as regards the claim that Cotton exerted his influence there from New England.[53] It is very likely, however, that Cotton was in correspondence with Hugh Peter in Rotterdam, whether or not he had a determining influence on Peter's understanding of Independency. The forced movements of the Puritans out of England ensured that an effort to stay in touch would often involve an international dimension, and this was certainly true in Cotton's case.

He considered going to Holland, only to be dissuaded by Hooker, whose letter from Rotterdam reported an absence of "heart religion" and "the power of godliness" there.[54] Hooker had been in Holland for two years, so his remark in the spring of 1633 that "my ague yet holds me" would have been enough by itself to prevent Cotton's following him to Holland, since Cotton had only recently recovered from a long siege of the same disease, a malarial affliction that had taken his wife Elizabeth's life. On October 2, 1630, Cotton mentioned having already suffered "ten fits" of "a quartane ague," and by early November he had counted "21 fits" with the illness "still continuinge."[55] Having recovered by early 1632, he probably felt little temptation to risk a relapse by moving to the Low Countries. Cotton was able to stay

53. Nuttall, *Visible Saints,* 15. Peter arrived in Rotterdam in the latter half of 1629. His biographer notes that "within a short time [he] was able to enlist Dutch financial support and to reorganize the church, now one of the largest English flocks in the Low Countries, upon a stricter Congregational model" (Raymond Phineas Stearns, *The Strenuous Puritan: Hugh Peter, 1598–1660* [Urbana, Ill., 1954], 56). Stearns does not mention Cotton's influence in this matter, nor does he mention Hoornbeeck. Cotton Mather, on the other hand, repays Hoornbeeck rather roughly for accepting Robert Baillie's criticisms of Cotton and publishing his own Latin secondhand account of Cotton's supposed transgressions; see Mather, *Magnalia,* I, 145–146.

54. See Hooker to Cotton, [c. April 1633].

55. See Cotton to Samuel Skelton, Oct. 2, 1630, and to Jeremiah Burroughes, [November 1630].

at his post in Boston somewhat longer than some through a combination of politically influential Boston laypersons, friends among the titled aristocracy, and a more indulgent bishop than colleagues were blessed with in East Anglia, where Bishop William Laud held sway before becoming archbishop of Canterbury. From the time that he finally joined up with Hooker and fled to New England in July 1633, he had another nineteen years of active service to give, all of it as teacher to the first church in the new Boston. He served that congregation only two years less than he had served in the first Boston, until his death in December 1652. His forty-year post-Cambridge career was thus neatly divided in half, in a manner of speaking, by the Atlantic Ocean. In both places, he played a key role in defining, strengthening, and consolidating the notion of what it meant to be a Nonconformist, an Independent, a Puritan. Letter-writing was always central to that mission.

1. Lincolnshire

Throughout his two decades as vicar of St. Botolph's Church in Boston, Cotton was deepening his understanding of the meaning of Nonconformity while practicing resistance to what he and other Puritans saw as human inventions in divine worship, which they believed ought to be fully governed by the dictates and example of Scripture. His first surviving letter, dated August 30, 1621, is written to the Welshman John Williams, who had just been appointed as the third—and last—bishop under whom Cotton would serve in the diocese of Lincoln. Williams was a favorite of James I.[56] The letter offers Cotton's own highly charged defense of his disagreements with the local and national church. When it was composed, Williams, recently invested as lord keeper of the great seal, had also been selected to become the new bishop of Lincoln but was not to be consecrated in that post until two months later. Cotton at this point was in his mid-thirties and had been at Boston for nine years. Having already experienced the oversight of two other bishops, and their attendant pressures on him to conform, his letter is an attempt to reach the new bishop with his own point of view on the critical subject of conformity before Cotton's opponents could get to him.[57] A sense of bitterness over the recent attacks upon him shows through Cotton's rather formal and deferential style. Cotton rehearses the charges that had already been made against him by his critics over the previous several years. It is a skillful piece

56. My "John Cotton's Correspondence: A Census," *Early American Literature,* XXIV (1989), 91–111, incorrectly recorded this letter to Bishop Williams as dating from 1631.

57. He was formally questioned on this issue in both 1616 and 1621; see Clive Holmes, *Seventeenth-Century Lincolnshire* (Lincoln, Lincs., 1980), 95–96.

of diplomacy and tact, pleading for the bishop's indulgence of Cotton's further inquiries into the truth as regards lawful forms of worship. Given that he had experienced severe stress from the effort to reconcile his own convictions with the church's requirement of conformity for some considerable time, it is amazing that Cotton was able to remain at his post for more than another decade—and that Williams was able to resist pressure from above for that long to close him down. Between 1621 and 1625, while James I remained in power, Cotton benefited from Williams's influence at court and indeed from James's admiration for scholarship.[58] John Norton reports that Cotton "was in great favour with Doctor *Williams,* the then Bishop of *Lincoln,* who much esteemed him for his learning, and (according to report) when he was Lord keeper of the great Seal, went to King *James,* and speaking of Mr *Cottons* great learning and worth, the King was willing notwithstanding his non-conformity, to give way that he should have his liberty without interruption in his Ministry, which was the more notable considering how that Kings spirit was carried out against such men."[59]

From the beginning of Cotton's tenure at St. Botolph's, the congregation was sharply divided on the question of conformity to prescribed forms of worship. In the spring of 1621 desecration of the church building signaled the severity of local divisions, focusing the attention of the church authorities more intently on Boston.[60] These Boston disagreements were thus at a high point when Williams took over the diocese. Over the next dozen years Williams's indulgence of Cotton's Puritan predilections became well known in English ecclesiastical circles. During those final twelve years of Cotton's Lincolnshire ministry he increasingly put his learning, his judgment, and his experience at the disposal of others in the Puritan movement. With remarkable consistency his correspondence for the 1620s and early 1630s indicates his growing importance as a pastoral counselor to clerical colleagues. In fact, he provides a classic example of those Puritans who were central to "the growth in the sense of solidarity and autonomy among the godly"

58. On Williams and court politics under James I, see Fincham, *Prelate as Pastor,* 35, 39–41. Fincham observes that Williams was a bishop "hungry for political power" (44).

59. Norton, *Abel Being Dead yet Speaketh,* 18.

60. Ziff, *Career of John Cotton,* 50–54. An aggressively Anglican critique of Cotton's Lincolnshire career appears in [Nicholas Hoppin], "The Rev. John Cotton, A.M.," *Church Monthly,* IV (1862), 161–167, V (1863), 40–54. Jesper Rosenmeier's recent work on this period sheds further light on the way local politics contributed to the church dissension. I am grateful to Professor Rosenmeier for sharing with me his unpublished essay, "'Eaters and Non-Eaters': John Cotton in Boston, Lincolnshire, 1621–22," delivered at the Modern Language Association meeting, Chicago, December 1990.

that characterized what Stephen Foster has called the middle period of the Puritan movement.[61]

He was gaining a reputation as a Nonconformist survivor at a time when others were not faring so well. Samuel Ward, the minister at Ipswich, Suffolk, confessed, "Of all men in the world I envy Mr. Cotton, of Boston, most; for he doth nothing in way of conformity, and yet hath his liberty, and I do everything that way, and cannot enjoy mine."[62] Ward was simply expressing a collective awareness of Cotton's special success in continuing his very popular ministry throughout a period of widespread silencing of his fellow Puritans. The combination of tact and strongly principled resolution seen in his early letters to Williams helps to explain how he survived the repression of Puritans as long as he did.

In that critical first letter to Bishop Williams, Cotton protests his loyalty to king and church, excepting only a few (not all) of the prescribed ceremonies of worship. But he is already speaking from the context of several years of scrutiny of his practices, inquiries that have threatened him, he says, with the ultimate penalty of silencing. He had, in fact, been temporarily suspended by both Bishop Richard Neile in 1616 and Bishop George Montaigne in 1621. The depth to which he felt that persecution, as he saw it, and his fear of the consequences are suggested in the list of epithets with which he tells the bishop he had lately been labeled: "enemy to the church," "rebel," "disrupter," and "revolutionary." His rhetorical eloquence climaxes in a flourish in which he laments that the ultimate danger is to be thrown "in invisum silentii sepulchrum," into the hateful tomb of silence. This, together with "exile," which he also mentions, was the ultimate threat for all Nonconformist Puritans, and at the beginning of the two decades of the Great Migration to New England it was very much on Cotton's mind. Still, the theme of resistance, tactfully registered here in his self-introduction to Bishop Williams, would be the theme of many of Cotton's exchanges for the next dozen years. He was already very much involved in the search for a workable balance between conscientious refusal to engage in certain of the ordinances of worship, a form of resistance that had characterized normal practice at Emmanuel College, and a literal carrying out of all the church's dicta on the subject. What he had experienced in the previous decade became the basis for his advice to numerous younger Puritan ministers in the decade to come. Even in its extremely precise handwriting—it is as neat a manuscript as Cot-

61. Foster, *Long Argument,* 97.

62. [Whiting], "Concerning the Life of the Famous Mr. Cotton," in Young, *Chronicles of the First Planters,* 427.

ton ever created—and its careful classical Latin, this first letter, unpublished until now despite its immaculate condition, clearly conveys to us Cotton's ability to show his respect for his new bishop's learning and his eminence in the church while also saying he did not expect to be able to conform to all of the church's requirements. It is a winning combination of flattery and self-revelation (Cotton to Williams, Aug. 30, 1621).

Cotton's ministry was drawing large numbers of congregants to St. Botolph's from Boston and the surrounding villages and countryside. That this is an important factor in the church's toleration of his Puritanism becomes evident in a second letter to Bishop Williams, written some three years later. Writing this time in English, Cotton is replying to an inquiry about reports of his "Inconformity." There had been a number of disruptive disagreements between conformist and Puritan elements in the church and community there in the late 1610s and early 1620s, including smashing of the church's stained-glass windows and statuary and mutilation of the mayor's ceremonial robe in 1621. Sermons of Robert Sanderson and of Cotton himself allude to these events.[63] Although Williams's responsibilities at court had kept him from close supervision of the Lincolnshire diocese thus far, Cotton's answer to inquiries about local worship practice suggests that Williams was by early 1625 feeling some pressure to supervise more closely independent-minded clerics like Cotton. In its deliberately punctilious, at times obsequious style and again in its extremely tidy handwriting, this second letter conveys one facet of Cotton's personality. He was careful, deliberate, and politic. In replying to his superior regarding his lack of conformity in some church ceremonies, Cotton cagily notes that "throngs" of worshipers are flooding in to St. Botolph's. However much Williams was hearing complaints from the more strictly conformist church members in Boston, it was clear that the "multitude of Com*m*unicants" were voting with their feet in flocking to Cotton's services from the surrounding countryside. As both bishop and vicar well understood, there was power as well as danger in popularity (Cotton to Williams, Jan. 31, 1624/5).

Cotton was not alone in feeling the conflict between Puritan principle and political reality. From at least the early 1620s on, as ecclesiastical scrutiny of

63. Jesper Rosenmeier, "'Eaters and Non-Eaters,'" considers Robert Sanderson's *XXXV Sermons* (London, 1681) and the political and ecclesiastical implications of Cotton's *Brief Exposition of the Whole Book of Canticles* . . . (London, 1642), published fifteen years later from an auditor's notes. See also Ziff, *Career of John Cotton*, 49–59. Sanderson's "Ad Clerum" also appears in his *X Sermons* (London, 1627), where he explains the unusual use of quotation marks in the sermons, an important factor for the scholar that was omitted in the 1681 edition.

the parish clergy intensified, Cotton increasingly became the counselor of troubled Puritan ministers around the nation. Among the surviving letters are many examples from junior and senior ministers who turned to Cotton with questions about difficult cases or practical problems they faced in their own churches or communities.

Meanwhile, students came to him from Cambridge, from Leiden and Franeker in the Netherlands, and Germany at the same time that others were going out to such locations from his informal Boston seminary. His letters tell of an overflowing household there near the end of his active English ministry. As a result, a considerable body of alumni of Cotton's seminary were spread around England and the Low Countries well before the early 1630s, when Cotton himself had to begin to think seriously about moving on. These students became some of the numerous correspondents he acquired over the years, bound to him by a kind of loving loyalty. To them, Cotton was a spiritual and ecclesiastical father. Such men, while getting their clerical feet under them, continued to look to him for advice on difficult questions of church practice. And he continued unstintingly to reply, usually speaking with certainty and authority of his understanding of contested issues. On at least one occasion, he is known to have admonished a former intern, Egbert Grim, who was ministering in Wesel, Germany, for falling away from the pure understanding of church ways that he had heard from Cotton. Thus his fatherly role, though usually evident in a positive, supportive form, could on occasion have a stern disciplinary force.[64]

Such contacts were an important part of the glue that united Puritans of various stripes and locales over many decades. Puritanism was a vast and extended "movement," evolving and changing in some of its dimensions but staying intact from the late sixteenth century in England to the mid-

64. Stephen Goffe to William Boswell, May 5, 1633, notes that Grim "was much misliked by our puritans . . . And by that thesis he gott the ill will of all that tribe. Mr. Cotton of Boston sent him a letter about it blaming his medling & Dr. Ames another" (Boswell Papers, B.L. I, 134, quoted in Raymond Phineas Stearns, *Congregationalism in the Dutch Netherlands: The Rise and Fall of the English Congregational Classis, 1621–1635*, Studies in Church History, IV [Chicago, 1940], 50). Grim (1608–1636) had gone from William Ames's tutelage at Franeker to Cotton's at Boston (Sprunger, *William Ames*, 237). He probably arrived at Wesel, near the Dutch border, in 1629 with the Dutch troops who liberated the town from the occupying Spaniards. He was engaged as a teacher at the grammar school in Wesel in 1632, where he reestablished the English church following the Spanish Catholic occupation. His period there was brief, however, as he died in 1636 at the age of twenty-eight. This information on Grim was generously provided by Dr. Roelen of the Stadtarchiev in Wesel. See *Festschrift zur Feier der Einweihung des neuen Gymnasialgebäudes am 18. Oktober 1882* (Wesel, 1882), 85, 162; Hermann Kleinholz and Wolfgang Petri, *Sitzungsberichte der Convente der reformierten weseler Classis, 1611–1662* (Cologne, 1980), 90, 108, 110.

eighteenth century in America.[65] The movement had its effect on its members in the way they conducted their personal lives and in the way they thought about community, from local to national levels. Like other historically powerful movements, Puritanism depended on key leaders to voice its values and principles. While the sermon was the most common form of discourse through which Puritan ideology received and sustained its fundamental identity, private channels of communication were also critical.

Just as this aspect of Cotton's calling was becoming more prominent, he began preaching that series of sermons on the First Epistle of John in which he reflected on the biblical example of a major letter-writer, analyzing for his congregation the different religious and rhetorical functions of the sermon and the letter. The pastoral function of prophecy was the sine qua non for bringing unbelievers to faith. Letters—even the apostles' letters—could not do this. *"Faith comes* not by reading, but by *hearing,* therefore the Apostle writes not to them that beleeve not, but to such as are beleevers."[66] As Cotton was preaching on the apostle's letters, he was also engaging in his own epistolary ministry. His letters to faithful ministers never presume to usurp the converting function of sermons, but consciously imitate the ancient models provided by John and Paul and their apostolic contemporaries.

65. The work of Patrick Collinson has led the way in establishing this view of English Puritanism; see especially *The Elizabethan Puritan Movement* (London, 1967), 11, where Collinson most comprehensively makes the case for a "puritan movement, as distinct from puritanism." Recently Stephen Foster has argued for continuity of this movement from England to New England in *The Long Argument.* This point of view has also characterized much of the work of Francis J. Bremer; in addition to his *Congregational Communion,* see Bremer, *The Puritan Experiment: New England Society from Bradford to Edwards* (New York, 1976); and Bremer, introduction, "Puritan Studies: The Case for an Atlantic Approach," in Bremer, ed., *Puritanism: Transatlantic Perspectives on a Seventeenth-Century Anglo-American Faith* (Boston, 1993), xi–xvii.

66. Cotton, *Christ the Fountaine of Life,* 181. These sermons were delivered at St. Botolph's Church and suggest that the context was the live issue of conformity to the officially sanctioned ordinances of worship in the place in which they were being delivered. They were probably preached in the latter part of the 1620s, and perhaps as late as 1632 (Emerson, *Cotton,* 138). The sermons in *Christ the Fountaine of Life* are full of reference to the need for believers to worship God through "the Ordinances" in a way consistent with their consciences. "If we cannot enjoy the liberty of the Ordinances, but with sinne against our soules, in this case the Ordinances of God are to be neglected, and omitted, if he cannot have them with innocency and purity to his soule, he must let them goe" (22–23). This is the language of Puritan resistance in England during the years of the Great Migration to New England. By at least September 1630, Cotton had been overtaken by serious illness, which caused him to take leave from his preaching duties for a time. He had largely recovered by the time of his remarriage in April 1632, but soon thereafter he was driven into hiding. The sermons in *Christ the Fountaine* could therefore have been delivered as late as 1632, but the pre-illness period seems more likely (Emerson, *Cotton,* 138).

Through preaching, ministers brought unbelievers to faith; through writing, they strengthened believers in their faith. The centrality of the epistolary function to the coherence of the Puritan movement had in the minds of its practitioners a clear biblical model.

During his remaining seven years at Boston, his importance to the strength of the Puritans' resistance to ecclesiastical coercion in the matter of ceremonies was reflected in the kind of requests for advice and counsel that he received. Single letters or exchanges with nineteen different individuals have survived for the years 1626–1632. These exchanges demonstrate the extent to which Cotton had become known as one whose wise counsel was available for the asking. Several of these individuals were younger ministers facing challenges at the outset of their careers or at moments of crisis or danger. Among the younger men who brought questions bearing on their Puritan identity to the more experienced Cotton were Ralph Levett (serving as a private chaplain in Lincolnshire), Herbert Palmer (later a famous catechist and leader at the Westminster Assembly), Edward Reyner (a lecturer in the cathedral city of Lincoln), Charles Chauncy (later the president of Harvard College), John Nicolaus Rulice (a German serving an English congregation), Timothy Van Vleteren (a Dutch Puritan and friend of several Cotton students), and Jeremiah Burroughes (later one of the five leading Independents at the Westminster Assembly). Mixed in with these men at early stages of their careers were veterans of Cotton's own age or older—the venerable Arthur Hildersham, for instance, along with archbishop of Armagh James Ussher, Nathaniel Ward, Nathaniel Rogers, and Thomas Hooker. Cotton was also in touch with a number of other men serving on the Continent, including Hugh Goodyear at Leiden, and a couple of acquaintances from Boston, John Dinley (then chaplain to the queen of Bohemia) and Colonel Sir Edward Harwood (one of the four English colonels serving in the Low Countries). These few surviving letters demonstrate Cotton's significance as an experienced veteran in the struggle against forced conformity.

Ralph Levett, a Yorkshire native and graduate of Christ's College, Cambridge, had been ordained in 1624. The opening sentence of his letter to Cotton, written March 3, 1625/6, indicates that Levett was one of the many recent students from Cambridge who spent some postgraduate time in Cotton's Boston household, preparing for formal entry into the ministry. In establishing an informal seminary in his household, Cotton was participating in a long-standing tradition that Patrick Collinson traces back at least to a 1580 conference of Puritan ministers that resolved that each minister ought to entertain a student of divinity, training him for the ministry. Among Cotton's known resident protégés were John Angier, Anthony Tuckney, Thomas

Hill, and Samuel Winter. There were many more. Indeed, John Preston recommended so many of his Cambridge graduates to Cotton that Cotton became known as "*Dr.* Preston's *seasoning vessel.*"[67]

Levett's case is interesting because at the time of his letter to Cotton he was serving as a private chaplain to the Wray family at Ashby-cum-Fenby in Lincolnshire. In such a position, he was protected from the direct oversight of the larger church and was more or less free to practice his Puritanism, subject only to the will of his employers. Nevertheless, the situation posed problems of conscience to a young Puritan cleric, and he writes to Cotton seeking advice on some very particular practical issues that have arisen. He wonders whether—and how—to pray for "my lady," his patroness, when she is present in the congregation. More tied to his Puritan inclinations is his doubt about entertainments, especially those he witnessed at Christmastime, where there was "cardinge" (card playing) and "mixt dancinge." Valentine's Day had also taken him unawares, as he was approached by the household's "2. young Ladyes" to draw a name out of a hat; "ev*ery* one drawes a Valentin (so they terme it)." His Puritan principles were clearly being challenged as he considered what was an appropriate response for him as a minister of God on the one hand and an employee of the family on the other. So he looked to his mentor for advice (Levett to Cotton, Mar. 3, 1625/6).

Cotton's answers are direct and detailed, providing just the sort of assistance and, in most cases, support for Levett's inclinations that the younger man had sought. He tells Levett how to pray in public so as not to invite the charge of flattering his patroness, opposes carding and drawing names for Valentines on the ground that they are lotteries, but finds no fault with dancing, opposing only "lasciuious dauncinge to wanton dittyes & in amorous gestures & wanton dalliances especially after great feasts." Levett clearly feels justified in troubling Cotton with these questions because of his experience of Cotton's "former love" in his household in Boston. Settling into his first ministerial post, not quite weaned from Cotton's tutorial nurture, Levett is somewhat uncertain in attempting to establish a ministerial presence that will make the right statement of principles while also meeting the needs of the family in whose service he ministers. Nothing in Cotton's answer could

67. See Patrick Collinson, *The Religion of Protestants: The Church in English Society, 1559–1625* (Oxford, 1982), 119; John Morgan, *Godly Learning: Puritan Attitudes towards Reason, Learning, and Education, 1560–1640* (Cambridge, 1986), 293–300. Bremer provides a long list of such "private schools" and their students (*Congregational Communion,* 37–40), as does Tom Webster (*Godly Clergy in Early Stuart England,* 15–35). On John Cotton's practice, see also Ziff, *Career of John Cotton,* 43–44; Mather, *Magnalia,* I, 238.

have given Levett any reason to think he had presumed too much in asking these questions. Cotton is available as a resource to help this young minister get firmly settled in the ministry (Cotton to Levett, [March 1625/6]).

The situation for the young Edward Reyner thirteen months later was similar in one respect: he too was conscious of being a neophyte in the matter of applying Puritan principles to his performance of his new duties. An exact contemporary of Levett, Reyner had become lecturer at Peters at the Arches, Lincoln, about six weeks before his letter to Cotton.[68] Like Levett, Reyner implies an ongoing acquaintance with Cotton and ends by saying, "My wife and I remembere our loue to you and yours," suggesting that this single letter is part of a larger context of friendship and, probably, counsel by the older minister. Unfortunately, Cotton's reply has not survived. Reyner's letter was written, however, in order to carry out the requests of two other ministers, both of whom had asked him to put a case of conscience before Cotton so that they in turn could advise troubled parishioners. They clearly knew that Reyner already had Cotton's ear; by now Cotton was receiving appeals from "far and near."

The first request, Reyner says, came from "Mr Langley of Treswel," Nottinghamshire, the adjacent county to the west. Langley was much older than Reyner, having received his bachelor's degree at Christ's College, Cambridge, in 1603, placing him very close in age to Cotton himself, though his approach to Cotton through Reyner suggests no immediate acquaintance between them. Langley's question is unknown to us, since it was detailed in an enclosure, now lost, which Reyner sent along with his cover letter. The other case was put to Reyner by "Good Mr. Wales (whom you know)," who "is much perplexed as you may understand by Mr Petchels Letter [another enclosure] and hath longed after your resolution of his doubt to help him out of *th*e briers." The inquirer is Elkanah Wales, who was perpetual curate at Pudsey, Yorkshire, from 1616 to 1662, but good Mr. Wales's question also remains unknown to us. Reyner then says, "Troubling you thus with *th*e doubts of others, I am not willing to trouble you further with my owne," though he proceeds to do so anyway, saying, "I haue beene put upon it in my self lately to study *th*e point, whether a man may be safely ignorant of *th*e lawfulnes or ~~Un~~lawfulnes of church-Ceremonyes in *th*e word." He concludes that he "must search *th*e Script*ure* for a Ground of doing or refusing them." Having expressed this much, of course, he has implied an invitation to Cotton to help him answer the question. Thus, in one brief letter, Reyner presents Cotton with three prickly questions from three different ministers. As was said

68. *Calamy Revised,* 408; Edmund Calamy, *Nonconformist's Memorial . . . ,* ed. Samuel Palmer (London, 1802–1803), II, 421–427.

of Thomas Hooker's role during this same period among the local ministers and students around Chelmsford, Essex, and as Reyner would later say of Cotton, he was their "living . . . Library" (Reyner to Cotton, Apr. 5, [1627?]).[69]

Less than a year later Cotton heard from a man just seven years his junior, Charles Chauncy, announcing, "I am now (by God's good hand) vickar of Ware, and desire your best direction how I may with most profit and edification of my charge proceed in the Lord's work." Such a sweeping request for assistance from a thirty-five-year-old vicar can be explained only by the fact that Chauncy had until then been protected from the real struggles of the parish ministry by his appointment as fellow of Trinity College, Cambridge, where he acquired a reputation as an outstanding scholar of both classical and oriental languages. He was briefly vicar of St. Michael's in Cambridge before taking the post at Ware in his home county of Hertfordshire. The inexperienced but brilliant minister, it seems, thought first of asking advice from John Cotton, whom he might well have known in Cambridge fifteen years earlier.

Chauncy complains of the "dissolute town" and of the previous lack of adequate instruction from which the people in this "barren wilderness" suffer. He is particularly concerned about the challenge his principles will meet "in regard to the government and discipline of our church." He expects he will face troubles because of his opposition to certain aspects of the Thirty-nine Articles, "which we are bound to read publicly and to yield our assent unto." He says, "The article concerning the ordination of bishops and ministers doth somewhat trouble me, as also the ceremonies which we are bound unto, which though I forbear myself, yet I know not how to avoid but that my curate must use if I will stand here." He then renews his request to Cotton: "I pray afford your wisest advice herein" (Chauncy to Cotton, Mar. 15, 1627/8).

Coming from this particular man, the letter is especially poignant, now that we know his subsequent history. Chauncy was well aware in early 1628 of the danger that lay before him in serving in the public ministry at just the time of the unleashing of the wrath of William Laud against the vile Puritans. His earnest plea to Cotton for advice was not idle. But Chauncy proved much less successful than his adviser in keeping clear of ecclesias-

69. Reyner, *A Treatise of the Necessity of Humane Learning,* 233. Hooker's opponents in Essex complained to the church authorities that he was especially influential with younger ministers; he was "an oracle and their principal library." Great Britain, Public Record Office, *Calendar of State Papers,* Domestic Series, *Of the Reign of Charles I,* ed. John Bruce, William Douglas Hamilton, and Sophia Crawford Lomas (London, 1858–1897), III, *1628–1629,* 554; T. W. Davids, *Annals of Evangelical Nonconformity in the County of Essex* . . . (London, 1863), 150–153.

tical justice. Three years later, on April 30, 1630, Chauncy was cited by the Court of High Commission for typical Puritan misdeeds: "the omission of Athanasius's Creed, the Lesson from the Old Testament, the Litany, the surplice, the cross in Baptism, and the exhortation in Matrimony, 'With my body I thee worship,' with various speeches in the pulpit and elsewhere, in praise of the Puritans, in disparagement of the authority of the church, and in anticipation of changes likely to ensue in church and state, in expectation whereof he asserted that some families were preparing to go to New England."[70] He ostensibly submitted to Bishop Laud's accusation six weeks later, buying himself time at Ware. Three years later, in October 1633, he would become vicar at Marston, St. Lawrence, in Northamptonshire, only to be fined, imprisoned, and finally humbled two years later following the High Commission's charge against him of contempt of ecclesiastical authority for opposing the building of a kneeling rail in his former church at Ware. Like Cotton and other Puritans, Chauncy preferred to have the congregants receive the Last Supper seated or standing. Laud on this occasion made an example of Chauncy, who finally succumbed by publicly reading a statement of submission to the prescribed forms of worship, including "kneeling at the receiving of the holy communion," and abjectly promising "never by word or deed to oppose either that or any other the laudable rites and ceremonies prescribed and commanded to be used in the church of England." The issues Chauncy raised with Cotton were absolutely central to him and to his fellow Puritans.[71]

We do not have Cotton's reply to Chauncy, but he doubtless offered his best advice on this and perhaps on some of the later occasions. Chauncy invited him to stop at Ware "in transitu" as he traveled south, it being exactly on the way from Boston to London. On his part, he promised to make personal contact with Cotton "once a year"; the importance of being a part of the Puritan network was very much on Chauncy's mind.

While Levett, Reyner, and Chauncy were all Cambridge-educated English Puritans, Cotton's seminary in the 1620s often included refugees from abroad, especially Germany and Holland, who had fled the Wars of the Palatinate. Other surviving letters include examples of Cotton's exchanges with four individuals closely connected with this experience. The earliest is a letter from John Nicolaus Rulice, a German minister from Heidelberg who had fled the Catholic persecutions in the early 1620s, apparently going first to Cambridge and then at some point to Boston before moving on to Kent and finally to Holland. His letter, written on November 29, 1628, as

70. *Cal. State Papers,* Dom. Ser., *Charles I,* IV, *1629–1631,* 233.

71. Ibid., IX, *1635–1636,* 123–124, 483, 490, 494–495.

he was preparing to embark for Holland, is mainly about his political maneuverings to obtain a lectureship in Kent. He goes into detail on this not so much to seek Cotton's help as to express his hopes to a mentor whose interest and encouragement he assumes. He concludes by asking for advice on how to conduct himself in his ministry once he is safely established in Holland. Other Cotton correspondents associated with Continental Puritanism include Hugh Goodyear, whom Cotton probably knew from Cambridge days and who had been at the English church in Leiden since 1616, and John Dinley, a Lincolnshire graduate of Christ's College, Cambridge, who was secretary to James's daughter Elizabeth, queen of Bohemia, in her forced exile in the Netherlands. Finally, there was Timothy Van Vleteren, a Dutch minister who had not been a member of Cotton's household seminary but who knew—and mentions—others who had. One thing characterizes all of these letters: the writer, whether it is Cotton or his correspondent, mentions other churchmen who are mutual acquaintances and share an interest in the Puritan movement. Their interdependence is one of the most striking features of these letters and is evidence of the community that existed among dispersed Puritans that ultimately spanned the Atlantic.

Both sides of Cotton's exchange with Timothy Van Vleteren have been preserved. Van Vleteren was from a Dutch family, though, like his father, he was born in England—at Sandwich, Kent, just across the channel from Holland. When he wrote to Cotton on October 26, 1629, he was the minister of the Dutch church in London (Austin Friars), though before that he had ministered at Souteland, near Middelburg in southwest Holland. His letter is written on the occasion of his forwarding a package of "papers" to Cotton from Maximilian Teelinck, whom Van Vleteren had known when Teelinck was minister at Vlissingen (or Fleissing) in 1627–1628 and Van Vleteren was at Souteland, just a few miles away. The other mutual friend is Isaac Bishop, Van Vleteren's successor at Souteland, "who hath vsed your table and rofe." Van Vleteren comments that "both these frindes have often spok of their ædification conversing *w*ith ijour reverence, and communicated their writinges from yoú vnto me namely Catechisme, on the Canticles, of predestination, sence witch time [I have] desired to be acquainted with súch a servant of Christ." His lack of acquaintance with Cotton does not prevent his putting a question to him: "It hath troubled me much in the matter of an oath, meditating on the 3 command*ment* whet[h]er a subiect is bound in Consience, when higher powers can affirme nothing against him, but súrmise or suspect of his faitfulness to sweare vpon interrgatories, or propositiones of their one [own] framing against him" (Van Vleteren to Cotton, Oct. 26, 1629).

Cotton's reply notes his pleasure at hearing of both Teelinck and Bishop: "I waite for an opportunity to write vnto *the*m both, as me*n* whom I much esteeme and affect, me[an]while let me intreate you w*hen* you write into those p*ar*ts Commend my deare affectio*n* to *the*m and tell *the*m *they* are both written in my heart though I can seldo*me* get liberty to write to *the*m, and many other good friends as I gladly would" (Cotton to Van Vleteren, Dec. 16, 1629). The fact that keeping up with his correspondence had become a burden reflects the role he was increasingly called on to play, that of adviser to his colleagues on points of discipline and interpreter of fundamental rules of Christian (and ministerial) behavior. His household seminary's alumni obviously held an important place in his memory, and he faithfully retained a recollection of their merits.

The training of such men and releasing them into the field to do their work was continuing. A 1630 letter to Hugh Goodyear at Leiden identifies the bearer of Cotton's letter as "Petrus Griebius, a German, who lived sometime here with vs, & whom God hath now gratiously fitted for publique service in his Church." Even as this "good yong man" leaves Cotton's household, another arrives, recommended by Goodyear. Cotton's seminary accommodations apparently had no vacancy at the time, but he found a way to welcome the unnamed newcomer from the Continent anyway, as he explains: "The yong man, whom you recom*m*end hither, is receyved to Table in my house, & (for want of roome w*i*th me) to lodging, in a neere neighbo*u*rs." Always remembering that the surviving fragments from Cotton's large correspondence must be just a small portion of the total, the recurrence of references to the young men whom Cotton nurtured at this critical early stage of their careers suggests the project must have occupied a considerable part of his energies (Cotton to Goodyear, Apr. 12, 1630).

With the arrival of the 1630s, Cotton's career was reaching a critical stage at the same time as the founding of the Massachusetts Bay Colony. His attentions were certainly drawn that way, as we know from his involvement in a planning conference in July 1629 at Sempringham Castle in Lincolnshire that was also attended by Hooker, Roger Williams, John Winthrop, and Emmanuel Downing.[72] Though he elected not to join the enterprise at that time, he was interested in the project, journeying all the way to Southampton in the next year to preach the farewell sermon to the Winthrop party. In a letter of October 3, 1630, to the Massachusetts Bay Company's Herbert Pelham in London, he arranged for a hogshead of meal to be sent to his Boston friend, William Coddington, already in New England at Naumkeak. Cotton's pre-emigration letter to Samuel Skelton at the same location (later Salem) is well known for its criticism of the church's early adoption of a selec-

72. George H. Williams, "The Life of Thomas Hooker in England and Holland, 1586–1633," in Williams et al., *Thomas Hooker,* 17.

tive membership practice and of the congregation's unwillingness to commune with other churches, a criticism he would recant just a few years later. While Cotton remained aware of the colonial experience, however, he was ever more conscious that political pressures were tightening, for him and for others (Cotton to Pelham, Oct. 3, 1630; Cotton to Skelton, Oct. 2, 1630).

Just a month after his letter to Skelton, he received one from Jeremiah Burroughes, who was then a lecturer in Bury St. Edmunds, Suffolk. He did not know Burroughes very well: "Though my acquaintance with you be small, yett the necessetie of the cause in which I shall desire your helpe, putts me on to repaire to you." This "cause" proves to be a major career decision, Burroughes having received an offer from "a gentlewoman, whom yett I neuer sawe, & I thinke she neuer sawe me, wherein she offred me a liuinge." Even though he senses he is no longer valued by community leaders in Bury, he is reluctant to take the new offer. Bury St. Edmunds "is a greate place & so perhapps some hope of more good then in a country village to which I am called." He wants to stay but fears he must go, so he appeals to Cotton to "helpe vs in our streights, & lett your answere be as full as it may conveniently," adding that "you & my tutor Hooker I esspecially rely on for Counsel vnder god" (Burroughes to Cotton, Nov. 1, [1630]).

Cotton's notes for an answer are brief. He explains, as he had done in the much longer letter to Skelton a month earlier, that he is weakened from having lately suffered greatly from ague. He does say, though, that one ought not "to pitch vpon a place, or remooue w*i*thout *th*e joynt app*ro*bac*i*on of your brethren mett together, to c*on*sider aduisedly of your Case." But he promises to write again soon and try to answer the question then "according to my weaknesse." Burroughes did indeed become installed at Tivetshall, Norfolk, on April 21, 1631, just under six months after this appeal for Cotton's advice. Despite Burroughes's fears, the move did not forever condemn him to anonymity. For Cotton, the prospect of removing from a large community offering the potential for influencing others to a remote and less isolated location was one he and other potential colonists were increasingly facing at just this time. In another year or so he would be following his own advice in consulting colleagues and friends regarding his position in Boston.

2. Silencing and Emigration

Another committed Puritan minister who achieved prominence of a different sort with his pen wrote to Cotton on December 13, 1631.[73] Nathaniel Ward was at a crucial point in his life when he wrote a strongly felt but brief

73. Ward published his rhetorically rambunctious satirical antitoleration tract, *The Simple Cobler of Aggawam,* in London in 1647.

note from his home at Stondon Massey, Essex. He addresses Cotton as his "Reverend and dear friend," telling him bluntly in the first sentence that the ultimately dreaded hand of the authorities had just been laid on his shoulder: "I was yesterday convented before the bishop, I mean to his court, and am adjourned to the next term." The bishop was Laud, who in the same year had already been responsible for Thomas Hooker's fleeing from Essex to Holland and indeed for a great deal of talk of emigration throughout East Anglia. Ward's spare prose emits a strong sense of emotional agony as he confronts the implications of the hardening of the lines of confrontation between bishops and Puritan preachers. The letter contains only eight sentences after an initial "Salutem in *Chris*to nostro," and just enough metaphoric enforcement to dramatize the very real fear and isolation that he feels. Ward writes to Cotton as a friend, to tell him about the fate of one of his dear clerical brethren. The letter summarizes much that has been implied in other letters discussed here regarding Cotton's centrality to a large circle of ministers who were attempting to preserve "purity in the ordinances" in their various locations throughout southeast England. Ward vividly conveys not only his expectation of personal suffering but also a sense of crisis and pain over the condition of the faithful in England (Ward to Cotton, Dec. 13, 1631). Unlike all of the above letters, Ward's is no questioning appeal, but simply a statement of heroic resolution. Ward knows who he is and how his previous actions in his ministry clearly identified him as an opponent of much that Bishop Laud stood for. He knows he will be harshly punished. Like any person facing adversity individually, he feels very much alone. He seems in effect to be saying good-bye to his past life and to those, like Cotton, who had helped him in it. Ward thankfully acknowledges Cotton's previous friendship, even as he prepares for enforced removal from the active ministry in England. They would soon meet again as fellow exiles in New England.

While we do not have Cotton's reply to Ward, we do have a copy of a letter he wrote to another unknown colleague who had been silenced, in which Cotton speaks sympathetically to the same problems faced by Ward: "It is a continuall heavynes to my heart, the Restray[n]t w*hi*ch (I perceyve by yo*u*r l*ette*re) is putt vpon y[ou]. The lively, & piercing, & powerfull Quickening, wherew*i*th *th*e heaven[l]y word of yo*u*r Ministery was w[o]nt to awaken yo*u*r People's hearts, how is it turned into a silent Deadnesse!" This letter of consolation is full of quoted phrases from Scripture, suggesting parallels between his correspondent's silencing and the silencing of great biblical preacher-prophets like the martyred Stephen and Zechariah. The letter borrows from the sermonic tradition of the jeremiad in sentences such as, "When wee say to seers, see not, & to Prophets, Prophesy not, doe wee not hereby cause *th*e Holy One [of] Izra[el] t[o c]ease fro[m] vs?" Cotton's letter, like many a Puritan sermon of the period, reads this silencing as an ominous sign for England: "I am m[o]re afraid of *th*[e] daunger w*hi*ch such Passages of Church-Officers threaten to o*u*r stat[e] then all of *th*e Power, & malice of Fraunce, or Spayne." This letter eloquently represents the state of mind of English Puritanism in the late 1620s and early 1630s. And, though making no specific suggestion of emigration, it anticipates the new beginning that New England would soon offer to many in its allusion to Revelation 3:8, reminding his friend that God "is able againe to sett before you an Open Doore" (Cotton to a Silenced Minister, [1628–1631?]).

Less than a year after receiving Ward's letter, Cotton was himself on the run. An exchange of letters with the earl of Dorset, unpreserved except in Cotton Mather's relation, apparently clinched Cotton's decision. On being summoned to appear before the Court of High Commission, he appealed to the earl of Dorset to intercede for him with Laud. The earl did try but wrote back to Cotton, as Mather tells it, "that if he had been guilty of *drunkenness,* or *uncleanness,* or any such *lesser falt,* he could have obtained his pardon; but inasmuch as he had been guilty of *non-conformity,* and *puritanism,* the crime was unpardonable; and therefore, said he, *you must fly for your safety.*"[74] Having lost his wife, Elizabeth, in April 1631, after a childless marriage of nearly two decades, Cotton had married a Boston widow, Sarah Hawkred Story, a year later.[75] On October 3, 1632, he wrote a letter to his bride of five months from a hiding place already apparently well removed from Boston. Cotton does not disclose his whereabouts but assures her he is "fitly & welcomely accom*m*odated." He regrets that his "Sweet Hearte" cannot yet join him but acknowledges his fugitive status in saying: "If you should now traveyle this way, I feare you will be watched, & dogged at *th*e heeles. But I hope, shortly God will make way for thy safe com*m*ing." That did indeed happen within six weeks (Cotton to Sarah Cotton, Oct. 3, 1632).

It is interesting that even during this undercover period, according to John Norton, "addresses . . . were made unto him privately by divers persons of worth and piety, who received from him satisfaction unto their Consciences in cases of greatest concernment."[76] Norton quotes John Davenport's account of his meeting with Cotton in London at about this time, a meeting that is said to have brought both Davenport and Thomas Goodwin over to the Puritan position on nonconformity.[77]

74. Mather, *Magnalia,* I, 241.

75. P. Thompson, *History of Boston,* 416.

76. Norton, *Abel Being Dead yet Speaketh,* 21.

77. Ibid., 32–33; see also Ziff, *Career of John Cotton,* 68. As noted below, Thomas Edwards

There are other traces of the Cottons' footprints as they slowly and cautiously moved farther south and eventually east from Lincolnshire during their last year in England. Cotton's 1637 letter to John Dod, written more than four years after his emigration, ends by saying, "My wife is still mindefull & sensible of yo*u*r gratious Counsell, when you kindely brought vs onward of o*u*r way, & *th*e Lord warmed o*u*r hearts with yo*u*r heavenly Conference." This would have been at the Dods' Fawsley, Northamptonshire, home. John Norton later wrote that after this Cotton "kept himself close for a time in and about *London*."[78] Another stop made by the Cottons as they followed a kind of Puritan underground railway was in Ockley, Surrey, where Henry Whitfield, later the first minister at Guilford, Connecticut, had been a conformist minister for many years. There, Cotton Mather writes, "such persecuted servants of Christ, as Mr. *Cotton,* Mr. *Hooker,* Mr. *Goodwin,* and Mr. *Nye,* then molested for their *non-conformity,* were sheltered under his roof."[79] Further, we know from a clue in a letter written still later that the Cottons' escape route from England probably led them through the household of Thomas Wilson, then a suspended minister in Otham, Kent, for whose "loving & Ch*ris*tian Intertaynm*ent*" Cotton was "so much beholding" still, in 1640. Cotton wrote to Bishop Williams resigning his post at St. Botolph's, and almost immediately the *Griffin,* carrying Cotton, Hooker, and Samuel Stone, among others, departed for New England from the Downs on the Kentish coast on about July 10, 1633. With this sailing, a major phase of his life and career was ended (Cotton to Dod, Dec. 19, [1637]; Cotton to [John] Elmeston, Aug. 26, 1640, n. 16).

The 1620s in England were a critical decade for the shaping of Puritan dissent, a decade in which a generation of ministers was forced to negotiate the narrow path in their own local circumstances between principled nonconformity and the limits of tolerance by ecclesiastical authority. As we have seen, John Cotton, through his household seminary and his correspondence with those who trusted his counsel, was a key figure in the training of a generation

---

would make the believable claim that converting Goodwin to Independency probably involved written arguments as well as oral suasion.

78. Norton, *Abel Being Dead yet Speaketh,* 21.

79. Mather, *Magnalia,* I, 541. Mather adds: "At last, being present at the conference between Mr. *Cotton,* and some other famous divines, upon the controversies of *church-discipline,* there appeared so much of *scripture* and *reason* on that side, that Mr. *Whitfield* also became a *non-conformist.*" Among his sources, Mather had Cotton's own brief comments on the meeting in *The Way of Congregational Churches Cleared . . .* (London, 1648) (see Ziff, *Cotton on the Churches,* 202–204); and John Norton, *Abel Being Dead yet Speaketh,* 20, 32–33, where Norton quotes Davenport's recollections. For analysis of the available information on this conference at Ockley, Surrey, see Webster, *Godly Clergy in Early Stuart England,* 157–164.

in England. He would continue to answer letters from clerical colleagues in England even during his errand into the wilderness, but his emigration permanently altered his relationship to the Puritan movement. Indeed, his flight and the flights of others from Laudian repressions signaled the change of the movement itself. Although he was no longer in a convenient position to help shape the Puritan posture in England, his reputation survived his departure so that in the next two decades—especially in the 1640s—he became a leading spokesman for New England's version of church polity.

Emigration was no easy thing for members of Cotton's generation. It was a central part of what Andrew Delbanco has called the Puritan Ordeal.[80] Cotton was in midcareer, age forty-eight, and surely would have preferred not to leave England for an unknown wilderness setting. Adding to the natural agonies of leaving many friends and family members and all that was familiar was the tendency of some respected friends and colleagues to question the propriety of deserting England at a critical juncture in the history of the church and commonwealth. They argued that powerful voices were needed, now more than ever, in the homeland. A year or so after their departure, Cotton and Hooker received a letter from a clergyman who had remained behind, challenging them to account for their departure.

Cotton replied at length on behalf of Hooker and himself, stating the rationale that must have guided most ministers who were threatened with silencing and other punishment for their Puritan ways in England. In the face of his correspondent's skepticism, he situated their emigration in a fully scriptural context, comparing himself and Hooker to the young Peter, who was still able to travel "& goe wither he would," even though as an old man he would (paraphrasing John 21:18) "suffer himselfe to be girt of others, & led along to Prison, & to death." In their midlife strength, Cotton argues, they are still able and willing to be of active service to God and, aware that there is in New England "more then enough [work] to fill both our handes, yea & the hands of many Bretheren moe," they committed themselves to two months'

80. On the human costs of the migration experience, see Delbanco, *The Puritan Ordeal;* Patricia Caldwell, *The Puritan Conversion Narrative: The Beginnings of American Expression* (Cambridge, 1983); Cressy, *Coming Over;* Virginia DeJohn Anderson, *New England's Generation: The Great Migration and the Formation of Society and Culture in the Seventeenth Century* (Cambridge, 1991); Stephen Fender, *Sea Changes: British Emigration and American Literature* (Cambridge, 1992). Generally, see also Nicholas Canny, ed., *Europeans on the Move: Studies on European Miration, 1500–1800* (Oxford, 1994). Kenneth W. Shipps discusses the interesting case of Samuel Rogers, who struggled with the question of whether to emigrate, finally deciding to stay put, in "The Puritan Emigration to New England: A New Source on Motivation," *NEHGR,* CXXXV (1981), 83–97. On the experience of emigrants from various European nations, see Ida Altman and James P. Horn, eds., *"To Make America": European Emigration in the Early Modern Period* (Berkeley, Calif., 1991).

sea travel in order to go where they could do that work in the full purity of the ordinances. What was sufficient reason for the biblical apostles was reason enough for their modern-day successors. Paul himself, says Cotton, finding that the Jews would not heed his testimony, chose "rather to depart quickly out of Hierusalem" than "to stay att Hierusalem to bear wittnesse to that cause vnto Prison." That prison would have been the consequence of staying in England, Cotton has little doubt. They weighed that option in the balance: "What service my selfe, o[r] Brother Hooker {m}ighte doe {to} o*u*r {people} or other bretheren, in Prison (especially in close Prison w*hich* was feared) I suppose, we bothe of vs (by gods helpe) doe the same, & much more, and with more freedome fro*m* hence" (Cotton to a Minister in England, Dec. 3, 1634).

His letter to England, thus depicting the futility of submitting to such punishment, was echoed many years later, still with strong emphasis, when he wrote that he and Hooker had both concluded, "By the free preaching of the word and the actual practice of our church discipline we could offer a much clearer and fuller witness in another land than in the wretched and loathsome prisons of London, where there would be no opportunity for books or pens or friends or conferences."[81] Given the concurrence of many of his congregation in Lincolnshire with his departure and the willingness of many to follow, the choice, as he recapitulates it eighteen months later in the first surviving letter after his emigration, was not a difficult one.[82]

The notion that Cotton came to think of himself, at some level of his consciousness, as an antitype, or latter-day version of the apostles Peter and Paul, is further supported in his writing at this point. Cotton expected that his role as teacher, prophet, and exemplum would continue in New England and perhaps increase. His letters for the rest of his career continued to convey this self-image. He remained a confident interpreter of scriptural authority to his peers and followers. The most striking example of this is his continuous correspondence with Peter Bulkeley, the minister at Concord, from the time of Bulkeley's settlement there in 1635 until at least 1650. Although they were in disagreement on some of the basic issues of the Antinomian controversy, Bulkeley was given to asking Cotton for help in resolving doctri-

81. Cotton, "The Foreword Written in New England," in John Norton, *The Answer to the Whole Set of Questions of the Celebrated Mr. William Apollonius* . . . (London, 1648), trans. Douglas Horton (Cambridge, Mass., 1958), 11.

82. Cotton, like several other ministers, was the center of a "clerical company" of emigrants from the Boston area. See Roger Thompson, *Mobility and Migration: East Anglian Founders of New England, 1629–1640* (Amherst, Mass., 1994), 186–189.

nal dilemmas as well as practical congregational challenges.[83] Others would turn to him for help. In 1639 the minister and the ruling elder at Plymouth, John Reyner and William Brewster, wrote to seek his professional advice on church matters. Some in New England, including Samuel Whiting, sought personal spiritual comfort, seeing Cotton as a minister to ministers. One of Whiting's letters to Cotton is, in fact, a brief spiritual autobiography, written to inform Cotton of Whiting's inner travail to the end of seeking his friend's pastoral counsel. Even the octogenarian minister Stephen Bachiler, accused of propositioning a married woman, sought counsel, and perhaps vindication, from Cotton (Reyner and Brewster to [Cotton and Wilson], Aug. 5, 1639; Whiting to Cotton, [?1637–1652]; Cotton to Bachiler, Mar. 9, 1641/2).

At the same time, those in England who had earlier valued Cotton's counsel continued occasionally to resort to him. John Elmeston, a schoolmaster in Kent, sought his advice in 1640 and again just a few weeks before Cotton died in 1652. His successor at St. Botolph's, Anthony Tuckney, whom Sarah Cotton considered virtually a brother, having been raised in the same household with him, was surely a regular correspondent of the Cottons, though only a fragment of a single letter survives (Cotton to [Tuckney], Oct. 5, 1635).[84] A prefatory epistle to *Of the Holinesse of Church-Members* (London, 1650) is truly a personal letter from Cotton to civic and church leaders "together with the whole Congregation and Church at Boston" in Lincolnshire. The book that this letter introduces was written as a direct response to letters from Boston and elsewhere in England, on the subject of church membership and what it entailed for the believer.[85]

He also worked at persuading other correspondents in England and Holland such as Thomas Goodwin, Philip Nye, and John Davenport to his views on church government and nonconformity. Thomas Edwards, an opponent of the Independents at the Westminster Assembly, made much use of letters that were circulated among the Puritans on both sides of the Atlantic. Edwards blamed Thomas Goodwin's "first comming to fall off from the Ceremonies" on his "having seen and perused the Arguments and Rea-

83. Thirteen letters or partial letters survive from the Bulkeley-Cotton correspondence, more than from Cotton's correspondence with any other person. On these letters, see Sargent Bush, Jr., "After Coming Over: John Cotton, Peter Bulkeley, and Learned Discourse in the Wilderness," *Studies in the Literary Imagination,* XXVII (1994), 7–21.

84. P. Thompson, *History of Boston,* 418, asserts, without citing evidence, that there was a continuing correspondence between the two. It seems a safe surmise.

85. Cotton wrote, "I have for the satisfaction of your selves, and of sundry others, who have written to me about the same, penned this ensuing Treatise." *Of the Holinesse of Church-Members* (London, 1650), sig A2v.

sons that past between him and M. *Cotton* and some others."[86] Cotton in his turn recalled receiving letters from Goodwin before and after leaving England in which their debates on the second commandment were an issue. "It is an usual thing with God," Cotton affirmed, "in times of reformation to enlighten his servants, though far distant one from another, with the same beams of light of divine truth, which the world interpreteth, they have learned one from one another. . . . But whether Mr. Davenport, and Mr. Goodwin received ought from me, I do not know, sure I am, I have received much from them." He thinks at this point of Paul's letter to the Ephesians, affirming that "the members of the body of Christ, are wont to minister supply one to another, according to the effectual working of the spirit of grace in every part, to the mutual edifying of themselves, and of the whole body in love, Ephes. iv,16."[87] Like Paul, Cotton firmly believed that a major element in his own contribution to strengthening the unity of the body of Christ was his letter-writing.

3. The Antinomian Controversy

Colonial life was very different from Cotton's former life as vicar of St. Botolph's but not necessarily simpler. There was a dramatic contrast between presiding over capacity congregations in the beautiful stone church at the old Boston and being teacher to a small group of struggling colonists in the primitive wooden structure that served as the first meetinghouse in the new Boston. The rhythms of his life in Massachusetts were decidedly different from those of his English experience. Travel had been a normal part of his premigration life. Both he and his English correspondents in the 1620s occasionally referred to his travels to London and to Hertfordshire, he visited his native town of Derby at least once a year, and we know he took the long journey to Southampton, where he preached to the departing Winthrop party in 1630. He in turn received visits from other Puritans at Boston. John Preston came to see him there once a year, Charles Chauncy promised to do the same, Arthur Hildersham sometimes visited and preached at St. Botolph's, and doubtless there were others who had regular contact with him.[88]

86. Thomas Edwards, *Antapologia; or, A Full Answer to the Apologeticall Narration of Mr Goodwin, Mr Nye, Mr Sympson, Mr Burroughs, Mr Bridge, Members of the Assembly of Divines* . . . (London, 1646), 14. See also 18–19, 31–32 on Cotton's correspondence with these men.

87. Cotton, *The Way of Congregational Churches Cleared,* in Ziff, *Cotton on the Churches,* 204.

88. See Charles Chauncy to Cotton, Mar. 15, 1627/8, and Timothy Van Vleteren to Cotton, Oct. 26, 1629. On his travel to Derby and on Preston's visits to Boston, see Mather, *Magnalia,* I, 238, 239. Passing references to Cotton's travels in England occur here and there in the writings of the Puritans. See, for instance, Ernest Axon, ed., *Oliver Heywood's Life of John Angier of Denton* (Manchester, 1937), which records Angier's recollection of travels on horseback in driving rain

In the Bay Colony, his opportunities—not to mention the temptations—for travel were drastically reduced. He made the occasional visit to Concord or Lynn, and his peers often made a point of traveling to Boston to hear Cotton's Thursday lectures, but these distances were small compared with his English travels. Yet, distinguished new immigrants often sought him out first on arrival. Henry Vane built an addition to Cotton's house, where he lived during his entire residence in the Bay Colony, and, not long after Vane's return to England, John Davenport immigrated and stayed with the Cottons until his departure for New Haven, probably living in the structure Vane had erected. Moreover, every incoming ship brought news from his native country, along with books and letters that required his attention and response. More than any other colonist, Cotton was regarded by friends and antagonists alike as a key commentator on the New England way. He was repeatedly addressed, either in his own right or as one of the leading ministers in the Bay, helping New Englanders to define themselves in relation to critical issues: church membership criteria, baptism, church polity, the place of women in the church, and even secular legal matters. His replies sometimes took the form of full-scale books, but more often of letters. He continued thus, on a transatlantic scale, to be a consultant, adviser, and, increasingly in the 1640s, spokesman for New England.

Davenport many years later recalled that Cotton, "that now blessed Servant of Christ, . . . wrote unto me, being then in *Holland,* to encourage my coming to *New-England,* that the Order of the Churches and of the Commonwealth was so settled, by common Consent; that it brought to his mind, the New Heaven and New Earth, wherein dwells Righteousness, advising me to come hither free from Engagements to others." This was in 1635 or 1636. Much later, in 1669, Davenport recalled that controversy had erupted by the time of his own arrival in New England: "Satan, in short time, stir'd up Strifes and Dissentions, to the great disturbance of the Churches and of the Countrey, which God at last mercifully quieted."[89]

Davenport's reference to the Antinomian controversy, which was occupying the attention of the leaders in Massachusetts Bay when he arrived in 1637, identifies a critical episode in Cotton's life that figures prominently in his correspondence for a period of six or seven years. Davenport's immediate sense of the force of the turmoil came from his living for several months

---

in the company of Cotton. A particularly significant occasion was Cotton's travel to Sempringham Castle in 1629 with Thomas Hooker and Roger Williams to meet with John Winthrop and others regarding the establishment of a new colony in Massachusetts.

89. John Davenport, *A Sermon Preach'd at the Election of the Governour, at Boston in New-England, May 19th 1669* ([Cambridge, Mass.?], 1670), 15.

in the Cottons' household until leaving to accept the New Haven church's call in early 1638. That controversy focused immediately on Cotton's views on the process of salvation and on the Covenants of Works and Grace.

Some of these letters are well known, most notably the exchange with Thomas Shepard at the beginning of the controversy. Soon after that exchange, with the pressure decidedly on Cotton for his apparent sympathy with the position of the radical "antinomians," Cotton wrote to Peter Bulkeley and his colleague, John Jones, to decline their invitation to attend their formal organizing of a church at Concord. Though he assured Bulkeley that he and Jones "are deare & pretious in my Affections," Cotton found himself "Restreyned by an vnexpected Occasion from Comming over to you this day (as I had verely purposed)." It seems likely that the pronounced suspicion of his views by many ministers in the Bay who would be in attendance deterred him, along with John Wheelwright and Henry Vane, from appearing there. He was not happy about his predicament, and his self-characterization in this letter is a telling revelation of the extent to which he was already deeply troubled by the disagreements in which he was embroiled: "Let me (desolate me) come in to yo*u*r mindes, *tha*t, noe weakenesse of mine may cast Dishono*u*r vpon *th*e Name & gr[ace] of Christ, who am Altogether vnworthy, *tha*t his Name should be called vpon me, or held forth by me." This is a very unusual instance of Cotton's self-admonition, while his agonized aside, "desolate me," is as direct an admission of the psychological stresses the Antinomian episode was placing upon him as any expression he would make for the rest of the drawn-out process. He was a man, as he confessed to Thomas Shepard, who did not like disagreements: "As for differences, & Jarres, it is my vnfeigned desire to avoide them with all men especially w*i*th Brethren." In the same year, writing to Lord Saye and Sele, Cotton revealed the extent to which he felt the crisis had compromised his ability to do his job. He complained of the "constant labors here (which the church is desirous to procure)," allowing him no time even for reading and pressing him "much beyond my strength either of body or minde." The extremity of Cotton's dismay and discouragement is also manifest in the fact that in the midst of the controversy, feeling such strong opposition to him and his expressed ideas on Redemption, he decided that he had no alternative but to leave the colony. He was on the verge of departing for New Haven by mid-1637 (Shepard to Cotton and Cotton to Shepard, [Feb. 1–June 1, 1636]; Cotton to Bulkeley and Jones, [July 5, 1636]; Cotton to William Fiennes, Lord Saye and Sele, [after March 1636]).[90]

90. As Cotton says in his letter to John Wheelwright, Apr. 18, 1640, in 1637–1638 he had "verely Purposed openly to have protested ag*ains*t all such proceedings as I took to be injurious

Thereafter, the issues of the controversy come more fully into view in certain of his letters. This is particularly so in his several exchanges with Bulkeley, in early 1637 and again in 1640–1642. In the latter period, Bulkeley was preparing his book on the Covenant of Grace, a plan on which Cotton congratulates him, and he sought Cotton's opinion on certain fine points of doctrine, most prominently the question of exactly when God created the Covenant of Works with Adam. These exchanges tell us more of Bulkeley's mind than Cotton's, perhaps, but they also indicate the extent to which Cotton was frequently reminded of the disagreements he had been enmeshed in at the height of the controversy.

One of the most interesting points in the letters bearing on the controversy is the assertion by Cotton—verified in at least one letter written to him—that the radical voices consciously sheltered themselves behind Cotton's reputation. He repeatedly says that he discovered too late that the "Ringleaders" agreed among themselves to claim publicly that they held only to the views that Cotton held, even though they knew very well that they departed from him in their extreme positions. Cotton was duped, in other words, until he finally understood the falsity of the claims of some of the leaders in his church.

This observation appears first in a letter of March 27, 1638, to Samuel Stone in Hartford. Written just five days after Anne Hutchinson's excommunication and the day before she was to leave Boston, it is the first statement of any kind that we have from Cotton after the formal end of the Antinomian controversy. He accepts Stone's overtures to "sweetely compose" the "Differences" between them and reports that already his "former Meetings" with his Boston-area colleagues "are often Renewed not w*i*thout mutuall Helpe & Comfort." While Cotton unambiguously confesses his "owne Iniquityes" through which "God was willing to bring me low at *tha*t time in *th*e Eyes of Brethren," he nevertheless is painfully aware of "*th*e Iniquityes of sundry members of o*u*r Church, who (like Achan, w*i*thout my Privety) had harboured & secretly disseminated such Erroneous & daungerous Opinions, as (like a Gangrene) would have corrupted & destroyed Faith & Religion had not they bene timely discovered, & disclaymed both by o*u*r owne & other Churches." He names Mistress Hutchinson here, but alludes to various others, some of whom had preceded Hutchinson to exile in Rhode Island, as equally guilty (Cotton to Stone, Mar. 27, [1638]).

A fragment of a letter to Davenport preserved in John Norton's biog-

---

& offensive & to have Departed into some other Parts of this Countrey." Cotton discusses this consideration and the reasons for his subsequent decision not to leave Massachusetts Bay in *The Way of Congregational Churches Cleared,* in Ziff, *Cotton on the Churches,* 241–243.

raphy of Cotton recalls those who had already gone to Aquidneck, saying, "The Lord pity and pardon them, and me also, who have been so slow to see their windings, and subtile contrivances, and insinuations in all their transactions, whilst they propagated their Opinions under my Expressions, diverted to their constructions." Sometime after late September 1642, he was still telling an English correspondent about the time "when some members of o*u*r Church did secretly nourish some grosse Erro*u*rs . . . but yet openly so carryed it to me, as if they had held forth noething, but according to *th*e Doctrine publickly taught by me touching o*u*r vnion w*i*th Christ, & evidencing of it to *th*e soule." Belatedly, he regretted that he had tried to make "a better Construction of their words then now I perceive *the*mselves intended." Perhaps Cotton Mather's description of Cotton's ministerial style sheds some light on how he failed to read the sentiments of his parishioners more promptly: "He chiefly gave himself to reading, and doctrine, and exhortation, depending much, on the ruling elders to inform him, concerning the state of his particular flock, that he might the better order himself in *the word and prayer.*"[91]

Cotton's fullest statement in the correspondence on this subject appears in his long letter to John Wheelwright (Apr. 18, 1640) in which he rehearses many of the specific stages of his and Wheelwright's "failings" in the development of the controversy.[92] He accuses himself especially of failing to understand that certain of his own church's members were knowingly going well beyond his own views. It was first in the synod in September 1637 that Cotton's eyes were opened to the "damnable opinions" that were abroad in the land. He admits "At first I was slow to beleive *tha*t any s[uc]h Erro*u*rs were extant in the countrey (b[u]t thought *the*m to be either some misexpressions of o*u*r men, or some misconstructions of the Countrey:)." But, he says, when he heard William Aspinwall and John Coggeshall ("Coxall") "& others . . . excusing & mainteyning *th*e opin[io]ns controverted about vnion, inhærent righteousnesse visibilitie & activity of indwelling Grace & the like, I tooke them aside & tolde them *tha*t if they were of *th*e Judgm*en*t w*hi*ch they stoode for, all those Bastard-opinions w*hi*ch were then de[live]red, would be fathered vpon the members of o*u*r church." He recalls advising them not to go forth as the messengers of the Boston church to spread such erroneous views. He had hoped to reclaim them through private counseling, "but all

91. Cotton to John Davenport, [after March 1638]; Norton, *Answer to the Whole Set of Questions,* trans. Horton, 37; Cotton to [unknown], [after Sept. 26, 1642]; Mather, *Magnalia,* I, 251.

92. A still longer statement by Cotton, a "publick and patient answer" to "a certain scandalous writer" is quoted by Cotton Mather (*Magnalia,* I, 244). He covers some of the same ground in *The Way of Congregational Churches Cleared,* in Ziff, *Cotton on the Churches,* 224–225, 242–243.

in vaine." He learned, in fact, that one of their number advised the others to keep their extreme opinions "private to themselves," while publicly claiming "to hold forth noe [m]ore [tha]n their Teacher might goe [alon]g w*i*th *the*m."[93]

Cotton connects his lament for his naïveté in the midst of deceptions by those around him in Boston to Jesus' parable of the sower of good seed who slept "whilest the enemy came [and] sowed Tares." But Cotton did not limit this self-accusation to private communications, going fully public with it, even to the point of showing the depth to which it touched an emotional nerve. Cotton "did publickly sometimes with *tears* bewail it, *that the enemy had sowed so many tares whilst he had been asleep.*"[94] Having admitted his own blindness to the extremity of these members' positions, and to their intentional deception of him while using his name and reputation as their shield, Cotton suggests that Wheelwright should also have picked up on the import of what "Mrs Hutchinson & Mr Coxall" were saying. "You had also sufficient grounds to suspect that if such Ringleaders were of *tha*t corrupt Judgm*en*t many moe were likely to be leavened & corrupted by them." Thus, his approach in the letter was to base his appeal for Wheelwright's confession to using poor judgment in the controversy by showing that he himself was also at fault. Mutual confession was needed, he believed, even though others had been more overtly malign in their intentions (Cotton to [Wheelwright], Apr. 18, 1640).

In reporting Cotton's own construction of the events of the Antinomian controversy, his grandson records Cotton's lengthy "publick and patient answer" to charges leveled at him by "a certain scandalous writer" who had "publickly reproached Mr. *Cotton,* with his former inclination to remove." Since Cotton's statement was a "publick . . . answer," it was apparently not a letter, but it was a written document to which Mather still had access. Since it was clearly meant by Cotton to present an important aspect of his side of the story, it is immediately relevant to his letters on the controversy. Mather quotes Cotton:

> There was a generation of *Familists* in our own, and other towns, who under pretence of holding forth what I had taught, touching union with Christ, and *evidencing* that union, did secretly vent sundry and dangerous

93. The statement quoted by Mather emphasizes the same points: "When they were questioned by some brethren about those things, they carried it, as if they had held forth nothing, but what they had received from me. . . . Yea, and I myself could not easily believe, that those erring brethren and sisters, were so corrupt in their judgments as they were reported" (*Magnalia,* I, 244).

94. Ibid., I, 245.

errors and heresies, denying all *inherent righteousness,* and all evidencing of a *good estate* thereby in any sort, and some of them also denying the *immortality of the soul,* and *the resurrection of the body.* When they were questioned by some brethren about those things, they carried it, as if they had held forth nothing, but what they had received from me: whereof, when I was advised to clear my self, I publickly preached against those errors. Then said the brethren to the erring party, *See your teacher declares himself clearly to differ from you. No matter* (say the other) *what he saith in publick, we understand him otherwise, and we know what he saith to us in private.* Yea, and I my self could not easily believe, that those erring brethren and sisters, were so corrupt in their judgments as they were reported; they seeming to me forward christians, and utterly denying any such tenents, or any thing else, but what they received from my self. All which bred in sundry of the country, a jealousie that I was in secret *a fomenter of the spirit of familism,* if not *leavened* my self that way. Which I discerning, it wrought in *me* thoughts (as it did in many other sincerely and godly brethren of our church) not of a *separation* from the churches, but of a *removal* to *New-Haven,* as being better known to the pastor, and some others *there,* than to such as were at that time jealous of me *here.* The true ground whereof was an *inward loathness to be troublesome unto godly minds,* and a fear of the unprofitableness of my *ministry* there, where my *way* was suspected to be doubtful and dangerous. I chose therefore rather to meditate a *silent departure* in peace, than by tarrying here, to make way for the breaking forth of *temptations.* But when, at the *Synod,* I had discovered the corruption of the judgment of the *erring brethren,* and saw their fraudulent pretence of holding forth no other, but what they received from *me* (when as indeed they plead for gross errors contrary unto *my* judgment) I thereupon did bear witness against them; and when in a private conference with some chief *magistrates* and *elders,* I perceived, that my removal upon such differences was unwelcome to them, and that such points need not to occasion any *distance* (neither in *place* nor in *heart*) amongst brethren, I then rested satisfied in my abode amongst them, and so have continued, by the grace of Christ unto this day.[95]

Among those who were trusted friends of Cotton in Lincolnshire and again in the new Boston but subsequently fell in with the Antinomian sectarian voices, William Coddington was surely one whose opposition ultimately hurt Cotton the most.[96] It was Coddington whose welfare as one of

95. Ibid., 244–245.

96. The large number of people punished in some way—disarmed, disfranchised, excommunicated, or in the most extreme cases banished—was by no means limited to people who had come from Lincolnshire, though, as Emery Battis has observed, the county providing the

the earliest colonial settlers in 1630 had concerned Cotton enough for him to buy a hogshead of meal that he had shipped to Coddington and his family. And in his letter to Samuel Skelton, Cotton had specifically objected to the Salem church's exclusion of Coddington and his family from full membership. Coddington had predictably risen to the magistracy in the Massachusetts Bay Colony, but by the end of the first decade he was an exile in Aquidneck and feeling severely wronged by the proceedings against him.

Two 1641 letters to Cotton reflect this sense of victimization. The first relates how Coddington and his wife hear reports of Cotton's recent preaching that strike them as so unlike him that "if we had not knowne w*ha*t he had holden forth before we knew not how to understand him." Coddington staunchly resists the Boston church's efforts to get him to admit his errors. He signs his first letter "yo*u*r neclected reiected afflicted frind." In August 1641, replying promptly to a letter from Cotton, Coddington is cordially grateful for the letter but somewhat insolently replies to Cotton's admonition that he needs to reform some of his ideas, saying, "I hope as speedely as yow may will discover to me what those wayes of heresy be that are to be avoyded," again signing off hyperbolically as "yo*u*r old & uselesse frind." There would be no further reconciliation between Coddington and his former spiritual guide (Cotton to Herbert Pelham, Oct. 3, 1630; Coddington to Cotton, [March–April 1641], Aug. 27, [1641]).

One of the most dedicated aristocratic friends of the New England Puritans in the 1630s was William Fiennes, Lord Saye and Sele, who knew the young Henry Vane and his unorthodox opinions even before he left for New England. After Vane had returned to England, Lord Saye and Sele wrote to Cotton in response to a letter Cotton had sent him dealing with the Antinomian controversy. Even as late as July 1638—almost a year after leaving New England—Vane was still claiming to have been in full agreement with Cotton's views all along. Cotton never named Vane as one of the "Ringleaders" in his congregation, but it seems likely that part of the conflict Cotton experienced stemmed from the fact that while Vane, the elected governor of the colony, was living in Cotton's house, attending his church and professing to be his devoted follower, he was also holding to views on grace and the covenants that Cotton would not have accepted. Lord Saye and Sele informed Cotton that Vane was claiming that "himselfe w*i*th others hear w*it*h

largest core group of individuals was Lincolnshire. Five of them came from Cotton's former church, and his former neighbors in England were among those identified as members of the Antinomian camp. The Lincolnshire group included, besides the Coddingtons, such prominent people as the large Hutchinson family, the Wheelwrights, and the magistrate Atherton Hough. Battis, *Saints and Sectaries,* 258–259, 304–307, 312–316, 322–328.

him, (whoe have bin very active to disperse & spread abroad theyr opinions) hold nothinge but what you approve of, and are of the same Judgement with them and this hath taken w*i*th many to your preiudice." Saye adds that he is glad Cotton's love follows Vane—indicating that Cotton has written to Vane—"for he may be recovered." He adds that even while Vane was in New England Saye had detected his radical views, "as might have appeared to you by my letters written to him into New England when I fyrst did perceave his delusions, if he had showed my letters to you" (William Fiennes, Lord Saye and Sele, to Cotton, July 1638).

Most of the letters disclosing Cotton's and others' perceptions about the extent to which at least some of those charged with Antinomianism practiced deception, by using Cotton's reputation as their shield, are published here for the first time. They make a telling contribution to our understanding of the complexity of the Antinomian controversy and reveal that the controlling of both public and private perceptions of people's opinions was very much an issue. In retrospect, Cotton admitted to personal failings, yet he was victimized by those whom he thought he was serving, members of his church fellowship. While his public humiliation arising from the criticism of his fellow ministers was a source of pain to him, it may be that in the long run he was more hurt by the deception practiced by his friends among the laity. That issue continued to trouble him as long as four years after the controversy was ended.

The controversy had had a disruptive effect on the Boston church, resulting in the voluntary departure to Aquidneck of a number of leaders and supporters of the dissident faction.[97] But the letters also show that dialogue with the departed church members continued. Cotton clearly hoped to reclaim at least some of them. Less than three months after Anne Hutchinson's departure for the island, he replied to a letter from an exiled "brother" at Aquidneck, both defending himself against the charge of having bowed or "condescended" to "the Opposite Part" in the course of the crisis and strenuously asserting the wrongheadedness of the worst of the dissidents. The leaders of the exiled group, he insists, actually "subvert[ed] *th*e Coven*an*t of Grace"

97. The largest island in Narragansett Bay, to which many of the Massachusetts Bay exiles went in the 1630s, was known by its Algonquian name, Aquidneck, which simply means "island." The inhabitants changed the name to Rhode Island in about 1644, a change made official in the colonial charter issued in 1663. See Irving Berdine Richman, *Rhode Island, Its Making and Its Meaning: A Survey of the Annals of the Commonwealth from Its Settlement to the Death of Roger Williams, 1636–1683,* 2 vols. (New York, 1902), I, 34; Samuel Greene Arnold, *History of the State of Rhode Island and Providence Plantations,* 2 vols. (New York, 1859–1860), I, 70.

when they claimed the Son of God's "Increated" being lived and worked in the souls of the blessed, a view from which Cotton vigorously separates himself. It is his "heavyest B[ur]den" that the doctrine of the Covenant of Grace, the theological crux of the controversy, "hath bene more grossely, & fundamentally opposed by {so}m{e} of o*ur* Brethren of *th*e Island, & others of their minde, then by all those, whom you {c}al{l the} Opposite Party of *th*e Countrey." If Cotton had occasionally been less than lucid in his statements in the Boston conferences with his fellow ministers early in the controversy, he is strikingly clear here in charging these members of his own church with gross error. He tempers this somewhat by explaining that his strong statements come, not from "Passion, but C[om]passion," in the hope that the offenders might still be "rescued" by "the mighty Redeemer of Izraell," though he urges his correspondent, as one possessing the "Ability to discerne *th*e Daunger of theire Tenents," to work to "Recover *th*em . . . into *th*e church" (Cotton to [Unknown] at Aquidneck, June 4, [1638]).

In 1640 the church was engaged in dialogue with these people. Messengers were dispatched from the church to travel to "the Island," where they were not well received. One of Anne Hutchinson's sons, Francis, tried to withdraw his membership from the Boston church, but his request was denied in Cotton's letter on behalf of the congregation on August 12, 1640. The next month, Cotton wrote to the absent members in a letter that John Wilson read to the congregation to obtain their endorsement. That letter, transcribed from Wilson's reading by Robert Keayne, stressed the strength—the "sacred & inviolable," even the "p*er*petuall & euerlastinge" quality—of the church covenant. Mere absence from the church was not sufficient reason to annul the bond of membership, he argued, urging their return to communion with the church (Cotton to Hutchinson, Aug. 12, [1640]; Cotton to Members of the Boston Church at Aquidneck, Sept. 20–26, 1640).

These various letters written after the end of the formal controversy show us a chastened Cotton. Unlike the much more stubborn, recalcitrant Wheelwright, Cotton sees that he made some mistakes, though he believes they were in the area of human relations rather than doctrine. He devoted significant energy in the next few years to healing the wounds the controversy had caused. As early as 1639, it was evident that Cotton was reclaiming his valued reputation as an arbiter of problem cases and as an authority on ecclesiastical matters. On March 21, 1638/9, just about a year after Anne Hutchinson's excommunication, Thomas Dudley wrote to Cotton asking for his help in counseling William Denison, a layman who had been expelled from the Roxbury church. The issue Dudley wanted Cotton to discuss with Denison was the relation between justification itself and evidence of justification, one of the prickly issues that had been at the heart of the controversy. One of the most uncompromising of the magistrates who had been publicly critical of Cotton at the examination of Anne Hutchinson in November 1637, Dudley now implied full confidence in Cotton's views.[98]

About a year after this, in the spring of 1640, Cotton was busy negotiating with Wheelwright and was prepared to serve as a go-between for him with the governor and General Court, trying to get Wheelwright restored to the full privileges of the community. In his letter of April 18, 1640, Cotton boldly outlined the terms of a "confession" by Wheelwright that he thought the General Court would accept, thus permitting Wheelwright's return to the Massachusetts Bay Colony, which had banished him in late 1637. (This belief that Wheelwright was definitely in the wrong was repeated in Cotton's letter five months later to the absent members at Aquidneck, who had argued a contrary view.) Wheelwright, proud, strong-willed, stubborn, perhaps even obstinate, indicated in his reply to Cotton that he was not yet ready to concede as much fault on his part as Cotton suggested he should. Not until four years later did he approach Governor Winthrop with a statement of regret for his lack of judgment and discretion in his Fast Day sermon in January 1637. His statement was accepted, and he was readmitted to the colony. In some degree, then, Cotton's efforts to persuade both Wheelwright and the court of the desirability of accommodation were successful. By then, there was no question that Cotton was fully restored to his leadership role in the church and commonwealth (Cotton to [Wheelwright], Apr. 18, 1640; Wheelwright to Cotton, June 3, 1640).[99]

98. In the traditional Reformed understanding of Redemption, sanctification was said to follow justification. That is, when God's saving grace was received through justification, the individual thus redeemed gave evidence of a changed spiritual condition in the quality of speech and acts performed. The Antinomian party had charged the local Massachusetts ministry with putting undue emphasis on evidence of grace, or the signs of one's justification. Emphasizing the signs of justification in one's external life was said by the Antinomians to represent inappropriate emphasis on works. They claimed that, as a result, the local ministry was preaching a Covenant of Works rather than the Covenant of Grace. Since this was directly counter to what the ministry held as a central point in their preaching, it became a major point of contention in the controversy. See "Introduction," in Hall, *Antinomian Controversy,* 16–19; and Stoever, *"A Faire and Easy Way to Heaven,"* 46–57, 69–76. Cotton's answers to "Sixteene Questions" from the other elders, "The Elders Reply," and "Mr Cottons Rejoynder" all deal repeatedly with these issues, especially in questions 10–13; see Hall, *Antinomian Controversy,* 43–151, 342.

99. For a fuller discussion of this exchange of letters, see Sargent Bush, Jr., "'Revising what we have done amisse': John Cotton and John Wheelwright, 1640," *WMQ,* 3d Ser., XLV (1988), 733–750.

4. The Final Decade

An abiding respect for Cotton's opinions and a rich variety of subject matter characterize those letters sent to him in the final ten years of his life. As was typical of the earliest period of his epistolary career, his correspondents in these final years ranged from the nationally prominent to the unknown and obscure, from Oliver Cromwell to Robert and Mary Burle of Maryland.

These letters defy any easy summary or categorization. They convey the deepening complexity and fullness of life in the colonies; despite occasional legislative attempts to limit the immigration of dissidents, the range of religious diversity among the colonists—and among Cotton's correspondents—grew appreciably.[100] During these years the intellectual leadership of the colonies became more actively interested in publication of its writings. This was partly the consequence of increasing challenges from home on issues of basic importance to the colonists; they were often simply required to provide their English colleagues with written explanations of their practice in church matters. The 1630s had seen a good many publications of works written or preached by New Englanders that they had not themselves approved for publication—usually sermons, but sometimes catechisms or studies of polity. One way to forestall the appearance of such unauthorized texts was for the authors to arrange the publication of their work themselves. Partly aided by the return of some colonists to England, who could serve as contacts with London printers, much more of this occurred in the 1640s than in the previous decade, as is evident in Cotton's correspondence.[101]

During these years, the publication of Cotton's own works became a more important issue for him and for others, as his correspondence shows. Thomas Allen's letter in late 1642 is a response to Cotton's request for feedback on his writings on New England church polity. Two years later Cotton's letter to one R. M.—probably Richard More, a New England mariner—

100. The variety of sectarian voices present in the colonies by midcentury has been amply demonstrated by Philip F. Gura in *A Glimpse of Sion's Glory: Puritan Radicalism in New England, 1620–1660* (Middletown, Conn., 1984); and David S. Lovejoy, *Religious Enthusiasm in the New World: Heresy to Revolution* (Cambridge, Mass., 1985), 1–134.

101. Though several men who had never left England published manuscripts by Cotton both before and after his death, one person who apparently had Cotton's cooperation was Thomas Allen, who had been the teacher of the church at Charlestown before returning to his native Norwich in England in 1651. Allen's prefaces typically mention details of Cotton's life in New England and attest to Cotton's entrusting manuscripts to him. Allen therefore had a hand in the posthumous publication of Cotton's *New Covenant* (1654), *Certain Queries* (1654), *An Exposition upon the Thirteenth Chapter of the Revelation* (1655), *The Covenant of Grace* (1655), and *A Treatise of the Covenant of Grace* (1659).

in England clarified the relationship between two of his books on church polity, *The Way of the Churches of Christ in New-England* and *The Keyes of the Kingdom of Heaven.* The latter provoked a letter in 1645 from Robert Jordan, a conformist non-Puritan minister who had recently arrived on Richmond Island off the coast of Maine and who had written a modest reply to Cotton's book, which he asked Cotton to read (Allen to Cotton, Nov. 21, 1642; Cotton to Master R. M., [late 1644]).

Other writing projects of his own and others were also occupying him during this period. In the early 1640s Peter Bulkeley was writing the sermons that would constitute *The Gospel-Covenant* and consulting Cotton on selected points. Like several other New England ministers, Cotton had preached on the Covenant of Grace in the 1630s, when covenantal theology was a major part of the controversy that temporarily divided them. Those sermons were not published until after his death, but another book, apparently based on more recent sermons, *The Covenant of Gods Free Grace,* was published in London in 1645. John Elmeston's letter raising the subject was thus timely—and probably based on Elmeston's awareness, even in distant Kent, of the debate that had involved Cotton so centrally in the late 1630s.[102] In 1646, Thomas Shepard was working on his book on the Sabbath, *Theses Sabbaticae,* and solicited Cotton's opinions on specific aspects of that subject. Two years later Cotton responded to Governor Winthrop's request for help in revising the preface to the laws of New England to be published in 1648. Later, in 1651, Richard Mather was working closely with Cotton to remove objections of some colonists to the published version of the colonial laws. Mather's hastily written letter of September 15, 1651, concerns final revisions to the Cambridge Platform.

Just three months before he died, Cotton explicitly affirmed the value of book publication when, on September 20, 1652, in his "Epistle to the Reader" of John Norton's *Orthodox Evangelist,* he wrote, "The Penning and Reading of godly Books, is a singular improvement of the Communion of Saints: as whereby we enjoy sweet and gracious conference with the Saints, though unknown to us." Norton was still more explicit on the permanent value of books as contrasted with the orally delivered word: "The speaker hasteth on, and cannot wait the leasure of the hearer; but the writer is always at hand, attending the Capacity of the Reader. . . . *Books* you have always with you, you may receive good from them when you will."[103]

102. See Cotton to Elmeston, Aug. 26, 1640. Elmeston's letter is not extant, but Cotton quotes from it and addresses issues raised by Elmeston.

103. Cotton, "Epistle to the Reader," in John Norton, *The Orthodox Evangelist* . . . (London, 1654), sig. [A3], and Norton, sig. [Av].

A good example of the growing acknowledgment of the importance and power of print is rehearsed in a letter written in the summer of 1651 by Cotton and four other ministers to unnamed ministers in England. The previous year a book written by William Pynchon, the founder of Springfield, Massachusetts, entitled *The Meritorious Price of Our Redemption,* had been published in London. When the book arrived in New England, the General Court was in session, and, based only on a reading of its title page, they determined that it was sufficiently "unsound" and ordered it burned on the Boston Common by the public executioner. They then called Pynchon to account and ordered, in effect, pastoral counseling by Cotton and two others. The learned Norton was requested to write and publish an answer to Pynchon's book; *A Discussion of That Great Point in Divinity, the Sufferings of Christ* (London, 1653) was the consequence. The letter from Cotton and four other elders reflects their interest in moderating the court's harsh reaction to Pynchon's book somewhat. But the whole episode indicates the importance of publication as a mode of communication (Cotton, Richard Mather, Zechariah Symmes, John Wilson, and William Thompson to Ministers in England, [Summer 1651]).[104]

In the same year Cotton replied to his old acquaintance John Elmeston, in Kent, who was trying to correct the wayward ideas of a local minister, Simon Hendon. Cotton took the time to enclose a written corrective to Hendon's ideas. When Elmeston later told Cotton Hendon was unimpressed, Cotton decided to say no more, but to leave Hendon to God. By that time (October 1652), Cotton had contracted what would prove to be his final illness and was conserving his strength (Cotton to Elmeston, Oct. 18, 1651, Oct. 12, 1652).

Cotton's old friend John Davenport was among those seeking his help with his own writings, with the aim of publication. He sent a manuscript to Cotton in May 1650, asking him to make revisions as he saw fit. The result was a volume of Davenport's New Haven sermons, *The Knowledge of Christ . . . ; or, Demonstrative Proofs from Scripture, That Crucified Jesus Is the Christ* (London, 1653). Davenport also sought urgently needed advice in a semilegal dispute in the New Haven church with the schoolmaster Ezekiel Cheever. Cheever moved on from New Haven soon thereafter, however, and, when he stayed temporarily in Hartford, Samuel Stone, the minister there, also wrote to Cotton to ask for his reactions to ten specific points related to Cheever's arguments with New Haven. Cotton the judge of difficult cases remained in much de-

104. Pynchon's *Meritorious Price* and its context have been described in introductory essays to a facsimile edition of the book by Michael W. Vella, Lance Schachterle, and Louis Mackey, eds., in Worcester Polytechnic Institute, *Studies in Science, Technology, and Culture,* X (New York, 1992). See also Michael P. Winship, "Contesting Control of Orthodoxy among the Godly: William Pynchon Reexamined," *WMQ,* 3d Ser., LIV (1997), 795–822.

mand, even among such able and clearheaded peers as Mather, Davenport, and Stone.

In these final years Cotton was very conscious of his duty to act as a defender of the faith as he and his colleagues knew it. A letter in mid-1645 from a leading Baptist in England, John Tombes, accompanied a lengthy treatise setting forth his opposition to infant baptism, in the hope of persuading the New England ministry. Though we do not have Cotton's reply to Tombes, we know that he did reply, and several other letters and partial letters indicate that baptism was a concern in the 1640s, when the subject was being hotly debated in England and New England.[105] One was to a Lydia Gaunt, recently removed from Lynn to Cape Cod, where she was falling in with people whose views were decidedly divergent from the orthodoxy of New England. Her letter, the loss of which is particularly regrettable, contained allusions to her family. As a mother of small children, she had asked Cotton questions about baptism, as Cotton's reply makes evident. Despite his warnings, she and her husband, Peter, became associated with a group of Anabaptists at Sandwich as early as 1651, suggesting that, however much she respected Cotton's views, she was drawn to the more radical views being adopted by her husband and their neighbors.[106] In addition, fragments preserved in Increase Mather's *First Principles of New-England* itemize another five letters dealing with baptism that were written by or to Cotton in the period 1647–1652 (Tombes to Wilson, Cotton, and Other New England Ministers, May 25, 1645; Cotton to [Gaunt], Sept. 14, 1648).

Cotton died ten years before New England churches formally adopted the so-called Half-Way Covenant, but as early as 1634 he confronted the issues that brought the churches to that compromise.[107] During the last decade of his life he saw the increasing pressure for the church to deal with this problem. As E. Brooks Holifield has put it, "Cotton and his clerical colleagues quickly discovered that unconverted parents were not invariably indifferent to the spiritual welfare of their children, and that some of those parents considered infant baptism as a desirable confirmation of spiritual potential."[108]

105. Philip J. Anderson has noted that "at least thirty-four pamphlets addressing the issue of baptism were published between 1640 and June 1645," with more following. "Letters of Henry Jessey and John Tombes to the Churches of New England, 1645," *Baptist Quarterly,* XXVIII (1979), 39 n. 14.

106. A few years later they identified with the Quakers, who were among the beneficiaries named in Lydia Gaunt's will, dated 1691. MacLean W. McLean, "Peter Gaunt (*ca.* 1615–*ca.* 1678) of Sandwich, Mass.," *National Genealogical Society Quarterly,* LXII (1974), 248, 249.

107. See Cotton, Thomas Oliver, and Thomas Leverett to Elders of the Dorchester Church, Dec. 16, 1634.

108. E. Brooks Holifield, *The Covenant Sealed: The Development of Puritan Sacramental Theology*

The synod of 1662 that passed the Half-Way Covenant arose from a need that developed throughout the 1640s to oppose the rule that baptism was the right only of the children of full church members.[109]

With the 1650s, New England began to be confronted more frequently with a variety of sectarian viewpoints. Cotton's letter to Lydia Gaunt acknowledged her desire to wait for the "New Apostles," a belief of the Seekers that, until the appearance of new preachers with apostolic power and authority, the church would remain corrupt. Predictably, Cotton curtly dismissed this hope for the arrival of newly empowered prophets. But he was given another opportunity to react to Seeker ideas when John Eliot in June 1651 passed along a book that he had received from Roger Williams, urging Cotton to read it and respond. Cotton did so, but with diminishing enthusiasm for the task, as his reply shows he failed to get even as much as one-third of the way into the anonymous work (Cotton to Eliot, June 1651).

Cotton's role as minister to ministers continued as well. Stephen Bachiler sent two letters to Cotton asking for guidance, one in 1642 and another in 1644. Cotton replied to the first with stern sympathy, clearly doubting Bachiler's innocence of the sexual indiscretions with which he was charged. That sexual matters required ministerial counsel is evident, also, from the letter of another agonized church member, Benjamin Keayne, who wrote to Cotton about his wife's sexual profligacy and his own resulting close call with "the French pox" (Cotton to Bachiler, Mar. 9, 1641/2; Keayne to Cotton, Mar. 12, 1646/7).

The matter of gender relations and the status of women in public contexts becomes explicit in the correspondence between Peter Bulkeley and Cotton on two occasions, about eight years apart. In February 1642 Bulkeley was dealing with a "few cases" that he sought Cotton's opinions on. One was a case in the Concord church in which a woman, "taking offence against a brother" (a male fellow–church member), had reason to speak out on the issue before the congregation. Bulkeley and his elders at Concord wonder what is the right procedure. That is, how much of a public voice should a woman have in such a case? Could she publicly admonish the man? The problem arose because, in general, a man was considered the superior of a woman, and her speaking out against him would be an inversion of this proper relationship, "an act of power," in fact, that would not be condoned in a secular setting. Bulkeley continues with the case of a woman charged

---

in Old and New England, 1570–1720 (New Haven, Conn., 1974), 169. For a discussion of Cotton's views on baptism in comparison with those of his New England peers, see 143–159.

109. On the Half-Way Covenant, see ibid., 168–186; Robert G. Pope, *The Half-Way Covenant: Church Membership in Puritan New England* (Princeton, N.J., 1969).

with some wrong that she wishes to defend herself against. Can she speak in her own defense, even when it is her husband who has complained against her? She would seem to be in a double bind in that women are subject to men's authority in general and, specifically, wives are subordinate to husbands. Cotton replies that in both cases the woman may speak out, though he adds that, if an extended debate ensues, it would be better if she had some male advocate. And, in the second case, the woman's answering the charges is not an act of power but an act of "subjection," in that she has been called to account and must reply.

These questions recurred for Bulkeley in 1650, and at that time he reminded Cotton of his previous opinions, pressing him once again to advise the Concord elders. The case is also vexed because it involves the complaint of a wife against a husband, both of whom are church members at Concord. Though in the 1642 instance Cotton's full reply is preserved, in the later case we have only Cotton's brief notes for a reply written on Bulkeley's letter. They are enough, however, to show that Cotton distinguishes between instances where the parties are married and where they are not. A wife, he reminds Bulkeley, does not have liberty to complain against a husband except in cases serious enough to lead to divorce, which would be either real danger to her life from the husband's abusive treatment of her or breach of conjugal fidelity. In lesser cases, the husband retains his "Husbandly Authority" over the wife. Where the parties are not married and both are church members, however, a woman's complaint against a man may cause him to lose "Church-Power" over her as a result of his offense. In such cases, the woman can speak out. Bulkeley reminds Cotton that he had said many years previously that, if a "brother" offends a "sister," he becomes a "debter, and soe in that respect, putts him into a degree of inferioritye, & makes the other his superiour," thus allowing her to admonish him in the public church forum. Cotton does not deny this, but points out that the married state of the two individuals in the case Bulkeley is citing alters matters. Gender hierarchy could be set aside in some instances, but not in all. The woman's "liberty" to speak in church is granted sometimes, but not in all circumstances. God's grace is equally available to women (Bulkeley quotes Scripture to the effect that "in Christ Jesus there is neither male nor female"), but not always the right to voice a grievance. Thus, in these previously unpublished exchanges, some light is shed on the theorizing of gender relations and the extent (and limits) of women's public voice during this period (Bulkeley to Cotton, Apr. 4, 1650; Cotton to Bulkeley, [after April 4, 1650]).[110]

110. The question whether women had the privilege of speaking in church was answered differently by different churches in New England. Since the churches required of every person

In his 1651 letter to Elmeston, before he became ill, Cotton referred to himself as one "whose businesses are more than my dayes," suggesting both his sense of carrying a heavy workload and his feeling that he was nearing the end. Interestingly, as he approached death, at least some of his correspondence must have reminded him of his earliest days as a letter-writer. The questions he was asked to settle sometimes looked very much like those of twenty-five years earlier from the likes of Levett, Reyner, and others in Lincolnshire. Nathaniel Norcross, a young man seeking a church in New England, wrote him in July 1648 with several requests for personal advice on his career, including the question whether the prospect of finding a wife in a particular location ought to enter into a decision whether to accept a given church's call. And the much older Richard Saltonstall posed a case of conscience at a point in his life when he was faced with having to break his earlier vow to spend the rest of his days in New England. His wife's illness had taken her back to England, and he was suffering considerable stress from his dilemma whether to keep his vow or return to England. Cotton's answer allowed him to join his wife in England with a clear conscience.

Adding to the variety of his contacts were exchanges with acquaintances to the south. He was probably one of the recipients of a letter from a married couple in Maryland, Robert and Mary Burle, expressing skepticism about the kind of sectarian religion they were hearing there—decidedly Antinomian, as they describe it, though they don't seem able to name it—and asking for reactions by New England clergymen to their summaries of various doctrinal points. It is not clear that Cotton actually knew the Burles, but he was well acquainted with Nathaniel White, another correspondent in this period. White's Puritan settlement on Eleutherea in the Caribbean was threatened by famine when Cotton wrote on behalf of his congregation and others, sending charitable relief in the form of money and supplies in April 1650,

---

seeking admission to membership a profession of faith in which one's knowledge of Scripture and one's experience of saving grace would be demonstrated, women were expected to make such a statement. In the Boston church, from the arrival of Sarah and John Cotton in September 1633, it was common for women to make private profession to the elders alone, as Sarah Cotton did, whereas in other churches, such as Salem, Cambridge, and Hartford, it was common for women to make their statements, like the men, before the full congregation. Cotton's views on this subject were thus on the conservative end of the spectrum—which was of course not a terribly broad spectrum by modern standards, even though it was broader than many modern accounts would allow. Much has been written bearing on the issue of the constraint of women's role and voice; for modern work, see Caldwell, *The Puritan Conversion Narrative;* Cohen, *God's Caress,* 142–144, 240–241; Mary Beth Norton, *Founding Mothers and Fathers;* Kamensky, *Governing the Tongue.* Hall, *Faithful Shepherd,* 93–101, discusses the varying practices of membership admission in different churches in New England.

which apparently arrived just in the nick of time, finding the colonists on the verge of starvation. This instance of Cotton's leadership in a charitable cause is consistent with his interest in the 1620s in efforts to relieve the sufferings of Swiss Protestant Grissons during the vicious Catholic-Protestant engagements in the Palatinate (Edward Reyner to Cotton, Apr. 5, [1627?]).

Cotton's contacts with England continued to the end as well. Besides his exchanges with Elmeston in Kent, we know he was corresponding with his friends in Boston as well as others in and around London. His contact with Thomas Goodwin, for instance, had continued to the point where Goodwin was on the verge of emigrating to New England. By 1647 the Independents had lost the struggle with the Presbyterians in the Westminster Assembly over the new shape church polity would take in England. Cotton and his colonial colleagues probably used that fact together with the established strength of congregational polity in New England to persuade Goodwin to make the move across the water. Goodwin's son told of how close a call it was:

> In the year 1647, he had invitations from the Reverend Mr John Cotton, in whom grace and learning were so happily conjoined, and other worthy ministers in New England, to come over thither, which he was so much inclined to do as he had put a great part of his library on shipboard. But the persuasions of some friends, to whose counsel and advice he paid a great deference, made him to alter his resolution.[111]

His remaining in England was not altogether a loss for the cause of New England Puritanism, however. Together with fellow Independent Philip Nye, Goodwin had already seen one of Cotton's books into print in London, and he would continue to perform the same role for others through the 1650s.[112]

Cotton's continued concern for developments in church and commonwealth in England is perhaps best seen in his 1651 exchange with Oliver Cromwell, who at that point was able to report on the final success of his battles in the English Civil Wars. While Cromwell's reply to Cotton has often

111. "Memoir of Thomas Goodwin, D.D. Composed out of His Own Papers and Memoirs, by His Son," in *The Works of Thomas Goodwin, D.D.* (Edinburgh, 1861–1866), V, lxxiii.

112. Goodwin had seen to the printing of Cotton's *Grounds and Ends of the Baptisme of the Children of the Faithfull* (1647) and (together with Philip Nye) *The Keyes of the Kingdom of Heaven* (1644). He had a hand in posthumously publishing Thomas Hooker, *A Survey of the Summe of Church-Discipline* (1648) and, again with Nye, Hooker's works, *The Application of Redemption . . . The First Eight Books* (1656), *The Application of Redemption . . . The Ninth and Tenth Books* (1656), and *A Comment upon Christ's Last Prayer* (1656). On Peter Bulkeley's admiration of Goodwin's influence with the press in England, see the postscript of his letter to Cotton, Apr. 4, 1650.

been reprinted, Cotton's half of the exchange is not so well known. What is remarkable about Cotton's letter to Cromwell, in fact, is the fullness with which he is able to cite the conditions under which Cromwell's decisive victory over the Scots at Dunbar occurred. This event was quite recent when Cotton wrote, and it is clear that he had excellent sources of information within Cromwell's circle. Although removed from the scene for some eighteen years, Cotton was still maintaining channels of communication with the sites of power (Cotton to Cromwell, July 28, 1651; Cromwell to Cotton, Oct. 2, 1651).

In short, Cotton's correspondence kept him active in the lives of a great many people on both sides of the ocean. While he complained in more than one letter of the burden of keeping up with his obligations, it is clear that letter-writing—and the receipt of letters—remained central to the intellectual and spiritual life he maintained from the beginning to the end of his career. He treated it as a part of his call to ministry, in the tradition of John, Peter, Paul, and other letter-writers in apostolic times. It was an important expression of his calling. Without this means of communication, John Cotton's ministry and his role in the Puritan movement would have been significantly diminished.

If the letters provide relatively little personal detail about Cotton and his family, they do help us to understand not only the esteem in which he was held by his professional peers but also the intensely intellectual quality of his spiritual life. He seldom shied away from answering a difficult question and usually delivered his opinion with striking confidence in his authority. Cotton was a dedicated scholar whose study of the Church Fathers and of more recent exegetical literature, together with his intimate knowledge of the Bible itself, gave him the foundation on which his authority was based. He was prepared to share the findings of his lifelong search for truth with his correspondents. He responded to those he disagreed with by saying, "Your argument will not hold," and explained the basis for saying so—usually resorting to scriptural exegesis. Nowhere in this correspondence does he deflect a question by suggesting the inquirer ask someone else. The writer had often already done that; Cotton's was the decisive voice. In offering his reactions, and typically basing those reactions firmly on Scripture—on the authority, that is, of God—his letters evince the manner, the speaker-audience relationship, of Pauline epistles. As Goodwin believed, Cotton functioned in Puritan circles as "Apostle of the Age."

Provenance

Some further comment on the provenance and the physical qualities of the manuscripts will perhaps assist the reader in understanding why some of the letters are broken and incomplete and also provide something of a biography of these remnants of early colonial history. It is not possible to reconstruct the story of survival for all of the manuscripts, but we do know a good deal about the provenance of the four largest collections: the Thomas Prince Collection at the Boston Public Library, the Hutchinson Papers in the Massachusetts State Archives, the Winthrop Papers at the Massachusetts Historical Society, and the Mather Papers at the American Antiquarian Society. Together, these four collections account for 85 percent of the surviving manuscripts in Cotton's correspondence.

The earliest period of survival is the most difficult to reconstruct, though the format of some of the letters tells us that Cotton himself was one of the reasons they have survived. He kept file copies of his letters—probably not all of them, but at least those he felt were particularly interesting or important. These include letters written to him as well as by him. Upon reading a letter he had just received, he often made notes for a reply immediately in empty space on the incoming letter. In such cases, these brief notes are all that remains of his reply; the full copies of the letters actually written are missing (see Cotton to Jeremiah Burroughes, [November 1630], and Cotton to John Davenport, [May 1650]). Other examples show that he worked over a draft, revising with deletions and interlinear insertions until he was happy with the result, of which he then made a fair copy to send, keeping the rough draft in his letter book as a file copy (see Cotton to John Dod, Dec. 19, [1637]). Sometimes, of course, the letter actually sent or received by Cotton survives, even occasionally with some of the author's sealing wax still present. In most cases, letters written *to* Cotton where a manuscript exists tend to be the actual document he received, while letters written *by* Cotton are usually preserved in full copies or notes that he retained. It is clear that, when the time came to leave Lincolnshire, he included at least some of these letters in the possessions he took to New England. That fact, in itself, says something about the value he placed on his correspondence.

A particularly interesting discovery revealed in the study of these and related manuscript materials is that Cotton had the help of others, who served as secretaries, or scribes, in both Lincolnshire and Massachusetts Bay. In the old Boston, he used the various young men who were a part of his household seminary to perform copying duties for him. These trainees made copies of his letters for his own files and also took notes on his sermons, which can be seen in a manuscript of the early sermon series that was published posthumously in 1656 as *A Practical Commentary . . . upon the First Epistle Generall of John.*[1] This manuscript is valuable evidence for understanding Cotton's use of his resident scholars. Different individuals took notes on different sermons, so that the manuscript consists of some ten different handwritings. One of them is identical with the handwriting in John Nicolaus Rulice's letter to Cotton dated November 29, 1628, by which time Rulice, a German who we know had lived for a time with Cotton, had already left Boston.[2] Clearly, Rulice and other members of Cotton's seminary were assigned duties as note-takers and copyists during their sojourns with their master. Of the eleven letters surviving in manuscript that were written by Cotton during the Lincolnshire period of his career, eight are in Cotton's own hand, and the other three are contemporary copies, each made by a different person. The handwriting of two of those individuals—the amanuensis of Cotton's November 12, 1628, letter to a "Beloved Sister" and of Cotton's brief notes (probably dictated) for a reply to Jeremiah Burroughes's letter of November 1630—are identical with two of the hands in the "First John" manuscript. Cotton himself often added his own signature or initials to these file copies, just as he inserted minor revisions in the "First John" manuscript.[3]

It appears that in New England in the early 1640s he resumed his practice of training young college students and graduates for the ministry. It has previously been suggested that Benjamin Woodbridge, in Harvard's first graduating class, in 1642, was one such trainee.[4] Cotton's own son, Seaborn,

1. The Bowdoin College Library calls the MS "John Cotton's Commentary on the First Epistle of John."

2. The identity of Rulice's handwriting is further confirmed by holograph letters in Amsterdam's Gemeente Archief: John Rulice to the English church at Amsterdam dated London, Oct. 1, 1635, and Rulice and four others (in Rulice's hand) to the elders and deacons of the English church at Rotterdam, May 18, 1636, Part Arch. 318, vol. XXVII.

3. This information enables us to state with fuller certainty than previously that the first drafting of the "First John" commentary began before November 1628 and seems likely to have occurred sometime during the period 1627–1628. Rulice's entries in the manuscript are very near the beginning. We do not know when he left Boston, but he was surely gone by November 1628, the date of his letter to Cotton. The completion date cannot be determined from this information, but the sermon series would have been of many months' duration, perhaps extending into 1629. Everett Emerson suggested the "First John" sermons date from 1629–1632, and Ann Kibbey has estimated a beginning in 1628. Emerson, *Cotton,* 27; Ann Kibbey, *The Interpretation of Material Shapes in Puritanism: A Study of Rhetoric, Prejudice, and Violence* (Cambridge, 1986), 153.

4. See Ziff, *Career of John Cotton,* 252–253.

was another. As a teenager, despite his somewhat immature handwriting, Seaborn occasionally served as copyist, as the manuscripts of two letters from 1648–1649—Cotton letters to Lydia Gaunt and Peter Bulkeley—clearly demonstrate.[5] Both are copies in Seaborn's hand. In the early 1640s, moreover, some five letters and two other documents by Cotton were preserved in yet another handwriting, which is decidedly not Cotton's or Seaborn's.[6] This copyist was not his wife, Sarah, nor could it be the hand of any of the other Cotton children, who were simply too young.[7] Though this particular hand is evident in Cotton's letters over a period of only about a year and a half, from late August 1640 to March 1642, it is evident that Cotton was by this time enjoying the same kind of scribal assistance that he had known in his Lincolnshire years.[8] It is likely that the establishment of Harvard College

5. Cotton to [Lydia Gaunt], Sept. 14, 1648, and [Cotton] to Peter Bulkeley, [early May] 1649. Seaborn's Latin letter to his father acknowledges Cotton's tutorial role in his son's early training. It also provides the comparative evidence to prove that the above two letters are in Seaborn's handwriting. See S[eaborn] C[otton] to John Cotton, [c. 1648–1651].

6. The letters in this handwriting are Cotton to [John] Elmeston, Aug. 26, 1640; Cotton to Peter Bulkeley, Jan. 16, 1640/1; Cotton to Bulkeley, Aug. 7, 1641; Cotton to [Bulkeley], [February 1641/2]; and Cotton to Stephen Bachiler, Mar. 9, 1641/2. The other documents are the preface to the *Bay Psalm Book* and "The Causes of Hen: Bull's Excommunication." All were in Thomas Prince's collection and are now in the Boston Public Library.

7. The exclusion of Sarah is based on comparisons of the letters and documents in question with her signature on her will in the Suffolk County Probate files (docket #806), a prenuptial agreement made before her marriage to Richard Mather in the Boston Public Library, and a lease in the Massachusetts Historical Society. I am grateful to Giuseppe Bisaccia, Elizabeth C. Bouvier, and Virginia H. Smith for assistance in making these comparisons.

An exception among the children in Cotton's household might be Sarah's daughter by her first marriage, Elizabeth Story. She was born in June 1622, so was old enough to have assisted her stepfather by 1640, but no example of her handwriting has been found. The handwriting in question is a very regular, mature hand. All are in the Prince Collection at the Boston Public Library.

8. This handwriting appears often enough in the Cotton Papers from the Prince Library that a former Keeper of Rare Books at the Boston Public Library, Zoltán Haraszti, made the mistaken assumption that it was in fact Cotton's hand, claiming as much in connection with a partial facsimile of one of the letters published in his book on *The Bay Psalm Book*. After providing persuasive internal evidence for his discovery that the preface to *The Bay Psalm Book* was written by Cotton and not Richard Mather, Haraszti adds an argument based on the identical handwriting of Cotton's letter to John Elmeston (whom he calls Elmerton) dated Aug. 26, 1640, and the manuscript of the final draft of the preface. What he failed to appreciate was that the handwriting in both was that of a scribe, not Cotton's at all. But it was the same scribe as the one who copied out other papers of Cotton's, so the proof of Cotton's authorship that Haraszti was interested in establishing is not altered by the present observations. See Zoltán Haraszti, *The Enigma of the Bay Psalm Book* (Chicago, 1956), 25–27.

in 1636 and the entrance of the first class in 1638 once again provided him with a pool of eager appprentices. In both Lincolnshire and Massachusetts, among the duties of Cotton's young seminarians was clerical assistance with the writing tasks of the master.

Whether they are in his own or a copyist's hand, most of Cotton's letters—and those from his correspondents—were initially preserved by Cotton himself. In a few instances, however, contemporary manuscript copies were made by others. His famous letter to Samuel Skelton in Salem, written on October 2, 1630, while Cotton was still in England, survives only in two such manuscript transcriptions, one made eight months later by Richard Mather, who was also still in England, and another, which is undated, made by Richard Bernard, an English minister who was about twenty years senior to Cotton.[9] Both copies—and probably others—were circulated among interested readers. The letter from Benjamin Keayne to Cotton in 1647 was almost immediately transcribed into a book containing deeds and related legal documents, and the transcription was then preserved along with such papers. As a result, it still resides at the Suffolk County Court House in Boston in a collection of early deeds. One letter was preserved because it was read aloud to the Boston congregation; Robert Keayne, who habitually took notes at Cotton's sermons and at church meetings, transcribed the letter as John Wilson read it to the congregation on September 26, 1640. Other letters were copied at later periods, but well before the present century, and survive now only because of those copies. Cotton's exchange of letters with Oliver Cromwell in 1651 is another well-known event in the Cotton correspondence, but, while Cromwell's holograph reply to Cotton is preserved in the holdings of the New York Public Library, Cotton's earlier letter to Cromwell exists only in manuscript transcripts made in the eighteenth and nineteenth centuries.

Another reason for the survival of texts of some of the letters where the manuscripts have been lost is that historians and antiquarians, recognizing their value, made copies for their own use; the copies survive while the originals do not. Both Increase and Cotton Mather were aware of the historical value of manuscript materials from the first generation of settlement, and they preserved in published works occasional fragments from Cotton's letters. Like the Mathers, the Winthrops also performed valuable service as conservators of such documents. Very early in the colony's history, John Winthrop began to retain copies of his family's correspondence, a practice that other Winthrops in succeeding generations imitated. Given their proximity as neighbors, there were probably not many times that Cotton and John Win-

9. At least one (other?) copy was in the possession of William Coddington at Aquidneck in 1641; see Coddington to Cotton, [March–April, 1641].

throp had occasion to exchange letters, but there are four instances in which the Winthrops preserved letters to or from Cotton.

In the eighteenth century, Ezra Stiles (1727–1795), the president of Yale College, saw and copied out many old manuscripts that have subsequently disappeared, some apparently in the British siege of Newport, Rhode Island, in 1776. Among them were two 1641 letters from Cotton's old Lincolnshire friend, William Coddington, then in exile in Rhode Island, which are extant now thanks only to Stiles's transcriptions.[10] Even earlier, in the seventeenth century, some letters were printed, both during and after Cotton's lifetime, that would otherwise now be lost. Sometimes adversaries such as Robert Baillie and Roger Williams published Cotton letters or excerpts from them in order to argue with them. On other occasions friends such as John Dod and John Elmeston saw them into print. Archbishop James Ussher's first editor and biographer, Richard Parr, included a Cotton letter to Ussher in his 1686 edition of Ussher's correspondence.

Among those we must thank for these efforts at preservation are the two major conservators and historians, Thomas Prince (1687–1758) and Thomas Hutchinson (1711–1780), both of whom collected books and documents from the earliest colonial period as they prepared their histories of New England. Both would be disappointed to know that, while their efforts did preserve to the present-day documents that would otherwise doubtless have been lost, their care has not been accorded full respect subsequently.[11]

Prince, as early as his tenth year, began a collection of books and manuscripts that he would call the New England Library. On his death in his seventy-second year, he bequeathed his collection to the Old South Church in Boston, of which he had been pastor for many years. He intended that his books and manuscripts be preserved and protected against loss, stipulating that the collection was to be maintained as a noncirculating library, though "any Person whom the Pastors & Deacons of s*ai*d Church for the Time being

10. Franklin Bowditch Dexter's *Extracts from the Itineraries and Other Miscellanies of Ezra Stiles, D.D., LL.D., 1755–1794, with a Selection from His Correspondence* (New Haven, Conn., 1916) included the two letters to Cotton. Stiles, like Thomas Hutchinson, was engaged in collecting primary materials for a history of New England. In fact, in 1766, Hutchinson, who had already published the first volume of his history, learned that Stiles had been preparing to write such a work. After offering flattering comments about Stiles's greater fitness for such a job, Hutchinson adds, "I have endeavoured for as much new material as I could from manuscripts of such authors as are quite forgot to tender a work so little interesting as this must be from the nature of it as entertaining as possible." Hutchinson to Stiles, Feb. 15, 1766, MSA, XXVI, fol. 80.

11. Both Prince and Hutchinson borrowed some of their collected materials from the Mathers. Since those materials were not all returned, the Mather family's subsequent view of these historians' handling of the materials was quite critical.

shall approve of may have access thereto, & take Copies therefrom." Historian though he was, Prince unfortunately failed to anticipate changing times and conditions. The first adverse circumstance was that of simple neglect. As Justin Winsor puts it: "The books and papers were deposited on shelves, and in boxes and barrels in a room in the steeple of the church, under the belfry, which according to tradition had been Prince's study. There this valuable deposit was left for many years without care, and subject to many vicissitudes."[12] It may be that it was then, perhaps owing to a leaky roof, that the water damage occurred that has marked many of the letters in the Cotton Papers portion of the Prince Library. Many of them apparently got wet when they were still folded, as the greatest loss of paper and text is often along the folds, which were subject to the wear and friction of rough treatment.

Political cataclysm was not anticipated by Prince, but it did occur nonetheless, and it bore directly on the fate of his collection. When Boston was occupied by the British in 1775–1776, South Church was used by British troops as a riding school. Winsor recounts this episode, observing that the building was frequented by idle spectators, who must have had access to the collection and might have been responsible for some of the loss it sustained. It is known that in heating the building the pulpit and pews were burned, and the adjoining parsonage, once the home of John Winthrop, was demolished to keep up the fires during the long winter. It is believed that many of these books and papers were used by the soldiers as kindling.[13] One letter in the Prince Collection, more nearly intact than many, contains grit that at some point was ground into the paper, whether by the boots of either British redcoats or patriot revolutionaries is unknown.[14]

Ironically, a decade before the British troops set about destroying Prince's collection, zealous colonial patriots had committed their own depredations nearby where another major collection of colonial manuscripts was held. Wrongly suspected of supporting the Stamp Act, the crown's lieutenant governor, Thomas Hutchinson, became the target of a vicious attack during the Stamp Act Riot of August 26, 1765, resulting in the complete gutting of his house and destruction of virtually everything in it. Money and plate

12. Justin Winsor, introduction, *The Prince Library: A Catalogue of the Collection of Books and Manuscripts Which Formerly Belonged to the Reverend Thomas Prince . . .* (Boston, 1870), ix. One person who did look into Prince's collection was Ezra Stiles, whose papers from 1770 include "Extracts from MSS in the Steeple Library of the South Chh of Boston collected by Mr Prince," including a transcription of a copy of Oliver Cromwell's letter to Cotton (Oct. 2, 1651). Papers of Ezra Stiles, Yale University: Itineraries, II, 403–404.

13. Winsor, introduction, *Prince Library,* ix–x.

14. John Cotton to John Reyner, Oct. 18, [1639].

were plundered; pictures, furniture, books, and papers were dragged into the street and trampled in the mud. Hutchinson later expressed gratitude that the king and the provincial government had replaced many items, "but," he added, "the loss of many papers and books, in print as well as manuscripts, besides my family memorials, never can be repaired." The manuscript of the second volume of Hutchinson's *History of the Colony of Massachusets-Bay* was among the papers that lay "in the street scattered abroad several hours in the rain," though most of that work was salvaged by neighbors. But Hutchinson himself lamented that "the most valuable materials were lost, some of which I designed to have published in the appendix."[15] For years Hutchinson had been engaged in collecting papers that would make up an archive of colonial history.[16] The Hutchinson Papers now in the Massachusetts State Archives are in particularly good condition and include some of the surviving Cotton papers. Like the Prince Collection, the portions of Hutchinson's collection that were preserved went first to the Massachusetts Historical Society. They were later the object of a successful replevin action and were transferred to the Massachusetts State Archives, where they remain today.[17] But most of the letters included in Hutchinson's *History* and his *Collection of Original Papers relative to the History of the Colony of Massachusets-Bay* are no longer extant in manuscript. What we cannot know in full detail is what else has been lost.

During the eighteenth century another famous collection of papers was also damaged. The collection in the possession of Samuel Mather, Cotton's great-grandson, rivaled Prince's collection in importance, especially as it related to the Cotton and Mather families. The two families had become intertwined after Cotton's death through two events. One was Richard Mather's becoming the third husband of Cotton's widow, Sarah, in 1656. The other was the marriage of Mather's eldest son, Increase, to the Cottons' only surviving daughter, Maria, on March 6, 1661/2.[18] These occurrences ensured that at

15. Thomas Hutchinson, *The History of the Province of Massachusets-Bay, . . . 1691 until . . . 1750,* 2d ed., II (London, 1768), x. On the Stamp Act Riot and the attack on Hutchinson's property, see Bernard Bailyn, *The Ordeal of Thomas Hutchinson* (Cambridge, Mass., 1974), 35–38.

16. Hutchinson was quite conscious of the importance of the act of preservation that he was performing. He theorized on the subject in a decidedly eighteenth-century vocabulary, but the preservationist values that he expressed still hold: "He who rescues from oblivion interesting historical facts is beneficial to posterity as well as to his contemporaries, and the prospect thereof to a benevolent mind causes that employment to be agreeable and pleasant which otherwise would be irksome and painful." Thomas Hutchinson, "The Preface," *Hutchinson Papers,* Prince Society, Publications (Albany, N.Y., 1865), I, i.

17. I am grateful to Martha Clark, Special Assistant to the Archivist, Massachusetts State Archives, for this information.

18. The Massachusetts Historical Society owns the copy of the Geneva Bible that John Cot-

least some of the first-generation Cotton papers would become part of the collection of family memorabilia preserved by the Mathers. The nineteenth-century historian Samuel G. Drake noted of the early eighteenth century: "There were few Persons engaged in collecting Materials for the History of the Past in New England. But there were a few splendid Exceptions, the most prominent (because best known) was the Collection of the Rev. Thomas Prince. That of the Mathers, though not less important, is less known." This Mather collection, Drake supposes, "must have been superiour to all others in New-England. It was accumulated during four Generations. It was commenced by Richard Mather of Dorchester, from whom it passed to his son, Dr. Increase Mather, and from him to his Son, Cotton Mather, from whom it passed with all its augmentations to Dr. Samuel Mather. A valuable part of it was given . . . to the American Antiquarian Society."[19] But before that delivery, which did, happily, preserve two items in the present collection, the Mather collection suffered major losses. Samuel Mather wrote on June 9, 1784, to his son, Samuel, in England, complaining: "There were several Letters I had, original Letters, written by the renowned Oliver Cromwell, to my Great-Grandfather, Mr. John Cotton, which I lent to your careless Uncle, Mr. Hutchinson, and, as I suppose, they are irrecoverably lost and gone: I furnished him, as I suppose you know, with most of his Materials, of which his History was composed."[20]

Dr. Mather neglects to mention another source of his loss, though the event was noted contemporaneously by Abigail Adams in one of her letters to her husband, John, then a member of the Continental Congress. Writing from their home in Quincy to John in Philadelphia, while describing the British army's 1775 occupation and burning of parts of Boston and surrounding towns, she writes, "Mr. [Samuel] Mather got out a day or two before Charlstown was distroyed, and had lodged his papers and what else he got out at Mr. Carys, but they were all consumed." John Adams knew the materials in question and understood the seriousness of the loss to history: "The Loss of Mr. Mathers Library, which was a Collection, of Books and Manu-

---

ton gave to his daughter, Maria. On the flyleaf Increase Mather entered: "I was marryed ^to Maria only daughter of the Rev[d] John Cotton^ *the* 6 day of *the* 1 month being *the* fifth day of *the* weeke 1661/2."

19. Samuel G. Drake, introduction, *The History of King Philip's War, by the Rev. Increase Mather, D.D.; Also, A History of the Same War, by the Rev. Cotton Mather, D.D.* (Boston, 1862), xv–xvi.

20. Ibid., xxii. Hutchinson himself, in his preface to the first volume of his *History,* acknowledged, "I am obliged to no person more than to my friend and brother the Reverend Mr. Mather, whose library has been open to me as it had been before to the Reverend Mr. Prince, who had taken from thence the greatest and most valuable part of what he had collected" (Hutchinson, *History,* I, [i]).

scripts made by himself, his Father, his Grandfather, and Greatgrandfather, and was really very curious and valuable, is irreparable."[21]

As another war with England was being waged in 1813, the Massachusetts Historical Society fortunately recognized the threat posed by leaving the Prince collection in the South Church and appealed to the church to house the collection in the society. This offer was accepted, and in 1814 the materials in Prince's New England Library that remained—still a considerable collection—were moved to the society. The church retained the legal right to recall the collection, however, and in fact did so in 1859. In 1866 the entire Prince Library was finally moved into the Boston Public Library, where the materials could be more generally accessible, with the understanding that the library would be put in good order and kept so and that a complete catalog would be prepared and printed, which was accomplished in 1870. Before the completion of this transfer, the Massachusetts Historical Society made the transcriptions of the Cotton Papers that remain in its collections today.[22]

Other collections have not escaped the ravages of time and events. One such collection whose loss is particularly lamentable was John Cotton's personal file of materials related to the Antinomian controversy. Hutchinson informs us: "Upon his death-bed [Cotton] ordered his son to burn all his papers relative to the religious disputes began in the time of Sir Henry Vane's year. He had bundled them all up, with an intention to do it himself, but death prevented his going into his study for that purpose. His son, loth to destroy what appeared to him valuable, made a case of conscience to Mr. Norton whether he was bound to comply. Mr. Norton determined against the papers." Although some valuable documents relative to that controversy have survived, including a few letters in the present volume, it is clear, nevertheless, that a major loss was suffered soon after Cotton's death.[23]

Other papers remained in the family's care somewhat longer. Cotton's will left his books to his sons Seaborn and John in equal portions but made

21. Abigail Adams to John Adams, June 25, 1775, and John Adams to Abigail Adams, July 7, 1775, in L. H. Butterfield, Marc Friedlaender, and Mary-Jo Kline, eds., *The Book of Abigail and John: Selected Letters of the Adams Family, 1762–1784* (Cambridge, Mass., 1975), 94, 95.

22. Justin Winsor, superintendent of the Boston Public Library when this final transfer was made, relates all of these details (Winsor, introduction, *The Prince Library,* xi–xiv). "Transcripts of the most important [manuscripts] were made under the supervision of the Rev. Chandler Robbins, D.D." (ibid., 142). Robbins was the society's recording secretary, 1857–1864, and then its corresponding secretary, 1864–1877 (Louis Leonard Tucker, *The Massachusetts Historical Society: A Bicentennial History, 1791–1991* [Boston, 1995], 540, 541). The actual transcribing was probably done by Edward Holden or John Appleton or both (see below, "Editorial Method," n. 3).

23. Thomas Hutchinson, *The History of the Colony and Province of Massachusetts-Bay,* ed. Lawrence Shaw Mayo (Cambridge, Mass., 1936), I, 152.

no mention of personal papers, which must have been at the disposal, therefore, of his widow, Sarah, who was his sole executrix. We know that ten years after Cotton's death John Davenport asked the younger John Cotton to return to him letters he had written to the young clergyman's father, which he did.[24] This suggests that there was probably a larger cache of Cotton's letters from which the Davenport letters were removed. Owing to the intermarriage of two generations of the Cotton and Mather families very soon after Cotton's death, at least some of Cotton's correspondence surely remained in the Mather family. Cotton Mather had such manuscripts in hand when writing *Johannes in Eremo* (Boston, 1695), which includes quotations from Cotton's correspondence. None of the letters quoted there, and subsequently in Mather's *Magnalia Christi Americana* (where the five *Johannes in Eremo* biographies were reprinted with minor changes), has survived to the present day. He also copied part of a Cotton letter into his unpublished "Biblia Americana."[25] Likewise, Increase Mather still earlier in *First Principles of New-England* (Cambridge, Mass., 1675) had quoted from several letters to and from Cotton, all of which have since disappeared. And John Cotton's great-grandson, Josiah Cotton, copied a part of a letter into his notebook, indicating that more than one branch of the Mather family in the fourth generation in America continued to own Cotton papers. The astute awareness by the Mather, Cotton, and Winthrop families of the historical value of materials from the first generation was critical to the preservation of many of the documents we now have, though it was often an insufficient safeguard.

This is not the first attempt to compile Cotton's letters. It stands on the shoulders of two previous beginnings. The first was called to my attention by Everett Emerson, who successfully aroused my interest in such a project by pointing me to the 1932 master of arts thesis (Columbia University) by Lawrance R. Thompson. Thompson's lectures on later American literature had been an inspiration to me as an undergraduate, but I had not known of his work on Cotton's manuscripts. His thesis was an edition of Cotton's correspondence as Thompson then knew it, forty-seven letters in all. Doing im-

24. John Davenport added a postscript to his letter to John Cotton, Jr., written in New Haven on Mar. 23, 1662/3: "I thanck you for my letters to your Father, which you sent me, according to my desire and your promise. Some I rec[eive]d by Edm[und] Toolie, and some by Jacob molines, with your letter. If any yet remaine with you; you will further oblige me, if you send them to me." Davenport's reference to two separate batches and his further intimation that he can think of still more that have not been returned suggest the considerable extent and importance of the Davenport-Cotton correspondence. Isabel MacBeath Calder, ed., *Letters of John Davenport: Puritan Divine* (New Haven, Conn., 1937), 212.

25. See Cotton to [Robert Harding?], [c. 1638–1644?].

pressive work for a master's student, Thompson had worked his way through many of the most difficult manuscripts (though he did not include all of those available to him), but, instead of returning to Cotton after completing his graduate work, he went on to a distinguished professorial career at Princeton University working successively on such later American writers as Henry Wadsworth Longfellow, Herman Melville, and Robert Frost. Nevertheless, the beginnings he had made on Cotton provided important encouragement at the earliest stage of the present project. Thompson's work seemed the logical starting point for a fuller edition, though his thesis proved somewhat erratic in its attention to details and had to be set aside as a model. Moreover, the half-century after his work on Cotton had been rich in advancements in both editorial methodology and historical scholarship. In the end, all letters in the present edition have been checked and rechecked against the manuscripts. Yet Thompson's early assay was a catalyst to this work. Without it, the present project would never have been undertaken.

A later and more comprehensive attempt to edit the Cotton correspondence also deserves mention. Some thirty years after Thompson completed his thesis, Robert Scholz began a new edition of the letters for his own master of arts thesis at the University of Minnesota under the direction of Darrett Rutman. Only an administrative decision that Scholz could bypass the master's degree altogether prevented his bringing to completion his impressive beginning. Late in the present project, I made contact with the Reverend Dr. Scholz, who very generously shared his findings with me. There were omissions in both of our lists of Cotton's correspondence at that point, but his work pointed me to a few items that I had either missed, questioned, or provisionally excluded and was thus an important factor in bringing this work to completion.

Persistent search for the primary documents over more than a decade has led to the collection of these 125 letters and 5 supporting documents. Direct inquiries at research libraries as well as at many smaller academic, municipal, and private libraries in England, Scotland, Wales, Northern Ireland, the Republic of Ireland, the Netherlands, Germany, France, Canada, and the United States has turned up these letters. In the end, only 3 of the manuscripts were found in England and 1 in Holland; the rest are in libraries in the United States. Of the total, 73 are by Cotton, and the remaining 52 were written to him. Manuscripts of 87 of these items survive, 49 of which are Cotton's letters (though in some instances not in his handwriting). This edition contains 54 letters that have never been published before and another 15 that have not been printed since the seventeenth century. Thus, a substantial portion of this volume—more than half the items—will be new material for anyone who has not studied the manuscripts or the seventeenth-century published texts in which a few have appeared. The editorial task in thus finding and, in many cases, reclaiming these texts for a wider readership has been immensely gratifying. But, in some cases, some work remains for the reader!

The materials presented in the following pages have survived some tumultuous years, a small remnant of a major collection, but a remnant that still speaks of the people and the times in clear and direct voices that are truly fascinating to hear more than 350 years later. The modern scholar can appreciate Thomas Hutchinson's confession that "the perusal of . . . the letters and papers of our first planters, afforded me a very sensible pleasure."[26] The obvious physical damage to many of the letters has left them fragmented, forcing them to speak to us sometimes in garbled sentences, as if with great effort and against great constraint. Yet speak they do, sometimes all the more eloquently for the scars they bear from their rough treatment through many periods of American history. The wonder is, not that so few have survived, but that we have as many letters from that distant day as we do. Although these 125 letters or partial letters are but a small fraction of the number Cotton wrote and received in his lifetime, we know of only three other contemporaries in New England (John Winthrop, Roger Williams, and John Davenport) for whom so many still exist. His fellow emigrant and equally famous colleague, Thomas Hooker, is represented, for instance, by fewer than a dozen letters today. Cotton's letters are among the treasures of early Anglo-American history, preserving the perspective of the leading Puritan intellectual of the generation of the Great Migration. It is high time they were more widely known.

The fragments of correspondence, surviving here sometimes like the shards of an ancient vase, tell a story that is only partially present, but that is strongly and clearly enough suggested by the remaining pieces of evidence so that we can infer, however dimly, the shape of the whole. But whether his correspondents, like Cotton, emigrated to establish new conditions for their spiritual lives or whether they remained behind to experience the troubles and triumphs of English Puritanism in the dramatic decades ahead, they knew that Cotton's loving advice filled a strongly felt need. Wise and sympathetic counsel from a fellow sufferer and fellow believer surely strengthened the bonds among the Puritans well beyond the limits of the life of any one person. The surviving fragments of Cotton's correspondence provide clear evidence of the importance of these personal, informal exchanges to the inner strength of the Puritan movement before, during, and beyond the period of the Great Migration.

26. Hutchinson, *History,* ed. Mayo, II, ix.

Editorial Method

This volume of letters represents an attempt to include all surviving vestiges of Cotton's correspondence. While the large majority are complete letters, a few are smaller scraps in the form of quoted excerpts from letters otherwise lost. These fragments are sometimes as brief as a single sentence. The assumption is that all glimpses of Cotton's written exchanges with his contemporaries contribute to our grasp of the range of topics in his correspondence, his positions on them, and the intensity of his engagement in them and thus help to fill out our picture of this important Puritan leader and inform our understanding of his place in the Puritan movement. The very fact that Cotton's private letters were quoted by people not among his correspondents, often not even contemporaries, suggests a general awareness of the significance of that correspondence.

Whether a given letter survives in manuscript or in published form, the earliest version has always been selected as the source text for this edition. Thus, when a manuscript survives, that manuscript, not a published version, has been used to establish its text in the present edition, even where modern (that is, nineteenth- or twentieth-century) editions have been produced. Where a manuscript no longer exists, the earliest published edition is always preferred, since, in virtually every instance, the editor of that publication had the manuscript in front of him. His editorial methods were typically different from those that a modern editor would use, and he probably modified the text in some degree, but that first edition is the nearest thing to the document itself; it therefore deserves preferred status.

The fundamental goal in editing the texts in this volume thus has been to present, as fully as possible, the original version of each letter. Texts are not modernized, the aim being to bring the reader as close to the letter and its moment of composition as possible. Letters are personal documents, seldom intended for public presentation, though there are occasional exceptions to this rule in Cotton's and his correspondents' practice. Since they thus are potential sources of information about a writer's uniquely personal thoughts and traits, it seems not only undesirable but unwise to alter them significantly.[1]

1. G. Thomas Tanselle argues that "if a private document is presented in clear text it loses part of its texture" ("The Editing of Historical Documents," *Studies in Bibliography,* XXXI [1978], 51).

A major problem in dealing with a good many of the manuscript letters is the damage they have incurred. As previously explained, before finding their present homes in climate-controlled conditions and under the care of trained and responsible manuscript curators in modern libraries, some of the letters suffered severe damage. The problem is chiefly evident in the manuscripts in the Thomas Prince Collection, which were surely damaged long before they were acquired in turn by the Massachusetts Historical Society and the Boston Public Library, though occasional manuscripts in other collections sometimes contain physical damage, usually less dramatic in its extent than that of Prince's materials. Some of the letters are torn, with significant loss of paper at the edges. Since they were obviously stored in their original folded state, when they became wet and suffered abrasion on the exposed portions—usually the corners and edges of the folds—the paper was physically worn or torn away, resulting in holes of various sizes, often in the center portions of the sheets. Water stains, faded ink, and ancient mildew are also frequent consequences. The worst example of this is the pitiful remnant of Cotton's personal draft of his very long letter to the Reverend Mr. [Edward] Naylor in Boston, Lincolnshire, but other examples of mutilation are numerous and sometimes almost as severe.

The result for the editor is that sometimes portions of text are unreclaimable. The struggle to extract such text has never been given up without repeated attempts to decipher it, using manipulations of incandescent, fluorescent, and black light, always aided by magnification. The results of such efforts have often been very gratifying, with words sometimes slowly emerging from portions of paper that at first glance had appeared quite blank; certain portions of Cotton's long letter to John Wheelwright, April 18, 1640, published here for the first time, provide a prime example. Happily, the quality of ink used in most instances in the early seventeenth century was excellent, having great staying power in the face of rigorous tests of its permanence. In fact, sometimes the strength of the ink can be the main problem, as in a key letter from Thomas Shepard to Cotton in 1636 that bled through the paper and blurred, making both sides of the paper very difficult to read.[2] Usually, the paper is also of very good quality, another factor in the survival of most of the manuscripts in question. (On one occasion when the paper was unusually absorbent, Thomas Dudley was provoked to complain of its inferior quality; he was obviously used to better stock.)

Fortunately, not all of the holograph letters are distressed. The collection also contains unpublished letters that are wonderfully whole and legible.

2. David D. Hall overcame those difficulties to include the letter in his important edition of papers related to the Antiomian Controversy: Hall, *Antinomian Controversy,* 25–29.

While the worst cases were truly daunting to a prospective editor, the fascination and challenge of a large body of papers that had come through very harsh conditions during three and a half centuries proved stronger than the suspicion that some of them might not be reclaimable for a broader reading audience at all. The attempt needed to be made.

Such efforts have in some instances been aided by the preservation in the Massachusetts Historical Society of transcriptions of some of the letters in the Prince Collection made just before those papers were transferred to the Boston Public Library. The society's account books record payments in 1862 and again in 1868 to Edward Holden for "copying" and to John Appleton in 1868 for "preparing papers." A memorial essay on Dr. Appleton mentions that he "rendered important service in copying ancient manuscripts for the Society's publications."[3] These attempted readings are often less than fully successful, and, although the transcriptions were made after the major mutilations had occurred to these materials, they do occasionally preserve letters, words, and sometimes phrases that have subsequently been lost to further crumbling at the edges. The society's preservation of a photostatic record of the state of the manuscripts in the 1920s has also been helpful in reclaiming occasional details. And a mid-twentieth-century microfilm copy made by the Boston Public Library has helped supplement readings of manuscripts in their present states. The latter library invested in a major reclamation project in the 1980s, during work on the present edition, which noticeably improved and stabilized the condition of the most precariously degenerated letters in the collection.

Editorial markers signal these manuscript problems. Breaks in the text are indicated by parallels: ||. When missing portions of text can be confidently restored, they are enclosed in square brackets: commu[nion].[4] When such restoration is conjectural, it is followed by a question mark: comm[onwealth?]. One or more unreclaimable words are indicated by a bracketed description: [two illegible words]. When details are supplied from the transcription of the manuscript or later photostats of it, they are included in braces, and the source is identified in the headnote to the letter in question: was s{trucke} be-

3. I am grateful to Brenda Lawson, of the Manuscripts Department at the Massachusetts Historical Society, for assistance in finding and interpreting these facts. Dr. John Appleton was Assistant Librarian of the society from 1854 to 1868; he died Feb. 4, 1869. MHS Accounts, VI, 10, X, 167; *Catalog of Manuscripts of the Massachusetts Historical Society* (Boston, 1969), I, 273; Louis Leonard Tucker, *The Massachusetts Historical Society: A Bicentennial History, 1791–1991* (Boston, 1995), 239, 474; Charles Deane, "Memoir of John Appleton, M.D.," MHS, *Procs.,* XV (1876–1877), 365–367.

4. Degrees of confidence will, of course, vary, but physical evidence such as the size of a hole or other obscurity in the text is always a factor, as is the context.

tweene. This fortunate preservation of earlier states has sometimes made it possible to read the various versions as a kind of palimpsest, filling in blanks in the texts that would otherwise remain silent patches. Usually, however, the damage occurred to the manuscripts at such an early point that all of the transcribers have had to deal with the same frustrating holes.

Contractions, very common in seventeenth-century informal written discourse, are usually expanded by using italics for the letters that were omitted in the contraction, thus retaining a clear indication that the author has written a contraction and, in the italics, showing which letters were omitted. This expansion of the author's contractions is done only where some orthographic or other symbol indicates that letters have been omitted.

Specifically, the tilde is replaced by the missing letter in italics: comõnwealth ⟩ com*m*onwealth. The crossed p is expanded with italicized letters: p*er,* p*ro,* p*ar,* p*re,* and so forth. When contractions include superscript letters, as they usually do, the raised letters are brought down to the line and missing letters supplied in italics: ag^{t} ⟩ ag*ains*t, w^{ch} ⟩ w*hi*ch, wth ⟩ w*i*th, X^{t} ⟩ *Chris*t, l^{re} ⟩ l*ett*ere, g^{o} ⟩ *er*go. The thorn, essentially an orthographic convenience in seventeenth-century written discourse, is replaced with italicized *th* and final letters are brought down to the line: y^{e} ⟩ *th*e, y^{m} or ỹ ⟩ *the*m, y^{t} ⟩ *tha*t, y^{y} ⟩ *the*y. Other less frequently encountered contractions and abbreviations and their expanded forms include: w^{n} ⟩ w*he*n, o^{r} ⟩ o*u*r, frõ ⟩ fro*m,* altho: ⟩ altho*ugh,* Lo: ⟩ Lo*rd.*

When a period is used at the end of an abbreviation, the word is not expanded, but printed just as written. If there is no final period or other diacritical signal at the end of a shortened form of a word, the word is left as written. Sometimes, where the writing is hurried or sloppy (Peter Bulkeley and Richard Mather are both frequently guilty of this), the final letter of a contraction is written more or less on the same line as the rest of the word. For instance, coven^{t} (for coven*an*t) sometimes becomes just covent. In such cases, the contraction is not expanded. Exceptions are abbreviations in signatures, as in Pet: Bulkeley, where the signature is left unchanged, and in the case of common titles of personal address, such as M^{r} or M^{rs}, where expansion would deviate from both seventeenth-century and modern practice. Otherwise, spelling, paragraphing, and capitalization are rendered just as they appear in the original text, except that ff is rendered as F, which is how it was understood in the period, and the long s is standardized to s. Ligatures (æ) are retained, as are the writers' uses of u and v, i and j, and the ampersand. Typically, there are no attempts to modernize or correct what now looks like nonstandard English, nor is [*sic*] inserted. But where there has been an obvious slip of the pen by the author—writing hope where home was intended, for instance—the error is corrected and a footnote mentions the change. In rare instances missing punctuation marks are inserted if needed for clarity. In such cases, the added detail is surrounded by square brackets. In the seventeenth century some writers still used a period to indicate something less than a full stop, giving it a value more like the semicolon. Textbooks called it a semiperiod. In these instances, the following clause begins with a lowercase letter.[5] Any explanation of meaning, as for archaic words or phrases or obscurely idiosyncratic spellings, is offered in the footnotes, not in the text itself. All translations of words or passages in Latin or Greek also appear in the footnotes, except in the case of entire letters, where the translation immediately follows the Latin version. The salutation of each letter is printed as it appears in the letter, whether run into the text or set off on a separate line.

In this period the new year was dated, not from January 1, but from March 25, which was the day commemorating the Annunciation of Mary, the mother of Jesus. So the letter-writers of the period covered in this collection began using the date of the new year only on March 25. All yearly dates between January 1 and March 25, therefore, are given in both Old Style (Julian calendar) and New Style (Gregorian calendar): February 15, 1625/6.

In keeping with the principle of preserving the letter-writer's act as well as product, deletions in the manuscripts, when they are legible, are rendered as they appear in the manuscript: ~~also tooke~~. When they are not decipherable, deletions are indicated in square brackets: [two words deleted]. Interlinear insertions are indicated by a caret before and after the inserted passage: ˆit seemeth you haveˆ; this closely approximates standard seventeenth-century practice, where the insertion written above the line was both preceded and followed by a caret.

In the first half of the seventeenth century the conventional way of indicating quotations was to put quotation marks in the left margin before every line that included any part of the quoted passage. This practice is found in both manuscripts and printed texts and is replicated here.

In texts edited from manuscripts, the beginning of a new manuscript page is indicated by a bracketed number. For instance, when the text on the first recto ends and the text on the reverse side, or verso, of the first sheet begins,

5. C[hristopher] Cooper, in a standard textbook late in the seventeenth century, wrote, "A *Period* . . . is placed at the bottom of the Line, and is markt thus, (.) A *Semiperiod* may have the same mark, but distinguisht from the former by a less breach in the line, and the word following beginning with a small Letter" (*The English Teacher; or, The Discovery of the Art of Teaching and Learning the English Tongue* [London, 1687; rpt. Menston, Yorks., 1969], 114–115). This passage is quoted by Noel Malcolm, ed., *The Correspondence of Thomas Hobbes* (Oxford, 1994), I, lviii, who encountered the same practice in that contemporaneous correspondence.

the printed text here inserts a bracketed marker: [IV]. When the text moves to the recto of the next sheet, the marker is: [2].

When a manuscript of a published letter has been lost, we must rely on the work of previous editors. The principle used here has always been to use the work of the first editor, who was usually working from the manuscript itself. In the course of four centuries, printing and editorial conventions have undergone considerable change, so that letters preserved through publication at different points in the intervening time reflect those varying customs. Some of the early transcribers held to a principle of preservation that aimed at retaining the seventeenth-century form of the letters, including what was already at the time of transcription archaic spelling, while others did not. Two late-eighteenth-century transcribers, Ezra Stiles and Thomas Hutchinson, for instance, both copied letters out in more or less their original form, though Hutchinson regularized or modernized some details. Hutchinson's own later editor, Lawrence Shaw Mayo, did not respect his efforts in this regard, however, so that Mayo's 1936 edition of the *History of Massachusetts-Bay,* now the standard edition, modernizes certain details, especially punctuation, in seventeenth-century letters quoted by Hutchinson. For this reason, the earliest editions of Hutchinson's *History* (London, 1764) and his *Collection of Original Papers* (Boston, 1769) are the sources of letters preserved in these books.

Since the edition attempts to render the letters as their authors wrote them, intrusive marks of earlier editors or collectors are removed. The most significant example of this is where underlinings occur in letters collected by Thomas Prince. Previous editors have sometimes shown those underlinings as if written into the letters by their authors. Even apart from the fact that early-seventeenth-century letter-writers rarely used underlining as a means of emphasis—and Cotton seems never to have done so—the physical evidence of the manuscripts offers ample proof that the underlinings were made by Prince in his efforts to date or otherwise contextualize the letters. His ink is typically lighter in color than the letter itself, having faded to a light brown while Cotton's ink usually remains quite black, or at least a darker brown. In addition, Prince preferred a broad point on his quill, broader than the points used by any of the authors, including Cotton, whose letters he has marked. So these underlinings are removed. At the same time, Prince's notes on the letters are preserved in footnotes.

Thus, the letters in this volume have sometimes been reclaimed from a precarious condition verging on extinction. The assumption is that the words of John Cotton and his correspondents are rare enough and valuable enough in our attempts to understand the history of his life and times and of the social and religious movements of which he was a part that even fragmentary texts are better than none. So an occasional text is included that some readers will find too broken to be worth the effort of reading. Such readers should skip over such admittedly frustrating moments in favor of the great majority of pages that present whole or nearly whole texts. While some of the texts that are interrupted by holes are less than fully coherent, and early publications preserving as little as a single sentence represent partial thoughts at best, those remnants can still make important contributions to the entire correspondence and are retained here in preference to suffering the decided loss of eliminating them simply because parts are missing. None is totally incoherent. The aim is to salvage whatever can be salvaged.

A few items have intentionally been omitted here that some might argue should have been included. These omissions have usually been of very lengthy texts published elsewhere that are arguably not letters at all. Some of the exchanges in the Antinomian controversy between Cotton and other ministers, for instance, certainly have the look of personal and immediate written exchanges between individuals. The letters exchanged in 1636 by Cotton and Thomas Shepard that served as the formal beginning of the controversy are included here. They are clearly letters exchanged between colleagues and contain, however briefly, acknowledgment of the personal regard that correspondence normally seeks to encourage. The exchanges that followed in the controversy included increasingly formal and distant discourses, though sometimes retaining the conventional guise of personal correspondence—formal questions from the elders, Cotton's answers in writing, followed by the elders' reply, and then by Cotton's "Rejoynder." At some point, however, personal correspondence spills over into another category of discourse. Because of the ballooning size of the contributions to this extended debate, after the exchange of letters between Shepard and Cotton, this collection includes only the one- or two-paragraph cover letters to which the controversial arguments were attached. The full documents are all present in the Prince Collection and are included in David D. Hall's invaluable volume, *The Antinomian Controversy*. The existence of excellent editions in Hall's collection makes it easier to exclude attachments to the correspondence that in any case do not fully qualify as legitimate letters. Other instances occur as well. The controversies with Roger Williams began as personal correspondence but quickly escalated into contributions to the period's pamphlet wars, especially in the "Bloody Tenent" writings by both Williams and Cotton. Those works, though often treated formally as if they were personal exchanges, are full-length books and clearly do not belong in a collection of letters such as this. On the other hand, a published prefatory epistle to Cotton's 1650 book, *Of the Holinesse of Church-Members,* is included here, even though it might never have been sent separately as a letter. Yet it is a legitimate letter, personally addressed by Cotton to his former congregation in Lincolnshire, a cover letter as it were, accompanying a book that he says he wrote specifically for them.

Another kind of document that sometimes verges legitimately into the category of correspondence is the transaction of official church business. For instance, a letter from one church to another, signed by multiple parties, such as Cotton, Wilson, and a ruling elder, is included. Sometimes, however, documents have been excluded because they seem to lack the signs of actual correspondence intentionally directed from one (or more) authors to one or more specific recipients. A case in point is a document in the Cotton Papers portion of the Prince Collection. It is a manuscript in the hand of the amanuensis who copied several items of Cotton's correspondence in the period 1639–1641. It bears the heading "The Causes of Henry Bull's Excom*m*unication" and is signed by the pastor and the teacher of the Roxbury church, Thomas Weld and John Eliot. It appears to be a testimonial that clearly provided information requested by an inquirer, but it is undated, and there is no specified or implied addressee or salutation. It is more an affidavit than a letter and is thus excluded. In another instance, Cotton signed a letter of attorney dated October 13, 1638, which is preserved in the notebook of Thomas Lechford, the lawyer who drew it up. But this document is not a letter in the familiar sense of the term at all and is accordingly excluded. Even harder to exclude is a thirty-line poem written by Cotton to (and about) Samuel Stone, praising its subject. It is more "occasional" composition than communication and thus seems to fall outside the working definition of a letter.[6]

6. "The Causes of Henry Bull's Excommunication" is in the Thomas Prince Collection at the Boston Public Library (Ms. Am. 1506, pt. 2, no. 25), while the manuscript of Lechford's Notebook for 1638–1641, containing the Letter of Attorney, is owned by the American Antiquarian Society. The latter was published in the American Antiquarian Society, *Transactions,* VII (1885). Cotton's "To My Reverend Dear Brother, M. Samuel Stone, Teacher of the Church at Hartford" was printed in Samuel Stone, *A Congregational Church Is a Catholike Visible Church . . .* (London, 1652), sig. [A4v]. It might have been written and sent to Stone in Hartford following the death of Stone's colleague there, Thomas Hooker, in 1647, since the final lines (25–28) address the need for Stone to carry on Hooker's work:

> To Brother *Hooker,* thou art next a kin,
> By Office-Right thou must his pledge Redeem.
> Take thou the double portion of his spirit,
> Run on his Race, and then his Crown inherit.

Occasionally it has been possible to identify the author or recipient of items previously misattributed or simply unidentified. A letter thought by Prince and later scholars to have been written to Cotton is actually his letter to a silenced minister ([1625–1631?]), as the handwriting unmistakably indicates. Other letters are now more definitively identified or dated than previously, though of course a number of items in the Boston Public Library's Prince Library remain anonymous, and a very few resist precise dating.

In a few cases, the letters offered here mention enclosures or related documents. Usually those have been lost. In one instance, however, Cotton's 1651 letter to John Elmeston, the enclosure is still extant and is therefore included in the Appendix. An earlier letter, Cotton's 1635 reply to John Hall, addresses questions that Hall had enclosed in his letter to Cotton. Since those questions are extant in a published form, they are also included in the Appendix. Similarly, the questions and conditions received from Lord Saye and Sele and Lord Brooke help a reader make sense of Cotton's 1636 reply. Likewise, Richard Mather's letter of September 15, 1651, about the public response to the Cambridge Platform is given fuller context by the list of "Exceptions" that Cotton himself made up at that time. Each of these documents thus helps to illuminate the particular details of the primary letter. In another, rather different instance, a letter by Cotton to Thomas Dudley raised questions for which Dudley sought assistance from John Eliot, who proceeded to annotate Cotton's letter. Cotton himself saw these annotations and added his own comments to Eliot's clarifications. The document is thus not itself a letter, but it provides a striking demonstration of the kind of dialogue that might well have been produced by many of the letters in the collection. In any case, it deepens the perspective on the Dudley-Cotton exchange and is included in the Appendix for that reason.

Each letter is preceded by up to five items of information: (1) the names of author and recipient; (2) the date, known or conjectured; (3) the type of manuscript, that is, signed autograph letter (ALS), initialed autograph letter (ALI), autograph draft (ADf), contemporary copy (Copy), and so forth; (4) the location of the manuscript, if known; and (5) citation to publication of the complete letter in the earliest known edition (abridged versions are usually omitted; reprints of earlier editions are not noted). When a letter has never before been printed, this "Published" line at the top of the headnote is simply omitted.

Headnotes to individual letters or occasionally to pairs of letters provide a context within which the letters can be read with fuller understanding than would otherwise be the case. Where the date is conjectural, the rationale for the dating is offered in the headnote. Where a manuscript has suffered some mutilation, the headnote includes a brief description of the state of the manuscript by way of explaining the cause of interruptions in the text. Endnotes intend to clarify specific details in the letters. In instances where a letter has been published recently in a modern edition that does not modernize the text (*Winthrop Papers,* Hall's *Antinomian Controversy,* LaFantasie's *Correspondence of Roger Williams,* for instance), when the present edition differs from the previous one, significant points of difference are itemized in endnotes, but differences in the interpretation of accidentals—punctuation and spelling—are not recorded. No attempt is made to record differences where a recent edition modernizes the text (Emerson's *Letters from New England,* for instance).

No printed text can substitute for the holograph itself as a source of information about the author and the conditions in which he or she wrote. So this edition has been prepared out of a full respect for the importance of using the manuscript—and only the manuscript—when one is available as the source text. Working with these rare and valuable documents has been a very special privilege for the editor. The results, one hopes, offer the reader the opportunity to hear the voices of these writers through the words they committed to paper some three and a half centuries ago. Insofar as this happens, it should help, however small the sample of evidence, to give meaningful shape to a key portion of our collective past. This, at least, has been the goal.

THE CORRESPONDENCE OF *John Cotton* 1621–1652

John Cotton to John Williams, Bishop of Lincoln

August 30, 1621

ALS. MS: Bodl, MS Add. D. 23, fol. 246

Translation by George Goebel

The only extant letter from Cotton written in Latin dates to two months before John Williams's consecration as bishop of Lincoln on November 11, 1621, but after James I had announced that Williams was his choice for the post. Knowing that Williams's authority would be critical in determining the limits of tolerance within which his own ministry would operate, Cotton was quick to lay the groundwork for what would prove to be a remarkable relationship for more than a decade, with Cotton always refusing to conform to the church's prescribed forms of worship in at least some respects, and the bishop periodically urging but never finally insisting upon conformity. Here, then, at the very beginning of our record of Cotton's extensive correspondence, we observe him cultivating that most crucial of ecclesiastical relationships for any English Puritan, his connection with his bishop.

Williams was a favorite of the elderly James, who, in 1621, appointed him not just bishop of Lincoln, which Williams had hoped for and even expected, but also keeper of the great seal, a valuable position in the king's court that came as a very welcome surprise to Williams.[1] When Charles I took the throne on his father's death in early 1625, Bishop Williams immediately felt the difference in the new king's policy toward nonconformity and, more directly, toward Williams himself. Prince Charles had argued against Williams's appointment to these posts, swayed by the animosity toward Williams of Charles's close friend and adviser, the duke of Buckingham. In 1625 Charles required Williams to give up the post of keeper of the great seal. Eventually, Williams was imprisoned in the Tower of London (long after Cotton had left England).[2] As long as Cotton remained at Boston, Williams was largely responsible for tolerating his departures from prescribed duties in the worship. "The huge diocese of Lincoln under Bishop Williams remained at least until 1637 . . . 'a great loophole in the Laudian system.' "[3]

We have no way of knowing whether there were other letters between the two during this period, though it is likely that there were. Nevertheless, these two earliest Cotton letters reflect a progression of the relationship between vicar and bishop. The first, punctiliously written in Latin, protesting loyalty to the king and bishop, is an attempt to strike a character with which the bishop would be sympathetic.[4] The second, responding to inquiries about his Nonconformist practices, is a diplomatic request for patience. Together, these first two letters show Cotton, the ecclesiastical politician and the principled Puritan, in action.[5]

Reverendissime Pater, amplissime Domine,

Divinitùs contigisse puto, vt quam honoris amplitudinem, literarum decus, atq*ue* præsidium Iacobus, tibi eximiæ eruditionis, candoris, atq*ue* prudentiæ præmium esse voluerit, eadem nunc mihi quoq*ue* asylum esse possit, & afflictis meis rebus opportunum perfugium. Enimverò si quid in municipali foro litigantem hominem comprimere duriùs, atq*ue* coarctare potuisset, si sum*m*o iure decerneretur, id omne protinùs ad almæ Cancellariæ tuæ æquitatem provocat, postulat ἐπιείκειαν.[6] Equidem litigare nescio, otij literarij cupientissimus: veruntamen, si pacis cultoribus æq*ue* ac litis sequacib*us* par gratia deferri æquum videatur (æquum autem tibi videbitur imprimìs) non gravatè feres, opinor (clementissime Domine) si quemadmodùm illi civilium, sic Ego Ecclesiasticarum legum rigore pressus, æquanimitatis tuae, clementiæq*ue* ianuam pulsavero.

Ecclesiam equidem, quæ apud nos viget Anglicanos, pio (vti par est) animi studio, & sum*m*â certè observantiâ prosequor: fidem, quam credit, credo: cultum, quem colit, colo: leges plerasq*ue* omnes veneror, nullas incuso: Authoritatem omnem, sive Ecclesiasticam, sive civilem, sive vtramq*ue* in nostrî omnium capite, serenissimo Principe Iacobo coniunctam, sive pro ipsius arbitrio demandatam, submissè revereor: Schismata omnia, sive Separatistarum fuerint, sive Anabaptistarum, ex animo detestor, & ex animis piorum omnium profligata cupio, adeò vt ausim dicere (quicquid contrà sugillent malè feriati homines) nè vestigium quidem huiusmodi sectæ per vniversam Hollandiam nostrâtem comparêre. Supersunt Ceremoniæ solæ (nec eæ quidem onmes) quas dùm Ego præ hæsitantiâ, non satis fidenti animo amplector, illæ me contrà tanquam Ecclesiæ infensum, tanquam potestatibus im*m*origerum, tanquam pacis publicæ perturbatorem, tanquam novatorem importunum, tanquam Schismatis flabellum, deniq*ue* tanquam telluris Ecclesiæ inutile pondus, è vineâ Domini eijcere, ex proprijs sedib*us* ἀνάστατον reddere, etiam ab aris Domini detractum, in invisum silentij sepulchrum proijcere satagunt.

Hijsce ingruentib*us* calamitatum vndis tantùm non obruto, quid mihi faciendum restat, colendissime Domine? Gratiam divinam supplex peto, veniam Principis Patriæ Patris, Matris Ecclesiæ indulgentiam, clementiam deniq*ue* Domini Episcopi, clementiam tuam. Nihil habet tua vel Episcopalis cathedra augustius, vel Cancellaria æquius, vel indoles ipsa magnificentius, quàm Evangelij cursum promovêre, Presbyterorum manus in opere Domini confirmâre, miseris solâmen, supplicib*us* gratiam elargiri. Titus (quem generis humani delicias insignitum noveris) neminem (nisi Aulu*m* Cecinnam, & huiusmodi maleficos) â se tristem dimittere solebat. Perîcles tametsi tonâre in concionib*us,* & fulgurâre diceretur, tamen in Reipublicæ administratione, eâ moderatione vsus est, vt nemo ipsius causâ, pullâ veste atrâtus incederet. Quid tibi Titum narro, & Perîclem, benignitatis scilicèt atq*ue* innocentiæ vmbras. Lex Spiritus vitæ in Christo Iesû Christianum pectus divinioris misericordiæ viscerib*us* perfundit, alios aliorum ^onera^ portâre edocet, & (tanquam Hippocratis gemellos, imò tanquam membra eiusdem corporis) alios aliorum curas, dolores, honores, gaudia, parili animorum affectû persentiscere.

Sed nolo tempora tua longo sermone morari, nè in publica com*m*oda imprudens pariter atq*ue* importunus peccem. Portio dupla Spiritus Domini, Sapientiæ, iustitiæ, æquitatis, timoris Domini quiescat super te: vt pro munerum amplitudine, amplificetur pectus tuum, velut arena maris. Ità iugi sacrificio litâre solet,

Amplitudinis tuæ

Bostoniâ: ii. Cal. cliens observantissimus,

Sept. 1621./ Joh*ann*es Cotton[us][7]

Most Reverend Father, most Eminent Lord:

It has been divinely ordained, I think, that the same eminence of office, honor of letters, and wardship which James meant to be the reward of your remarkable learning, honesty, and foresight, should now be to me also an asylum, and a timely refuge for my afflicted affairs. For if someone pleading a case in the civil courts had been especially severely afflicted and constrained, if his case were being judged by the letter of the law, he appeals the whole thing straightaway to the equity of your kindly Chancellory,[8] and begs for fair treatment. Indeed I do not know how to plead a case; my only desire is for literary retirement. But if it seems fair to show equal favor to those who cultivate peace as to those who pursue litigation (as to you especially it will seem fair) you will not take it ill, most clement Lord, if I, subjected to the rigors of ecclesiastical law, as they of civil, knock at the door of your patience and clemency.

The church which flourishes among us English I support with—as is only right—pious zeal in my heart and the most scrupulous observance. The creed it believes, I believe; whom it worships, I worship; its laws—nearly all—I respect, none do I condemn. All authority, whether ecclesiastical, or civil, or both united in our common head, the most serene prince James, or delegated by his authority, I humbly revere. All schisms, whether of Separatists or Anabaptists, I heartily detest, and wish that they were driven completely from the hearts of the faithful; so much so that I should dare to say—whatever idle fools may allege to the contrary—that not even a trace of such a sect is to be found in all of our Holland.[9] Only ceremonies remain—and by no means all of them. Because in my doubt I do not embrace them with a confident enough spirit, they in turn—as if I were an enemy to the church, a rebel against the authorities, a disrupter of the public peace, a troublesome revolutionary, a scourge of schism, in short, as if I were a useless burden on the Church's land—they seek to drive me out of the vineyard of the Lord, to render me exiled from my own home, and even to tear me from the altars of the Lord and cast me into the hateful tomb of silence.

All but overwhelmed by these threatening waves of calamity, what else is there for me to do, most reverend Lord? I humbly beg for divine grace, for the forgiveness of the Prince, the father of his country, for the indulgence of our mother, the church, and finally for the clemency of the Lord Bishop—your clemency. Your Episcopal See has nothing more venerable, your Chancellory nothing more equitable, your own nature nothing more glorious, than to advance the course of the Gospel, to strengthen the hands of the priests for the Lord's work, and to bestow solace on the suffering and grace on the suppliant. Titus (who, as you know, was famous as the darling of the human race)[10] would never send anyone away (unless it were Aulus Caecina, and evildoers of that sort)[11] unhappy. Pericles, though he was said to thunder and lighten his speeches, was so moderate in conducting public business that no one ever went about in mourning garments because of him.[12] But why do I tell you of Titus and Pericles, mere shadows of kindness and integrity? The law of the spirit of life in Jesus Christ fills the Christian heart with the very flesh of a more divine mercy, teaches us to bear each other's burdens, and (like Hippocrates' twins, or rather, like parts of the same body) to feel each other's cares, pains, honors, and joys with an equal affection of the soul.[13]

But I do not want to waste your time with long discourse, lest I sin against the public good both in my imprudence and my persistence. Let a double share of the Lord's spirit, of wisdom, of justice, of equity, of fear of the Lord rest over you, that in proportion to your services your heart may be enlarged like the sands of the sea. Such is the constant prayer of

Your eminence's

Boston: 30th day most humble servant,
Aug. 1621./[14] John Cotton

1. Williams's biographer quotes his letter to James I in response to the appointment as keeper: "I am quite astonish'd at your Favour and Goodness. I do not therefore trouble my Head to find out the Reasons of this advancement, because I take it for no ordinary Effect, but an Extraordinary Miracle." B. Dew Roberts, *Mitre and Musket: John Williams, Lord Keeper, Archbishop of York, 1582–1650* (London, 1938), 46–47. He had reason for surprise. As Kenneth Fincham points out, "Williams became the first churchman to hold the Great Seal since Archbishop Heath in 1558" (*Prelate as Pastor: The Episcopate of James I* [Oxford, 1990], 35).

2. Dew Roberts, *Mitre and Musket,* 99–104.

3. Clive Holmes, *Seventeenth-Century Lincolnshire* (Lincoln, Lincs., 1980), 113–114, quoting H. R. Trevor-Roper, *Archbishop Laud: 1573–1645* (London, 1940).

4. Williams's surviving letters contain several examples of letters both by him and to him in Latin, especially exchanges with individuals at St. John's College, Cambridge. See John E. B. Mayor, ed., *Letters of Archbishop Williams, with Documents Relating to Him* (Cambridge, 1866). No letters to or from Cotton are included in Mayor's edition.

5. Larzer Ziff discusses this letter and its context in *Career of John Cotton,* 55–59.

6. Cotton mistakenly placed the acute accent over the third epsilon rather than the second iota.

7. Here the page has been trimmed, removing the bottom portion of several letters and everything after the letter n.

8. A reference to Williams's oversight of the Court of Chancery, a function of his role as keeper of the great seal.

9. "Our Holland" is the southern region of Lincolnshire, where Boston is located.

10. Titus Flavius Vespasianus (39–81) was the Roman emperor from 79 until his death in 81. Suetonius, in his *Lives of the Caesars,* calls him "the darling [or favorite] of the human race," the description to which Cotton is referring here.

11. Aulus Caecina Alienus (d. A.D. 79) was a Roman general who used his power to bestow authority on various rulers and then successively to betray them. When Titus became emperor, he had Caecina executed as a conspirator.

12. Pericles (c. 494–429), an Athenian ruler, was famous as a stirring orator, but was known during his rule for moderation and stability. Cotton doubtless knew the accounts of him in Plutarch's *Life of Pericles* and in Thucydides' *History of the Peloponnesian War.* The latter work was in the Emmanuel College Library during Cotton's period there (see Sargent Bush, Jr., and Carl J. Rasmussen, *The Library of Emmanuel College, Cambridge, 1584–1637* [Cambridge, 1986], 206). The original source of the "thunder and lightning" characterization of Pericles' oratory may be Aristophanes' *Acharnians* 531, but it is repeated in Plutarch, *Life of Pericles* 8). The "mourning garments" reference is also in Plutarch (*Pericles* 38). (I am grateful to George Goebel for these details on Plutarch and Aristophanes.) On Pericles, see Donald Kagan, *Pericles of Athens and the Birth of Democracy* (New York, 1991).

13. Conjoined twins. I have not found such a reference in Hippocrates. Roger Williams provides a useful gloss in writing that church and state are "like Hi*ppocrates twinns,* they are borne together, grow up together, laugh together, weepe together, sicken and die together." *The Bloudy Tenent of Persecution,* in *The Complete Writings of Roger Williams,* 7 vols. (New York, 1963), III, 333, and quoted in Timothy L. Hall, *Separating Church and State: Roger Williams and Religious Liberty* (Urbana, Ill., 1998), 62.

14. I have converted the Roman dating system, "second day before the calends of September," to the English system.

John Cotton to John Williams, Bishop of Lincoln

January 31, 1624/5

ALS. MS: BL Add. MS 6394, fols. 29–30

Published: P. Thompson, *History of Boston,* 418–420; *NEHGR,* XXVIII (1874), 137–139; MHS, *Procs.,* XLII (1908–1909), 204–207; Champlin Burrage, *The Early English Dissenters in the Light of Recent Research (1550–1641)* (Cambridge, 1912), II, 261–264

In L. Thompson, "Letters of John Cotton," 20–25

Cotton addressed the letter:

To *th*e right honourable & Reverend
father in God, my very honourable
good Lord, Lord Bishop
of Lincolne, Lord Keeper of
the great Seale, d*el*
this w*i*th Speede.

An endorsement acknowledges receipt in two different hands, one for the first two lines, another for the remainder, written downward at the foot of the sheet:

Cotton. 31. Jan. 1624.
to Lo: Keep*er*. Boston.
1. Wherin himself, his cu=
rat, & his Parish*ion*ers con=
formable. Ob*jecti*ons ansuered.

My honourable & very good Lord,

As yo*u*r Lordship hath dealt honourably, & Christianly w*i*th me: so might I iustly be esteemed impiously vngratefull, if I should deale otherwise, then ingenuously, & honestly w*i*th yo*u*r Lordship. When my cause first came before yo*u*r Lord*shi*p, yo*u*r Lord*shi*p wisely and truely discerned, *tha*t my forbearaunce of *th*e Ceremonyes was not from wilfull Refusall of Conformity, but from some doubts in my Iudgem*en*t (w*hi*ch I confesse is very shallow) & from some scruple in Conscience, w*hi*ch is indeede as weake. And therefore vpon mine humble, & instaunt Petition, yo*u*r Lord*shi*p was pleased in much goodnesse, to graunt me time to consider further of these things for my better satisfaction. Yo*u*r Lord*shi*ps gentlenesse hath not since bred in

THE RIGHT HON:BLE & RIGHT
REV:D JOHN WILLIAMS DD.
LORD KEEPER OF THE GREAT
SEAL OF ENGLAND & LD
BISHOP OF LINCOLN
1621.

PLATE 1. John Williams, Bishop of Lincoln. Oil painting by C. Johnson, dated 1621, the year of his accession to the bishopric of Lincoln and of Cotton's first letter to him. *Private collection. Photograph Courtauld Institute of Art, London. Published with the kind permission of the owner*

me any obstinacy in mine owne Opinion: much lesse emboldened me to depart the further from *th*e receyved Iudgem*en*t & practise of *th*e Church in any point. The point of kneelinge in Receyvinge *th*e holy Com*m*union, was noe lesse doubtfull to me (if not more) in *th*e dayes of yo*u*r Lord*shi*ps Prædecesso*u*r,[1] then it is now. His Lord*shi*p knoweth, that in Westminster by his Com*m*aundm*en*t, I propounded my doubts about it before himselfe, & the Reverend & learned Bishop of Sarisbury, *tha*t now is.[2] Vnto whom I

My honourable & very good Lord

As yor Lordship hath dealt honourably, & Christianly wth me: so might I iustly be esteemed impiously ungratefull if I should deale otherwise, then ingenuously, & honestly wth yor Lordship. When my cause first came before yor Lordp, yor Lordp wisely & truely discerned, yt my forbearance of ye Ceremonyes was not from wilfull Refusall of Conformity, but from some doubt in my Iudgemt (wch I confesse is very shallow) & from some scruple in Conscience, wch is indeede as weake. And therefore upon mine humble, & instant Petition, yor Lordp was pleased in much goodnesse, to graunt me time to consider further of these things for my better satisfaction. Yor Lordps gentlenesse hath not since bred in me any obstinacy in mine owne Opinion: much lesse emboldened me to depart the further from ye receyved Iudgemt & practise of ye Church in any point. The point of Kneelinge in Receyvinge ye holy Comunion, was not lesse doubtfull to me (if not more) in ye dayes of yor Lordps Predecessor, then it is now. His Lordp knoweth, that in Westminster by his Comandemt, I propounded my doubts about it before himselfe, & the Reverend & learned Bishop of Sarisbury, yt now is. Unto whom I did so freely open my selfe, out of deepe desire to helpe my selfe by their deeper Iudgemts, yt my Lord discerninge my simplicity, became (as I conceyved it) ye more favourable & willinge not onely to beare wth me, but also to give some way to my Restitution, & in the meane tyme to leave me in such Estate, as yor Lordp found me. I humbly beseech yor Lp think not I have so abused yor Lordps Patience, as to harden my selfe by yor Lordps Lenity. Noe, I assure yor Lordp, out of an unfeigned Desire, to improve yor Lordps Gentlenesse to mine owne Peace, & the Churches satisfaction, I have thus farre gayned (what by Conference, what by study, what by seekinge unto God) as of late to see the weakenesse of some of those groundes against Kneelinge wch before seemed too stronge for me to dissolve. The Experience of ye faylinge of my Iudgemt in some of these things, maketh me the more to suspect it in other Argumts & grounds of like nature. Besides I shall never forgett, what yor Lordp gravely & wisely once said unto me; The Ceremonyes I doubted of were not when expresly forbidden in Scripture: the Argumts brought against ym were but by Consequence deducted from Scripture: deduction of Consequences was a worke of ye Iudgemt: other mens Iudgemts (so many, so learned, so godly) why should I not conceyve, did as infallibly deduce iust Consequences, to allowe these thinges, as mine owne, to doubt of ym. Alas, alas, (my deare Lord) I see by often Experience, the shallownesse of mine owne Iudgemt, especially in comparison of many Centuryes of Godly-Learned who doubt not of the Lawfull liberty of these Ceremonyes, especially of this Gesture. Their Consent herein hath further strongly perswaded me, to suspect the motions of mine owne minde, when I see my selfe in any thinge to dissent from ye receyved Iudgemt of so many Reverend Fathers, & Brethren in ye Church, whom I doe not onely highly reverence, but admire. I see, it is comonly a Palsey-distemper in any member of ye Body, when it is carryed by a motion different from ye rule of ye rest of ye members. And I iustly suspect yt Spirit, in my selfe, or in another, yt breatheth a motion different from ye rest of ye members of ye body of Christ, ye Church of God.

Thus may yor Lordp well perceyve, how little, yor Lps forbearance of me hath hitherto stiffened me in any private Conceyte. And though it hath bene suggested to yor Lordp (as I heare) yt it hath emboldened or Parish to Inconformity, & induced divers others to come from other Parishes, to Comunicate wth us in ye like Liberty: Yet surely yor Lordp hath done honourably & Christianly, & well beseeminge the equity of yor High & Honourable Court, Not to give Credit to such a Suggestion, till yor Lordp hath Enquired, & heard or Answer. The truth is, the Ceremonyes of ye Ringe in Marryage, & standinge at ye Creede, are usually performed by my selfe: & all ye other Ceremonyes of

PLATE 2. Cotton to Bishop John Williams, January 31, 1624/5, recto. The sample shows a particularly neat and meticulous example of Cotton's handwriting. *British Library, Additional MS 6394. Published with the kind permission of the British Library*

did so freely open my selfe, out of deepe desire to helpe my selfe by their deeper Iudgem*en*ts, *tha*t my Lord discerninge my simplicity, became (as I conceyved it) *th*e more favourable & willinge not onely to beare w*i*th me, but also to give some way to my Restitution, & in the windinge vp to leave me in such Estate, as yo*u*r Lord*shi*p found me. I humbly beseech yo*u*r L*ordshi*p thinke not I have so abused yo*u*r Lord*shi*ps Patience, as to harden my selfe by yo*u*r Lord*shi*ps Lenity. Noe, I assure yo*u*r Lord*shi*p, out of an vnfeigned Desire, to improve yo*u*r Lord*shi*ps Gentlenesse to mine owne Peace, & the Churches satisfaction, I have thus farre gayned (what by Conference, what by study, what by seekinge vnto God) as of late to see the Weakenesse of some of those groundes against kneelinge, w*hi*ch before seemed too stronge for me to dissolve. The Experience of *th*e faylinge of my Iudgem*en*t in some of these thinges, maketh me the more to suspect it in other Argum*en*ts & grounds of like nature. Besides I shall never forgett, what yo*u*r Lord*shi*p gravely and "wisely once said vnto me, The Ceremonyes I doubted of, were noe where "expresly forbidden in Scripture: the Argum*en*ts brought against *th*em were "but by Consequence deducted from Scripture: deduction of Consequences "was a worke of *th*e Iudgem*en*t: other mens Iudgem*en*ts (so many, so learned, "so godly) why should I not conceyve, did as infallibly deduce iust Conse-"quences, to allowe these thinges, as mine owne, to doubt of *th*em. Alas, alas, (my deere Lord) I see by often Experience, the shallownesse of mine owne Iudgem*en*t, especially in comparison of many Centuryes of Godly Learned, who doubt not of the Lawfull liberty of these Ceremonyes, especially of this Gesture. Their Consent herein doth further strongly persuade me, to suspect the motions of mine owne minde, when I see my selfe in any thinge to dissent from *th*e receyved Iudgem*en*t of so many Reverend Fathers, & Brethren in *th*e Church, whom I doe not onely highly reverence, but admire. I see, it is com*m*only a Palsey-distemper in any member of *th*e Body, when it is carryed by a motion different from *th*e rule of *th*e rest of *th*e members. And I iustly suspect *tha*t Spirit, in my selfe, or in another, *tha*t breatheth a motion different from *th*e rest of *th*e members of *th*e body of Christ, *th*e Church of God.

Thus may yo*u*r Lord*shi*p well perceyve, how little, yo*u*r L*ordshi*ps forbearaunce of me hath hitherto stiffened me in any private Conceyte. And though it hath bene suggested to yo*u*r Lord*shi*p (as I heare) *tha*t it hath emboldened o*u*r Parish to Inconformity, & induced divers others to come from other Parishes, to Com*m*unicate w*i*th vs in *th*e like Liberty: Yet surely yo*u*r Lord*shi*p hath done honourably & Christianly, & well beseeminge the æquity of yo*u*r High & Honourable Co*u*rt, Not to give Credit to such a Suggestion, till yo*u*r Lord*shi*p hath Enquired, & heard o*u*r Answer. The trueth is, the Ceremonyes of *th*e Ringe in Marryage, & standinge at *th*e Creede, are vsually performed by my selfe: & all *th*e other Ceremonyes [fol. 29v] Of Surplice, Crosse in Baptisme, Kneelinge at *th*e Com*m*union are frequently vsed by my fellow-Minister in o*u*r Church,[3] & w*i*thout disturbance of *th*e People.[4] The People on Sabbaths, & sundry other Festivall dayes, doe very diligently, & throngly frequent *th*e Publique Prayers of *th*e Church, appointed by Authority in *th*e Booke of Com*m*on Prayer: neyther doe I thinke, *tha*t any of *the*m ordinarily (vnlesse it be vpon iust occasion of other buisinesse) absenteth himselfe. It is true indeede, *tha*t in Receyvinge the Com*m*union, sundry of *the*m doe not kneele: but (as I conceyve it, & as they Expresse themselves) It is not out of scruple of Conscience, but from *th*e store & multitude of Com*m*unicants, w*hi*ch often doe so thronge one another in this great Congregation, that they can hardly stand (much lesse kneele) one by another. Such as doe forbeare kneelinge out of any doubt in Conscience, I know not, how very few, they be: I am sure, in comparison of *th*e rest, they be nullius numeri.[5] That divers others come from other Parishes for *tha*t Purpose, to Receyve w*i*thout kneelinge, is vtterly vnknowen to me, & (I am persuaded) vtterly vntrue. All *th*e neighbo*u*r Parishes, Ministers & People rounde about vs, are wholly Conformable[.] Once indeede (as I heard) one of *th*e Inhabitaunts of o*u*r neighbo*u*r Parish, com*m*inge to visit his wife (who then nourced a Gentlemans child in o*u*r Towne) did here Com*m*unicate w*i*th vs. And whether for his not kneelinge, or for some further Cause, I know not, but (as I heard) *th*e Co*u*rt beinge Informed of Him, did proceede severely against Him. But otherwise, the man (as I have since bene certefyed) hath alwayes vsed to receyve kneelinge, both before, & since. Yet his Case beinge further bruited abroade, then well knowen, might easily breede such a Suspicion, & afterwards a Report, w*hi*ch in time might come to yo*u*r Lord*shi*ps eares, *tha*t divers did come from other Parishes to vs, for this purpose, To Receyve Inconformably. But yo*u*r Lord*shi*p is wise, easily discerninge betweene Reports & Evidences.

Let me now therefore humbly intreate yo*u*r Lord*shi*p, in *th*e bowells of Christ Iesus, since yo*u*r Lord*shi*ps Lenity hath hitherto neyther hardened me to any selfe-conceyted Obstinacy, nor wrought any Præiudice, eyther to yo*u*r Lord*shi*p, or to *th*e Church of God: Yo*u*r Lord*shi*p will therefore be pleased To allowe me yet further time, for better Consideration of such doubts, as yet remayne behinde[.] That if vpon further search, I can finde theim too weake to deteyne me, as I have done *th*e former I may then satisfy yo*u*r Lord*shi*ps Desire, & Expectation: If Otherwise, yet I trust yo*u*r Lord*shi*p shall ever finde me (by *th*e helpe of God) a peaceable, & (to my best endeavo*u*rs, accordinge to my weake abilityes) a serviceable member of *th*e Church of God.

I dare not præsume, w*i*th more wordes to Presse yo*u*r Lord*shi*p, whom *th*e store & weight of so many important Affayres, presse continually. The Lord of Heaven & Earth give me still to finde fav*ou*r in y*ou*r Lord*shi*ps Eyes: And even He Prosper y*ou*r Lord*shi*p w*i*th Longe life, & Happynesse[,] & Fav*ou*r w*i*th God, & man. So humbly cravinge Pardon for my great boldnesse I desire leave to rest

Y*ou*r Lord*shi*ps exceedingly much bounden Orat*ou*r,

Boston. Jan. 3i. i624./ Iohn Cotton./

1. George Montaigne was bishop of Lincoln from 1617 to 1621. He was an orthodox supporter of Anglican forms of worship and was later a strong backer of Archbishop William Laud.

2. John Davenant (1576–1641) was bishop of Salisbury from 1621 to 1641. Cotton's spelling, Sarisbury, was a common alternative spelling from at least the time of the Norman invasion. The town is listed as Sarisberie in the Domesday Book (1086). John Field, *Place-Names of Great Britain and Ireland* (Totowa, N.J., 1980), 151–152.

3. Edward Wright was appointed Boston's mayor's chaplain in 1618 and served with Cotton in the worship service at St. Botolph's Church. See Nicholas Hoppin, "The Rev. John Cotton, A.M., Vicar of Old Boston," *Church Monthly,* IV (1862), 40–54, V (1863), 161–167; mentioned in Ziff, *Career of John Cotton,* 50–51.

4. Others have noted that these exceptions can be explained from practical realities rather than from Cotton's theological or ecclesiastical theories. The Puritans viewed the marriage ceremony as a secular or civil ceremony, so that the ring symbolism did not carry the significance of a religious act. On the other hand, standing at the time of the recitation of the creed, required by the official church but resisted in Puritan practice, was perhaps necessitated for the preacher, Cotton, because at that moment in worship he needed to stand and move to the pulpit, where he would be prepared to pray and preach immediately afterwards. So "cynics could suggest," writes Ziff (*Career of John Cotton,* 57); in fact, one skeptical nineteenth-century historian had done so; see Hoppin, "The Rev. John Cotton, A.M.," *Church Monthly,* IV (1862), 48.

5. Nullius numeri: of no account.

R[alph] Levett to John Cotton

March 3, 1625/6

ALS. MS: MSA, CCXL, Hutchinson Papers, I, fol. 1

Published: MHS, *Colls.,* 2d Ser., X (1823), 182

In L. Thompson, "Letters of John Cotton," 36–37

Ralph Levett was a little-known, minor figure in the Puritan movement, but his case is all the more interesting for that, as we see him here at the beginning of his career struggling to find his way as a Puritan while ministering, apparently, as the private chaplain to the Wray family at Ashby-cum-Fenby in Lincolnshire. Levett was from a Yorkshire family but after his Cambridge education (Christ's College, bachelor of arts, 1621/2; master's, 1624) and his ordination at York (1624), he spent his ministerial career in nearby Lincolnshire, moving to Grainsby in 1635, where he was instituted by Lady Frances Wray. More than five years after this letter was written, on January 25, 1632, Ralph Levett would marry Anne, the daughter of Anne and Edward Hutchinson, at Bilsby, Lincolnshire, the village where John Wheelwright was minister from 1623 until 1632. Wheelwright also had married a Hutchinson—Mary, the aunt of Levett's wife and sister-in-law of the elder Anne, who was later prominent in the Massachusetts Antinomian controversy. The small circle of Lincolnshire Puritans was thus linked in various ways well before some of them emigrated to New England.[1]

This letter and Cotton's reply, which have survived in excellent condition, clearly indicate the extent to which Puritans were troubled about the appropriate response to games and folk customs that had no scriptural precedent and were even, in some cases, of pagan origin. Levett, a young minister still feeling his way on such matters, not fully certain how to react to worldly practices that he has discovered in the household of his patroness such as card playing, dancing, and exchanging valentines, turns to the older, more experienced Cotton for advice.

Fully as interesting as the questions asked by Levett, however, are the answers Cotton gives in his reply. The subject of card playing and choosing valentines by drawing lots was an issue that, even as Levett and Cotton exchanged thoughts on the subject, "continued to excite debate among puritans."[2] The issue of lots had been prominent in the expulsion of Williams Ames from Cambridge in 1609. Ames took the relatively conservative Calvinist position that resorting to lots for frivolous amusements or games was blasphemous, the "prophaning of a holy thing."[3] Cotton agreed, indicating in his letter to Levett that "carding" and selecting valentine recipients by lots is "a takeinge of Gods name in vaine." There was room for disagreement on this point, however, even among Puritans. Samuel Ward, a fellow at Emmanuel when Cotton was there, and since 1610 the master of Sidney Sussex College, was much more liberal on this issue than Cotton.[4] Likewise, Thomas Gataker, in a key work on the subject, *Of the Nature and Use of Lots . . .* (London, 1619), argued that, although God's general providence governs all events, there is a category of casual events not tied to the notion of God's special providence. Drawing lots in sport or as a pastime or to divide property was, in Gataker's view, harmless and perfectly lawful.[5]

On the subject of dancing, however, Cotton's mind was more open to its acceptability under certain conditions. His was a more liberal position, in fact, than that taken by Increase Mather in New England more than half a century later. Whereas in 1626 Cotton said that he "would not simply condemne" dancing, "yea though mixt," his son-in-law, Increase Mather, wrote in 1685, "*Gynecandrical Dancing,* or that which is commonly called *Mixt* or *Promiscuous Dancing, viz.* of Men and Women (be they elder or younger persons) together: Now this we affirm to be utterly unlawful, and that it cannot be tollerated in such a place as *New-England,* without great Sin."[6] The subject had been debated in Puritan circles for decades. It was sometimes frowned upon for competing with churchgoing and thus drawing youth away from sermons. In 1577,

John Northbrooke had been more direct in warning of the physical dangers of dancing. As they dance, he wrote, "maydens and matrones are groped and handled with unchast handes and kissed and dishonestly embraced."[7]

The letter also indicates Levett's acquaintance with Cotton's wife, Elizabeth, and other people in the Boston area, suggesting that he was probably one of the students and recent graduates from Cambridge who spent some time living in Cotton's house before taking up a position in a church elsewhere. As is evident in other letters from this period of Cotton's career, Levett was not the only one to seek Cotton's advice after leaving his immediate tutelage.

Levett used a separate sheet to address the letter:

> To my much respected and very
> kind freind Mr Cotton
> preacher of the word
> at Boston give
> these.

Sir/

first, i give you thanks for your kindnes to me at my being with you both first & last; as also for your kind letter, wherby i am somtymes restreined from unseasonable reproofes, as after i conceive they would have beene:

Now (being ~~being~~ *th*e more bold upon *th*e consideration of your former love) i desire to be troublesome to you for the resolution of these questions. First whether it be convenient *tha*t i sho. pray for my good lady[8] in the publick assembly, being then the mouth of *th*e people to god[,] such a petition seems to be heterogenral, & lik a string out of tune; if convenient whether w*he*n she is present, & in w*ha*t words./

Another question is concerning their toyes they use at *tha*t tyme, which they say they celebrate in remembr*an*ce of Christs birth (tho. they nev*er* less rem*em*b*er* him) viz: carding, dancinge[.] i wo. know w*ha*t my duty is *tha*t i may discharge a good conscience; i have oft upon occasion spoken against mixt dancinge after feasts litle thinking there had ben any such suffered & practised here.

A third is this. On valentines day they have a custom to writ names in papers & put *the*m tog*ethe*r in an hatt, & then ev*er*y one drawes a Valentin (so they terme it)[.] i wo. k*no*w wheth*e*r it be lawful;

Our 2. young Ladyes came to me being sick on an ague to draw one, w*hi*ch since hath not once troubled me & *ergo*[9] the rather i desire yo*u*r judg*men*t in this case, that if it be a sin i may humble mys. for my negligence, & may upon occa*s*ion speak ag*ain*st it./

Remember i pray you my best love to M[ris] Cotton, M[r] Holden,[10] & M[r]

Vicars[.][11] So i com*m*end you & yours to *th*e peace of God, desiri[ng the] continuance of your prayers for us.

Ashby March 3. yours in al christian affection
1625./ R. Levett

1. There has been much valuable work in the area of migration and mobility studies, especially for the period of the Great Migration (1620–1640). Roger Thompson provides a carefully focused and detailed examination of the sizable cluster of emigrants to America from "Greater East Anglia," including kin connections in Cotton's Lincolnshire (*Mobility and Migration: East Anglian Founders of New England, 1629–1640* [Amherst, Mass., 1994], 14–27, 184–185).

2. Margo Todd, "Providence, Chance, and the New Science in Early Stuart Cambridge," *Historical Journal,* XXIX (1986), 699. Sir Simonds D'Ewes recorded an instance in 1607/8 in which a young fellow commoner (gentleman) at Jesus College, Cambridge, was involved in controversy as a result of drawing a valentine by lots and shortly thereafter had to deal with the rumor that he was betrothed to his "valentine" (*The Autobiography and Correspondence of Sir Simonds D'Ewes* . . . [London, 1845], 163–164).

3. Todd, "Providence, Chance, and the New Science," *Historical Journal,* XXIX (1986), 705.

4. See ibid., 697–711.

5. See Barbara Donagan, "Providence, Chance, and Explanation: Some Paradoxical Aspects of Puritan Views of Causation," *Journal of Religious History,* XI (1981), 395–398.

6. Increase Mather, *An Arrow against Profane and Promiscuous Dancing,* in Joseph E. Marks III, ed., *The Mathers on Dancing* (Brooklyn, N.Y., 1975), 31. Mather quotes John Cotton's *Briefe Exposition with Practical Observations upon the Whole Book of Ecclesiastes* (London, 1654), with its later comments opposing mixed dancing, specifically at weddings. Cotton might have preached the sermon first in England, later revising it in New England. See Ziff, *Career of John Cotton,* 262, where the work's composition is dated between 1612 and 1632, and Emerson, *Cotton,* 141, where it is dated 1644.

Bruce C. Daniels takes up the issue of dancing and Puritan attitudes toward it in *Puritans at Play: Leisure and Recreation in Colonial New England* (New York, 1995), 109–113, where he misdates the letter 1635, also mistakenly claiming that it was written to one Richard Levett, mysteriously describing him as the "young minister" of the congregation in Salem, Massachusetts, where "a controversy concerning the probity of dancing" had arisen. Since none of these asserted details are correct, the letter needs to be reconsidered in its actual context of the conscientious struggles of a young English Puritan minister within an English gentry household.

7. John Northbrooke, *Spiritus Est Vicarius Christi in Terra: A Treatise Wherein Dicing, Dauncing, Vaine Playes or Enterluds with Other Idle Pastimes etc. . . . Are Reproved* (London, [1577?]), 143, quoted in Patrick Collinson, *The Religion of Protestants: The Church in English Society, 1559–1625* (Oxford, 1982), 225.

8. Probably Lady Frances Wray, daughter of Sir William Drury, and wife of Sir William Wray of Ashby, Lincolnshire. Their daughter, Frances, married Sir Henry Vane, Jr., in 1640. See Charles Dalton, *History of the Wrays of Glentworth, 1523–1852* (Aberdeen, 1880–1881), II, 65.

9. Levett wrote gô, a standard abbreviation of ergo, Latin for therefore.

10. Possibly Thimbleby Holden, official of the archdeaconry of Stow and rector of St. Peter at Arches, Lincoln, 1615–1627 (Clive Holmes, *Seventeenth-Century Lincolnshire* [Lincoln, Lincs., 1980], 60).

11. John Vicars was the longtime minister at St. Mary's, Stamford, Lincolnshire, who, for offenses such as holding conventicles and making "the pulpit of Stamford a place to vent his malice," was called before the Court of High Commission in 1631, suspended from his ministry for seven years, and deprived of his living. Stamford is about thirty-five miles southeast of Boston. See Samuel Rawson Gardiner, ed., *Reports of Cases in the Courts of Star Chamber and High Commission* (Winchester, 1886), 198–238; Holmes, *Seventeenth-Century Lincolnshire,* calls him a "Puritan zealot" (42–43, 62).

John Cotton to R[alph] Levett

[March 1626]

DfL. MS: MSA, CCXL, Hutchinson Papers, I, fol. 2

Published: MHS, *Colls.,* 2d Ser., X (1823), 183–184

In L. Thompson, "Letters of John Cotton," 38–39

Cotton's reply to Levett's letter is written on the verso of the sheet that Levett had used as an envelope. It is written in a hand other than Cotton's—probably one of the young scholar-ministers under Cotton's care—but the interlinear insertions are in his own hand. The letter lacks a signature, although more than two inches of blank space remain at the bottom of the sheet.

Good Mr Levett, I am glad to heare of your recovery & of the constancy of my Ladies good affectio*n* & respect to you, the Lord goe on still to establish both vnto you, that you may haue the more opportunity to doe God and that family faithfull seruice accord*in*ge to your desire./

To pray in p*ar*ticular ˆfor freindsˆ by name euen in publique, is not vnlawfull; Paul desired it for himselfe as well of the whole Church of Ephesus, as of the priuate members. Eph. 6.19.[1] Nayther is it inexpedient, ˆso to Prayˆ for kings, or any other, in Authority or ˆinˆ any eminency eyther for place or distresse. And though themselues be present, yet there will be no suspicio*n* of flattery or other inconvenience, if we doe not so much praise the*m* to God for their styles & vertues as pray for his mercy ˆ& blessingeˆ to the*m* & theirs. If I were to pray in any great mans family I would vsually craue some or other mercy & blessinge fro*m* God vpon his seruant the gouernour of this family: & In the publique congregatio*n* in prayinge for the nobility ~~&~~ ˆorˆ Gentry, I would also mentio*n* his seruant or seruants then assembled, w*i*th some title of their p*r*eference to the congregatio*n*.

Cardinge[2] I take to be vnlawfull as conteyninge in it a lottery, at least in the shufflinge & cuttinge & dealinge. And a lottery also it is to choose valentines in that sort you mentio*n*. Where man and his actio*n* is only c*au*sa p*er* accidens[3] of an euent (as in cardinge & in choice of valentines) God is the only & im*m*ediate c*au*sa p*er* se,[4] now to appeale to him & his Im*m*ediate p*ro*uidence for dispensinge thes ludicras,[5] seemeth to me a takeinge of Gods name in vaine.[6]

Dauncinge (yea though mixt) I would not simply condemne. For I see two sorts of mixt dauncings in vse w*i*th Gods people in the Old Test*am*e*n*t. The one religious Exod. 15.20.21.[7] The other ciuill, tendinge, to the praise of conquerors, as the former of God. 1 Sam. 18.6.7.[8] Only lasciuious dauncinge to wanton dittyes & in amorous gestures & wanton dalliances especially after great feasts I would beare witnes ag*ains*t, as ag*ains*t Flabella Libidinis.[9]

Your witnes bearinge ag*ains*t such th*in*gs, is (I take it) best done in openinnge some scripture, & fro*m* thence instructinge in the truth & dissuadinge the contrary.

1. Eph. 6:18–19: Praying always with all prayer and supplication in the Spirit, and watching thereunto with all perseverance and supplication for all saints; And for me, that my utterance may be given unto me, that I may open my mouth boldly, to make known the mystery of the Gospel.

2. Card playing.

3. Causa per accidens: the accidental cause; see note 6, below.

4. Causa per se: the cause per se; see note 6, below.

5. ludicras: The Latin *ludicra* means amusements, diversions, toys, jokes. *Ludicra* is the correct nominative plural for *ludicrum,* so that "ludicras" does not make sense as a Latin word and is not seen in classical or postclassical sources. Cotton (or his amanuensis) seems to have coined an English word, *ludicra,* which is used here in a plural form. The *OED* records the rare adjectival form, *ludicral* (1656), and the more common *ludicrous,* which is first noted in 1619 in a book Cotton might well have known, Thomas Gataker's *Of the Nature and Use of Lots* (iii, 34). Since *ludicrous* was newly derived from the Latin, Cotton's nominal coinage here seems likely, though the word, unlike *ludicrous,* seems to have had no subsequent history.

6. In a sermon delivered between three and six years later (1629–1632), Cotton paraphrased this sentence: "in all kind of lottery, whatsoever it bee about, wee appeal to God, who is disposer of all things, *Prov.* 16.33. for man being but *causa per accidens* of the event of the lot, there must bee some cause *per se,* and that is God; so that whatsoever it bee about, though matters of pastime or lusory, it is a religious ordinance, because it appeals to divine providence, and therefore to bee avoided" (*A Practical Commentary . . . upon the First Epistle Generall of John* [London, 1656], 127).

7. Exod. 15:20–21: And Miriam the prophetess, the sister of Aaron, took a timbrel in her hand; and all the women went out after her with timbrels and with dances. And Miriam answered them, Sing ye to the Lord, for he hath triumphed gloriously; the horse and his rider hath he thrown into the sea.

8. 1 Sam. 18:6–7: And it came to pass as they came, when David was returned from the slaughter of the Philistine, that the women came out of all cities of Israel, singing and dancing, to meet king Saul, with tabrets, with joy, and with instruments of musick. And the women

answered one another as they played, and said, Saul hath slain his thousands, and David his ten thousands.

9. Flabella Libidinis: a fan of lust. Some fourteen years later in New England Cotton preached on the dangers of mixing dancing with feasting. Preaching on Mark 6, which contains the story of the dancing of Herodias's daughter and the consequent beheading of John the Baptist, Cotton (as recorded by Robert Keayne, an auditor) said: "Next note how uncomely and unseasonable a thinge it is, for weomen to dance befor men, or with men in times of publike and plentifull feastinge. It is of very dayngerows Conseqwence. The Kinge was taken with her dawnce, and he was Soe well pleased with it that he will give a Kingdom for a dance, halfe a Kingdom for a dance, John Baptist head, for a dance. Yea it did Cost him his whole kingdome, as stories report. It Cost him not only his kingdome, but his life and his soule. Use[:] Therfor, take heed of dancinge, of dalliance of wanton behavior, It is of ill Conseqwence." Transcribed from Keayne's manuscript in Helle M. Alpert, "Robert Keayne: Notes of Sermons by John Cotton and Proceedings of the First Church of Boston from 23 November 1639 to 1 June 1640" (Ph.D. diss., Tufts University, 1974), 230–231.

John Cotton to James Ussher, Archbishop of Armagh

May 31, 1626

Published: Richard Parr, *The Life of the Most Reverend Father in God, James Usher, Late Lord Arch-Bishop of Armagh . . . with a Collection of Three Hundred Letters . . .* (London, 1686), 338–339; Charles Richard Elrington, ed., *The Whole Works of the Most Rev. James Ussher, D.D.* (Dublin, 1847–1848), XV, 330–331; *NEHGR,* XXIV (1870), 356–357

In L. Thompson, "Letters of John Cotton," 40–42

James Ussher (1581–1656), who was appointed archbishop of Armagh by James I just four days before the king died in 1625, was perhaps above all else a scholar. After becoming archbishop, he delayed returning to take up his duties in Ireland for at least a year while he pursued scholarly inquiries, working toward completion of his *Bibliotheca theologica,* which nevertheless was unfinished at his death. He was generally sympathetic to the Puritans, but diplomatic enough not to have offended James. At the time of this letter from Cotton, Ussher had just returned to England from a brief visit to Ireland that began in March 1626. His modern biographer shows that he was back in England in late May and was in London "for the month of June and most of July" 1626.[1] That he continued to ponder the complexities of predestination theology is indicated by his publication in Dublin five years later of his Latin work on a ninth-century monk, *Gottschalci et praedestinationae controversiae . . . historia . . .* ("History of Gottschalk and the Controversies of Predestination Occasioned by Him").[2]

Cotton indicates in this letter, which is a cover letter to the enclosure of his manuscript on predestination, that he had written it just a year earlier, or in early 1625, and that it was apparently an elaboration of some catechetical questions on predestination composed still earlier than that. This makes the treatise a somewhat later creation than has previously been assumed.[3] It was a work others were to see as well, as we know from the offhand remark by Timothy Van Vleteren in his letter to Cotton of October 26, 1629, that he had read and admired his catechism and his works "on the Canticles" and "of predestination." In this context, it is important to recall that since 1622 ministers had been under the king's admonition forbidding clergy from handling "in any popular auditory the deep points of predestination, election, reprobation, or of the universality, efficacy, resistability, or irresistability of God's grace."[4] Insofar as it was not written to be delivered orally to a "popular auditory," Cotton's work was not technically in violation of this royal injunction, but, since he apologizes to Ussher for the "plain and popular" style, it would seem he did intend the work for a broad readership, thus testing at least the spirit, if not the letter, of the king's injunction.

The enclosed manuscript on predestination (which has not survived) would remain a text provoking discussion and disagreement throughout Cotton's lifetime. One who would have such disagreements, apparently not long after Ussher saw it, was William Twisse, who took it on himself to write a rejoinder to some of Cotton's positions. So, while it was a text that many ministers, including Ussher, consulted, it was never published as a full, complete statement of Cotton's final views on this thorny topic. His appeal to Ussher to tell him the points on which he might have different views was probably a sincere expression of his desire to be further enlightened on the subject before committing his thoughts to print. We cannot know whether, or how much, Cotton revised the text that Ussher saw before William Twisse was tempted to write out his own differences with Cotton in response to the request of a young minister named Bets who was living at Broughton, the seat of Lord Saye and Sele. Lord Saye, according to Twisse, read his rejoinder, "liked well of it, and communicated it unto *Mr. Cotton,* who carried it with him into *New-England.*"[5] The work of both men remained in manuscript another thirteen years after that. Finally, when Twisse was serving as moderator of the Westminster Assembly, and just a year before his death, his work appeared with the title *A Treatise of Mr Cottons, Clearing Certaine Doubts concerning Predestination, Together with an Examination Thereof.* This work is often taken as a full expression of Cotton's work on predestination, but it clearly is not. It is, rather, just those portions of Cotton's thought on the subject with which Twisse wished to express disagreement. Even in that respect, Cotton's views are very briefly stated, presumably in his words, while Twisse's "examination" of them is much fuller. The effect, both in tone and argument, is to show Cotton up. Twisse goes so far as to suggest Cotton's views at some points "embrace the sower leaven of Arminianisme" or, more strongly still, "In all this wee have as pure Arminianisme tendred unto us, as could drop from the pen of *Arminius* himselfe." Such summary characterizations are in direct opposition to Cotton's reputation—and the broader evidence of his writings—as a vehement opponent of the liberality of the Arminians on the nature of grace and salvation.[6]

Right Reverend,

My beloved Neighbour-Minister Mr. *Wood,*[7] acquainted me with your desire to hear from me, how I conceived of the way of God's eternal Predestination, and the Execution of it: I should not have hearkned to him herein (tho I love him well) were it not for the deep Affection and Reverence I bear to your Person and Gifts, which hath constrained me (together with his importunacy) to yield to the sending of this Discourse to you, which I was occasioned to write a year ago for the satisfaction of a Neighbour-Minister in Points of this nature. The Questions and Answers in the beginning of the Book, I delivered and opened by way of Catechism long ago; which a Neighbour-Minister having afterwards gotten from some of my Hearers, he wrote those Doubts, which follow in the Book, the better to inform either himself or me: Whereupon as I could get any time in the midst of other continual Employments (too heavy for me) I wrote to him the Discourse following, the more fully to acquaint him with the grounds of my Judgment, as knowing well his sufficiency to object fully, if he found himself unsatisfied in any Passage thereof. The Style (I confess) is unmeet for you to read, as being plain and popular, and therefore too large, and withal empty of variety of reading, which store of other Occurrences in my Calling here, inforceth me too often to intermit.

Thus much let me humbly intreat at your Lordship's hands, by the honour which you owe to Christ, and by the Love you bare to his poorest Servants, stick not (I beseech you) to advertise me freely of any such tenent herein, as you shall think less safe. I trust you shall find me conscious of mine own Slenderness, and glad to receive such Light, as God shall be pleased to impart to me by you.

Yet this one thing more let me also add. Tho I yield some degree of Efficacy in Christ's Death unto all; yet I conceive it far short, both of Impetration[8] and Application of that gracious Atonement, which is thereby wrought to the Elect of God; whence also it is that I dare not preach the Gospel indifferently unto all, before the Law; nor the worth of Christ, before the need of Christ. Childrens Bread is not meet for Whelps; and full Souls will despise Hony-Combes. I see *John Baptist* was sent to humble, before Christ to heal; and Christ himself preached Repentance, before Faith in the Promises, *Mark* 1. 15.[9] Neither do I remember in the Gospel any Promise of Grace, pardoning Sin, nor any Commandment to believe Sin pardoned, but to the broken, the bruised, the poor, the weary, the thirsty, or the like. Faith in the Promises, before the Heart be changed from Stoniness to Brokenness, I fear is no better than the Temporary Faith, which is found in the stony Soil; *Luke* 8. 13.[10]

But I cease your Lordship's further Trouble. Now the Lord Jesus, who hath delighted in you to fill your Heart with the Riches of his manifold precious Graces, be pleased to enlarge you to the Employment of them to his best advantage, guide all your Ways in his Faithfulness, and Wisdom, and sustain you with his Mercy and Power unto the end. So I humbly take leave, and rest;

Earnestly desirous to be directed by your
Boston, May 31. Lordship, or confirmed in the Truth,
1626. *John Cotton.*

1. R. Buick Knox, *James Ussher: Archbishop of Armagh* (Cardiff, 1967), 34. On his lifelong scholarly pursuits, see Hugh Trevor-Roper, "James Ussher, Archbishop of Armagh," in Trevor-Roper, *Catholics, Anglicans, and Puritans: Seventeenth-Century Essays* (London, 1987), 120–165.

2. Trevor-Roper, *Catholics, Anglicans, and Puritans,* 145–146.

3. Everett Emerson suggests 1618 as the date of composition (*Cotton,* 83).

4. Edward Cardwell, ed., *Documentary Annals of the Reformed Church of England* . . . , 2d ed. (Oxford, 1844), II, 202, quoted in Foster, *Long Argument,* 68.

5. William Twisse, "The Authors Epistle unto the Reader," in *A Treatise of Mr. Cottons, Clearing Certaine Doubts concerning Predestination, Together with an Examination Thereof* (London, 1646), sig. A3.

6. Ibid., 234, 242. Cotton Mather comments on the vehemence of the attacks on Twisse's work by others, including Daniel Cawdry, Robert Baillie, and Roger Williams. See Mather, *Magnalia,* I, 256. For discussion of these theological issues, see David Como, "Puritans, Predestination, and the Construction of Orthodoxy in Early Seventeenth-Century England," in Peter Lake and Michael McGiffert, eds., *Conformity and Orthodoxy in the English Church, c. 1560–1660* (Rochester, N.Y., 2000), 64–87.

7. Probably Geoffrey (also Geffrey) Wood, vicar at Anwick, Lincolnshire, a village about seventeen miles west of Boston, near Sleaford. He earned his bachelor of arts degree at Emmanuel College in 1603/4 and received the master's degree in 1607, thereafter moving to Oxford. He was ordained a priest at Lincoln in 1608 and became vicar at Anwick in 1612, the same year Cotton went to Boston. Geoffrey Wood was still living in 1637, when he made a will that was not proved until 1658. J. E. Swaby, "Lincolnshire Parish Clergy in the Seventeenth Century," MS, Lincolnshire County Archives 83/176; see also Venn, *Alumni Cantabrigienses,* and *Alumni Oxoniensis.*

8. Impetration: "an obtaining by request and prayer" (T[homas] B[lount], *Glossographia* . . . [London, 1656]).

9. Mark 1:14–15: Now after that John was put in prison, Jesus came into Galilee, preaching the Gospel of the kingdom of God, And saying, The time is fulfilled, and the kingdom of God is at hand: repent ye, and believe the gospel.

10. Luke 8:13: They on the rock are they, which, when they hear, receive the word with joy; and these have no root, which for a while believe, and in time of temptation fall away.

Herbert Palmer to John Cotton

October 25, 1626

ALS. MS: MSA, CCXL, Hutchinson Papers, I, fol. 3

In L. Thompson, "Letters of John Cotton," 43–46

Herbert Palmer (1601–1647), from Wingham, Kent, was a student at St. John's College, Cambridge, from 1616, taking his bachelor of arts in 1619, and his master's in 1622. He became a fellow of Queen's College, Cambridge, in 1623 and in the next year took church orders. His appointment in 1626 as lecturer at St. Alphage's, Canterbury, in Kent, occurred shortly before he wrote this letter, and the appointment, as his questions and comments indicate, motivated him to write to Cotton. He was a moderate Puritan who would later become the master of Queen's College and an influential member of the Westminster Assembly. Described by Robert Baillie as "the best catechist in England," he played a key role in the creation of the Westminster Shorter Catechism, probably the assembly's most influential document.[1]

The manuscript is well preserved, with two exceptions, which account for the breaks in the text. In the lower right corner of the recto, paper is torn away, causing the loss of words at the end of eighteen successive lines. There is also some badly faded ink around a fold about three-quarters of the way down the sheet and near the mutilations at the right edge. The text is all written on one side of the sheet. The braces enclose details supplied by the transcription in the Massachusetts Historical Society. In sending it to Cotton, Palmer folded it inside a second sheet, which bears the address block, in Palmer's hand:

To the Reuerend & his most
Esteemed Friend Mr John
Cotton Minister of *th*e
word at Boston
in Lincolneshire
these

Reuerend S*i*r

I haue receiued by my Vncle Humfry[2] your most Wellcome Letter; For w*hi*ch I desire to returne all thankfulnesse to God first, & then to your selfe; whose many imployments I know take you so vp; as but *tha*t I felt a want of good Directions in my selfe being young and vnexperienced, I should scarce haue aduentured to haue Disturbed you w*i*th my sute. But your Satisfying it, is a good signe you haue pardon'd my boldnesse; & so I will not striue further to excuse it. But yet methinkes I find *tha*t in your Letter w*hi*ch encourages me ˆfurther, to wit,ˆ againe to adventu[re] & to craue not only satisfaction of my present doubts expressed in this Letter, but admittance to haue recourse to you this way on occasions ˆhereafterˆ as I shall haue need[.] W*hi*ch If it shall seeme to you too importune a request, either now or at any other tyme; I refuse not to be punished w*i*th your sylence: My solliciting of you shall witnesse how highly I prise this Fauour from you; And yet I haue learnt more manners then to thinke my Desires ought to be pressed to any Præiudice of your more important affaires: I will therefore bound my sute w*i*thin this limit, to have leaue to repayre to you by writing on Occasion; & to craue answeres as your selfe shall Judge me & my businesses to deserue; & your leysure permit. In your Letter you make mention of *tha*t Place: mat: 20.[3] *tha*t in our entrance into Gods Vineyard euery Labourer agreeth w*i*th God for some penny or other: so applying *th*e whole parable to Ministers. Now because I haue formerly heard you make some mention of this Place before, Give me leaue to ~~desire~~ put these Questions to you concerning *th*e meaning of it. First how *th*e Parable can be restrained to Ministers? Since *th*e Context of *th*e Latter part of *th*e 19 Chap*ter* to w*hi*ch this ~~is~~ seemes to be Joyned is vttered of all Christians particularly v 29 & 30.[4] *th*e words of w*hi*ch last Verse are againe repeated in the Close of this Parable v.16.[5] where is likewise Added, many are called but few chosen; w*hi*ch seemes euidently to be ment of all *tha*t are called outwardly to be Christians, *tha*t only few of them are elected! 2. How may it appeare *tha*t *th*e meaning of men being call'd at the 3 6 9 & 11th houres [deleted word] is, *tha*t men are called to *th*e Ministery w*i*th Variety o[f] Gifts, some meaner some greater,? (for such as I remember was your Interpretation[6] of *tha*t) .3. Since *th*e Parable sayth euery man receiued a penny *tha*t seemeth to imply, *tha*t all hau[e] *th*e same specificall Reward & no Difference betweene them; rather then *tha*t each man {had} a Distinct Penny of a diuerse kind, to wit according as he hath agreed w*i*th God: & So much *th*e rather because no mention is made *tha*t *th*e Lord made any Particular agreement {with} any of *th*e Labours but those whom he hired early in *th*e morning, to the others he onl{y sayd} Goe; & whatsoeuer is right *tha*t you shall receiue .1. as I giue to others. W{*hi*ch} I {yet} most of all desire satisfaction in because on *th*e one side I haue read some w[o]rkes [tha]t auouch *tha*t whosoeuer is a Faithfull Minister doth conuert some or other, & to || Jer. 23.22.[7] On *th*e other side I haue heard credibly of a Religious Minister of great || after well nigh 4[0][8] yeeres continuall paynes, complayned g{reauously *tha*t he} || *tha*t he had conuerted all *tha*t tyme; according to *tha*t Esay 49. [deleted number] 4 & 5:[9] So *th*{at}|| to be resolued in, whether conuersion of Soules be a propriety to a faith || Omni & Soli. Next I desire to be satisfyed whether a Lecturer ought || his manner of Preaching from *tha*t of a Pastour, at least wise be more sparing || Reproofe but euen in exhortation: Vpon wh*i*ch Supposition I see not but ~~g~~ *th*e gre{at}|| of doing good vpon *th*e Peoples Soules he is restrained from; especially if *tha*t Ru{le}|| vniuersall as *tha*t a Lecturer should be tyed thereby euen when he is to preach to a || Towne as I am to doe who haue not one Pastour but Diuerse: W*i*thall *th*e Inte|| *th*e People who call men to be Lecturers hath not any such Restriction, but re|| the most Profitable way, not conceiueing any Difference betweene their Le[cturer] & Pastor requisite in *th*e manner of their Preaching. Lastly whether *tha*t of ou|| concerning Dogs & swine be to be vnderstood of Priuate Counsayle & Repr{oofe} or extend also *th*e Publike Ministery. Thus w*i*th my best Respects to your || wife & earnestly Praying God to continue you Long a Light in his Church I {take} || & rest

Your vnfained Friend in {all christian observance}
Herb{ert Palmer}

Queenes Camb: Oct 25 1626.

[10] Mr Aldrich[11] liues not in Kent but in Sussex, whom ^yet^ I shall I thinke see when I ~~goe~~ ^am^ in ~~to~~ *th*e Country, for *tha*t he liues w*i*th some of my neere Friends whom I haue promised to visit; I shall then remember you to him. I suppose I shall stay here till after Christs Natiuity:

1. On Palmer, see *DNB;* William Urwick, *Nonconformity in Herts. . . .* (London, 1884), 772–777; John Edwin Cussans, *History of Hertfordshire . . .* (London, 1870–1881), I, 41–43; Carlton A. Palmer, Jr., comp., "The Ancient Family of Palmer of Plymouth Colony," typescript (Livermore, Calif., 1988), 25–26. Both Urwick and *DNB* quote Baillie's remark.

2. John Humfrey was at this time married to his second wife, Elizabeth Pelham, the half sister of Herbert Palmer's mother, Margaret Pelham Palmer. Frances Rose-Troup, "John Humfry," Essex Institute, *Historical Collections,* LXV (1929), 293–308, esp. 293–295; Joseph Lemuel Chester, *Herbert Pelham, His Ancestors and Descendants* [Boston, 1879], 3–4; Palmer, comp., "The Ancient Family of Palmer," 25–26.

3. Matthew 20 contains Jesus's parable of the householder who hires workers at different times of the day but pays them all the same wage.

4. Matt. 19:29–30: And every one that hath forsaken houses, or brethren, or sisters, or father, or mother, or wife, or children, or lands, for my name's sake, shall receive an hundredfold, and shall inherit everlasting life. But many that are first shall be last; and the last shall be first.

5. Matt. 20:16: So the last shall be first, and the first last: for many be called, but few chosen.

6. The capital I is written over an e.

7. Jer. 23:22: But if they had stood in my counsel, and had caused my people to hear my words, then they should have turned them from their evil way, and from the evil of their doings.

8. The second digit is illegible, but Cotton's reply to Palmer (see below) confirms that the number is 40.

9. Isa. 49:4–5: Then I said, I have laboured in vain, I have spent my strength for naught,

and in vain: yet surely my judgment is with the Lord, and my work with God. And now, saith the Lord that formed me from the womb to be his servant, to bring Jacob again to him, Though Israel be not gathered, yet shall I be glorious in the eyes of the Lord, and my God shall be my strength.

10. This was written in three lines along the left margin, top to bottom.

11. Probably Simon Aldrich, whose years at Trinity College, Cambridge, had partially coincided with Cotton's there. He matriculated in 1596, received bachelor of arts, master of arts, and bachelor of divinity degrees in 1596/7, 1600, and 1607, respectively. He became a fellow at Trinity in 1599, and was vicar at Ringmer, Sussex, from 1611 to 1627. Venn, *Alumni Cantabrigienses,* I, 14.

John Cotton to Herbert Palmer

November 8, 1626

Copy. MS: MSA, CCXL, Hutchinson Papers, I, fols. 3a, 4

In L. Thompson, "Letters of John Cotton," 47–50

The first page of this letter is on the verso of Palmer to Cotton, October 25, 1626; the second page is the recto of a second sheet. The manuscript is not in Cotton's hand, an amanuensis apparently having made this copy for Cotton's own files.

Good Sir.

My other Occasions are not such but that I hope I shall be willing at any time to returne answer to your vsefull l*ette*res though I am indeed comstrayned to write the more cursorily, w*hi*ch I desire you to impute ether to insufficiencie in my selfe or to vrgency in other buisinesse and not to any willinge neglect of you or of your l*ette*res.

Though that place Math: 19. 29. 30.[1] may be well conceiued to reach to all Chr*ist*ians yet the words were spoken to ministers, & vpon Occasio*n* of *th*e Ministers refusall of all to follow him. It is not vnvsuall to intersect[2] generall Epiphonema's[3] vpo*n* Particular Occasions, & yet to retourne againe to p*r*osecute a p*ar*ticular argument in hand. And indeed in Math: 20. who can so fitly be called Labourer in Gods vineyard as the Ministers of *th*e word. I Cor. 3. 9.[4] Howsoeuer I easiely graunt *th*e Parable may be applyed further then to Ministers (though cheifely to them) euen to all Chr*ist*ian[s] *tha*t labo*u*r in any Calling ^w*i*th^in *th*e Church; though p*ro*perly none are said to labo*u*r in the vineyard but them that labo*u*r about the vineyard, either in digging it or dressing it or gathering the stones out of it &c: But it is generally true *tha*t euery man in his Calling aymeth at some end w*hi*ch God calleth *th*e Agreeing w*i*th him for a Pennye: Men called at the, 6, 9, ^&^ 11 houres may fitly imply men called to *th*e Minist~~ry~~^ery^ w*i*th variety of gifts. For the Talent of Time is one gift & one gift may easiely by Synechdoche be put for many there being the like Reason of [one or two letters deleted] all as of One. And indeed the murmurring is often most found amongst men of auntient standing against young men of lesse time & Ordinarily of lesse outward Gifts. Though all receiued a Peny it doth not imply they all receiued *th*e same specificall reward w*i*thout Difference. For God in cleareing his Dealeing ag*ains*t the murmurers reformeth them to *th*e Agreem*en*t v*erses* 13. 14.[5] w*hi*ch implyeth *th*e Peny was the Price agreed vpon betweene god and the Labourers. And albeit onely those who were first sent foorth agreed w*i*th God exp*re*ssly for a Peny, yet *tha*t Onely implyeth that a certaine sort of Labourers in the ministery (& vsually those who are afterwards most apt to murmure against God & their Brethren) doe capitulate w*i*th God & Man about certainety & security of mainetenance. But the Labourers *tha*t were afterwards hired had secret thoughts & desires about some ends w*hi*ch they p*ro*pounded vpon their labours, though they did not so exp*re*ssly indent[ure][6] with God or man about them.

And yet I deny not w*hi*ch is the point of yo*u*r 2d Quæstio*n* *tha*t a Godly & painefull Minister may sometimes be lesse fruietefull (,yea it may be altogether barren) in conuersion of soules. Though the place you quote out of Isay doe not verify it either in Isay himselfe (for he had his spirituall Children whom God had giuen him Isay 8.18.)[7] or in Christ. The Place onely argueth an vnfruitefullnesse of the Ministery of both to *th*e body of *th*e Nation. But if a good Minister complayne (as you say) of not conuerting one soule in 40 yeares. First Consider he might conuert some & never know it; as Elijah turned many to Righteousnesse who knew not of one. Againe sometimes he that is now a Godly minister was at his first entraunce into his Calling a meere Scholler, & then he agreed with God vpon another Penny then *th*e Conv*er*sion of soules. Thirdly before God he is said to begett soules *tha*t doth vnfeighnedly desire & endeauo*u*r it; God accepting *th*e will for the Deed. Fourthly Sometimes a Minister (though of a Godly Spirit) weakeneth his spirit by some defilement either at his first entrance into *tha*t calling or in his after p*ro*gresse; that may afterwards much euacuate the Power of his ministery. But Ordinarily a Faithfull Minister making the conversio*n* of soules the scope of his Labours p*re*uayleth w*i*th good successe to *th*e accomplishm*en*t of his desires, and [s]eldome doth a worldling attaine heereto. For as Solomon saith (Pro: 11.30) He that [IV] winneth soules is wise. But my hast will not p*er*mitt me ~~to~~ heerein to enlarge my selfe at this time.

To [two letters deleted] your 3[d] Quæstion I haue answered in my former l*ett*ere. The Difference betweene Pasto*u*r & Teacher inferreth a difference in their ~~ad~~Ministratio*n*. Rom: 12.7.8.[8] But yet I deny not, If god haue giuen to any the gifts of both; he may (seasonably) dispense both. The Peoples

Intentio*n* in Calling a man to teach or Exhort may iustly incline a man to fullfill their honest desires. For before God it is not *th*e setlednesse or vnsetlednesse of mainetenance that maketh a man a Psto*u*r or a Teacher; but the worke whereto he is called.

The Place of Doggs & swine (which is your last Quæstion) I vnderstand generally. And therefore The Ap*ost*les forbore to speake to publique Congregations as well as to priuate p*er*sons; when they found them of a malignant spirit Act: 13: 45. 46.[9]

The Lord Jesus guide & blesse all yo*u*r wayes to the prayse of his grace in Christ.

Com*m*ende me heartily to M[r] Goodwin,[10] M[r] Perne,[11] M[r] Arrowsmith.[12]

Boston. Nov: 8. Yo*u*rs heartily in the Lord
1626. J Cotton

1. See Palmer to Cotton, Oct. 25, 1626, n. 4.

2. Though the manuscript clearly reads "intersect," it is possible the copyist misread Cotton's interject.

3. A term in rhetoric for an exclamatory sentence or a striking reflection.

4. 1 Cor. 3:9: For we are labourers together with God: ye are God's husbandry, ye are God's building.

5. Matt. 20:13–14: But he answered one of them, and said, Friend, I do thee no wrong: didst not thou agree with me for a penny? Take that thine is, and go thy way: I will give unto this last, even as unto thee.

6. The writer wrote indent- at the end of a line, but neglected to complete the word in the next line.

7. Isa. 8:18: Behold, I and the children whom the Lord hath given me are for signs and for wonders in Israel from the Lord of hosts, which dwelleth in Mount Zion.

8. Rom. 12:7–8: Or ministry, let us wait on our ministering: or he that teacheth, on teaching; Or he that exhorteth, on exhortation: he that giveth, let him do it with simplicity; he that ruleth, with diligence; he that sheweth mercy, with cheerfulness.

9. Acts 13:45–46: But when the Jews saw the multitudes, they were filled with envy, and spake against those things which were spoken by Paul, contradicting and blaspheming. Then Paul and Barnabas waxed bold, and said, It was necessary that the word of God should first have been spoken to you: but seeing ye put it from you, and judge yourselves unworthy of everlasting life, lo, we turn to the Gentiles.

10. Probably John Goodwin (1594?–1665), who was a fellow at Queen's College from 1617 to 1627 and thus a colleague of Palmer's at the time of this letter. But possibly Thomas Goodwin (1600–1680), who was a fellow at the neighboring Catharine Hall (now St. Catharine's College) from 1620 to 1632. Both men are said to have been influenced by Cotton to become Independents.

11. Andrew Perne (1596–1654) was a fellow at Catharine Hall, Cambridge, from 1622 to 1627, when he was made rector at Wilby, Northamptonshire. He was later a representative of Northampton at the Westminster Assembly. *DNB;* Venn, *Alumni Cantabrigienses,* III, 348.

12. John Arrowsmith (1602–1659) received his master of arts degree from St. John's College, Cambridge, in 1623, when he became a fellow at Catharine Hall. He was later a member of the Westminster Assembly. See *DNB;* Venn, *Alumni Cantabrigienses,* I, 42.

Edward Reyner to [John Cotton?]

April 5, [1627?]

ALS. MS: MSA, CCXL, Hutchinson Papers, I, fol. 84

Edward Reyner (1600–1668) was educated at St. John's College, Cambridge (bachelor of arts, 1620/1; master's, 1624/5). He taught school in Lincolnshire, first at Aserby and then, through an offer from the countess of Warwick, at Market-Rason, about sixteen miles northeast of Lincoln. After four years at the latter post, the countess bestowed on him the lectureship at Welton, five miles north of Lincoln. After this he was made lecturer at Benedicts in Lincoln on August 13, 1626, and then at St. Peter at Arches in Lincoln on February 17, 1626/7. Since this letter asks how to deal with the issue of conformity in church worship, it was probably written early in Reyner's experience as a lecturer in Lincoln, very likely in 1627. He became a Nonconformist and eventually suffered persecution for this, causing him to flee to Norfolk, where he ministered for a few years during the interregnum, returning finally to Lincoln in 1654. He remained a lifelong resister of church-enforced subscription to forms of worship, very likely urged to such a course by Cotton's reply to this letter, which has not survived.[1]

The manuscript is written in a small, deliberate hand, on one side of a single sheet, and is addressed on a separate sheet:

> To my Reverend and worthy Freind
> Mr Cotton Minister of *th*e Gospel
> at Boston these deliver

Reverend S^ir.

I returned by *th*e hand of Mr Tilson[2] all *th*e Letters commendatory of Andreas a Salis, together with our Contributions towards *th*e Grisons releife,[3] amounting, as I remember, to *th*e Summe of 9^li.2^s. w*hi*ch is as much as my best Indevours ˆthrough *th*e Grace of Godˆ could extend it to. Mr Langley of Treswel[4] writ to me diverse weekes agoe, desiring me to get *th*e judgments of some Divines with us (and of you by Name) about this case here inclosed; w*hi*ch I desire you to resolue as soone as your leisure will permit, becaus *th*e letter hath beene with me many weeks, you being not returned from farre till of late: and I know not what speede *th*e Gentlman whom *th*e Case concerns (who desires to be conceal'd) ~~he~~ requires of *th*e Answer. Good Mr. Wales (whom you know)[5] is much perplexed as you may understand by Mr Petchels Letter and hath longed after your resolution of his doubt to help him out of *th*e briers. Troubling you thus with *th*e doubts of others, I am not willing to trouble you further with my owne. All my Suite to you at t[hi]s present is that you would pray earnestly for me that God may guide me in *th*e Disquisitio*n* of his Truth. I haue beene put upon it in my self lately to study *th*e point, whether a man may be safely ignorant of *th*e ~~Un~~lawfulnes or Unlawfulnes of church-Ceremonyes [two words on the line and an interlinear insertion deleted] ˆinˆ *th*e word: and *th*e Conclusion is I must search *th*e Script*ure* for a Ground of doing or refusing ˆthemˆ: *th*e Lord direct me herein, and by his Spirit leade me into all truth, for I enter into this way with a trembling foote. I know you are pressed with Multitudinous Imployments, I cease to detaine you from them any longer: Help me with your prayers and I haue my desire. The Lord Jesus be with your spirit. Amen.

Lincolne.

April. 5.

My wife [deleted word] and I remembere our loue
to you and yours.

I would gladly heare when her Brother
*th*e watch-maker comes to Boston.

Yours in *th*e Lord Jesus
Ed: Reyner

1. For biographical summaries on Reyner, see Brook, *Lives of the Puritans,* II, 421–427; *Calamy Revised,* 408; *DNB.*

2. Edward Tilson, a linendraper, woolendraper, and property owner was mayor of Boston in 1625 and 1642. In 1643 he was one of many men "of good estate" in Lincolnshire indicted for treason for supporting Parliament against the king. See P. Thompson, *History of Boston,* 84 n. 7, 455, 773–774.

3. The Grisons were residents of an area of southern Switzerland that was the scene, throughout the 1620s, of violent reversals of ecclesiastical jurisdiction between the Catholics and Protestants, as part of the struggle in Europe during the Thirty Years' War. Famine and plague (there were four bad harvests in a row, from 1625 to 1628), together with the burning of villages, rape, and murder, visited this area and caused their appeal to English Protestants for relief. Reyner's comment here indicates that he had been trying to raise funds for the Grisons, with very limited success. He mentions this briefly, indicating that Cotton already knew about it and might in fact have been involved in related charitable efforts himself, as was another of his correspondents, John Nicolaus Rulice.

Andreas à Salis is probably Rudolf-Andreas von Salis (1594–1668), whose family were leaders in the county of Chiavenna in southern Switzerland. He was instrumental in achieving the peace settlement with Spain in a mission to Madrid in 1637–1639. C. V. Wedgwood, *The Thirty Years War* (New Haven, Conn., 1939), 255; Hubert G. R. Reade, *Sidelights on the Thirty Years War* (London, 1924), II, 320–321, 446–447; Victor Attinger, ed., *Dictionnaire historique et biographique de la Suisse . . .* (Neuchatel, 1921–1933), III, 699.

4. Henry Langley was a Puritan rector of the West Moiety at Treswell, Nottinghamshire, from February 11, 1610/1, to 1636. He was educated at Christ's College, Cambridge, receiving the bachelor of arts in 1602/3(?) and the master's in 1606. Thoroton Society, Record Series, XX (1961); Ronald A. Marchant, *The Puritans and the Church Courts in the Diocese of York, 1560–1642* (London, 1960), 308; Venn, *Alumni Cantabrigienses,* III, 44.

5. Elkanah Wales (1588–1669) was a graduate of Trinity College, Cambridge, who in 1616 became perpetual curate at Pudsey, Yorkshire, where he remained for his long ministry until ejected in 1662. He was well known as a preacher and a Nonconformist, often preaching successfully in nearby Leeds and Halifax, where his brother Samuel was curate until his death about 1626. The acquaintance of Reyner with the older Wales seems likely, given the comment by Brook that Reyner, who was born in Morley, near Leeds, and grew up in that region, "greatly frequented sermons in his childhood, and constantly attended the Monthly Exercise . . . at Leeds, Pudsey, Halifax, and other places." Brook, *Lives of the Puritans,* II, 421–422; Marchant, *The Puritans and the Church Courts,* 289.

Charles Chauncy to John Cotton

March 15, 1627/8

Published: Hutchinson, *History,* I, 259–260

The long career of Charles Chauncy (1592–1672) was full of highs and lows, some of them epitomizing the experience of the nonconforming Puritans when faced with the power of bishops and archbishops insisting on conformity. But his own personality and frame of mind also contributed to both his failures and his achievements. The following letter was written only two weeks after Chauncy had been presented by his college, Trinity College, Cambridge, to the vicarage of Ware in Hertfordshire on February 27, 1627/8. An accomplished orientalist as well as classicist, he had taught both Hebrew and Greek at Cambridge, where he was also vicar of St. Michael's.

Chauncy's instincts in seeking Cotton's advice on how to deal with the requirements of formal submission to the Thirty-nine Articles, originally written during the reign of Elizabeth I and reaffirmed in 1604 under James I, were sound. Cotton had already survived as a known Puritan for a decade and a half in Boston, and Chauncy realized he would have difficulties at Ware on the issue of conformity. Three years later, on April 30, 1630, the Court of High Commission did indeed make him a target, charging him on several counts with Nonconformity and praise of the Puritans. He apparently satisfied the court on this occasion, but again in November 1635, after his move to Marston St. Lawrence in Northamptonshire, he was called to account for his nonconformity in refusing to build a communion kneeling rail at his former church in Ware.[1] He was fined and imprisoned on this occasion until abjectly submitting to the church's authority, promising conformity thereafter, very much against his Puritan principles.[2]

Chauncy arrived in New England in 1638. He was one of the ministers at Plymouth for some three years, though his preference for full immersion in infant baptism might have led to his removal to Scituate, where he served from 1641 to 1654.[3] During the Protectorate in England, he was invited to return to his former church at Ware, but was dissuaded from doing so by the offer of the presidency of Harvard College, an office he held from 1654 to 1671.[4] The importance to Chauncy of the issues raised in the letter was demonstrated by their reappearance as the cause of a still-agonized conscience in his last will and testament.[5]

Salutem in fonte salutis.[6]
Good Sir,

My kindest respects and most loving salutations to yourself and your wife. The present convenience of a messenger from Ware makes me bold to trouble you with these few lines. I am now (by God's good hand) vickar of Ware, and desire your best direction how I may with most profit and edification of my charge proceed in the Lord's work. I have a very large parish and a dissolute town to deal with (as you may well guess) and which is worse, we have little government in the place to assist us. The people have wanted instruction for many years (such I mean as might build them up in the faith and make them wise unto salvation) besides, the places round about me are a barren wilderness, and so must undergo much opposition. I have already sustained *aliqua gravamina conscientiæ,*[7] to go thus far in regard to the government and discipline of our church, and am likely to undergo more in the book of articles, which we are bound to read publicly and to yield our assent unto; the article concerning the ordination of bishops and ministers doth somewhat trouble me,[8] as also the ceremonies which we are bound unto, which though I forbear myself, yet I know not how to avoid but that my curate must use if I will stand here. I pray afford your wisest advice herein. *Hæc sub sigillo.*[9]

I shall be glad to see you at my poor vickarage, *in transitu,*[10] and for my part (if God permit) I will not fail to see you once a year. I pray salute Mr. Johnson[11] and Mr. Bellingham[12] with their wives in my name, and the rest of my christian friends in your town or family, and I beseech you remember me unto the Lord in your prayers, and the Lord give a blessing to your person and labors.

Your's in the Lord with all hearty affection,
Ware, March 15. 1627. Charles Chauncey.

1. Great Britain, Public Record Office, *Calendar of State Papers,* Domestic Series, *Of the Reign of Charles I,* ed. John Bruce, William Douglas Hamilton, and Sophia Crawford Lomas (London, 1858–1897), IV, *1629–1631,* 233.

2. Ibid., IX, *1635–1636,* 123–124, 483, 490, 494–495.

3. The Plymouth church, in fact, sought and received advice from the Boston elders—Cotton in particular—regarding Chauncy's ideas on baptism. Cotton's review and refutation of Chauncy's position was recorded by Robert Keayne on June 21, 1640 (MS, "Notes of Sermons or Expositions of Rev. John Cotton, First Church, Boston, Nov. 23, 1639, to May 22, 1642 . . . By Robert Keayne," MHS). James F. Cooper, Jr., comments on this entry in *Tenacious of Their Liberties: The Congregationalists in Colonial Massachusetts* (New York, 1999), 29-30.

4. On Chauncy, see Mather, *Magnalia,* I, 418–430; Brook, *Lives of the Puritans,* III, 451–455; *DNB; DAB;* John Edwin Cussans, *History of Hertfordshire* . . . (London, 1870–1881), I, 152–153; William Urwick, *Nonconformity in Herts.* . . . (London, 1884), 713–715; Samuel Eliot Morison, *The Founding of Harvard College* (Cambridge, Mass., 1936), 37–40; Mark A. Peterson, "Charles Chauncy (1592–19 Feb. 1672)," *American National Biography.*

5. In his will he expressed penitence for his "so many sinful compliances with and conformity unto vile human inventions, and will-worship and hell-bred superstition" (Mather, *Magnalia,* I, 421). Laud's humiliation of Chauncy had even more serious repercussions, however, in that it was introduced at the archbishop's trial as evidence of his oppression of the clergy. William Prynne, *Canterburies Doome* (London, 1646), 93–96.

6. *Salutem in fonte salutis:* Greetings in the source of salvation. Chauncy probably intended a pun here on the two senses of *salus* (salutem and salutis); I owe thanks to George Goebel for this observation.

7. *aliqua gravamina conscientiæ:* some burdens of conscience.

8. Article 36 of the Thirty-nine Articles, "Of Consecration of Bishops and Ministers," said: "The Book of Consecration of Archbishops and Bishops, and ordering of Priests and Deacons, lately set forth in the time of Edward the Sixth, and confirmed at the same time by authority of Parliament, doth contain all things necessary to such Consecration and Ordering; neither hath it anything that of itself is superstitious or ungodly. And therefore whosoever are consecrated or ordered according to the Rites of that Book, since the second year of the aforenamed King Edward unto this time, or hereafter shall be consecrated or ordered according to the same Rites; we decree all such to be rightly, orderly, and lawfully consecrated and ordered."

9. *hæc sub sigillo:* these things under seal, that is, for your eyes only.

10. *in transitu:* in transit; en route. Ware is about twenty miles due north of London, directly on the route from Boston to London. It seems very likely that Cotton did indeed visit Chauncy at Ware, *"in transitu,"* on one or more of his periods of absence from Boston in the late 1620s and early 1630s.

11. Probably Isaac Johnson (d. 1630), a native of Rutland but resident in Boston, Lincolnshire, after his marriage to Lady Arbella Fynnes, daughter of the earl of Lincoln. He and Lady Arbella later accompanied Winthrop to Massachusetts, both dying there within four months of their arrival.

12. Richard Bellingham (1592–1672) was a lawyer who held the office of recorder of Boston from 1625 to 1633. He was elected a member of Parliament in 1628. In 1634 he followed Cotton to Massachusetts, where he held the offices of deputy governor in 1635, 1640, and 1655–1660, and governor in 1641, 1654, and 1665–1672. He had a major hand in writing the first body of civil laws in the Bay Colony.

 John Cotton to Arthur Hildersham

[Spring 1628?]

ALS. MS: BL Add. MS 4275, fols. 154–155

Published: MHS, *Procs.,* XLII (1909), 204

In L. Thompson, "Letters of John Cotton," 54–55

This is the only surviving complete letter from Cotton to the elderly battle-scarred and much-respected veteran of the Puritan movement, Arthur Hildersham (Hildersam) (1563–1631). He had begun preaching at Ashby-de-la-Zouch, Leicestershire, in 1588, where he ministered, with various enforced interruptions, for the remaining forty-three years of his life. He was silenced and exiled for his radical Puritanism on various occasions, during the reigns of both Elizabeth I and James I. According to Benjamin Brook, Hildersham occasionally preached at his friend Cotton's church in Boston.[1] In fact, the opening sentence, referring to the occasion on which the Cottons "last enjoyed" the Hildershams, implies such a visit had taken place at the Cottons' home in Boston.

The date of this letter is based on the enclosure, Cotton's introductory epistle "To the Godly Reader . . . ," which was published in Hildersham's *Lectures upon the Fourth of John* (London, 1629).[2] Hildersham dates his own "Dedicatory Epistle" from "Ashby Delazouch, June 1, 1628," and the work was entered in the Stationers' Register on June 11, 1628. Cotton's prefatory epistle was probably with the manuscript at that time. Since the title page bears the date 1629, the book appeared only after March 25, 1629, and it would have been possible for Cotton's epistle to be added up until shortly before publication. It seems more likely that it was sent to Hildersham in the preceding year and that he sent the work to London only after having Cotton's letter in hand.

The letter carries the broken impression in red wax of Cotton's circular signet with the image of a bird. This appears with Cotton's address block on a separate leaf in Cotton's hand:

To my Reverend &
deare freind M[r] Hildersam
Preacher of *th*e word
at Ashby, del*iver* these
w*i*th speede./

Reverend & Deare S*i*r

My wife & selfe com*m*end o*u*r hearty love to you, & to M[res] Hildersam, w*i*th thankes to you both, since wee last enioyed you. M[r] Winters[3] Iourney into yo*u*r parts, giveth me this Opportunity, to send by so safe & ready a Bearer, what you called me to write, by M[r] Sharpe,[4] an Ep*ist*le to *th*e Reader of yo*u*r Booke,[5] addressed to *th*e Presse. I have expressed therein my true thoughts, & what I desire might be of some vse to stirre vp yonge men like my selfe, to a more advised & fruitefull Reading of those labo*u*rs of yo*u*rs, w*hi*ch I doubt not will much increase *th*e fruite of yo*u*r Reckoning, when you are gathered to Rest.[6]

It is now late at night, & this Bearer departeth early in *th*e morning: Therefore let me in a word Intreate you, to goe on in com*m*unicating what other of yo*u*r labo*u*rs you may, to *th*e hands of all. Noe fishing, like to *tha*t in *th*e broade Sea.

W*i*thall, I pray you, helpe this Bearer in his suite to M[res] Martha Temple, so farre as you shall see Gods hand making way for him.[7] As his learning is beyond *th*e Ordinary measure of his time, & his Grace, more: so this argueth noe com*m*on mercy of God to Him, that his moderation & Industry in his Calling, hath generally found Approbation of all here (for ought I heare) even of those who are not wont to thinke well of every good man.

The Lord Jesus still establish yo*u*r Peace, & prosper all his worke in yo*u*r hand, till y*ou*r chaunge come. Helpe vs, I pray you, w*i*th yo*u*r faithfull Requests before *th*e Throne of Grace. / So I rest,

The vnworthyest of yo*u*r poore brethren,
John Cotton./

1. For biographical data on Hildersham, see Brook, *Lives of the Puritans,* II, 376–388; Stuart Barton Babbage, *Puritanism and Richard Bancroft* (London, 1962), 183–186. Stephen Foster ascribes the importance of Hildersham's career to the "middle period" of the Puritan movement, between Elizabethan Puritanism and the period of Archbishop Laud's ascendancy (*Long Argument,* 103–104).

2. Benjamin Brook incorrectly records the date of the first edition as 1628 and says Cotton's preface first appeared in the second edition (*Lives of the Puritans,* II, 382). The *Short-Title Catalogue* lists four editions, the first dated 1629, followed by a "Second Edition" in 1632.

3. Samuel Winter (1603–1666) had been admitted sizar at Emmanuel College in 1622/3 and later "placed himself under John Cotton" at Boston. He might at this time have been master of the Boston Grammar School (Venn, *Alumni Cantabrigienses,* IV, 440). From 1651 to 1660 he was provost of Trinity College, Dublin.

4. The specific identity of Mr. Sharpe is unknown, but Sharpe is one of thirteen surnames that Pishey Thompson said were "among the most common among parish officers" in Boston, Lincolnshire, between 1600 and 1650 (*History of Boston,* 571).

5. Arthur Hildersham, *Lectures upon the Fourth of John* (London, 1629). These were sermons preached at Ashby-de-la-Zouch between January 31, 1608/9, and November 12, 1611.

6. Cotton's epistle is full of praise for Hildersham's sermons, explaining how they are useful to ministers and "private Christians" alike, emphasizing his age and the benefits of his long

career to many, and expressing satisfaction that Hildersham "doth now at last adorne his hoarie head with this Crowne of glory, to bring forth his works to more publike light."

7. Cotton's efforts on Martha Temple's behalf apparently went for naught. Winter eventually married twice, first to Anne Beeston of Boston and later to Elizabeth Weaver. Samuel Clarke's early account of Winter says that "he left *Cambridg* and went to *Boston* in *Lincolnshire,* where he lived under the Ministry of Holy and Learned Mr. J*ohn Cotton,* out of whose Family (somtime after) he married a Wife, one Mr*s. Ann Beeston,* a Gentlewoman of a good Extraction, and one that had a considerable Portion, that Match being of Mr. *Cotton*'s contrivance." *The Lives of Sundry Eminent Persons in This Later Age* (London, 1683), 95.

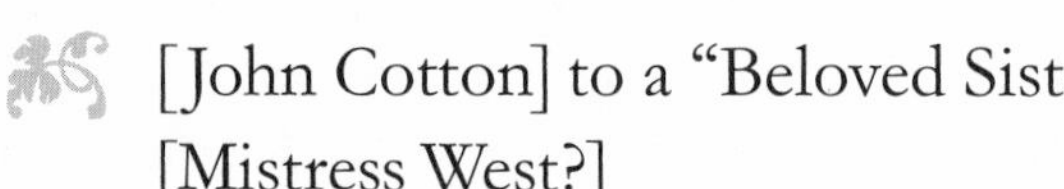

[John Cotton] to a "Beloved Sister" [Mistress West?]

November 12, 1628

Copy. MS: MSA, CCXL, Hutchinson Papers, I, fol. 7

Although this letter is unsigned and not in Cotton's hand, the handwriting is identifiable as that of one of the scribes who contributed to the manuscript of Cotton's book of sermons on 1 John that is now in the Bowdoin College Library. Knowing that Cotton employed his apprentices in just this way, we can assume that it is a copy made for Cotton's personal files by one of his seminarians. The addressee is not named, but the closing remarks, commending the love of Cotton and his wife to the addressee, with Mr. West and other friends, indicate that the correspondent may be the wife of Mr. West. She has not been identified.[1] I am grateful to Robert F. Scholz for calling this letter to my attention.

Beloved Sister in o*u*r blessed Savio*u*r,

The fact of *tha*t young Couple, w*hi*ch you mentioned to mee (concealing there names) hath beene a continual greife of hearte to mee, soe oft as I have thought of it ever since.

Many of Gods servants have heretofore conceived some hope of *th*e continuanc[e] of his patience & mercy towards those churches of England, because of *th*e growth of sundry young Christians in these dayes. But now when younge Christians defile themselves w*i*th *th*e lusts of youth, such as should have helped to stand in the gappe,[2] to holde off gods heavy Judgments, will by this meanes hasten to kindle his feirce displeasure, and plucke downe vpon vs his vengance w*i*th Cartropes of vanity. Besides it greiveth mee *th*e more for this younge Couple because this filthines was wrought by them vpon occasion of giving & asking spirituall Counsaille, w*hi*ch was to abase a gratious ordinance of god to wantonnesse. God will not hold such guiltlesse, as take

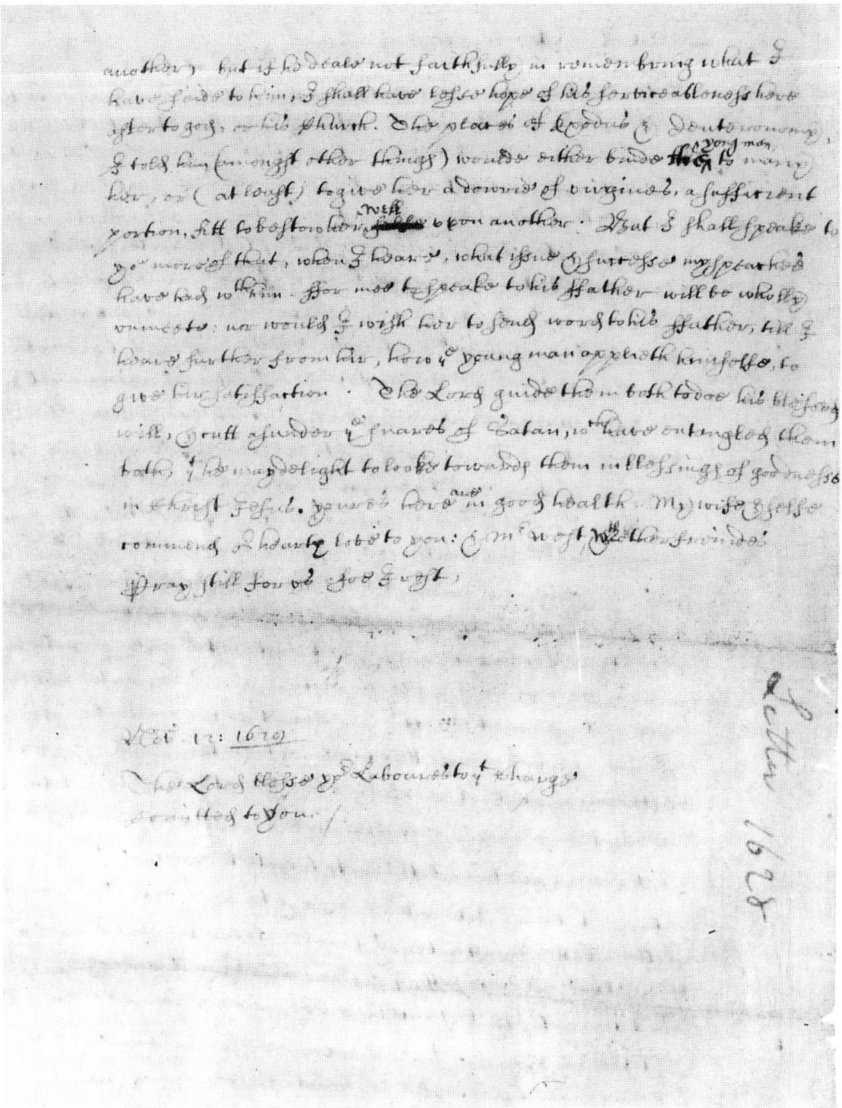

PLATE 3. Cotton to a "Beloved Sister," November 12, 1628, ending. Perhaps directed to one Mistress West, a Lincolnshire neighbor, the letter is unsigned because it is Cotton's letter book copy. The handwriting is that of one of Cotton's young ministerial scholars in his household seminary, though the corrections are Cotton's. The same hand reappears in the contemporary manuscript of Cotton's *Practical Commentary on the First Epistle Generall of John,* published posthumously, but recorded by many scribal hands in the late 1620s (Bowdoin College MS Collection). *Massachusetts State Archives, CCXL, Hutchinson Papers, I, fol. 7. Published courtesy of Massachusetts Archives*

such an holy name of his in vaine. I am afrayed *th*e maide is ^yet^ more solicitous to recover *th*e love of this lustfull youth & marriage w*i*th him, then to recover *th*e love of her first husband, *th*e Lord Jesus, in enioying of whom, it was better w*i*th her, then it is now. As therefore shee & *th*e younge man have sinfully ioyned & combined them selves togeather in vncleanesse soe it may be iust w*i*th god to seperate them now as farre asunder one from another, soe as hereafter never to enioy mutuall honest Affection, or Christian communion togeather. Simeon & levi because they combined togeather in sin & soe became bretheren in evill,[3] it pleased god therefore to punish them both, w*i*th dividing them asunder, & scattering them in Israell Gen*esis* 49. 5.6.7.[4] But *th*e Lord give them both, hearts to loath themselves, *tha*t hee may returne to them in loving kindnesse, & tender mercyes & dispose of them better for after tymes, then heretofore they have done of themselves. I much pitty *th*e maide whose body is wronged, & spirit corrupted by this vncleane Carrage of *th*e younge man.

But tell her, I feare, god will never give her any hope of enioying *th*e young man in mercy, till her hearte be soe weaned from him, *tha*t shee frely can resigne her selfe vnto gods good pleasure, to have him, or have him not. M^r^. Ja: Fi: came over to mee & acquainted mee w*i*th *th*e same case, to whom I spake my mind fully, more fully then I can now write, he spake to mee in the name of [IV] another, but if he deale not faithfully in remembring what I have saide to him, I shall have lesse hope of his serviceableness here after to god, or his Church. The places of Exodus & Deuteronomy,[5] I told him (amongst other things) woulde either binde the[6] ^yong man,^ to marry her, or (at least) to give her a dowrie of virgines, a sufficient portion, fitt to bestow her ^well^ ~~selfe~~ vpon another. But I shall speake to yow more of that, when I heare, what issue & successe my speaches have had w*i*th him. For mee to speake to his Father will be wholly vnmeete: nor would I wish her to send word to his Father, till I heare further from hir, how *th*e young man applieth himselfe, to give her satisfaction. The Lord guide them both to doe his blessed will, & cutt asunder *th*e snares of Satan, w*hi*ch have entangled them both, *tha*t he may delight to looke towards them in blessings of goodnesse in Christ Jesus. Youres here ^are^ in good health. My wife & selfe commend o*u*r hearty love to you: & Mr West, w*i*th[7] other freindes.

Pray still for vs. soe I rest

Nov. 12: 1628

The Lord blesse yo*u*r Laboures to *tha*t Charge
Committed to you./

1. West was a common name in Lincolnshire. Venn, *Alumni Cantabrigienses,* lists some four different Cambridge graduates named West who were ministers in Lincolnshire in 1628. It seems

unlikely that any of them is the Mr. West mentioned by Cotton, since he offers no suggestion that West is a clergyman.

2. The scribe here first wrote gape; Cotton then later added the second p in a darker ink.

3. Simeon and Levi, in avenging their sister Dinah's rape, deceived and murdered the men of Shechem, as described in Gen. 34, earning their father Jacob's chastisement.

4. Gen. 49:5–7: [Jacob speaks:] Simeon and Levi are brethren; instruments of cruelty are in their habitations. O my soul, come not thou into their secret; unto their assembly, mine honour, be not thou united: for in their anger they slew a man, and in their selfwill they digged down a wall. Cursed be their anger, for it was fierce; and their wrath, for it was cruel: I will divide them in Jacob, and scatter them in Israel.

5. See Exod. 22:16–17 and Deut. 22:28–29.

6. Here the is written over the word him.

7. Here w*i*th is written over &.

John Nicolaus Rulice to John Cotton

November 29, 1628

ALS. MS: MSA, CCXL, Hutchinson Papers, I, fols. 5, 5a, 6a

John Nicolaus Rulice was a German-born divine from Heidelberg who had fled the war-torn Palatinate in the early 1620s, one of "a band of young Germans who," in Larzer Ziff's words, "as Protestant fortunes waned in their homeland, found it necessary to come to England for their training."[1] According to Keith L. Sprunger, he "spoke English though not well enough to preach in it at first."[2] Recommended by the (deposed) king of Bohemia, he apparently went first to Cambridge, where he studied with John Preston, master of Emmanuel College. Subsequently, he was one of the scholars sent by Preston to stay with Cotton after leaving Cambridge.[3] At the time of this letter he appears to have been between that period in Boston and a soon-to-begin residence with John White in Dorchester, Dorset, though some accounts place him in Dorchester from as early as 1627.[4] Rulice's comments in this letter about his recent sojourn in Kent and his imminent trip to Holland suggest that he had not yet begun his Dorchester period. Later, from June 1634 until late 1635, he was in England as the representative of the refugees from the Palatinate, promoting the third and last royal collection for that cause. In the course of that work he ran afoul of Archbishop Laud, as his friend Samuel Hartlib would testify in witnessing against Laud at his trial.[5] He served the English Reformed Church at Amsterdam from 1635 to 1639, then moved to the German Reformed Church in the same city. According to Hartlib, Rulice became "a perfect Englishman, and hath preached in English for many years both in England and at Amsterdam."[6]

The manuscript is slightly water-damaged, written on both sides of a single folio sheet. The breaks in the text are from loss of paper along the bottom half of the right margin of the recto and a small hole affecting two lines on the verso. Text enclosed in braces has been supplied from the nineteenth-century transcription in the Massachusetts Historical Society.

Address block written on a separate sheet, used as envelope:

> To the Reverend & my much
> respected friend Mr Cotton
> minister of the word of God at
> Boston these w*i*th speed.

Reverend Sir,

I had a great desire to see you, before I departed out of the country: but Gods prouidence will not permitt it; in giving me now a faire opportunity (:there being some i3 Hollandish ships ready to goe over, onely staying for a convoy:) w*hi*ch If I should lett slip, may be could not be had againe a good while, specially this winter season. I have beene in Kent at Maidestone, & came but hether two dayes agoe. I have cause to blesse God for the continued wisedome & mercy of his prouidence about me.

If I should ˆstayˆ in England, I thincke Kent were the place, God calleth me to: The people being very earnest, their necessity great, & my heart not (as it was) ag*ains*t, but if God should make way, for it. They were unwilling to lett me ~~to~~ goe; but that they hope, my goeinge over may be a meanes of settling me amongst them. Two of their Knights, Maideston Burgesses, dwelling in the towne, great w*i*th the Arch Bishop have their sonnes in our Kings court at the Hage; & by their & Mr Wings (Cha{playne} to the queene of Bohemiah;[7] ˆ&ˆ well Knowne to some of Maidestone) meanes, w*i*th a letter from an Ambassadour now in the Hage (; to whom I was ~~first~~ commended at my first comming over, who is very great w*i*th the Archbishop:)[8] to the Arch Bishop; & specially Gods blessing they hope it may easily be brought about, that I be settled amongst them as a lecturer; without subscription.[9] And truly it is as fayre as may be, in my apprehension; onely I doubt much, whether The Arch Bishop would be willing notw*i*thstanding all these to conn[iv]e to my not conformity: ˆas conceyuing it might be a gate to lett in by little & little our Church discipline;ˆ[10] they answered againe, that he had done as much for Mr Throgmorton[11] now dead, who had 5 yeares a lectureship in those places.

I desire to take notice of all the prouidences of God; & to follow him in the use [of] lawfull meanes to my uttmost. I would entreate you to send me your Ju[dgment] about this buisinesse, what you conceyve of the probalitie[12] of it; & whether it wou[ld do?] for me to desire the Ambassadour to intreate the Arch Bishop to connive me {in} || [not] conforming; or onely to putt him in mind of his former favour to me, & {to crave} || same, for giving ~~me a~~ licence ^to me^ to accept of a lecturship in his Dio{cese} || Gentlewoman in London (For she should have the name, though she doe bu|| least it seeme a plot of those of Maidestone:) is willing to bestow upon {me} || subscription then might be bought out? & further, I pray, Sir, add || to this quæstion, often comming in my mind; whether it were lawfull ~~to~~ ^upon^ || w*i*th the Church government to accept a license without subscript|| seeing I can not enioy your præsence, I entreate you to adde som|| w*hi*ch may be usefull to me beyond the sea, how I should carry my|| walking, & specially if God should call me sometimes in publique; || [fol. 5v] others in their courses by my familiarity; & yet not discourage them from comming on to the wayes of God by my solitarinesse? but doe them most good, glorify most God, & comfort most my owne soule? I dare adde noe more; I made to bold already:

I pray, Sir, remember my seruice to Mr Maior & his wife, Mr Tilson, Mr Askom (from whom I would willingly carry a letter to Mr Dinely:) Mr Whiting, Mr Browne Mr Leverit, Mr & Mris Wacot[13] & the rest; & thus w*i*th my hearty respect & seruice to your selfe & Mris Cotton, & ^great^ thanckes for those manifold favour[s] || from you; I take my leave, beseeching you not to forgett me in your pray[ers] || to send them w*i*th a blessing after me, & to remember me allwayes in your dayes of humiliation; expecting w*i*th the next opportunity an answer; & remaine

London 29. Nov.
1628.

Yours in the lord to be commanded
John Nicolaus
Rulice.

1. Ziff, *Career of John Cotton,* 44.

2. Sprunger, *Dutch Puritanism,* 120.

3. Samuel Hartlib to John Worthington, October 1661, in James Crossley, ed., *The Diary and Correspondence of Dr. John Worthington,* Chetham Society, *Publications* (Manchester, 1855), II, 58–61.

4. Rose-Troupe, *John White,* 44; David Underdown, *Fire from Heaven: Life in an English Town in the Seventeenth Century* (New Haven, Conn., 1992), 94.

5. Ole Peter Grell, *Dutch Calvinists in Early Stuart London: The Dutch Church in Austin Friars, 1603–1642* (Leiden, 1989), 206–208, 246.

6. Hartlib to Worthington, October 1661, in Crossley, ed., *Correspondence of Worthington,* II, 58–61. In addition to sources already mentioned, brief comments on Rulice's career appear in G. H. Turnbull, *Hartlib, Dury, and Comenius: Gleanings from Hartlib's Papers* (Liverpool, 1947), 93, 97, 120; Alice Clare Carter, *The English Reformed Church in Amsterdam in the Seventeenth Century* (Amsterdam, 1964), 84, 94–95, 99, 167; Harold Jantz, "The German-American Tricentennial: A Closer Look," *Yearbook of German-American Studies,* XVIII (1983), 15.

7. The queen of Bohemia was Elizabeth, daughter of England's James I, who had married Frederick, elector of the Rhine Palatine in 1613. They were crowned king and queen in 1619 but were deposed and exiled the next year, taking up residence in Holland.

8. The archbishop of Canterbury, George Abbot (1562–1633).

9. Lectureships were not funded by the church and thus enjoyed an independence from hierarchical administration. They were supported either by contributions from local laity, by bequests, or by a combination of the two. Since the passing of the Constitutions and Canons of 1604 under James's authority, all ministers had been required to subscribe to three articles before admission to any church position. The second of these included the statement that "the Booke of Common prayer, and of ordering of Bishops, Priestes and Deacons, containeth in it nothing contrary to the word of God, and that it may lawfully so be vsed, and that he himselfe will vse the forme in the saide Booke prescribed in publike prayer, and administration of the Sacraments, and none other" (*Constitutions and Canons Ecclesiasticall . . . Agreed upon with the Kings Maiesties License in Their Synode Begun at London Anno Dom. 1603* [London, 1604], no. 36). Subscription to such a statement was anathema to Puritans, though many, including Cotton, did submit, however halfheartedly. A lectureship "without subscription" relieved a Puritan preacher of the need to compromise his conscience by ingenuously subscribing.

In the 1620s the lectureships offered Puritan preachers a refuge from the increasing pressures felt by incumbents in church positions to conform to prescribed forms of worship. In 1628, when this letter was written, there were 121 lectureships in London alone, about half of them held by Puritans. See Paul S. Seaver, *The Puritan Lectureships: The Politics of Religious Dissent, 1560–1662* (Stanford, Calif., 1970), esp. 214–215, 220–221, 238; Nicholas Hoppin, "The Rev. John Cotton, A.M., Vicar of Old Boston," *Church Monthly,* IV (1862), 164.

10. The inserted clause here is added in four short lines in the left margin, keyed to the place in the main text by a raised letter F.

11. Job Throgmorton (also Throckmorton and Throkmorton), who had died earlier in 1628. See the biographical sketch in Brook, *Lives of the Puritans,* II, 361–362.

12. The b in this word is written over a p.

13. This list of names includes people of prominence in Boston, most of them identifiably Puritan in their ecclesiastical or political leanings. Mr. Maior may be the "Mr Mayor" of Boston who in 1631 paid the funeral expenses of Cotton's wife, Elizabeth, as indicated in the Boston Corporate Records (P. Thompson, *History of Boston,* 415, 416). Mr. Tilson: Edward Tilson was mayor of Boston in 1625 and again in 1642; he was a linendraper who in the Civil War became a strong Parliamentarian. Mr. Askom: Thomas Askham was mayor of Boston in 1627. Mr. Dinley: John Dinley (Christ's College, Cambridge, bachelor of arts, 1610/1; master's, 1613) was a member of a Boston family who was apparently employed by the queen of Bohemia in Holland at this time, possibly as her secretary, and was also a Cotton correspondent (see Dinley to Cotton, January 1630/1; John Peile, *Biographical Register of Christ's College, 1505–1905 . . .* [Cambridge, 1910], I, 258). Mr. Whiting: Samuel Whiting, a cousin of Cotton's by marriage, minister at nearby Skirbeck, was a close sympathizer with Cotton and later a correspondent (see Whiting to Cotton, [Late January–Early February 1649/50], and [1637?–1652]); Rulice, however, may be referring to Samuel's brother, John, who was mayor of Boston in 1626 and again in 1633, 1644, and 1645. Another brother, James, is also possible (mayor in 1640), and Robert Whiting was a lesser officeholder in the town in the early 1630s. Mr. Browne: possibly John Browne, who had witnessed the will of William Pury at Boston on September 24, 1624 (Lady Elizabeth C. Cust, *Records of the Cust Family of Pinchbeck, Stamford, and Belton in Lincolnshire, 1479–1700* [London, 1898], 315). Mr. Leverit: Thomas Leverett held several civil posts in Boston, though he resigned his office as alderman on the same day Cotton resigned as vicar of St. Botolph's Church, to sail with him to New England, where he became the ruling elder of the first church in Boston,

Massachusetts. He is credited with shielding Cotton from harassment for nonconformity in old Boston. Mr. and Mistress Wacot: probably Humphrey Walcott, Esq., and his wife, of Walcot, Lincolnshire, about ten miles northwest of Boston. Walcott is described by Venn as "a staunch Parliamentarian" (*Alumni Cantabrigienses,* IV, 313).

Timothy Van Vleteren to John Cotton

October 26, 1629

ALS. MS: MSA, CCXL, Hutchinson Papers, I, fol. 16

In L. Thompson, "Letters of John Cotton," 56–57

Timothy Van Vleteren was born in Sandwich, Kent, but was of Dutch upbringing and identity. He had matriculated at the University of Leiden in 1622. He became the minister at Souteland in 1624 and remained there until early 1628, when he took up the position as minister to the Dutch congregation in London at Austin Friars. He held that position until his death in London on July 23, 1641. While at Austin Friars, Van Vleteren became an important contact for exiles from the war in the Palatinate.[1]

His Dutch background is evident in his orthography, where he writes the letter y in the Dutch equivalent, ij, and he often puts a diacritical mark over the letter U: ú. Despite its peculiar appearance to English speakers, Van Vleteren's spelling is retained to demonstrate his decided "accent."

The letter is written on a single side of the sheet. Cotton's draft reply is on the verso (Cotton to Van Vleteren, Dec. 16, 1629). The page is intact except for a small section on the left margin, causing some loss in three lines of Van Vleteren's letter (more in Cotton's), and some fraying of the bottom edge of the sheet that removes part of the postscript. The address block is written on the verso:

> Too his reverend Learned
> frind Mr John Cotton
> faitfull mynister of
> Christ at
> Boston
> with a letter.

Reverende frind, these papers I have received from Max*imilian* Teeling[2] to direct them vnto ijoú, who is mij very good frind not for his fathers sake onlij, bút for inward christian familiaritie betwixt vs both, having lived many dayes to gether in the schole, vnivirsitie, and not farre distant from places in our ministry in Zeeland, he at Flissinge, I at Soúteland. where Isaak Bishop is mij súccessor,[3] who hath vsed ijour table and rofe, both these frindes have often spok of their ædification conversing w*i*th ijour reverence, and communicated their writinges from yoú vnto me namely Catechisme, on the Canticles, of predestination,[4] sence witch time || desired to be acquainted with súch a servant of Christ || good in his ministrie, the more sence it hath pleased || to call me from thence to the Dutch chúrch at London where I have lived 2 Jeares, wherefore if ijoú have a sparing hoúre now and then, to intreat ijour reverence, use this time to propounde a divine (of no other matter is mij Calling) question, or ecclesi|| as I see how manij rubbes and doúbts I meet with in my high Calling, and having occasion to see your face at London shall be verij glad, or to doe anij kindnesse here for ijoú or ijoures. it hath troubled me much in the matter of an oath, meditating on the 3 command*ment*[5] whet^e^r a subiect is bound in Consience ~~to~~ [deleted word], when higher powers can affirme nothing against him, but súrmise or suspect of his faitfulness to sweare vpon interrgatories, or propositiones of their one framing against him. I pray let me heare of yoú and of the receiving of the papers. thús commende your reverence to the word and grace of god in London 26 octo 1629.

Timotheús van Vlet[ere]n
your frind and servant in ||

I dwel at mij fathers hoúse in S'Magnes parish
neare London bridge a house or twoo in tems streth[6]
his name is || {Herrelly}[7] ||útch mar||ant

1. On Van Vleteren, see Ole Peter Grell, *Dutch Calvinists in Early Stuart London: The Dutch Church in Austin Friars, 1603–1642* (Leiden, 1989), 59–60, 189, 199–201; on his death, see William John Charles Moens, ed., *The Marriage, Baptismal, and Burial Registers, 1571 to 1874 . . . of the Dutch Reformed Church, Austin Friars, London . . .* (Lymington, 1884), 208.

2. Maximilian Teeling (or Teelincks) (1602–1653) was the oldest son of Willem Teeling, who was well known to English Puritans and is considered the father of Dutch Pietism. Maximilian studied at the University of Leiden before becoming the minister at the English church at Vlissingen (Fleissing; sometimes Flushing), where he served from 1627 to 1628. He later served as minister of the Dutch churches at Zieriksee (1628–1640) and Middelburg (1640–1653). Irvonwy Morgan, *Puritan Spirituality, Illustrated from the Life and Times of the Rev. John Preston . . .* (London, 1973), 50; Pieter Jacobus Meertens, *Letterkundig Leven in Zeeland in de Zeistiende en de eerste Helft der zeventiende Eeuw . . .* (Amsterdam, 1943), 182–184; F. Nagtglas, *Levensberichten van Zeeuwen . . .* (Middelburg, 1893), 747–749.

3. Isaac Bishop was minister at Souteland from 1627 to 1638, when he left for Vlissingen. These details appear in a handwritten volume at Middelburg's Gemeente Archief: W. M. C. Regt, "Naam lijsten der predikanten van Zeeland, c. 1572–c. 1938." Bishop (also Biskop and Biscop) served at Vlissingen until his death in 1661. On Bishop, see "Isaak Biscop," in Godewardus Vrolikhert, *Vlissingsche Kerkhemel . . .* (Vlissingen, 1758), 112–117. Thanks are due to A. Meerman, Vlissingen's Municipal Archivist, for the latter reference and for the information that Bishop himself usually signed his name Biscop.

4. These writings of Cotton were all still in manuscript at this time.

5. The third commandment: "Thou shalt not take the name of the Lord thy God in vain; for the Lord will not hold him guiltless that taketh his name in vain." Exod. 20:7, Deut. 5:11.

6. St. Magnes Church still stands at the north end of London Bridge; Thames ("tems") Street, which is now Lower Thames Street, runs parallel to the river one block to the north. See G. E. Mitton, ed., *Maps of Old London* (London, 1908), which contains "The Panorama of 'London, Westminster, and Southwark, in 1543' by Anthony Van den Wyngaerde" and "A Large and Accurate Map of the City of London" at the time of the Stuarts.

7. This name is visible (but not fully legible) in an old negative photostat of the manuscript at the Massachusetts Historical Society.

John Cotton to Timothy Van Vleteren

December 16, 1629

Copy. MS: MSA, CCXL, Hutchinson Papers, I, fol. 16a

In L. Thompson, "Letters of John Cotton," 58–60

Although no other letters in Cotton's correspondence with Van Vleteren have survived, we know that Van Vleteren answered this letter. Samuel Clarke, in introducing his excerpt of a Cotton letter to Arthur Hildersham, states that in the letter Cotton referred to Van Vleteren's reply (see headnote to Cotton to Hildersham, Feb. 3, 1629/30).

This is written on the upper half of the verso of Van Vleteren to Cotton, October 26, 1629; neither the letter nor the signature is in Cotton's hand. It was probably copied from Cotton's manuscript for his files by one of the ministers-in-training in Cotton's household. There is loss of text in the first line from fraying at the top edge of the sheet and just before and into the signature block, where paper is lost at the end of a fold.

Reverend S*i*r. I thanke you of yo*u*r || [three illegible words] you doe soe kindly salute. I receiued fro*m* Mr Teelincks l*ette*re and therewith an Epicedium vpo*n* his fathers death.[1] I was also glad to heare ~~of~~ ˆbyˆ you, both of him and Mr Isaack Biscop. I waite for an opportunity to write vnto *the*m both, as me*n* whom I much esteeme and affect, me[an]while[2] let me intreate you w*hen* you write into those p*ar*ts Commend my deare affectio*n* to *the*m and tell *the*m *the*y are both written in my heart though I can seldo*m*e get liberty to write to *the*m, and many other good friends as I gladly would. Let me also desire you to enquire of Mr Teelinck whether his father receiued a little discourse fro*m* me (shewing how farre *th*e strongest endeauours of me*n*, and Commo*n* Graces fall short of Conuersio*n*) w*hi*ch his father desired me to write to him:

w*hi*ch also I sent him but neuer heard of the receipt. His losse haue I much lamented though I neuer saw his face: and *th*e lord double his spirit vpo*n* his so*m*ne and vpon many more such to make vp the breach w*i*th yo*u*rs*elf* (Louing S*ir*) I shall be ready (as god shall give leaue) to Communicate w*i*th you in w*ha*t Conferences you shall require rather to helpe mys*elf tha*n you. In *thi*s yo*u*r quæstio*n* of an oath I am rather a Learner *tha*n a teacher as being yet vnacquainted w*i*th the oath. onley these two *thi*ngs can I say about it. i. That w*hen* god Commandeth vs to sweare (Jer.4.2.)[3] in truth (w*i*thout falshood) In iudgm*ent* (w*i*thout rashnes) in righteousnesse (w*i*thout iniury to o*u*rs*elf* or others[)], this last conditio*n* seemeth to me ˆplainelyˆ to forbid vs to accuse ether o*u*rs*elf* or others (vnlesse in case it may be done w*i*thout danger of Iniury to o*u*rs*elf* or our brethre*n*[)]. 2 otherwise, where the former Conditio*n*s of an oath may be obserued I thinke I may not onely lawfully take an oath put vpo*n* me by *th*e Magistrate, but also vpo*n* mine oath confesse some such *thi*ngs as otherwise I would choose to conceale. w*hen* the High-preist put many Interrogatories to o*u*r sauio*u*r touching his disciples and his doctrine he answered nothing. But w*hen* he aduised him by *th*e liuing god, to tell him whether he were the sonne of god, ˆheˆ *the*n answered plainly and freely as conceiuing hims*elf* sent into the world to beare witnesse to the truth (though vpo*n* his Confessio*n* sentence was forthw*i*th giuen ag*ains*t him)[4] the truth being such the confessio*n* whereof would more aduan~~tage~~ˆceˆ *th*e Glory of god and *th*e churches good *tha*n *th*e danger of open confessio*n* could endammage him. Michaiah was at first loath to answer to Ahabs demaund (i kings 22. 15.[)][5] || he s[p]eakes f*u*lly though it cost him impriso*n*m*en*t. To draw consectaried[6] fro*m* these two || still in my exp*er*ience or p*r*esent leisure will reach. The lord teach vs euer || his ?p*ar*take with in *Chris*t Jesus [illegible word] whose guidance and gracious blessing I ||

Desirous of yo*u*r p||
*Christ*ian loue
John. Cotto*n*.

Bosto*n* Decemb. i6. i629.
I was a month in a late londo*n* jorney w*hi*ch kept me so long fro*m* hearing or answering of yo*u*r l*ette*re I being on my way before yo*u*r l*ette*re came to me, else I should (god willing) haue answered sooner.

1. Epicedium: a funeral song. Willem Teeling had died earlier in 1629; on his career, see F. Ernest Stoeffler, *The Rise of Evangelical Pietism* (Leiden, 1965), 127–133.

2. End-line hyphenation: mean-while, but frayed paper on the right margin interrupts the word.

3. Jer. 4:2: And thou shalt swear, the Lord liveth, in truth, in judgment, and in righteousness; and the nations shall bless themselves in him, and in him shall they glory.

4. See Matt. 26:62–66.

5. 1 Kings 22:14–15: And Micaiah said, As the Lord liveth, what the Lord saith unto me, that will I speak. So he came to the king. And the king said unto him, Micaiah, shall we go against Ramoth-gilead to battle, or shall we forbear? And he answered him, Go, and prosper: for the Lord shall deliver it into the hand of the King.

The Geneva Bible's marginal gloss suggests that Micaiah was mockingly quoting Ahab's false prophets to Ahab, who consequently imprisoned Micaiah.

6. The scribe probably meant to write consectaries.

John Cotton to Arthur Hildersham

February 3, 1629/30

Published: Samuel Clarke, *A Generall Martyrologie, Containing A Collection of All the Greatest Persecutions Which Have Befallen the Church of Christ from the Creation to Our Present Times, Whereuto Are Added, The Lives of Sundry Modern Divines* . . . (London, 1651), 382

Samuel Clarke's account of Hildersham's life makes use of various items from Hildersham's correspondence, including the following fragment, which is not otherwise preserved. Clarke introduces the excerpt with these remarks: "In a private Letter of his from *Boston* February 3. 1629. he [Cotton] mentioneth a Letter he received from a *Dutch* Minister in *London,* (one *Timotheus Van Vleren*) who telleth him, he had sent sundry of the books on *John* 4.[1] to Ministers beyond the Seas, who do read them with such great satisfaction, that the said *Dutch* Minister did in the name of many others intreat Master *Cotton* to beseech Master *Hildersam* to put forth his Sermons of *Psal.* 51. and other his lucubrations. And accordingly Master *Cotton* in that Letter writeth thus." Clarke then quotes the following excerpt from Cotton's letter to Hildersham, adding the remark, "This his request he renewed in another Letter of *July* 23. 1629."

Since Van Vleteren's letter to Cotton of October 26, 1629, seems to be the first in their correspondence, the letter of February 3 must be dated in the Old Style. According to our calendar, therefore, the year is 1630, by which time the Van Vleteren correspondence had begun. The passage referring to Van Vleteren's testimonials about the value of Hildersham's book of sermons on John 4 is not preserved. What little we do have from the letter is in the same spirit as Cotton's 1628 letter to Hildersham, urging him in his old age to make his sermons available through publication.

The unpreserved letter from Cotton to Hildersham, dated July 23, 1629, in which Clarke says Cotton "renewed" his request that Hildersham publish his sermons on Psalm 51, was thus presumably written *before* the present letter.

PLATE 4. Portrait 2. Arthur Hildersham. Oil painting by an unknown artist, 1619.
By courtesy of the National Portrait Gallery, London

Since the Sermons already on part of the Psalme, do arise to a just and full volume, be entreated to hearken to the desires of so many at home and abroad, and give them leave to be doing good, whilst the rest are preparing. You have cause to love the Lord your God with all your might; and therefore since those Sermons might be shewing your love to God in working his work, before their fellowes, do not hold back any part of their service to the Church, for the present time:[2]

1. Arthur Hildersham's *Lectures upon the Fourth of John* (London, 1629), to which Cotton had contributed an "Epistle to the Reader."

2. This advice, that Hildersham's very long series of sermons on Psalm 51 be published in two installments in order to get some of them before readers immediately, was ignored. Hildersham died on March 4, 1632, with the sermons still unpublished. His *CLII Lectures upon Psalme LI* was entered in the Stationers' Register August 26, 1633, but not published until 1635, edited by his son, Samuel Hildersham.

John Cotton to Hugh Goodyear

April 12, 1630

MS. LGA: Weskamer 1355, gg

Published: D. Plooij, *The Pilgrim Fathers from a Dutch Point of View* (New York, 1932), 86–87 (this printing includes both a facsimile of the manuscript and a transcription)

Hugh Goodyear (c. 1590–1661), born in Lancaster, was a graduate of Emmanuel College (bachelor of arts, 1612/3; master's, 1616), which is where he came to know Cotton, who stayed there until 1612. Goodyear became the minister of the English church at Leiden in 1616, where he remained until his death forty-five years later. He was an important link between English and Dutch Puritanism for that entire period. Among the papers in the archives of the English church at Leiden's Gemeente Archief is an inventory of Goodyear's sizable library at the time of his death.[1] His Calvinist Puritan sympathies are evident in the volumes by not only Cotton (*The Bloudy Tenent, Washed* [1647] and *A Practical Commentary upon the First Epistle Generall of John* [1658]) but also numerous contemporary Puritans such as Thomas Hooker, Richard Mather, Thomas Shepard, Richard Sibbes, John Preston, John Rogers, John Dod, John Paget, Jeremiah Burroughes, Thomas Goodwin, and many others, including Calvin and Baynes. As Cotton indicates, this was his first letter to Goodyear; it is not known whether the correspondence between them continued. It is worth noting that Goodyear was apparently one of the sources of young ministerial scholars from the Continent who went to live and study with Cotton in Boston. Just as one left Cotton's seminary, bearing this letter, another arrived, recommended by Goodyear (Venn, *Alumni Cantabrigienses,* II, 240; Sprunger, *Dutch Puritanism,* 125–128).

To my Reverend and very loving freind
Mr. Goodyeare Minister of *th*e Word at Leyden[2]
Reverend,

& beloved in o*u*r blessed Savio*u*r, I was sory *tha*t in my first l*ette*re to you, I should be thus cast vpon straites of time, *tha*t I could noe way expresse my selfe to you. But I had rather onely salute you, then send away this good yong man empty by you, Petrus Griebius,[3] a German, who lived sometime here with vs, & whom God hath now gratiously fitted for publique service in his Church. The yong man, whom you recom*m*end hither, is receyved to Table in my house, & (for want of roome ˆw*i*th meˆ) to lodging, in a neere neighbo*u*rs./ I wonder not at *th*e Arminian Tumults;[4] A spirit vnquiet in it selfe, will not easily suffer others to Rest. What Rest (thinke you) can such Doctrines yeild to vnstable soules, w*hi*ch bottome *th*e foundation of their Peace vpon *th*e Constancy of their owne wills, w*hi*ch are so free to mutability?/ What deteyneth *th*e Separatist from ioyning w*i*th you, I desire to know at your leasure.[5] Vnfeigned fellowship w*i*th Christ would easily admitt, yea gladly seeke fellowship w*i*th his members, *tha*t walke before him in *th*e simplicity & purity of his Ordinaunces.

My wife & selfe com*m*end o*u*r hearty love to you, & yo*u*rs: & so desiring a part in yo*u*r holy prayers, I rest

Yo*u*rs ever in *th*e Lord Jesus,
John Cotton./

Boston. Apr*il*
12. 1630./

The holograph version of this letter has been lost since at least 1982, according to the staff at Leiden's Gemeente Archief, so has not been seen for this edition.

1. See the facsimile edition, *The Auction Catalogue of the Library of Hugh Goodyear* (Utrecht, 1985), with an introduction by J. D. Bangs.

2. These two lines do not appear on the photographic copy of the manuscript printed in Plooij, but they are printed before the transcription of the letter. They are doubtless transcribed from either a separate envelope sheet or, more likely, the verso of the letter, where they served as the instructions to the messenger who carried the letter, Peter Gribius.

3. Peter Gribius was trained by Cotton at Boston after studying under William Ames at Franeker. He refused the earl of Oxford's orders to use the prayer book and Anglican ceremonies in 1630–1631 when serving as chaplain at the English garrison at Bois-le-Duc in the Netherlands, after which he became the pastor at Oost-Duiveland (1633–1642), Middelburg (1642–1652), and finally the German church in Amsterdam. In 1645 he translated the Dutch liturgy into English. B. Glasius, *Biographisch Woordenboek van Nederlansche Godgeleerden* (Te'sHer-

togenbosch, 1851–1856) I, 561–562; Raymond Phineas Stearns, *Congregationalism in the Dutch Netherlands: The Rise and Fall of the English Congregational Classis, 1621–1635,* Studies in Church History, IV (Chicago, 1940), 13, 50, 86, 87, 139; Sprunger, *Dutch Puritanism,* 188, 193, 278, 283, 322; Sprunger, *William Ames,* 224, 237.

4. Jacobus Arminius (1560–1609) had been on the faculty of the University of Leiden for the last six years of his life, and his doctrines, anathema to the more strictly Calvinist Puritans, continued to inspire partisan supporters.

5. The Separatist church in Leiden was the remnant of the church from which the Plymouth colonists had departed some ten years earlier. Though dwindling in numbers, they clung to their differences from Goodyear's non-Separatist congregation in Leiden. See Sprunger, *Dutch Puritanism,* 139.

John Cotton to Samuel Skelton

October 2, 1630

Copy. MS: AAS, copy by Richard Mather dated June 13, 1631, Mather Family Papers. PH, another copy, with annotations by Richard Bernard

Published: Thaddeus Mason Harris, *Memorials of the First Church in Dorchester, from Its Settlement in New England, to the End of the Second Century* (Boston, 1830), 53–57; David D. Hall, "John Cotton's Letter to Samuel Skelton," *WMQ,* 3d Ser., XXII (1965), 478–485

In L. Thompson, "Letters of John Cotton," 61–69

Cotton's letter to the pastor of the newly formed church at Salem quickly became a well-known statement on the issues of Separatism, congregational autonomy, administration of the sacraments, and the very nature of a church. The fact that it is preserved today in a manuscript copy transcribed by Richard Mather some eight months after it was written indicates that copies were made and circulated in England before Cotton's emigration. Six years later, when preaching in Salem, he acknowledged his awareness that copies had also been circulated in New England ("seeing my letter, as I understand, is in many of your hands . . .").[1]

The letter's interest to a broader audience than the addressee, both then and subsequently, was owing to its treatment of issues that remained central to the colonists' concerns about their desire to purify church practice and membership in the larger Church of England. The ministers who remained in England tended to see the practice of New England churches as too exclusive, thus casting aspersions on the quality and even legitimacy of conforming churches in England. In 1630, while still in Lincolnshire, though already thinking about the possibility of his own emigration, Cotton took this stance, sharply criticizing the practice of the Salem church for seeming to follow the Separatist lead of the Plymouth church. He later revised this opinion, minimizing Plymouth's influence on Massachusetts Bay churches, an important point in that the Massachusetts Bay clergy almost uniformly insisted that they were not Separatists, but remained firmly within the body of the English Church, while the Plymouth colonists, from the time of their Leiden establishment in 1608, had always been a Separatist church.[2]

After Cotton arrived in New England, his own views took a 180-degree turn, so that in 1636, when he went to Salem to preach, he opened his discourse with a "confession." He recalled that "at the first coming over of some of our honored magistrates," one of whom had had a child born on the ship bringing them over, they found that in Salem "they themselves could neither be admitted to the Lord's Table, nor their child to baptism." Cotton related how, "doubting of the lawfulness of that practice," he had written to Skelton, even in spite of the debilitating illness he was suffering at the time. Skelton had "sent me a large and loving answer," but, unfortunately, "through the extremity of sickness then upon me, I could not read it; and afterwards being shuffled among other papers, I could never find it to this very day: but what might have been for instruction to me from his letters, the Lord hath since shewed unto me by diligent search of the Scriptures."[3] Once in New England, he not only changed his mind about the practice of requiring a full confession of faith from each aspirant to membership, regardless of previous church affiliations, but he became a leading promoter of it. As Cotton's contemporary, William Hubbard, wrote, Skelton and his colleague, Francis Higginson, "walked something in an untrodden path" in the early years, but when Cotton and Hooker arrived in 1633, they "did clear up the order and method of church government, according as they apprehended was most consonant to the Word of God. And such was the authority they (especially Mr. Cotton) had in the hearts of the people, that whatever he delivered in the pulpit was soon put into an Order of Court, if of a civil, or set up as a practice in the church, if of an ecclesiastical concernment."[4] The letter to Skelton and Cotton's subsequent change of mind acquired enough notoriety, however, that as long as eighteen years later Cotton was still having to defend his altered opinion against English and Scottish critics of the New England Way.[5]

The following text transcribes Richard Mather's copy. The Richard Bernard transcription at Pilgrim Hall Museum, Plymouth, is less complete and differs in a myriad instances in spelling, punctuation, and capitalization while also omitting occasional words, one major clause, and the final sentence and signature and date blocks. When the letter was first published by Thaddeus Mason Harris, he reported that he used the Mather holograph copy, but then "collated it with an original in Mr. COTTON's own handwriting, in a small quarto volume of his *adversaria* in the possession of the Hon. JOHN DAVIS, of Boston" (*General History,* 53). The John Davis Papers are now owned by the Massachusetts Historical Society, but the "small quarto volume" that Harris had in hand was apparently the one now owned by the Pilgrim Society in Pilgrim Hall, Plymouth, Massachusetts, which does contain another copy of Cotton's letter to Skelton. It is in Bernard's hand, not Cotton's. Harris also modernizes the spelling, punctuation, and capitalization. David D. Hall's edition, on the other hand, offers an exact transcription, though it differs from the present edition in eliminating all indications of abbreviations, contractions, deletions, and interlinear insertions; modernizes the usage of the letters v and u (but not of ff for F); changes Mather's -cõn to -tion; eliminates the u in Cotton's chaunge, demaund, and covenaunt; separates into two words Cotton's compounds aseale, afew, welbeing, and avayne; and changes z to s in the word Baptize and its variants. Minor differences in spelling, capitalization, and punctuation between Hall's and the present edition are ignored, but occasional substantive differences are noted.

To m^{r} Sk: in N.E./
Beloved S*i*r

I am glad to heare of your health by others; though I do not heare *tha*t you haue written to any of yo*u*r frends in these parts by this last returne. I thank you for yo*u*r loving entertainm*en*t of mr Coddington & his wife (my loving & *Chris*tian neighbo*u*rs) into yo*u*r house.[6] onely as *th*e death of so many of *th*e former plantac*i*on hath bene grievous to mee, so hath it not a little troubled mee *tha*t you should deny *th*e Lords Supper to such godly & faithfull S*er*va*n*ts of *Chris*t as m^{r} Gou*er*no*u*r m^{r} Johnson, m^{r} Dudley,[7] m^{r} Codington; whereof *th*e 3 latter were well knowne vnto you to bee men of an vpright heart & vnblameable life; & *th*e first might haue bene evidenced vnto you to be no lesse by their approoved testimony. my griefe increased upo*n* mee when I heard you denyed Baptisme vnto m^{r} Codingtons child, & *tha*t upo*n* a reason worse then *th*e fact; because hee was no member of any p*ar*ticular reformed church, though of *th*e Catholike.[8] And *tha*t w*hi*ch added wonder to my griefe was *tha*t I heard you admitted one of m^{r} Lathrops congregac*i*on,[9] not onely to *th*e Lords Supper, but his child vnto Baptisme, upo*n* sight of his testimony fro*m* his church: whereas m^{r} Codington bringing *th*e same fro*m* *th*e chiefe of o*u*r congregac*i*on was not admitted.

A quartane ague (ten fits wherof I haue already borne) hath so weakened my body & p*ro*strated my Spirits, *tha*t I am not fitt to wryte my mynd of these things: yet *th*e vnfained loue I beare you, & *th*e desyre I haue *tha*t peace & truth may dwell amongst you, hath constrained mee to beare witnesse against this yo*u*r judgm*en*t & practise in a word or two.

Two things herein I conceiue to bee erroneous. First *tha*t you think *tha*t no man may be admitted to *th*e Sacrament, though a member of *th*e catholike church, vnlesse hee be also a member of so*m*e p*ar*ticular reformed church: 2ly *tha*t none of o*u*r congregac*i*ons in England are p*ar*ticular reformed churches, but mr Lathrops & such as his.

For *th*e first, we ^doe^ not find (neither is it credible) *tha*t *th*e Eunuch (Act. 8) was a member of any p*ar*ticular congregac*i*on, yet Philip baptized him. neither yet did hee baptize him into any p*ar*ticular congregac*i*on w*hi*ch hee should betake himselfe vnto after his Baptisme, his calling (it may bee) requiring his necessary absence in a forraine court. But you will say, hee made p*ro*fession of his faith before Baptisme v*ers* 37. neither do I deny *tha*t it is meete for parents (whether *the*y bee members of a p*ar*ticular church or no) to p*ro*fesse their covenaunt w*i*th god to *the*ms*elves* & their seed, whereof Baptisme is aseale, & you know all English congregac*i*ons require it. but this I deny *tha*t he made p*ro*fession to beco*m*e a member of Philips p*ar*ticular church: & besides such a p*ro*fession as hee made to Philip I dare say the S*er*va*n*ts of God who*m* you haue refused [1v] haue made as great, yea & larger to your selfe.

you will say (p*er*haps) such an example was extraordinary & not imitable: but say not so; for though his rapture was extraordinary, yet all *th*e Acts of the ap*ost*les & evang*eli*sts & brethren touching doctrine or sacram*en*ts or discipline are presidentiall[10] vnto all churches in all ages; & to *tha*t end was *tha*t booke written. w*hi*ch further to evidence in this point see Act. 10.47, 48.[11] what p*ar*ticular congregac*i*on was *th*e Centurion or his devout soulidiers or his frends of, when Peter baptised *the*m? it may bee you will say *the*y were proselytes to *th*e Jewish Synagogue, but I beleeue not, for then had *the*y bene circu*m*cised, & then *th*e *Chris*tian Jewes would not haue contended with Peter for eating with *the*m, Act. 11.3. where *th*e [12]church plainly calleth *them* vncircu*m*cised.[13] & yet when Peter saw *the*y had rec*eive*d *th*e holy gh*ost* hee openly pleadeth for *them* v*ers* 47. Can any man forbid water, why these should not be baptized *tha*t haue receiued *th*e holy gh*ost* as well as wee? And if no man can forbid ~~water~~ *the*m *th*e water of Baptisme, who then can forbid *them* *th*e Lords Supper? when men haue ~~forbidden~~ receiued Baptisme & *th*e holy gh*ost* & haue examined & judged *the*ms*elves* who can forbid *the*m to eate & drinke *th*e body & blood w*hi*ch is given for *them?* or who can forbid their children to be baptized?

Yo*u*r other errour requires a booke rather then a l*ett*er to answere it: you went hence of another judgm*en*t, & I am afraid yo*u*r chaunge hath sprung fro*m* new=Plim*m*outh=men, who*m* though I much esteeme as godly & loving *Chris*tians, yet their grounds w*hi*ch *the*y receiued for this tenent fro*m* mr Robinso*n,* do not satisfye mee; though *th*e man I rev*er*ence as godly & learned.[14] Cyprian[15] of old laboured vnder a like kynd of errour, yet held his integrity & zeale in *th*e maine. His grounds of dischardging all o*u*r congregac*i*ons are 3.[16]

First hee saieth, wee want *th*e matter of a visible church, w*hi*ch are Saints by calling. but I demaund where had hee or all *tha*t[17] deny *th*e right hand of fellowshipp to vs, their calling to be saints if not in o*u*r English congregac*i*ons? say not all *th*e godly here begotten are begotten of adultery; for god is not wont to blesse *th*e bedd of an adulteresse w*i*th greater increase then *th*e bed of *th*e married wiues. And if Paul justified his calling to *th*e ministery & Ap*ost*leshipp fro*m* *th*e successe of his labours in this kynd (as hee doth 1 Cor. 9.2. Gal. 2.7.)[18] why may not *th*e Saints of God justifye *th*e Congregac*i*ons in w*hi*ch *the*y are called & in w*hi*ch *the*y find *th*e power of gods grace in word & sacram*en*ts, to be *th*e churches of god by *th*e like gracious & ordinary p*re*sence of *Chris*t there? Say not (as hee doth) *tha*t Saints are gathered out of *th*e world; for though *tha*t bee true in *th*e first plantac*i*on of *th*e church, yet first *the*y *tha*t so gather *them* are *th*e ministers of *Chris*t; now if o*u*r congregac*i*ons bee no churches, then are wee *tha*t preach to *them* no ministers, & so no likely instrum*en*ts to bee blessed of god in such a worke. Againe, when men p*ro*fesse *the*ms*elves* to bee *th*e churches of god & are not, god is not wont to blesse *th*e labours of such preachers to such people; but will rather blesse *th*e labours of private *Christ*ians amongst a world of Pagans. What though many [2] scandalous gospellers bee tollerated amongst vs? *tha*t argueth *th*e neglect of discipline, not *th*e nullity of a church: Sardis had but afew names in her,[19] and *th*e churches of Corinth & Galatia had sundry scandalous p*er*sons both for life and doctrine, yet are still styled by *Chris*t & his ap*ost*les churches; yea & *Chris*t described as walking in *th*e midst of *the*m: as praised bee his name hee hath not w*i*thdrawen his pr*e*sence fro*m* vs; & where hee vouchsafeth his pr*e*sence, who are wee *tha*t wee should deny ours? are wee purer then hee?

His 2[d] ground is taken fro*m* o*u*r want of *th*e essentiall forme of a church, w*hi*ch (as hee conceiveth) is a right constituc*i*on by mutuall coven*an*t betweene pastour & people to yeeld p*ro*fessed subjecc*i*on to *th*e gospell of *Chris*t. whereto I answere *tha*t this explicite & solemne covenaunt is rather a solemne vow to bind *th*e members of *th*e church together in neerer fellowshipp w*i*th god & one another, then any such essentiall cause of *th*e church w*i*thout w*hi*ch it can not bee. and therefore wee read *tha*t in *th*e church of *th*e Israelites it was often renewed whereas their constituc*i*on was sett vp at first. twise was this coven*an*t renewed in Moses tyme, afterward in Asa's & Joash ˆhisˆ time, in Josiahs & Nehemiahs &c nor haue wee any menc*i*on of such a coven*an*t in *th*e new Testam*en*t in *th*e first constituc*i*on of any church, vnlesse very obscurely. for indeed *th*e n*at*ur*e* & definition of a church lyeth in this: It is a flocke ^(1)^ of saints (2) called by god into *th*e fellowship of *Chris*t (3) meeting together in one place (4) to call vpo*n* *th*e name of *th*e Lord (5) & to edify *th*ems*elves* in com*m*unicating spirituall gifts (6) & p*ar*taking in *th*e ordinances of *th*e Lord (7). (1) Act 20.28. (2) 1 Cor. 1.2. (3) 1 Cor. 1.9. (4) 1 Cor. 14.23. (5) 1 Cor. 1.2. ^1 Tim. 2.1.^ (6) 1 Cor. 14.12, 31. (7) 1 Cor. 14.26.[20] where these things are found there is nothing wanting to *th*e n*atu*re or essence[21] or constitu*ci*on of a church. Neu*er*thelesse, I easily graunt you such a covenaunt is very requisite for *th*e welbeing & continuance of a church. & therefore I answere secondly such a cove*na*nt is not so much wanting to our churches as you suppose: For, first it is not avayne thing, *tha*t *th*e whole state in Parliam*en*t in *th*e beginning of Q*ueen* Elizabeths raigne did renounce popery vnder a penalty to embrace *th*e gospell of *Chris*t. for such a thing was Asa his coven*ant*, even a law of *th*e chiefe members of *th*e state in *th*e name of *th*e rest (2 Chron. 15.12, 13)[22] & in this Act of Parliam*en*t all *th*e people of *th*e land are conceiued (as in all other lawes) to giue their free consent, because *th*e law makers are chosen & appointed by *th*em, even *th*e whole lower house w*i*thout whose consent nothing passeth. 2 neither is it a vayne thing *tha*t g*ene*rally all *th*e people of *th*e Kingdo*m*e offer their children vnto Baptisme, & therein openly p*ro*fesse their repentance faith & desyre to haue their children baptized in *tha*t faith. 3[ly] in many congrega*ci*ons *th*e people chuse *th*eir ministers & in many others willingly accept *them,* wherein is implyed a mutuall engagem*en*t to p*er*fourme *th*e duties of minister & people. 4[ly] there be w*i*th you & euen so*m*e of *them* who*m* you haue refused, *tha*t can tell you *tha*t in so*m*e congrega*ci*ons in England, *th*e ministers & all the [2v] p*ro*fessours among *th*e people haue entered into such a covenaunt to yeeld p*ro*fessed subjec*ci*on to *th*e gospell of *Chris*t, so farre as *th*ey conceiue *Chris*t requireth of *th*em in their places in these tymes.[23]

His 3[d] ground is taken fro*m* *th*e state of our church gou*er*nm*en*t, w*hi*ch hee reporteth to putt a heavy yoake vpo*n* gods people. What is amisse in any of *th*em or their wayes, I will not take vpo*n* mee to justifye; but to omitt other questions, too large for this piece of paper, & to joyne issue w*i*th him vpo*n* his owne principles; it is neither a false nor a tyrannicall gou*er*nement (as hee calleth it) of *th*e prelates of *th*e church *tha*t can disanull *th*e being of a church. what more Antichristian then to sett vp two *Chris*ts? & yet so did *th*e church of Israel in expresse type, when *th*ey admitted 2 high priests together, Annas & Caiaphas Luk. 3.2.[24] And was it not more then a heavy yoake when *th*e priests & *th*e pharisees put vpo*n* *th*e people not onely their owne tradi*ci*ons (Mat. 23.4)[25] but also made a law *tha*t whosoeu*er* p*ro*fessed *th*e name of *Chris*t should be excom*m*unicated (Joh. 9.22)?[26] & yet did not *Chris*t com*m*unicate w*i*th *tha*t church? & send his disciples to it mat. 23.3?[27] yea & yet called it Gods vineyard mat. 21.39?[28]

I say no more. reject not *th*e wombe *tha*t bare you nor *th*e paps *tha*t gaue you sucke: till *Chris*t giue[29] vs a bill of divorcement, do not you divorce yo*u*rselfe from vs. The Lord Jesus shew you as much mercy as hee hath done to vs & still doth; & so may hee do to you & vs more & more for euer.

Haue pitty also vpo*n* those poore creatures *tha*t dye among you, & (as it is said) some for lacke of necessaryes: call upo*n* *th*e richer sort for a compassionate heart & hand: wee do *th*e like here for yours & ours as we may.[30] my wife & self com*m*end our hearty loue to you, & all our good frends w*i*th you, w*i*th your wife.[31] So I rest in much weakenesse, yet

Boston octob. 2. 1630. desyrous of your best comfort

J:C./

Copied out June 13. 1631
by mee
Rich: Mather.

1. "A Sermon Delivered at Salem, 1636," in Ziff, *Cotton on the Churches,* 43.

2. Cotton himself, replying to Robert Baillie's *Dissuasive from the Errours of the Time . . .* (London, 1645), denied that the Massachusetts Bay colonists, in Salem or elsewhere, modeled their practice on Plymouth, insisting that "the men were such as were not wont to attend to the patterns of men in matters of religion . . . but to the pattern of the Scriptures." In particular: "Sure I am, Mr. Skelton . . . was studious of that way, before he left Holland in Lincolnshire." *The Way of Congregational Churches Cleared* (1648), in Ziff, *Cotton on the Churches,* 193, 195.

The modern debate began in Perry Miller, *Orthodoxy in Massachusetts, 1630–1650: A Genetic Study* (Cambridge, Mass., 1933), 102–147, and continued in Larzer Ziff, "The Salem Puritans in the 'Free Aire of a New World,'" *Huntington Library Quarterly,* XX (1957), 373–384; David D. Hall's introduction to his edition, "John Cotton's Letter to Samuel Skelton," *WMQ,* 3d Ser., XXII (1965), 478–480; George D. Langdon, Jr., *Pilgrim Colony: A History of New Plymouth, 1620–1691* (New Haven, Conn., 1966), 107–114; Lewis M. Robinson, "The Formative Influence of Plymouth Church on American Congregationalism," *Bibliotheca Sacra,* CXXVII (1970), 232–240; Hall, *Faithful Shepherd,* 78–86; Slayden Yarbrough, "The Influence of Plymouth Colony Separatism on Salem: An Interpretation of John Cotton's Letter of 1630 to Samuel Skelton," *Church History,* LI (1982), 290–303.

3. "A Sermon Delivered at Salem, 1636," in Ziff, *Cotton on the Churches,* 41–42.

4. William Hubbard, *A General History of New England from the Discovery to 1680* (1815), 2d ed., ed. William Thaddeus Harris, MHS, *Colls.,* 2d Ser., V–VI (Boston, 1848), 181–182.

5. See especially his answers to Robert Baillie, in *The Way of Congregational Churches Cleared* (1648), in Ziff, *Cotton on the Churches,* 195–199, 209–211.

In discussing "Cotton's censorious letter," Edmund S. Morgan says that this letter "is one more indication that nonseparating Puritans, who inclined toward a Congregational polity, had not yet worked out the details of it as fully as the Separatists had. One detail that Cotton had obviously not thought through was that of establishing proper qualifications for receiving the sacraments" (*Visible Saints: The History of a Puritan Idea* [New York, 1963], 87). Morgan's discussion is the definitive statement of the establishment of New England's church membership practices. Cotton's letter to Skelton is central to that discussion (80–106).

6. William Coddington (1591–1678) and his wife, Mary Mosely (d. 1630), had left Boston, Lincolnshire, to sail with Winthrop's company in the spring of 1630.

7. John Winthrop, Isaac Johnson, and Thomas Dudley. Unknown to Cotton, Isaac Johnson had died two days before this, on September 30, 1630, about a month after his wife, Lady Arbella Johnson. Coddington's wife was also one of the many casualties in 1630 (Winthrop, *Journal,* 39). Dudley, on the other hand, lived long, often serving the colony as governor, deputy governor, and magistrate.

8. Coddington was, in fact, a member of St. Botolph's, Cotton's own church.

9. John Lathrop (d. 1653) was the minister of a London church that, while formally a non-Separatist congregation, was known to have Separatist leanings. Lathrop was imprisoned in 1632 and banished by Archbishop Laud in 1634, whereupon he emigrated to Scituate, within the colony of Plymouth. Brook, *Lives of the Puritans,* III, 163–165.

10. That is, precedential, or serving as precedent.

11. Acts 10:47–48: Can any man forbid water, that these should not be baptized, which have received the Holy Ghost as well as we? And he [Peter] commanded them to be baptized in the name of the Lord. Then prayed they him to tarry certain days.

12. Here Mather inserted an asterisk just before the word church, and in the left margin, wrote: * text. Harris accordingly replaced church with text in Cotton's sentence.

13. Acts 11:2–3: And when Peter was come up to Jerusalem, they that were of the circumcision contended with him, Saying, thou wentest in to men uncircumcised, and didst eat with them.

14. John Robinson (1576?–1625) was pastor of the Separatist congregation in Leiden from which the settlers of the Plymouth Colony chiefly came. He received his bachelor of arts degree at Cambridge in 1596 and was chosen fellow of Corpus Christi College, Cambridge, in 1597, where he remained until 1604.

15. Caecilius Cyprianus (c. 200–258), bishop of Carthage from c. 248 and an important Church Father, the first African Christian martyr, debated issues of church membership, baptism, and congregational autonomy with his contemporaries. In his discussion of these and related issues in both *The Keyes of the Kingdom of Heaven . . .* (London, 1644) and *The Way of Congregational Churches Cleared . . .* (London, 1648), Cotton cited Cyprian's *Epistolae* to support his positions. See Ziff, *Cotton on the Churches,* 102, 138, 299–301, 319–320, 327. See also Cotton to [Edward?] Naylor, [1651–1652].

16. John Robinson's defense of the Leiden church's differences with the Church of England appear in several of his writings; see Robert Ashton, ed., *The Works of John Robinson . . .*, 3 vols. (London, 1851). Cotton may be referring to Robinson's *Just and Necessary Apology of Certain Christians . . .*, II, 13, 34, 68, 69, 73–74, 77, where, in sections titled "Of the Largeness of Churches," "Of the Ecclesiastical Presbytery," and "Of the Church of England," he discusses the issues Cotton describes here as Robinson's three "grounds."

17. all *that*] Hall: all they that

18. 1 Cor. 9:2: If I be not an apostle unto others, yet doubtless I am to you: for the seal of mine apostleship are ye in the Lord. Gal. 2:7: But contrariwise, when they saw that the gospel of the uncircumcision was committed unto me, as the gospel of the circumcision was unto Peter.

19. Rev. 3:4: Thou hast a few names even in Sardis which have not defiled their garments; and they shall walk with me in white: for they are worthy.

20. (1) Acts 20:28: Take heed therefore unto yourselves, and to all the flock, over the which

the Holy Ghost hath made you overseers, to feed the church of God, which he hath purchased with his own blood.

(2) 1 Cor. 1:2: Unto the church of God which is at Corinth, to them that are sanctified in Christ Jesus, called to be saints, with all that in every place call upon the name of Jesus Christ our Lord, both theirs and ours.

(3) 1 Cor. 1:9: God is faithful, by whom ye were called unto the fellowship of his son Jesus Christ our Lord.

(4) 1 Cor. 14:23: If therefore the whole church be come together into one place, and all speak with tongues, and there come in those that are unlearned, or unbelievers, will they not say that ye are mad?

(5) 1 Cor. 1:2: see above. 1 Tim. 2:1: I exhort therefore, that, first of all, supplications, prayers, intercessions, and giving of thanks, be made for all men.

(6) 1 Cor. 14:12. Even so, forasmuch as ye are zealous of spiritual gifts, seek that ye may excel to the edifying of the church. 31:12: For ye may all prophesy one by one, that all may learn, and all may be comforted.

(7) 1 Cor. 14:26: How is it then, brethren? when ye come together, every one of you hath a psalm, hath a doctrine, hath a tongue, hath a revelation, hath an interpretation. Let all things be done unto edifying.

21. n*atu*re or essence] Hall: nature essence

22. 2 Chron. 15:12, 13: And they entered into a covenant to seek the Lord God of their fathers with all their heart and with all their soul; That whosoever would not seek the Lord God of Israel should be put to death, whether small or great, whether man or woman.

23. Here Cotton doubtless refers to Isaac Johnson and William Coddington, members of Cotton's St. Botolph's Church in Lincolnshire, who must have been among those who had joined in a church covenant. In *The Way of Congregational Churches Cleared,* Cotton wrote: "There were some scores of godly persons in Boston in Lincolnshire . . . who can witness, that we entered into a covenant with the Lord, and one with another, to follow after the Lord in the purity of his worship." In Ziff, *Cotton on the Churches,* 198.

24. Luke 3:2: Annas and Caiaphas being the high priests, the word of God came unto John the son of Zacharias in the wilderness.

25. Matt. 23:4: For they bind heavy burdens and grievous to be borne, and lay them on men's shoulders; but they themselves will not move them with one of their fingers.

26. John 9:22: These words spake his parents, because they feared the Jews: for the Jews had agreed already, that if any man did confess that he was Christ, he should be put out of the synagogue.

27. Matt. 23:3: All therefore whatsoever they bid you observe, that observe and do; but do not ye after their works: for they say and do not.

28. Matt. 21:39: And they caught him, and cast him out of the vineyard, and slew him.

29. giue] Hall: gives

30. See Cotton's letter of the next day, Oct. 3, 1630, to Herbert Pelham, for an example of his charitable action on behalf of a friend who had emigrated to Salem.

31. Susanna Travis Skelton (d. Mar. 15, 1630/1). Anderson, *Great Migration,* 1685–1686.

John Cotton to Herbert Pelham

October 3, 1630

ALS. MS: MHS, Winthrop Papers, Au. 41

Published: MHS, *Colls.,* 5th Ser., I (1871), 195; *Winthrop Papers,* II, 315–316

In L. Thompson, "Letters of John Cotton," 70

The first contingent of settlers in the Massachusetts Bay Colony sailed from England in late March 1630. Although John Cotton preached the farewell sermon at Southampton not long before that departure, he did not accompany them, delaying his own commitment to the enterprise for another three years. At the time the following letter was written, both Cotton and the addressee, Herbert Pelham, were still in England. Pelham (1600–1673) was a member of the Massachusetts Bay Company from 1629 but did not emigrate until about 1635, serving the company in the meantime as a valuable agent in London, handling the supply line from England to the colony. It is in this capacity that Cotton addresses him here. When he did emigrate, he settled first in Sudbury and afterward in Cambridge, where he remained until 1647, when he returned permanently to England. He served as the first treasurer of Harvard College from December 27, 1643, and was elected an assistant each year from 1645 to 1649 even though for the last two years he was not in the colony.

John Winthrop's letters from New England to family members in England in the late months of 1630 convey news of "the vnexpected troubles and necessities which are fallen vpon vs," including a pressing shortness of supplies and the sickness and deaths of many.[1] Cotton's sending a hogshead of meal to William Coddington was part of an informal relief effort by friends in England. Just a month later, for instance, John Rogers, the famous Puritan preacher of Dedham, Essex, wrote to John Winthrop, Jr., who was still in England, enclosing twenty shillings "to provide such a Barrell of meale as this mony will reach vnto and direct it over to John Page," "late of Dedham," from whom Rogers had just received "so lamentable a letter" saying he and his family in New England were "like to starue" unless someone could send supplies.[2] Rogers appended a note to "good Mr. Pelham" asking him in case John Winthrop, Jr., was away to see to Rogers's request himself. Clearly, it was understood that Pelham was the man who saw to such details for the Winthrops.

On November 18, 1630, Captain William Peirce sent a bill for provisions loaded at Bristol for shipping to Massachusetts Bay. The largest item on the bill is £115 2s. for thirty-four hogsheads of wheat meal.[3] This probably included the one ordered by Cotton for his friend Coddington in this letter.

M[r] Pelham;

I pray you, let me intreate you, w*i*th these 3 pieces of Gold, to buy an Hogshead of Meale, or what else you can most conveniently gett, & send it to M[r] william Coddington[4] in New England, for *th*e vse I have specifyed in his l*ett*ere, & in my l*ett*ere to Elizabeth Mason. &c./ I take leave, & rest,

Yo*u*r wor*sh*ips in *th*e Lord

John Cotton./

Boston. Oct. 3.
1630./

1. John Winthrop to John Winthrop, Jr., July 23, 1630, *Winthrop Papers,* II, 305.

2. John Rogers to John Winthrop, Jr., [November 1630], ibid., 316.

3. Ibid., 317–318.

4. William Coddington (1591–1678), a friend from Boston who had sailed to New England with Winthrop's company in the spring of 1630, was a magistrate and treasurer of the colony. See Anderson, *Great Migration,* 395–401.

Jeremiah Burroughes to [John Cotton]

November 1, [1630]

ALS. MS: MHS, John Davis Papers, 012.3

Unpublished but transcribed in Kenneth Wayne Shipps, "Lay Patronage of East Anglian Puritan Clerics in Pre-Revolutionary England" (Ph.D. diss., Yale University, 1971), app. 13, 404–405

Jeremiah Burroughes (1599–1646), who ultimately became a strong proponent of congregational church government, was at the time of this letter a lecturer at Bury St. Edmunds, Suffolk. An Emmanuel College graduate (bachelor of arts, 1620/1; master's, 1624), he had gone to Bury in the spring of 1627, the same year that Edmund Calamy (1600–1666) accepted a position as lecturer to a different congregation in the same town, a situation that contributed to the dilemma Burroughes describes here. Faced with the question whether to leave his position, Burroughes subsequently decided the issue by becoming rector at Tivetshall, Norfolk, where he was instituted to the rectory on April 21, 1631. He was later deprived of that office by Bishop Matthew Wren's visitation articles of 1634 and went to Holland, where he became minister at the English church in Rotterdam in 1637.[1] When he returned to England, he became one of the five Independent divines who were delegates to the Westminster Assembly and was the author of several books, some posthumous.

Dating of the letter to 1630 is deduced from the date of his installation at Tivetshall.

Written at the top of the recto:

Mr Jer. Burroughs
l*ett*ere to great Grandfather
Cotton.

Worthy S*i*r
Though my acquaintance with you be small, yett the necessetie of the cause in which I shall desire your helpe, putts me on to repaire to you.

There is some question about my remouinge from Bury. The cause standes thus; I was at first called thither by the people, & my maintenance depended on them, but now very shortely, the condition of the place wilbe altered, my maintenance almost wholy, if not altogether, will depende vppon the company of our corporation; it is to come out of their hall. There is a 100^{li} p*er* annu*m* to be setled vppon each parish, & vppon that we must expect no more collection from mens purses, now there lately was a rumor in the towne that the corporation intended to setle this 100^{li} vppon Mr White[2] who is joined with me, & that I should be at his dispose for my meanes, at the first heareinge of it I had 2 arguments that made me to feare such an intention, 1. Their general contempt of me formerly, & cleauinge to Mr White, 2. Because he that is preacher in the other parish[3] shall haue the whole 100^{li} setled on him because the other that is with him does onely reade, & I haue greate cause to thinke that now vppon the alteration of the conditions of the place they would gladly bringe our parish to this that Mr White should be the preacher & chuse some curate to helpe him. Besides lately those men haue manifested themselues excedingely vexed at a sermon I preached that touched their last Alderman who was ~~an~~ an enimie to all good; These thinges beinge thus, it pleased god now in this shire to offer me another place, I had a fortnight since a letter from a gentlewoman, whom yett I neuer sawe, & I thinke she neuer sawe me, wherein she offred me a liuinge,[4] I know of no meanes that euer was made to her but by hearesay from others. It semed by her letter that the predecessor who was a godly man by reporte, desired her vppon his death bed to thinke on me. yett I neuer was halfe an houre in the mans company nor knew of any such thin[g]e[5] till a good while after his death. vppon this I thought I should know what the intentions of o*u*r men, were, I called a meetinge of the parish, & signified vnto them, That I was to giue an answere to such a one who offred me such a place, yett I would not till I had consulted with them, & I told them, That I was willinge to refuse that offer & still to abide with them, & all that I would demaunde should be this, That whereas the meanes of the place is now shortely to come out of the Hall, That I might haue their promise that when it comes I might haue my meanes from thence proportionably with him that is joined with me that does but the same worke. vppon which They begane first to shuffle, & sayde it was not

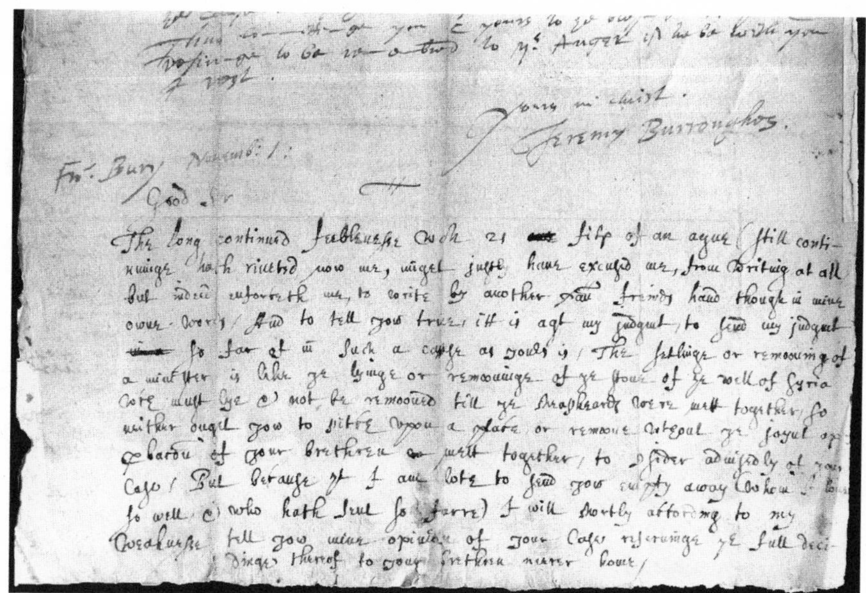

PLATE 5. Jeremiah Burroughes to Cotton, November 1, [1630], verso, with Cotton's notes for a reply at the bottom of the page. Composed, as Cotton says, during the period of his severe malarial illness, his words are written by one of his household seminarians, whose hand is prominent in the manuscript of Cotton's *First John* volume. *Massachusetts Historical Society manuscript: Davis Papers, 012.3. Courtesy of the Massachusetts Historical Society*

to be done presently, I answered but promise that when it shall come That I may haue my meanes there as well as the other shall haue his. Then they answered but perhapps the sole powre will not be ours, I replyed, but promise thus farre that if you shall haue any powre that you will vse it for this ende, Then they begane to breake out, & one bad me remember such a sermon & threatned me, a 2d sayde The would further see how mens deseruinges would be, a 3d that they must not see their cheife gouernour abused, a 4th That it was fitt satisfaction should be giuen for the sermon I preached, & Thus *th*e meetinge brake of. There were ^but^ 6 of *th*e 12 who are *ou*r choise burgesses, at the meetinge & all ioined together & but one of their company ~~namely~~ of ther 24. which are inferior Burgesses spake one worde in my behalfe.

Now yett for all this I Thinke feare of shame & *th*e speach of people will moue them not wholy to depriue ^me^ of meanes at least presently but for a while It may be some meanes wilbe allowed. but what wilbe hereafter I doe not know, in priuate some of these men were more moderate, but I cannot gett The promise of this reasonable demaunde.

Now yett if I know my harte I am more willinge to abide then to goe if I might haue cleared to me any thinge that might vphold me in those stronge suffringes I am like to goe vnder, if I tarry I had need s[ee] clearely that god is with me.

[IV] If I should continue, & after meete with much trouble & many suffringes & then should wauer in my thoughts, whether god did not shew me another way that he would rather haue had me wrought in another place, Then I know not how I should be able to goe vnder them, But on the other syde if you thinke I may goe, I pray open the cause as clearely as you canne, that I may haue arguments to build on to assure me that god sendes me & wilbe with me.

I pray open The groundes of a ministers setlinge in a place or remouinge, lett these 2 quest*ions* especially be cleared

1. Whether vncertainty of meanes, if a man haue convenient for the present & any probability for continuance at least for a time, be a good cause for a ministers remouinge.

2. Whether opposition of the people & of those esspec*ially* that haue the powre of *th*e meanes in their handes & willingnesse of a greate parte of other of *th*e people to be ridde of a minister be a good cause.

The causes that might moue stayinge I suppose Mr Chaplin[6] will fully certifie, These 2 thinges may be sayde

1. It is a greate place & so perhapps some ~~more~~ hope of more good then in a country village to which I am called. I confess one would thinke their might be more good, but in regarde of *th*e straunge disposition of the people & that yokefellow with whom I am joyned I see little hope. I haue bene neare 3 yeares & a halfe with them with little successe.

2. If I goe There is feare of the succession.

I confesse for myne owne parte I could wish that the arguments for my stayinge might preuaile[.] I would they had but so much force in them as that I might without doubtinge conclude That god would haue me stay.

Thus I haue bene longe & wearied you but the cause require[s] it, I must giue in my [an]swere[7] very spedily[.] I pray therefore helpe vs in your[8] streights, & lett your answere be as full as it may conveniently, you & my tutor Hooker[9] I esspecially rely on for Counsel vnder god. I haue bene longe [deleted word] openinge *th*e cause because I cannot sende to you any more.

Thus committinge you & yours to *th*e blessinge of god & Desiringe to be remembred to Mr Anger[10] if he be with you I rest.

Yours in Christ.
Jeremy Burroughes.

Fro*m* Bury Nouemb*er* 1:

1. John Browne, *A History of Congregationalism and Memorials of the Churches in Norfolk and Suffolk* (London, 1877), 69, 115.

2. Henry White (d. 1661), a graduate of Gonville and Caius College, Cambridge, and a native of Suffolk. After his time at Bury, he was rector at Rougham, Suffolk, from 1636 until his death. Shipps, "Lay Patronage of East Anglian Puritan Clerics," 314; Venn, *Alumni Cantabrigienses,* IV, 386.

3. Edmund Calamy.

4. Shipps notes that it was Lady Jane Bacon who offered him an advowson at Tivetshall ("Lay Patronage of East Anglian Puritan Clerics," 176).

5. The missing letter is obscured by an ink smudge.

6. Mr. Chaplin is probably the messenger who carried this letter to Cotton.

7. A hole in the paper and a stain have removed the first two letters.

8. The o is written over a y.

9. Thomas Hooker (1586–1647) had held a lectureship in Chelmsford, Essex, since 1625, but in July 1630 he was cited for his nonconformity to the Court of High Commission. He chose not to obey that summons and was thus in hiding by the time Burroughes wrote to him and Cotton, though he remained in England until July 1631, when he went to Holland. See George H. Williams, "The Life of Thomas Hooker in England and Holland, 1586–1633," in G. H. Williams et al., *Thomas Hooker,* 19–24; Frank Shuffelton, *Thomas Hooker, 1586–1647* (Princeton, N.J., 1977), 131–135; Sargent Bush, Jr., *The Writings of Thomas Hooker: Spiritual Adventure in Two Worlds* (Madison, Wis., 1980), 53–57.

10. John Angier (1605–1677), who grew up in Dedham, Essex, and attended Emmanuel College, Cambridge (bachelor of arts, 1625/6), had gone in 1627 to live with Cotton in Lincolnshire. He stayed there three years, until "the beginning of *September* 1630," when he took up a position as minister in Ringley, Lancashire. He had thus just recently left Boston, as Burroughes seems to have suspected. See Ernest Axon, ed., *Oliver Heywood's Life of John Angier of Denton . . .* (Manchester, 1937), 53–54.

[John Cotton] to Jeremiah Burroughes

[November 1630]

Copy. MS: MHS, John Davis Papers 012.3

This note is written on the verso of Burroughes to Cotton, November 1, [1630]. It is clearly and carefully written, but not in Cotton's hand. The slash marks are in the manuscript and do not indicate line endings.

Good S[i]r[1]

The long continued feeblenesse w*hi*ch 21 [deleted word] fits of an ague (still continuinge[)] hath riueted, now me, might justly haue excused me, from writing at all / but indeed enforceth me, to write by another *Christi*an freinds hand though in mine owne words / And to tell yow true, itt is ag*ains*t my judgm*ent*, to send my judgm*ent* ~~in a~~ so far of in such a ca~~u~~se as yours is / The setlinge or remoouing of a minister is like *th*e lyinge or remoouinge of *th*e stone of *th*e well of Syria w*hi*ch must lye & not be remooued till *th*e sheapheards were mett together,[2] So neither ought yow to pitch vpon a place, or remooue w*i*thout *th*e joynt app*ro*baci*o*n of your brethren [deleted word] mett together, to c*on*sider aduisedly of your Case / But because *tha*t I am loth to send yow empty away (whom I loue so well, & who hath sent so farre) I will shortly according to my weaknesse tell yow mine opinion of your Case reseruinge *th*e full decidinge thereof to your brethren neerer home/

1. The i falls directly on a vertical fold in the paper and is worn away.

2. Gen. 29:1–10 tells of Jacob's coming into "the land of the people of the east." Verses 7–8: And he said, Lo, it is yet high day, neither is it time that the cattle should be gathered together: water ye the sheep, and go and feed them. And they said, we cannot, until all the flocks be gathered together, and till they roll the stone from the well's mouth; then we water the sheep.

John Cotton to N[athaniel] Rogers

1630

Published: Cotton Mather, *Magnalia Christi Americana . . .* (London, 1702), book III, 27; A. W. M'Clure, *The Life of John Cotton* (Boston, 1846), 266–267

Nathaniel Rogers (1598–1655), son of the famous preacher at Dedham, Essex, John Rogers, was well known to Cotton in both England and New England. Rogers had been educated at Emmanuel College (bachelor of arts, 1617/8; master's, 1621), after which he served as domestic chaplain in an unknown aristocratic family for a couple of years. He then became curate under Dr. John Barkham at Bocking, Essex, for about five years before being dismissed by the strongly conformist Dr. Barkham. He was subsequently rector at Assington, Suffolk, from 1630 to 1636, when he resigned his post to avoid ecclesiastical censure for his Puritan ways, and sailed for New England with his wife of eight years, Margaret Crane, and at least two children. He became copastor with John Norton at Ipswich, succeeding Nathaniel Ward in February 1638.[1]

This letter was probably written to Rogers after he had assumed the post at Assington, but this cannot be known with certainty. It is a statement on Cotton's application of his Sabbatarian principles, some of which were expressed in his earlier treatise on the duration of the Sabbath and his later exchange of letters with Thomas Shepard (Cotton to Shepard, [Apr. 3, 1646]).[2]

The source text is the first edition of Mather's *Magnalia*. Mather's printing of this fragment of a longer letter is laced with his usual frequent italics. Since it was not Cotton's habit to use underlining, it is safe to assume the italics were Mather's addition. They are retained, however, since occasionally Mather used italics where documents contained quotation marks. This might be the case here, since Cotton is clearly replying to specific inquiries from Rogers, whose wording he may be incorporating into his answer. It should be noted that, although Mather's biography of Cotton appears as the first of five biographies of first-generation New England ministers in *Johannes in Eremo* in 1695, this passage from Cotton's letter to Rogers does not appear there, being added in the version in the *Magnalia* seven years later.

Studying for a Sermon upon the Sabbath-day, so far as it might be any wearisome Labour to I*nvention* or *Memory,* I covet (when I can) willingly to prevent it; and would rather attend unto the quickning of my *Heart and Affections,* in the Meditation of what I am to deliver. My Reason is, much *Reading* and *Invention,* and *Repetition* of things, to commit them to *Memory,* is a weariness to the *Flesh* and *Spirit* too; whereas the *Sabbath day* doth rather invite unto an holy Rest. But yet if God's Providence have straitned my time in the *Week-days* before, by concurrence of other Business, not to be avoided, I doubt not, but the Lord, who allowed the *Priests* to employ their *Labour,* in killing the *Sacrifices* on the *Sabbath-day,* will allow us also to labour in our Callings on the Sabbath, to prepare our Sacrifice for the People.

1. On Rogers's biography, see Brook, *Lives of the Puritans,* III, 238–241; Venn, *Alumni Cantabrigienses,* III, 479; *DNB.*

2. See Winton U. Solberg, "John Cotton's Treatise on the Duration of the Lord's Day," in Frederick S. Allis, Jr., and Philip Chadwick Foster Smith, eds., *Sibley's Heir: A Volume in Memory of Clifford Kenyon Shipton,* CSM, *Publs.,* LIX, *Colls.* (Boston, 1982), 505–522.

John Dinley to John Cotton

January 1, 1630/1

ALS. MS: MSA, CCXL, Hutchinson Papers, I, fols. 17, 17a
Translation by George Goebel

John Dinley (also Dinely/Dyneley/Dingley) was a member of a Boston family and was apparently acquainted with Cotton from that context, though he had been at Christ's College, Cambridge (bachelor of arts, 1609/10; master's, 1613), when Cotton was a fellow at the neighboring Emmanuel. When he wrote this letter from Leiden, Dinley was probably serving as secretary to Elizabeth, queen of Bohemia, who was living in The Hague.[1]

D*omi*no Cottonio: Jo. Dinleius. Sa*lutem*

Ab Aschamo fratre te intellexi valere, meiq*ue* retinere memoriam, quo nil mihi gratiús aút optatius contingere possit, nam salute et benevolentia tua et ipse rectius valeo. Iam mihi occasionem scribendi dat, misera rerum facies, et perditissima Jesuitarum consilia, quibus nonsolum imperia, Eccelsiasq*ue* in ijs hospitantes everterúnt, sed etiam fidem, pacem, conscientiasq*ue* hominum evertere pergent. Animo quidem flebam, quum audirem, quanta fit Gallia et Germanica animarum strages, ijs in locis ardet persecutio, sed novo commento, non ulterius in vitas sanctorum sæviunt, út superiori seculo, non bestijs, aút equuleis, aut flammis obijciuntur, paucæ cædes, parca sanguinis effúsio: hunc norúnt esse semen Ecclesiæ. Propterea̒ quos crudelitate vincere non potuerúnt, in eos dolis et insidijs grassantur. Gallijs quotquot Panitium Deum non adorant, a Rep. ab honoribus arcentur, sordidi habentur et despicatui. Palatinatú, ubi regnant Jesuitæ, etiam uxoribus, liberis, bonis, cognationibús, patriâ exuuntur. rapiuntur filij invitis parentibus in seminaria fraudis et mendaciorum disciplina et si qui sint, qui mordente conscientiâ renituntur; rem miram ajunt. magnu*m* facinus: quid in Missa est mali? accedite modo, hoc petimus, mentes quoad vultis intemeratas servate, scimus enim vos corpore præsentes, animis abesse, et in hæresi vestrâ permansuros. quin ind[e] cum lege cautum sit, omnes punitum iri, qui proferre testimonium nequeunt, se Missæ interfuisse, sunt Jesuitæ nonnulli, qui accepto munere tabulas concedunt, licet non interfuissent. sic omnes dolis implent vaferrimè, et venantur meticulosos lepores. huiusmodi astu plurimi in casses eorum inciderúnt; uti in urbibus nonnullis, vix decem supersint, qui non ad Missam accedúnt, aut eludúnt, et mundo capti, etiam mentibus capiuntur. quot postea in eorum animabus plagæ! qualis vellicatio, quantus horror et bella intestina! id Jesuitæ quærunt, ut obliteratâ Dei imagine, et extincto diuino lumine, quod in hominibus micat, vel callum conscientijs vel laqueum collis inducunt. A te peto, ut sententiam tuam hac in re mihi communicares; An tutâ conscientiâ liceat Missæ interesse, an coacti excusentur, an potius bonis omnibús amissis tradere se debeant diuinæ providentiæ, aut si quid amplius, ad hanc rem pertinere putaveris. Aliud est, in quo non nihil cæcutio. quid sentiendum sit de Paganis, penè dixeram, pijs. Legi Phocionem cicutam carcere bibentem, amico respondisse interroganti, quid ulterius vellet. jube inquit filium meum, ne mortem patris, à civibus meis [IV] ulciscetur, in quo responso, quis non vocem sancti hominis agnoscit. quid aliud orabat Stephanus, ne persecutoribus suis statueretur peccatum; plurima in omni virtutum genere exempla produci possunt, quæ cum optima sint, an absq*ue* gratiâ diuinâ effici potuerúnt, nescio: dicitur quicquid ex fide non est, esse peccatum: an itaq*ue* castitatem, fortitudinem, sapientiam, temperantiam, iustitiam, patientiam eorum mirabilem, peccata dicemus, quoniam illis indultúm non fuit, cui crederent, si datúm fuisset, proculdubio credidissent: dicuntur Deum ignotum coluisse, quod non fecissent, nisi cuperint scire. palpando etiam eum quærebant, et Deus temporibus ejús ignorantiæ connivisse dicitur. quorsum hæc, si probi viri luent pœnas cum perditissimis! Hæ mihi tenebræ sunt, diu multumq*ue* mecum cogitavi, sed me extricare nondum possum, opus mihi est filo tuo, nam ex te pendeo. Quod reliquum est, neq*ue* ego scribere, neq*ue* tu legere sine dolore possumús. Ecclesia Gallicana quæ Hagæ constituitur (cuius Princeps Auricus pars est) grave vulnus nuper accepit. duo ministri erant, qui ejusdem curam gesserúnt; unus Espanius, cælebs, doctus eloquens, qui stupri accusatus reliquit Provinciam, et in Angliam secessit; Alter Sanassonius [two illegible words][2] adulterio deprehensus. uterq*ue* exutus non sine Religionis scandalo. operâ Andreæ Riueti Galli Professoris his Theologiæ, pij et prudentis viri Ecclesia illa utitur, donec Pastores saniores invenerint. Ita omnibus modis insidiatur Satan Ecclesiæ; vi dolis, scandalis; sed inferorum portæ prævalere nunquam poterint si nos crediderimus. Finesius tuus domum revocatus a nobis discessit. Inclita stirps nobilissimarum ædium. Lectissimam tuam conjugem amicissimè saluto. Vale vir optime, et quantam vis occupatissimus sis, sepone horúlam modò in gratiam meam. Lugduni Batav*orum* Calend*is*[3] Januar*iis* 1630

John Dinley to Master Cotton, greeting:

From brother Ascham[4] I learn that you are well and still remember me. Nothing could be more pleasing and welcome to me, for I am more truly well because of your good health and good wishes. The occasion of my writing now is the wretched outlook of affairs and the wicked devices of the Jesuits, by which they have not only overthrown nations and the churches they harbored but continue to overthrow the faith, peace, and consciences of men. My heart wept to hear how great the destruction of souls in France and Germany was. A persecution rages there, but on a new scheme. No longer is their savagery directed at the lives of the saints, as in the past; the victims are not subjected to the wild beasts, the rack, or the flames; few are slaughtered; little blood is shed—they know that this is the seed of the church. Therefore those that they could not overcome with cruelty, they attack with craft and deceit. In France, those who do not adore the breaden god[5] are excluded from public office and are held mean and contemptible. In the Palatinate, where the Jesuits rule, they are stripped of wives, children, goods, kin, and country.[6] Children are carried off against their parents' will to seminaries of fraud and an education of lies. And if there are some who, at the gnawing of conscience, resist, they say it is astonishing. A terrible crime? What harm is there in the mass? All we ask is that you go; preserve your minds as untouched as you will (for we know that, though present in body, you will be absent in spirit, and will persist in your heresy.) Indeed, since the law decrees that anyone who cannot produce evidence of having attended mass will be punished, there are some Jesuits who will supply affidavits, for a price, even to those who have not attended. Thus with great cunning they fill everyone with deceit, and hunt the timorous hares. With this sort of guile they catch many in their nets, so that in some cities scarce ten remain who do not either attend mass or evade it dishonestly. Distracted by worldly things, they are also distracted in their minds; how many scars will there be afterwards on their souls! What rending! What horror! What internal battles! This is what the Jesuits want: by obliterating the divine image and extinguishing the divine light that glows in men, to put a callus on their souls or a noose about their necks. Please tell me what you think about this matter: that is, whether one may attend mass with a safe conscience, and if those who are forced may be excused, or if they should rather sacrifice all their goods and entrust themselves to divine providence, and anything else that you think relevant to this matter.

There is another matter in which my sight is not a little dim: what are we to think of the—I almost said pious—pagans? I have read that when Phocion was drinking the hemlock in prison, and a friend asked what his last wish was, he answered, "Tell my son not to avenge my death on my fellow citizens."[7] Who does not recognize the voice of a saintly man in this answer? What else was Stephen praying, when he asked that the sin be not held against his persecutors?[8] Many examples could be produced in every species of virtue, so outstanding that I am doubtful whether they can have been achieved without divine grace. It is said that whatever does not arise from faith is sin; are we then to call their wonderful chastity, fortitude, wisdom, temperance, justice, and patience sins, because to them had not been vouchsafed that in which they might believe? Had it been given, they would certainly have believed; they are said to have worshipped the unknown god, which they would not have done, had they not desired to know. Indeed, they were groping in search of him, and it is said that God turned a blind eye to the ignorance of that time. What follows, if honest men are to be punished with the most wicked? These are dark matters to me; I have pondered long and often, but I cannot extricate myself. I need your guidance, for it is you I follow.

What is left I cannot write, nor you read, without pain. The French church established at the Hague (to which the prince of Orange[9] belongs) has recently suffered a severe blow. There were two ministers who undertook its care. One, Espanius, unmarried, a learned and eloquent man, was accused of fornication and has left the province and gone to England.[10] The other, Sanisson, having been caught in adultery, [two illegible words].[11] Both have been defrocked—not without scandal to religion. The church is making use of the services of Andreas Rivet, a Frenchman, their professor of theology,[12] until they can find some sounder pastors. Thus in all ways does Satan scheme against the church—with force, deceits, and scandals. But the gates of Hell will never prevail if we have faith.

Your Finesius[13] was summoned home and has left us—renowned scion of a noble house! My friendliest greetings to your most excellent wife. Farewell, best of men, and, however busy you may be, take a few minutes on my behalf. Leyden, 1 January 1630

1. Cotton's friendship with Dinley and the latter's location in Holland had been acknowledged two years earlier by John Nicolaus Rulice (see Rulice to Cotton, Nov. 29, 1628).

2. A worn fold in the paper here causes this interruption.

3. In the Roman dating system, the first day of each month was called the Calends of that month. Thus, the date of this letter is January 1.

4. Thomas Askham, sometime mayor of Boston, Lincolnshire.

5. Dinley's "Panitium Deum" appears to be a translation of the locution *breaden god,* described in the *OED,* with citations from 1579 into the nineteenth century, as "a polemical term for the consecrated host."

6. Citizenship.

7. Phocion (402–317) was an Athenian general and statesman who had studied under Plato. The story is in Plutarch's *Life of Phocion* 36.

8. See Acts 7:60.

9. Princeps Auricus, or the prince of Orange, at this time was Prins Frederik Hendrik.

10. The offender was a French Protestant pastor, Jean d'Espagne (1591–1659), who had come to the French church at The Hague in 1621. Dinley's statement helpfully fills out the vague allusion in the *DNB,* which simply observes that Espagne "seems to have left in 1629, under disagreeable circumstances." He went to London, where he became the pastor to a French congregation. See *DNB;* P. C. Molhuysen, *Nieuw Nederlandsch biografisch Woordenboek* (Leiden, 1918), 578–579; and "Beschryving Naamen der Walsche Predikanten," in Jacob de Riemer, *Beschryving van's-Graven-hage . . . ,* I (Delft, 1730), 401. I am grateful to Keith L. Sprunger for his generous assistance in identifying Espagne.

11. Sanassonius was Jean Sanisson, who had been called to the French church on September 12, 1618, and had to leave in 1630 because of what one contemporary source kindly called bad conduct ("quad gedrag"). "Beschryving Naamen der Walsche Predikanten," in Riemer, *Beschryving van's-Graven-hage,* I, 401.

12. André Rivet (1572–1651). See J. J. Woltjer, "Foreign Professors," in Th. H. Lunsingh Scheurleer and G. H. M. Posthumus Meyjes, eds., *Leiden University in the Seventeenth Century: An Exchange of Learning* (Leiden, 1975).

13. Probably a member of the Fiennes family, whose head was William Fiennes, Lord Saye and Sele, a friend of the Puritans, supporter of the New England colonial enterprise, and correspondent of Cotton. Several members of the Fiennes family studied at Leiden during this period, apparently supplementing their degree work at Cambridge or Oxford. University of Leiden records indicate that Nathaniel Fynnes, Josephus Fynnes, and Johannes Fynnes were all students in "Philosophiae" in May 1631. Nathaniel and Johannes (John) were probably the second and third sons of Lord Saye and Sele. In addition, the records show that one Petrus Fine

had apparently left the University of Leiden in November 1629. See *Album Studiosorum Academiae Lugduno Batavae, 1575–1875 . . .* (The Hague, 1875), 222, 235; Edward Peacock, *Index to English Speaking Students Who Have Graduated at Leyden University* (London, 1883), 35, 98.

Nathaniel Ward to John Cotton

December 13, 1631

Published: Hutchinson, *History,* I, 120–121; Nathaniel Ward, *The Simple Cobler of Aggawam in America,* ed. David Pulsifer (Boston, 1843), 93. Also included in Shirley Wilcox Harvey, "Nathaniel Ward: His Life and Works" (Ph.D. diss., Boston University, 1936), 68–69; and in Judith B. Welles, "John Cotton, 1584–1652, Churchman and Theologian" (Ph.D. diss., University of Edinburgh, 1948), 296–297

Nathaniel Ward's letter to Cotton at a time of great personal stress is self-explanatory, both in objective content and subjective force. In its distant brevity, having the quality of a cry in the wilderness, it speaks eloquently of the crisis in the church at the beginning of a very hard decade for English Puritans. Ward had been at Emmanuel College from 1596 until at least 1603, the year of his master of arts degree and of Cotton's arrival there from Trinity College. Ward became the rector at Stondon Massey, Essex, in February 1625/6. Only eight months before Ward wrote this letter, in April 1631, Thomas Hooker, just before fleeing to the Netherlands under the pressure of ecclesiastical courts in Laud's bishopric of London, had warned his congregation of the dire consequences of the silencing of the ministry: "I will deal plainly with you. As sure as God is God, God is going from England."[1] Hooker, at least, had gone, despite a petition in his defense signed by Ward and forty-eight other Essex clergymen, while other Puritan leaders—the most outspoken, forceful voices in the movement—were also being cast into what Cotton himself had called "the hateful tomb of silence."

Bishop Laud's January 1632 visits to parishes in Essex would result in the excommunication of Thomas Weld, the suspension of Nathaniel Rogers, and the expulsion from the diocese of Thomas Shepard, all of whom would soon emigrate to Massachusetts Bay.[2] Ward escaped in this round with just a dressing-down by the bishop, but later "he was suspended on Sept. 27, 1632, excommunicated on Oct. 30, and deprived of his benefice on Dec. 16."[3] He followed Cotton and others to New England in 1634.

Ward's admiration for Cotton was undimmed more than a decade later. Edward Winslow, in *Hypocrisie Unmasked,* reported Ward's saying to him: "Concerning Mr. *Cotton,* were I worthy, I would presume to speake that now of him, which I have said more then many times of him elsewhere, That I hold him such an eminent Worthy of Christ, as very few others have attained unto him; and that I hold my selfe not worthy to wipe his slippers for matters of grace, learning, and industry in the worke of God."[4]

Salutem in *Chris*to nostro.[5]
Reverend and dear friend,

I was yesterday convented before the bishop,[6] I mean to his court, and am adjourned to the next term. I see such giants turn their backs that I dare not trust my own weak heart. I expect measure hard enough[7] and must furnish apace with proportionable armour. I lacke a friend to help buckle it on. I know none but Christ himself in all our coast fitt to help me, and my acquaintance with him is hardly enough to hope for that assistance my weak spirit will want and the assaults of tentation call for. I pray therefore forget me not and believe for me also if there be such a piece of neighbourhood among Christians. And so blessing God with my whole heart for my knowledge of you and immerited[8] interest in you, and thanking you entirely for that faithful love I have found from you in many expressions of the best nature, I commit you to the unchangeable love of God our Father in his son Jesus Christ in whom I hope to rest for ever.

Stondon Mercy, Your's in all truth of heart,
Dec. 13. 1631. Nath[l] Warde.

1. "The Danger of Desertion," in G. H. Williams et al., *Thomas Hooker,* 244.

2. Harvey, "Nathaniel Ward," 70, notes this cluster of Laud's actions.

3. John J. Teunissen, "Nathaniel Ward (c. 1578–1652)," in James A. Levernier and Douglas R. Wilmes, ed., *American Writers before 1800: A Biographical and Critical Dictionary* (Westport, Conn., 1983), III, 1517. See also Giles Firmin, *Presbyterial Ordination Vindicated* . . . (London, 1660), 38; Edward H. L. Reeve, *Stondon Massey* (Colchester, 1906), 72; Harvey, "Nathaniel Ward," 68–71; Mary Janette Bohi, "Nathaniel Ward, Pastor Ingeniosus, 1580?–1652" (Ph.D. diss., Univ. of Illinois, 1959), 70–72; and Jean Béranger, *Nathaniel Ward (ca. 1578–1652)* (Bordeaux, 1969), 56–59.

4. Edward Winslow, *Hypocrisie Unmasked: A True Relation of the Proceedings of the Governor and Company of the Massachusetts against Samuel Gorton of Rhode Island* (1646), with introduction by Howard Millar Chapin (New York, 1968), 77.

5. Salutem in *Chris*to nostro: Greetings in our Christ. "The Second Edition" of Hutchinson's *History* (London, 1760 [i.e., 1765]) introduces an error in changing Salutem to Salutum (104). Lawrence Shaw Mayo's edition (Cambridge, Mass., 1936) repeats the error.

6. In his Essex church, Ward was in the ecclesiastical domain of William Laud, bishop of London.

7. Barely a year later, on January 2, 1633, Laud, by then archbishop of Canterbury, reported to Charles I that "afte longe patyence and often Conference, proceeded ag*ain*st Nathanyel Warde Parson of Stondon in Essex, to Excom*m*unicac*i*on and Depriuac*i*on, for refusing to subscribe to *th*e Articles established by *th*e Canon of *th*e Church (of which I certifyed the last yeare)

I haue now left him still vnder *th*e Censure of Excom*m*unicac*i*on." Lambeth Palace Library MS 943.247.

8. Immerited, meaning unmerited or undeserved, with its various cognates, is a usage strictly of the seventeenth and early eighteenth centuries (*OED*).

John Cotton to a Silenced Minister

[1628–1631?]

AL. MS: BPL, Ms. Am. 1506, pt. 2, no. 1

Though unsigned, this letter is entirely in Cotton's own handwriting. An eloquent expression of agonized sympathy for a recently silenced colleague, it is heavily scriptural in its phrasing. Thomas Prince wrote on the top of the first recto: "This seems to have been written in England upon *th*e silencing of Mr Cotton in *th*e beginning 1633." That it was written in England seems clear from the fact that the addressee had recently visited Cotton. But Prince's date may be a bit too late, and in any case the letter deals, not with Cotton's silencing, but with the addressee's. The letter probably dates from the late 1620s or very early 1630s, a period of increased pressure on Puritan ministers after Charles I took the throne in 1625. The terminal point of the likely period of this letter's creation is probably the death of Cotton's wife, Elizabeth, in April 1631.[1] He refers to her in the pronoun "mine" when he says, "Commend me (with mine) to yo*u*r good yokefellow." Although Cotton was remarried in April 1632 and thus could have been referring to his second wife, Sarah, by that time he was the subject of closer surveillance by the church authorities himself and went into hiding by early autumn 1632. Had Cotton been writing in 1632, it is likely he would have mentioned the difficulties he was encountering, but he does not. Moreover, since other letters from late 1630 speak of his weakness from his long illness with ague, the malaria that eventually took Elizabeth's life, and Cotton is said to have taken leave to recuperate at the earl of Lincoln's estate by February 1631,[2] it seems most likely that the letter is no later than late summer of 1630, but certainty in this case is unattainable.

This manuscript was restored in 1987 as part of an important reclamation project at the Boston Public Library involving the Cotton Papers. Its condition is much improved, as a comparison with the earlier microfilm reveals, but the paper is badly deteriorated, especially along the right margin, and contains numerous small holes and tears throughout. It consists of one sheet written on both sides in Cotton's characteristically dark black ink. Prince's occasional underlinings are omitted here.

Deare freind,

& brother in o*u*r blessed Savio*u*r, It is a continuall heavynes to my heart, the Restray[n]t w*hi*ch (I perceyve by yo*u*r l*ette*re) is putt vpon y[ou]. The lively,

& piercing, & powerfull Quickening, wherewith the heaven[l]y word of your Ministery was w[o]nt to awaken your People's hearts, how is it turned into a silent Deadnesse! The comfortable Sabbaths [whi]ch were wont to give Rest vnto your Peoples Soules, what Greife, || & Anguish of Heart doe they now yeild to all your well-|| Hearers! When wee say to seers, see not, & to Prophets, Prophesy not, doe wee not hereby cause the Holy One [of] Izra[el] t[o c]ease fro[m] vs? Yea is not this Iniquity, as a [b]reach ||[in the] High [w]all, ready to fall, whose breaking com[eth] [s]odainely vn||erably Isay 30. 10, to: 14.[3] I am m[o]re afraid of th[e] daunger which such Passages of Church-Officers threaten to our stat[e] then of all the Power, & malice of Fraunce, or Spayne. While[s]t the Lord our sheild is with vs, what could the Arme of flesh doe ag[ains]t vs?[4] but when w[e]e cause the Holy One of Izrael to Depa[rt] from vs, who shall save vs?[5] Horses, & ships, & men, & weapons of warre, are v[a]ine things for safety: neyther can they deliver any by their great streng[t]h. The Lord is the saviour of his Peop[le] & yet he it is, whose Presence wee grow weary of, whose word wee stoppe our Eares against,[6] & the mouthes of them that speake it, & w|| servants & Ministers, wee evill intreat, till there be noe Re||[.] The Lord be mercifull to vs, that wee perish not in o[ur] Iniqu[ity.] Mourne therefore for the Church of God (good Brother:) but mourn not for your self. [For unto you] it is given, not onely to beleive, [but] also to suffer for his || sake,[7] who loveth Purity, & s[peaks?] in his Ordinaunces. Y||[rejo]yce, & be gl[ad], when you see your selfe lye like a stone, ca[st] asi[d]e of the Builders, that you m[a]y more fully partake in [Fellow]ship with the Lord Jesus, who b[ein]g in like sort cast aside, [beca]me the Head-stone of the Corner.[8] Take [h]eede, you discourage n[o]t [your]selfe, nor be dismayed with sence|| s||e [suf]f[eri]ng, sin[ce y]ou know the Deservings of Christ [IV] become yours, & the Chastisements of our Peace are vpon Him.[9]

Commend me (with mine) to your good yokefellow: tell hir, she must now abound in thankfulnesse to God, & in Comfort to you, especially now when other outward Comforts fayle. If a freind love[th] at all times, & a brother be borne for Adversity:[10] how much more a Christian freind, a beloved sister, a faithfull wife?

Commend me also to your good neighbour, who was here with you. Helpe vs still with your Prayers: our Poore Desires are for you, vnto Him [who] holdeth the starres in his right hand,[11] & is able againe to sett before you an Open Doore.[12] Even He worke it for his [N]ame sake, & [for] the Comfort & safety of his poore Church. In Him I re[st,]

Partaker of your Greifes, & Hopes in Christ,

1. P. Thompson, *History of Boston,* 416.
2. Ibid.

3. Isa. 30:10–14: Isaiah is charging that the people of Israel "will not hear the law of the Lord": Which say to the seers, See not; and to the prophets, Prophesy not unto us right things, speak unto us smooth things, prophesy deceits: Get you out of the way, turn aside out of the path, cause the Holy One of Israel to cease from before us. Wherefore thus saith the Holy One of Israel, Because ye despise this word, and trust in oppression and perverseness, and stay thereon: Therefore this iniquity shall be to you as a breach ready to fall, swelling out in a high wall, whose breaking cometh suddenly at an instant. And he shall break it as the breaking of the potters' vessel that is broken in pieces; he shall not spare: so that there shall not be found in the bursting of it a sherd to take fire from the hearth, or to take water withal out of the pit.

4. See 2 Chron. 32:8.

5. See Isa. 30:12.

6. The language here is borrowed from scriptural passages about the silencing of two of God's prophets, Zechariah and Stephen; see Zech. 7:11 and Acts 7:57.

7. See Phil. 1:29. The phrase, "For unto you," is added from Philippians 1 because all of Cotton's wording immediately following a break in the paper at that point quotes that verse.

8. This language appears many times in the Bible. See, for instance, Psalm 118:22, Matt. 21:42, Mark 12:10, Luke 20:17, Acts 4:11, 1 Pet. 2:7.

9. See Isa. 53:5.

10. See Prov. 17:17.

11. See Rev. 1:16, 1:20, 2:1.

12. See Rev. 3:8.

John Cotton to [Colonel Sir Edward Harwood]

[Probably 1629–1631, but possibly 1624–1632]

ADfI. MS: MSA, CCXL, Hutchinson Papers, I, fol. 86

In L. Thompson, "Letters of John Cotton," 51–53

Sir Edward Harwood (1586?–1632), a Lincolnshire native, was a professional soldier admired for his military skills by both James I and Charles I, despite his Puritanism.[1] He had seen military duty in the Low Countries at least as early as 1616, by which time he had already been knighted. He had regular contact and correspondence with England's ambassador to The Hague, Sir Dudley Carleton. He took part in the ill-fated English expedition against Cádiz in 1625 under the duke of Buckingham, where he was in charge of the rear guard, leading to a safe and orderly retreat. Remembering his value at Cádiz, Buckingham lamented Harwood's absence in the disastrous 1627 English defeat at the Isle of Rhé, crying out, "Oh Ned Harwood, Ned Harwood, that I had had thee here."[2] Though we know he returned to England occasionally, as in late 1617 and early 1618, after the Cádiz expedition in early 1626, and again in 1630,[3] and doubtless on other occasions, at the time of this letter Harwood was apparently in the service of the queen of Bohemia in the Netherlands. He was one of four colonels commanding English troops in the Netherlands in fulfillment

PLATE 6. Colonel Sir Edward Harwood. Large oil painting (84 by 43¾ inches) by an unknown artist of the Anglo-Flemish School, early seventeenth century. The first owner of this portrait was Sir Horace Vere, commander of English forces in the Low Countries when Harwood served as one of the four English colonels there. Vere and his wife, Lady Mary, were Puritan sympathizers. The portrait of Harwood remained in the possession of the descendants into the twentieth century. *Published with the kind permission of Sotheby's, London*

of the terms of the Dutch Treaty of 1624.[4] He was killed in action at Maastricht in August 1632.

This letter is the second instance in the correspondence when Cotton has taken on the role of matchmaker (see Cotton to Hildersham, [Spring 1628?]). He also played a role in the marital fortunes (or misfortunes) of various other acquaintances; he assisted John Reyner in Plymouth and in unhappy cases served as counselor to a woman in Lincolnshire, a troubled minister in New England, and a layman in Massachusetts Bay (Cotton to John Reyner, Oct. 18, [1639]; Cotton to a "Beloved Sister," Nov. 12, 1628; Cotton to Stephen Bachiler, Mar. 9, 1641/2; Benjamin Keayne to Cotton, Mar. 12, 1646/7). Edward Harwood was the eldest of the five surviving children of William and Elizabeth Harwood.[5] His sister, Susan, had married one Richard Draper of Boston. Mary Draper, the subject of Cotton's benevolent interest here, was a daughter of that marriage.[6] It is uncertain whether Mary's marriage to Mr. Brett that is proposed by Cotton was allowed, but the surviving marriage records for Boston do not record such an event.[7]

The dating of the letter is somewhat uncertain. Cotton mentions his wife, probably meaning Elizabeth, who died in April 1631, though he remarried in April 1632, some four months before Harwood's death. Since Cotton says Mary Draper has "soiourn[ed] awhile w*it*h my wife," the former spouse seems the more likely referent. The most useful information for establishing the approximate date of the letter is genealogical data. The four children of Richard and Susannah Draper included Marie Draper, baptized October 14, 1604. Since Cotton suggests she will soon be past the best age for marrying, she was probably at least in her mid-twenties at the time of this letter, which would place it in approximately 1629. The period 1629–1631 seems most likely for this letter, but 1624–1632 is possible.

The manuscript is entirely in Cotton's own hand and is a draft with revisions from which a fair copy was made to send to Harwood. The MS was apparently Cotton's file copy. It is frayed at the top and bottom, cutting off most of Cotton's signature, and has a hole in the middle of the right margin, where paper is lost along a fold; parts of six lines suffer some loss of text at that point. The only appearance of Harwood's name is where the letter is endorsed on the verso in a later hand: "Mr Cotton to Edw. Harwood." The reference to the recipient's "warlike employments" and Cotton's military tropes reinforce this identity. A nineteenth-century transcription in the Massachusetts Historical Society provides some assistance with missing text; those readings are enclosed in braces.

Worthy S*i*r,

In *th*e middest of y*o*ur warlike employm*en*ts (w*hi*ch *th*e Lord goe on to p*ro*sper to his Churche's succo*u*r) give me leave, I pray you, to intreate yo*u*r consideration of a motion of peace. Yo*u*r niece Mary Draper (whom I heartily wish well vnto as for ~~your sake &~~ hir neerenesse to you, & to other freinds, so for hir soiourninge awhile w*it*h my wife) is desired in marryage by a yonge man ^(knowen to yo*u*r selfe, though not at all to me)^ a servant to yo*u*r Brother Mr George Harwood,[8] one Mr. Brett, ~~better knowen to yo*u*r selfe than me~~ & (as I heare) w*it*h *th*e consent of his freindes, & w*it*h some acceptaunce also of yo*u*r Niece, so farre as may stande w*it*h *th*e good likinge of yo*u*r selfe, & other freinds. If you conceyve *th*e match to[9] be meete for hir, I desire you to further it, both w*it*h yo*u*r owne helpinge hand (of whom she cheifely dependeth for ^guidance &^ maintenaunce:) as also w*it*h p*ro*curem*en*t of yo*u*r brothers acceptaunce of *th*e buisinesse. If she passe this flower of hir age vnmarryed, hir body is like to [deleted word] settle into ^distemper^ weakenesse, & hir spirit into vnseasonable sadnesse, & softnesse. The disioyntinge of affectionate yonge couples, leaveth ^often^ a snare vpon *the*m, & breedeth an vndisposednesse ^afterwards^ to kindly cleavinge vnto any other. I pray ^you^ therefore consider hir yeares, hir neerenesse to you, hir dependaunce on you, hir weakenesse, ^hir affection gone out,^ hir p*re*sent opportunity (as is reported to me) ~~of hir conveniently~~ helping hir selfe by *th*e match: & vnlesse yo*u*r selfe (who are better acquainted w*i*th both p*ar*tyes) see such vnmeete{nesse}[10] in it, as might dissuade you from yeildinge to *the*m, I pray you then e{xercise yo*u*r}[11] fatherly love & care of hir, in ^answeringe^ [one or two words deleted] ~~forwarding among~~[?]|| w*i*th yo*u*r acceptaunce & fartheraunce. But if you conceyve this motion || I pray, thinke timely of some other, whom you shall thinke more suita[ble to hi]r[12] best good. I should be glad to see hir setled in some good condition, w*hic*h *th*e Lord reach out vnto hir in his due time.

And now (good S*i*r,) let me take my leave, in stirringe you vp to goe on still to ~~vse~~ *tha*t ^rich Talent of^ wisedome & courage w*hic*h you have receyved of *th*e Lord, to his best advantage, in fightinge his battayles, & cuttinge out a way for his Churches peace. I know not what times God hath reserved for his Church to meete w*i*thall (O*u*r sinnes, ~~I know~~ ^it is confessed^, & the sinnes of *th*e Times, deserve ill:) but yet sure, *th*e ^wayes^ ~~lives~~ of *th*e Enemyes are not more holy, their cause not so iust, their consciences not so peaceable, their Religion not so gratious, their lives not so righteous, their deathes not so comfortable. The Lord therefore guide you w*i*th ^the counsayle of^ his owne wisedome, & encourage you w*i*th *th*e ^strength^ ~~wisdome~~ of his owne ^right^ ~~strength~~ arme. The Lord Jesus hath overcome Hell, & Death, & *th*e Devill for vs: Onely He helpe vs to deny o*u*r selves, & ^to^ cleave to Him, *tha*t in his victory you may goe forth conqueringe to overcome. / So w*i*th my owne, & wives due respect of hono*u*r to you; I take my leave, & rest

Yo*u*r wo*rshi*ps in Chri*sti*an service & love,

J C[13]

1. A letter of June 8, 1623, from Lady Carleton to Sir Dudley Carleton remarked that "Sir Edw. Harwood would marry Lady Smith, if she were Puritan enough." He never married. Great Britain, Public Record Office, *Calendar of State Papers,* Domestic Series, *Of the Reign of James I, 1619–1623,* ed. Mary Anne Elizabeth Greene (London, 1858), 600.

2. Hugh Pe[ter], "The Life and Death of Collonell *Harwood,*" in *The Advice of That Worthy Commander, Sir Ed: Harwood, Collonell* (London, 1642), sig B2. This biographical sketch was reprinted in *The Harleian Miscellany,* V (London, 1810), 198–201. The book is prefaced by an elegiac poem with six lines in Latin and twelve in English by the subject's "Nephew," *"M. Draper,"* thus a brother to Mary, who is the subject of this letter.

3. On February 23, 1618, Harwood, already in England, asked Ambassador Lord Carleton for an extension of his leave of absence (*Cal. State Papers,* Dom. Ser., *James I, 1611–1618,* ed. Greene [London, 1858], 523). For his presence in England on January 3, 1626, see *Of the Reign of Charles I,*

1625, 1626, ed. John Bruce (London, 1858), 214. He was released from other duties to participate in the Cádiz expedition from at least October 1625, when the expedition sailed. More than four years later John Barrington, writing to his mother, Lady Barrington, from London on April 28, 1630, noted that he did "this day . . . confer with Sir Edward Horwood," who left for the Continent within the week, as Barrington recorded in another letter nine days later, May 7, 1630 (Arthur Searle, ed., *Barrington Family Letters, 1628–1632,* Camden Society, 4th Ser., XXVIII [London, 1983], 146, 147–148). I am grateful to my colleague, Johann Sommerville, for assistance in tracing Harwood's movements in England and the Netherlands.

4. Raymond Phineas Stearns writes: "The British soldiers of the 'four standing Colonels in the Low Countries' consisted of some sixty-eight companies. . . . Nearly every major town contained a group of British people" who formed English churches which "almost without exception . . . were puritanically inclined." *The Strenuous Puritan: Hugh Peter, 1598–1660* (Urbana, Ill., 1954), 53, 54.

5. The available information on the Harwood family during this period is somewhat contradictory. While *Lincolnshire Pedigrees* lists five siblings of Edward and Susan's generation, it indicates Edward is the eldest. But the baptismal records of the parish of Thurlby, near Bourn, Lincolnshire, the Harwoods' home, suggest that Susan was baptized January 15, 1574/5, making her the oldest by a full ten years of the seven children of William and Elizabeth Greenham Harwood whose baptisms are listed. The picture is confused, however, by the appearance of a second Susan's baptism in "about 1594" and by the record of Edward's baptism on December 30, 1597, after the baptisms of all of his siblings, including his brother George, whose daughter's marital fate is being left up to Edward in the present letter. A. R. Maddison, ed., *Lincolnshire Pedigrees* (London, 1902–1906), II, 458.

6. Although I have not found a record of the marriage of Susan Harwood and Richard Draper (who was from Boston), the Boston records of births and christenings, 1557–1834, show four baptisms of children of "Richarde Draper": Anna (Jan. 23, 1597), Richarde (May 1, 1602), Marie (Oct. 14, 1604), and Mathewe (Sept. 27, 1607). These dates would be consistent with the mother's birth in 1574/5 and marriage in her early twenties, if not sooner. These records were consulted in the genealogical files of the Church of Latter-Day Saints at the Stake Family History Center, Madison, Wis. I am also grateful for assistance by Lynda Hotchkiss, Genealogist at the Lincolnshire Archives of Licolnshire County Council.

7. Other records show that one Mary Draper married a Christopher Shackleton in Heptonstall, Yorkshire, on December 21, 1630, but whether she was Mary Draper, niece of Col. Sir Edward Harwood, is unknown (Thomas Waln-Morgan Draper, *The Drapers in America . . .* [New York, 1892], 5).

8. George Harwood, a London haberdasher and younger brother of Edward, served as treasurer of the Massachusetts Bay Company from May 1628 to September 1634, though he did not emigrate. Rose-Troup, *John White,* 111–113, 189–191, 248–249.

9. The word to is written over another word.

10. The Massachusetts Historical Society's transcription shows this word as vnmeetednesse. The missing text here and subsequently results from loss of paper at the center of the right margin.

11. The Massachusetts Historical Society's transcription includes brackets at this point, so the text here was already lost at the time the transcription was made. The text in braces therefore is simply an earlier reader's reasonable conjecture.

12. The Massachusetts Historical Society transcription has suita[ble for hir].

13. The bottom edge of the paper is frayed, leaving only the top half of these two letters in the signature, though, since this is a draft, Cotton might only have signed his initials.

John Cotton to Nathaniel Rogers

March 9, 1631/2

Published: Cotton Mather, "*Eulogius:* The Life of Mr. Nathaniel Rogers," in *Magnalia Christi Americana* . . . (London, 1702), book III, 107; A. W. M'Clure, *The Life of John Cotton* (Boston, 1846), 278–279. This fragment is also printed in Brook, *Lives of the Puritans,* III, 240, where the phrasing is changed in several instances. Since Brook cites Mather's *Magnalia* as his source for the text, his version appears to be simply a rather free rendering of Mather's text rather than an independent reading of the manuscript, which, in any case, is now lost. Mather appears to have been the only editor to have had the manuscript in hand; his is therefore the source text here.

The second of only two brief fragments surviving from Cotton's correspondence with Rogers, this letter, written during a period of Cotton's own extended illness, addresses the matter of Rogers's poor health. Cotton Mather later recalled that Rogers "was much troubled with Spitting of *Blood*" and that "he was also subject unto the *Flatus Hypocondriacus,* even from his *Youth;* wherewith when he was first surprized, he thought himself a *dying Man;* but a good Physician, and a long Experience, convinced him, that it was a more *Chronical* Distemper."[1] Mather adds that Rogers was "under the early Discouragements of this Distemper" when Cotton wrote this letter.

I bless the Lord with you, who supporteth your *feeble Body,* to do him Service, and mean while perfecteth the *Power* of his Grace in your *Weakness.* You know who said it, *Unmortified Strength posteth hard to Hell, but sanctified Weakness creepeth fast to Heaven.* Let not your *Spirit* faint, tho' your *Body* do. Your *Soul* is precious in God's sight; your *Hairs are numbred,*[2] and the number and measure of your *fainting Fits,* and wearisome Nights, are weighed and limited by his Hand, who hath given you his Lord Jesus Christ, to *take upon him your Infirmities,* and *bear your Sicknesses.*[3]

1. Mather, *Magnalia Christi Americana* (1702), book III, 107. For a discussion of Rogers's affliction published in 1621 by an authority of his own generation, see Robert Burton, *The Anatomy of Melancholy,* ed. Thomas C. Faulkner, Nicholas K. Kiessling, and Rhonda L. Blair (Oxford,

1989), part 1, sect. 2, memb. 5, subsect. 4, "Causes of Hypocondriacall or Windie Melancholy," also called "flatuous Melancholy," 378.

2. Cotton is paraphrasing two biblical passages, both of which are part of Jesus' instructions to his disciples: Matt. 10:28–30: And fear not them which kill the body, but are not able to kill the soul: but rather fear him which is able to destroy both soul and body in hell. Are not two sparrows sold for a farthing? and one of them shall not fall on the ground without your Father. But the very hairs of your head are all numbered. Luke 12:4–7: And I say unto you my friends, Be not afraid of them that kill the body, and after that have no more that they can do. But I will forewarn you whom ye shall fear: Fear him, which after he hath killed hath power to cast into hell; yea, I say unto you, Fear him. Are not five sparrows sold for two farthings, and not one of them is forgotten before God? But even the very hairs of your head are all numbered.

3. Matt. 8:16–17: When the even was come, they brought unto him many that were possessed with devils: and he cast out the spirits with his word, and healed all that were sick: That it might be fulfilled which was spoken by Esaias the prophet, saying Himself took our infirmities, and bare our sicknesses.

William Coddington to John Cotton

June 4, 1632

Published: Hutchinson, *History,* I, 24; Emily Coddington Williams, *William Coddington of Rhode Island: A Sketch* (Newport, R.I., 1941), 10; Young, *Chronicles of the First Planters,* 337 (partial printing)

This letter survives only in the single-sentence paragraph printed by Hutchinson. In this, as in other instances, he had access to the manuscript, which has subsequently been lost. It verifies the existence of a friendship between Cotton and Coddington before they emigrated to New England. At this point, Coddington had been in New England and had returned to England, one of those whom Hutchinson says "went over [to England] to fetch their families and returned with them" while others were quickly discouraged and returned permanently to England.[1] In 1632 Cotton had not yet emigrated. Coddington's enthusiasm for the place, clearly indicated in this fragment, might have encouraged Cotton to think about migration. Coddington became a magistrate in Massachusetts Bay but would later be among those who left the colony in reaction to the Antinomian controversy. He settled in quickly at Aquidneck, however, where he became a magistrate and, later, governor.

The text is that of the 1764 edition of Hutchinson. Lawrence Shaw Mayo's 1936 edition of that work and Emily Coddington Williams both modernize the punctuation, as does Young, who also omits the final sixteen words. In fact, to judge from

Coddington's unorthodox spelling in his later surviving letters, it would appear that Hutchinson probably standardized the spelling in printing this fragment.

I am I thank God in bodily health yet not enjoying that freedom of spirit, being withheld from that place which my soul desireth and my heart earnestly worketh after, neither I think shall I see it till towards the next spring, my wife being with child and all her friends unwilling she should go in that condition.[2]

1. Thomas Hutchinson, *The History of the Colony and Province of Massachusetts-Bay,* ed. Lawrence Shaw Mayo (Cambridge, Mass., 1936), I, 23.

2. Coddington's first wife had died, and in 1632, on his return trip to England, he married Mary Mosely, of Owsden, Bury St. Edmunds, Suffolk. They returned to New England almost a year after this letter was written (Williams, *William Coddington of Rhode Island,* 9–10). On Coddington, see also Anderson, *Great Migration,* 395–401.

John Cotton to Sarah Hawkred Story Cotton

October 3, 1632

ALS. MS: BPL, Ms. Am. 1502, pt. 1, no. 1

Published: Young, *Chronicles of the First Planters,* 432–433; MHS, *Colls.,* 4th Ser., VIII (1868), 543–544

In L. Thompson, "Letters of John Cotton," 71–72

The only surviving Cotton letter to a member of his immediate family, this has special value and significance for its reference to conditions suffered by Cotton during the period when he was forced into hiding and before his resignation from his Boston vicarage a few months later. Sarah Story was Cotton's second wife. In July 1613, he had married Elizabeth Horrocks, sister of James Horrocks, whom Cotton Mather called "a famous minister in *Lancashire.*"[1] They had been married almost eighteen years, without children, when she died in April 1631.[2] Cotton's marriage to Sarah Story, "a vertuous widow, very dear to his former wife,"[3] took place April 25, 1632. This letter, from Cotton to his "Sweete Heart," is poignant in his tender expression of regret in his opening paragraph that husband and wife must be separated so soon after their marriage. His real awareness of personal danger is evident in various ways, especially in his unwillingness to mention details of his whereabouts or to have his wife mention his letter to "many other freinds" in Boston. Secrecy was the order of the day.

The page has stitch holes on the left, as if it had been sewn into a letter book (by

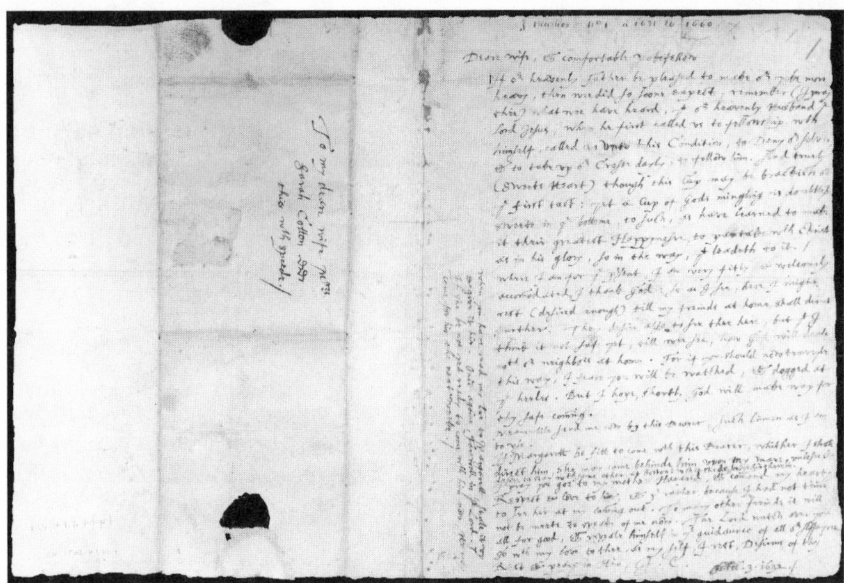

PLATE 7. Cotton to Mistress Sarah Hawkred Story Cotton, October 3, 1632. Written while Cotton was in hiding and just five and a half months after their marriage. The letter is entirely in Cotton's own hand, except for the line across the top, which is Thomas Prince's handwriting. *Boston Public Library Ms. Am. 1502, I, no. 1. Courtesy of the Trustees of the Boston Public Library*

Sarah Cotton?). Prince's note at the top of the first recto, "I. Mather no 1 a 1631 to 1660," suggests that it had been in Increase Mather's papers. Addressed on back of a second sheet in Cotton's hand:

> To my deare wife M*ist*res*s* / Sarah Cotton
> del*iver*/ this w*i*th speede. /

Deare wife, & comfortable yokefellow

If o*u*r heavenly Father be pleased to make o*u*r yoke more heavy, then wee did so soone expect, remember (I pray thee) what wee have heard, *tha*t o*u*r heavenly Husband *th*e Lord Jesus, when he first called vs to fellowship w*i*th himself, called vs vnto this Condition, to Deny o*u*rselves, & to take vp o*u*r Crosse dayly, to follow him. And truely (Sweete Heart) though this Cup may be brackish at *th*e first tast: yet a Cup of Gods mingling is doubtless sweete in *th*e bottome, to such, as have learned to make it their greatest Happynesse, to partake w*i*th Christ as in his glory, so in the way, *tha*t leadeth to it. /

Where I am for the p*re*sent, I am very fitly & welcomely accom*m*odated, I thank God: so as I see, here I might rest (desired enough) till my freinds at home shall direct further. They desire also to see thee here, but *tha*t I think it not safe yet, till wee see, how God will deale *wi*th *ou*r neighbo*u*rs at home. For if you should now traveyle this way, I feare you will be watched, & dogged at *th*e heeles. But I hope, shortly God will make way for thy safe com*m*ing.[4]

Meanewhile send me now by this Bearer, such linnen as I am to vse.

If Margarett[5] be fitt to come *wi*th this Bearer, whither I shall direct him, she may come behinde him vpon my mare*, ^vnlesse she desire to stay *wi*th some other, at Boston: *whi*ch if she do, helpe hir therein.^

I pray you goe to my mother Haucred,[6] & com*m*end my hearty Respect & love to hir; & *th*e rather, because I had not time to see hir at my com*m*ing out. To many other freinds it will not be meete to speake of me now. The Lord watch over you all for good, & reveale himself in *th*e guidaunce of all *ou*r Affayres.

So *wi*th my love to thee, as my self, I rest, Desirous of thy Rest & peace in Him, J.C.

Octob. 3. 1632./

*When you have read my l*ett*re to Margarett, seale it vp & give it hir.[7] Once againe, Farewell in *th*e Lord. If she be not yet ready to come *wi*th him now, He may come for hir the next weeke. /

1. Mather, *Magnalia,* I, 237.

2. The Boston *Corporation Records* indicate a payment on November 1, 1631, to Mr. Mayor for £7 pounds, 10 shillings, to repay him for expenses in connection with Mrs. Cotton's funeral. The exact date of the funeral is not recorded. See discussion of these details in P. Thompson, *History of Boston,* 415, 416.

3. Mather, *Magnalia,* I, 240.

4. Sarah did join him sometime within the next six weeks. Cotton Mather's biography of his grandfather Cotton notes that his voyage with her to New England took seven weeks, ending on September 3, 1633. Their first child, aptly named Seaborn, arrived after four weeks at sea, August 12, 1633. Conception would therefore have been in mid-November 1632, or just five to six weeks after Cotton wrote this letter. The urgency of the need to leave England is demonstrated in the couple's willingness to put to sea with Sarah Cotton eight months pregnant. Savage, *Genealogical Dictionary,* I, 462.

5. Margaret was apparently a servant who had lived in Cotton's house.

6. Sarah's stepmother, Elizabeth Hawkred (or Haucred, Hawkridge). Sarah's parents were Anthony and Isabel Dowse Hawkred. Isabel had died in June 1614, after which Anthony married Elizabeth Ayscough in 1615. LaVerne C. Cooley, *A Short Biography of the Rev. John Cotton of Boston and a Cotton Genealogy of His Descendants* (Batavia, N.Y., 1945), 14.

Alexander Young, in printing this letter, misread Haucred as Havered and mistakenly tried to connect the name to the family of Cotton's first wife, the Horrockses.

7. He refers to an enclosure addressed to Margaret, probably requesting her attendance on him. Cotton wants Sarah to know the contents before it is delivered to Margaret. This footnote is inserted vertically, in four lines along the lowest part of the left margin.

Thomas Goodwin to John Cotton

[Spring 1633?]

Published: John Cotton, *The Way of Congregational Churches Cleared: In Two Treatises* (London, 1648), 24; Ziff, *Cotton on the Churches,* 204

In answering Robert Baillie's *Dissuasive from the Errours of the Time* (1645), which cites Thomas Edwards's attacks on the Independents as one of Baillie's chief sources of damning evidence against Cotton,[1] Cotton gives a little information about his contacts with Thomas Goodwin and John Davenport shortly before his departure for New England. Edwards had said Cotton was "a misleader" of his two colleagues in persuading them to desist from the ceremonies in episcopal worship. Cotton replied that they were not "misled by me, [but] led by the Spirit and Word of Grace in their own judgments and consciences. It is true, Mr. *Davenport,* Mr. *Goodwin,* with some other godly Brethren had some conference with me at *London,* about the cause of my sufferings, and of my purpose to leave the Land; which they said, they desired the rather, because they did not look at mee as a passionate man, though the Disswader [Baillie] (who knoweth me not) be pleased so to represent me to the world. . . . And upon their motion two Points were chiefly debated: 1. Touching the limitation of Church-power, to matters of commandement, not of indifferency. . . . The 2. touching the office of Bishops, whether the Scripture Bishops bee appointed to rule a Diocesse, or a particular Congregation."[2] He continued, indicating that "presently after, I received Letters from Mr. *Goodwin,* (and as I take it, before I left *England*) signifying, that":[3]

as in our former conferences, wee had debated much of the negative part of the 2. Commandement, so [I have] since meditated much, and seriously of the affirmative part of it, the positive institutions of Gods Divine Worship in opposition to humane inventions.[4]

1. Baillie's source is Thomas Edwards, *Antapologia* . . . (London, 1644).

2. Cotton, *The Way of Congregational Churches Cleared,* 24.

3. The authority for the following as a fragmentary quotation from an actual letter is Cotton's own use of quotation marks in the left margin—the standard printing convention of the day for marking quotations—indicating that he was quoting directly from a letter still in his possession. Where the present text has "[I have] since," Cotton wrote "hee had since" to fit the quotation in to his narrative. It should be noted that Ziff's modern printing of *The Way* (in *Cotton on the Churches*) omits the quotation marks altogether.

4. The second commandment as recorded in Exod. 20:4–6: Thou shalt not make unto thee any graven image, or any likeness of any thing that is in heaven above, or that is in the earth beneath, or that is in the water under the earth: Thou shalt not bow down thyself to them: for I

the Lord thy God am a jealous God, visiting the iniquity of the fathers upon the children unto the third and fourth generation of them that hate me; And shewing mercy unto thousands of them that love me, and keep my commandments.

"The affirmative part of it" is obviously the concluding clause ("And shewing mercy . . .").

Thomas Hooker to John Cotton

[About April 1633]

Published: Mather, *Johannes,* 20–21; Mather, *Magnalia Christi Americana* . . . (London, 1702), book III, 62; G. H. Williams et al., *Thomas Hooker,* 297–298

Thomas Hooker had fled from the summons of Bishop Laud in the spring of 1631, embarking for Holland, where he had been invited to preach at the English church in Amsterdam's Begijnhof. Failing to reach agreement with the incumbent minister there, John Paget, on matters of church polity—Hooker being too pronounced a congregationalist—he went south to Delft, where he joined the Scottish minister, John Forbes, at the Prinsenhof church. He is also believed to have spent at least part of the spring and perhaps early summer of 1633 in Rotterdam, where William Ames was living.[1] George H. Williams has argued that this letter was written about April 1633, just three months before Hooker and Cotton embarked on the same ship, the *Griffin,* from the Downs in early July, arriving in Boston Harbor on September 3. The letter from which Cotton Mather quoted this fragment was an important document in the developing plans of Cotton and Hooker alike to establish their ministries away from England.

Williams's edition modernizes the capitalization and occasionally the punctuation. Even though Cotton Mather himself altered capitalization and added italics, the present text follows Mather's earliest printing (1695). The differences from Williams's edition are all in punctuation, spelling, and capitalization.

In introducing his quotation from the letter, Mather stated, "I have at this time in my Hands, his Letter from *Rotterdam* to Mr. *Cotton,* wherein are these words:"

The State of these Provinces to my weak eye, seems wonderfully ticklish and miserable. For the better part, *Heart-Religion,* They content themselves with very Forms, tho' much Blemished; but the Power of Godliness, for ought I can see or hear, they know not; and if it were thoroughly pressed, I fear least it will be fiercely opposed. My Ague yet holds me; the wayes of Gods Providence, wherein He has walked towards me, in this long time of my Sickness, and wherein I have drawn forth many wearyish Hours, under His Almighty Hand (Blessed be His Name) together with Pursuits and Banishment, which have waited upon me, as one Wave follows another, have driven me to an Amazement: His Paths being too secret and past finding out by such an Ignorant, Worthless Worm as my self. I have Looked over my Heart and Life, according to my measure; aimed and guessed as well as I could: and Entreated His Majesty to make known His Mind, wherein I missed; and yet methinks I cannot spell out readily the Purpose of His Proceedings; which I confess have been wonderful in Miseries, and more than wonderful in Mercies to me and mine.

1. On Hooker's years in Holland, see George H. Williams, "The Life of Thomas Hooker in England and Holland, 1586–1633," in G. H. Williams et al., *Thomas Hooker,* 22–35; Frank Shuffelton, *Thomas Hooker, 1586–1647* (Princeton, N.J., 1977), 121–158; Sargent Bush, Jr., *The Writings of Thomas Hooker: Spiritual Adventure in Two Worlds* (Madison, Wis., 1980), 56–73.

John Cotton to John Williams, Bishop of Lincoln

May 7, 1633

Published: Hutchinson, *Collection,* 249–251 (reprinted, with minor changes, in *The Hutchinson Papers,* Prince Society, Publications [Albany, N.Y., 1865], I, 280–282); Young, *Chronicles of the First Planters,* 434–437; P. Thompson, *History of Boston,* 417–418

In L. Thompson, "Letters of John Cotton," 73–76

This letter, in which Cotton resigns his post of nearly twenty-one years as vicar of St. Botolph's Church, Boston, was apparently sent to the bishop of Lincoln at his residence at Buckden in Huntingdonshire. The resignation was not formally accepted for another two months, by which time Cotton was either safely on board the *Griffin* bound for New England, or about to be. Although the records of the Corporation of Boston for July 22, 1633, report that Cotton submitted his resignation on July 8 and that the "lord Bishop did the same day, at his house in the College of Westminster, accept of the same resignation," the date of Cotton's letter suggests a longer interval, perhaps purposely allowed by Bishop Williams to give Cotton some time to flee. Once the resignation was accepted, the mayor and burgesses of Boston quickly recommended Sarah Cotton's cousin, Anthony Tuckney, then the mayor's chaplain of Boston, to be his successor as vicar.[1]

The three published versions of the letter are all slightly different, though it seems likely that only Hutchinson had access to the manuscript. Thompson remains truer to the spellings recorded by Hutchinson, but he omits one long sentence (which he indicates with elipses) and a few other phrases in the first paragraph, whereas Young includes the full text but modernizes and Americanizes the spellings and punctuation throughout. Hutchinson's 1769 edition is preferred, therefore, as being closest to Cotton's now lost holograph letter. Hutchinson heads the letter with Cotton's address block:

> To the right reverend and my very honourable good Lord, John Lord Bishop of Lincoln, at his pallace in Buckden,[2] present these.

My very good Lord,

It is now above twenty yeares agoe, since by the goodnes of God and (for a good part of this time) by your Lordships lawfull favour, I have enjoyed the happines to minister to the church of God at Boston, a remote corner of your Lordships diocesse. What I have done there, all this while, and how I have spent my time and course, I must ere long give account to the great shepherd of the sheep, the bishop of our soules. Meane while, give me leave to make your Lordship this short account: The bent of my course hath been (according to my weake measure) to make and keep a 3 fold christian concord amongst the people; between God and their conscience; between true hearted loyaltie and christian liberty; between the fear of God and the love of one another. That wherein I have most seemed to your Lordship to fayle (to witt in not discerning christian liberty to practise some commands of authority, in some circumstances) I doe humbly thanke your Lordship, and freely acknowledge, your Lordship hath not been wanting freely and often to admonish me thereof, and that with such wisdom and gravity, and with such well tempered authority and mildness, that I profess unfeynedly noe outward respect in the world could have deteyned me from requesting your Lordships favour with ready subjection to your Lorships counsell, that I might have prolonged myne owne peace and your Lordships favour together, but so it is (my good Lord) though I doe unfeynedly and deservedly honour your Lordship, and highly esteem many hundreths of other reverend divines, great lights of the church (in comparison of whom what am I poore sparke?) who doubt not of their liberty in those matters; yet to this day (I speake in the simplicity of my heart) I can only follow your Lordship with observance, and them with reverence, but not with that plerophory of fayth in these thinges which in such cases the apostle requireth, Rom. 14.5.[3] Your Lordship well knoweth it is both the apostles and prophets principle (and it holdeth in every righteous man from the meanest to the greatest) *Justus ex fide suâ vivit, non alienâ,*[4] and therefore, howsoever I doe highly prize and much preferre other mens judgment and learning, and wisdom, and piety, yet in thinges pertaining to God and his worship, still, I must (as I ought) live by mine own fayth, not theirs. Nevertheless, where I cannot yeeld obedience of fayth, I am willing to yeeld patience of hope.

And now, my good lord, I see the Lord who began a yeare or two agoe to suspend (after a sort) my ministry from that place by a long and soare sickness (the dregs whereof still hang about me) doth now putt a further necessity upon me, wholly to lay down my ministry there, and freely to resigne my place into your Lordships hands. For I see neither my bodily health, nor the peace of the church will now stand with my continuance there. I doe now therefore humbly crave this last favour at your Lordships hand, to accept my place as voyd, and to admitt thereto such a successor as your Lordship shall finde fitt, and the patron (which is the corporation of Boston) shall present to you therefor. The congregation is great, and the church duetyes many, and those, many times, requiring close attendance, and I would be very loth the service of God, or the helpe of the people should be in any sort neglected by my long discontinuance.

What though this resignation of my place into your Lordships hands may be defective in some forme of law; yet I trust your Lordship will never forgett the auncient moderation and æquity of that honourable and high court of chauncery, whereunto your Lordship was advanced,[5] to temper the rigour of legall justice, to the relief of many distressed. Never (I thinke) came there any cause before your Lordship more distressed, nor more justly craving christian æquity.

Now the Lord of heaven and earth soe guide and keep and blesse your Lordship on earth, that he may delight to crown your Lordship with honour in heaven, at the end of your dayes, through Jesus Christ. Thus at once commending my humble sute and late vicarage, and the comfort of the whole congregation to your Lordships honourable favour and integrity, I humbly take leave and rest

A bounden suppliant to your Lordship and for you,

May 7. 1633. J. C.

1. James Savage quoted excerpts from the Municipal Records of Boston regarding actions taken at the meeting of mayor, aldermen, and Common Council on July 22, 1633, including the acceptance of Cotton's resignation; see "Gleanings for New England History," MHS, *Colls.*, 3d Ser., VIII (1843), 343–344. See also Nicholas Hoppin, "The Rev. John Cotton, A.M., Vicar of Old Boston," *Church Monthly*, V (January 1863), 49–50.

2. Hutchinson misread this word as Kurkden, which both Pishey Thompson and Alexander Young corrected to Buckden, the name of the bishop of Lincoln's residence in Huntingdonshire.

3. Rom. 14:5: One man esteemeth one day above another: another esteemeth every day alike. Let every man be fully persuaded in his own mind.

4. *Justus ex fide suâ vivit, non alienâ:* The just man lives by his own faith, not another's.

5. Cotton refers to Williams's service as lord keeper of the great seal from 1621 to 1625, a post giving him authority over the courts of chancery. Given the language used by Cotton here,

S. R. Gardiner's comment in his *DNB* biography of Williams is germane: "In times when the court of chancery demanded the shrewdness which would qualify a judge to administer equity on general principles, it would probably have been difficult to make a better choice" (quoted in Barrie Williams, *The Work of Archbishop John Williams* . . . [Appleford, Eng., 1980], 37).

John Cotton to a Minister in England

December 3, 1634

ALS. MS: MSA, CCXL, Hutchinson Papers, I, fols. 18, 18a

Published: Hutchinson, *Collection,* 54–58; Young, *Chronicles of the First Planters,* 438–444; *Hutchinson Papers,* Prince Society, Publications (Albany, N.Y., 1865), I, 60–65; Emerson, *Letters,* 127–130

In L. Thompson, "Letters of John Cotton," 77–82

A year and a half after leaving England, Cotton was challenged by a minister there to justify his and Thomas Hooker's emigration. His reply, the first surviving letter postdating his departure from England, seems to suggest that the request expressed skepticism about the wisdom or validity of a minister's leaving England and thus escaping accountability and punishment from the authorities when others remained behind to face such consequences. The reply is a justly famous one, defending the values on which the emigrants usually based their departures, a desire for liberty to worship in the purity of the ordinances always being uppermost. Cotton would again state some of the points he makes in this letter when writing—probably in the winter of 1646–1647—a preface to John Norton's *Responsio ad totam quaestionum syllogen* . . . [*Answer to the Whole Set of Questions of the Celebrated Mr. William Apollonius, Pastor of the Church of Middelburg*] (London, 1648). He especially stressed the fact that he and other emigré ministers had sought the counsel both of their congregations and of their fellow ministers before finally deciding not to stay to face a church trial.[1]

The identity of the addressee remains a mystery. Alexander Young speculated that it was "perhaps John Davenport, Richard Mather, or Thomas Shepard," and Everett Emerson also suggests that it was "perhaps John Davenport." All three of these men were considering or had already decided on emigration to New England, but their whereabouts at this time suggest that none seems likely to have been Cotton's correspondent. In December 1634 Davenport had been in the Netherlands for about a year. Thomas Shepard was spending the winter of 1634–1635 in Bastwick, Norfolk, having already decided to emigrate.[2] Richard Mather, who also sailed for New England in the spring of 1635 and was at this time apparently thinking about that decision, was still at Toxteth in Lancashire, although he had been suspended from his ministry there. We know that letters from both Cotton and Hooker played a part in Mather's decision, so it is possible that this letter was seen by Mather.[3] But it is unlikely that he was the intended recipient, since the minister in question appears to have been in or near Northamptonshire, to judge from the Midlands locations of the neighbors and acquaintances to whom Cotton sends greetings at the close of the letter.

Because the manuscript has lost some paper and ink since first being edited a century and a half ago, the Hutchinson and Young editions provide occasional details that can no longer be deciphered in the manuscript. At such points, except where otherwise noted, Hutchinson's readings, being earlier, are adopted and enclosed in braces. The manuscript is in the hand of an amanuensis, with the exception of the final two lines, which include only the date lines and Cotton's complimentary close with his signature, all in Cotton's hand.

Reverend & Beloved Brother in o*u*r blessed Savio*u*r,

That w*hich* you observe touchinge the wonderfull goodnesse of the L*or*d to my wife, & childe in the midst of deepe dangers,[4] I desire never to forgett it, but to walke (as the L*or*d shall be pleased to helpe me) accordinge to that aboundant faithfullnesse of his to one soe vndeserving, all my dayes. Helpe me with your faythfull prayers soe to doe: That as by the prayers of your selfe, & other Bretheren, I acknowledge the former mercy to have bene graunted me, soe by the same a faithfull, & fruitfull vse of it may be graunted to me likewise; otherwise I may say it w*i*th shame, I see a frame of spirit in my selfe ready to turne every grace of god into vnprofitablenesse, yea & forgettfullnes of the most high god, the god of our salvation; Howsoever god dealt otherwise with my Cosigne Tuckney[5] (it might give vnto some whom it nearly concerned, a seasonable Advertism*ent*) yett I am p*er*swaded it was in much faithfullnes to hir, that god tooke hir away to p*r*event the disquietnes, & discouragem*ent* of hir spirit, w*hich* the evills ensueinge, evills Hasteninge vpon the Towne would otherwise have brought vpon hir; The L*or*d is wise, & gratious, & knoweth how to deliver his, out of the Houre of Temptation; blessed for ever be his name in *Chr*ist.

The Quæstions you demaund, I had rather Answer by worde of mouth, then by l*ette*re yett I will not refuse to give you account of my Brother Hookers Remoovall, & mine owne, seinge you require a Reason thereof from vs bothe; we bothe of vs concurre in a 3 fold ground of our removeall. 1. god haveinge shutt a dore ag*ains*t both of vs fro*m* ministringe to him, & his people in our wonted congregations, & callinge vs by a Remnant of our people, & by others of this Countrye to Minister to them here, & openinge a dore to vs this way, who are we that we should strive ag*ains*t god & refuse to follow the concurrence of his ordinance, & providence together, callinge vs forth to Minister here. If we may & ought to follow gods callinge 3 hundered myles, why not 3 thousand? 2. O*u*r Savio*u*rs warrant is {clear and strong (as we} conceyve [it])[6] in o*u*r case, that when we are dist{ressed in our} course in one country (ne q*ui*d dicam gravius)[7] we should flee {to} ano{ther.} To choose rather to bear wittnes to the truth ~~rather~~ by imprisonm*en*t t{han} by Banishm*en*t, is indeede sometimes gods way, but not in case men have ability of body, & opportunity to remoove, & noe necessary Engagm*en*t for to stay. Whilst Peter was yong, he might gird himselfe, & goe wither he would Joh: 21: 18.[8] but when he was old, & vnfitt for traveyle, then indeed god called him, rather to suffer himselfe to be girt of others, & led along to Prison, & to death. Nevertheles in this point I conferred with the ch{efe} of our people, & offered them to beare wittnesse to the trueth I had Preached, & practised amongst them even vnto bonds, if they conceyved it mighte be any confirmation to their fayth, & patience, but they diswaded me that course, as thinkeinge it better for themselves, & for me, & for *th*e Church of god, to with drawe my selfe fro*m* the p*r*esent storme, & to Minister in this countrye to such of their towne as they had sent before hither, and such others as were w{il}linge to goe alonge with me, or to followe after me; the most of the[m] choosinge rather to dwell in the T[9]|| there. What service my selfe, o[r] Brother Hooker {m}ighte doe {to} o*u*r {people} or other bretheren, in Prison (especially in close Prison w*hich* was feared)[10] I suppose, we bothe of vs (by gods helpe) doe the same, & much more, and with more freedome fro*m* hence, as occassion is offered: Besides all o*u*r other service to the people here, w*hich* yett is enough, & more then enough to fill both our handes, yea & the hands of many Bretheren moe, such as your selfe, should god be pleased to make way for your comfortable passage to vs. To have tarryed in England for the end you mention, to appeare in defence of *tha*t cause for w*hich* we were Quæstioned, had bene (as we conceyve it in our case) to {l}imitt wittnessebearinge to the cause (w*hich* may [be] done more wayes then one) to one onely way, & *tha*t such away, as we doe not see god callinge vs vnto. Did not Paul bear wittnesse ag*ain*st the Leviticall {cerem}onyes, & yett choose rather to depart quickly out of Hierusalem, because [18v] Because the most of the Jewes would not receyve his Testimony concerninge *Chri*st in that Quæstion, (Acts. 22.18:)[11] then to stay att Hierusalem to bear wittnesse to that cause vnto Prison, & death? Not that we came hither to strive ag*ain*st Ceremonyes (or to fight ag*ain*st shadowes:) there is noe neede of our further labo*u*r in that course; o*u*r people here desire to worship God in spirit, & in trueth, & o*u*r people left in England know as well the groundes, & reasons of o*u*r sufferings ag*ain*st these things, as o*u*r sufferings themselves, w*hich* we beseech the L*or*d to accept, & blesse, in o*u*r blessed Savio*u*r. How farre our Testimony there hath p*r*evayled with any others, to search more seriouslye into the cause, we doe rather observe in thankefullnesse, & silence, then speake of to the P*r*eiudice of our Bretheren.

3 It hath bene noe small inducem*en*t to vs, to choose rather to remoove hither, then to stay there, *tha*t we mighte enioy *th*e libertye, not of some ordinances of god, but of all, & all in Puritye. For though we blesse the L*or*d with you for *th*e gratious meanes of salvation w*hich* many of your Congregations doe enioy (whereof our owne soules have founde the blessinge, & w*hich* we desire may be for ever continued, & enlarged to you,) yett seeing *Chri*st hath instituted noe Ordinance in vayne, (but all to the p*er*fectinge of the body of *Chri*st) & we knowe *tha*t our soules stand in neede of all to *th*e vttmost, we durst not soe farre be wantinge to the grace of *Chri*st, & to the necessity of o*u*r owne soules, as to sitt downe some where else, vnder the shadowe of some ordinances, when by two monthes travayle we mighte come to enioy *th*e libertye of all.

To your 2d Quæstion, howe farre ministers are bound to bear wittnesse ag*ains*t corruptions cast vpon the face of gods ordinances, It is too large a point for me to give Answer to it, in the heele of a l*ett*ere. But thus much breifely, wittnes is to be borne ag*ains*t corruptions, 1. By keepinge a mans owne {g}arm*en*ts cleane; I meane his owne outward practise, Rev: 16.15.[12] 2. By de{clar}inge the whole counsell of god to his people, not shunninge any part of it, {as} [se]asonable[13] occasion is offered, to pr*e*vent sinne in them. Acts. 20. 26. 27.[14] {3. By} avoydinge appearances of evill, as well as evill it selfe, 1 Thes: 5. 22.[15] {Ele}azerus durst not eate mutton, or bre{ad}, or {an}y oth{er cleane foode, when it had} an appearance of eatinge swines flesh, but choose death rather then deliveran{ce} by such meanes. 2. Maccab*ees* C*hapter* 6: v*erse* 21. to 25.[16] whose story though it be Apochryphall, yett the example is Authenticall, as beinge ratifyed by the Ap*ost*les Testimonye, amongst the rest of like nature, Heb: 11: 35:[17] where by the others he speaketh of, he meaneth not other wemen,[18] but other men, for the word is ἄλλοι, masculine;[19] Howsoever, Peters dissemblinge is evidently blamed by Paul in a like case, when by this example he countenanced the imposinge of ceremonyes ~~by Paul in a like case,~~ vpon the gentiles, to whom god never gave them; gal: 2: 11 to 14.[20] 4. By contendinge for the trueth in an holy manner, when others contend w*i*th vs ag*ains*t it, Jude: 3. 4. 5.[21] By givinge Account of our fayth before magistrates, if they call vs to it Publiquely, requiringe to be informed of our doctrine & manner of life, 1 Pet: 3. 14.[22] otherwise if they call vs to knowe our opinions in private (intendinge to bringe vs into trouble) or Publiquely, rather as captious Quæstionists, then Judiciall governo*u*rs, in such a case I suppose, we may conceale our mindes, & putt o*u*r Adversaryes vpon proofe, as o*u*r savio*u*r did, John. 18. 19.{20.} 2{1}.[23] {But w}hy doe I spend time, & wordes to you in these thinges, who {know them as well as I can tell you?[24] I rather desire} you may be kepte {in} a peaceable {way} of bearinge w{itt}nesse to the trueth (if the will of g{od be} such) then exposed to Hazards, by such confessions as mighte p*re*iudice your liberty.

My poore requests are to Heaven for you, as I desire you mighte not forgett me, & mine, & all vs here. Now the god of peace, & power guide, & support your spirit, in all your holy endeavours, blesse, & prosper your labo*ur*s & keep you as a chosen vessell in the shadowe of his hand through him that hath loved vs.

P*re*sent my humble service to my righte Honourable L*or*d as alsoe my deare affectyon to Mr Ball, Mr Slater, & all the Bretheren with you, especially to Mr Dod, Mr Cleaver, Mr Winston, Mr Cotton,[25] with earnest desire of the continuance of all their prayers (with your owne) in o*ur* behalfe. So I rest

Boston: Dec 3, 1634./

Yo*ur* very loving brother in o*ur* blessed savio*ur*,
J. C[otton][26]

1. See Cotton's foreword in Douglas Horton's translation of Norton's *Answer to the Whole Set of Questions* . . . (Cambridge, Mass., 1958), 10–18.

2. On Davenport, see *DAB*, V, 86; on Shepard, see Thomas Werge, *Thomas Shepard* (Boston, 1987), 9.

3. Increase Mather, in his biography of his father, describes Richard Mather's discussions with his parishioners about "his call to *New-England*" and includes his "Arguments tending to Prove the Removing from *Old-England* to *New*," adding that "hereunto he was the more inclined, by some Letters of Mr. *Cottons* and Mr. *Hookers* who were lately arrived in *New-England*, and wrote (as then there was cause) very encouragingly unto godly people to come after them." *The Life and Death of That Reverend Man of God, Mr. Richard Mather* . . . (Cambridge, Mass., 1670), in Dorchester Antiquarian and Historical Society, *Collections* (Boston, 1850), 68.

4. See John Cotton to Sarah Hawkred Story Cotton, Oct. 3, 1632, and n. 4.

5. Mary, the wife of Anthony Tuckney, Cotton's successor as vicar at St Botolph's, Boston, had died in October 1633 (*Calamy Revised*, 496). Since Anthony Tuckney, a cousin of Sarah Hawkred Story, was raised in the home of the Hawkreds as an adoptive son, his relation with Sarah was especially close.

6. A fold in the paper meets a hole at this point. Young's reading (AY) here is fuller than Hutchinson's (TH) and is adopted in this instance. Part of the text omitted by Hutchinson is, in fact, still legible. TH: warrant is in our case. AY: warrant is clear and strong (as we conceive,) in our case.

7. ne quid dicam gravius: lest I say something worse, that is, to put it mildly; to say the least.

8. John 21:18: Verily, verily, I say unto thee, When thou wast young, thou girdest thyself, and walkedst whither thou wouldest: but when thou shalt be old, thou shalt stretch forth thy hands, and another shall gird thee, and carry thee whither thou wouldest not. The Geneva Bible differs from this version only in having the word "lead" in place of "carry" in the final phrase; Cotton's use of "led" may suggest his use of the Geneva Bible in this instance.

9. A line and a half of text is lost at the fold here (as it was when both Hutchinson and Young edited the letter).

10. The adjectival intensifier "close," as it is used here to modify "prison," was a common

usage in Cotton's day indicating a particularly secluded, secret, or "strictly confined" condition (*OED*). The same phrase appears in Shakespeare's *Two Gentlemen of Verona,* 3.1.235: "To close prison he commanded her," as it does in the heading on page 1 in Cotton's *Controversie concerning Liberty of Conscience in Matters of Religion, Truly Stated, and Distinctly and Plainly Handled* . . . (London, 1646), which explains that the questions were "*written long since by a . . . close prisoner in* Newgate." Cotton's usage probably means something like what is now called solitary confinement.

In his later foreword to John Norton's *Answer to the Whole Set of Questions,* Cotton gave renewed emphasis to their belief that prison would have meant suffering and death. There he asserted that to submit to trial and to continue to refuse conformity would simply result in one's being slapped into prison forthwith. "There would be left to you no chance to discuss the matter or make a witness, but only the unavoidable necessity of wasting away in the unbroken silence of a dark and filthy dungeon. Since this was the situation—that we either had to perish uselessly in prison or leave the country—under the leadership of Christ and not by ourselves alone, and only after we had called our brethren into council, we made the decision to leave the country. Those brethren. . . . came to the judgment that by the free preaching of the word and the actual practice of our church discipline we could offer a much clearer and fuller witness in another land than in the wretched and loathesome prisons of London, where there would be no opportunity for books or pens or friends or conferences." Norton, *Answer to the Whole Set of Questions,* trans. Horton, 10–11.

11. Acts 22:18: And saw him [Ananias] saying unto me, Make haste, and get thee quickly out of Jerusalem: for they will not receive thy testimony concerning me.

12. Rev. 16:15: Behold, I come as a thief. Blessed is he that watcheth, and keepeth his garments, lest he walk naked, and they see his shame. The Geneva Bible's translation of the final word as "filthiness" is closer to Cotton's meaning here than the "shame" of the Authorized Version.

13. seasonable] TH and AY: reasonable.

14. Acts 20:26, 27: Wherefore I take you to record this day, that I am pure from the blood of all men. For I have not shunned to declare unto you all the counsel of God.

15. 1 Thess. 5:22: Abstain from all appearance of evil.

16. 2 Macc. 6:21–25: But they that had the charge of this wicked banquet, for that old friendship of the man, took him aside prively, & prayed him, that he would take such flesh, as was lawful for him to use, & as he would prepare for him self, & dissemble as though he had eaten of the things appointed by the King, even the flesh of the sacrifice, That in so doing he might be delivered from death, and that for the old friendship that was among them, he would receive this favor. But he began to consider discreetly, & as became his age, and the excellency of his ancient years, and the honor of his gray hairs, whereunto he was come, & his most honest conversation from his childhood, but chiefly the holy law made and given by God: therefore he answered consequently, and willed them straightways to send him to the grave. For it becometh not our age, said he, to dissemble, whereby many young persons might think, that Eleazar being four score year old and ten were now gone to another religion, And so through mine hypocrisy (for a little time of a transitory life) they might be deceived by me, and I should procure malediction, & reproach to mine old age (Geneva Bible).

17. Heb. 11:35: Women received their dead raised to life again: and others were tortured, not accepting deliverance; that they might obtain a better resurrection.

18. wemen] TH and AY: women.

19. ἄλλοι: others

20. Gal. 2:11–14: But when Peter was come to Antioch, I withstood him to the face, because he was to be blamed. For before that certain came from James, he did eat with the Gentiles: but when they were come, he withdrew and separated himself, fearing them which were of the circumcision. And the other Jews dissembled likewise with him; insomuch that Barnabas also was carried away with their dissimulation. But when I saw that they walked not uprightly according to the truth of the gospel, I said unto Peter before them all, If thou, being a Jew, livest after the manner of Gentiles, and not as do the Jews, why compellest thou the Gentiles to live as do the Jews?

21. Jude 3, 4, 5: Beloved, when I gave all diligence to write unto you of the common salvation, it was needful for me to write unto you, and exhort you that ye should earnestly contend for the faith which was once delivered unto the saints. For there are certain men crept in unawares, who were before of old ordained to this condemnation, ungodly men, turning the grace of our God into lasciviousness, and denying the only Lord God, and our Lord Jesus Christ. I will therefore put you in remembrance, though ye once knew this, how that the Lord, having saved the people out of the land of Egypt, afterward destroyed them that believed not.

22. 1 Pet. 3:14: But and if ye suffer for righteousness' sake, happy are ye: and be not afraid of their terror, neither be troubled.

23. A hole in the left margin of the sheet and obliteration along a fold running into the hole result in loss of the numbers here, but both TH and AY show verses 20 and 21 as part of Cotton's reference.

John 18:19–21: The high priest then asked Jesus of his disciples, and of his doctrine. Jesus answered him, I spake openly to the world; I ever taught in the synagogue, and in the temple, whither the Jews always resort; and in secret have I said nothing. Why askest thou me? ask them which heard me, what I have said unto them: behold, they know what I said.

24. Here TH has a period where AY has a question mark.

25. The six ministers to whom Cotton sends greetings are all in Midlands locations, most of them in Northamptonshire, suggesting that the unnamed addressee probably also had a Northamptonshire address. This suggests that "my righte Honourable L*ord*" was probably Sir Richard Knightley, the "great patron of Northamptonshire Puritanism." Equally pertinent, he was "a long-standing patron and protector of John Dod." J. T. Cliffe, *The Puritan Gentry: The Great Puritan Families of Early Stuart England* (London, 1984), 92; Carol G. Schneider, "Roots and Branches: From Principled Nonconformity to the Emergence of Religious Parties," in Francis J. Bremer, ed., *Puritanism: Transatlantic Perspectives on a Seventeenth-Century Anglo-American Faith* (Boston, 1993), 175, 188.

Thomas Ball (1590–1659) was a former student of John Preston's at Queen's College, Cambridge, later a fellow at Emmanuel when Preston was master there, and ultimately the author of a biography of Preston (unpublished until 1885). He had been vicar at Northampton's All Saints' Church from 1629 and in 1634 became rector there and at St. Gregory's in Northampton as well. See Venn, *Alumni Cantabrigienses,* I, 77, and Henry Isham Longden, *Northamptonshire and Rutland Clergy from 1500* (Northampton, 1938–1952), I, 169; *DNB.* John Ball (1585–1640), known to be a friend of both Cotton and Dod, is also possible, though he was a minister at Whitmore, Shropshire, while the others named here, including Thomas Ball, were Northamptonshire neighbors. On John Ball, see Brook, *Lives of the Puritans,* II, 440–444; *DNB;* Samuel Clarke, *A Generall Martyrologie* . . . (London, 1651), 442–451.

Mr. Slater is probably Christopher Slater (sometimes Sclater) (1584–1646), vicar at Leighton Buzzard, Bedfordshire, from 1624. See Venn, *Alumni Cantabrigienses,* IV, 88.

John Dod (1550–1645), a longtime Nonconformist, had been silenced while in various ministerial posts. He was a venerable resource for English Puritans. In 1634 he was ministering at Fawsley, Northamptonshire. When Cotton had been contemplating the question of emigration, he consulted Dod, who purportedly told him, "The removing of a Minister, was like the draining of a Fish-pond; the good Fish will follow the Water, but Eels, and other Baggage Fish, will stick in the mud" (Cotton Mather, *Magnalia Christi Americana* . . . [London, 1702], book III, 20). On Dod, see Brook, *Lives of the Puritans,* III, 1–6; Foster, *Long Argument,* 105.

Robert Cleaver, perhaps the son of the Robert Cleaver (d. 1613) who had been a collaborator with Dod on several popular books of biblical exegesis. The young Robert Cleaver had inherited the family property in Boddington, Northamptonshire. George Baker, *The History and Antiquities of the County of Northampton* (London, 1822–1830), I, 480.

John Winston was curate of Canons Ashby, Northamptonshire. Longden, *Northamptonshire and Rutland Clergy from 1500,* XV, 149.

Nathaniel Cotton had been minister of Adston, in the parish of Canons Ashby, Northamptonshire, since 1630. Ibid., III, 265.

26. All but the top portions of the J and C is lost where the paper has been trimmed. It is possible that he signed only J.C., as on other copies of letters kept for his own files.

John Cotton, Thomas Oliver, and Thomas Leverett to the Elders of the Dorchester Church

December 16, 1634

Published: I. Mather, *First Principles,* 2–4

In L. Thompson, "Letters of John Cotton," 83–87

In view of the great interest historians have demonstrated in the so-called Half-Way Covenant (a title coined only in the eighteenth century), this letter from the Boston church to the Dorchester church claims special status as an overlooked and significant document, for it anticipates the ruling of the Half-Way Synod twenty-eight years later. The letter is preserved only in Increase Mather's *First Principles of New England* (1675), a work that served Mather's political purpose of confirming that his own views were thoroughly consistent with those of the original generation of New England's founders.[1] The letter, which Mather says was "written with Mr. *Cottons* own hand," indicates that the elders and members of the Dorchester church had written to their Boston counterparts to ask their opinion whether the child of baptized parents who had never confirmed their possession of God's grace as adults might nevertheless be granted baptism on the grounds of the full church membership of the grandfather. This is exactly the question that was repeatedly raised from the late 1640s until the synod of March 1662 finally answered it—for Massachusetts churches—in the affirmative. Though it has often been assumed that the question did not arise until a new generation had grown up in New England, the Dorchester church conceived the question almost immediately. More than a decade later the synod meeting in Cambridge in 1646–1648 was asked to resolve the question of what to do with the children of baptized but unconverted parents, but the synod did not rule on the matter, leaving churches to their own devices for many years to come.[2]

The letter makes plain that the question from the Dorchester church was duly discussed by the entire congregation of the Boston church. Unfortunately, this is not confirmed in the *Records of the First Church in Boston,* where entries for 1634 consist almost entirely of lists of new members, so this letter is the closest thing we have to actual minutes of the congregational meeting. Cotton was the only one of the two ministers present for the discussion, the pastor, John Wilson, being then on a trip to England. The other two signers of the letter were laymen, Thomas Oliver and Thomas Leverett, the ruling elders of the Boston church.

Richard Mather, who would be a strong advocate for the Half-Way Covenant, had not yet arrived in New England. He became the minister of a newly organized church at Dorchester only after many of the original church members and ministers had moved to Connecticut in 1635 and 1636.

Increase Mather's text, prepared from Cotton's manuscript, is the only source for this document. Mather's italics are preserved throughout, though reflecting late-seventeenth-century printing practice rather than Cotton's own style.

To our Reverend and Beloved Brethren the Elders[3] with the rest of the Church of *Dorchester.*

Grace and peace from God our Father and from the Lord Iesus Christ our Saviour.

The Case of Conscience which you propounded to our Consideration, [to wit, whether a Grand Father being a member of a Christian Church, might claim Baptism to his Grand-Child, whose next Parents be not received into Church Covenant][4] has been deliberately treated of in our Church Assembled together publickly in the name of Christ. And *upon due and serious discourse about the point, it seemed good unto us all with one accord,* and agreeable (as we believe) to the word of the Lord, that the Grand-Father may lawfully claim that priviledge to his Grand-child in such a Case, yet with these two Cautions. First, that the Grand-child baptized by right of the Grand-fathers Covenant, be Committed to the Grand fathers education; for as God in the Covenant of Grace undertaketh to be a God, unto the Believer and his seed, so by the Rule of Relatives, the Tenour of the Covenant requireth that the Believer, do undertake that himself and his Seed do give up themselves to become the people of the Lord, which he cannot undertake, in behalf of his Seed, unless they be committed to his education. 2. This other Caution also we conceive to be requisite, that the Parents of the Child, do not thereby take occasion to neglect the due and seasonable preparation of themselves for entrance into Covenant with God and his Church: these Cautions premised and observed, the Baptisme of the Grand-child by right of his Grand-fathers Covenant, we believe to be warranted from the nature and tenour of the Covenant of Grace by this Reason, where there is a Stipulation of the Covenant on Gods part, and restipulation of the Covenant on mans part, there may be an obsignation[5] of the Covenant on both parts, or in plainer words, where there is an offer of the Covenant on Gods part, and a receiving and undertaking of the Covenant on mans part, there may be a sealing of it on both parts.[6] But here is an offer of the Covenant on Gods part, *Gen 17.7.*[7] where God says, that he will be a God to *Abraham,* that is, to the Believer and his Seed, and by Seed is not there meant the next Seed only, but Seeds Seed also to many Generations, *Isai. 59.21.*[8] And here is likewise a receiving and undertaking of the Covenant on mans part, seeing the Grand-father receiveth the Covenant by his faith, and by the profession of his faith, and by his desire of the Seal of the Covenant to strengthen his faith, and he undertaketh also the keeping of the Covenant, in bringing up his Grand-child as much as in him lies to live and walk as himself does, as one of Gods people, according to the Tenour of the Covenant, from whence the Conclusion evidently followeth, that therefore Baptisme may there be Administred to Seal up the Covenant, where the Grand-father receives the Covenant, & undertakes to bring up his Grand child in the faith and obedience of the Covenant.

Against this Argument it was objected by some what the Apostle writes, *1 Cor.7.14.*[9] where if both the husband and the wife, who are the next Parents of the Child be unbelieving, the Child is pronounced unclean, and therefore uncapable of the holy Covenant, and of the holy Seal of it, whereto it was answered that the word in the Text translated *unbelieving* is in the Original *Infidel.* Now *there is a difference between an Infidel and a Carnal Christian, as then was amongst the Jews a difference between an Heathen and a Carnal Israelite.* Though the Child be unclean where both the Parents are Pagans and Infidels, yet *we may not account such Parents for Pagans and Infidels, who are themselves baptized, and profess their belief of the Fundamentall Articles of the Christian Faith, and live without notorious Scandalous Crime, though they give not clear evidence of their regenerate estate,* nor are convinced of the necessity of Church Covenant. After this Answer given, there was no farther reply against the point in hand, but on the contrary, some of the Brethren expressing their Consents with Addition of other Reasons, and all of them by their silence, *we do therefore profess it to be the judgement of our Church,* and as we believ agreeable to the word of God (such Cautions being observed as hath been mentioned) *that the Grand-Father a member of the Church, may claim the priviledge of Baptisme to his Grand-Child, though his next Seed the Parents of the Child be not received themselves into Church Covenant.* Wherein nevertheless we desire, so to be understood, not as presuming to judge others, who happily may be of different opinion in this point, or to direct you, who are by the grace of God given to you, able to direct your selves and us also in the Lord, but as willing in meekness of wisdome to search out the truth of God with you, and in brotherly Love to satisfy your request and demand touching this Question.

Now the God of truth and peace Lead you into all truth, and go on to build up his holy Kingdome in the midst of you in the gracious Administration of all his holy Ordinances amongst you in the Lord Jesus, In whom we rest.

Boston Decemb. Your loving Brethren
the 16*th*. 1634. *John Cotton*
Tho. Olliver.
Tho. Leveret

In the Name of the Church

1. Increase Mather had opposed the revision of baptismal policy that the Half-Way Synod approved, even though his father, Richard Mather, then the minister at Dorchester, was a chief proponent of the changes. A year after his father's death in 1669, however, Increase changed his view of the matter, so that by 1675, when he published *First Principles,* he supported the more liberal baptism policy. See Robert Middlekauff, *The Mathers: Three Generations of Puritan Intellectuals* (1971; Berkeley, Calif., 1999), 85–86; Michael G. Hall, *The Last American Puritan: The Life of Increase Mather, 1639–1723* (Middletown, Conn., 1988), 140.

2. Two indispensable books deal with these matters. Edmund S. Morgan, *Visible Saints: The History of a Puritan Idea* (New York, 1963), presents the fundamental description of membership practices in the New England churches; and Robert G. Pope, *The Half-Way Covenant: Church Membership in Puritan New England* (Princeton, N.J., 1969), follows Morgan's treatment with a detailed examination of the dilemma created by baptizing infants but requiring a confession of faith by each fully confirmed adult member. In Morgan, see esp. 125–138 on the debates over baptism. James F. Cooper, Jr., argues that the crisis surrounding the Half-Way Covenant "surpassed all others in the seventeenth century in its breadth and lasting consequences" (*Tenacious of Their Liberties: The Congregationalists in Colonial Massachusetts* [New York, 1999], 89). Although Pope cites other documents quoted in Increase Mather's *First Principles,* he does not discuss this letter, the first document that Mather takes up.

3. The ministers at Dorchester in 1634 were John Warham and John Maverick. They had been chosen the ministers of the congregation before the settlers of the town left England. Roger Clap wrote of a day of fasting at Plymouth in England that was concluded by the people's choice of these two as ministers and their acceptance of the people's call. See *Memoirs of Capt. Roger Clap* (Boston, 1731), rpt. in Dorchester Antiquarian and Historical Society, *Collections* (1843; rpt. Freeport, N. Y., 1971), 34; William Dana Orcutt, *Good Old Dorchester: A Narrative History of the Town, 1630–1893* (Cambridge, Mass., 1893), 23; Rose-Troup, *John White,* 200–202.

4. The brackets are in Mather's printing.

5. This word, "now *rare,*" in the sixteenth and seventeenth centuries (and later) meant "formal ratification or confirmation of something, as by sealing" (*OED*).

6. Mather's text prints a question mark here instead of a period. In the absence of a manuscript it is impossible to know whether this was a typographical error or whether Cotton (or an

amanuensis) wrote the question mark himself. It is removed here to be consistent with both the sense and the sentence structure.

7. Gen. 17:7: And I will establish my covenant between me and thee and thy seed after thee in their generations for an everlasting covenant, to be a God unto thee, and to thy seed after thee.

8. Isa. 59:21: As for me, this is my covenant with them, saith the Lord; My spirit that is upon thee, and my words which I have put in thy mouth, shall not depart out of thy mouth, nor out of the mouth of thy seed, nor out of the mouth of thy seed's seed, saith the Lord, from henceforth and for ever.

9. 1 Cor. 7:14: For the unbelieving husband is sanctified by the wife, and the unbelieving wife is sanctified by the husband: else were your children unclean; but now are they holy.

John Cotton to [John Hall]

[Late 1634–Early 1635]

AL. MS: MSA, CCXL, Hutchinson Papers, I, fols. 88–94a

Published: Roger Williams, *The Bloudy Tenent, of Persecution, for Cause of Conscience, Discussed* . . . (London, 1644), 7–14; John Cotton, *The Controversie concerning Liberty of Conscience in Matters of Religion, Truly Stated, and Distinctly and Plainly Handled* . . . (London, 1646), 7–14; Edward Bean Underhill, ed., *The Bloudy Tenent of Persecution . . . and Mr. Cotton's Letter Examined and Answered* (London, 1848), 19–30; Samuel L. Caldwell, ed., *The Bloudy Tenent of Persecution* . . . , in NC, *Publs.,* III (1867), 41–54; Emerson, *Letters,* 155–166

In L. Thompson, "Letters of John Cotton," 88–100

Although an unsigned manuscript in Cotton's hand has been preserved, the origin and context of the present letter must be constructed from external evidence. The document was published, along with the inquiry to which it is a reply, in Roger Williams's *Bloudy Tenent, of Persecution* (1644). Williams's book is a lengthy reply to Cotton's "Answer" (the present letter) and to another document, a "Treatise" to which Cotton refers at the end of his letter. These texts provided Williams the occasion to initiate his public debate with Cotton on the issue of persecution for conscience, a debate that has held much interest for successive generations of readers in the nineteenth and twentieth centuries.[1] Cotton's letter appeared in Williams's book—published during Williams's 1643–1644 visit to England—without introduction or date. When in 1647 Cotton replied to *The Bloudy Tenent,* he tried to reconstruct how he came to write the "Answer": "*Mr. Williams* sent me about a dozen yeares agoe (as I remember) a letter, penned (as he wrote) by a Prisoner in *Newgate,* touching persecution for Conscience sake: and intreated my judgement of it for the satisfaction of his friend."[2] Williams's next installment, *The Bloody Tenent Yet More Bloody,* contains a denial that he had been the one who asked Cotton to reply to the prisoner's arguments. Calling himself "the discusser," Williams claimed, "To my *knowledge* there was no such letter or *intercourse* passed between Master *Cotton* and the discusser; but what I have heard is this: One Master *Hall* of *Roxbury,* presented the prisoners Arguments against persecution to Master *Cotton,* who gave this present controverted *Answer;* with the which Master *Hall* not being satisfied, he sends them unto the *discusser,* who never saw the said *Hall,* nor those *Arguments* in writing; (though he well remember that he saw them in print some yeers since.)."[3] This statement was published the year Cotton died, so it is the last word on the matter. Given his denial that he provoked Cotton's letter, it seems reasonable to accept Williams's identification of John Hall as the source of the inquiry. Hall was, as Williams says, a resident of Roxbury and member of the Roxbury church.[4]

If Cotton's estimate of when he was asked for his thoughts on the Newgate prisoner's arguments are accurate—twelve years before he wrote the preface to *The Bloudy Tenent, Washed*—the date of his response would be 1635 or perhaps late 1634. Cotton also says, "When I wrote that Letter, [Williams] (for ought I can remember) did then keepe communion with all his Brethren, and held loving acquaintance with my selfe."[5] At least by July 8, 1635, as Winthrop notes, it was clear that Williams was at odds with the magistrates and ministers of the Bay on fundamental issues.[6] Cotton's letter was presumably written before then.

The following text is based on the author's manuscript, which is in good condition except for wear at the bottom of most pages, causing some loss of text. At such points, the text is provided in braces from the first printed edition, *The Bloudy Tenent* (1644). Cotton numbered his pages in the upper right corner of each recto (his odd-numbered pages) and in the upper left of the verso (his even-numbered pages). Some of these numbers have been trimmed off; where they remain, they are here indicated just before the bracketed Hutchinson Papers folio numbers, as in i/88, which indicates Cotton's number on the first recto (i), which is folio 88 in the Hutchinson Papers. The enclosure in Hall's letter to which Cotton is responding is printed in the Appendix, below.

[i/88] The Quæstion you putt, is, whether Persecution for Cause of Conscience, be not ag*ains*t *th*e Doctrine of Jesus Christ *th*e king of kings? Now by Persecution for Cause of Conscience I conceive you meane, eyther for Professing some point of Doctrine, w*hi*ch you beleive in Conscience to be *th*e Trueth: or for Practising some worke, w*hi*ch in conscience you beleive to be a Religious Duety. Now in points of Doctrine some are fundam*en*tall, w*i*thout right Beleife whereof a man cannot be saved: others are circumstantiall, or lesse principall, wherein men may differ in Judgem*en*t w*i*thout Præiudice of salvation on eyther part. In like sort, in points of Practise some concerne *th*e weightyer Duetyes of *th*e Law, as what God wee worship, & w*i*th ˆwhatˆ kinde of worship, whether[7] ˆsuch,ˆ as if it be right, Fellowship w*i*th God is held: if corrupt, Fellowship w*i*th him is lost. Againe in ˆpoints ofˆ Doctrine ˆ& worshipˆ lesse principall, eyther they are held forth in a meeke & peaceable way, though the things be erroneous & vnlawfull: or they are held forth w*i*th such arrogance, & impetuousnesse, as tendeth & reacheth (even of it self) to *th*e Disturbance of Civill Peace. Finally, let me make[8] this one distinction more, when men are Persecuted for Conscience sake, It is eyther for Conscience rightl{y} informed, or for erroneous ˆ& blindeˆ Conscience.

[88a] These things p*re*mised, I would lay downe mine Answer to *th*e Quæstion in certaine Conclusions:

1. It is not lawfull to Persecute any for Conscience sake, rightly enformed. For in Persecuting such, Christ himself is persecuted in *th*em, Acts. 9.4.[9]

2. For erroneous ˆ& blindeˆ & [deleted word] Conscience ˆeven in fundam*en*tall & weighty points,ˆ It is not lawfull to persecute any, till after Admonition once, or twise.

And so *th*e Ap*ost*le directeth, Tit. 3. io,[10] & giveth *th*e Reason, *tha*t in fundam*en*tall & principall points of Doctrine or worship, ˆthe word of God in such thinges is so cleare, *tha*tˆ He cannot but be convinced in Conscience of *th*e daungerous Erro*u*r of his way, after once or twise Admonition, wisely & faithfully dispensed. And then if an one persist, it is not out of Conscience, but ag*ains*t his Conscience, as *th*e Ap*ost*le saith v. ii,[11] He is subverted, & sinneth being condemned of himself, *tha*t is, of his owne Conscience. So *tha*t if such a man, after such Admonition shall still persist in *th*e Erro*u*r of his way, & be therefore punished, He is not persecuted for Cause of Conscience, but for sinning ag*ains*t his owne Conscience.

3 In things of lesse moment, whether Points of Doctrine or worship, if a man hold *th*em forth in a spirit of Chri*sti*an meekenesse[12] & love (though w*i*th zeale & Constancy) He is not to be persecuted, but tolerated, till God may be pleased to manifest his Trueth to Him. Phil. 2.i7. Rom i4. i,2,3,4.[13] [3/89]

4. But if a man hold forth & Professe any Erro*u*r, or false way, w*i*th a boisterous, & arrogant spirit, to *th*e disturbance of Civill Peace, He may iustly be punished according to *th*e quality, & measure of *th*e Disturbance caused by Him.

Now let vs consider of yo*u*r Reasons, or Objections to *th*e contrary: Yo*u*r first Head of Objections is taken from *th*e Scripture.[14]

"Ob. i. Because Christ com*m*aundeth, to let alone *th*e Tares & wheate to grow "together to *th*e Harvest, Mat. i3. 30, 38.[15]

Ans*wer* Tares are not Bryars & Thornes, but partly Hypocrites (like vnto the Godly, but indeede Carnall, as *th*e tares are like to wheate, but are not wheate:) or partly such corrupt Doctrines or Practises, as are indeede vnsound, but yet such as come very neere the Trueth (as Tares doe to *th*e wheate) & so neere *tha*t good men may be taken w*i*th *th*em, & so the Persons w*i*th whom they grow cannot be rooted out, but good wheate will be rooted vp w*i*th *th*em. And in such a Case, Christ calleth for Toleration, not for pœnall[16] Prosecution, according to *th*e 3[d] Concl{usion}.

"Ob.2. In Mat*thew* i5. i4:[17] Christ com*m*aundeth his Disciples to let *th*e Blinde "alone, till they fall into *th*e Ditch: therefore He would have their Punishm*en*t deferred till their finall Destruction.

[89a]

Ans. He there speaketh not to publique officers, whether in Church, or Com*m*on-wealth, but to his private Disciples concerning *th*e Pharisees, over whom they had no Power. And *th*e Com*m*aund He giveth to let *th*em alone, is spoken in regard of troubling *th*emselves, or regarding *th*e Offence, w*hi*ch they tooke at *th*e holesome Doctrine of the Gospell. As who should say, Though they be offended at this saying of mine, yet doe not you feare their feare, nor be troubled at their Offence, w*hi*ch they take at my Doctrine, not over[18] sound Judgem*en*t, but out of ˆtheirˆ blindenesse. But this maketh noething to *th*e Cause in hand.

"Ob.3. In Luk. 9. 54,55:[19] Christ reprooveth his Disciples, who would have had "Fyre come downe from Heaven to Consume *th*e Samaritans, who refused to "Receyve him.

"[O]b.4. And Paul teacheth Timothy, Not to strive, but to be gentle towards "all men, suffering evill men patiently, &c.[20]

Ans. Both these are directions to Ministers of *th*e Gospell, how to deale not w*i*th obstinate Offendo*u*rs ˆw*i*thin *th*e Churchˆ that sinne ag*ains*t Conscience, [deleted word] ~~church way,~~ but eyther w*i*th men w*i*thout, as *th*e Samaritans were, & many vnconverted Chri*sti*ans in Crete, whom Titus (as an Evangelist) {was} to seeke to Convert: or at best, w*i*th some Jewes, or Gentiles in *th*e Church, who though carnall, yet were not convinced of *th*e Erro*u*r of their way. A{nd} it is true, It became not *th*e Spirit of *th*e Gospell {to} Convert aliens to *th*e Faith (such as *th*e Samaritans [5/90] were) by fyre & Brimston: nor to deale harshly in publique Ministery or private Conference w*i*th all such contrary minded men, as eyther had not yet entred into Church Fellowship: or if they had, yet did hitherto sinne of Ignorance, not ag*ains*t Conscience. But neyther of both these Texts doe hinder *th*e Ministers of *th*e Gospell to proceede in a Church way ag*ains*t Church-members, when they become scandalous Offend*ou*rs eyther in life or Doctrine. Much lesse doe they speake at all to Civill Magistrates.

"Ob.5: From the Prædictions of *th*e Prophets, who foretold *tha*t Carnall weap-
"ons should Cease in *th*e Dayes of *th*e Gospell, Isay. 2.4. ^& ii.9:^ Micah.
"4.3,4.[21] And the Ap*ost*le p*r*ofesseth *th*e weapons of o*u*r warfare are not Car-
"nall, 2. Cor. io:4.[22] And Christ is ^so^ farre from Persecuting those *tha*t
"would not be of their Religion, *tha*t He chargeth *th*em, when they are Perse-
"cuted *th*emselves [about five words deleted] they should Pray & when they
"are cursed they should blesse: The Reason whereof seemeth to be, they who
"are now Persecut*ou*rs, & wicked Persons may become true Disciples & Con-
"verts &c.

Ans. Those Prædictions in *th*e Prophets doe onely shew ^i.^ w*i*th what kinde of weapons, He will subdue *th*e Nations to *th*e Obedience of *th*e Faith of *th*e Gospell, not by fyre & sword, & weapons of warre, but by *th*e Power of his word & Spirit [90a] w*hi*ch noe man doubteth of.

2. Those Prædictions of *th*e Prophets shew what *th*e meeke & Peaceable Temper will be of all *th*e true Converts to Chri*sti*anity, not lions, or leopards &c., not cruell Opress*ou*rs, nor malignant Opposers or biters of one another. But doeth not forbid *th*em to drive ravenous wolves from *th*e sheepefold, & to Restrayne theim from Devouring *th*e sheepe of Christ.

And when Paul saith, the weapons of o*u*r warfare are not Carnall, but spirituall, He denyeth not Civill weapons of Justice to *th*e Civill Magistrate Rom. i3.[23] but onely to Church-Officers. And yet[24] *th*e weapons of Church-Officers, He acknowledgeth to be such, as though they be spirituall, yet are ready to take vengeaunce of all Disobedience, 2. Cor. io.6:[25] w*hi*ch hath reference (amongst other Ordinaunces) to *th*e Censures of *th*e Church ag*ains*t scandalous Offend*ou*rs.

3. When Christ com*m*aundeth his Disciples to Blesse *th*em that curse & persecute *th*em, He giveth ^not^ therein a Rule ~~not~~ to Publique Officers whether in Church or Com*m*onwealth to suffer notorious sinnes either in life or Doctrine to Passe away w*i*th a Blessing: but to private Chri*sti*ans to suffer Persecution patiently, yea & to Pray for *th*eir Persecut*ou*rs. Againe It is true Christ would have his Disciples ^to^ be farre from Persecuting (for *tha*t is a sinfull Oppression of men for Righteousnesse sake:) but *tha*t hindreth not, but *tha*t He would have *th*em Execute vpon all Disobedience *th*e Judgem*en*t {& vengeance} required in *th*e word, 2. Cor. [7/91] io.6. Rom*ans* i3.4.[26]

4. Though it be true *tha*t wicked Persons now may by *th*e Grace of God become true Disciples & Converts, yet wee may not doe Evill *tha*t good may come thereon. And Evill it would be to Tolerate ^notorious^ Evill Doers, whether seducing Teachers, or scandalous livers. Christ had some-

thing ag*ains*t the Angell of *th*e Church of Pergamus for tolerating *th*em *tha*t held *th*e Doctrine of Balaam: & ag*ains*t *th*e Church of Thyateira, for tolerating Jezebel, to teach, & seduce, Revel*ation* 2. i4,20.[27]

Your 2d Head of Reasons is taken from *th*e Profession & Practise of famous Princes, ag*ains*t Persecution for Conscience.[28] Whereto a treble[29] Answer may breifely be returned:

i. Wee willingly Acknowledge *tha*t none is to be Persecuted at all, noe more then they may be oppressed for Righteousnesse sake.

Againe wee acknowledge *tha*t none is to be punished for his Conscience though misenformed, as hath bene said, vnlesse his Erro*u*rs be fundamentall, or seditiously & turbulently promoted, & *tha*t after due Conviction of his Conscience, *tha*t it may appeare he is not punished for his Conscience, but for sinning ag*ains*t his Conscience. Furthermore, wee Acknowledge none is to be Constrayned to beleive, or p*ro*fesse *th*e T{rue} Religion, till he be convinced in Judgem*en*t of *th*e Trueth of it: but yet Restrayned he may be from Blaspheming *th*e Trueth & ˆfromˆ seducing any vnto pernicious Erro*u*rs{.}

[91a] 2. Wee Answer, What Princes professe or practise is not a Rule of Conscience: they many times tolerate *tha*t in point of state Pollicy, w*hi*ch cannot iustly be tolerated in point of true Chri*sti*anity.

Againe, Princes many times tolerate Offenders out of very necessity, when ˆthe Offendo*u*rs are eitherˆ ~~eyther they are~~ too many or too mighty for *th*em to punish; in w*hi*ch respect David tolerated Joab & his Murders, but ag*ains*t his will.

3. Wee Answer further, *tha*t for those 3 Princes ˆnamed by youˆ who tolerated Religion, wee can name you more & greater who have not tolerated Hæretiques & schismatiques, notw*i*thstanding their P{ret}ˆenceˆ of Conscience, & Arrogating *th*e Crowne of Martyrdome to their sufferings. Constantine *th*e great at *th*e Request of *th*e generall Councell at Nice, Banished Arius, w*i*th some of his fellowes.[30] Sozemeni Lib*er* i. Ecclesiastiæ histor*iae* C.i9, & 20.[31] The same Constantine made a severe law ag*ains*t *th*e Donatists: & *th*e like Proceedings ag*ains*t *th*em were vsed by Valentinian, Gratian, & Theodosius, as Augustine reporteth in Ep*isto*la, i66.[32] Onely Julian *th*e [deleted word] Apostata graunted liberty to Hæretiques as we{ll} as to Pagans, *tha*t He might by tolerating all w{eed}es to grow, choake *th*e vitalls of Chri*stiani*ty:[33] ˆw*hi*ch was also {the} P{racti}se & sinne of Valens *th*e Arian:ˆ[34] Q{u}e{en} Elizabeth as famous for hir Governm*en*t as [m]ost[35] of *th*e former, it is well knowen {what law}es she made & executed ag*ains*t Papists. {Yea and King James (one} of yo*u*r owne witnesses) [9/92] though he was slow in p*ro*ceeding ag*ains*t Papists (as you say) for Conscience sake: yet you are not ignorant how

sharpely & severely He punished those whom the malignant world calleth Puritans, men of more Conscience, & better Faith, then the Papists whom he tolerated.

I come now to yo*ur* 3d & last Argum*en*t taken from *th*e Judgem*en*t of auntient, & later writers, yea even of Papists theimselves, who have condemned Persecution for Conscience sake.

You begin w*i*th Hilary,[36] whose Testimony wee might admitt, w*i*thout any "Præiudice to *th*e Trueth, for It is true, the Chri*sti*an Church doeth not Perse-"cute, but is persecuted. But to Excom*m*unicate an Hæretique is not to Persecute, *tha*t is, It is is not to Punish an innocent, but a culpable, & damnable person, & *tha*t, not for Conscience, but for persisting in Erro*ur* ag*ains*t light of Conscience, whereof he hath bene convinced.

It is true also what he saith That neyther *th*e Ap*ost*les did, nor may wee "p*ro*pagate Chri*sti*an Religion by *th*e sword. But if Pagans cannot be wonne "by *th*e word, they are not to be compelled by *th*e Sword. Neverthelesse, this hindereth not, but if they or any others should blaspheme the true God, & his true Religion, they ought to be severely punished: & noe lesse doe they deserve, if they seduce from *th*e Trueth to damnable Hæresy, or Idolatry.

[10/92a] Yo*ur* next writer (w*hi*ch is Tertullian)[37] speaketh to *th*e same Purpose, in the Place alledged by you. His intent is onely to Restrayne Scapula *th*e Romane Governo*ur* of Africa from *th*e Persection of Chri*sti*ans ~~& for *tha*t ende, fetcheth an Argum*ent*~~ for not Offering sacrifice to their Gods. And for *tha*t end fetcheth an Argum*en*t from *th*e law of Naturall æquity, Not to Com-"pell any to any Religion: but ^to permitt *the*m^ eyther to Beleive willingly, or "~~to permitt *them*~~ not to Beleive at all: w*hi*ch wee acknowledge, & accordingly permitt the Indians to continue in their vnbeleife. Neverthelesse, It will not therefore be lawfull openly to tolerate *th*e worship of Devills, or Idolls, " or *th*e seduction of any from *th*e Trueth. When Tertullian saith [That an other "mans Religion neyther hurteth nor profiteth any][38] It must be vnderstoode of private worship, & religion professed in private: Otherwise a false Religion professed by *th*e members of *th*e Church or by such as have given their Names to Christ, will be the Ruine & Desolation of *th*e Church, as appeareth by *th*e Threates of Christ to *th*e Churches of Asia. Rev. c.2.

Yo*ur* next Author Hierome[39] crosseth not *th*e Trueth nor advantageth yo*ur* Cause. For wee graunt what he saith, that Hæresy must be cutt off w*i*th *th*e sword of *th*e Spirit. But this hindreth not, but *tha*t beinge so cutt downe, if *th*e Hæretique still persist in his Hæresy to *th*e seduction of others, He may be cutt {off} also {by} *th*e Civill sword, to p*r*event the p{erdi}tion [11/93] of others. And *tha*t to be Hieromes meaning, appeareth by his note vpon *tha*t of "*th*e Ap*ost*le, A little leaven, leaveneth *th*e whole lumpe: Therefore (saith he)

"A sparke assoone as it appeareth, is to be extinguished, & *th*e leaven to be re- "mooved from *th*e rest of *th*e Dowe. Rotten pieces of flesh are to be cutt off, & "a scabbed Beast is to be driven from *th*e sheepe-folde, lest the whole house, "masse of dow, body, & flock, be sett on fyre w*i*th the sparke, be sowred w*i*th "*th*e dow, be putrifyed w*i*th *th*e rotten flesh, perish by the scabbed beast.

Brentius[40] (whom you next quote) speaketh not to yo*u*r Cause. Wee willingly graunt him, & you, That men have noe Power to make lawes to binde Conscience. But this hindereth not, but *tha*t men may see the lawes of God observed, w*hi*ch doe binde Conscience.

The like Answer may be returned to Luther, whom you next Alledge. i. "That the Governm*en*t of *th*e Civill Magistrate extendeth noe further then over "*th*e Bodyes & Goods of their Subjects, not over their soules. And therefore "they may not vndertake to give lawes vnto *th*e soules, & Consciences of men. "2. That *th*e Church of Christ doeth not vse the Arme of secular Power t{o} "compell men to *th*e Faith, or Profession of the Trueth: for this is to be done "by spirituall weapons, whereby Chri*sti*ans are to be exhorted not compelled.

But this hindreth not, that C{hri*sti*ans sinning} [93a] ag*ains*t light of Faith & Conscience, may iustly be censured by *th*e Church w*i*th Excom*m*unication, & by *th*e civill sword also, in case they shall corrupt others to *th*e Perdition of their soules.

As for *th*e Testimony of *th*e Popish Booke, wee weigh it not, as knowing whatsoever they speake for Toleration of Religion, where theimselves are vnder Hatches, when they come to sitt at sterne they iudge & Practise quite contrary, as both their writings, & Judiciall Proceedings have testifyed to *th*e world these many yeares.

To shutt vp this Argum*en*t from Testimonyes of writers It is well knowen, Augustine Retracted this Opinion of yo*u*rs, w*hi*ch in his yonger time he had held, but in after riper Age reversed, & refuted, as appeareth in *th*e 2d Booke of his Retractations, c.5: & in his Ep*ist*les, 48, & 50. And in his i. booke ag*ains*t the Ep*ist*le of Parmenianus, c.7. he sheweth, that if *th*e Donatists were punished w*i*th Death, they were iustly punished. And in his ii. Tractate vpon John, They Murther[41] (saith he) Soules, & *th*emselves are afflicted in Body: they putt men to everlasting Death, & yet they complaine, when theimselves are putt to suffer temporall Death.[42] Optatus in his 3d Bo{ok}[43] iusifyeth Macharius, who had putt some Hæretices to Death, That He had done noe more herein, then what Moses, Phineas, & Elias, had done before Him.

{Bernard[44] in his} 66. sermon in Cantica, Out of doubt [13/94] (saith he) It is better, *tha*t they should be restrayned by *th*e sword of him who beareth not *th*e sword in vaine then *tha*t they should be suffered to draw many others into their Erro*u*rs. For he is *th*e minister of God for wrath to every evill Doer. &c

Calvines Judgem*en*t is well knowen, who procured the Death of Michael

Servetus for pertinacy in his Hæresy ˆ& defended his fact by a Booke written of *tha*t Argum*en*t.[45] Beza also wrote aˆ ~~Beza wrote a Booke~~ Booke de [deleted word] Hæreticis morte plectendis[46] ˆ*tha*t Hæretiques are to be punished w*i*th Death.ˆ Aretius ~~also tooke~~ ˆlikewise tookeˆ *th*e like Co*u*rse ˆabout the Death ofˆ ~~in pursuing~~ Valentinus Gentilis ~~to the death~~ & iustifyed the Magistrates Proceeding ag*ains*t Him in an History written of *tha*t Argum*en*t.[47]

Finally you come to Answer some ˆmaineˆ Objections, as you call *th*em: w*hi*ch yet are but one, & *tha*t One objecteth noething ag*ains*t what wee hold. "It is (say you) noe Præiudice to *th*e Com*m*onwealth, if liberty of Conscience "were suffered to such as feare God indeede, w*hi*ch you proove by *th*e Examples of *th*e Patriarchs & others.

But wee readily graunt you liberty of Conscience is to be graunted to men *tha*t feare God indeede, as knowing they will not persist in Hæresy, or turbulent Schisme, when they {are} co{nvinc}ed in Conscience of *th*e sinfullnesse thereof. But *th*e Quæstio{n i}s, whether an Hæretique after once or twise Admonition (& so, after Conviction) or any other scandalous, & {h}eynous Offendo*u*r, may be tolerated eyther in *th*e Church w*i*thout Ex{c}om*m*{unication} [94a] or in *th*e Com*m*onwealth w*i*thout such Punishm*en*t, as may p*re*serve others from daungerous & damnable Infection. Thus much I thought needefull to be spoken for Avoyding *th*e grounds of yo*u*r Erro*u*r. I forbeare Adding Reasons to justify the Trueth, because you may finde *tha*t done to yo*u*r hand in a Treatise sent to some of *th*e Brethren late of Salem,[48] who doubted (as you doe) of *th*e same point.

The Lord leade you by a spirit of Trueth
into all Trueth, through Jesus Christ./
[no signature][49]

1. Some commentaries on the Williams-Cotton debate have been more soundly based in the seventeenth-century historical and intellectual contexts than others. For a helpful contextualizing of the language of the Williams-Cotton debate, see Conrad Wright, "John Cotton Washed and Made White," in F. Forrester Church and Timothy George, eds., *Continuity and Discontinuity in Church History: Essays Presented to George Huntston Williams* . . . (Leiden, 1979), 338–350.

2. John Cotton, *The Bloudy Tenent, Washed, and Made White* . . . (London, 1647), 1–2.

3. Roger Williams, *The Bloody Tenent Yet More Bloody* . . . (London, 1652), 4. Williams was recalling seeing the prisoner's arguments (which had been addressed directly to King James I) in *A Most Humble Supplication of Many of the King's Majesty's Loyal Subjects . . . Who Are Persecuted (Only for Differing in Religion) contrary to Divine and Human Testimonies* (London, 1620), chaps. 6–9. See Appendix, below.

4. Boston, Record Commissioners, [Sixth Report], *A Report of the Record Commissioners, Containing the Roxbury Land and Church Records* (Boston, 1884), 4, 84. James Savage (*Genealogical*

Distionary, II, 333–334) lists more than one individual named John Hall, concluding that "no little confusion, after long scrutiny, exists as to the men of this name," but verifies the one cited in the Roxbury church records where his name "has prefix of respect" and is a freeman as of May 6, 1635. Anderson (*Great Migration,* 840–844) clarifies the matter, crediting a note by Donald Lines Jacobus in Dwight Brainerd, *Ancestry of Thomas Chalmers Brainerd,* ed. Donald Lines Jacobus (Montreal, 1948), 142–143.

5. Cotton, *The Bloudy Tenent, Washed,* 15.

6. Winthrop, *Journal,* 149–150.

7. The w in whether is written over the word as.

8. The word make is written over the word add.

9. Acts 9:4: And he fell to the earth, and heard a voice saying unto him, Saul, Saul, why persecutest thou me?

10. Titus 3:10: A man that is an heretick after the first and second admonition reject.

11. Cotton quotes from Titus 3:11.

12. meekenesse is written over two words, which are probably: & loving.

13. Phil. 3:17: Brethren, be followers together of me, and mark them which walk so as ye have us for an ensample.

Rom. 14:1–4: Him that is weak in the faith receive ye, but not to doubtful disputations. For one believeth that he may eat all things: another, who is weak, eateth herbs. Let not him that eateth despise him that eateth not; and let not him which eateth not judge him that eateth: for God hath received him. Who art thou that judgest another man's servant? to his own master he standeth or falleth. Yea, he shall be holden up: for God is able to make him stand.

14. "Yo*ur* . . . Scripture." appears to have been added after the following line of text was written.

15. Matt. 13:30, 38: Let both grow together until the harvest: and in the time of harvest I will say to the reapers, Gather ye together first the tares, and bind them in bundles to burn them: but gather the wheat into my barn.

The field is the world; the good seed are the children of the kingdom; but the tares are the children of the wicked one.

16. The e in penall is written over two letters.

17. Matt. 15:14: Let them alone: they be blind leaders of the blind. And if the blind lead the blind, both shall fall into the ditch.

18. The word over is written over the word at.

19. Luke 9:54, 55: And when his disciples James and John saw this, they said, Lord, wilt thou that we command fire to come down from heaven, and consume them, even as Elias did? But he turned, and rebuked them, and said, Ye know not what manner of spirit ye are of.

20. Cotton is here paraphrasing 2 Tim. 2:24: And the servant of the Lord must not strive; but be gentle unto all men, apt to teach, patient.

21. Isa. 2:4: And he shall judge among the nations, and shall rebuke many people: and they shall beat their swords into plowshares, and their spears into pruning hooks: nation shall not lift up sword against nation, neither shall they learn war any more.

Isa. 11:9: They shall not hurt nor destroy in all my holy mountain: for the earth shall be full of knowledge of the Lord, as the waters cover the sea.

Mic. 4:3–4: And he shall judge among many people, and rebuke strong nations afar off; and they shall beat their swords into plowshares, and their spears into pruninghooks: nation shall not lift up a sword against nation, neither shall they learn war any more. But they shall sit every man under his vine and under his fig tree; and none shall make them afraid: for the mouth of the Lord of hosts hath spoken it.

22. 2 Cor. 10:4: (For the weapons of our warfare are not carnal, but mighty through God to the pulling down of strong holds.)

23. Cotton left a space here as if he meant to return and insert a verse number.

24. The letter y is written over a letter w.

25. 2 Cor. 10:6: And having in a readiness to revenge all disobedience when your obedience is fulfilled.

26. Rom. 13:4: For he is the minister of God to thee for good. But if thou do that which is evil, be afraid; for he beareth not the sword in vain: for he is the minister of God, a revenger to execute wrath upon him that doeth evil.

27. Rev. 2:14, 20: But I have a few things against thee, because thou hast there them that hold the doctrine of Balaam, who taught Balac to cast a stumblingblock before the children of Israel, to eat things sacrificed unto idols, and to commit fornication.

Notwithstanding I have a few things against thee, because thou sufferest that woman Jezebel, which calleth herself a prophetess, to teach and seduce my servants to commit fornication, and to eat things sacrificed unto idols.

28. Here the published version deletes ag*ains*t persecution for Conscience, and inserts instead, King *James, Stephen* of *Poland,* King of *Bohemia.*

29. The word treble is written over the word double.

30. Arius was exiled and excommunicated as a heretic for his controversy with Bishop Alexander over whether Christ was equal to God the Father or the Father's creation.

31. Salmaninus Hermias Sozomenus (early fifth century), *Ecclesiasticae historiae libri novem,* continued Eusebius's *Church History* through the period 323–425.

32. The Donatists were a Christian group in North Africa formed by Donatus, bishop of Carthage, that broke off from the Roman Church in 312; they opposed state interference in church affairs and were denied civil and ecclesiastical rights in the period 412–414. Valentinian I (321–375) was emperor of Rome from 364 to 375. Gratian was Valentinian's son and coemperor who was put to death by the usurper Magnus Maximus in 383. Theodosius overthrew Maximus in 388, restoring Valentinian II (372–392) to power. These events appear, as the author indicates, in Augustine's *Epistolae,* no. 166. See Augustine, *Opera* (Venice, 1552), II, fol. 156.

33. Julian the Apostate (331–363) was the last Roman emperor (361–363) who tried to replace Christianity with polytheism.

34. Valens the Arian (328–378), younger brother of Valentinian I, who appointed him emperor of the Roman Empire in the East (364–378). He adopted Arianism, which denied the divinity of Jesus, and persecuted orthodox Christians. After defeating them, he tolerated the pagan Visigoths, allowing them to settle in Roman territory; they rebelled in 378 and defeated his army—and him.

35. The first printed version changes this word to any.

36. St. Hilary of Poitiers (c. 315–367), was the leading Christian theologian of his day and a defender of orthodoxy against Arianism, especially in *De trinitate.*

37. Tertullian (c. 155–160 to post 220), early Christian theologian and polemicist and leader of the African church, wrote and spoke strongly against heresies and in particular the pagan culture of Rome, where he had been raised.

38. Cotton's brackets.

39. Jerome (c. 347–420) was the learned Church Father and translator of the Bible into Latin.

40. Johann Brentz (1499–1570) was leader of the Reformation in Württemberg, a supporter of Luther's views.

41. Murther is written over the word kill.

42. The writings of Augustine (354–430) that Cotton cites here are *Retractationes, Epistolae, Contra epistolam Parmeniani,* and *Tractatus CXXIV in Johannis Evangelium.*

43. Optatus (d. 384?), bishop of Milevi in North Africa, flourished under Valentinian and Valens (c. 370). He wrote *De schismate donatistarum adversus parmenianum,* which by 1635 had been published in two Latin editions: Leiden, 1613, and London, 1631.

44. St. Bernard, abbot of Clairvaux (1090–1153). Cotton refers to his *Sermones super Cantica Canticorum,* which had been published in at least six different editions in the late fifteenth century.

45. Calvin's *Defensio orthodoxae fidei de sacra trinitate, contra prodigiosos errores Michaelis Serueti Hispani . . .* ([Geneva], 1554).

46. Theodore Beza (1519–1605), successor to Calvin, defended the 1553 Geneva burning of Michael Servetus in *De hæreticis a civili magistratu puniendis.*

47. Benedictus Aretius (1505–1574), *Valentini gentiliis iusto capitis supplicio Bernæ affecti breuis historia . . .* (1567).

48. This "Treatise" no longer exists and was probably a manuscript that was never published. It can be partially reconstructed, however, since Williams answers it point by point in the final fifty-six chapters of *The Bloudy Tenent.*

49. The published version of 1646, however, does print his name at this point.

Roger Williams and Samuel Sharpe to the Boston Elders

[Between July 22 and September 1, 1635]

MS. BPL, Ms. Am. 1506, pt. 2, no. 3

Published: John Russell Bartlett, ed., *The Letters of Roger Williams, 1632–1682,* in NC, *Publs.,* VI (1874), 71–77 (Charles Deane's transcription), reissued in *The Complete Writings of Roger Williams* (New York, 1963), VI, 71–77; Williams, *Correspondence,* I, 23–29

Roger Williams's (1603–1683) sojourn in New England had taken him from Boston to Salem to Plymouth and back to Salem, where he was called as teacher of the church in 1634, at a time when he was in trouble with the colonial government for objecting to civil authorities' meddling in spiritual matters. The Salem congregation's action in calling Williams caused the magistrates to react strongly against the Salem church. In early July 1635, as Winthrop described the matter, "*Salem* men had preferred a petition at the last general Court for some land in marble head necke, which they did challenge as belonginge to their towne, but because they had chosen mr williams their Teacher while he stood vnder question of Authoritye & so offered contempt to the magistrates &c: their petition was refused till &c: vpon this the Churche of Salem wrote to other Churches to admonishe the magistrates of this as a haynous sinne, & likewise the Deputyes."[1] As the following letter indicates, the Boston ministers had received Salem's letter but had chosen not to present it to the congregation. That information provoked this letter from the Salem church, signed by Williams and Samuel Sharpe (d. 1658), the Ruling Elder of the Salem church. It is in Williams's handwriting.

The dating of the letter is based on the fact that it is in response to one from Boston dated July 22 (now lost), together with the knowledge that this letter from Salem was censured by the General Court at its meeting on September 2 and 3, 1635.[2] Thus, it must have been written between those two dates. Thomas Prince's note at the top of 2v reads: "This letter I suppose censured by *th*e Gen. Ct. of the M. col. Sept. 2. 1635."

The following text is a transcription from the manuscript, which consists of two large sheets. The letter is written on both sides of the first sheet and the recto of the second sheet. Both sheets contain holes in the center and fraying at the bottom and the sides, though the first is more severely damaged than the second, having lost most of the lower right quadrant, severely affecting the text on both sides. At other points, the ink is faded and the paper water-stained or otherwise damaged so that legibility is sometimes problematic, even where paper and ink survive. Portions of the missing text—letters, words, and phrases—are sometimes preserved in Charles Deane's transcription, which was published in *The Complete Writings of Roger Williams* (1874), where Deane's note says that he "copied this letter some years ago from the original," which was then housed at the Massachusetts Historical Society. Since Deane made his transcription—probably in the late 1860s—more paper has been lost, so his text is often useful, though even then, as he said, "the letter was considerably imperfect, many of the words quite obliterated and gone" (77). He modernized spelling and punctuation throughout. In the present text, braces enclose material no longer present in the manuscript and therefore taken from Deane's version. Square brackets appearing within the braces were inserted by Deane to indicate his guesses about missing text. They are retained here, though such bracketed passages are necessarily less authoritative than text not within square brackets. The present edition occasionally departs from the Deane text and from the LaFantasie edition of Williams's *Correspondence* in reading particular details in the manuscript. Where these differences are substantive, they are indicated in the notes.

The text of this letter in Glenn W. LaFantasie's edition of *The Correspondence of Roger Williams* (designated CRW in textual notes to this letter) uses a 1924 photostat of the letter as the source text. For the present edition, consultation of the manuscript has enabled a fuller recovery of certain details. In addition, CRW offers an "eclectic text" of this letter, not attempting to indicate what portions are taken from the Deane transcription. While there are advantages to the reader in such an approach, the present edition, here and elsewhere, attempts to show what the surviving manuscript contains and what it does not.

I am especially grateful to Glenn LaFantasie for sharing his text of this letter with me before it was published. The headnotes and annotation of LaFantasie's edition are invaluable in contextualizing Williams's letters.

The Church of Jesus Christ at Salem, to o*ur* dearly beloved, & much Esteemed in Jesus, *th*e Elders of *th*e Church of Christ, at Boston./

{Y}our letters (dear & welbeloved in Christ) dated *th*e 22 of this 5th moneth, have been read openly before vs, wherin we vnderstand you see not your way clear before you, for delivering of o*ur* humble complaint vnto *th*e Church of Christ ˆwith youˆ as also your reasons why you dare not publish to *th*e bodie our letters; o*ur* Dear Brethren according to your loving & Christian desire, we dare not but gently & tenderly interpret this your delay as springing from your holy care & feare lea{s}t[3] dishonour should redound to o*ur* Lord & King, in these waightie affaires of hi{s}[4] holy goverment, We giue you many & hartie thankes for your loving & f{ai}thfull dealing in returning vs a reason of your holie fears & Jealou{sies};

And we beseech you {[in the bow]}els of christian tendernes to bear with vs while we first adde {a} wo{rd} vnto your ~~rea~~ selues, & afterwards to your reasons{.}

We have not yet apprehe{n}ded it to be *th*e choyce of *th*e officers of a church when Publicke letters are sent from {sis}ter churches, to deliver or not to deliuer the letters vnto *th*e bodie; we acknow{l}edge it their libertie & dutie to order wisely for convenience & due season of presenting *th*e church with them, but wholly to conceal or suppress *th*e letters of *th*e church we yet see not, o*ur* Reasons are amongst others these 2: {1s}t, because they are *th*e churches, not {the} officers. *Th*e church hath *th*e right w*hi*ch *th*e officers may not assume vnto themselv{es and} *ther*fore it hath been questioned whether publick letters sent ~~sent~~ to {[a Church of]} Christ ought not to be de{li}vered publi{cly} to *th*e Elders, in the face of *th*e Church met togither according to what is writte{n, [Acts]} 15:30.[5] when they had gather{ed} the Multitude (*tha*t is *th*e Church) {toget}her then they {[deliv]e}red the letters. If this be *th*e power & libertie of *th*e officers, for ought we see {[if there]} be but one Elder in *th*e church, *th*at he may privately p{ut u}p the {pub}lick letters of *th*e who{le.}

Our 2^{d} R{eason} is because *th*e presence of o*ur* Lord Jesus is {most} especially promise{d} & attends?[6] to the whole bodie met togither, in his name, {than to one} or all the Elde{rs; and} therfore in sollemne seeking of Gods face by *th*e who{le Church (h}is spowse & wife) we conceiue a more clear & distinct apprehension o{f the mind of} Christ concerning an Answer to be returned back ˆdoth ordinarily ariseˆ then from *th*e offic{ers apart from [the Church.]}

For however it hath been the Prælat{e[s p]le}a, [that] {the people are weak}||

giddie & rash, & therfore shold not enjoy suc{h liberties, we con[ceive per]s}ones truly g{ather}ed in his name shall find {a wisdom great[er than theirs]} in *th*e midst among{st} them, even Jesus Christ who {himself is made their wis[dom]}|| 1 Cor. 1.30.[7] {Y}our reasons of not reading are {three; two against reading a[t all, the third,]} ag*ain*st reading it on[8] *th*e Lordes day. The first mo{re expressly concerning}|| o*u*r admonition (you say) is a g{i}ft w*hi*ch shold not be {offered up [until we have]} reconciled o*u*r selues to o*u*r much h{ono}ured & beloved *th*{e majistrates [who are]} [IV] against us.

Now we beseech you humbly o*u*r dear Brethren consider || a gift, o*u*r praiers, & thankes, & offrings, are also gifts Mat. {5.[23,24.],}[9] & then if no gift may be offred while a case of offence dep{[endeth, then surely]}

1 Brethren,[10] ^A brother^ yea a whole church must intermit their holy mee{t[ings, and]} for a while *th*e ordinances, yea for *th*e present be vn-churched.

2 And so 2dly If we shold meet togither ^to consider^ about, & finde out *th*e offence, we sh{[ould not]} offer vp *th*e incense of o*u*r praiers, to the Lord for *th*e discouerie of *th*e offence vn{to [our brethren.]}

3 further for ought we see we shold not at all come togither, for *th*e pres[ence] of o*u*r soules & bodies together in *th*e presence of *th*e Lord is a gift.

4 Nay more by *tha*t rule no church in her members might haue fellowship with vs, nor our selues with them, in case we haue not power to offer vp a gift while {a} matter of offence dependeth, th{ou}gh o*u*r selues are readye to receiue light from o*u*r Brethren concerning *th*e[11] offence.

5^{thly} If this rule be absolute, y{e h}aue fayled so farre to communicate with vs a{s}[12] to send vs these your letters, if {[we cannot]} meet together to read them & consider & seek *th*e Face of o*u*r God in Chris{t} for {an}swer.

6^{thly}[13] since *tha*t some times Brethren may be offended at a good & righteous Act, pleasing to Christ as some were, Actes 11. {[17,18],}[14] by this ground it will follow *tha*t *th*e churches shall offer vp no gift to God n{o}r[15] man vntill they haue repented of their duties, & confest them as sinne both to God & man in case others be offended.

Lastly be you pleased to remember *tha*t hitherto in a Church way (the way o{f} Christ for Church faylinges) {we ha}ue no{t} heard of any one Brother off{ended} with vs, w*hi*ch should haue been, in ||ou might any way have held forth A{rg}um*en*t[16] vnto us, o*u*r reason is bu|| {[gre]}at[17] difference between a ch{urch} way, & *th*e ~~pleading~~ ^proceeding^ of a Common weale;

Your {second} Argum*en*t seems to be, *th*e Act of *th*e Magistrates gaue || {[pub]}lick {of}fence, & beside *tha*t, a Publicke action offensive may be but a priv{ate} offence{: un}to thi{s} with all due submission we conceive *th*e court of Justice is a{s} publicke {[as the]} gate of *th*e citie,[18] Amos. 5.12. they turn aside *th*e poore from their ri{ght in th}e gate;[19] 2dly we acknowledge in some obscu{re and} darke passages, {one or two} may spie a blemish where thowsands doe not, this is a secret, {and we desire} to walke by the rule: Prov. 25.9: debate the cause with {thy neighbor himse}lfe & discover not a secret to another,[20] but to punish {[befor]e she hath been} conve{n}ted, to deal with a Church out of a Church way{, [to] punish two or three hundred of our town}e for the conceiued fayling of *th*e Church we s{ee [not] how any cloud of} obscuritie can hide this Evill from *th*e Eyes of all; {and therefore not two or three of} our selues but many of *th*e p{rese}nt Court, & many {others, and ourselves [of the] Ch}urch of Christ who crie to *th*e Lord for mercie to ex|| {see a failing, yea} some hundreds of *th*e whole town smarting in thei{r}|| {and the whole} land may, & other {la}nds hearing of it cannot choose {[but be bli]nded, weaken}ed, stumbled; & therefore we conceiue as *th*e sunne {[cannot] be shut up in a} chamber Pub{li}cke failings[21] must be openly [2] {[complain]}ed of: i tim 5.20. them *tha*t sinne rebuke before all *tha*t others may fear.[22]

{[Yo]u} say you cannot Judge of *ou*r right & title, for our matters, are onely {[st]}ayd, we signifie thus much to your selues & humblie request if there be {c}ause, you will signify so much to *th*e brethren *tha*t we ˆareˆ farre from arguing {o}ur right with any in a church way. we hoped *th*e proofe *tha*t was desired by *th*e Court wold have giuen satisfaction might they haue had leave to speake & furthermore *th*e delay of a Peticion in cases of present necessitie, (as ye well know) may be as greivous as[23] the delay of a few moneths (such stood *th*e present state of *th*e towne ~~then~~) as if it was a whole yeer,: & therfore the Lord ~~deli~~ provides against delayes of a poore mans wages, deutr. 24:14:15. not onely because of his present need but also because of *th*e ~~pres~~ greife of his spirit. w*hi*ch would[24] make him crie vnto God ˆfor redressˆ against the ~~injuries~~ iniurious.[25] We doubt not but a peticion may be both delayed & rejected, but we must needs profess *ou*r exceeding greif *tha*t a church of Christ shall vnder goe a punishm*en*t before convented, be punished (if there were due cause) before exhorted to repentence in a rule of Christ, & hundreds of innocents punished of *th*e town|| as the conceiued nocents of *th*e Church.

This to *ou*r apprehensions is such an euill, as which (whether we respect *th*e Persons, or the Publick nature of *th*e Evill, as) God is not wont to expiate without some p{u}blicke stroake of Jealousie[26] & displeasure.

We hope we shall ever be with *th*e formost in all humble respect & service to all higher powers, according to God, we speak now of *ou*r much honoured Brethren as Brethren, whose soules are deer & pretious to vs, in holie Couenant, & therin conceiue the onely way to honour them in *th*e Lord, is to beseech them to wash away *th*e dishonour of *th*e most high, by true, godly sorrow & repentance, & in this your service we conceiue in *th*e e{nd} you will finde *tha*t most true w*hi*ch *th*e spirit of G{[od]} writes, open rebuke is better then secrett loue.

Your 3d Argum*ent* is *tha*t you dare not vpon the Lords day deal in a worldly busines, nor {[bring a]} Ciuill busines in *th*e church; first pleas you to remember (o*u*r dear & welbeloued in Ch{rist)} that for any Ciuill matter we open not o*u*r mouth, we speak of a spirituall offence ag{ainst} o*u*r Lord Jesus & ag*ain*st *th*e holy Couenant of Brethren, & so we doubt not though uncleannesse [illegible word] vsurie oppression[27] be offenses ag*ain*st *th*e C{[ivil st]}ate w*hi*ch *th*e chu{rch} medles {[not]} with, yet the church deals with members lawfullie for their breach {[of cove]}nant [deleted word] ˆ&ˆ disobedience ag*ain*st *th*e Lord Jesus.

Againe, we are not bold to limit you (o*u*r beloued) to *th*e Lords day. We leaue {[it to your]} wisdome & *th*e wisdome of *th*e church, when to consider of *th*e matter: yet hither{[to]} we haue conceiued that *th*e kingly office of o*u*r Lord Jesus ought to be as well administred on *th*e Lords day as his preistly & prophetic [offices,][28] & that[29] he is as much honoured in *th*e censuring[30] or pardoning of sinners from his throne (Zach 6.13.)[31] in case of transgressio*n* ag*ain*st his croun, as {against} *th*e administration of other in[32] sweet & blessed ordinances.

Now o*u*r blessed {C[hrist Jes]}us who holdeth his starrs in his right hand, & out of whose mouth goes a sha{[rp two-]}edged sword, & whose Countenance shines a{s} *th*e sunne in his strength Rev. 1.16.[33] shine mercifully and clearly vpon your soules in all holy ||rections consolati{on}s & [sa]lvations. Your most vnworthy Brethren, unfaine{dly} respecti[ng?][34] & affecti{on}ate in Christ Jesus.

Roger William{s} Samuel Sharpe
||ams & *th*|| Encs||

1. Winthrop, *Journal,* 151.

2. The General Court meeting at Newtown, September 2, 1635, ordered "that the deputies of Salem shalbe sent backe to the Freemen of their towne that sent them, to fetch satisfact*i*on for their le*tte*res sent to the seu*er*all churches, wherein they have exceedingly rep*roa*ched & vilifyed the magistrates & deputyes of the Generall Court." The next day, September 3, the court "ordered that if the major p*ar*te of the Freemen of Salem shall disclaime the le*tte*res sent lately from the church of Salem to seu*er*all churches, it shall then be lawfull for them to send deputyes to the Gen*er*all Court." The same day, the court gave Roger Williams six weeks to get "out of this jurisdicc*i*on, not to returne any more without licence from the Court," mentioning among his offenses that he had "writt le*tte*res of defamac*i*on, both of the magistrates & churches here." Samuel Sharpe, Williams's cosigner, was "enioyned to appeare" at the next court. *Records of Massachusetts Bay,* I, 156, 158, 160–161.

3. lea{s}t] CRW: lea, with the footnote: "Faded ink has made the complete word unreadable." Actually, there is a small hole in the paper that removes the s.

4. hi{s}] CRW: hi, with the footnote: "RW neglected to write the final letter in this word." In fact, a hole in the paper has removed the s.

5. Acts 15:30: So when they were dismissed, they came to Antioch: and when they had gathered the multitude together, they delivered the epistle.

6. Deane and CRW omit this word, which is badly blurred, though surviving portions of each letter suggest this speculative reading.

7. 1 Cor. 1:30: But of him are ye in Christ Jesus, who of God is made unto us wisdom, and righteousness, and sanctification, and redemption.

8. reading it on] Deane: reading on.

9. Matt. 5:23, 24: Therefore if thou bring thy gift to the altar, and there rememberest that thy brother hath ought against thee; Leave there thy gift before the altar, and go thy way; first be reconciled to thy brother, and then come and offer thy gift.

10. Deane omits this word.

11. *the*] Deane and CRW: our.

12. CRW omits this word.

13. 6[thly]] Deane: 6th.

14. Acts 11:17, 18: Forasmuch then as God gave them the like gift as he did unto us, who believed on the Lord Jesus Christ; what was I, that I could withstand God? When they heard these things, they held their peace, and glorified God, saying, Then hath God also to the Gentiles granted repentance unto life.

15. n{o}r] CRW: or.

16. forth A{rg}um*ent*] Deane: forth . . . argument.

17. is bu|| {[gre]}at] Deane: is . . . [gre]at; CRW: is best [*illegible*] great. A hole in the paper causes the break in the text.

18. {[as the]} gate of the citie] Deane brackets this entire phrase, even though the last four words are quite legible in the manuscript. Deane himself actually caught this error, but too late to have the correction incorporated by the printer. Charles Deane to John Russell Bartlett, Mar. 31, 1874 (copy), and Bartlett to Deane, Apr. 3, 1874 (copy), in working papers file of the editors of *The Correspondence of Roger Williams,* Rhode Island Historical Society.

19. "they turn aside . . ." is the final clause in Amos 5:12.

20. This is a quotation of the verse in Proverbs.

21. failings] Deane and CRW: sinnings.

22. This is a quotation of 1 Tim. 5:20.

23. The a in this word appears to have been written over a semicolon.

24. would] Deane: will.

25. Deut. 24:14–15: Thou shalt not oppress an hired servant that is poor and needy, whether he be of thy brethren, or of thy strangers that are in thy land within thy gates: At his day thou shalt give him his hire, neither shall the sun go down upon it: lest he cry against thee unto the Lord, and it be sin unto thee.

26. Jealousie] Deane: jealously.

27. uncleannesse [illegible word] vsurie oppresion] Deane: unclean . . . oppression; CRW: uncleanne [*illegible*] oppression.

28. [offices,]] Deane: [office,]; CRW: office,.

29. & that] Deane: and [also] that; CRW: and also that.

30. in the censuring] Deane: in the [act of] censuring.

31. Zech. 6:13: Even he shall build the temple of the Lord; and he shall bear the glory, and

shall sit and rule upon his throne; and he shall be a priest upon his throne: and the counsel of peace shall be between them both.

32. in] Deane and CRW: his.

33. Rev. 1:16: And he had in his right hand seven stars: and out of his mouth went a sharp twoedged sword: and his countenance was as the sun shineth in his strength.

34. Respecti[ng]] Deane and CRW: respective.

John Cotton to [Anthony Tuckney]

October 5, 1635

Published: Robert Ba[il]lie, *A Dissuasive from the Errours of the Time* . . . (London, 1646), 66–67

The following fragments of this letter survive only as they are included by the Scottish Presbyterian, Robert Baillie, in a list of items of evidence of what he viewed as the New Englanders' lack of adequate control over heretical and separatist practices and viewpoints. Baillie says the letter was written by Cotton "*from* New-England *to his friends at* Boston, October 5. 1635." Cotton helped identify the recipient more precisely when he remarked in *The Way of Congregational Churches Cleared* . . . (London, 1648), "My letter, which Mr. *Baylie* quoteth amongst his testimonies . . . was not written to [Thomas Goodwin], but to a brother of mine (by Mariage) in *Boston*" (26). This describes Anthony Tuckney (1599–1670), Cotton's successor as vicar at Boston in 1633. When Tuckney was about eleven years old, his father, William, died, and he was placed in the care of his uncle Anthony Hawkred, husband of his father's sister. Hawkred's daughter, Sarah, in 1632 had become John Cotton's second wife. Thus, Sarah Hawkred Cotton and Anthony Tuckney were cousins, raised in the same household. As Cotton implies in calling Tuckney his "brother of mine (by marriage)," Sarah Cotton apparently thought of Tuckney as her brother.[1]

Baillie prints these fragments from Cotton's letter as two separate items in a long list of items of complaint against New England practices or reports of such practices. The two fragments printed below might have been contiguous in Cotton's letter, but Baillie treats them as separate items, indicating that they were extracted from a fuller context, now lost.

Some other things there be, which were I again with you, I durst not take that liberty which some times I have taken: I durst not joyn in your Book-Prayers.

* * *

I durst not now partake in the Sacraments with you, though the Ceremonies were removed. I know not how you can be excused from Fellowship of their sins, if you continue in your place. While you and some of my other friends continue with them, I fear the rest will settle upon their Lees with more securitie. The wise-hearted that left their Stations in *Israel,* I doubt not, were some of them, if not all, usefull and serviceable men in their places; yet they did themselves and their Brethren more good service in going before their Brethren, as the Goats before the Flocks, *Jerem. 50.8*[2] then if they had tarried with them to the corrupting of their own wayes. *2 Chro. 11.14,16.*[3]

1. The individual and family relations are clearly charted in Horatio G. Somerby's handwritten "Genealogical account of the Families of Cotton, in England" (1859), MHS; see "Pedigrees of Hawcred, Tuckney, Story, Cony, Horrocks, and Others," 140–141. Somerby later published a pamphlet summarizing his findings in which he concludes that "Anthony Tuckney . . . was . . . first cousin to Cotton's wife, Sarah Hawkridge." *The English Ancestry of Rev. John Cotton of Boston* (Boston, 1868), 12.

2. Jer. 50:8: Remove out of the midst of Babylon, and go forth out of the land of the Chaldeans, and be as the he goats before the flocks.

3. 2 Chron. 11:14–16: For the Levites left their suburbs and their possession, and came to Judah and Jerusalem: for Jereboam and his sons had cast them off from executing the priest's office unto the Lord: And he ordained him priests for the high places, and for the devils, and for the calves which he had made. And after them out of all the tribes such as set their hearts to seek the Lord God of Israel came to Jerusalem, to sacrifice unto the Lord God of their fathers.

John Cotton to Roger Williams

Early 1636

Published: *A Letter of Mr. John Cottons, Teacher of the Church in Boston, in New-England, to Mr. Williams a Preacher There . . .* (London, 1643); NC, *Publs.,* I (1866), 295–311, rpt. in *The Complete Writings of Roger Williams* (New York, 1963), I, 295–311; Williams, *Correspondence,* I, 31–52

On October 9, 1635, Roger Williams was banished from the Massachusetts Bay Colony. He was given until spring to leave, but was about to be arrested for violating the admonition "not to goe about to drawe others into his opinions," in Winthrop's words, when he left the colony in January 1635/6, and made for Rhode Island.[1] There were apparently exchanges, both in speech and in writing, between him and Cotton both before and after his departure. Williams later recalled receiving the following letter from Cotton in *"a time of my distressed wandrings amongst the* Barbarians" after leaving Massachusetts. Being then in *"an howling Wildernesse in Frost and Snow,"* he did not immediately reply. Later, he says, he did write a reply but forebore sending it, perceiving that Cotton was not in a receptive frame of mind or, as he put it, in the hope that time would *"mollifie and soften, and render more humane and mercifull, the eare and heart of that (otherwise) excellent and worthy man."*[2] Meanwhile, they apparently kept up an exchange regarding the issue of toleration which ultimately led to their *Bloody Tenent* writings. The present disagreement, however, had to do with Williams's Separationist views, the primary cause of his banishment.[3]

The New England Puritans insisted that their aim regarding the "purity" of church fellowship was, not to condemn the individual churches of England, with which they wanted to continue their fellowship and communication, but to establish a more scripturally pure example of church organization and membership from which others could learn. At the same time, they did find fault with the English congregations that formally declared a separation from the established church there, and they took the position that one should not commune with such churches. Cotton makes this argument here, pronouncing his strong opinion on the politics of the church in England. He finds the government and church officials in England have "winked at" the Separatists' meetings, whereas "the Conventicles of the puritans (as they call them)" are "hunted out with all diligence, and pursued with more violence then any law will justifie." And yet, Cotton says, the Separatist churches are not blessed with peace, but are characterized by dissension. The New Englanders' policy of not associating with the Separatist congregations in England, he affirms, is well advised. While the churches' practice in England is still characterized with "pollutions," Cotton believes (in accord with most of his New England colleagues) that this is not grounds for condemning them or dissociating from them. Williams's approach was to insist more strenuously on maintaining purity by refusing to affiliate with the corrupt.

This letter is a significant statement on New England church membership practices, taking Williams's objections to the presence of sinful people in those congregations as an occasion for confirming the churches' methods of evaluating their members. In New England practice, each prospective member presented a statement of his or her faith and religious knowledge and experience before being accepted into membership. Most church spokesmen in New England admitted that this was not an infallible method for eliminating the sinful. Cotton here replies to Williams's exclusionary preferences by suggesting that it is appropriate to admit into church membership those "who doe truely repent and confesse their greatest and most notorious sins" even though there are still some "superstitions" in their former practice the sinfulness of which they remain uncertain about. He observes approvingly that many confessed that they came to New England to escape the "bondage" of "humane inventions" in the churches' practices and that they profess "their hearty sorrow" for having been previously defiled by it. They are, in other words, seeking purity in the churches, though the level of purity may be lower than that which Williams is holding out for.

When Williams was in London in 1643–1644 he seems to have shown Cotton's letter to acquaintances there, one of whom took it upon himself to publish it as *A Letter of Mr. John Cottons to Mr. Williams*. This was quickly followed by Williams's own *Mr. Cottons Letter Lately Printed, Examined and Answered,* which answers Cotton point by point, quoting Cotton piecemeal throughout.[4] The following text is that of the first edition, though all quotation marks are here rendered as double rather than the single quotation marks in the 1643 printing.

Beloved in Christ,

Though I have little hope (when I consider the uncircumcision of mine owne lips, *Exod.* 6.12.)[5] that you will hearken to my voyce, who hath not hearkened to the body of the whole Church of Christ with you, and the testimony, and judgement of so many Elders and Brethren of other Churches, yet I trust my labour will be accepted of the Lord; and who can tell but that he may blesse it to you also, if (by his helpe) I indevour to shew you the sandinesse of those grounds, out of which you have banished yours from the fellowship of all the Churches in these Countries? Let not any prejudice against my person (I beseech you) forestall either your affection or judgement, as if I had hastened forward the sentence of your civill banishment; for what was done by the Magistrates, in that kinde, was neither done by my counsell nor consent, although I dare not deny the sentence passed to be righteous in the eyes of God, who hath said that he that with-holdeth the Corne (which is the staffe of life) from the people, the multitude shall curse him, *Prov.* 11.26.[6] how much more shall they separate such from them as doe with-hold and separate them from the Ordinances, or the Ordinances from them (which are in Christ the bread of life.) And yet it may be they passed that sentence against you not upon that ground, but for ought I know, upon your other corrupt doctrines, which tend to the disturbance both of civill and holy peace, as may appeare by that answer which was sent to the Brethren of the Church of *Salem,* and to your selfe. And to speake freely what I thinke, were my soule in your soules stead, I should thinke it a worke of mercy of God to banish me from the civill society of such a Common wealth, when I could not injoy holy fellowship with any Church of God amongst them without sin.[7] What should the Daughter of *Zion* doe in *Babell?* why should she not hasten to flee from thence? *Zach.* 2.6,7.[8]

I speake not these things (the God of Truth is my witnes) to adde affliction to your affliction, but (if it were the holy will of God) to move you to a more serious sight of your sin, and of the justice of Gods hand against it. Against your corrupt Doctrines, it pleased the Lord Jesus to fight against you with the sword of his mouth (as himselfe speaketh, *Rev.* 2.16.)[9] in the mouthes and testimonies of the Churches and Brethren. Against whom, when you overheated your selfe in reasoning and disputing against the light of his truth, it pleased him to stop your mouth by a suddaine disease, and to threaten to take your breath from you. But you in stead of recoyling (as even *Balaam* offered to doe in the like case) you chose rather to persist in your way, and to protest against all the Churches and Brethren that stood in your way: and thus the good hand of Christ that should have humbled you, to see and turne from the errour of your way, hath rather hardned you therein, and quickned you onely to see failings (yea intolerable errours) in all the Churches and brethren, rather then in your selfe. In which course though you say you doe not remember an houre wherein the countenance of the Lord was darkned to you, yet be not deceived, it is no new thing with Satan to transforme himselfe into an Angell of light, and to cheare the soule with false peace, and with flashes of counterfeit consolation. Sad and wofull is the memory of Master *Smiths* strong consolations on his death-bed, which are set as a Seale to the grosse and damnable Arminianisme and Enthusiasmes delivered in the confession of his faith, prefixed to the story of his life and death.[10] The countenance of God is upon his people when they feare him, not when they presume of their owne strength; and his consolations are found not in the way of presidence in errour, but in the wayes of humility and truth.

Two stumbling blockes (I perceive by your letter) have turned you off from fellowship with us. First, the want of fit matter of our Church. Secondly, disrespect of the separate Churches in England under afflictions, who doe our selves practise separation in peace.

" For the first, you acknowledge (as you say) with joy that godly persons are "the visible matter of these Churches, but yet you see not that godly persons "are matter fitted to constitute a Church, no more then trees or Quarries are "fit matter proportioned to the building.

Answ. This exception seemeth to mee to imply a contradiction to it selfe, for if the matter of our Churches be as you say godly persons, they are not then as trees unfelled, or stones unhewen. Godlinesse cutteth men downe from the former roote, and heweth them out of the pit of corrupt nature, and fitteth them for fellowship with Christ and with his people.

" You object, first, a necessity lying upon godly men before they can be "fit matter for Church fellowship, to see, bewaile, repent, and come out of "the false Churches ministry, worship, and government, according to Scripturs, *Isa.* 52.11. 2 *Cor.* 6.17. *Revel.* 18.4.[11] And those this to be done[12] not by a "locall remoovall or contrary practise, &c. but by a deliverance of the soule, "understanding, minde, conscience, judgement, will and affections.

Answ. 1. We grant it is not locall remoovall from former pollutions, or contrary practise, that fitteth us for fellowship with Christ and his Church, but that it is necessary also that we doe repent of such former pollutions wherein we have beene defiled and inthralled.

Wee grant further that it is likewise necessary to Church-fellowship, we should see and discerne all such pollutions as doe so farre enthrall us to Antichrist, to separate us from Christ.

But this wee professe unto you, that wherein we have reformed our practise, therein have we endeavoured unfainedly to humble our soules for our former contrary walking. If any through hypocrisie are wanting herein, the hidden hypocrisie of some will not prejudice the sinceritie and faithfulnesse of others, nor the Church estate of all.

And that we doe (by the grace of Christ) see and discerne all such pollutions as doe so farre enthrall us to Antichrist as to separate us from Christ; your selfe doth acknowledge in acknowledging the visible members of these Churches to be godly persons; for godly persons are not so enthralled to Antichrist, as to separate them from Christ, else they could not be godly persons.

Answ. 2. We deny that it is necessary to Church-fellowship (to wit, so necessary as that without it, a Church cannot be) that the members admitted thereunto should all of them see, expressely bewaile all the pollutions which they have beene defiled with in the former Church-fellowship, ministery, worship, government. If they see and bewaile so much of their former pollutions as did enthrall them to Antichrist, as to separate them from Christ, and be ready in preparation of heart, as they shall see more light, so to hate more and more every false way, we conceive it is as much as is necessarily required to separation from Antichrist, and to fellowship with Christ and his Churches. The Churches of *Iudea* admitted many thousand Jewes that believed on the name of Christ, although they were still zealous of the Law, and saw not the beggerly emptinesse of *Moses* his ceremonies, *Act.* 21.20.[13] And the Apostle *Paul* directeth the Romans to receive such unto them as are weake in the faith, and see not their liberty from the servile difference of meats and dayes, but still lie under the bondage of the Law, yea he wisheth them to receive such upon this ground, because Christ hath received them, *Rom.* 14.1. to 6.[14]

Say not, there is not the like danger of lying under bondage to *Moses* as to Antichrist, for even the bondage under *Moses* was such, as if they continued in after instruction and conviction, would separate them from Christ, *Gal.* 5.2.[15] And bondage under Antichrist could doe no more.

Answ. 3. To the places of Scripture which you object, *Isa.* 52.11. 2 *Cor.* 6.17. *Revel.* 18.4. we answer, two of them make nothing to your purpose, for that of *Esay* and the other of the *Revelation,* speake of locall separation, which your selfe knoweth we have made, and yet you say you doe not apprehend that to be sufficient. As for that place of the *Corinths,* it onely requireth comming out from Idolaters in the fellowship of their Idolatry. No marriages were they to make with them: no feasts were they to hold with them in the Idols Temple: no intimate familiaritie were they to maintaine with them: nor any fellowship were they to keepe with them in the unfruitfull workes of darkenesse; and this is all which that place requireth. But what makes all this to prove that we may not receive such persons to Church-fellowship as our selves confesse to be godly, and who doe professedly renounce and bewaile all knowne sinne, and would renounce more if they knew more, although it may be they doe not yet see the utmost skirts of all that pollution they have sometimes beene defiled with; as the Patriarchs saw not the pollution of their Polygamie? But that you may plainely see this place is wrested besides the Apostles scope, when you argue from it that such persons are not fit matter of Church-fellowship, as are defiled with any remnants of Antichristian pollution; nor such Churches any more to be accounted Churches, as doe receive such amongst them; Consider I pray you, were there not at that time in the Church of *Corinth* such as partaked with Idolaters in their Idols Temples? and was not this the touching of an uncleane thing? and did this sinne reject these members from Church fellowship before conviction? or did it evacuate their Church estate for not casting out of such members?

2. Your second objection is taken from the confession of sinnes made by "*Johns* Disciples, and the proselyte Gentiles before admission into Church-"fellowship, *Matth.* 3.6. *Act.* 19.18.[16] whence you gather that Christian Churches "are constituted of such members as make open and plaine confession of "their sinnes; and if any sinnes be to be confessed and lamented, (Jewish, or "Paganish) then Antichristian drunkennesse, and whoredome much more, of "all such as have drunke of the whores cup, or but sipt of it. And therefore "as persons, though godly, are not made fit for the Church, if open drunk-"ennesse or whoredome lie upon them, yea or but one act of either, untill "conviction, true repentance, confession, and renunciation of their wayes be "discerned: so here.

And yet as if you had grasped more then you could hold, you let fall some part of what you had assumed, and doe grant, that

" Such a confession and renunciation is not absolute necessary to the admis-"sion of members, (though the want of it be a grievous offence) if the substance "of true repentance be discerned.

Answ. 1. If such a confession and renunciation be not of absolute necessity to the admission of members when the substance of true repentance is discerned, then such Congregations may be true Churches (by your owne confession) who doe admit for their members such godly persons as doe professe and hold forth the substance of true repentance; for such persons professing their repentance for all their knowne and open sinnes, doe withall professe their readinesse to repent of and forsake whatsoever further sinnes shall be discovered to them.

Ans. 2. When you judge that godly persons are not matter fitted for the Church, untill first they be illuminated and convinced of the sinfulnesse of every sipping of the whores cup;[17] you take away with the one hand what you granted with the other, and withall you impose a burthen upon the Church of Christ, which Christ never required at their hands nor yours.

For we deny that it is necessary to the admission of members that every one should be convinced of the sinfulnesse of every sipping of the Whores cup, for every sipping of a drunkards cup is not sinfull; and though the cup of the whore doe more intoxicate the mind then the drunkards cup doth the body, yet you know bodily drunkennesse and whoredome are such notorious and grosse sinnes that no man that hath any true repentance in him, cannot but bee convinced of the sinfulnesse of them, and of the necessity of repentance of them in particular. But the Whores cup being a mystery of iniquity,[18] the sinfulnesse of it, is nothing so evident and notorious as that every true repentant soule doth at first discerne the filthinesse of it: and therefore as those three thousand Jewes and Proselytes were admitted into the fellowship of the first Christian Church, when they repented of their murther of Christ, although they never saw nor confessed all the superstitious leavenings wherewith the Pharisees had bewitched them, *Act.* 2. 37 to 47.[19] so doubtlesse may such godly persons be admitted into the fellowship of our Churches, who doe truely repent and confesse their greatest and most notorious sins, although they be not yet convinced of every passage of Antichristian superstition, wherewith they have beene defiled in their former walkings.

The Disciples of *John* (whom you instance in) did indeed confesse their sinnes, the Publicans their sinnes, the Souldiers theirs, the People theirs, but yet it doth not appeare that they confessed their Pharisaicall pollutions, but rather the notorious sinnes, incident to their callings, as did also those Gentiles of whom you speake, *Act.* 19.18,19.[20] Conjurers confessed their curious Arts, and others their deeds, but whether all their deeds, is not expressed.

Answ. 3. But to satisfie you more fully (and the Lord make you willing in true meekenesse of Spirit to receive satisfaction) the body of the members whom we receive, doe in generall professe, the reason of their comming over to us was, that they might be freed from the bondage of such humane inventions and ordinances as their soules groaned under, for which also they professe their hearty sorrow, so far as through ignorance or infirmity they have beene defiled.[21] Besides, in our daily meetings, and especially in times of our solemne humiliations, we generally all of us bewaile all our former pollutions, wherewith we have defiled our selves, and the holy things of God, in our former Administrations and Communions, but wee rather choose to doe it, than to talke of it, and wee cannot but wonder how you can so boldly and resolutely renounce the Churches of Christ, for neglect of that, which you know not whether they have neglected or no, and before you have admonished us of our sinfulnesse in such neglect, if it be found amongst us.

" *Object.* 3. Your third Objection is taken from *Hag.* 2. 13,14,15.[22] a place "which you desire may be throughly weighed, and that the Lord would hold "the scales himselfe. The Prophet there tels the Church of the Jewes, that if "a person uncleane by a dead body, touch holy things, those holy things be- "come uncleane unto him, and so, saith he, is this Nation, and so is every "worke of their hands, and that which they offer there is uncleane. And this (as "you conceive) argueth that even Church Covenants made, and Ordinances "practised by persons polluted through spirituall deadnesse and filthinesse of "Communion, they become uncleane unto them, and are prophaned by them.

Answ. Now surely if your selfe had hearkned to your owne desire, and had throughly weighed the Scripture, and had suffered the Lord to have held the scales himselfe, you would never have alledged this place to your purpose. Your purpose was to prove that Churches cannot be constituted by such persons as are uncleane by antichristian pollutions, or if they be so constituted, they are not to be communicated with, but separated from: To prove this you alledge this place; when the Prophet acknowledgeth the whole Church of the Jewes to be uncleane, and yet neither denyeth them to be a Church truely constituted, nor stirreth up himselfe or others to separate from them.

If you say, why but they were uncleane? I Answer, be it so, but were they therefore no Church truely constituted, or to be separated from? yea did not *Haggai* and *Zachary* themselves communicate with them, and call others also to come out of *Babell* to communicate with them, even whilest *Joshua* the High Priest was still polluted with his unclean garments, *Zac* 2.6,7. with 6.3. 8.3.[23] But if indeed you desire to know, what upon due weighing of the place, I conceive to be the meaning of it, you shall finde it to be this; The occasion of the words arise from a worldly distemper, which the time grew upon, all sorts of the members of that Church, who were so farre carryed away with care of their owne outward accommodations, that while every man looked to his owne house, and the seiling of it, the Temple of the Lord and the building thereof was generally neglected of them all, Prince, Priest, and People, whence it was that God neither delighted in their spirituall services, nor in their bodily labours, but left them without a blessing in both, *Hagg.* 1. 6. to 11.[24] Now to cleare the justice of Gods proceeding against them in that case, he alledgeth a secondable law for it, out of *Moses;* The former is written in *Levit.* 6.27.[25] where the Law saith, that a garment touching any holy flesh of the sin offering should be holy. But if the garment which toucheth holy flesh shall touch other things, as the person that weareth it, or any pottage, or Bread, or wine, or any touch of other common thing, the thing touched is not thereby hallowed by the touch of such a garment.

Againe, there was another Law, that whosoever touched any uncleane body, should be uncleane seven dayes, and if in that time hee touched the

Tabernacle, or the holy things thereof, they shall be uncleane, *Numb.* 19.13.[26] Now (to apply these Lawes to the scope of the Prophet) the touch of a dead body did type out either fellowship with dead workes, as *Ephes.* 5.11.[27] or dead persons, 2 *Cor.* 6.14,15,16,17.[28] or dead world, *Gal.* 6.14.[29] but of these three, it was the dead world wherewith Priest and Prince and all the people were at that time generally defiled, in that they tooke more care and paines for worldly conveniences, then for the Lords holy Ordinances. Whereupon according to the answer of the Priest, agreeable to the Law, the Prophet pronounceth them, in the sight of the Lord, all to be uncleane.

From both these Lawes, and the Interpretation of them by the Priest, and the application of them by the Prophet, it appeareth that there were two sorts of these people, and both uncleane. Some that did not touch the holy flesh, or offerings, but on the outside of their garments onely, to wit, in bodily presence (and the body is but the garment of the Soule) 1 *Cor.* 5.4.[30] and such were all the Hypocrites amongst them: Others were sincere, as worshipping God in firme Truth, as *Zorobabell, Jehoshua,* and many more, but yet now defiled with touching a dead body, that is, with laying hold on a dead world, their worldly accommodations, which made their hearts and hands slow or dead to set forward the Temple worke, and in this condition both sorts, their persons, their oblations, their bodily labours, were all uncleane, and found neither acceptance nor blessing from the Lord, till the Lord stirred up the Spirits of them all to addresse themselves more seriously to the Temple worke, *Hag.* 1.12,13,14.[31]

This I take to be the true and genuine meaning of the place, which if you apply to the point in hand, will reach nothing neare to your purpose. Hypocrites in the Church, and godly Christians themselves, whilst they attend to the world more then to the things of God, their persons, their labours, their civill oblations are all uncleane in the sight of God; therefore the Church of Christ cannot be constituted of such, or if it doe consist of such, the people of God must separate from them. You might well have gathered, therefore, the Church of Christ and the members thereof must separate themselves from their hypocrisie, and inordinate love of this world, or else they and their duties will still be uncleane in the sight of God, notwithstanding their Church estate. This collection tendeth to edification, the other to dissipation and destruction of the Church, and of them that wrest blood in stead of milke from the breasts of holy Scripture.

The second stumbling blocke or offence which you take at the way of these "Churches is, that you conceive us to walke betwixt Christ and Antichrist.

" First, in practising separation here, and not repenting of our preaching "and printing against it in our owne country.

" Secondly, in reproaching your selfe at *Salem* and others for separation.

“ Thirdly, in particular, that my selfe have conceived and spoken, that sepa-
“ration is a way that God hath not prospered, as if (say you) the truth of the
“Churches way depended upon countenance of men, or upon outward peace
“and liberty.

Answ. 1. In stead of halting betwixt Christ and Antichrist, wee conceive the Lord hath guided us to walke with an even foote betweene two extreames; so that we neither defile our selves with the remnant of pollutions in other Churches, nor doe wee for the remnant of pollutions renounce the Churches themselves, nor the holy ordinances of God amongst them, which our selves have found powerfull to our salvation. This moderation, so farre as we have kept it in preaching or printing, wee see no cause to repent of, but if you shew us cause why we should repent of it, wee shall desire to repent that we repented no sooner.

2. I know no man that reproacheth *Salem* for their separation, nor doe I beleeve that they doe separate. Howsoever if any doe reproach them for it, I thinke it a sinne meet to be censured, but not with so deepe a censure as to excommunicate all the Churches, or to separate from them before it doe appeare that they doe tolerate their members in such their causelesse reproachings. Wee confesse the errours of men are to be contended against, not with reproaches, but the sword of the Spirit; but on the other side, the failings of the Churches (if any be found) are not forthwith to be healed by separation. It is not Chirurgery, but Butchery, to heale every sore in a member with no other medicine but abscission from the body.

3. For my selfe, I acknowledge the words which you mention, that the way of separation is not a way that God hath prospered. But you much mistake, when you thinke I speake it for want of their outward countenance, peace and liberty. The truth is, they finde more favour in our native country then the way of reformation wherein we walke, which is commonly reproached by the name of Puritanisme. The meetings of the Separatists may be knowne to the Officers in the Courts and winked at, when the Conventicles of the puritans (as they call them) shall be hunted out with all diligence, and pursued with more violence then any law will justifie. But I said that God had not prospered the way of separation, because he hath not blessed it either with peace amongst themselves, or with growth of grace; such as erring through simplicitie and tendernesse of conscience have growne in grace, have growne also to discerne their lawfull liberty to returne to the hearing of the word from English Preachers.

Object. But this (you feare) is to condemne the witnesses of Jesus (the separate Churches in London and elsewhere) and our jealous God will visit us for such arrerages, yea the curse of his Angel from *Meroz* will fall upon us, because we come not forth to helpe Jehovah against the mighty,[32] we pray not for them, wee come not at them, (but at Parishes frequently) yea we reproach and censure them.

Answ. The Lord Jesus never delivered that way of separation to which they beare witnesse, nor any of his Apostles after him, nor of his Prophets before him. So farre as in that way they hold or practise any holy truths, wee beare witnesse to them both in our profession and practise. The Angels curse in this case (wee blesse God) we doe not feare, because we doe come forth (according to the measure of grace given us) to helpe the Lord against the mighty, although we doe not come forth to helpe them against Jehovah. It is not to helpe Jehovah, but Satan against him, to withdraw the people of God from hearing the voyce of Christ which is preached in the evidence, and simplicity, and power of his Spirit in sundry Congregations (though they be Parishes) in our native Country. In which respect, though our people that goe over into England, choose rather to heare in some of the Parishes where the voyce of Christ is lifted up like a trumpet, then in the separated Churches (where some of us may speak by experience we have not found the like presence of Christ, or evidence of his Spirit) do not you marvaile, or stumble at it: Christs sheepe heare his voyce.[33] If any carelessely heare at randome, making no difference betwixt the voyce of Christ and the voyce of strangers, or if they shall stoope to any defilements of themselves, that so they may heare a good Preacher; as I know none such, so neither doe any of us approve them in so doing.

That wee doe not pray for the separate Churches by name, it is because we cannot pray in faith for a blessing upon their separation, which we see not to be of God nor to be led to him. If any reproach them, I will not goe about to excuse it, onely they may doe well to consider, whether they also have not reproached others.

If there bee so many separate Churches in London and in other parts of the Kingdome (as you write) it is little comfort to the true servants of Christ to heare that either such inventions of men are multiplyed, as like stumbling blockes doe turne any well minded men out of the way, or that such men being desirous of reformation, should stumble, not onely at the inventions of men, but for their sakes at the ordinances of the Lord; which appeareth the more evidently, because they separate not onely from hearing the word in all the Parishes, but also from fellowship (as your selfe say) both of the Church of *Plymouth,* and of that whereof Master *Lathorpe* was Pastor,[34] and yet they refuse all the inventions of men, and choose to serve the Lord in his owne Ordinances onely. Now truely Sir, (to use your owne words) I feare this newes pleaseth not the Lord Jesus, and therefore the more inwardly sorry I am, that it pleaseth you rather to returne to them, not to helpe the Lord against the mighty, to wit, either against the high Prelates, or against the inventions of men, as you suppose, for that you might have done here, or in *Plymouth,* or in Master *Lathorpes* Congregation; but to helpe erring though zealous soules against the mightie Ordinances of the Lord, which whosoever stumble at shall be broken; for whosoever will not kisse the Sunne, (that is, will not heare and imbrace the words of his mouth) shall perish in their way, *Psal.* 2.12.[35]

1. Winthrop, *Journal,* 158, 163.

2. Roger Williams, "To the Impartiall Reader," in *Mr. Cottons Letter Lately Printed, Examined and Answered* (London, 1644), 31, ed. Reuben Aldridge Guild, in *The Complete Writings of Roger Williams* (New York, 1963), I, 315, 316.

3. On this subject, see Edwin S. Gaustad, "Roger Williams and the Principle of Separation," *Foundations,* I, (1958), 55–64; Ziff, *Career of John Cotton,* 88–97; Hugh Spurgin, *Roger Williams and Puritan Radicalism in the English Separatist Tradition* (Lewiston, Maine, 1989); Emerson, *Cotton,* 103–109; Timothy L. Hall, *Separating Church and State: Roger Williams and Religious Liberty* (Urbana, Ill., 1998), 17–47.

4. Glenn LaFantasie's edition of this letter offers a meticulous series of footnotes quoting parts of Williams's responses to points in Cotton's letter. See Williams, *Correspondence,* 44–52.

5. Exod. 6:12: And Moses spake before the Lord, saying, Behold, the children of Israel have not hearkened unto me: how then shall Pharaoh hear me, who am of uncircumcised lips?

6. Prov. 11:26: He that withholdeth corn, the people shall curse him: but blessing shall be upon the head of him that selleth it.

7. Here Cotton, with a touch of irony, paraphrases an opinion of Williams's—that the churches of New England were corrupt and that to belong to them enmeshed one in their corruption.

8. Zech. 2:6, 7: Ho, ho, come forth, and flee from the land of the north, saith the Lord: for I have spread you abroad as the four winds of the heaven, saith the Lord. Deliver thyself, O Zion, that dwellest with the daughter of Babylon.

9. Rev. 2:16: Repent; or else I will come unto thee quickly, and will fight against them with the sword of my mouth.

10. John Smyth (c. 1554–1612), a minister at Gainsborough, infamous among the Puritans as a Separatist, had emigrated from England to Holland in about 1608 with his Separatist congregation. He soon adopted Anabaptist views, ultimately falling out with his own church over his desire to merge with a Mennonite congregation. See Philip F. Gura, *A Glimpse of Sion's Glory: Puritan Radicalism in New England, 1620–1660* (Middletown, Conn., 1984), 40–41, 98–100; Gertrude Huehns, *Antinomianism in English History, with Special Reference to the Period 1640–1660* (London, 1951), 61. Cotton refers to T[homas] P[iggott], *Propositions and Conclusions, concerning True Christian Religion, Conteyning A Confession of Faith of Certaine English People, Livinge at Amsterdam . . . The Life and Death of John Smith* ([The Netherlands?], 1613).

11. Isa. 52:11: Depart ye, depart ye, go ye out from thence, touch no unclean thing; go ye out of the midst of her; be ye clean that bear the vessels of the Lord.

2 Cor. 6:17: Wherefore come out from among them, and be ye separate, saith the Lord, and touch not the unclean thing: and I will receive you.

Rev. 18:4: And I heard another voice from heaven, saying, Come out of her, my people, that ye be not partakers of her sins, and that ye receive not of her plagues.

12. This repeats the wording of all previous editions, but Cotton probably wrote—or meant to write—And this to be done. . . .

13. Acts 21:20: And when they heard it, they glorified the Lord, and said unto him, Thou seest, brother, how many thousands of Jews there are which believe; and they are all zealous of the Lord.

14. Rom. 14:1–6: Him that is weak in the faith receive ye, but not to doubtful disputations. For one believeth that he may eat all things: another, who is weak, eateth herbs. Let not him that eateth despise him that eateth not: and let not him which eateth not judge him that eateth: for God hath received him. Who art thou that judgest another man's servant? to his own master he standeth or falleth. Yea, he shall be holden up: for God is able to make him stand. One man esteemeth one day above another: another esteemeth every day alike. Let every man be fully persuaded in his own mind. He that regardeth the day, regardeth it unto the Lord; and he that regardeth not the day, to the Lord he doth not regard it. He that eateth, eateth to the Lord, for he giveth God thanks; and he that eateth not, to the Lord he eateth not, and giveth God thanks.

15. Gal. 5:2: Behold, I Paul say unto you, that if ye be circumcised, Christ shall profit you nothing.

16. Matt. 3:6: And were baptised of him in Jordan, confessing their sins.

Acts 19:18: And many that believed came, and confessed, and shewed their deeds.

17. See description in Rev. 17:1–4: the great whore that sitteth upon many waters: With whom the kings of the earth have committed fornication, and the inhabitants of the earth have been made drunk with the wine of her fornication. . . . And the woman was arrayed in purple and scarlet colour, and decked with gold and precious stones and pearls, having a golden cup in her hand full of abominations and filthiness of her fornication.

18. Rev. 17:5: And upon her forehead was a name written, MYSTERY, BABYLON THE GREAT, THE MOTHER OF HARLOTS AND ABOMINATIONS OF THE EARTH.

19. Acts 2:37–47 tells of the conversion and baptism of some three thousand members of "the house of Israel."

20. Acts 19:18, 19: And many that believed came, and confessed, and shewed their deeds. Many of them also which used curious arts brought their books together, and burned them before all men: and they counted the price of them, and found it fifty thousand pieces of silver.

21. Here Cotton refers to the substance of some of the confessions he had heard from propsective church members. Those confessions from the first church of Boston have not been preserved, but others have. See, for instance, Edmund S. Morgan, ed., "The Diary of Michael Wigglesworth," CSM, *Publs.,* XXXV, *Trans.* (1951), 426–444; Robert G. Pope, ed., *The Notebook of the Reverend John Fiske, 1644–1675,* in CSM, *Publs.,* LXVII, *Colls.* (1974); George Selement and Bruce C. Woolley, eds., *Thomas Shepard's "Confessions,"* in CSM, *Publs.,* LVIII, *Colls.* (1981); Mary Rhinelander McCarl, "Thomas Shepard's Record of Relations of Religious Experience, 1648–1649," *WMQ,* 3d Ser., XLVIII (1991), 432–466. These documents have been the subject of significant discussions regarding the spiritual life of the laity in New England; see, for instance, Charles E. Hambrick-Stowe, *The Practice of Piety: Puritan Devotional Disciplines in Seventeenth-Century New England* (Chapel Hill, N.C., 1982), 84–90; Patricia Caldwell, *The Puritan Conversion Narrative: The Beginnings of American Expression* (Cambridge, 1983); Charles Lloyd Cohen, *God's Caress: The Psychology of Puritan Religious Experience* (New York, 1986); Kathleen M. Swaim, " 'Come and Hear': Women's Puritan Evidences," in Margo Culley, ed., *American Women's Autobiography:*

Fea(s)ts of Memory (Madison, Wis., 1992), 32–56; Michael McGiffert, *God's Plot: Puritan Spirituality in Thomas Shepard's Cambridge,* rev. ed. (Amherst, Mass., 1994), 135–148.

22. Hag. 2:13–15: Then said Haggai, if one that is unclean by a dead body touch any of these, shall it be unclean? And the priests answered and said, It shall be unclean. Then answered Haggai, and said, So is this people, and so is this nation before me, saith the Lord; and so is every work of their hands; and that which they offer is unclean. And now, I pray you, consider from this day and upward, from before a stone was laid upon a stone in the temple of the Lord.

23. Zech. 6:3: And in the third chariot white horses; and in the fourth chariot grisled and bay horses.

Zech. 8:3: Thus saith the Lord; I am returned unto Zion, and will dwell in the midst of Jerusalem: and Jerusalem shall be called a city of truth; and the mountain of the Lord of hosts the holy mountain.

24. Hag. 1:6–11: Ye have sown much, and bring in little; ye eat, but ye have not enough; ye drink, but ye are not filled with drink; ye clothe you, but there is none warm; and he that earneth wages earneth wages to put it into a bag with holes.

Thus saith the Lord of hosts; Consider your ways. Go up to the mountain, and bring wood, and build the house; and I will take pleasure in it, and I will be glorified, saith the Lord. Ye looked for much, and lo, it came to little; and when ye brought it home, I did blow upon it. Why? saith the Lord of hosts. Because of mine house that is waste, and ye run every man unto his own house. Therefore the heaven over you is stayed from dew, and the earth is stayed from her fruit. And I called for a drought upon the land, and upon the mountains, and upon the corn, and upon the new wine, and upon the oil, and upon that which the ground bringeth forth, and upon men, and upon cattle, and upon all the labour of the hands.

25. Lev. 6:27: Whatsoever shall touch the flesh thereof shall be holy: and when there is sprinkled of the blood thereof upon any garment, thou shalt wash that whereon it was sprinkled in the holy place.

26. Num. 19:13: Whosoever toucheth the dead body of any man that is dead, and purifyeth not himself, defileth the tabernacle of the Lord; and that soul shall be cut off from Israel: because the water of separation was not sprinkled upon him, he shall be unclean; his uncleanness is yet upon him.

27. Ephes. 5:11: And have no fellowship with the unfruitful works of darkness, but rather reprove them.

28. 2 Cor. 6:14–17: Be ye not unequally yoked together with unbelievers: for what fellowship hath righteousness with unrighteousness? and what communion hath light with darkness? And what concord hath Christ with Belial? or what part hath he that believeth with an infidel? And what agreement hath the temple of God with idols? for ye are the temple of the living God; as God hath said, I will dwell in them, and walk in them; and I will be their God, and they shall be my people. Wherefore come out from among them, and be ye separate, saith the Lord, and touch not the unclean thing: and I will receive you.

29. Gal. 6:14: But God forbid that I should glory, save in the cross of our Lord Jesus Christ, by whom the world is crucified unto me, and I unto the world.

30. 1 Cor. 5:4: In the name of our Lord Jesus Christ, when ye are gathered together, and my spirit, with the power of our Lord Jesus Christ.

31. Hag. 1:12–14: Then Zerubbabel the son of Shealtiel and Joshua the son of Josedech, the high priest, with all the remnant of the people, obeyed the voice of the Lord their God, and the words of Haggai the prophet, as the Lord their God had sent him, and the people did fear be-

fore the Lord. Then spake Haggai the Lord's messenger in the Lord's message unto the people, saying, I am with you, saith the Lord. And the Lord stirred up the spirit of Zerubbabel the son of Shealtiel, governor of Judah, and the spirit of Joshua the son of Josedech, the high priest, and the spirit of all the remnant of the people; and they came and did work in the house of the Lord of hosts, their God.

32. Williams is incorporating the language of Judg. 5:23.

33. In John 10:11–30, Jesus characterizes himself as the good shepherd; Williams has verse 27 particularly in mind.

34. John Lathorpe (also Lothropp, Lathrop) (1584–1653) was the Separatist pastor of the church at Scituate (1635–1639) and later at Barnstable (1639–1653), both in Plymouth Colony. His last position in England had been as successor to Henry Jacobs as pastor of a London church often mentioned as a key Separatist congregation. See *DAB; DNB;* Brook, *Lives of the Puritans,* III, 163–165; Venn, *Alumni Cantabrigienses,* III, 104.

35. Ps. 2:12: Kiss the Son, lest he be angry, and ye perish from the way, when his wrath is kindled but a little. Blessed are all they that put their trust in him.

Either Cotton or the typesetter obviously intended to write Sonne, not Sunne. The printed book ends with the word FINIS just under the last line of Cotton's text. It seems more likely a printer's addition than Cotton's conclusion to this letter.

Thomas Shepard to John Cotton

[Between February 1 and June 1, 1636]

ALS. MS: BPL, Ms. Am. 1506, pt. 2, no. 4

Published: Hall, *Antinomian Controversy,* 25–29

In L. Thompson, "Letters of John Cotton," 101–107

David D. Hall has suggested that this letter from Thomas Shepard (1605–1649) and Cotton's reply to it "are perhaps the earliest documents of the Antinomian Controversy."[1] As subsequent letters show, Cotton's reputation for close association with antinomian ideas would be a lingering problem for him for many years.

Shepard's autobiography records his dismay at the emigration from England of "diverse families of my Christian friends" and revered senior ministers; as he put it, he "saw the Lord departing from England when Mr. Hooker and Mr. Cotton were gone."[2] About twenty years younger than they were, Shepard had enrolled at Emmanuel College, Cambridge, after both Cotton and Hooker had left; he received his bachelor of arts degree in 1623 and his master's in 1627 when he began his ministry at Earles-Colne, Essex, until being silenced by Bishop Laud in 1630. He was later chaplain to the Darley family at Buttercrambe, Yorkshire, but, when he tried to take up a call in Northumberland, was again forced into hiding. He eventually arrived in New England in October 1635. When Hooker's company left Newtown for Hartford, Connecticut, at the end of May 1636, Shepard became the minister at Newtown (soon to be renamed Cambridge) and married Hooker's eldest child, Joanna. Hall convincingly suggests the dates for the correspondence between Shepard and Cotton, based on Shepard's reference to "our church," which was formally organized on February 1, and Cotton's sending greetings to Hooker, who left for Hartford on May 31.

The manuscript is a single sheet folded once, making four pages. The letter is written on the two halves of the recto and the left-hand half of the verso. The address block appears on the right-hand side of the verso:

> To the reuerend his deare
> freind Mr Cotton teacher
> at Boston be
> these d*eliver*ed.

The ink has bled through the paper, and there is some loss of paper where the sharp nib of Shepard's pen cut through the page. Hall's edition is an invaluable guide through this difficult manuscript. The notes to this letter and Cotton's reply identify substantive differences between Hall's edition and this one, though differences owing simply to the adoption of different editorial conventions are not noted, nor are differences in initial capitalization and compounding. Braces enclose material taken from the nineteenth-century transcription at the Massachusetts Historical Society. Both Hall and the present editor have used these transcriptions, though Hall's text does not identify them as such. Thomas Prince wrote a note below the address block: "1635. Oct. 3. R. Mr. Tho. Shepard w*i*th his pp arrive at Boston, a few days after came to Newtown. Not called Cambridg till May. 2. 1638."

Dear S*i*r

It is the earnest desire not only of my selfe, but of diuerse of our members, whose harts are much endeared to yow, that for the farther clearing up of the truth, yow would be pleased to giue vs satisfaction by way of wrighting rather then speech for this on time to these p*ar*ticulars

1: Whether the man Christ Jesus in suffring the death of the soule, did not only loose the life of Joy; but also (to his own feeling) the life of righteousnes, or of the first Adam, & so liued by faith in the Diety;[3] & hence he puts out the life of legall righteousnes & extinguisheth Adams righteousnes in all his members, & causeth him to liue by that faith of the son of god.

2: Whether A Christian finding a qualification of a promise sauingly wrought[4] in him; can, or should lay hold or close with the Lord Jesus according to that p*ro*mise; but rather to stay for a more full, & clearer Reuelation of the spirit: for if he is thus to set that promise by, & ^so^ to wait for the spirit; then doth he not refuse to giue present honour to gods truth & loue reuealed in the p*ro*mise; & on the other side; if he is to stay & rest his soule vpon the promise before the spirit comes, doth he not then build on somewhat in himselfe, & receiues the p*ro*mise before god giues it to him? I doe gladly consent {in}[5] that which yow deliuered last Thursday, that he that stayes his soule vpon the p*ro*mise is bound to wait for a further[6] reuelation or declaration of gods mind to him by the spirit in the ordinances & in the promise; & I thinke there is little loue in that woman to [he]r absent husband, that is quieted with his letters of his purpose to returne; & [lon]gs not the more from the receiuing of them, to see & enjoy himselfe; but my question if you obserue[7] it, is different from this;/

3: Whether this reuelation of the spirit, is a thing beyond & aboue the woord; & whether tis safe so to say; because the spirit is not seperated from the word but in it & is euer according to it:/

4: Whether a man can Truly lay hold on any promise, but that either he must be de facto in Christ, or in fieri,[8] immediatly & nextly preparing for Christ: for if he truly lay hold on a p*ro*mise & neuer meet with Christ, then I would gladly know, [how] yow can free the Lord & his {promise from} Falshood; for the promise speakes plainly that Christ is come to seeke & saue the lost; now if he that is truly lost beleeues this promise, & yet Christ neuer come to saue him, then where is the truth of the p*ro*mise? & on the other side: if he cannot truly lay hold {on} it, then I doe humbly desire you, to cleare your owne speeches this last Thursday; for yow sayd (if I mistook not) a man might be truly lost (mentioning the p*ro*mise first) & yet Christ neuer seeke nor saue him, for then yow sayd all the woorld ~~sh~~ which is lost, should be saved; & then Judas who not only was lost but felt himselfe also lost, is saued: to which I conceiued I had no call publikely to reply; that Judas was not lost nor yet felt [himself] lost, in the sence & meaning of the promise; for lost men are wil[ling and] glad, to follow there guide; which he was not; therefor is it not safer to say that a man may misapply the promise, & so thinke he doth truly close with Christ & the promise, rather then to say plainly that a man may truly lay hold on a promise, & yet misse of Jesus Christ? for vnder correction I doe p*er*ceiue that the inferences made vpon such speeches, will be very dangerous; not that I goe about to instruct yow, whom god hath so greatly enriched what you should speake; for the Lord knowes I account it one of the greatest New England mercies that the prouidence of the Lord hath placed me so neare vnto you; to be taught & to learne of yow; but this that I speake tis from that due respect I beare to your selfe, and loue and tendernes to your precious ministry, that it may suffer no blur; & also to cut off all seeming differences & jarrs; I make no question, with yow, but a man may not only lay hold vpon a promise, [bu]t also vpon Christ himselfe, yet loose and misse of Christ; yet the truth is cleare to me that whosoeuer Truly layes hold of or closeth with a promise; but that either he hath Christ, or shall haue Christ & the p*ro*mise./

5: Whether a Christian hauing once his sonship sealed to him by the spirit euer doubts agayne of Gods loue to him as a son, though he fall into diuerse grosse & scandalous sins:

6: Whether a Christian may be so far clensed by the blood of *Christ*, that although he comes not to the p*er*fection of Adams {righ}teousnes, yet he may come to attayne the same essence & truth of righ[teou]snes that Adam had, & yet fall away: for I doe willingly consent thus far with yow,

1: That by Christs blood a man may be sanctified, & set apart ~~from prophane~~ from p*ro*phane & common vse, to speciall vse in the church, in the judgement of which he may be truly sanctified, as all the churches Paul writ to were Saints and sanctified: yet many reall hypocrites among them that were visible Saints.

2: [That] a man may not only outwardly & in the judgement of the church be s[anctifi]ed, but he may[9] in his own feeling & in the sight of god himselfe be inwardly sanctified, or made lega[ll]y righteous; but yet Inward legall righteousnes seemes to me to be far different, in Essence from Adams righteousnes. Jehues inward zeale was far different from Adams zeale;[10] tis true Adams righteousnes was not immortall seed, but the same true holines & righteousnes, those that are in Christ are only renewed vnto and being sown agayne in their harts by Christ it is so far cherished by Christ that its made now immortall seed; of which true holines & [righteou]snes I know no grounds as yet to thinke that any vnregenerate man {is renewed vnto.}

3: I [d]oe also grant that many p*ro*fessors do cozen themselues with inward legall righteousnes, either wrought in them by vertue of the spirit of bonda[ge] or fetcht from Christ himselfe, & take legall acts & dispositions as sure signes and markes of being in *Christ*; but yet still I desire to know of yow whether this is the same righteousnes that Adam had for essence, differing from it only in degree; & whether tis the same holines & righteousnes that true beleeuers haue differing on from another only in the efficient, faith woorking the on, the law and the spirit of bondage woorking the other: I beseech yow for speedy satisfaction send a speedy answer to these; for we shall not be able to stir out this weeke many sad imployments being now vpon our church; on thing more I doe with submissio*n* desire yow not to [be] mistaken in; ~~viz.~~ ˆas ifˆ that the Familists[11] doe not ~~not~~ care for woord or ordinances but only the spirits motion; for I haue bin with many of them & hence haue met with many of there bookes; & I doe know thus much of them, that scarce any people honour woord and ordinances more, for they will professe that there they meet with the Spirit & there sup*er*latiue raptures; H.N:[12] the author of them cites scripture abundantly, & Jesabell Reuel*ation* 2: who hath her depths, calls herselfe a prophetesse,[13] tis her glory to interpret scripture; & but that I should hold yow too long I could send yow diuerse of there Theses de Sacra Scriptura,[14] by which yow might soone see what honour they put vpon the woord; & if your seruant, after his mariage would not heare yow, because the spirit moued him not; it was not its likely out of any contempt to the woord, but because he might happily account your selfe a legall preacher; so (as they tearme them) to heare whom the spirit neuer mooues them; or if he did not thus judge of yow, he had not fully learned his lesson; & he may well stand for an exception agaynst a generall rule; this I speake from the enforcement of my conscience, least vnder this colour of aduancing woord together with the spirit, yow may meet in time with some such members (though I know none nor judge any) as may doe your people & ministry hurt, before yow know it; & thus I haue plainly writ my hart vnto yow, being ~~s~~ p*er*swaded that in the spirit of meeknes, yow will not thinke I haue thus writ to begin or breed a quarrell; but to still & quiet those which are secretly begun & I feare will flame out vnles they be quenched in time; I desire therefore that yow would answer me in wrighting as soone as euer yow can; & I do beleeve we shall not differ when things are hereby ripened, for we are desirous & glad to learne; thus beseeching the god of all grace and peace to fill blesse & prosper yow; with remembrance of my respect to that precious gentleman with yow,[15] and to your wife I rest.

Yours in the L. Jesus

Tho. Shepard:

From Newtown:/

1. Hall, *Antinomian Controversy,* 24. For analysis of the theological positions of Cotton and Shepard in the controversy, see Stoever, *"A Faire and Easy Way to Heaven,"* 34–80.

2. *The Autobiography,* in Michael McGiffert, ed., *God's Plot: Puritan Spirituality in Thomas Shepard's Cambridge,* rev. ed. (Amherst, Mass., 1994), 57.

3. Diety] DH: Duity.

4. sauingly wrought] DH: saving [wrought].

5. {in}] DH: [to].

6. further] DH: farther.

7. obserue] DH: observd.

8. de facto: in reality; in fieri: in the process of becoming.

9. he may] DH: the man.

10. Jehues] DH: Aehues; zeale] DH: seale; zeale] DH: seale.

11. The Family of Love, a group who followed the writings of a Dutch mystic of the sixteenth century, Hendrik Niclaes (1502–c. 1580). Although they tended not to write down their beliefs in a way to make them readily reconstructed, a recent investigator of their English construction offers this summary:

> The Familist's faith comprised a complex set of beliefs, moderate and radical in equal measure. In H.N.'s own dualistic terms, conservatism and restraint normally characterised the "outward man," while the "inward man" was bolder and more ambitious. He aspired to be

as sinless as Christ, and believed he could attain spiritual perfection in this life. He knew he could share in Christ's resurrection, even as the "outward man" went about his business. He came very close to rejecting the literal validity of Scripture, and he probably conceived of heaven primarily as an illuminated state of mind. Finally, he scorned and threatened all who disagreed with him. (Christopher W. Marsh, *The Family of Love in English Society, 1550–1630* [Cambridge, 1994], 48, and see esp. chap. 2)

Christopher Hill offers a slightly different summary of the Familists, stressing their finding heaven and hell on earth, their belief that Christ was within every believer, and their communal property ownership (*The World Turned Upside Down: Radical Ideas during the English Revolution* [New York, 1972], 22, 29). Their tendency to emphasize the presence of the spirit within gave them links in their opponents' minds with Antinomians and Quakers. Continental Familism is discussed in Alastair Hamilton, *The Family of Love* (Cambridge, 1981); and Jean Dietz Moss, *"Godded with God": Hendrick Niclaes and His Family of Love,* in American Philosophical Society, *Transactions,* N.S., LXXI, pt. 8 (Philadelphia, 1981).

12. Hendrik Niclaes.

13. See Rev. 2:20, where St. John the Divine, writing to the church at Thyatira, says, "Notwithstanding I have a few things against thee, because thou sufferest that woman Jezebel, which calleth herself a prophetess, to teach and to seduce my servants to commit fornication, and to eat things sacrificed unto idols."

14. Scriptura] DH: Scriptera.

15. Prince annotates this reference: "Henry Vane Esq. rec^{d} into Boston Ch. Nov. 1. 1635." Vane was living in Cotton's house.

John Cotton to [Thomas Shepard]

[Between February 1 and June 1, 1636]

Copy. MS: BPL, Ms. Am. 1506, pt. 2, no. 5

Published: Hall, *Antinomian Controversy,* 29–33

In L. Thompson, "Letters of John Cotton," 108–114

This letter is written on one large leaf folded in half, making four sides. The letter occupies the first three sides. It is not in Cotton's hand.

Deare brother,

I thanke you vnfeignedly for this labor of yo*ur* love, to acquaint me with such passages in my ministery, as through eyther misexpression on my Part, or misconstruction, or misreport of others, might hinder the worke of christ amongst vs. The particulars you enquire of are many, & the Returne of yo*ur* messenger is short, & therefore I shall (god Helping) returne you (as I may) short, & plaine Answer[1] there vnto.

1. Yo*ur* i. Quære concerneth me not, nor any Doctrine or opinion of mine.

I have sometimes heard it, & pleaded ag*ains*t it, as not safe if it should be receyved; But I know noe man *tha*t holdeth it, or even mentioned it, but by way of Inquiry, & Disputation.

2. To yo*u*r 2d. I looke at all Promises as given vs by the coven*an*t of grace, & the coven*an*t of grace as given vs by christ. So *tha*t I doe not satisfy my selfe in closeing with a Promisse, or with the coven*an*t of grace but as I first close with christ, in whom the coven*an*t, & the Promise is made, & confirmed, Isay: 42:6:, Gal: 3:16: 2:Cor: i.20:[2]

And I conceyve the soule closeth with christ, by feeling himself {a poore} desolate soule, lost for want of christ, sensible of his owne Insuffic{iency} to reach him, & vnworthynesse[3] to receyve him, yet seeking & longi[ng][4] for him in every ordinaunce, & spirituall Deuty, though finding it selfe vnable to beginne, or continue seeking or waiting, farther then christ shall helpe, & worke with him.

Thus closeing with christ wee safely close with every Promise so farre as the Lord revealeth it, & applyeth it to vs: w*hi*ch also stayeth the soule though not from[5] searching further[6] after christ, & the seale of his spirit, yet from sinkeing. I suppose David closed with the Promise applyed to him by Nathan: 2. Sam. 12.13.[7] & so gave hono*u*r to the trueth, & love of god revealed in the promise, yet rested not so, but searched after further[8] sence of the sprinkeling of the blood of christ, & comfort of the spirit Psal: 51. 7.8.[9]

3. The word, & Revelation of the spirit, I suppose doe as much differ, as letter, & spirit. & therefore though I consent to you, *tha*t the spirit is not separated[10] from the word, but in it, & ever according to it: yet above, & beyond the letter of the word it reacheth forth comfort & Power to the soule, though not above the sence, & Intendm*en*t of the Word.

4. I doe not conceyve, that any man can truely lay hold of a sav{ing} Promise, till he lay hold of christ, & so the promise never fayleth him, nor his takeing hold of it.

As for *th*at Promise, that christ came to seeke, & to save that w*hi*ch is lost, if he that is truely lost doe truely beleive this Promise, I doubt not, christ certainly came to save him; the promise to such is a word of trueth.

Nor doeth this crosse (to my Remembrance) any speach delivered by me the last lecture. for though I saide, A man might be truely lost (as I saide, all men were by the fall) yea & feele himselfe to be lost (as I saide, Judas did, & others doe by a spirit of bondage, or Despayre) yet I spake not of men truely lost according to the full meaning of the promise, but according to the com*m*on app*re*hension of it, when sundry fee[l]ing[11] their lost estate by a spirit of bondage, hearing *tha*t word doe fo[rth]with[12] beleive, it belongeth to them. As for *the*[13] sence w*hi*ch you give of truely lost, I refuse it not: though I conceyve the promise may reach lower then to such. For what if the soule can not finde it selfe glad to follow his guid{es}[14] but feeleth it selfe lost for want of a guide, & of grace to follow him; [then?][15] is it in such an estate as christ will seeke & save if it feele it selfe lost {for want} of Ch{r}i{st? I doe not remember nor} doe I beleive {that [I] hath saide that [any one] may} truely {lay hold of a Promise and yet misse of christ. [It is]}[16] [2] ag*ains*t mine owne Judgm*en*t who doe not see how a man can truely lay hold of any promise before he have layde hold of christ.

I blesse the L*or*d for your love to me, & tender resp*e*ct to my vnworthy lab*ou*rs: & I truely returne you this office of thankfullnesse, yo*u*r p*er*son & worke findeth a large roome in my heart, though my heart it selfe be straite, & narrow. As for differences, & Jarres, it is my vnfeigned desire to avoide them with all men especially w*i*th Brethren: but I doe not know, I assure you, any difference, much lesse Jarres, betweene me, & any of my Brethren in o*u*r Publique ministery, or otherwise, to any offence.

5. Yo*u*r 5th Quære I never affirmed, but doe conceyve *tha*t a childe of god sealed by the spirit falling into divers grosse, & scandalous sinnes may doubt againe of gods love; onely this I would say, *tha*t the sonnes of god so sealed doe more rarely fall into such sinnes (for it is somewhat contrary to their sealing) (w*hi*ch stampeth a character of christs Nature vpon them:) yet sometimes such as doe ˆsoˆ fall may yet reteyne a[17] doubtlesse clayme vnto gods fatherly love, as Isay. 63: 16:17.[18] Neverthelesse I have found by some experience (more wayes then one) *tha*t god doeth leave his sealed children some times to such renewed doubtings, the better to rayse vp their hearts rather to lay vp all o*u*r ioy in christ, then in o*u*r owne songs in the Night.

6. In yo*u*r 6th Quære you grant in yo*u*r 3 propositions as much (in a manner) as I desire to hold forth, for it is the desire of my heart by the grace of christ to p*ro*[vo]ke chri*sti*ans (in this Countrey of vniversall Profession) not to rest in any such changes or graces, or Deutyes, or ordinances (as church-fellowship &c.) as may leave them short of saveing fellow-ship with Jesus christ. But whether the com*m*on graces, & gifts of temp*or*ary beleivers differ onely in degree, & in the efficient, I am not for the p*re*sent able to determine. All *tha*t I have saide about it, is this, *tha*t I would not wish chri*sti*ans to build the signes of their Adoption vpon any sanctification, but such as floweth fro*m* faith in christ Jesus; for all other holynesse, & righteousnes, though it were as true as that of Adams in Innocency may be as his was a mortall seede, & fall short of p*er*severance: whereas the least seede of fayth, & of that holynes w*hi*ch floweth fro*m* it abideth for ever.

As for *th*e Familists, I onely expressed what I have found, not onely fro*m* my man, but from a Ring Leader of *tha*t sect Mr Townes of Notinghamshire[19] who is wont to say, he knowes how farre our scripture learning can leade vs, as haveing himselfe fou[nd] a more p*er*fect way; also in the confession of fayth published w*i*th the Life & Death of Mr John Smyth[20] I finde they abuse *tha*t Place in .2. Pet: 1:19:[21] to say, *tha*t chri*sti*ans doe well to hearken to the word as to a light shining in a Darke Place, till *th*e Day Starre arise in their hearts: but then they are free from the wo[rd] & sacram*en*ts &c: save onely for offence sake. If they please th[em]selves[22] in their Revelatyons, & Raptures, com*m*ing vpon them in the word but not from the word, their delusion is manyfest, but go[od] Brother, doe not Resemble such a Delusion to the faithfull Practis[e] of such chri*sti*ans, as feeling[23] their neede of christ, & finding a Pro[mise] of {grace applyed[24] to them by his word, though they close therewith} [3] give god the glory of his trueth, & love, yet doe not rest therein till they have gott this Promise sealed vnto them by the further Annoyntm*en*t of the spirit. I persuade my soule without doubting, it is farre fro*m* yo*u*r Intention so to doe, though yo*u*r expressions seeme to feare some such danger in this manner of holding out of christ, w*hi*ch I have applyed my ministery vnto these many yeares both in old Boston, & in New; wherein if any erro*u*r be discovered to me, God forbid I should shutt mine eyes ag*ains*t it, but I suppose wee differ not herein, nor any of my Brethren if wee vnderstand one another. Nor doe I discerne (though after diligent search) *tha*t any of o*u*r members, (brethren or sisters) doe hold forth christ in any other way, so *tha*t if my ministery be hurt by this kinde of Declaration of *th*e way of christ, or if any quarrells or stirrs be breed thereby, I hope even this also will tend to the farther service of christ in the issue.

Meane while I hartily thanke you for this p*re*tious fruite of yo*u*r vnfeigned brotherly love, desireing you to helpe me further, w*i*th any such advertisem*en*ts as may p*re*vent any hindrance of the worke of christ in my hand, & may advance his kingdome who is god over all blessed for ever.

Yo*u*r salutations to Mr Vane[25] I will god willing p*re*sent to him anon, who hath bene abroade all this Day.

Remember my Deare affection to yo*u*r selfe, Brother Hooker & others with you whom I deepely hono*u*r in the Lord; the lord Jesus fill vs with him selfe, & leade vs in his owne way to his heavenly kingdome. In him I rest,

Yo*u*r affectionate though weake
Brother

J C

1. Answer] DH: Answers.

2. Isa. 42:6: If the Lord have called thee in righteousness, and will hold thine hand, and will keep thee, and give thee for a covenant of the people, for a light of the Gentiles.

Gal. 3:16: Now to Abraham and his seed were the promises made. He saith not, And to seeds, as of many; but as of one, And to thy seed, which is Christ.

2 Cor. 1:20: For all the promises of God in him are yea, and in him, Amen, unto the glory of God by us. DH reads this as 2 Cor. 2.20.

3. vnworthynesse to receyve] DH: unworthy also to receyve.

4. longi[ng]] DH: [1 word mutilated].

5. Cotton originally wrote for. In the word *from,* the ro is written over or.

6. further] DH: farther.

7. 2 Sam. 12:13: And David said unto Nathan, I have sinned against the Lord. And Nathan said unto David, The Lord also hath put away thy sin; thou shalt not die.

8. further] DH: farther.

9. Ps. 51:7, 8: Purge me with hyssop, and I shall be clean: wash me, and I shall be whiter than snow. Make me to hear joy and gladness: that the bones which thou hast broken may rejoice.

10. First written seperated; the second e is overwritten with an a.

11. fee[l]ing] DH: seeing. This word was end-line-hyphenated in the manuscript, with the first syllable, feel-, running to the edge of the page, which has suffered wear and loss.

12. This word was end-line-hyphenated, with loss of part of the first syllable where the paper's edge is worn away.

13. *the*] DH: that.

14. Here the Massachusetts Historical Society transcript provides the word guides, though the context seems to call for guidance or perhaps guiding. DH: guide

15. him; [then?] is] DH: him: is.

16. Crumbling at the bottom of the page has caused progressive loss of paper, beginning even before the MHS transcription was made. That transcription enables us to reclaim text here. The square brackets enclose words supplied by the present editor. Filling blank spaces in the MHS transcription, they fit both the sense and the physical space in the line, but they are in the end conjecture.

17. a] DH: or.

18. Isa. 63:16, 17: Doubtless thou art our father, though Abraham be ignorant of us, and Israel acknowledge us not: Thou, O Lord, art our father, our redeemer; thy name is from everlasting. O Lord, why hast thou made us to err from thy ways, and hardened our heart from thy fear? Return for thy servants' sake, the tribes of thine inheritance.

19. Robert Towne was author of *The Assertion of Grace* . . . (London, 1645). For brief comment on Towne, see Philip F. Gura, *A Glimpse of Sion's Glory: Puritan Radicalism in New England, 1620–1660* (Middletown, Conn., 1984), 56, 252–253. "Nottingham-shire" is hyphenated in the MS.

20. See Cotton to Roger Williams, early 1636, n. 10.

21. 2 Pet. 1:19: We have also a more sure word of prophecy; whereunto ye do well that ye take heed, as unto a light that shineth in a dark place, until the day dawn, and the day star arise in your hearts.

22. This word is end-line-hyphenated, with loss of part of the first syllable at the edge of the sheet.

23. chri*sti*ans, as feeling] DH: christians [why by?] feeling.

24. a Pro[mise] of {grace applyed] DH: a [Promise applyed.

25. Vane is underlined, presumably by Thomas Prince, whose note at the end of the letter reads, "Mr Henry Vane was Rec[d] into Boston Ch. Nov. 1., 1635./ chosen Gov. of *the* M Col. May 25, 1636."

John Cotton to Peter Bulkeley and John Jones

[July 5, 1636]

ALI. MS: MSA: CCXL, Hutchinson Papers, I, fol. 41

In L. Thompson, "Letters of John Cotton," 115–116

This letter is Cotton's reply to an invitation to attend the ceremony at which a church for the new town of Concord was to be organized. In the congregational system, the church had to be created before a minister could be called. So there were typically two ceremonies, one to organize the church, the next at a later date to ordain a minister. The first was the more important event.[1] Just five months earlier "a great Assembly" had gathered at Newtown to create a new church there, where the congregation of Thomas Hooker and Samuel Stone was about to depart for Connecticut. Thomas Shepard had duly announced plans for the organizational gathering, which Winthrop reports was well attended. On that occasion it was Cotton who had extended the right hand of fellowship to Shepard on behalf of the other churches in the Bay. This recent event at the same location as the Concord church's organizing clearly served as a touchstone in the minds of Winthrop and others.[2] The short notice given by Peter Bulkeley and John Jones made an unfortunate contrast with Shepard's coming in person to inform the magistrates of his plans and having "also sent to all the neighbor Churches for their Elders to give their assistance at a certaine daye at New towne, when they should constitute their bodye" (Winthrop, *Journal,* 168–169). In the case of the Concord church's gathering, several key figures in the colony, both clerical and political, stayed away, excusing themselves on the ground of insufficient advance notice. On the day Cotton wrote this reply to Bulkeley and Jones, John Winthrop made the following entry in his *Journal:*

> mr *Buckly* and mr Iones 2: Englishe ministers appointed *this daye* [July 5] to gather a Churche at *N: towne* to settle at *Concorde:* they sent word 3: dayes before to the Governor [Henry Vane] & deputye [Winthrop] to desire their presence, but they tooke it in ill parte & thought not fitt to goe because they had not come to them before (as they ought to have doone & as others had doone before) to acquaint them with their purpose. (179)

Though the short notice might have posed practical problems for Cotton and others, the developing rift between what would become the Antinomian faction, centered in the membership of Cotton's Boston church, and others may well be part of the reason for the poor attendance at the Concord church's inception. Some fourteen months later, Bulkeley, with Thomas Hooker, was a moderator at the synod held at Newtown to consider the Antinomian dissension, a meeting at which Cotton was first called to account. It is perhaps understandable, therefore, that the following April, when Bulkeley and Jones were ordained, there were again some attendance problems: "The governour [Vane], and Mr. Cotton, and Mr. Wheelwright, and the two ruling elders of Boston, and the rest of that church, which were of any note, did none of them come to this meeting. The reason was conceived to be, because they accounted these as legal preachers, and therefore would not give approbation to their ordination" (Winthrop, *Journal,* 212).

To Mr Bulk*eley* & Mr Joh*nes*

Deare Brethren,

Being my self Restreyned by an vnexpected Occasion from Com*m*ing over to you this day (as I had verely purposed) Impute not I pray you my necessary Absence to voluntary Estrangem*en*t. As yo*u*r persons are deare & pretious in my Affections: so is it *th*e earnest Desire of my soule, *tha*t yo*u*r Entrance vpon yo*u*r great Calling this day, & *th*e Guidance of all yo*u*r after-Administrations in it may be carryed along by *th*e gratious [&] mighty hand of God, to *th*e blessed Enlargem*en*t of *th*e kingdome of h[is] Grace in Jesus Christ. The Right hand of his Fellowship is able to bring mighty things to passe, & to give vs this Blessing also amongst others, *tha*t wee & all o*u*r fellow brethren may (in his Name) sett forwad *th*e Lords worke w*i*th one shoulder. Pray for this Blessing, & Pray againe for it, & for the Pardon of such Sinnes, as doe w*i*thhold this Blessing for vs: *tha*t so wee & all o*u*r Brethren may mutually give *th*e Right hand of Fellowship, not in complem*en*t (*th*e hand being [with] vs, but *th*e Power of the hand ag*ains*t vs) but in Trueth: heart[,] hand & power, & all concurring in holy stedfastnesse of love || & one minde (according to yo*u*r old Boston Text, Phil. i.27:)[3] to Advaunce together *th*e Fayth of *th*e Gospell, in *th*e hearts & lives of alle People. And let me (desolate me) come in to yo*u*r mindes, *tha*t, noe weakenesse of mine may cast Dishono*u*r vpon *th*e Name & gr[ace] of Christ, who am Altogether vnworthy, *tha*t his Name should be called vpon me, or held forth by me.[4]

Together w*i*th yo*u*r selves & wifes, I salute *th*e Brethren. The Grace of o*u*r Lord Jesus be w*i*th you all. Amen. In Him I r[est,]

Yo*u*rs in Him,

J. C.

1. See J. William T. Youngs, Jr., "Congregational Clericalism: New England Ordinations before the Great Awakening," *WMQ,* 3d Ser., XXXI (1974), 482.

2. This key meeting was held at Newtown probably to enable more of the Bay-area ministers and magistrates to attend, since the more remote site in Concord would have been inconvenient for most. If so, the absences would have been all the more disappointing.

3. Phil. 1:27: Only let your conversation be as it becometh the gospel of Christ: that whether

I come and see you, or else be absent, I may hear of your affairs, that ye stand fast in one spirit, with one mind striving together for the faith of the gospel.

4. There is more than mere modesty on Cotton's part here. The degree to which he had already, in July 1636, felt the sting of criticism from his fellow ministers for what struck them as questionable views on the process of spiritual regeneration, is evident here. The parenthetical phrase "desolate me" may be as direct an expression of the psychological cost of the Antinomian episode to Cotton as any expression he made for the rest of the drawn-out process.

John Cotton to a Minister in England

[After January 1635/6]

Published: *A Coppy of a Letter of Mr. Cotton of Boston, in New-England, Sent in Answer of Certaine Objections Made against Their Discipline and Orders There, Directed to a Friend, with the "Questions" Propounded to Such as Are Admitted to the Church-fellowship, and the Covenant It Selfe* ([London], 1641); Emerson, *Letters,* 196–198

The identity of the addressee as a minister is indicated in Cotton's concluding reference to himself as the correspondent's "brother in Christ." In the letter Cotton is fulfilling a semiofficial duty in answering basic questions about the way churches in New England were being conducted, so this is not a familiar letter like many others by Cotton. It addresses the issue of Separatism and New England's attitude toward it. In particular, did they believe the English church was corrupt? Roger Williams's extreme position on the corruption of the English Church and the need for a truly pure church (in New England or elsewhere) to declare a firm separation from it was clearly at issue for the English correspondent here, and Cotton is glad to reassure him that Williams is deviant from standard New England practice. Such questions from England and answers from New England became increasingly common in the wake of the Antinomian controversy, repeatedly occupying the attention of several of the New England clergy in the 1640s; this answer to four concerns voiced from the home country was a very early instance of that process.

The dating of the letter is based on internal evidence. In particular, since it mentions Williams's departure under the sentence of banishment, which occurred in January 1636, we know the letter postdates that time. But, since Cotton stresses the relative infrequency of excommunication in New England churches, implying a more or less harmonious situation, it seems likely that the letter predates the disturbances caused by John Wheelwright's Fast Day sermon in January 1637 and his subsequent banishment from the civil jurisdiction of the colony of Massachusetts Bay, late in 1637, along with some of his followers. In the same year, the trial of Anne Hutchinson was under way, which resulted in her excommunication and banishment. Winthrop's *Journal* in late April 1636 notes that the Salem church, "still infected with mr willms his opinions," had recently questioned other ministers in New England about Salem's opinion that members should not attend "any false Church" in England.[1] The issues raised by Cotton's correspondent in England were thus under discussion in New England—and doubtless reported in England—in the spring and summer of 1636.

The text that follows is that of the 1641 printing, the only form in which the letter survives. It is transcribed from the copy owned by the Boston Public Library.

There have been things (as it seemeth) reported unto you;

First, that we receive none into our Church-fellowship untill they first disclaime their Churches in *England* as no Churches, but as limbs of the devill; now, I answer, God forbid, God forbid: It is true, one *Sheba* of *Bickry* blew a Trumpet of such a seditious Separation;[2] I meane, one Mr. *Williams* late Teacher of *Salem,* but himselfe and others that followed stiffely in that way, who were all excommunicated out of the Church and banished out of the Common-wealth,[3] for men in that way, and of such a spirit are wont not onely to renounce the Churches of *England,* but ours also, because we held communion with them in *England* in the things which are of God; see therefore how unjustly wee are slandered for renouncing communion with you, as is mentioned, and for it they themselves are punished in our Common wealth, censures[4] in our Churches; for such Antichristian exorbitures: by this you may see the Objection clearely answered.

The second Calumny is, that our members must professe their repentance for all former communion with the Churches among you: Now for the answer, wee professe no such things, but onely in generall so farre as we have polluted our selves with any corruptions or inventions of men, or defiled Gods Ordinances with any corruption of their owne, whereby you may gather answer[5] from the second Calumny.

The third Calumny is, that we enter into covenant solemnly, never to have communion with the present Churches of *England,* whereas in truth we never have such words or meaning in any part of our Covenant, but that we professe to walke in all the Ordinances of the Lord, according to his will revealed in his Word.

Of the fourth report you mention, there is some ground for it, our practise, power indeed is given among us to the people to chuse their Ministers, so likewise to receive any member unto the Church fellowship, and to joyne in the excommunication of such as grow scandalous, which yet is very rare. Among us through the goodnesse of God scarce two or three have beene excommunicated out of our Churches, which is more for rejecting communion with the Churches, than for any other crime: It is true also, that we allow any members of the Church to complaine of an offence given him by any brother, if a private way of Admonition according to the rule have not reformed him, *Matth.* 18.17.[6] but that hath fallen out very seldome since I came hither, for ought I have heard, either in our owne or other Churches, they much wrong both you and us who told you that Master *Wilson* was suspended from his Ministry for his Journey into *England,*[7] or for any Communion he had with the Churches there; nor to my remembrance did any of the Brethren question him about it, till of himselfe he began to give some account of his journey to the Church, and then indeede two or three grave and godly men desired him to cleare a passage or two; first, how he could leave the whole Congregation above twelve moneths together without their consent, and how he could leave his wife (as I remember) without her consent; to both which he gave a satisfactory answer, and was not at all suspended by the Church, but of himselfe he forbare one day, or at the least halfe a day, till hee had declared both the particulars; that which you adde of grace and gifts of Christ, or of his presence in the Ministry of his servants among you, we willingly & thankefully acknowledge, and do professe, that the hope which most of us have obtained of the common salvation wee received from the preaching of Gods faithfull Ministers among you, wee cannot, we dare not deny to *Blesse the Wombe which bare us, and the Paps wich gave us sucke;*[8] and long may these Lights shine among you, with all peace, purity, and power, *Amen.*

What you speake of Separatists and Brownists; wee generally here doe consent with you, that the bitternesse of Separation whereby men doe not onely cut themselves from the inventions of men, but also from the Ordinances of God, and fellowship of his servants; for who so have done, they never were blessed with peace: As for those scruples you pray me to weigh without prejudice, we here doe consent with you therein, only there is a passage or two which I crave leave to explaine my self in first, that you say our Pastor M. *Wilson* affirmes among you that wee did not follow *Calvins* platforme as an Episcopall he saith, he doth not remember any such word to have fallen from him, onely thus much he confesseth, as we doe all here, that wee doe not transact all things so reservedly in a consistory, but though wee bee prebestary,[9] doe prepare all things for the Church, yet wee transact no publique act, but in their presence, and with their consents, unlesse any of their brethren can give a reason from the Scripture to the contrary, or some better intelligence of his owne, which latter sometimes falls out; secondly, what you speake of prophesying, I neede not say much of it, it is very warily used here, unlesse it be in absence, and weakenesse of Ministers,[10] and for any abuse herein allow it not, but dislike it as you doe: Now you have shewed so much for to inquire the truth of these matters, I pray you informe others also what answer you have received, which will be a further testimony of your love; pray for us, as we doe for you, so taking leave I rest,

Your unworthy weake
Brother in Christ,
Iohn Cotton.

Questions put to such as are admitted to the Church-Fellowship.

How it pleased God to worke in them, to bring them home to Christ, whether the law have convinced them of sinne, how the Lord hath wonne them to deny themselves and their owne righteousnesse, and to rely on the righteousnesse of Christ, then they make a briefe confession, or else an answer to a few questions about the maine fundamentall points of Religion, that it may appeare indeed whether they be competently endued with the knowledge of the truth, and sound in the faith, and about the Godhead, the Trinity, the worke, our first estate of innocency, the fall, our redemption, Christ his Natures, his Offices, Faith, the Sacraments, the Church, the Resurrection, the last judgement, such as every Christian man is bound to learne and give account of; we refuse none for weakenesse, either knowledge or grace, if the whole be in them, and that any of the Church can give testimony of their Christian and sincere affections, and then the Church consenting to their admission, one of the Elders propounded to the party, the covenant that hee must enter into with God and the Church, whereunto the party expresly covenants, then is reciprocally received the Churches covenant backe againe by the voyce of the elder. This is all the secret we have among us, neither have we any more secret carriage, than this which no godly man that ever came over to us have ever disliked, you come not more willingly to have communion with us, then we receive you, upon no harder termes then have been declared.

The Covenant *it selfe.*[11]

"Since it hath pleased God to move you brethren to hold forth the right hand of fellowship; It is your part, and that which I am to require of you in the name of the Lord, and of his Church, before you can be admitted thereunto, whether you be willing to enter a holy Covenant with God,[12] and with them and by the grace and helpe of Christ be willing to deny your selfe, and all your former polutions, and corruptions, wherein in any sort you have walked, and so to give up your selfe to the Lord Iesus, making him your onely priest and attonement, your onely profit, your onely guide and King, and Lawgiver, and to walke before him in all professed subjections unto all his holy Ordinance, according to the rule of the Gospell, and to walke together with his Church and the members thereof in brotherly love, and mutuall edification and succor according to God; then doe I also promise unto you in the name of this Church, that by the helpe of Christ, we likewise will walke towards you in all brotherly love and holy watchfulnesse to the mutuall building, up one of another in the fellowship of the Lord Iesus," Amen, Amen.

FINIS.

1. Winthrop, *Journal,* 175.

2. Sheba of Bickry: 2 Sam. 20:1–22 tells of the rebellion against King David by one Sheba of Bichri, a rebellion that ends in Sheba's beheading. The chapter begins: "Then there was come thither a wicked man (named Sheba the sonne of Bichri, a man of Iemini) and he blewe the trumpet, and said, We haue no parte in Dauid. . . ." (Geneva Bible). Cotton's "God forbid, God forbid," is a conscious imitation of Joab's speech in the same story (2 Sam. 20:20), as translated in the Geneva Bible; when asked why he and his men are besieging the city of Abel of Beth-maacah, Joab answers, "God forbid, God forbid it me, that I shulde deuoure, or destroy it," offering to stop if the inhabitants will give up Sheba of Bickry. Since the "God forbid, God forbid" wording does not appear in the King James version (which has "Far be it, far be it from me"), the Geneva Bible translations are quoted elsewhere in this letter as well.

3. Roger Williams was in Salem for a few months in 1631 just after arriving from England. He then went to Plymouth until late 1633, when he became an assistant to the pastor at Salem, Samuel Skelton. When Skelton died in 1634, Williams was called as the congregation's teacher, much to the dismay of the colonial authorities. In July 1635 he was summoned before the General Court, examined regarding his teachings, and was finally—at the October session of the General Court—ordered out of the colony. At first he was told to depart within six weeks; but, considering the coming of winter, the court relented and permitted him to stay until spring, provided he would stop disseminating his ideas. He did not stop, so the court decided to ship him to England immediately, whereupon he escaped to Rhode Island in January 1636. See *Records of Massachusetts Bay,* I, 160–161; Winthrop, *Journal,* 149–150, 158, 163.

The "others that followed stiffly in that way" were named in a letter from Williams's successor as minister at Salem, Hugh Peter, to the church at Dorchester on July 1, 1639. In addition to "Roger Williams & his wife," Peter listed:

> John Throckmorton & his wife.
> Thomas Olney and his wife.
> Stukely Westcot and his wife.
> Mary Halliman.
> Widdow Reeues.

Others who voluntarily joined Williams in exile during 1636 and 1637 were, respectively, William Harris and Joshua Verrin. For a facsimile copy as well as transcription of Peter's letter and discussion of the numerous Salem migrants to Williams's Providence, see Sidney Perley, *The History of Salem, Massachusetts,* 3 vols. (Salem, Mass., 1924–1928), I, 268–272. See also James Duncan Phillips, *Salem in the Seventeenth Century* (Boston, 1933), 106–108; Richard P. Gildrie, *Salem, Massachusetts, 1626–1683: A Covenant Community* (Charlottesville, Va., 1975), 35–38.

4. Probably a misprint for censured.

5. The 1641 edition has auswer.

6. Matt. 18:15–17: . . . if thy brother trespace against thee, go, and tell him his faute betweene thee & him alone: if he heare thee, thou hast wonne thy brother. But if he heare thee not, take yet with thee one or two, that by *th*e mouth of two or thre witnesses euerie word may be co*n*firmed. And if he wil not vouchesaue to heare the*m,* tel it vnto the Church: & if he refuse to heare the Church also, let him be vnto thee as an heathen man, and a Publicane (Geneva Bible).

7. John Wilson had already made two return trips to England since his emigration to New England in 1630. The first return was from March 29, 1631, to May 26, 1632. On this trip he returned with his wife. The second was a trip begun in the company of John Winthrop, Jr., sometime between early October and early November 1634 and concluded a year later, on October 6, 1635. The reference here, however, is to the first trip, when Wilson was still the only minister in the Boston church and when he was in fact gone for "above twelve moneths together." Winthrop, *Journal,* 48–49, 69, 156; Robert C. Black, III, *The Younger John Winthrop* (New York, London, 1966), 79, 89–90.

8. See Luke 11:27.

9. Probably a misprint for presbetary (presbytery), which for Cotton would have referred, not to a formal administrative body as in the Presbyterian Church, but to the elders of an individual parish church (see *OED,* s.v. "Presbytery," 4c). He contrasts this informal consultation of local elders with the English Church's formal consistories presided over by a bishop and having formal jurisdiction over certain aspects of church life.

10. On the occasion of John Wilson's departure for England, he left the Boston church in the charge of certain key laymen. Winthrop records his parting admonition on March 29, 1631: "About 10: of the Clocke, mr Coddington & mr Willson & diverse of the Congregation mett at the Gouernors, & there mr Willson prayinge & exhortinge the Congregation to Love, &c, Comended to them the exercise of prophesey in his absence, & designed those whom he thought most fitt for it. viz. the Gouernor, mr dudly & mr Noell the elder." Winthrop, *Journal,* 48.

11. The following text of the Covenant is printed in italics in *A Coppy.* Quotation marks here replace that archaic convention.

12. At two places in the Boston church's early records, the church covenant is recorded. In the first of these instances, the wording is very close to that which is included in the text accompanying this letter, suggesting that Cotton was copying from the same source text, or perhaps quoting from his memory of regular usage. In the church records, the text begins with a "Query": "Whether you be willing to Enter into a holy Covenant with God and his people in this Church," and is followed by a declarative statement, which begins, "You promise, by the grace and help of Christ, to deny your selffe and all your former pollutions . . . ," continuing with a version of the text of the Covenant printed here. After the concluding phrase, "the mutuall buldinge up of one another in the Fellowship of the Lord jesus," the *Records* include a benediction or prayer, which is omitted in Cotton's text: "And Even he the good Lord our God that keepeth Covenant and mercy with Thousands of his people make us all herein Faithfull unto him and one unto another for his one name sake." *Records of the First Church,* 4–5, 10.

John Cotton to William Fiennes, Lord Saye and Sele

[After March 1636]

Published: Hutchinson, *History,* I, 496–501; Edmund S. Morgan, ed., *Puritan Political Ideas, 1558–1794* (Indianapolis, Ind., 1965), 167–173; Emerson, *Letters,* 190–194. Abridged versions appear in Perry Miller and Thomas H. Johnson, eds., *The Puritans* (New York, 1938), 209–212; George M. Waller, ed., *Puritanism in Early America* (Lexington, Mass., 1950), 11–14; and later editions of both

In L. Thompson, "Letters of John Cotton," 125–133

In the mid-1630s, certain titled members of the English gentry who supported the Puritan movement and its settlements in America considered emigrating. William Fiennes, Lord Saye and Sele, and Robert Greville, Lord Brooke, wishing to prepare the way for playing prominent roles in the government of New England, sent over a list of ten "demands," which laid out a plan of government under which the primary power and influence would be granted to "gentlemen of the country." They asked, further, that their authority be hereditary. Moreover, they wanted the franchise to depend upon property ownership alone, not church membership. In making these and other demands—which amounted to conditions for their coming to the colonies—Lords Saye and Sele and Brooke reminded the colonists that they personally had "already been at great disbursements for the public works in New England." Cotton, as one historian aptly puts it, was "assigned the unenviable job of answering them."[1]

Hutchinson printed the ten demands and Cotton's answers as the second appendix to the first volume of his *History*.[2] Hutchinson's third appendix was the following letter, which might have accompanied Cotton's formal list of answers back to England, though the letter alludes to it only briefly. The upshot was that Lords Brooke and Saye lost interest in moving to New England. Cotton's letter is thus an important document in the determination of a new political system, free of the allegiance to hereditary nobility that the English Parliament, with its upper and lower houses, incorporated.

The following is a transcription of the text as printed by Hutchinson in 1764, except where changes are noted. Hutchinson was the last editor to have access to the manuscript of this letter, which might have been a casualty of the destruction of his household in the Stamp Act riot on August 26, 1765. Hutchinson describes the item as a "Copy of a Letter from Mr Cotton to Lord Say and Seal in the Year 1636." He omits any date from the text of the letter itself.

Right honourable,

What your Lordship writeth of Dr. Twisse his works *de scientiâ mediâ,* and of the sabbath, it did refresh me to reade, that his labors of such arguments were like to come to light;[3] and it would refresh me much more to see them here: though (for my owne particular) till I gett some release from some constant labors here (which the church is desirous to procure) I can get litle, or noe oppertunity to reade any thing, or attend to any thing, but the dayly occurrences which presse in upon me continually, much beyond my strength either of body or minde. Your Lordships advertisement touching the civill state of this colony, as they doe breath forth your singular wisdome, and faithfulness, and tender care of the peace, so wee have noe reason to misinterprite, or undervalue your Lordships eyther directions, or intentions therein. I know noe man under heaven (I speake in Gods feare without flattery) whose counsell I should rather depend upon, for the wise administration of a civill state according to God, than upon your Lordship, and such confidence have I (not in you) but in the Lords presence in Christ with you, that I should never feare to betrust a greater commonwealth than this (as much as in us lyeth) under such a *perpetuâ dictaturâ*[4] as your lordship should prescribe. For I nothing doubt, but that eyther your Lordship would prescribe all things according to the rule, or be willing to examine againe, and againe, all things according to it. I am very apt to believe, what Mr. Perkins hath, in one of his prefatory pages to his golden chaine, that the word, and scriptures of God doe conteyne a short *upoluposis,*[5] or platforme, not onely of theology, but also of other sacred sciences (as he calleth them) attendants, and hand maids thereunto, which he maketh ethicks, eoconomicks,[6] politicks, church-government, prophecy, academy.[7] It is very suitable to Gods all-sufficient wisdome, and to the fulnes and perfection of Holy Scriptures, not only to prescribe perfect rules for the right ordering of a private mans soule to everlasting blessednes with himselfe, but also for the right ordering of a mans family, yea, of the commonwealth too, so farre as both of them are subordinate to spiritual ends, and yet avoide both the churches usurpation upon civill jurisdictions, *in ordine ad spiritualia,*[8] and the commonwealths invasion upon ecclesiasticall administrations, *in ordine*[9] to civill peace, and conformity to the civill state. Gods institutions (such as the government of church and of commonwealth be) may be close and compact, and coordinate one to another, and yet not confounded. God hath so framed the state of church government and ordinances, that they may be compatible to any commonwealth, though never so much disordered in his frame. But yet when a commonwealth hath liberty to mould his owne frame (*scripturæ plenitudinem adoro*)[10] I conceyve the scripture hath given full directjon for the right ordering of the same, and that, in such sort as may best mainteyne the *euexia*[11] of the church. Mr. Hooker[12] doth often quote a saying out of Mr. Cartwright[13] (though I have not read it in him) that noe man fashioneth his house to his hangings, but his hangings to his house. It is better that the commonwealth be fashioned to the setting forth of Gods house, which is his church: than to accommodate the church frame to the civill state. Democracy, I do not conceyve that ever God did ordeyne as a fitt government eyther for church or commonwealth. If the people be governors, who shall be governed? As for monarchy, and aristocracy, they are both of them clearely approoved, and directed in scripture, yet so as referreth the soveraigntie to himselfe, and setteth up Theocracy in both, as the best forme of government in the commonwealth, as well as in the church.

The law, which your Lordship instanceth in [that none shall be chosen to magistracy among us, but a church member][14] was made and enacted before I came into the countrey; but I have hitherto wanted sufficient light to plead against it. 1st. The rule that directeth the choice of supreame governors, is of like æquitie and weight in all magistrates, that one of their brethren (not a stranger) should be set over them. Deut. 17. 15.[15] and Jethroes counsell to Moses was approved of God, that the judges, and officers to be set over the people, should be men fearing God. Exod. 18. 21.[16] and Solomon maketh it the joy of a commonwealth, when the righteous[17] are in authority, and their mourning when the wicked rule, Prov. 29. 2;[18] Job 34. 30.[19] Your Lordship's feare, that this will bring in papal excommunicatjon, is iust, and pious: but let your Lordship be pleased againe to consider whether the consequence be necessary. *Turpius ejicitur quam non admittitur:*[20] non-membership may be a iust cause of non-admission to the place of magistracy, but yet, ejection out of his membership will not be a iust cause of ejecting him out of his magistracy. A godly woman, being to make choice of an husband, may iustly refuse a man that is eyther cast out of church fellowship, or is not yet receyved into it, but yet, when shee is once given to him, shee may not reject him then, for such defect. Mr. Humfrey was chosen for an assistant (as I heare) before the colony came over hither: and, though he be not as yet ioyned into church fellowship (by reason of the unsetlednes of the congregation where he liveth) yet the commonwealth doe still continue his magistracy to him, as knowing he waiteth for oppertunity of enioying church-fellowship shortly.[21]

When your Lordship doubteth, that this corse will draw all things under the determination of the church, *in ordine ad spiritualia* (seeing the church is to determine who shall be members, and none but a member may have to doe in the government of a commonwealth) be pleased (I pray you) to conceyve, that magistrates are neyther chosen to office in the church, nor doe governe by directions from the church, but by civill lawes, and those enacted in generall corts, and executed in corts of iustice, by the governors and assistants. In all which, the church (as the church) hath nothing to doe: onely, it prepareth fitt instruments both to rule, and to choose rulers, which is no ambition in the church, nor dishonor to the commonwealth, the apostle, on the contrary, thought it a great dishonor and reproach to the church of Christ, if it were not able to yield able judges to heare and determine all causes amongst their brethren. i. Cor. 6. i. to 5.[22] which place alone seemeth to me fully to decide this question: for it plainely holdeth forth this argument: It is a shame to the church to want able judges of civill matters (as v. 5.) and an audacious act in any church member voluntarily to go for judgment, other where than before the saints (as v. i.) then it will be noe arrogance nor folly in church members, nor preiudice to the commonwealth, if voluntarily they never choose any civill judges but from amongst the saints, such as church members are called to be. But the former is cleare: and how then can the latter be avoyded. If this therefore be (as your Lordship rightly conceyveth one of the maine objections if not the onely one) which hindereth this commonwealth from the entertainment of the propositions of those worthy gentlemen, wee intreate them, in the name of the Lord Jesus, to consider, in meeknes of wisdome, it is not any conceite, or will of ours, but the holy counsell and will of the Lord Jesus (whom they seeke to serve as well as wee) that overruleth us in this case: and we trust will overrule them also, that the Lord onely may be exalted amongst all his servants. What pittie and griefe were it, that the observance of the will of Christ should hinder good things from us!

But your Lordship doubteth, that if such a rule were necessary, then the church estate and the best ordered commonwealth in the world were not compatible. But let not your Lordship so conceyve. For, the church submitteth it selfe to all the lawes and ordinances of men, in what commonwealth soever they come to dwell. But it is one thing, to submit unto what they have noe calling to reforme: another thing, voluntarily to ordeyne a forme of government, which to the best discerning of many of us (for I speake not of myselfe) is expressly contrary to rule. Nor neede your Lordship feare (which yet I speake with submission to your Lordships better judgment) that this corse will lay such a foundation, as nothing but a mere democracy can be built upon it. Bodine confesseth, that though it be *status popularis,*[23] where a people choose their owne governors; yet the government is not a democracy, if it be administred, not by the people, but by the governors, whether one (for then it is a monarchy, though elective) or by many, for then (as you know) it is aristocracy.[24] In which respect it is, that church government is iustly denyed (even by Mr. Robinson) to be democratical,[25] though the people choose their owne officers and rulers.

Nor neede wee feare, that this course will, in time, cast the commonwealth into distractions, and popular confusions. For (under correction) these three things doe not undermine, but doe mutually and strongly mainteyne one another (even those three which wee principally aime at) authority in magistrates, liberty in people, purity in the church. Purity, preserved in the church, will preserve well ordered liberty in the people, and both of them establish well-ballanced authority in the magistrates. God is the author of all these three, and neyther is himselfe the God of confusion, nor are his wayes the wayes of confusion, but of peace.

What our brethren (magistrates or ministers, or leading freeholders) will answer to the rest of the propositions, I shall better understand before the gentlemans returne from Connecticutt, who brought them over. Mean while, two of the principall of them, the generall cort hath already condescended unto. 1. In establishing a standing councell, who, during their lives, should assist the governor in managing the chiefest affayres of this little state.[26] They have chosen, for the present, onely two (Mr. Winthrope and Mr. Dudley) not willing to choose more, till they see what further better choyse the Lord will send over to them, that so they may keep an open doore, for such desireable gentlemen as your Lordship mentioneth. 2. They have graunted the governor and assistants a negative voyce, and reserved to the freemen the like liberty also.[27] Touching other things, I hope to give your Lordship further account, when the gentleman returneth.

He being now returned, I have delivered to him an answer to the rest of your demands,[28] according to the mindes of such leading men amongst us, as I thought meete to consult withall, concealing your name from any, except 2 or 3, who alike doe concurr in a joynt desire of yeilding to any such propositions, as your Lordship demandeth, so farre as with allowance from the word they may, beyond which I know your Lordship would not require any thing.

Now the Lord Jesus Christ (the prince of peace) keepe and bless your Lordship, and dispose of all your times and talents to his best advantage: and let the covenant of his grace and peace rest upon your honourable family and posterity, throughout all generations.

Thus, humbly craving pardon for my boldnesse and length, I take leave and rest,

Your Honours to serve in Christ Jesus,

J. C.

1. Stephen Foster, *Their Solitary Way: The Puritan Social Ethic in the First Century of Settlement in New England* (New Haven, Conn., 1971), 38. This exchange is also discussed in T. H. Breen, *The Character of the Good Ruler: A Study of Puritan Political Ideas in New England, 1630–1730* (New

Haven, Conn., 1970), 50–51, 54, 74–75; and Karen Ordahl Kupperman, "Definitions of Liberty on the Eve of Civil War: Lord Saye and Sele, Lord Brooke, and the American Puritan Colonies," *Historical Journal,* XXXII (1989), 20–26.

2. "Certain Proposals made by Lord Say, Lord Brooke, and other Persons of quality, as conditions of their removing to New-England, with the answers thereto," in Hutchinson, *History,* I, 490–495, app. 2; Thomas Hutchinson, *The History of the Colony and Province of Massachusetts-Bay,* ed. Lawrence Shaw Mayo (Cambridge, Mass., 1936), I, 410–413, app. 2.

3. William Twisse (1578–1646) wrote *Dissertatio de scientia media* . . . (Arnheim, 1639), and *Of the Morality of the Fourth Commandment* . . . (London, 1641). The fourth commandment (Exod. 20:8): Remember the sabbath day to keep it holy.

4. *perpetuâ dictaturâ:* a permanent dictatorship.

5. *upoluposis:* the fourth letter is probably an error in Hutchinson's transcription. The l should be a t. The Greek word is ὑποτύπωσις: model, pattern.

6. Hutchinson's "eoconomicks" is probably an alteration of Cotton's use of the *oe* ligature: œconomicks.

7. William Perkins (1558–1602) first published *A Golden Chaine* . . . in Latin (London, 1591), and subsequent editions in both Latin and English in 1591, and in English in 1592, 1595, 1597, and beyond. The first of these to include the list of "attendants" or "hand maids" of theology was the London, 1595, edition, where it appears in a Ramistic table on the unnumbered recto page just preceding p. 1. Cotton omits one of the seven "handmaides" listed by Perkins, namely "The Jewes commonweale."

8. *in ordine ad spiritualia:* in regard to spiritual matters.

9. *in ordine:* literally, in order; here Cotton means in regard to.

10. *scripturæ plenitudinem adoro:* I honor/marvel at the fullness of Scripture.

11. *euexia:* εὐεξία: good health, vigor.

12. Thomas Hooker.

13. Thomas Cartwright (c. 1535–1603), an influential Cambridge Puritan, was deprived of the Lady Margaret Professorship of Divinity and expelled from the university for his Puritan views on ecclesiastical governance. On Cartwright and the Puritan movement, see Peter Lake, *Moderate Puritans and the Elizabethan Church* (Cambridge, 1982), 77–92, 287–291.

14. The brackets are included in Hutchinson's printing of the letter, suggesting that they were in Cotton's manuscript. Since the clause in brackets appears to be a quotation from Lord Saye's letter to Cotton, the brackets might have been substituted by Hutchinson for Cotton's usual method of indicating a quotation with quotation marks in the left margin before every line that is quoted.

15. Deut. 17:15b: One from among thy brethren shalt thou set King over thee: thou mayest not set a stranger over thee, which is not thy brother.

16. Exod. 18 tells of Moses' attempt to settle all disputes and answer all questions for his people; his father-in-law, the priest Jethro, advises him to set up a better system, saying in verse 21: Moreover thou shalt provide out of all the people able men, such as fear God, men of truth, hating covetousness; and place such over them, to be rulers of thousands, and rulers of hundreds, rulers of fifties, and rulers of tens.

17. Hutchinson (1764) prints righteons.

18. Hutchinson incorrectly prints Prov. 29.21. The mistake could be either Cotton's or Hutchinson's. Assuming the latter, it is here printed correctly in the body of the letter. Prov.

29:2: When the righteous are in authority, the people rejoice: but when the wicked beareth rule, the people mourn.

19. Job 34:30: That the hypocrite reign not, lest the people be ensnared.

20. *Turpius ejicitur quam non admittitur:* He is more shamefully ejected than not admitted, that is, it is more shameful that he be ejected than that he not be admitted.

21. John Humfry (1593–1653?) was an original patentee of the Massachusetts Bay Colony and was selected deputy governor on October 20, 1629, but gave up the post on deciding to stay in England. On May 8, 1632, however, he was elected as assistant to the General Court of the colony in anticipation of his emigration. He finally arrived in July of 1634, settling in Salem. See Frances Rose-Troup, "John Humfry," Essex Institute, *Historical Collections,* LXV (1929), 293–308.

22. Hutchinson's Cor, is corrected here to Cor. 1 Cor. 6:1–5: Dare any of you, having a matter against another, go to law before the unjust, and not before the saints? Do ye not know that the saints shall judge the world? and if the world shall be judged by you, are ye unworthy to judge the smallest matters? Know ye not that we shall judge angels? how much more things that pertain to this life? If then ye have judgments of things pertaining to this life, set them to judge who are least esteemed in the church. I speak to your shame. Is it so, that there is not a wise man among you? no, not one that shall be able to judge between his brethren?

23. *status popularis:* a popular constitution.

24. I[ean] Bodin, *The Six Bookes of a Commonweale,* trans. Richard Knolles (London, 1606), 250.

25. John Robinson (1576?–1625), the Separatist English pastor at Leiden.

26. In March 1635/6 the General Court established a "Standing Council," a group of former governors who would be magistrates for life, without any need of annual reelection (see *Records of Massachusetts Bay,* I, 167, 174, 195). This ruling proved controversial and was altered in May 1639, under pressure from the deputies. From then on, all magistrates were subject to annual election. See Robert Emmet Wall, Jr., *Massachusetts Bay: The Crucial Decade, 1640–1650* (New Haven, Conn., 1972), 13–15.

27. In September 1634, the magistrates asserted the principle that a simple majority of magistrates and deputies combined was not enough to create a law. They claimed the magistrates, voting separately, had to have a majority among them—a smaller number of men than the deputies—before an act became law. The deputies objected, and the court called in John Cotton for consultation. His sermon counseled compromise, according to Winthrop (Winthrop, *Journal,* 128), but in 1635/6 the General Court nevertheless decided that "noe law, order, or sentence shall passe as an act of the Court, without the consent of the greater parte of the magistrates on the one parte, and the greater number of the deputyes on the other parte" (*Records of Massachusetts Bay,* I, 170). See Wall, *Massachusetts Bay: The Crucial Decade,* 11–13.

28. See "Certain Proposals," in Hutchinson, *History,* I, 490–495, app. 2.

Massachusetts Ministers to John Cotton

[December 1636]

Published: *Sixteene Questions of Serious and Necessary Consequence, Propounded unto Mr. John Cotton of Boston in New-England, Together with His Answers to Each Question* (London, 1644), 1; Hall, *Antinomian Controversy,* 46

Cotton's exchange with Thomas Shepard in 1636 led to further written exchanges with a growing number of ministers in the Bay.[1] What began as person-to-person correspondence escalated into an extensive formal written debate between Cotton and the other ministers. Except for John Wheelwright, any supporters he had apparently found it unwise or impolitic to speak out. If they did, their statements have been lost. The exchange that does survive began with the Shepard-Cotton letters, then progressed to a request from the other elders that Cotton reply to sixteen written questions, to his extended answers to those questions, then to the "Elders' Reply" to his answers, and finally to "Cotton's Rejoynder," a statement of more than seventy pages in Hall's modern edition. The present edition, rather than reproducing all of this public debate, which certainly grew beyond the bounds of normal correspondence, includes only the three brief cover notes to the "Sixteene Questions," Cotton's "Answers," and finally the "Elders' Reply." Cotton's lengthy "Rejoynder" to the latter is preceded by a curt "Reuerend and Beloued," and is all business thereafter.

Deare and Reverend Sir,

Wee doe humbly and earnestly desire a short and plaine Answer of those Questions under-written, and at the hand of you, those things we desire your speedy Answer unto: and though some of these wee know your judgement in, yet not for ourselves onely, but for others sakes we put them all in.

1. The progress of this increasingly formal and elaborate investigation into Cotton's ideas is documented in Hall, *Antinomian Controversy,* where the full texts of all of the documents mentioned here may be found.

John Cotton to Massachusetts Ministers

[December 1636]

Copy. MHS: MS notes in a seventeenth-century hand on the verso of the title page in *Severall Questions of Serious and Necessary Consequence, Propounded by the Teaching Elders, unto M. Iohn Cotton of Boston in New-England, with His Respective Answer to Each Question* (London, 1647)

Published: *Sixteene Questions of Serious and Necessary Consequence, Propounded unto Mr. John Cotton of Boston in New-England, Together with His Answers to Each Question* (London, 1644), 1–2; Hall, *Antinomian Controversy,* 46

The following text is based on a manuscript note in the copy of *Severall Qvestions* owned by MHS. It also contains interlinear corrections in the same hand throughout the printed text, including an explanatory comment below the MS copy of Cotton's brief cover letter: "The printed Part I corrected by *th*e MSS. Original," indicating the copyist's belief that he had in hand an authoritative manuscript copy.

Reverend & beloved Brethren

For an Answer unto your (Interrogatories, shall I call them or) Questions, Tho I might without sin refer you (as our Saviour did the High Priest when his doctrin was questioned) to what I have ever taught & spoken openly to the World, as having in secret said nothing else (John 18.20.21.) Yet because you are much dearer ~~to me~~ & precious to me than the High Priest was to Him and because Love thinketh no evil & Truth feareth not *th*e Light I have (by the help of Christ) sent you (according to your desire) a plaine & homely[1] Answer to each particular.

Wherein if I err, let me see mine error, and try if I shut mine eyes against the Light. If in your judgment I hold forth the Truth, then bear witness with me to *th*e Truth for *th*e honour of the name of Christ, & for *th*e Peace & salvation of the Churches in our Lord Jesus, your Lord & ours.

1. *Sixteene Questions* prints short instead of homely.

Massachusetts Ministers to John Cotton

[January 1636/7]

Copy. MHS: MS, "The Elders Reply," copied into the back of *Severall Questions of Serious and Necessary Consequence, Propounded by the Teaching Elders, unto M. Iohn Cotton of Boston in New-England, with His Respective Answer to Each Question* (London, 1647), [11], in the same hand as the previous letter and the interlinear corrections in the same volume

Published: Hall, *Antinomian Controversy,* 61–62

This letter and the written replies to Cotton's answers that followed it are given the heading "The Elders Reply." It was not written immediately on receipt of Cotton's answers to the elders' questions, as the authors indicate in the first paragraph. As Hall suggests, they probably wrote it in January.[1]

Reverend and Beloved in the God of Love!

These few things that we have replyed to your Answer we entreat you to accept of, as fruits of our love to your self, & of our desires of the establishing of Truth & peace in the Churches of Christ. We have the rather embarked ourselves in a busines of this nature because of your own desire, & of *th*e offense of diverse who have made account that our silence all this while, hath spoken our consent to all you said. The truth is, we have been tender of your honour, & have made conscience of dissenting in the least from you, wherein Truth might not be wounded: And for this, we appeal to the Searcher of all hearts. You cannot be ignorant which way the stream of most Divines, both of our own Country & others runs. From whose steps if any turn aside, they had need bring sound proof from the Scripture, or else fear they tread awry in so doing. Now Dear Sir, we leave these things with you, hoping that *th*e Lord will honour you, with making you a happy Instrument of calming these storms & cooling these hot contentions & paroxysmes that have begun to swell & burn in these poor Churches. We had written sooner, but that we were delayed partly by *th*e expectac*i*on of your grounds, & partly by *th*e difficulty of our meeting & staying together this Winter season, to advise of what we should do herein. The God of Peace create peace for us, and help us to love his Truth together in Christ Jesus our Prince of Peace, Even so Amen.

To your Preface

Which we desire to take in the best part, tho*ugh* we see no ground why you should conceive we gave you the Questions as so many High=priest=like

Interrogatories, contrary to our free ingenuous profession made in private to you. viz. That sundry opinions (intimated in those Questions) going up & down as yours in the repute of some, we might have from your own hand what you held, whereby to stop their mouths that raise up any slander of you, or prejudice against the Truth. And this the Lord knows was the true intent of our Hearts. Nor see wee, why you should conceive it needless to answer sith you say nothing privately, which you have not publickly preached, as neither *Christ* had. For tho you speak nothing, yet others might publicly conceive you to be of this or *tha*t Opinion, which they father on you. and sundry things which you have publickly uttered, were darkly & doubtfully delivered; whereof as we have privately besought you to consider, so we desire to see them interpreted: Nor know we why you should so express yourself, as to profess us dearer to you, than was the High Priest to *Christ.* Should we so have mentioned our affection to your self, it would have come very short of that which we find in our hearts. But to conclude, as you desire us to bear witness to what we shall apprehend you hold forth as true, which we have done & are resolved in *th*e Lord for ever to do; so we beseech you to bear witness with us against those Opinions which shall appear to be false, & the defenders thereof: for we need, not only your consent with us in the truth, but your seasonable reproof of those that dissent.

1. Hall, *Antinomian Controversy,* 60.

Peter Bulkeley to John Cotton

[March 31, 1637]

ALS. MS: BPL, Ms. Am. 1506, pt. 2, no. 7

This letter is written on a single quarto-sized sheet (12″ × 7.5″), folded once to divide it into two leaves, or four pages. The text is written on the first three pages. Though there is some staining from water damage, the paper is unbroken except for a small hole at the bottom of the first page, causing breaks in the text in three lines at the end of both the first recto and its verso. Thomas Prince's note appears at the end of the letter: "I suppose this was written in 1637 before *th*e Synod set on[.] Began on Aug. 30. 1637." Prince's characteristic underlining is present on a few lines on each page and is omitted here.

The dating of the letter is determined by the reference to the imminent ordination of Peter Bulkeley and John Jones as ministers to the Concord church, which took place on April 6, 1637, at Newtown.[1] This event should not be confused with the gathering of the church, which had occurred on July 5, 1636. As J. William T. Youngs, Jr., observes, "The formation of the religious community was of primary importance; the formal installation of a pastor, although desirable, was less consequential."[2]

Bulkeley's paragraphing is sometimes problematic. He does not indent, but begins all paragraphs at the left margin. When a paragraph ends with a line extending to the far right side of the page, he starts the next paragraph on a new line, so that some blank space may (or may not) appear at the end of the previous line, marking his paragraph separation. When a paragraph ends on a short line, however, he simply skips an inch or so to the right, indicating a paragraph break by the blank space in the middle of the line, and starts the next paragraph on the same line. Modern indentation is adopted here, but the paragraph breaks are those indicated by Bulkeley.

Bulkeley's seal is still intact on the verso of page 2, where he wrote the address block in three lines:

> To his reuerend & deare frend
> M[r] Cotton att Boston giue
> these.

Deare S*i*r,

your complaynt of *th*e want of brotherly loue, I must needes say is too iust, w*hi*ch I haue often lamented to see ~~in~~ soe much wanting amongst those *tha*t p*ro*fesse the fayth of the Lord Jesus. I doe confesse I haue found as ~~much wanting~~ ˆlittle toward myselfeˆ here, as euer I did in any place *tha*t god brought me vnto. It is the place that I haue desired to shew loue vnto, for his sake whoe had putt his name here; and yett haue I found soe much strangenes, alienation, and soe much neglect from some whoe would sometimes haue visited me w*i*th diuerse myles going, (yett here, will passe by my dore, as ˆifˆ I were *th*e man that they had nott knowen,) ~~in soe much~~ that I haue sometimes maruelled where the cause of the change should be: whether in myselfe or in them. As concerning myne owne respect and vnfeyned loue vnto yourselfe, I hartily desire yow to lay aside all Jealousys concerning the same, assuring yow before him whoe knoweth our harts, my soule is knitt vnto yow, as it hath bin (in some measure) euer since god brought me into acquayntance w*i*th yow, though in some things there may be some difference of apprehensions and of iudgm*en*t. And herein I doe hartily beseech him, *tha*t is *th*e god of peace and is one in hims*elf* *tha*t he would please ~~him~~ to worke peace & vnitye of iudgm*en*t in vs all, *tha*t we may all thinke and speake *th*e same thing and make vs one in him, as he and his Christ are one. Butt Dear S*i*r, admitt that there were lesse of this grace of loue then there is ~~any~~ among those *tha*t professe *th*e name of Christ. yett the vnrighteousnes and sin*n* of man, doth nott disanull *th*e veritye & truth of god. I meane though loue may be wanting among vs, yett god[s][3] truth stands firme still, *tha*t where brotherly loue is ^in truth^ it is an euidence of translating fro*m* death to life. It can be noe euidence where it is nott, but where it is, there it doth euidence. In the poynt of euidencing iustificat*ion* by sanctificat*ion:* There is one arg*umen*t w*hi*ch to me [ink blot] yett is vnanswerable; It is termed a going vpon couent of workes to goe this way. I confesse it, [i]f ^we^ goe about to proue it by *tha*t sanctificat*ion* or legall reformation w*hi*ch the fora|| conuiction of *th*e law doth bring vs vnto. but if the sanctificat*ion* ~~be an||rue, be there~~ ^be true|| [one word lost]^ I reason thus, &c./ [IV]

The same couent of grace which p*ro*miseth iustificat*ion* p*ro*miseth sanctificat*ion* also *er*go to euidence one of these by the other, is noe turning aside to another couent, but an euidencing of one p*ar*te of the couent ^of grace^ by another. This is one arg*umen*t. I will adde but one more. I thinke you doe allow this, *tha*t after *tha*t a man hath knowen his iustificat*ion* by the wittnes of the sp*iri*t then he may afterwards take euidence fro*m* his sanctificat*ion*./ Suppose then one truly iustifyed, whose iustifyed estate is yett hid from him. This man is sanctifyed w*i*th *th*e same sanctificat*ion* for kinde, (though p*er*haps nott for measure) as afterwards when his iustificat*ion* is cleared vp vnto him. if then the p*er*son b[e] iustifyed, (before he see it, as well as after, if w*i*thall, his sanctificat*ion* be the sa[m]e, before and after, ~~why it~~ I cannott conceaue any reason why it should[4] a going vpon (or aside to) a couent of workes before, more then afterwards.

Concerning that other passage *tha*t was betwixt vs concerning Mr Wheelewrights assertion, *tha*t (To beleeue) should belong to *th*e Couent of workes, It is to me very strange. I doe confesse there is a fayth w*hi*ch men doe make vnto thems*elves* w*hi*ch doth leaue them *tha*t haue it, vnder a couent of workes, and till they haue a better fayth, they will neuer come w*i*thin a better couent. Butt yett this will nott make good his assertion. I should thinke it a benefitt, to see any thing *tha*t might giue me light in this poynt. for *th*e p*re*sent I haue many things ag*ains*t it. I will name but one or two. 1t. if (beleeue) belong to *th*e couent of workes, then the law doth nott reueale *th*e whole couent of workes. but the law doth reueale *th*e whole. *er*go. the reason of the consequence is bec*ause* the law doth nott reueale nor require fayth. gal: 3.12.[5]

2d. if (beleeuing) were of the couent of workes, then a beleeuer could nott be saued, (for by the couent of workes noe flesh can be saved.) but the beleeuer may & shall be saued. Joh: 3.16 &c. go.[6]

I will adde noe more. if I may see *tha*t these will nott hould, I shall *th*e more suspect the rest.

One word more touching one word in your sermon of this day which was this. *tha*t both our iustificat*ion* and the fayth ^of^ our iustificat*ion* must ~~depend~~ ^be built^ onely vpon the righteousn*ess* of Chr*ist* (as for iustificat*ion* its*elf* ~~we~~ I[7] doubt nott. concerning the fayth (that is, the assurance) of my iustificat*ion* this must alsoe ~~build~~ ^be built^ vpon the right*eousness* of Chr*ist*) wh*ic*h I pray yow explayne. for to my vnderstanding; ~~the words~~ the words import this much, That if being iustifyed, ^I^ doe aske the question how I may be assured of my iustificat*ion* the answ*er* is, I must be assured by *th*e righteousnes of Christ. I doe easily see how my iustificat*ion* doth spring fro*m* Christs right*eousness* but how doth assurance? or thus 1. my iustificat*ion* must be built vpon the right*eousness* of Christ. this I affirme w*i*th || [one word lost] The fayth (1. the assurance) of my iustificat*ion* must be built vpon Christs right*eousness*. i[f]|| [one word lost] I aske, how may I be assured *tha*t I am iustifyed by Christs [2] righteousnes, (or ~~assured~~ *tha*t his right^eousnes^ ~~right:~~ is myne,) how shall I be assured hereby? &c.

I doe assure you it troubles my sp*irit* th*a*t I cannott goe along w*i*th yow in these ~~lesser~~ things. yett shew me the light *tha*t may helpe me to see. I trust the Lord will open myne eye, and giue me an hart nott to deteyne his truth in vnrighteousnes. These sorry lines I scribble after supper, since my com*m*ing ho[m]e[8] fro*m* Boston. I am now going to rest. The L. Jesus whoe is *th*e rest & peace of his peo*ple* rest in our harts by *th*e presence of his grace & sp*irit* & helpe vs to rest our*selves* vpon him, laying downe our soules in his lappe, & bosome, in w*hi*ch is sweete peace. Rem*em*ber my loue to good M[rs] Cotton. The L. be w*i*th yow all. Amen.

Yours euer in Christ,

This present Thursday night.

Pet: Bulkeley /

There must be some difference betwixt Christs righteousnes, and that w*hi*ch doth manifest it vnto me as mine. but those 2 yow seeme to confound./

I should haue acquaynted yow yesterday, that the ordination of the Elders of the Church ~~of~~ at Concord is to be ^on^ Weddensday ~~se~~ come-senight. It is to be here at Newtowne. I pray take notice of it. if it be necessary to giue any other notice, to other p*er*sons or in another way, we would nott be wanting ^therein^ for auoyding ^of^ offence. &c I haue spoken of it alsoe to M[r] Wilson &c/

1. John Winthrop records the date of the meeting and comments on the absences of all the leading figures in the Boston church. *Journal*, 212.

2. J. William T. Youngs, Jr., "Congregational Clericalism: New England Ordinations before the Great Awakening," *WMQ*, 3d Ser., XXXI (1974), 482. William K. B. Stoever comments on this letter's relation to theological issues in the Antinomian controversy (*"A Faire and Easie Way to Heaven,"* 236 n. 53).

3. Bulkeley wrote god.

4. Bulkeley omitted the verb here. He probably meant to write be or seem or appear immediately after should.

5. Gal. 3:12: And the law is not of faith: but, The man that doeth them shall live in them.

6. John 3:16: For God so loved the world, that he gave his only begotten Son, that whosoever believeth in him should not perish, but have everlasting life.

7. The I is written over the word we.

8. Bulkeley wrote hope.

Richard Bernard to [John Cotton]

April 1, 1637

ALS. MS: PH, "Cotton Families Collection: Writings of Mr. John Cotton," Collections of the Pilgrim Society, fols. 125–127

Richard Bernard (1567–1641) had been a Nonconformist as early as the first decade of the seventeenth century. His handbook on preaching, *The Faithfull Shepheard* . . . (London, 1607; rev. eds. 1609, 1621), had a wide circulation among Puritans. In it he sided with those ministers who adapted their thinking on nonconformity to their larger sense that it was their duty, as God's ministers, to tend their flocks, which they could only do if they avoided silencing.[1]

As Bernard acknowledges at the outset, he and his unnamed correspondent had previously exchanged letters on issues of church practice in New England. Given his seniority and reputation, Bernard's challenge here to the notion of a church covenant incorporating a concept of exclusivity in the acceptance of members must have seemed an especially important one to Cotton and his colleagues. An anonymous West Country correspondent of John Winthrop's who was clearly sympathetic with the New England cause reported rumors in England as to how Cotton might answer Bernard, expressing some fear that he would be insufficiently politic in his reply.[2] This assumption that Cotton would reply to Bernard helps us identify Cotton as Bernard's likely addressee. The inclusion of Bernard's letter in a manuscript volume of items related to Cotton now in the possession of the Pilgrim Society reinforces the idea that Cotton is the intended recipient. The New Englanders answered Bernard in 1639; the reply was later published as an anonymous book, now attributed to Richard Mather, *An Apologie of the Churches in New England for Church Covenant* (London, 1643).[3] It appears that Bernard's treatise was never published.

An answer to some passages in your Letter to mee, which I in my treatise I haue not touched.
Sir/

You say that Circumcision (in roome whereof baptisme succedeth) was not administred to Beleivers and theire seed, as Such; vnless *w*ithall they ioyned themselus in Com*m*union with the people of ˆ*th*eˆ God of Abraham; And therefore wee never reade, that Melchisedech, or Job, or his freinds (and theire seed) were circumcised and yet doubtless all of them Beleevers and Heires of life. And why not circumcised? Were they not fellow-heires with Abraham of the grace of Christ? Yes verily. but yet because they had not opportunity to ioyne *w*ith Abrahams family and posterity (*w*h*i*ch were then the ˆonlyˆ visible Church of God) neither did God put Circumcision upon them, neither did they require it for themselus, or theire seed.

Therefore what? You haue not made your inference, as I wish you had your self: but I conceiue it to be this. Therefore men may be Beleevers and heires of life, and yet baptisme not administred vnto them, nor theire seed, vnlese they ioyne themselus in Com*m*union *w*ith some p*ar*ticular Church by your Church Covenant.

First to answer to the inference. I. I say there is noe such Covenant to let in, or to hold out, B~~e~~eleevers or theire seed: for this see the Treatise.

II[ly] Answer, I pray you, your self, how came it that the Eunuch was baptised by Phillip?[4] ˆtoˆ what particular Church did he ioyne himself in Com*m*unio*n?* [125v] or Cornelius *w*ith the rest in Acts: 10: when they were ~~b~~ baptized?

III: I desire to know what it is that maketh men Christian Beleevers, now, and heires of heaven? To make one a Christian Beleever I take it to be the preaching of the word of Promise, called the Gospell, by which through *th*e holy Ghost, faith to beleiue in Ch*ris*t is wrought in the hˆeˆart so, as *w*ith the mouth confession is made to salvation: and such a Beleever is of vs judged one ordained to eternall life, and an Heire of heaven.

VI. If this be so, as it is in truth, then who dare deny baptisme to such, and to theire seed? Sure I am Phillip durst not. Act: 8. 37. 38.[5] nor Peter Act: 10. 47. 48.[6] For such a Beleever taketh hold of the p*ro*mise, is a partaker of Gods Covenant, and therefore hath vndeniably a right to Gods seal: If he beleiue, he is to be baptized, and his seed also: els he hath wrong offered him, and Gods worke also in him is neglected, *w*h*i*ch how it can be answered to God I for my parte cannot tell. This great sinne both ag*ains*t God and man cannot be excused by an vnwarrantable Covenant made to bring them into a particular Church. Take it into y*ou*r serious consideratio*n,* I doe beseech you; Let not our owne inventions, overthrow the way of God so plainely chalked out before vs, as is the admittance of a Beleiver and his seed vnto baptisme.

Secondly to answer to the p*r*emises. I. I acknowledge that baptisme is in stead of Circumcision; but it will not therefore follow, that because some Beleevers then, and heires of heaven with theire seed were not circumcised;

that therefore now Beleevers should not be ~~p~~ baptized. For ~~your~~ your self put, by your owne words, an answer into my mouth.

[fol. 126] God put not then Circumcision vpon all, Beleevers Circumcision was ~~was~~ imposed vpon Abraham and his seed (neither yet that so onely, for some bor*n*e in Abrahams house, and other bought w*i*th monie were at the first w*i*th Abraham circumcised.) Gen: 17.[7] but baptisme is imposed vpon all Beleivers in Ch*ris*t,—Jew and Gentile, of any kindred, people, or Natio*n* vnder heaven. II. Concerning your instances in Melchisedech and Job w*i*th his freinds, that they were not circumcised; and yet were fellow Heires w*i*th Abraham of the grace of Ch*ris*t.

1. Its' vncertaine at what time Job, and his freinds lived; that they were not circumcised, how can it be p*ro*ved? If Job came out of Abrahams line by Keturah,[8] he was circumcised. or if he came of Esau, w*h*o is Edom, in the land of Vz, lam: 4.21. Job. 1.1.[9] its like he was circumcised. But graunt that [deleted letter] neither he nor his freinds were circumcised: What then? You say they had not opportunity to joyne w*i*th Abrahams family; God did not put circumcision vpon them, neither did they require it for themselus or theire seed; so as partly they could not, and partly they minded it not, because God required it not. Whats this to our peoples comeing to you, and haveing opportunity to joyne w*i*th you; yea they offer theire children, and are refused. So as your instance for Job and his freinds help you not in this matter.

Now for Melchisedech he was more auncient then Abraham, a Preist of the most high God, & if a Preist, without controversie, he had a Church of his owne, and was not tyed to submitt to the outward speciallities of Abrahams Covenant: he beeing Preist of an other order, greater then that of Levi, who was in the loynes of Abraha*m* who payed tythes to this Melchisedech, by whom Abraham was blessed, and wee know the lesser to be blessed of the greater.[10] If he had not beene exempt from the law of Circumcision, he had [126v] opportunity to haue ioyned in Com*m*union w*ith* Abraham, and with the people of God p*ro*ceeding fro*m* Abraham. This instance also is to little purpose.

If you would p*ro*duce fit instances, and to purpose, they should be such as were Beleevers, and heires of salvation, to whom the seale of the Covena*n*t belonged, by the will of God, who had opportunity to receiue the seale, who also desired it, and yet were denyed it by the Church of God, either of *tha*t in the old, or by any one in the New Testament. but such Instances are yet to seeke, and never will be found. I desire better Arguments for your tenents, or let me beseech you in the Lord Jesus feare to maintaine your vncooth wayes, and vntroden paths, by such weake proofes.

Vpon my Confession that I haue beene notoriously cousened by some p*ro*fessours; you inferr that therefore you will not receiue all as soone as they offer themselus into Church fellowshipp.

I. The scope ^of my speech^ was to shew that men of excelle*n*t parts, w*i*th Com*m*on gifts, may p*ro*ue in time notoriously wicked, and therefore such Persons soe qualified, theire future condition not discernable for the p*r*esent, at theire admittance into Church fellowshipp, giues noe good assurance, of theire inward sanctity, ~~and~~ ^~~as~~^ ^as^ if such only were worthy of admittance, and others who can make noe such demonstration of theire guifts ^were to be^ left out.

II. Why you should not receiue all that offer the*m* selues into your Congregations, I see noe ground. If they offer themselus, you may enquire of the*m* the reason of theire willingness, and theire answere being Ch*ris*tianlike, at that p*r*esent, though weake, and discovering much ~~weakeness~~ ignorance yet theire will expressed to learne, and liue well whatsoever, they p*ro*ue after, you are not aforehand to surmise, to withhold them from your fellowshipp, as I conceiue.

[fol. 127] Wheras I said, that by baptisme they entred into the Covenant (meaning our people com*m*eing to y*o*u) I vnderstood by baptisme, the seale with the precedent Confession, of theire faith, as wee vse at baptisme in our Church; for without the Covena*n*t the seale is nothing, but as a seale to a blanke.

You like it not, that I call your Covenant a particular Covenant, ~~of grace~~, and our Covenant in baptisme a general Covenant of grace. But whether our confession of faith in Ch*ris*t, ~~or~~ ^our^ renuntiation of sinn, vowing to forsake the Devill, *th*e world and the flesh, and our p*ro*fessed obedience to the revealed will of God, be more vniversall at all times, and to all Ch*ris*tians more knowne, or fro*m* the begining hitherto kept of all, then this your late devised, and in former ages vnheard of, and in all Ch*ris*tian Churches els vnpractised Covena*n*t, let every one judge.

You cannot call ours a parsonall Covenant, except you meane bec*ause* one person, at one time maketh it, as one person doth with you, ~~w~~ vpon the admittance, and so yours is personall. For our Covenant is the Catholike p*ro*fession of the Christian faith, into w*hi*ch all Ch*ris*tians are admitted. Againe as you make it an act of the Church in admitting any member into it, so of any baptised,[11] it is said; wee recieue this Child into the Congregation of Christs flocke. By w*hi*ch the baptised[12] beeing one of Ch*ris*ts flocke, hath a right and interest in,—Christ his Church wheresoever. for beeing baptised into Ch*ris*t, Christ is put on, and Ch*ris*t they carry with them, and who dare deny Ch*ris*t admittance into any of your Congregations when such offer themselus? for letters com*m*endatorie wanting is noe good reason to hold them out: se the Treatise of this matter: for confirmation, how you bring it in to disanull the right of interest by baptisme, I see not. of Job and his freinds, and of Melchisedech, before. For the magnifying of your church Covenant, and the invalidity thereof [127v] it's shewed in the treatise. What you haue said, out of Justine Martyre,[13] wee require the same of ours to be baptised, before baptisme administred[.] What Justine speaketh, was of such as were to be Christened. Its nothing to this our case, concerning the already with vs baptised; I haue not Justine by me at this p*r*esent, if I miss his meaning, the text will discover it, but I take it I am in the right.

Deare S*i*r, let the scattered Christians be more deare to you; Let the sprinkling of Ch*ris*ts bloud on them sacramentally moue your compassion towards them, Take them in, if bad to make them good, if godly minded, to make them better. They are all in the Church, for who ever cast them out? & if within, why keep you them out, by your, I say still, vnwarrantable Covenant, as you make it, and esteeme it. So[14] wishing my heartie requests prevalent w*i*th y*o*u/ I rest/

Batcombe — Yours, in *th*e lord
April 1. — Jesus.
1637

Ric. Bernard

I am grateful to Jeremy Bangs, who, while serving as Visiting Curator of Manuscripts, the Pilgrim Society, Pilgrim Hall Museum, in Plymouth, Massachusetts, called this manuscript to my attention.

1. Hall, *Faithful Shepherd,* 48. Janice Knight associates Cotton with this attitude, though she makes no mention of Bernard; see *Orthodoxies in Massachusetts: Rereading American Puritanism* (Cambridge, Mass., 1994), 35, 41–52. On Bernard, see Brook, *Lives of the Puritans,* II, 459–462; Venn, *Alumni Cantabrigienses,* I, 141; *DNB;* Hall, *Faithful Shepherd,* 42, 48–71.

2. "We heare of a letter that Mr. Cotton should write (how true the report is, I knowe not yet) in answere to a lettre written to him by one Mr. Bernard of Botcombe in Sommersetshire, a man though vpright in the mayne, yet of very greate weaknesses; wherein, as we heare, Mr. Cotton should write, that we are a true Church Implicitè but not Explicitè, which if it be soe (as you may soone vnderstand) will doe not a little hurt among vs . . . ; yet suppose the distinction admitted, we doe wonder if a reuerend and wise minister of Christ should vpon the letter, or perhaps prouocation of Mr. Bernard, or indeed of any, send ouer your opinions to vs in such a point, which can doe vs little or noe good, your selues very much disadvantage many wayes." Unknown to John Winthrop, [1637], *Winthrop Papers,* III, 399–400.

3. The title page of this book includes the statement, "Sent over in Answer to Master Bernard, in the Yeare 1639." The letter's arrival in mid-1637 was awkward, as Winthrop noted in a journal entry for October 8, 1638: "About two years since one Mr. Bernard, a minister at Batcomb in Somersetshire in England, sent over two books in writing, one to the magistrates, and the other to the elders, wherein he laid down arguments against the manner of our gathering of our churches, etc., which the elders could not answer till this time, by reason of the many troubles about Mrs. Hutchinson's opinions, etc." Winthrop, *Journal,* 268.

4. See Acts 8:27–39.

5. Acts 8:37, 38: And Philip said, If thou believest with all thine heart, thou mayest. And he answered and said, I believe that Jesus Christ is the Son of God. And he commanded the chariot to stand still: and they went down both into the water, both Philip and the eunuch; and he baptized him.

6. Acts 10:47, 48: Can any man forbid water, that these should not be baptized, which have received the Holy Ghost as well as we? And he commanded them to be baptized in the name of the Lord. Then prayed they him to tarry certain days.

7. This scriptural citation appears in the right margin. Gen. 17 tells of God making the covenant with Abraham and of instituting circumcision as a sign of the covenant.

8. Keturah was Abraham's second wife. Gen. 25:1.

9. These citations appear in the right margin. Lam. 4:21: Rejoice and be glad, O daughter of Edom, that dwellest in the land of Uz; the cup also shall pass through unto thee: thou shalt be drunken, and shalt make thyself naked. Job 1:1: There was a man in the land of Uz, whose name was Job; and that man was perfect and upright, and one that feared God, and eschewed evil.

10. On Melchisedec, see Heb. 7.

11. The s is written over z.

12. The s is written over z.

13. Justin Martyr (100?–165?), Palestinian Church Father.

14. This entire sentence and the full signature and date blocks that follow are in a different ink and handwriting—presumably Bernard's—from those in the rest of the letter.

John Dod and Twelve Other Ministers in England to New England "Brethren"

[About June 1637]

Copy. BPL, Ms. Am. 1506, pt. 2, no. 9

Published (without the signatures): *A Letter of Many Ministers in Old England, Requesting the Judgement of Their Reverend Brethren in New England concerning Nine Positions, Written Anno Dom. 1637, Together with Their Answer Thereunto Returned, Anno 1639, and the Reply Made unto the Said Answer, and Sent over unto Them, Anno 1640, Now Published . . . by Simeon Ash, and William Rathband* (London, 1643), sig. A2v–[A3]; John Ball, *A Tryall of the New-Church Way in New-England and in Old . . .* (London, 1644), sig. A2v–[A3]

In L. Thompson, "Letters of John Cotton," 134–138

Thomas Prince noted on the verso at the end of this manuscript: "This seems to have been wrote in *th*e spring of 1638," but on the recto he guessed the "spring or summer of 1637." The dating mentioned in the above title (1637) is more authoritative, however, especially as one of the signatories, Simeon Ashe, was responsible for the

Ob. An.
Ch.1645.
Ætatis
suæ 96.
A Grave Divine; precise, not turbulent,
And never guilty of the Churches rent:
Meek even to sinners; most devout to GOD:
This is but part of the due praise of DOD.
C.B.
T. Cross sc.

PLATE 8. John Dod. Line engraving by T. Cross, 1645. *National Portrait Gallery Engravings Collection. By courtesy of the National Portrait Gallery, London*

letter's publication. Moreover, Cotton's letter to John Dod dated December 19, 1637 (see below), begins by mentioning that this letter from the English ministers was received "in *th*e latter end of *th*e last sum*m*er." If we understand this to mean in late August or early September, then it was probably not written later than early July 1637.[1]

In this copy of the original, the signatures are all written in a single hand, the same one that copied out the letter. This manuscript differs from the published version (which was printed from the same plates in 1643 and 1644) in numerous particulars of spelling and punctuation. Those differences are not recorded here, but, where wording in the manuscript differs from that in the published version, the changes are noted. A microfilm copy of the manuscript made earlier in this century by the Boston Public Library occasionally preserves details that have subsequently been lost at the edges of four holes along a horizontal center fold and in stains from water damage. Details are supplied from the microfilm copy of the manuscript wherever possible and are enclosed in braces. Where text is missing in both the manuscript and the microfilm, it is supplied from the published 1643 edition and enclosed in brackets. Prince's characteristic underlining, in lighter ink than the letter, is omitted here.

Reuerend and Beloved[2]

Whilstt wee lived togeather in *th*e same Kingdo*m*e wee p*ro*fessed the same faith, joyned in *th*e same ordenances, laboured in *th*e word[3] of god to gaine soules vnto his kingdome, and maintaned *th*e purity off gods worship[4] againstt corruptions, booth on the rightt hand & on the lefte, Butt since your departure into New England we heare (& partly beleiue itt) *tha*t divers haue embraced certaine new[5] opinions, such as yow disliked formerly: & we judge to be groundeles & vnwarantable. As thatt a stinted forme of prayer & sett leiturgie is vnlawfull, Thatt it is not lawfull to Joyne in prayer, or resceiue[6] the sacram*en*tt where a stinted lyturgie is vsed, Thatt[7] *th*e children off godly & approoved Christians are nott to be baptized vntill there parents be sett members off some perticular Congregatio*n,* That[8] the parents themselues though of approoved piety are nott to be received to *th*e lords supper, vntill they be admitted as sett members, Thatt[9] *th*e power of excomunicatio*n*. &c. is soe in the body of *th*e church *th*at what *th*e major partt shall allowe that mustt be donne, though *th*e pasto*u*rs & governers & p*ar*t of *th*e assemblie be of another minde, & peraduenture vpon more substantiall reasons, Thatt[10] none are to be admitted as sett members, butt they mustt p*ro*misse nott to departt or remooue vnlesse *th*e congregation will giue leaue, Thatt[11] a minister is soe aminister to a perticular congregation, thatt if they dislike him vnjustly or leaue him he sceaseth to be aminister, yea thatt one Minister[12] can performe noe ~~spirituall~~ ^ministeriall^ actt,[13] in any other[14] congregatio*n,* & thatt[15] members of one congregatio*n* may nott com*m*unicate in another, These[16] & other such like w*hi*ch we omitt to reckon vp: aree written & reported to be the comune teanents in New England, w*hi*ch are resceiued w*i*th greatt applause, maintaned w*i*th greatt confidence, & applauded as *th*e onely church way wherein the lord is to be worshiped, And letters fro*m* New England haue soe taken w*i*th diuers in many p*ar*ts of this kingdome, thatt they haue leftt ou*r* assemblies, because of a stinted lyturgie & excomunicated them selues fro*m* the lords supper because such as ought ~~nott~~ are ^not^ debared[17] fro*m* itt, & being turned aside them selues they labour to ensnare others to *th*e greife of *th*e godly *th*e scandall of religion *th*e wounding of there owne soules (if they did aduisedly consider *th*e [matter]) & greatt aduantage of them *tha*t are wily to espie & ready to make vse of all aduantages to pr*e*judice the trueth, Beloued Breethren, if yow stood in ou*r* places we are well assured itt would be noe small greife vnto yow to heare & see the people lead aside to *th*e disgrace of *th*e gospell vppon weake & groundlesse jmaginations & in rash & inconsiderate Zeale to deale w*i*th thatt w*hi*ch is off god as if itt weare of man, And if it be to vs some greife[18] of heartt to heare *tha*t yow haue changed fro*m* thatt trueth w*hi*ch yow did p*ro*fesse & to embrace[19] thatt for trueth w*hi*ch in forme[r] tymes vpon sounde grounds ye did condemne as erronious, wee hope yow will nott b[e offen]ded. Yow knowe how oftt itt [h]{ath bene obiected} thatt Nonconformists in pra{c}tis{e ar}e sepratists in hearte butt thatt {they} goe crosse to [their] owne positions or smother [the tr]ueth for sinis{ter} ends: they of *th*e Sep[aration] boast that [they stand] vpon *th*e nonconformists [groun]ds, {A v}[ainglo]{r}ious florish & [slight pretense. But] booth these and *th*e other, [are much][20] {countenan}[ced b]{y} your sodaine [chan]{ge, i}f yow be changed as itt is reported how shall you{r breethren b}[e a]ble to stand vp [in t]{he} defence of their in{n}ocencye & the vprightnesse of their c{ause} [w]hen your example & opinion shalbe cast in their dish, Must they leaue yow now w*i*th who*m*e they haue held sosietye, or will yow pleade for seperatio*n* w*hi*ch yow haue condemned as rash & inconsiderate[?] Yow knowe that they whoe haue runne this way, haue fallen into manyfoald diuisions & may nott yow Justly feare leastt the same befaull yow, some warnings ye haue had alredy[21] & haue yow nott cause to feare every day more & more. Errour is very fruitfull, & will spreade apace: A crack in *th*e foundation, may occasio*n* a wide breach in *th*e buildinge, when[22] there will nott be meanes or minde to mende[23] itt, experience every day may tutor vs herein Butt to lett passe all inconveniences: our request in all meekenesse & loue is Thatt if these or anye of *th*e forementioned opinions, be indeede you*r* teanents yow would be pleased to take a seacond review of you*r* grounds & send vs you*r* strongest reasons *tha*t haue swayed yow in these matters, & if ^wee^[24] shall finde them vpon due examination to be such as will carry weightt we shalbe ready to giue yow the right hand of fellowshipp: if otherwise yow shall receiue our justt & modestt animaduersions in whatt we conceiue yow haue erred fr*om* the trueth. Yow will nott Judge if we cannott apprehend the strength of you*r* grownds itt is because we loue nott the trueth, or be carryed w*i*th by-respects (though these conseits prevaile to much) such riged & harshe censures cannott lodge in meeke & humble breasts, weighty reasons p*ro*mote the trueth, nott vnaduised Judgeing. You*r* selues haue Judged thatt to be errour, w*hi*ch now yow take to be trueth when yett yow we[re] nott blynded w*i*th by respects,[25] nor hudwincked you*r* eyes thatt yow mightt nott see *th*e lightt. & if yow haue just warrantt fro*m* god to pull downe whatt yow haue builded & to build what yow haue pulled downe we desire yow would lovingly & maturely imparte itt for as yett we haue seene none w*hi*ch we are nott ready to prooue & shew by the rule [of] trueth [2r] to be too weake to carry ~~bur~~ any burden. We [26] adore w*i*th yow the fullnesse of *th*e scripture & we knowe the Counsell of the lord shall stand, If yow can shew thatt yow walke in the wayes of god we shall hartely rejoyce to walke w*i*th yow, butt if yow haue turned aside we shall earnestly desire yow [27] would be pleased seariously to consider the matte[r] & speedely reforme whatt is outt of order, Thus nott doubtinge of you*r* fauorable interpretation of this ou*r* motion for the preuention [28] of distraction, maintainence ˆofˆ [29] peace & scearching outt of *th*e trueth whereby we may be directed to liue to the praise of god the good of his people & comforte of our selues Beeseching god to leade & guide vs into all trueth & holynesse & keepe vs blameles vntill his gloryous appearance we restt.

You*r* louing breethren

Although I haue nott heard soe fully as my breethren of those perticular opinions, yett doe I Joyne w*i*th them in the Request:[30]

John Dodd [31]
Robertt Cleauer
Ralph Shearrard
Timothy Dodd
Sim Ash

William Bourne
Thomas Pagett
Julius Harringe
John Ball
Thomas Langley
John Winstone
Natha: Cottons
Ephraim Huitt

1. This letter is discussed in Carol G. Schneider, "Roots and Branches: From Principled Nonconformity to the Emergence of Religious Parties," in Francis J. Bremer, ed., *Puritanism: Transatlantic Perspectives on a Seventeenth-Century Anglo-American Faith* (Boston, 1993), 167–200. Schneider particularly focuses on John Ball's role in the transatlantic dialogue of which this letter was a part. On the signers of the letter, see 175–177. Schneider notes that Thomas Shepard and John Allin in their *Defence of the Answer Made unto the Nine Questions* . . . (London, 1648) gave 1636 as the date of the letter. Tom Webster discusses this letter, arguing for William Ames's influence on the thinking of the English signers, especially Ball, in *Godly Clergy in Early Stuart*

England: The Caroline Puritan Movement, c. 1620–1643 (Cambridge, 1997), 301–305. See also Hall, *Faithful Shepherd,* 80–85.

2. In both of the published versions of the letter the salutation reads "Reverend and beloved Brethren."

3. word] 1643: worke

4. off gods worship] 1643: of worship

5. new] 1643: vain

6. or resceiue] 1643: or to receive

7. vsed, Thatt] 1643: used. 3. That

8. Congregatio*n,* That] 1643: congregation. 4. That

9. members, Thatt] 1643: members. 5. That

10. reasons, Thatt] 1643: reasons. 6. That

11. leaue, Thatt] 1643: leave. 7. That

12. aminister, yea thatt one Minister] 1643: a Minister. 8. That a Minister

13. can performe noe ~~spirituall~~ ˆministeriallˆ actt] 1643: cannot performe any ministeriall act

14. in any other] 1643: in another

15. congregatio*n,* & thatt] 1643: Congregation. 9. That

16. 1643: new paragraph starts here.

17. such as ought ~~nott~~ are ˆnotˆ debared] 1643: such as are not debarred.

18. to vs some greife] 1643: to us griefe.

19. & to embrace] 1643: and embrace.

20. booth these and *th*e other, [are much]] 1643: both these are much

21. Prince underlined "some warnings ye haue had alredy" and noted in the margin: "By this it seems this was wrote in *th*e spring or summer of 1637, before *th*e synod sat, w*hich* was Aug. 30, 1637."

22. when] 1643: where.

23. mende] 1643: amend.

24. Inserted in different color ink.

25. by respects] 1643: by-respects.

26. 1643: new paragraph starts here.

27. desire yow] 1643: desire that you.

28. preuention] 1643: preventing.

29. First written maintain, the text was revised with the addition of ence of in a different-color ink.

30. 1643: omits this postscript and all the names.

31. On John Dod, Cleaver, Winston, and Nathaniel Cotton, see above, John Cotton to a Minister in England, Dec. 3, 1634, n. 25. The other signers are as follows:

Ralph Shearrard: unidentified.

Timothy Dodd: (d. 1665) The son of John Dod of Fawsley, he was educated at Emmanuel College, Cambridge (bachelor of arts, 1615–1616; master's, 1619). Lecturer at Daventry, Northamptonshire, from at least 1640 on. *DNB;* Venn, *Alumni Cantabrigienses,* II, 51.

William Bourne: (d. 1643) A graduate of Christ's College, Cambridge (bachelor of arts, 1589; master's, 1592), he was the venerable and popular preacher at Manchester, where he was fellow of Manchester College and preacher at the Collegiate Church from 1605. By 1633 he had been cited six times for Nonconformist practices. See Robert Halley, *Lancashire: Its Puritanism and*

Nonconformity (Manchester, 1869), I, 133, 171–172, 236, 384–385; R. C. Richardson, *Puritanism in North-west England: A Regional Study of the Diocese of Chester to 1642* (Manchester, 1972), 24, 43, app.; Schneider, "Roots and Branches," in Bremer, ed., *Puritanism: Transatlantic Perspectives,* 176.

Thomas Pagett: (d. 1660) Educated at Trinity College, Cambridge (bachelor of arts, 1608/9; master's, 1612). About 1639 he became rector of St. Chad's, Shrewsbury. Venn, *Alumni Cantabrigienses,* III, 296.

Julius Harringe: Julines Herring (1582–1644) was a graduate of Sidney Sussex College, Cambridge, and had been minister at Coventry, Warwickshire, then at Caulk, in Derbyshire. For seventeen years, starting in 1618, he was lecturer at St. Alkmund's in Shrewsbury, Shropshire, though frequently suspended for his Puritanism. In 1636, he accepted a call to succeed John Paget at the English church in Amsterdam, where he would assist John Nicolaus Rulice, but he could not get out of England until September 1637; he arrived in Amsterdam September 20. See Samuel Clarke, *A Generall Martyrologie . . .* (London, 1677), 161–167; Brook, *Lives of the Puritans,* II, 489–492; *DNB;* Peter Lake, "Puritanism, Arminianism, and a Shropshire Axe-Murder," *Midland History,* XV (1990), 47–49.

John Ball: (1585–1640). Entered Brasenose College, Oxford, in 1602. He was minister for many years at Whitmore, Shropshire. During his numerous brushes with the church authorities, he was protected by Lady Bromley, of Sheriff-Hales, Shropshire. He was a committed Nonconformist, but opposed to the New England Way. He was the author of numerous books; some of his posthumous works were edited and published by Simeon Ashe, including his ninety-page reply to the New Englanders' answers to the questions posed in this letter. Brook, *Lives of the Puritans,* II, 440–444; *DNB.*

Thomas Langley: Probably Thomas Langley, vicar of Middlewich, Cheshire (bachelor of arts, 1604/5, Jesus College College, Cambridge; master's, 1608). Venn, *Alumni Cantabrigienses,* III, 45; *Calamy Revised,* 314.

Ephraim Huit: Minister at Wroxhall, Warwickshire. He was silenced and emigrated to New England in 1639. He became pastor at Windsor in Connecticut, "where [Thomas] Hooker's Amesian government held the field." Webster, *Godly Clergy in Early Stuart England,* 304.

Sim Ash: (d. 1662) Simeon Ashe entered Emmanuel College in 1613, where he studied with Hooker, who later sent him to Arthur Hildersham's household seminary. He was ejected from his vicarage at Rugeley, in Staffordshire, and later served at Wroxhall. During the Civil War, he was chaplain to the earl of Manchester. *DNB; Calamy Revised,* 16; Venn, *Alumni Cantabrigienses,* I, 43; Webster, *Godly Clergy in Early Stuart England,* 25.

John Cotton to John Dod

December 19, [1637]

ADfI. BPL, Ms. Am. 1506, pt. 2, no. 11

Published: Emerson, *Letters,* 215–218

In L. Thompson, "Letters of John Cotton," 139–143

Although the following letter is a reply to the previous one from John Dod and twelve other ministers, it does not contain the answers to their questions. Those

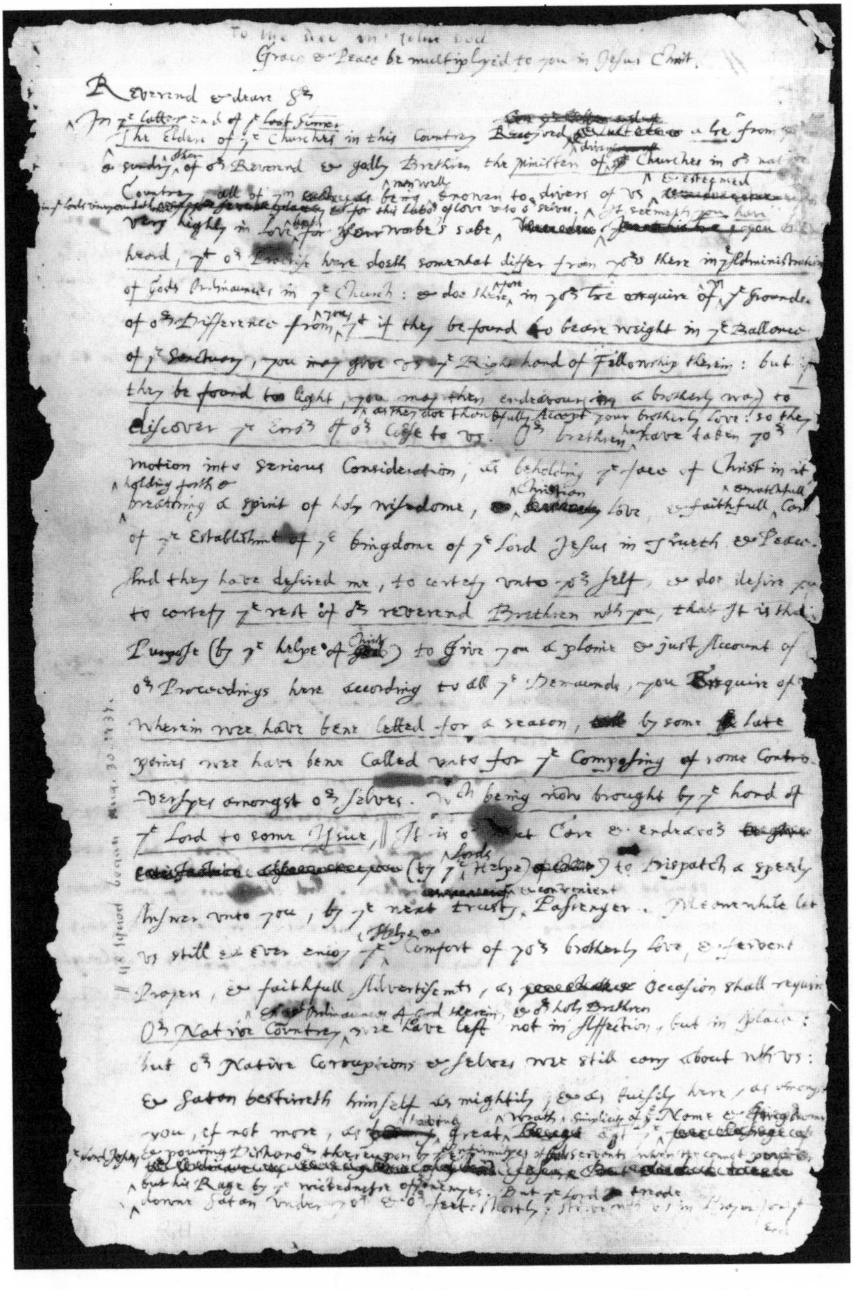

PLATE 9. Draft of Cotton to John Dod, December 19, [1637], recto. This is entirely in Cotton's hand, including the deletions and interlinear insertions. The underlinings, however, are the work of Thomas Prince a century later. *Boston Public Library Ms. Am. 1506, pt. 2, no. 11. Courtesy of the Trustees of the Boston Public Library*

answers were not sent until 1639 and were in turn answered by the English ministers. The English questions and New England answers were collected and published in London twice in 1643, once in a volume called *Church-Government and Church-Covenant Discussed, in an Answer of the Elders of the Severall Churches in New-England unto Nine Positions, Sent over to Them (by Divers Reverend and Godly Ministers in England) to Declare Their Judgements Therein* . . . and again in *A Letter of Many Ministers in Old England, Requesting the Judgement of Their Reverend Brethren in New England concerning Nine Positions, Written Anno Dom. 1637, Together with Their Answer Thereunto Returned, Anno 1639, and the Reply Made unto the Said Answer, and Sent over to Them, Anno 1640*. The latter was reissued as *A Tryall of the New-Church Way in New-England and in Old* . . . (London, 1644) and contained the English ministers' further responses to the New Englanders' answers. The English ministers assigned the task of writing these replies to John Ball, one of the signers of the first letter in the series. He received authorial credit on the title page of *A Tryall.* It is not known to what extent Cotton was responsible for the New Englanders' answer, but the present letter indicates that it would be a truly cooperative effort. John Ball's book combines his "reply" and the New Englanders' "answer" to produce a volume of some ninety quarto pages, more a work of controversy than a personal letter. The present letter was not published in any of the aforementioned volumes.

This manuscript is a heavily revised draft in Cotton's hand and is clearly not the copy he sent to England. Many phrases and clauses have been underlined with Thomas Prince's recognizable pen and ink, emphasizing passages which bear upon his attempt to date the letter. His underlinings are omitted here.

The letter is addressed in Cotton's hand on what is now a small separate sheet of paper:

> To my reverend & deare freind
> & brother in Christ Mr Joh*n* Dod.

On the same sheet, Thomas Prince noted to himself:

> See the answer of *th*e elders of *th*e sever*al* Ch*urch*es in NE ˆunto 9 positions:ˆ—written in 1639 & printed at London in 1643.

Grace & Peace be multiplyed to you in Jesus Christ.
Reverend & deare S*ir*,

ˆIn *th*e latter end of *th*e last sum*m*erˆ The Elders of *th*e Churches in this Country ˆ~~In *the* latter end of~~ˆ ~~the last sum*m*er~~ Receyved a l*ett*ere from y[ou] & sundry ˆotherˆ of o*u*r Reverend & godly Brethren the Ministers of ˆdivers ~~several~~ˆ ~~the~~ Churches in o*u*r nat[i]ve Countrey, all of *th*em ~~each as~~ being ˆmen wellˆ knowen to divers of vs ˆ& esteemedˆ [two or three deleted words] very highly in love ˆbothˆ for ~~their~~ your[1] worke's sake ˆin *th*e lords vineyard at home [deleted word] ~~severall places~~ & for this lab*ou*r of love vnto o*u*r selves.^ [deleted word] ^It seemeth you have^ ~~In this l*ett*ere you have~~ heard, *tha*t o*u*r Practise here doeth somewhat differ from yo*u*rs there in *th*e Administration of Gods Ordinaunces in *th*e Church: & doe there^fore^ in yo*u*r l*ett*ere require of ^vs^ *th*e Grounds of o*u*r Difference from ^you,^ *tha*t if they be found to beare weight in *th*e Ballence of *th*e sanctuary, you may give vs *th*e Right hand of Fellowship therein: but if they be found too light, you may then endeavour (in a brotherly way) to discover *th*e Erro*u*r of our Co*u*rse to vs. O*u*r brethren ^here as they doe thankfully Accept your brotherly love: so they^ have taken yo*u*r motion into serious Consideration; as beholding *th*e face of Christ in it, ^holding forth &^ breathing a spirit of holy wisedome, ^Christian^ ~~brotherly~~ love, & faithfull ^& watchfull^ Care of *th*e Establishm*en*t of *th*e kingdome of *th*e Lord Jesus in Trueth & Peace. And they have desired me, to certefy vnto yo*u*r self, & doe desire you to certefy *th*e rest of o*u*r reverend Brethren w*i*th you, that It is their Purpose (by *th*e helpe of ~~god~~ ^Christ^) to Give you a plaine & just Account of o*u*r Proceedings here according to all *th*e Demaunds, you Require of [vs.] Wherein wee have bene letted for a season, [deleted word] by some ~~p~~ late paines wee have bene Called vnto for *th*e Composing of some Controversyes amongst o*u*r selves. W*hi*ch being now brought by *th*e hand of *th*e Lord to some Issue, It is o*u*r next Care & endeavo*u*r ~~to give satisfaction alsoe vnto you~~ (by *th*e ^Lords^ Helpe) ~~of all)~~ to Dispatch a speedy Answer vnto you, by *th*e next trusty ^[deleted word] & convenient^ Passenger. Meanewhile let vs still & ever enioy *th*e ^Helpe &^ Comfort of yo*u*r brotherly love, & fervent Prayers, & faithfull Advertisem*en*ts, as [one or two deleted words] Occasion shall require[.] O*u*r Native Countrey ^& *th*e Ordinaunces of God therein, & o*u*r holy Brethren^ wee have left not in Affection, but in place: but o*u*r Native Corruptions & selves wee still carry about w*i*th vs: & Satan bestirreth himself as mightily, & as buisily here, as amongst you, if not more, as ~~being~~ ^having^ great ^wrath^ ~~Rage~~ ag*ains*t *th*e ^simplicity of *th*e Name & kingdome^ [two deleted words] [of] *th*e Lord Jesus, & pouring Dishono*u*r thereupon by *th*e Infirmityes of Gods servents when He cannot pour [entire line deleted] ^out his Rage by *th*e wickednesse of [our] enemyes. But *th*e lord treade^ downe Satan vnder yo*u*r & o*u*r feete shortly: strive w*i*th vs in Prayer for *tha*t end, as (by his Grace) wee doe for you.

Wee doe all heartily salute you in *th*e Lord w*i*th *th*e rest of o*u*r Reverend & beloved Brethren by Name; Mr Cleaver, Mr Bourne, Mr Winston, Mr Ball, & *th*e rest. My wife is still mindefull & sensible of yo*u*r gratious Counsell, when you [deleted word] kindely brought vs onward of o*u*r way, & ~~God~~ *th*e Lord warmed o*u*r hearts with yo*u*r heavenly Conference.[2] Wee both of vs com*m*end o*u*r hearty thanks & love to you, & yo*u*r wife, w*i*th yo*u*r sonne

Timothy. The Lord Jesus still give you to abounde in holy fruitefulnesse to Him & to his People, till you have finished yo*u*r Co*u*rse in his Peace.

In Him I rest, desirous of y*ou*r continuall Prayers,

Yo*u*r very loving freind & brother in o*u*r Lord Jesus,

J. C.

Boston. this *19*th of *10*th

One thing, let me intreate ~~you~~ further of you: I heare there is a written Booke goeth vp & downe in England vnder my Name, as my Catechisme. I did indeede goe over the Principles of Religion in way of Catechisme here according to *th*e five Heads ~~received~~? expressed in Hebr: 6. And therew*i*th I handled also *th*e Principles of Church-Governm*en*t. But what Notes h[ave] bene ta[ke]n of it from my mouth, I know not: sure I am I nev[er] perused any Copy ^to be^ sent for England. And therefore if you heare of such a writing, I pray you, doe me this Chri*sti*an favo*u*r, to beare witnesse ^from me,^ I doe not owne it, as having never seene it: although may be, sundry things in it, were delivered by me, w*hi*ch I doe Acknow[ledge.]

1. your is written over their.

2. A reference to Dod's giving shelter and advice to the Cottons as they were fleeing ecclesiastical punishment. John Norton noted, "The envy of his maligners having procured Letters missive to convent him before the High-Commission . . . Mr. *Cotton* having intelligence thereof, and well knowing that nothing but scorns and imprisonment were to be expected, conformably to the advice of many able heads and upright hearts (amongst whom that holy man Mr. *Dod* of blessed memory had a singular instance) he kept himself close for a time in and about *London*." *Abel Being Dead yet Speaketh* . . . (London, 1658; rpt. Delmar, N.Y., 1978), with an introduction by Edward Gallagher, 20–21.

John Cotton to Samuel Stone

March 27, [1638]

ALI. MS: BPL, Ms. Am. 1506, pt. 2, no. 12

In L. Thompson, "Letters of John Cotton," 144–147

Samuel Stone had sailed on the *Griffin* with Cotton and Thomas Hooker in the summer of 1633. On arriving in New England, he and Hooker established the church at Newtown (later Cambridge) while Cotton joined John Wilson at the Boston church. Hooker, Stone, and most of their congregation left Newtown in May 1636 to go to Hartford, Connecticut, where both ministers spent the rest of their lives, though both returned on occasion to the Boston area. Despite their disagreements, which were dramatized during the Antinomian disturbances of the preceding two years, Stone and Cotton were old acquaintances with much in common.

This letter to Stone in Hartford, written just five days after Anne Hutchinson's excommunication from the Boston church and the day before her actual departure from Boston, is Cotton's first known communication with Hartford after the end of the Antinomian problems. It is, in fact, the first known statement of any kind from him following that episode.

The manuscript is one folio sheet written on both sides, water-stained, slightly frayed on the right edge of the recto.[1]

To Mr Stone.

Beloved br. in o*u*r Lo*r*d Jes.

O*ur* br. Shep.[2] did (according to yo*ur* l*ette*re) tender me 20[s] for my saddle: but I would by noe meanes Receyve it: but prayed him to Returne yo*ur* money to you againe. The sadde was old: & had it bene better, yet being lost, it was not a pennyworth for a Penny.

Touching *th*e Differences ˆ~~Teacher~~ˆ, w*hi*ch you hope God will sweetely compose betweene o*ur* Brethren & my self, I doe also hope, & vnfeignedly desire *th*e same w*i*th you. O*ur* former Meetings are often Renewed not w*i*thout mutuall Helpe & Comfort, through *th*e Blessing of God: & eyther God will give vs in all things jdem sentire, & jdem loqui,[3] or (at least, I hope) placidè ferre contrà sentientes.[4]

I willingly heare yo*ur* Counsell of becom*m*ing so wise, & fearefull of my self, as not to vent new things w*i*thout sufficient Argum*en*ts. I may truely Confesse (as Agur,[5] a wiser man *tha*n I, did) surely I am more foolish *tha*n any man: Prov. 30.2.[6] But for Fearefullnesse of my self, though I have just & sad Cause ˆto observeˆ[7] an vnmortifyed selfishnesse still remayning: yet I may truely tell you, God hath so often exercised me w*i*th renewed Feares & Agonyes about mine owne spi*rit*uall Estate, & *th*e Estate of some others Depending on me, *tha*t I could not Rest mine owne Sp*iri*t vpon every signe thereof (though otherwise good in itselfe:) but have bene forced, ~~though~~ not to seeke out new wayes of Peace, but those w*hi*ch as I have sometime here & elsewhere delivered, so I have thought *th*em to be *th*e Path beaten out by others of o*ur* best Professours. ˆSee Zanchii Miscellanea in Respons. ad 2du*m* Postulatu*m* Marbachij pag. 599 &c.ˆ[8] Onely *th*e want of cleare discerning of *th*e Difference betweene *th*e Imputation of Christs Righteousnesse, & o*ur* Justification, did ˆ(in *th*e Conference)ˆ[9] putt me vpon some incongruous Apprehension, & Disorderly Expression of *th*e Order & Place of Fayth vnto *th*em both. W*hi*ch as God helped me by *th*e Endeavours of some of you better to discerne, I thought it my duety then more clearely to Expresse, & acknowledge.

That God was willing to bring me low at *tha*t time in *th*e Eyes of Brethren, I doe Acknowledge his Righteous Hand therein: as bearing vpon me, not onely myne owne Iniquityes (w*hi*ch make me justly lower then any Debasem*en*t from m[en)] but also *th*e Iniquityes of sundry members of o*u*r Church, who (like Achan,[10] w*i*thout my Privety) had harboured & secretly disseminated such Erroneous & daungerous Opinions, as (like a Gangrene) would have corrupted & destroyed Faith & Religion had they not bene timely discovered, & disclaymed both by o*u*r owne & other Churches. M[res] Hutchinson[11] (of whom you speake) though she publiquely Revoked *th*e Erro*u*rs, yet affirming hir Judgem*en*t was never otherwise, though hir Expressions were contrary, she was Excom*m*unicated by o*u*r whole Church. Nemine Contradicente.[12] Some others of o*u*r members *tha*t joyned w*i*th hir in *th*e Opinions, we[re] gone away before, to seeke ~~out~~ other Plantations elsewhere, as P*re*saging *th*e Ce[nsure] [IV] w*hi*ch otherwise was likely to overtake *th*em. I had signifyed to o*u*r Brethren (*th*e Elders) before *th*e Conference, That if such Erro*u*rs could be prooved to be held by hir, or any other of o*u*r members, God forbid, wee should Neglect[13] to beare witnesse ag*ains*t *th*em ~~according~~ according to God. But *tha*t w*hi*ch could not then be prooved by 2 witnesses hath bene since prooved by many, to more generall satisfaction of vs all.

Helpe vs still w*i*th yo*u*r Prayers, & Advice, as Occasion shall serve. Com*m*end my hearty love, to my br. H. & his w.[,] br War[,] br. Goodw. w*i*th my due Respect to Mr Hay.[14] w*i*th like love to yo*u*r self, & yo*u*rs w*i*th yo*u*r Fath. & moth. The Lord guide & blesse all yo*u*r labo*u*rs to his best Advantage in Christ Jesus. In whom I rest

Yo*u*r very loving br. in Ch.

J. C.

Wee were not worthy of Mr D.[15] & his People here, but o*u*r losse is yo*u*r Gaine: the Lord Pitty vs, & Increase you w*i*th *th*e Increasing of God.
B.[16] this 27. of i[st]./

1. Thomas Prince appears to have been particularly interested in this letter. He marked the manuscript extensively as follows: (1) over Cotton's phrase "Excom*m*unicated by o*u*r whole Church" in the fourth paragraph, Prince wrote "March. 22. 1637/8."; (2) under the date line at the end, he noted, "Suppose March. 27. 1638."; (3) after Cotton's "Mr D." in the postscript, Prince placed two parallel lines (||) and at the end of the letter wrote, "|| I suppose *th*e R. Mr Davenport"; (4) below all other writing on the verso he wrote, "1637. Aug. 30. *th*e 1st NE synod meets at Cambridge."; (5) he underlined the following words and phrases: in the second paragraph: "Differences," "Brethren," "my self," and "former Meetings are often Renewed"; in the third paragraph: "in *th*e Conference"; in the fourth paragraph: "God was willing to bring me low at *tha*t time in *th*e Eyes of Brethren," "M[res] Hutchinson," "publiquely Revoked *th*e Erro*u*rs,"

"was Excom*m*unicated by o*u*r whole Church," "before *th*e Conference"; in the fifth paragraph: the abbreviated names: "H.," "War," "Goodw."; and, in the postscript: "D."

2. Thomas Shepard, minister at Cambridge and son-in-law of Stone's Hartford colleague, Thomas Hooker.

3. idem sentire, & idem loqui: to think the same and speak the same.

4. placidè ferre contrà sentientes: peacefully to bear with those contrary opinions.

5. Agur was the non-Israelite author of Prov. 30:1–14.

6. Prov. 30:2: Surely I am more brutish than any man, and have not the understanding of a man.

7. David D. Hall, quoting excerpts from this letter, reads this phrase: "Cause to abhor sin and unmortifyed. . . ." *Antinomian Controversy,* 428 n. 35.

8. Girolamo Zanchi (1516–1590), a Calvinist reformer at Strasbourg, had a theological dispute centering on grace and predestination with Johann Marbach (1521–1581), a leader in the "Lutheranizing" of Strasbourg. Zanchi describes the dispute in his posthumous *Miscellaneorum tomus alter* (Neustadt, 1608). Cotton's page reference is to this edition.

9. The synod held at Newtown, beginning August 30, 1637, and continuing three weeks, to investigate the Antinomian opinions in the colony, was jointly presided over by the Reverends Peter Bulkeley and Thomas Hooker. The careful scrutiny and challenging of Cotton's opinions by the other elders made him realize more clearly than he had before the overwhelming opposition to his views. As he implies in this passage, this realization drove him to public adjustment of his statements. See Hall, *Antinomian Controversy,* 340–342.

10. At the capture of Jericho, Achan disobeyed the ban on stealing when he hid a Babylonian garment and a wedge of gold. This brought God's wrath against all the Israelites, and they were defeated in battle at Ai. When Achan's transgression was discovered, he was stoned to death. See Josh. 7:1–26. Achan means troublemaker.

Blair Worden comments on the way the story of Achan took hold on the mind not only of Cromwell but of Puritans generally, in "Oliver Cromwell and the Sin of Achan," in Derek Beales and Geoffrey Best, eds., *History, Society, and the Churches: Essays in Honour of Owen Chadwick* (Cambridge, 1985), 125–146. Worden notes a number of publications by Puritans in which the sin of Achan provides a way to understand contemporary political or ecclesiastical wrongdoing (145 n. 88). None of his examples are as early, however, as this use of the reference by Cotton.

11. Anne Hutchinson, about whom much of the controversy swirled in 1637–1638.

12. Nemine Contradicente: no one disagreeing, that is, unanimously.

13. Cotton obviously meant to write: wee should *not* Neglect. . . .

14. my br. H.: Thomas Hooker, pastor of the Hartford church; br War: John Warham, minister at Windsor, Connecticut; br. Goodw.: William Goodwin, the ruling elder in the Hartford church, as he had been previously at Newtown; Mr Hay.: John Haynes, a wealthy and influential layman in Hartford, former governor of Massachusetts Bay and sometime governor of Connecticut.

15. John Davenport (1597–1670) had arrived in New England in June 1637 and had lived in Cotton's house at Boston. According to an entry in Winthrop's journal dated March 30, 1638, just three days after this letter, Davenport "went by water to Quinepiack," or New Haven, where he would be the minister and a near neighbor of Stone and other settlers in Hartford. Winthrop, *Journal,* 251.

16. Boston.

John Cotton to [Unknown] at Aquidneck

June 4, [1638]

Copy. MS: BPL, Ms. Am. 1506, pt. 2, no. 13

Neither the author nor the addressee is identified anywhere in this document. Nor does the catalog of the *Prince Library* attempt to identify either party. At least two modern scholars have identified Cotton as the author.[1] Authorship can only have been by a very limited number of people, as the letter takes up theological issues surrounding the recent Antinomian controversy debates over the Covenant of Grace. It is unlikely it would have been written by a secular elected official like Winthrop or Dudley. The content indicates a Boston resident closely connected to the recent Antinomian debates. The writer is defending himself against charges of being a cause of the troubles the exiled people have had. Cotton's centrality in the controversy and his ending up, by the spring of 1638, decidedly on the side of the majority are consistent with his being addressed as one who has "condescende[d]" to "the Opposite Party." Moreover, the writer's expression of affectionate concern for "yo*u*rself w*i*th *th*e rest of o*ur* Brethren & Sisters" at Aquidneck suggests that they are members of the letter-writer's church. The exiles were, in fact, mostly members of the Boston church. For all of these reasons, Cotton seems the most likely candidate. The handwriting, however, is not his. It is the work of an amanuensis not otherwise represented in the Cotton correspondence.

The addressee is less clear, though the possibilities can be sharply limited. The contents strongly indicate the letter was written to one of the nineteen men who founded the settlement on the island of Aquidneck. The person chosen as leader, or judge, by that group was William Coddington, Cotton's old Boston friend. He, at least, might be a reasonable choice as the likely recipient of this letter, but this is far from certain, as there are other possibilities, including William Aspinwall and the Edward Hutchinsons (Sr. and Jr.). Others in the inner core of the Aquidneck group can be eliminated because they are mentioned in the letter: William Hutchinson, John Clarke, John Coggeshall, and William Baulston.

This letter adds important evidence of epistolary dialogue between Cotton and the Antinomian exiles shortly after closure on the matter had been reached in Boston, while also offering some comments by Cotton to a third party about other principals in the controversy, most notably Anne Hutchinson. His strong assertion of his conviction that the leaders of the exiled faction were deeply in the wrong and his related bristling at the suggestion that he had betrayed them confirm statements he made in other letters and in subsequent published recollections. He remains deeply troubled that these members of his church had so "grossely, & fundamentally opposed" the

Covenant of Grace, especially in claiming they possessed in their hearts "*th*e Increated life of *th*e sonne of God," a position that Cotton himself has been charged with holding in concord with the Hutchinsonians. He denies the validity of such a claim decisively here. The letter is a significant addition to the literature of the controversy.

This is a very difficult manuscript, owing chiefly to water damage and some loss of paper. The color of the ink varies from very dark to very badly faded. A transcription in the Massachusetts Historical Society has provided some details now lost. Such details are enclosed in braces. The following rendering, however, contains many passages that the MHS transcriber failed to decipher. I am particularly grateful for assistance in dealing with this letter to Michael P. Winship, Michael McGiffert, and Charles L. Cohen.

Beloved brother,

I have Received 2 l*ette*rs from you out of *th*e Island, & had returned {Answers} to *th*em both, [(]to {the} former long before now) if they *tha*t went out hence to you had given m{e timely} Notice of the{eir} Departure)[.] In yo*u*r
"former, you say, you consider me as Sam[pson] made of God for a tim[e of]
" storming ag*ains*t *th*e Philistines to foyle many of *th*em w*i*th *th*e Jawbone of
"{an Ass}, till at last Dalilah discoverin[g] his strength, *th*en his Eyes were putt
"out, vntill in time his {stre}ngth beginning to grow againe, he slew more att
"his Death, than in his life. The Explanat[io]n herein (you say{) yo}u omi{t} for Brevity sake.

Vnwelcome Brevity to me (I may we[ll s]ay) w*hi*ch brevity [illegible word] in a m[is]t of Obscurity. Whom you may meane by Philistines, I may haply guesse: but in my guessing so hav||vns|| *th*em I shall wrong both *th*em & you to make such a Construction of yo*u*r Words. But who {this} [Dalilah][2] should be, I am not able to divine, nor wherein she hath discovered my strength, nor in what Respect mine Eyes are said by you (like his) to be putt out. All *th*e hint you give me to search out your meaning is, *tha*t you s[ay], you suggest this to my thoughts touching my ||ing or Condiscend[ing] to *th*em on *th*e Opposite Part. I must Professe I want Sampsons Hei[f]er to plough w*i*thall, that I ||[might?] vnderstand yo*u*r Riddle.[3] If you speake to me (as you say) this in Faithfulnesse, then let me in[treat] you in *th*e name of *th*e Lord, to speake in Plainenesse. Apollo's Riddles are not f{itt} Dispensations of Gods Oracles, & Counsells. I thanke God, I know not wherein I have Cond[escended?] in *tha*t w*hi*ch is evill, Corrupt or vnsound. In any Vnsafe tenents of them *tha*t Difference of Judgm*en*t, & Profession is still *th*e same, as it was; If you thinke I condescende to *th*e Opposite part, because I beare witnesse ag*ains*t a more opposite Part (to wit ag*ains*t o*u*r Brethren, who have abolished *th*e Coven*an*t of Grace). ~~by blotting out *th*e Law written in o*u*r [heart]s & being~~ || ~~in~~ I wish you a better Spirit of Discerning, then to Inferre such a Conclusion vpon such ||. It is one thing to Invert a Breach[4] or two of *th*e Coven*an*t of Grace (by setting *th*e sight of wo[rks] before *th*e sight of Christ:) another thing to subvert *th*e Coven*an*t of Grace, by blotting out *th*e Law written in o*u*r hearts, & bringing in (instead thereof) *th*e Increated[5] life of *th*e sonne of God, to live, & worke in vs, & so make all New creatures eyther Gods, or Hypocrites. I must ever be forced to speake (what my soule deepely groaneth vnder as my heavyest B[ur]den) *th*e Doctrine of *th*e Coven*an*t of Grace hath bene more grossely, & fundamentally opposed by {so}m{e} of o*u*r Brethren of *th*e Island, & others of their minde, then by all those, whom you {c}al{l the} Opposite Party of *th*e Countrey. The Lord lay it not to *th*e Charge {of a}ny wh[o seek?] for some Direction in moulding *th*e Platforme of Church & Com*m*onwealth; but [unless] the Foundation of *th*e Coven*an*t of Grace, as it is in Trueth, be truely & soundly [estab]lished amongst you, I know not, how you can build vp eyther Church, or Com*m*onwealth, but as an house w*i*thout a Foundation. I heare of some Rents & Breaches amongst you, & wonder not at it. For laying such a Foundation of a Coven*an*t, w*hi*ch w[h]osoeve[r] in trueth cleaveth to, recedeth himselfe from Christ, how shall he be able to [keep him]selfe from Receding from his Brethren. Beare w*i*th my Plainenes [which] not Passion, but C[om]passion forceth from me. The mighty Redeemer of Izraell res[cue] all his chosen || from such strong Delusions.

To *th*e Queries w*hi*ch you propound to me in yo*u*r latter l*ett*er, I shall give you a short & p{laine} Answere. To 1, & 2: Hir Acknowledgem*en*t in *th*e Church I did never ˆcallˆ or Publici[se]: I [sought?] a iust Retractation of sundry daungerous Erro*u*rs: nor did I ever wish she[6] sh|| all about it eyther in any Iudiciall, or [in] any Church way; but this farm[?] onely || thems[elves]||ay (if it might be) to bring hir to see hir sinne. In affirming before *th*e Church *tha*t in all *th*e Retractation she had changed onely her Expresions, but not hir Iudgm*en*t.[7]

To 3[d], I deny any particular Invectives ag*ains*t her, or any other, so farre as she remaineth[?] stedfastly in *th*e Doctrine p*ro*fessed by hir in hir Retractation: & to yo*u*r 4th I deny also any such Purpose of mine of Coming to *th*e Island, though she, & goodwife Hawkins[8] || parted from me[.]

Yo[*u*r] 5th, I cannot vnderstand, *Tha*t I should tell Serjeant Boston[9] || said to me. They had those things from ˆhirˆ, & that she would [illegible word] to satisfy theim. Nor can I well interprete yo*u*r 6th what I meant, when in speach w*i*th hir [hus]band,[10] I ioyned hir & M[r] Coxall,[11] M[rs] Dyer[12] &c. in Iudgem*en*t together, & yet p*ro*[posed] to *th*em, I || conceyve a great deale of Difference betweene *th*em[.] Possibly, I might speake of them [IV] {as sometimes} of one minde & Judgem*en*t in sundry things: but if she stand to hir Retractation there [is (I] doubt not) a broade difference of Iudgem*en*t betweene *th*em.

Touching [good]wife Hawkins[13] (of whom you lastly enquire) I have heard of some of those complaints against hir, w*hi*ch came to yo*u*r Eares; but I have had noe occasion to search *th*e trueth or *th*e {Bottom of} *th*em. I to[ld] hir selfe my feare, lest hir Judgem*en*t should be vnsound in some Funda[me]ntal poynts (but, *tha*t I onely feare I cannot proove:) but if it be so (as I have told hir) I feare she might doe much hurt in corrupting *th*e Iudgem*en*ts of yong women.

For yo*u*rself, be willing in all oth[er m]atters to keepe corresponding w*i*th || were willing to runne deepe hazard w*i*th you, *tha*t rather for yo*u*r sake, you should stand out ag*ains*t *th*em too much in point of Civill Libertyes or Rights. As God hath given {more} Ability to discerne *th*e Daunger of theire Tenents, so God requireth of you, to take more paines in employing of yo*u*r talents to Recover *th*em (if it be *th*e will of God) into *th*e || church. The like Earnest suite[?], I pray you com*m*end from me, together w*i*th my love, to M{r Clarke & his} wife[14] & yo*u*rs. Yo*u*rself w*i*th *th*e rest of o*u*r Brethren & Sisters, I heartily wish {(as God helpeth} me) all true Good vnto, in *th*e Lord, Especially *th*e light of his Trueth, & Grace {& Peace} in *th*e Fellowship, & Acknowledgem*en*t of Christ Jesus God & Man. In whom I rest

Yo*u*r Compassionate Brother

{I pr}ay you let me heare, if you had *th*e like Earthquake, {as wee} had *th*e last 6th day being *th*e 1st of 4th.[15]
Boston 4th of 4th./

1. See Darrett B. Rutman, *American Puritanism: Faith and Practice* (Philadelphia, 1970), 107, and *Winthrop's Boston,* 125; Michael P. Winship, "'The Most Glorious Church in the World': The Unity of the Godly in Boston, Massachusetts, in the 1630s," *Journal of British Studies,* XXXIX (2000), 71–98.

2. The MHS transcription has Phylistine instead of Dalilah.

3. Cotton here cleverly extends his correspondent's use of the analogy to Samson's story. Calling the correspondent's likening of himself to Samson a "Riddle," he alludes to the account in Judg. 14 of the early part of Samson's life when Samson married an unnamed Philistine woman and later posed a riddle to her people. She persuaded Samson to tell her the answer, which she then related to her countrymen. When they correctly answered his riddle, Samson said (verse 18): If you had not plowed with my heifer, you would not have found out my riddle.

4. Or possibly: Branch.

5. Uncreated; not created, thus inherent or essentially a part of the nature of God Himself. William K. B. Stoever discusses created and increated grace, as understood by Reformed theologians and as an issue in the Antinomian controversy. He places Cotton with Hutchinson as favoring increated grace, however, a position that Cotton here strenuously opposes (Stoever, *"A Faire and Easie Way to Heaven,"* 170–174).

6. Presumably Anne Hutchinson.

7. "A Report of the Trial of Mrs. Anne Hutchinson before the Church in Boston" quotes her as saying, "My Judgment is not altered though my Expression alters" (Hall, *Antinomian Controversy,* 378).

8. Jane Hawkins was a midwife, friend, and fellow exile of Anne Hutchinson. In Winthrop's opinion, Mistress Hawkins was a "rank Familist." *Journal,* 153.

9. William Baulston had held the title sergeant in Boston before his exile. He was one of the group of nineteen men who had established the government of Aquidneck in March 1638. Irving Berdine Richman, *Rhode Island, Its Making and Its Meaning: A Survey of the Annals of the Commonwealth from Its Settlement to the Death of Roger Williams, 1636–1683* (New York, 1902), 117.

10. William Hutchinson.

11. John Coggeshall.

12. Mary (Mrs. William) Dyer, whose stillbirth or miscarriage of a "Monster" on October 17, 1637, had become a matter of much interest in connection with the inquiries into the Antinomians' beliefs and activities. See Winthrop's comments in *A Short Story of the Rise, Reign, and Ruin of the Antinomians, Familists, and Libertines* . . . (London, 1644), in Hall, *Antinomian Controversy,* 280–282.

13. Jane Hawkins had been accused of delivering trance prophecies attacking the bishops in extemporaneous "Verses in Rythm" in England before emigration. As Winthrop later noted, "Hawkins's wife (who continued with [Mrs. Hutchinson] and was her bosom friend) had much familiarity with the devil in England, when she dwelt at St. Ives" (*Journal,* 330), a comment that he repeated in *A Short Story* (Hall, *Antinomian Controversy,* 281). She was the midwife who delivered Mistress Dyer's "monster." Cotton later wrote of her that "though she offered her self to the Elders of our Church, yet was not received, upon discovery of some unsound principles in her judgement. Being then no member, the Church had no power to deale with her. But when suspition grew of her familiarity with the Devill, especially upon that occasion, which the short story relateth, shee was convented before the Magistrates, and diligently examined about that, and other evills. But though no familiarity with the Devill could be proved against her; yet because of some other offences in dealing with young women, she was forbidden to stay in the Countrey" (*The Way of Congregational Churches Cleared* [1648], in Hall, *Antinomian Controversy,* 437). John Wheelwright, Jr., dismisses her as "a poore silly woman" incapable of understanding Mrs. Hutchinson's "weekly *Lecture,*" (*Mercurius Americanus* . . . [London, 1645], 7–8). For an account of her exposure as a false "Prophetess" and a "Cheat" by Cotton's bishop, John Williams, in April 1629, see John Hacket, *Scrinia Reserta: A Memorial Offer'd to the Great Deservings of John Williams, D.D.* . . . (London, 1693), pt. II, 47, cited in Keith Thomas, *Religion and the Decline of Magic* (New York, 1971), 138; and Thomas S. Freeman, "Worlds of Wonder, Days of Demons?: Puritan Exorcisms in England and New England," paper delivered at "The Worlds of John Winthrop: England and New England, 1588–1649," conference at Millersville University, Millersville, Pa., September 1999. Michael P. Winship gave valuable advice on developing these references to Jane Hawkins.

14. John and Elizabeth Clarke. Clarke, a doctor, had arrived in the Bay only in 1637, but elected to join the exiles going to Aquidneck, where he was one of the nineteen founders. Battis, *Saints and Sectaries,* 231, 272-3, 332.

15. Prince's note: "June 1. 1638 a terrible Earthquake thro *the* Countrey." Prince treated this subject at some length in *Earthquakes the Works of God and Tokens of His Just Displeasure: Two Sermons on Psalm xviii. 7* . . . , 2d ed., corr. (Boston, 1727), 40, where he quotes Nathaniel Morton's dramatic eyewitness account of the same earthquake in *New England's Memorial.*

William Fiennes, Lord Saye and Sele, to [John Cotton]

July 1638

ALS. MS: BPL Ms. Am. 1506, pt. 2, no. 14

William Fiennes, Lord Saye and Sele, who two years earlier had received Cotton's transmission of the New Englanders' answers to his and Lord Brooke's questions on colonial government, is now concerned about reports in England on Cotton's views on grace. The Antinomian controversy had recently been quelled in New England, but reports of it were circulating in England, as they would continue to do for years. The English Puritans, including Lord Saye, were alarmed at reports that the New England brethren were taking positions more radical in one way or another than their own. Here Saye, having heard or perhaps seen in print Cotton's insistence on inward assurance of grace as opposed to trusting primarily in external signs of grace, argues for the value of such external signs. This gets to the heart of a central issue in the Antinomian controversy, and Saye seems to want Cotton to know that English supporters of the New Englanders need to believe they still see eye to eye on such central issues as grace and salvation. Since Henry Vane, unaware of "the danger of his way," is assuring his listeners that his views are also Cotton's, Saye apparently feels compromised as a defender of Cotton and his colleagues. The references to Vane are themselves valuable, given the absence of very much concrete information on this period of Vane's life.[1] Echoing John Winthrop's famous phrase of eight years earlier, Saye reminds Cotton that "you . . . are a Citty sett vppon a hill."[2] Saye's remarks are those of a committed but practical layman, urging his friend as spiritual leader in New England to remember the experience of the struggling believer. In a more general way, the letter also indicates the level of concern expressed by Puritans in England for the developing patterns of practice and belief in New England. These concerns would not soon disappear.

This letter was written when Lord Saye had other weighty matters on his mind, as he briefly indicates in his postscript in mentioning Scotland, where in recent months the Covenanters had drawn the ire of the crown by resisting the imposition of English forms of worship and church structure. Both Lords Saye and Brooke had strong sympathies for the Scottish Presbyterians, as opposed to the English bishops.[3]

The entire letter is written on one side of the sheet; the verso is blank. Much of the top of the page is torn away, removing more than half the text of the first twelve lines and thus depriving the present reader of the context that Saye doubtless provided. A smaller tear at the bottom has removed parts of seven lines. The top and bottom of the page are water-stained.

PLATE 10. William Fiennes, First Viscount Saye and Sele. Oil portrait by Adam de Colonne, 1628. *Collection at Broughton Castle, Oxfordshire. Published with the kind permission of the present Lord Saye and Sele*

Reve[rend]||

|| whearin it doth || your owne hand testyfy || in those opinions of || very evill consequence & || of bitternes when they are sprung vp || I have made some vse of your lette[r]|| occasion is offered for your receavinge. In || w*hi*ch I have se[e]ne, somthings I have founde that ||pre taken, at least in my apprehension, that I might || to consent vnto them; yet most I could assent vnto ||, rather then to somtymes hold on the other syde, but that pa[ssa]ge

of steppinge asyde to Hagar[4] I knowe not howe to excuse: for to make our callinge & election sure to our selves by ˆaddinge one grace to anotherˆ [, by] growinge from grace to grace, & by reflectinge vppon those graces ˆin their growthˆ to gather the life of the hed by the foote, and the cause, by the effect is a followinge the direction of the scripture & showinge our fayth by our workes to our selves & others: and not a steppinge out of the way to Hagar from impatiency of waytinge for comfort from a free promise. Allusions many times out of a prettines and aptness w*hi*ch they seeme to carry w*i*th them for what ~~they~~ ˆweˆ want exprest, carry vs alsoe along w*i*th them farther then will stande w*i*th truth. It is a dangerous thinge to deprive our selves of the direction and consolation of any part of the scripture, and in punishment therefore we may be putt to call it hence agayne to helpe vs, as they did Jeptath,[5] though we conceave it fayth, to be borne of a bound woman. You will give leave to my boldnes, since it proceades from love, & is ioyned w*i*th much reverence of your graces. I am the more glad you wrott as you did because M^r^. Vane[6] seames to me to assume this, and as I remember speakes it directly, that himselfe w*i*th others hear w*it*h him, (whoe have bin very active to disperse & spread abroad theyr opinions) hold nothinge but what you approve of, and are of the same Judgement ˆwith themˆ and this hath taken w*i*th many to your preiudice and noe question Satan hath had an effectual workinge in all this to the blemishinge & cloudinge of the truthes of this present time [deleted word] in their fyrst revivinge and raysinge out of the Grave, whear the pryde and covetousnes of men had buryed them, and Satan woud now cast a stone vppon them that they might neaver ryse, it behooveth you in that place whoe are a Citty sett vppon a hill[7] to vse all meanes to prevent his slights & subtletyes, whearof this was not the least, that after the castinge of of Bishopes & reducinge the Churches to theyr primitive & true power, he had opportunity to showe vnto the world the rents & devisions that presently fell amongst you. What vse will be made hearof amongst vs, I neade not write. For the young man M^r^. Vane whome your love followinge, & it is well it ~~should~~ doth soe, for he may be recovered; I have not bin wantinge to doe my indeavour to showe him the danger of his way, and what hath bin the sad issue thearof in others, from whence I think it cometh, and wheather Satans ayme is to drive it: as might have appeared to you by my letters written to him into New England when I fyrst did perceave his delusions, if he had showed my letters to you.[8] I shall be glad to doe my best to that ende still, but I have not that frequent converse w*i*th him now as heartofore, nor the rest of his frendes whearof thear are the most in Hollande, & the rest will shortely be thear alsoe, M^r^. Goodwin beinge thear; & M^r^. Ny now ˆvpponˆ goinge.[9] I shall much desyre to see the answere you write of, vnto the objections of M^r^.||[10] and others hear w*i*th vs agaynst your church

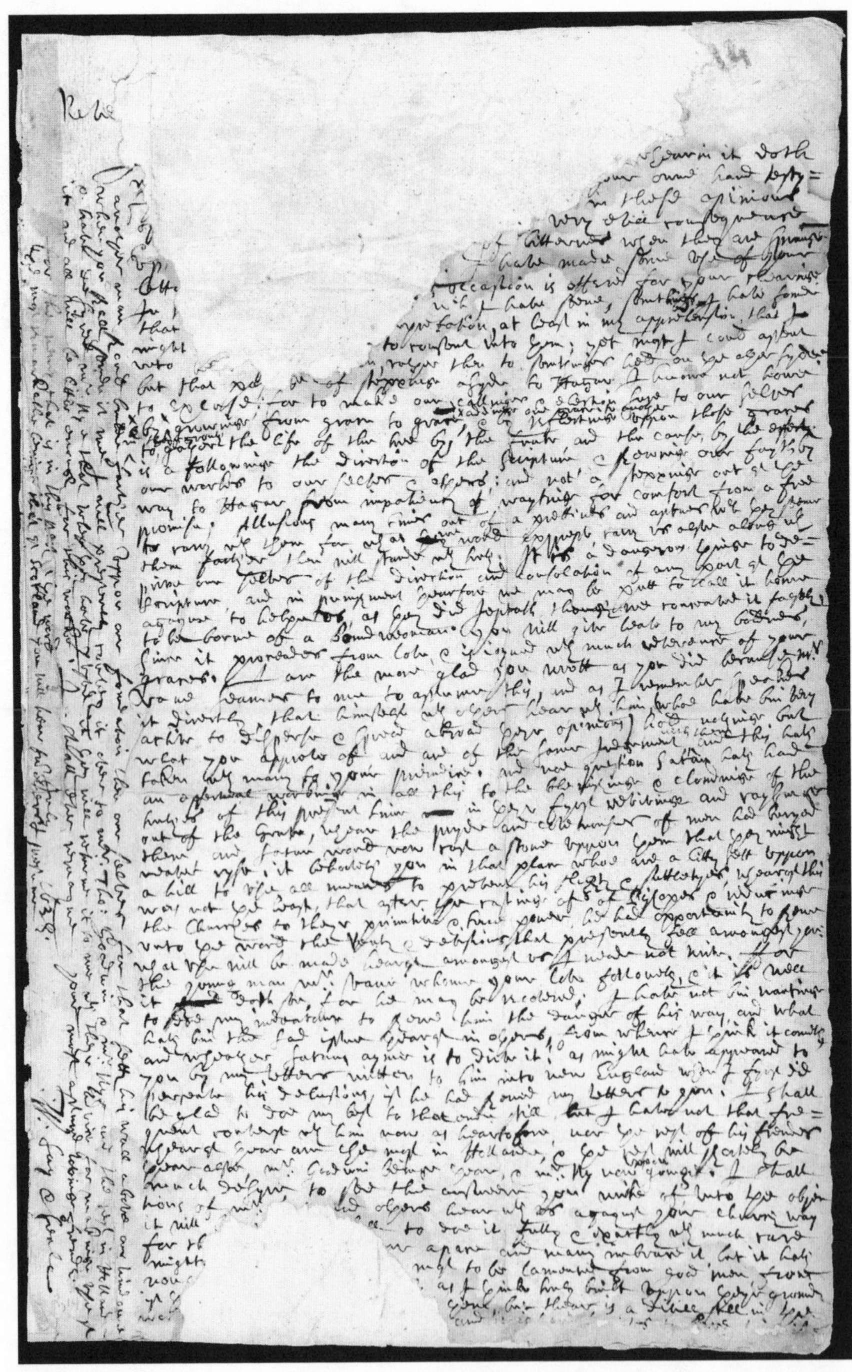

PLATE 11. William Fiennes, Lord Saye and Sele, to Cotton, July 1638. *Boston Public Library Ms. Am. 1506, pt. 2, no. 14. Courtesy of the Trustees of the Boston Public Library*

way it will || to doe it fully & exactly w*i*th much care for th[e]|| apace and many embrace it, but it hath might|| most to be lamented from good men, from vou|| as I thinke truly built vppon theyr ground if th|| them, but thear is a divil still in the wor|| and it is hard f[or] us to haue ||[11] another man should builde farther vppon our foundation then our selves for that setts his wall above our windowe. When you shall sende it me I will presently convey it over to Mr. Tho: Goodwin & Mr. Nye and the rest in Holland & have desyred Mr. Nye that when they have p*er*vsed it they will returne it to me w*i*th theyr advice for makinge vse of it and all will be better enough for this worke. I shall ever remayne your most assured lovinge frende.

July 1638. W: Say & Seale

for the news that is in this part of the world the most remarkable beinge that of Scotland you will hear fro*m* others I presume.[12]

1. See James K. Hosmer, *The Life of Young Sir Henry Vane* . . . (Boston, 1889); John Willcock, *Life of Sir Henry Vane the Younger: Statesman and Mystic (1613–1662)* (London, 1913); Margaret A. Judson, *The Political Thought of Sir Henry Vane the Younger* (Philadelphia, 1969); Violet A. Rowe, *Sir Henry Vane the Younger: A Study in Political and Administrative History* (London, 1970). For a careful study of Vane's religious thought and writings, see David Parnham, *Sir Henry Vane, Theologian: A Study in Seventeenth-Century Religious and Political Discourse* (Madison, N.J., 1997). Parnham discusses Vane's theology of grace in relation to various contemporaries', including Cotton's (232–257).

2. Similar phrasing occurs in several other contemporary writings and speeches, most of them consciously based on the passage in Jesus' Sermon on the Mount in Matt. 5:14, as was Winthrop's in "A Model of Christian Charity." See discussion of such references in Francis J. Bremer, "To Live Exemplary Lives: Puritans and Puritan Communities as Lofty Lights," *Seventeenth Century,* VII (1992), 27–39, esp. 31.

3. For the current political state of affairs between England and Scotland, see Conrad Russell, *The Fall of the British Monarchies, 1637–1642* (Oxford, 1991), 27–90.

4. Hagar was Sarah's Egyptian slave, who bore Ishmael to Abraham. She was thus an outsider, not a part of the chosen community of God. "Steppinge asyde to Hagar" implies the abandonment of the covenant. In the context of the Antinomian controversy, it suggested placing one's hope in worldly signs. This tendency in turn indicated fidelity to a Covenant of Works, the very fault with which the Antinomians had charged most of New England's ministry. By urging Cotton not to be too skeptical of the value of external signs of grace, Saye is striking a moderate and balanced position that holds to the value of works as signs of an indwelling grace.

5. Jephthah was a Gileadite who, because he was his father's illegitimate child, was cast out by his stepbrothers. He was later recalled to lead Israel's army successfully against the Ammonites, which resulted in his judgeship over Israel for six years (see Judg. 11–12). Paul refers to him as a man of faith (Heb. 11:32–34). Henry Snyder Gehman, *The Westminster Dictionary of the Bible,* rev. ed. (Philadelphia, 1944), 289.

6. Henry Vane the younger had returned to England just two and a half months after his failure to be reelected following his one-year term as governor of the Massachusetts Bay Colony; he

left New England on August 3, 1637 (Winthrop, *Journal,* 228–229), so had been back in England approximately nine months when Saye wrote the present letter to Cotton.

7. See Matt. 5:14: Ye are the light of the world. A city that is set on a hill cannot be hid.

8. Henry Vane had lived in Cotton's house during his stay in New England, from October 1635 to August 1637, building his own adjoining house during this period. See Ziff, *Career of John Cotton,* 115.

9. Thomas Goodwin (1600–1680) and Philip Nye (1596?–1672), two of the leading Independents in England, were strong supporters of the New England Way of church government. They were both forced to flee to the Netherlands at about this time, but returned as delegates in the Westminster Assembly early in the next decade. In the 1650s, these two men often combined to assist in the publication of books by New Englanders, including both Cotton and Thomas Hooker.

10. Although the name here is lost to the hole in the MS, it is probably Dod. Cotton had apparently mentioned in a previous letter to Saye that he and his fellow New England ministers were finally preparing their answer to the questions by John Dod and other ministers in England. It was sent in the next year, 1639 (see John Cotton to Dod, Dec. 19, [1637]). Saye's close acquaintance with Dod is indicated in a life of Thomas Dudley attributed to Cotton Mather, where the author writes that Dudley, before migration, "by being a follower of Mr. Dod . . . came into the knowledge of the Lord Say & [of] Lord Compton, & other persons of quality" ("The Life of Mr. Thomas Dudley, Several Times Governor of Massachusetts Colony, in New England," MHS, *Procs.,* XI [1869–1870], 211–212).

11. Here the part of the bottom line on the page that is not torn away is obliterated by water damage. The rest of the letter is written along the left margin.

12. In the spring of 1637, the English Church had tried to impose the English Prayer Book, a uniform worship service, and bishops on the Scottish Kirk, intending to supplant the strong Scottish Presbyterian tradition stemming from John Knox, which emphasized the Word in sermons and extemporaneous prayer, without the hierarchy of bishops. The Scots reacted violently, first at St. Giles Church in Edinburgh, but ultimately more widely. In late winter and early spring of 1638, the Scottish Covenant was signed by thousands, declaring opposition to the English forms and episcopacy in favor of traditional Scottish Calvinist ways. The consequence was war with the king and bishops, beginning in late 1638. Although Saye chose not to comment on Scotland in this letter, he had strong sympathies for the Scottish Presbyterians. In fact, as Conrad Russell observes, when the peers "were summoned collectively to York to serve in the war, only Saye and Brooke refused. Their initial replies were a plain refusal from Saye, and a call for a Parliament from Brooke, but after consultation, they sent a second reply claiming that they were only obliged to serve the King within the kingdom of England, and not beyond the borders." Russell, *The Fall of the British Monarchies,* 84; see also C. V. Wedgwood, *The King's Peace, 1637–1641* (New York, 1956), 173–282.

John Cotton to John Davenport

[After March 1638]

Published: John Norton, *Abel Being Dead yet Speaketh; or, The Life and Death of That Deservedly Famous Man of God, Mr. John Cotton . . .* (London, 1658), 36–37; Sa[muel] Clarke, *A Collection of the Lives of Ten Eminent Divines . . .* (London, 1662), 77

John Norton (1606–1663), Cotton's successor as teacher in the Boston church, was the first to publish a biography of him. In that work, Norton included this fragment from a letter to John Davenport, who had lived with Cotton after arriving in Massachusetts Bay in June 1637. Davenport left to help found New Haven and to become the minister there at the end of March 1638.[1]

The full text of this letter, now lost, might have been among the papers pertaining to the Antinomian controversy shown to Norton by Cotton's son (probably the eldest, Seaborn, then nineteen years old) when Norton advised the young Cotton to carry out his father's dying request and destroy them.[2] The complaint registered here by Cotton against members of his church who claimed to espouse his views while actually holding views he considered unacceptable appears in his other letters and writings of the period.[3]

The truth is . . .[4] the body of the Island[5] is bent to backsliding into error and delusions: The Lord pity and pardon them, and me also, who have been so slow to see their windings, and subtile contrivances, and insinuations in all their transactions, whilst they propagated their Opinions under my Expressions, diverted to their constructions.

1. Winthrop, *Journal,* 251. See also Cotton to Samuel Stone, Mar. 27, [1638].

2. Citing simply *"MS Letters,"* Thomas Hutchinson records this loss: "Upon his death-bed [Cotton] ordered his son to burn all his papers relative to the religious disputes began in the time of Sir Henry Vane's year. He had bundled them all up, with an intention to do it himself, but death prevented his going into his study for that purpose. His son, loth to destroy what appeared to him valuable, made a case of conscience to Mr. Norton whether he was bound to comply. Mr. Norton determined against the papers." Lawrence Shaw Mayo, ed., *The History of the Colony and Province of Massachusetts-Bay* (Cambridge, Mass., 1936), I, 152n.

3. See, for instance, Cotton to [John Wheelwright], Apr. 18, 1640; and his remarks in *The Way of Congregational Churches Cleared* (1648), in Ziff, *Cotton on the Churches,* 246.

4. Here Norton inserted (saith he).

5. Aquidneck, where most of those at odds with the Massachusetts authorities over religious issues had gone.

Thomas Dudley to John Cotton

March 21, 1638/9

ALS. MS: BPL, Ms. Am. 1506, pt. 2, no. 15

Published: Augustine Jones, *The Life and Work of Thomas Dudley, the Second Governor of Massachusetts* (Boston, 1900), 257–258

Thomas Dudley (1576–1653), sometime governor and deputy governor, had emigrated from England with Winthrop's party in 1630. Soon after their arrival, he and Winthrop had a disagreement on where the governor would live, Winthrop (who prevailed) preferring Boston and Dudley Newtown, "a division that later cut deep during the Antinomian crisis."[1] The following exchange of letters between Dudley and Cotton is directly related to that controversy. At the three-week synod that began on August 30, 1637, Dudley—who generally favored taking a hard line and who considered Winthrop too lenient a ruler—had occasionally been rather hard on Cotton. Yet in this letter Dudley requests that Cotton counsel William Denison, a layman expelled from the Roxbury church, on the relationship between evidence of justification and justification itself. This was a key issue on which Cotton had had great difficulty in satisfying his brother elders as to his orthodoxy in the preceding two years. In seeking Cotton's help in this matter, Dudley signals the degree to which Cotton had finally satisfied his neighbors on this point and the extent to which his reputation as valued teacher and counselor was recovering.[2]

Fourteen of the twenty-two lines of the body of this water-damaged and mutilated letter are interrupted by a hole averaging about one inch in width. A single leaf is folded once into two half-sheets; the bottom third of the right-hand half-sheet is cut away. The entire message is on the recto of the left-hand half-sheet. Braces indicate readings adopted from the nineteenth-century MHS transcription.

Addressed on verso of right-hand half-sheet:

To the Reverend my good
freind M[r] Cotton Teacher
of the Church at
Boston.

Reverend S*ir*,

I appointed my bro[ther] Denison[3] the bearer hereof ~~should~~ ˆtoˆ haue ˆbeneˆ mett mee at the Court at B[ost]on[4] about what I now wryte, but it fell out otherwise. The vprightnes I p{erceive} to be in him stirreth mee vpp to desire his reconciliacon to the [Chur]ch, and one thinge that hindreth is his opynion about the f[irst ev]idence:[5] Hee graunteth that the Spiritt can giue noe first evide{nce unless} it worke grace, and I assent that there can be noe grace {without the} Spiritt worke it, w*hi*ch agreeth w*i*th what passed at my hou[se betwee]ne yo*u*r selfe and mee: herein I p*er*ceave noe difference be{tween us},: But when their premisses are drawen to a conclusion the ||es back and affirmeth that yet the Spiritt giues the first evid[ence abo]ut the sight of grace. If two things goe togeather neyth[er can be] first or last, and if the Spiritt work not grace, that Spir[itt is] delusory, then I cannot know it to be the Spiritt of God until I see it hath wrought grace, For evidence (about w*hi*ch the question is) implyeth sight ˆbothˆ in the significacon and ordinary vse of the word: I am not able to see but that he contradicteth himself, If you soe also conceaue I pray you S*i*r help him,: This I would this day haue spoken to you if I had not bene hindred: you see how badd my pap*er* is,[6] and it is tyme for the bearer to begone towards Boston[.] I pray you beare w*i*th hast, pap*er,* &c. I shall vnderstand by my Bro*ther* Denison at his retourne w*i*thout yo*u*r trouble of wrytinge what you say, I therefore forbeare yo*u*r further trouble resting:

Rocksbury the 21. of the .1. month *1638*[7]

yo*u*r old vnprofitable freind
Tho: Dudley./

1. Andrew Delbanco, "Thomas Dudley (1576–1653)," in James A. Levernier and Douglas R. Wilmes, eds., *American Writers before 1800* (Westport, Conn., 1983), I, 476.

2. On Dudley, see ibid., 475–477; Jones, *The Life and Work of Thomas Dudley;* Edmund S. Morgan, *The Puritan Dilemma: The Story of John Winthrop* (Boston, 1958), 86–87, 103–107, 115–116; Hall, *Antinomian Controversy,* 311–348.

3. William Denison (d. 1654) had held the offices of deputy and constable in Roxbury but was disarmed in 1637 for supporting John Wheelwright in the Antinomian disputes. Dudley uses the term "brother" here because Denison's son, Daniel, had married Dudley's daughter, Patience, on October 18, 1632. This use of "brother" is described in a passage in Winthrop's *Journal* for April 24, 1638, that makes reference to another marriage of one of Dudley's children: "The governour [Winthrop] and deputy [Dudley] went to Concord to view some land for farms, and, going down the river about four miles, they made choice of a place for one thousand acres for each of them. . . . At the place where the deputy's land was to begin, there were two great stones, which they called the Two Brothers, in remembrance that they were brothers by their children's marriage, and so did brotherly agree" (Winthrop, *Journal,* 256–257). On William Denison, see Daniel Denison Slade, "Daniel Denison," CSM, *Publs.,* I, *Trans.* (1892–1894), 116–120.

4. A Quarter Court was held on March 5, and the General Court was held at Boston on March 13, 1638/9, at both of which Deputy Governor Thomas Dudley was present. *Records of Massachusetts Bay,* I, 248–255.

5. That is, evidence of justification, or grace.

6. The paper is somewhat porous, so that the ink had a tendency to run and blur.

7. Thomas Prince's note: that is, 1638/9.

John Cotton to Thomas Dudley

[About March 22, 1638/9]

ADfL. MS: BPL, Ms. Am. 1506, pt. 2, no 15a

Cotton ignored Dudley's suggestion that he not bother to reply in writing, with the result that Dudley felt the need to seek help from his church's teacher, John Eliot, in interpreting Cotton's answer. Eliot broke down the final two paragraphs of this letter, phrase by phrase, giving his own gloss of Cotton's meaning in each phrase. Eliot's interpretation then came to Cotton, who added his own clarifications to Eliot's interpretations. These agonized notes do not constitute actual letters, but they bear immediately on this exchange between Dudley and Cotton, so they are included here in the Appendix.

This draft is written in Cotton's hand in two separate blocks at the bottom of each folded half-sheet on the verso of Dudley to Cotton, Mar. 21, 1638/9. The break in the text is where paper is torn away from the bottom of the sheet, causing the loss of one or two words. A few characters subsequently lost, enclosed here in braces, are preserved in the BPL microfilm copy of the manuscript.

The Spirit witnesseth directly Gods free love to me in *th*e Gospell, & thereby begetts faith & love in me to God:

By begetting faith & love in me to God, it evidenceth his owne witnesse of Gods love to me to be noe Delusion. Now this is a reflexe Act, & therefore in o{r}d{er} ||re followeth *th*e direct Act.

When my soule is humbled, *th*e Spirit of God by Applying *th*e Gospell to me declareth & witnesseth the Grace & favo*u*r of God to me: & by so doeing worketh at once saving Grace in me towards God: & thereby declareth *tha*t his witnesse of *th*e Grace of God to me, is noe Delusion.

And yet because these be two witnesses, the One of Gods love to me, the other, of my faith & love to God, I give the first place to *th*e Spirits witnesse of Gods love to me: *th*e latter, to *th*e witnesse of my faith & love to God.

John Reyner and William Brewster to [John Wilson and John Cotton]

August 5, 1639

Copy. MS: BPL, Ms. Am. 1506, pt. 2, no. 16

Published: William Bradford, *History of Plymouth Plantation, 1620–1647,* ed. Worthington Chauncey Ford (Boston, 1912), II, 275–276

John Reyner (d. 1669), a Yorkshireman, studied at Magdalene College, Cambridge, earning a bachelor of arts in 1625. He arrived in New England ten years later and became teacher at Plymouth church, where he served until 1654, when he was encouraged to resign, thereafter ministering at Dover until his death. William Brewster (1567–1644), the venerable Pilgrim father, had been involved in the formation of the Separatist community at Scrooby, which later moved to Leiden. He became ruling elder in the church there in 1609 and remained a central figure in it after the community's removal to Plymouth in New England, where he was ruling elder from 1620 until his death. The quavering handwriting in his signature betrays his advanced age.[1]

Their letter raises an important issue for the churches at both Boston and Plymouth at a time when the growing population meant that residents in the towns had to travel longer distances to get to their farms, encouraging a desire to establish new homes and churches near the farms. This had become an issue in the Boston church in 1636 with the desire by some members to create a new church at Mount Wollaston. Four years earlier, in 1632, the Plymouth colony had experienced the same thing as Miles Standish and others moved to Duxbury, where a new church was formed. William Bradford later observed that "as their stocks increased and the increase vendible, there was no longer any holding them together, but now they must of necessity go to their great lots," something which he feared would be "the ruin of New England, at least of the churches of God there."[2] In 1635, Hingham was settled, and there would be more spin-off communities after this exchange of letters between the Plymouth and Boston churches. That the issue struck home with its recipients is registered in the note at the end of the letter stating that it was read to the Boston congregation immediately upon Wilson's making it available. We do not have the reply from Wilson and Cotton to this letter, but a passage in Cotton's *Powring out of the Seven Vials* (1642), where he offers advice to those who "plant townes or villages," is relevant: "Sit downe no where without good Ministers. . . . Never make a beginning, but where you may come and partake of the waters of Gods house every Lords day. . . . You have seene when some have made a beginning without Ministers . . . let it be the wisdome of sincere hearted

Christians, that come from old England for liberty and purity of Ordinances, not to leave them now for fresh meadows and fountaines."[3]

This letter is written on one side of a single sheet; the verso is blank. It is written in a scribal hand, not in that of either Brewster or Reyner, though they both signed it. Addressed, on a separate half-sheet in Reyner's hand:

> To ohr reverende brethren
> *the* church of christ at Boston,
> to the Elders there these be
> d*elivere*d

And, immediately following, in a different hand:

> L*ette*re from Plymoth about the
> Keeping of Farmes./ & *the*
> Answer therevnto.

Reu*er*end and welbeloued in o*ur* com*m*on Sauio*ur*: The Lord haueing called you w*i*th vs in the fellowship of the Gospell to mutuall helpfullnes in the Lord as occasion is ministred we craue yo*ur* serious thoughts and resoluc*i*ons in some questions on foote among us concerneing the holding of farmes of w*hi*ch there is noe lesse frequent vse w*i*th yo*ur* selues then w*i*th vs. The p*ar*ticulers we desire to com*m*end to yo*ur* serious consideracon are these.

1 Whether in these parts especially in some placs, and where people haue continued for some space of tyme it bee not needfull for the comfortable and welbeing euen of the churches that places for husbandry be made use of; though distant from the place of a mans habitacon and of the churches assembling three or foure miles or there abouts?

2 Seing by meanes of such farmes a mans famylie is diuided so that in busie tymes they cannot (except vpon the Lords day) all of them joyne w*i*th him in famylie duties, whether to make use of them because of the forenamed needfulnes be not to doe evell that good may come of yt?

3 Whether a master in the absence of some part of his famylie by occasion of his farme may not lawfully appoynt a sonne or servant whoe is in some measure fitted to performe duties among them in his absence?, or whether such a one be not as a substitute to o*ur* church officer in his non=residencye?

4 Whether a man not haueing wherew*i*th to mayntaine his stock & estate & place the Lord hath called him in, neare hand, may vndertake & retaine such a farme abroad as abouesaid, when for the p*re*sent hee wants & cannot p*ro*cure such a servant in his famyly as may be helpfull there, w*i*th the rest of his servants by prayer & instruccon?

It is p*re*supposed & p*ro*vided in all these cases that such servants or others as on the weeke day are employed abroad at farmes doe resort duly before the Lords day to the famylies they belong too, & continue there till the second day, except some one whoe is necessaryly detayned there, though not usually from the publike assemblies.

Some of us after agitacon of these things remayneing darke & doubtfull in them, if you shall by imparting to us what light you haue receiued concerneing them from the true light be meanes of guideing our feete in the wayes of truth & peace we shall haue occasion hereby ministred of returneing thanks to the father of lights in yo*u*r behalfe. Now the Lord himself giue vs w*i*th you vnderstanding in all thinges through him whoe is the way, the truth & the life. Farewell

Plym*m*outh Moneth. 6th *th*e 5th day Y*ou*rs in *th*e faith & fellowshippe of *th*e Gosp*ell*
1639

John Reyner.
Will*ia*m Brewster.
in *th*e name & w*i*th *th*e consent of *th*e rest.[4] ———

Rec. this of o*u*r Pasto*u*r *th*e 24th day of *th*e 6th Moneth 1639 & read to *th*e Congregation *th*e day following./[5]

1. For biographical details on Reyner, see Venn, *Alumni Cantabrigienses,* IV, 430. On Brewster, see Anderson, *Great Migration,* 227–230; Dorothy Brewster, *William Brewster of the Mayflower: Portrait of a Pilgrim* (New York, 1970).

2. William Bradford, *Of Plymouth Plantation, 1620–1647,* ed. Samuel Eliot Morison (New York, 1959), 253, 254.

3. John Cotton, *The Powring out of the Seven Vials* . . . (London, 1642), "3rd Vial," 23, 24. Darrett B. Rutman discusses this letter briefly in the context of the pressure to establish a church at Mount Wollaston (*Winthrop's Boston,* 96–97). Various historians of Plymouth comment on the issue there; see, for instance, George D. Langdon, Jr., *Pilgrim Colony: A History of New Plymouth, 1620–1691* (New Haven, Conn., 1966), esp. 39; Rutman, *Husbandmen of Plymouth: Farms and Villages in the Old Colony, 1620–1692* (Boston, 1967), 14–15; Crispin Gill, *Mayflower Remembered: A History of the Plymouth Pilgrims* (New York, 1970), 130–131.

4. "Plym*m*outh . . . rest." is all in John Reyner's hand, except for Brewster's signature. Horizontal lines are drawn just above and below 1639.

5. Written in the same hand as "L*ette*re from Plymoth . . . ," noted above.

 John Reyner to John Cotton

October 15, 1639

ALS. MS: BPL, Ms. Am. 1506, pt. 2, no. 17

Although John Reyner, minister at Plymouth from 1636 to 1654, begins here by talking about church matters—the qualifications for church office—his letter turns in its long central paragraph to a matter of intimate concern to Reyner, who inquires about a "party spoken of at our pa[rtin]ge." Reyner wants to know whether this unnamed person has yet been admitted to membership in the Boston church, inquiring further whether the church's examination of the individual for membership has revealed anything to suggest that "we may be vnmeete for one another." He goes on to suggest that he is trying to be very careful that he permit his judgment to guide him rather than allowing only "phansy & aff[ect]ion" to be "pleased." Reyner's voice is the voice of a suitor making delicate inquiries into the spiritual qualities of a woman to whom he is attracted. Cotton's reply mentions that the person has in fact not yet been taken into membership, owing to the great number of applicants the Boston church had recently had to deal with. All of this lends special interest to the fact that the Boston church *Records* indicate that on the "1st Day of the 1st Moneth 1640," or about four and a half months after this exchange, the church admitted one "Francis Clarke one of our pastors Mr John Wilson maid servants." Later in the same *Records,* under the entry for "the 18th Day of the 7th Moneth 1642," it reads, "Our sister Francis Clarke now wife of Mr John Rayner teacher of the Church of Plumworth hath letters of Recommendation and Dismission granted her unto the Church of Plumworth."[1] Thus, one catches Mr. Reyner focusing his interest on the woman who would in due course become his second wife. Cotton, in his turn, plays the role of confidant and perhaps, to some degree, matchmaker, a role he took on in his earlier correspondence in England (see Cotton to Arthur Hildersham, [Spring 1628?], and Cotton to [Col. Sir Edward Harwood], [prob. 1629–1631]).

This letter is a single badly damaged sheet, with a row of large and small holes resulting from folds in the paper. The entire sheet is also water-damaged, with consequent fading of the ink in several places, especially near the right margin.

Addressed, on a separate slip:

To the Reverend his very louing
brother M[r] Cotton Teacher
of the church of Boston
these Del*iver.*

Welbeloved in *th*e Lord and much respected, in experience [wi]th [r]emembrance of youre lovinge readynes to tender my good though least deseruinge [so]e many wayes expressed; I am emboldened to trouble you w*i*th these few lines also at this time. first Whereas when I was last w*i*th you, you seemed to holde forth, that onely such contradictinge & blasphemenge [as] we reade of Act. 13.45:[2] & sininge against *th*e holy ghost did cause a church once v[isib?]ly con[st]itute to cease to be a true church; How may it appeare that Isr[ae]l to whome *th*e Lord then [gives a] bill of divorce, & whome he puts away. Jer.3.8.[3] & calls Lo—ammi, ^[lo-]^ruhamah Hos: i.6–9[4] therefore in such

PLATE 12. John Reyner to Cotton, October 15, 1639. Reyner, the minister at Plymouth Colony, inquires about a woman in Cotton's congregation who would later become his wife. The condition of this manuscript indicates the effect of water damage and abrasion of the paper when folded in the spotting, discoloration, faded ink, and mildew, all probably incurred during the Prince Library's storage in the belfry of Old South Church in the late eighteenth and early nineteenth centuries. *Boston Public Library, Ms. Am. 1506, pt. 2, no. 17. Courtesy of the Trustees of the Boston Public Library*

estate noe true church had soe sin*n*ed; or if they had, whether it may not [be] as surely affirmed of those concerninge whome the controversy is, whether they be true Churches, that they haue sin*n*ed as deeply & generally, especially consideringe *th*e light which hath soe clearely & longe shined amonge them.

Further I desire also a worde || quaere, In case (for I speake onely vpon supositi*on*) some few brethren in a church, not seeing || qualifications w*hi*ch are mentioned as requisite in an elder or Bishop, as suppose that || .3.3 or *ἀνεξικακία*[5] or *πραοτης προς τους αντιδιαθεμένους*[6] 2 Tim.2.24.25.[7] or all of them, || may they not, w*i*th expressinge thereof, comfortably goe alonge w*i*th *th*e rest, & *th*e rest safely pro[ceed]e to election by vertue of that submission enjoyned Eph.5.21.[8]

Finally since the season of *th*e yeare drawes on, I desire (if you thinke it meete) to heare from you, how the party spoken of at our pa[rtin]ge, is approued by you for church com*m*unio*n*. if it be soe, that any thinge ~~any thinge~~ hath faln out to hinder, or appeared to you, for w*hi*ch we may be vnmeete for one another, the will of *th*e Lord [be] done; its not sui[ta]ble soe much as to weare gloues, that are not fellowes, as you know p[a]res cu*m* parib*us* et bi[9] || soe be that you conceyue competent fitnes, if *th*e Lord knit a [faded word], & likwise that distance of *th*e p||r people || [faded word] may not be p*re*iudiciall to our proceedinge, if other thinges accorde; I shall vpo[n]|| *th*e first opportunity be w*i*th you; for as I would not hasten to such a bl[essing?]|| out-run*n*inge (if I may soe say) gods providence soe I desire w*i*th David || *τοῦ θεοῦ βουλῇ*;[10] & then even he, *th*e father of spirits[,] doe what seemeth good in h||hes; I *th*e rather desire in these thinges thus to be informed for *th*e present; because though [judg]ment & phansy & affection must all of *the*m be satisfyed; yet there is roume enough ˆleftˆ for phansy & affe[ctio]n to worke, when *th*e judgment is in some measure satisfyed [with] speciall thinges requisite, but to much experience witnesseth, in what danger *th*e judgment is to be bribed, when phansy & aff[ect]ion are onlie pleased, & how hard a thinge it is to lay them asleepe when they are once a[wakened?]|| & ˆto say noe moreˆ if they be not asleepe a hundred to one but they will disturbe the judgment; thus daringe to loke vp to him w*i*th whome I must obtaine favour if I finde such a blessinge; & des[iri]nge *th*e continuance of youre prayres for me & direction of [faded word] such weighty occasi[ons]|| I beseech *th*e Lord, to returne into youre owne bosome even seven fold all *th*e labour || and to holde you as a starre in his right hande many & many dayes to *th*e glory of his name || of his church. farewell.

[Ply]mouth. *th*e 15th of *th*e 8th M.
1639

Youre lovinge brother in *Chris*t Jesus
John Reyner.

I have intreated *th*e bearer hereof George Watso*n*[11] a brother w*i*th vs, to call for your Answ. at his returne, w*he*n he hath laden his boate, or if you please you may sende by o*u*r brother M.r Smith,[12] if he be not already come away, & if he come w*i*th this boate.

1. *Records of the First Church,* 28, 37.

2. Acts 13:45: But when the Jews saw the multitudes, they were filled with envy, and spake against those things which were spoken by Paul, contradicting and blaspheming.

Reyner is clearly using the Authorized (King James) translation of the Bible here. The final phrases of this verse read rather differently in the Geneva Bible: . . . which were spoken *of* Paul, *contrarying them, and railing on them.*

3. Jer. 3:8: And I saw, when for all the causes whereby backsliding Israel committed adultery I had put her away, and given her a bill of divorce; yet her treacherous sister Judah feared not, but went and played the harlot also.

4. Hos. 1:6–9: And she conceived again, and bare a daughter. And God said unto him, Call her name Lo-ruhamah: for I will no more have mercy upon the house of Israel; but I will utterly take them away. But I will have mercy upon the house of Judah, and will save them by the Lord their God, and will not save them by bow, nor by sword, nor by battle, by horses, nor by horsemen. Now when she had weaned Lo-ruhamah, she conceived, and bare a son. Then said God, Call his name Lo-ammi: for ye are not my people, and I will not be your God.

5. ἀνεξικακία: forebearance.

6. πραοτης προς τους αντιδιαθεμένους: gentleness toward (one's) opponents.

7. 2 Tim. 2:24, 25: And the servant of the Lord must not strive; but be gentle unto all men, apt to teach, patient, In meekness instructing those that oppose themselves; if God peradventure will give them repentance to the acknowledging of the truth.

8. Eph. 5:21: Submitting yourselves one to another in the fear of God.

9. pares cum paribus: a common expression meaning, figuratively, birds of a feather. The complete expression from which the phrase is taken would be pares cum paribus facillime congregantur, which means, literally, like persons most readily crowd together. See Eugene Ehrlich, *Amo, Amas, Amat, and More* . . . (New York, 1985), 216.

10. τοῦ θεοῦ βουλῇ: by / according to the will of God.

11. Watson (c. 1602–1689), a mariner, was resident in Plymouth by 1634; see Anderson, *Great Migration,* 1944–1947.

12. The Reverend Ralph Smith, whose service of the Plymouth church had ended, at the request of church members, in 1636.

John Cotton to John Reyner

October 18, [1639]

Copy. MS: BPL: Ms. Am. 1506, pt. 2, no. 17a

In L. Thompson, "Letters of John Cotton," 152–153

Like Reyner's letter of October 15, to which it is a reply, this letter is in poor condition. It is written entirely on one side of a sheet that was used as an envelope sheet for a letter sent to Cotton.[1] It appears to be Cotton's file copy written in an unidentified hand; neither the handwriting, the signature, nor the pattern of abbreviation is Cotton's. The sheet was folded once vertically and twice horizontally. The greatest loss of paper is at these folds, in the center of the sheet, and on the entire left margin, where several letters are missing or badly faded in each line. All twenty-eight lines in the body of the letter are broken by holes in the paper. Water damage is considerable, and dirt and grit are ground into the back of the sheet.

Beloved broth*er*

||[I]f onelie sining ag*ains*t *th*e Holy Sp*irit*(w*hi*ch y*o*u know is *th*e si[nne] w*it*h ||) ||e rebellio*n* ag*ains*t *th*e Lo*rd* especially in gross & notorious sin|| co*n*ceivi*ng* || w*hi*ch doeth discover a Church on mans p*ar*t, altho*ugh* I can*n*ot say, *th*at *th*e forfeit*ure* ||tak||[o]n gods p*ar*t, till with*al* hee take his ordina*n*ces fro*m th*em, or give *th*em vp to such [d]ispensatio*n* of *th*em, as maketh *th*em of none effect. The Church of Israel (w*ho*m y*o*u m|| in) had broke forth into such obstinate rebellio*n,* as *th*e Lo*rd* declareth in justi[fy]ing his p*ro*ceedinge ag*ains*t *th*em to cast *th*em out of his sight 2. Kings i7: i2 to i8,[2]

[We] can*n*ot charge *th*e like sin*n*es, nor *th*e like rebellious obstinacie in *th*em ag*ains*t co*n*ceiving || *th*e Churches q*ue*stio*n*ed: much less can I say *tha*t *th*e Lo*rd* hath vtt*er*lie w*i*thdrawen [the] ordinan[ces f]ro*m th*em, or all his powerfull & gracious p*re*sence fro*m* ev*er*ie ordina*n*ce ||st *th*em, co*n*sid*er*ing still *th*e sincerity & power of some p*rea*ching.

To y*ou*r next [quæ]re, I shold answ*er* affirmatiuely, *tha*t if ||[f]ew breethr*en* in a Churc[h sh]all [se]e some such defecte, as y*o*u [me]ntio?[n] in a p*er*so*n* eligible to office (||[m]easure of ἐπιείκεια,[3] ἀνεξικακία:[4] [π]ραότης[5] as were to be wished) || notice therof duely, & yet *th*e rest of *th*e bodie bee still satisfied in p*ro*ceeding to electio*n,* those few may co*m*fortably goe [al]ong w*i*th *th*e rest. For I p*re*suppose [th]ose q*ua*lificatio*n*s are in some measure fou*n*d in an eligible p*er*so*n* or els trueth [&] saving grace is wa*n*ting. Where *th*e p*er*so*n* is truely caled to an estate [of] saving grace, y*o*u know *th*e seedes of al grace are found in him, in some meas[ure]. And thogh it were much to be desired, *tha*t ev*er*y p*er*son chose*n* to Church office excell in ev*er*y gift of grace: yet seldo*me* [do]eth it so fall out, *tha*t *th*e same p*er*s[on doth] excell in zeale & meeknes togeth*er*.

*Th*e p*er*so*n* y*o*u enquire of,[6] is not yet || church, by reaso*n* of *th*e store of oth*er*s w*h*o p*re*sented *th*emselues[7] ||att; ˆasˆ app*rov*e more fully || shall (god willing) mor||

I co*mmen*d my*ne* hearty loue to y*o*u, to M[r] [Chau]ncy,[8] & *th*e Eld*er*[9] w*i*th my due service & respect to y*our* Gov*ernor*[10] &c. And so co*m*me*n*ding [yo]u to *th*e gracious guiding, keeping, & blessing of *th*e Lo*rd* I rest

Yo*ur* very loving broth*er* in him

[Bo]sto*n th*is i8 of *th*e 8th/ Jo: Cotto*n*

1. The verso has the address: To [the] Reverende & much esteemed/ freinde Mr John Cotton/ Teacher of *th*e church at/ Boston.

2. 2 Kings 17:12–18: For they served idols, whereof the Lord had said unto them, Ye shall not do this thing. Yet the Lord testified against Israel, and against Judah, by all the prophets, and by all the seers, saying, Turn ye from your evil ways, and keep my commandments and my statutes, according to all the law which I commanded your fathers, and which I sent to you by my servants the prophets. Notwithstanding they would not hear, but hardened their necks, like to the neck of their fathers, that did not believe in the Lord their God. And they rejected his statutes, and his covenant that he made with their fathers, and his testimonies which he testified against them; and they followed vanity, and became vain, and went after the heathen that were round about them, concerning whom the Lord had charged them. And they left all the commandments of the Lord their God, and made them molten images, even two calves, and made a grove, and worshipped all the host of heaven, and served Baal. And they caused their sons and their daughters to pass through the fire, and used divination and enchantments, and sold themselves to do evil in the sight of the Lord, to provoke him to anger. Therefore the Lord was very angry with Israel, and removed them out of his sight: there was none left but the tribe of Judah only.

3. *ἐπιείκεια*: fairness, equity.

4. *ἀνεξικακία*: forbearance.

5. [*π*]*ραότης*: mildness. The first letter of this word is missing because of paper loss at the left margin, and the rest of the word is less than fully legible, but this reconstruction seems the likeliest possibility. Goeorge Goebel's assistance has led to this reconstruction.

6. The anonymous "party" in Reyner to Cotton, Oct. 15, 1639.

7. More than fifty people had been admitted to membership in the Boston church between March 1 and October 1, 1639. Yet in the five months from October 1639, through February 1640, the church records show only two people admitted to membership: "Katherine Pollard a mayd" and "Mrs. Marye Hudson widdowe," on December 15, 1639, and January 19, 1639/40, respectively. *Records of the First Church,* I, 24–26.

8. Charles Chauncy. On Chauncy, see Chauncy to Cotton, Mar. 15, 1627/8.

9. William Brewster.

10. William Bradford.

 John Cotton to [John Wheelwright]

April 18, 1640

ALS. MS: BPL, Ms. Am. 1506, pt. 2, no. 18

This letter is the longest in Cotton's surviving correspondence. It is no longer intact, but, as originally written, it was more than five thousand words long, filling both sides of four large sheets in a neatly written hand. Cotton's letter and Wheelwright's reply, which follows, are important documents in the history of the Antinomian controversy, offering a retrospective analysis by these key players in that drama of exactly what went wrong for each of them. For both writers, Wheelwright's Fast Day sermon of January 19, 1637, is a central interest.[1] The two letters represent the second stage of a discussion initiated in at least one previous exchange of letters, as Cotton indicates by quoting the Wheelwright letter to which he is replying, which in its turn was a reply to one from Cotton. Although other letters between the two do not appear to have survived, we know that the correspondence continued, since Thomas Prince recorded the fact that they included a fragmentary letter from Wheelwright to Cotton dated October 2, 1640.[2] The crux of Cotton's appeal is to encourage Wheelwright to construct a "Confession" to the colonial magistrates that would reconcile their differences and pave the way for removal of his banishment. As a result, these letters—and others now unknown—gradually led up to Wheelwright's direct appeal to Governor Winthrop and the General Court's revocation of his penalty in May 1644.[3]

A central issue in Wheelwright's situation, as Cotton argues here and as Wheelwright eventually came to realize, is the need to be sensitive to the influence a preacher can have on his audience. Wheelwright's letter, to which Cotton is here replying, apparently argued strenuously that his conviction for sedition and contempt of authority in his Fast Day sermon was unjust, since he did not intend to encourage his listeners to seditious or heretical actions or thoughts. Cotton does not want to let him off the hook, however, and argues that a minister must be aware of how his words are apt to be taken by a particular audience. Though his exact words are not quoted in the letter, Wheelwright had preached that his message condemning those under a Covenant of Works—and he implied that this was nearly all the magistrates and ministers in the colony—could "cause a combustion." "What then? did not Christ come to send fire upon the earth," so that if it comes to it, we must "be willing to be killed like sheepe," and the like.[4] Cotton knows that in Wheelwright he is dealing with a man of a contentious, even volatile nature. He employs tact and his own confession to errors in this letter as a way of getting Wheelwright to think about where he might back down. It took Wheelwright a while—he was not willing to concede much in his reply to this letter—but in his letter to Winthrop on September 10, 1643, he finally acknowledged "mine own distempered passions" as a source of the problems and of his present regret, admitting that he thereby "had such an hand in those sharp and vehement contentions raised . . . to the great disturbance of the churches of Christ. It is the grief of my soul that I used such vehement censorious speeches in the application of my sermon."[5] How sincere he was in such a confession may be subject to debate, but it is clear that his correspondence with Cotton in 1640 and probably later was the beginning of his awareness of a need to take fuller responsibility for his rhetoric.

As in so many other examples in this volume, these letters have both suffered severe mutilation. But the fragments that survive amply repay the effort to read through the numerous interruptions in the text from loss of paper or ink. The loss of ink, even where the paper survives, is at some points so severe as to leave paper that at first inspection looks quite blank but that, with careful scrutiny and manipulation of lighting and magnification, gradually reveals faint writing. The letters tell their own story, but for fuller discussion of the exchange and its relation to the controversy, see Sargent Bush, Jr., "'Revising what we have done amisse': John Cotton and John Wheelwright, 1640," *WMQ,* 3d Ser., XLV (1988), 733–750.

The manuscript is not in Cotton's hand, but he read over the copy carefully, as is evidenced in his occasional changes in spelling, capitalization, and punctuation. On rare occasions he also added a phrase or word. Some paper is lost from each of the four sheets of this manuscript, especially on the right margin of the rectos (and thus the left margin of the versos). But there are also both bleaching in small spots and large areas of staining from water damage, together with mildew. The second sheet, containing pages 3 and 4, is the most severely damaged page, with about two-fifths of the sheet torn away, from top to bottom, creating greatly fragmented text on those two pages. In this case, the nineteenth-century transcription partially preserved at the Massachusetts Historical Society is of relatively little help.[6] Though occasional words and letters are present in that transcription that have since crumbled away from the manuscript—and are here incorporated in braces—for the most part that transcriber elides many difficult passages that have here been successfully deciphered. The present edition is thus—for all of its lacunae—a much more coherent text than that of the earlier transcriber.

Reverend and beloved Brother

Yo*u*r acceptance in good part of my former l*ette*re (though plaine & v||g to Argue of sin[)]||[7] doeth encourage me to pro[c]eede yet further in the same cause, *tha*t by *th*e helpe of *th*e grace of Christ (||[8] the will of God) we may yet further disco[v]er & discerne o*u*r owne failings (f[or] wherein you have failed, I have in some sort failed also) that both of vs revising what we have done amisse, may give Glory to God & remoove the o[ffe]nces *tha*t have bene given by vs by humble & sincere judg[in]g of o*ur* selves befo[re] the Lord & his people so farre as hee shall call vs therevnto. If there wer[e] any failing in the Application of yo*ur* sermon, I account it a failing also in [my] selfe, that being demaunded in open Co*ur*t my Judgm*en*t of yo*ur* sermon, I did [not] finde any fault in it. For though I thought yo*ur* Application very sharp yet rem*em*bring *tha*t it had b[een] d[ir]ected ag*ains*t such as confounded the Doctrine of *th*e Co[ve]n*an*ts of workes & gr[ace]|| feared many in the countrey did because of the great opposition || to arise ag*ains*t the Doctrine of the Coven*an*ts delivered by vs) I suppo[sed] yo[u] m[igh]t have some Reason for *th*e vehemency of yo*ur* Expressions ag*ains*t such. But s[o]m[e] p*er*ceiving *tha*t all the heate of the gr[eat] opposition was kindl[ed]||[by] divers opin[io]ns of M[r] Vane, M[rs] Hutchinson, M[r] || & M[r] Coxall[9] & thos[e] [f]ollowers (who indeede vnder Prætence of ma|| the Cove*na*nt of Grace ||thren the Grace of the Co[ve]*na*nt)[10] I then p*er*ceive[d] the vehemency of y*ou*r Reproofes should rather have bene directed ag*ains*t such as fundamentally subverted the Coven*an*t of Grace, [tha]n [a]g[ainst] such as opposed them especially seeing the opposers erred not fundamentally but onely brought some disorder into *th*e Coven*an*t of "grace, yet reteyning all the Integralls of it[. Mr.] P[e]t[11]|| openly professed "before the church that the speech [he made] in *th*e Co*ur*t (ag*ains*t the Differ- "encing of men lying vnder *th*e Coven*an*t of workes, & grace || holding forth "of a false Coven*an*t & of a fancy-Christ) was not bent ag[ainst the] Doctrine "of Christ & the Coven*an*ts delivered by *th*e Trueth: but ag*ains*t such a Christ "& such a Coven*an*t of Grace wherein Christ is so made all in all to vs as *the*y "[that] have noe Faith nor hope of any sanctifying grace inhærent in vs, but " Christ is all these to vs & in vs that Graces are onely found in the Coven*an*t " of works, not of Grace: *tha*t such Graces as are found in the Coven*an*t of "Grace are neither seene nor active (no, not instrumentall in Christs hand) but "passive onely.[12]

This expression of his tooke off noe small sparke[?] from my spirit especially when both o*ur* Governo*ur* & [Deputy] Governo*ur* p*ro*fessed to my selfe in a serious conference of mine with them [that] they did not looke at *th*e Differences betweene the Elders & me (tou[ching] vnion or evidencing of vnion) to be fundamentall matter, but such as wherein Difference of notion might stand with trueth of Grace, & peace of churches & Comon-wealth.[13] These p*ro*fessions of theirs eased my b[ur]den that whereas before [I] conceived more hardly of their p*ro*ceedings then there was Cause & therefore could see noe safe co*ur*se but in a quiet Se[c]ession without [p]rotestation ag*ains*t some injurious Proceedings ag*ains*t the Trueth of *th*e Gospell, now I saw their zeale had kindled & burst forth ag*ains*t th|| & corrupt opinions w*hi*ch had subverted the Coven*an*t of Grace, & ag*ains*t || the greatest part of the tyme in the synod at Newtown[14] || Synod where I heard those damnable opinions agitated & co|| [IV] at first I was slow to beleive *tha*t any s[uc]h Erro*ur*s were extant in the countrey (b[u]t thought *the*m[15] to be either some misexpressions of o*ur* men, or some misconstructions of the Countrey:) yet when I saw the Messeng[ers] of o*ur* church (Mr Aspinall[16] Mr Coxall, & others) still pinching & excepting ag[ainst th]e Proceedings of the Synod [a]bout those points & excusing & mainteyning *th*e opin[io]ns controverted about vnion, inhærent righteousnesse visibilitie & activity of indwelling Grace & the like, I tooke them aside & tolde them *tha*t if they were of *th*e Judgm*en*t w*hi*ch they stoode for, all those Bastard-opinions w*hi*ch were then de[live]red, would be fathered vpon the members of o*ur* church. And therefore I expressed my greife *tha*t they who were not cleare in such poynts should offer to go[e fo]rth in the Churches name, as o*ur* messengers, when they differed so ^much^ fro[m] o*ur* church in Judgm*ent*.[17] Afterwards I hoped *tha*t o*ur* [brethr]en though Erring might be recovered by some further pr[ivate?] Po|| Conference with *the*m. But all in vaine: they had bene [ver]y long [setl]ed in them & I found a l*ett*er from one of *tha*t Judgm*en*t who sent st||ed & advised *the*m to keepe such opinions private to themselves, || freinds but publiquely before [one illegible word] witnesses to hold forth noe [m]ore [tha]n their Teacher[18] might goe [alon]g w*i*th *the*m. So then I plainely saw tha[t they] had run a co*ur*se of hæresie a long tyme together before o*ur* Pasto*ur*s speach in the Co*ur*t,[19] & before yo*ur* sermon. I saw also by good Proofe at last *tha*t though they looked at you & mee as com*m*it[ted] on to their way & so hopefull for o*ur* estates in Grace; yet || so many as knowing their opinions [be]tter, opposed them more, they looked at as legallists & enemyes of free Grace. And a[f]ter this censure were cast all *th*e Elders (save you & me) & all the Magistrates save two or three. In so much as they disswaded any *tha*t were affected to o*ur* Judgm*en*ts to heare the Elders or to give those com*m*on respects of due hono*ur* to Magistrates dissenting from them w*hi*ch true Chri*sti*ans have in tymes past not denyed to Pagans. Hence also sprung their troublesome Questionings in every Church where any of them came to heare: And likewise from thence sprung the counsell & desire (though vnknown to me) both to remoove o*ur* [church?][20] to *th*e Mount & to get Mr Vane to procure the Im*m*unity of Boston from [the] [j]urisdiction & *th*e making of it an House-towne.[21]

Now then Consider I pray you ([dear][22] Brother) in the feare of God; If there was at *tha*t tyme when you Preach[ed] yo*ur* sermon a strong faction in o*ur* Towne, *tha*t runne out into a co*ur*se of Hæresie, sedition & contempt of Authority, & censured all *th*e enemyes of free grace who opposed them in their way: & withall, If yo*ur* sermon did animate & encourage promiscuously all *tha*t held forth in the Bulke the Doctrine of free Grace, [&] did censure their opposers p*ro*miscuously as enemyes to free Grace, scribes, Pharisees,

Philistines, Herods, Pilates, Antichr*ist*ians, then (for aught I see) It will vnavoydably follow *tha*t you in yo*u*r sermon (I meane in the Application of it) were an Abetto*u*r of those *tha*t run a co*u*rse [of] Hæresie sedition & Contempt of Authority & so vnawares became Accessary [with the]m in these great [e]vills. But the former of these is true in both the p*ar*ts [of it.] And therefore I see not, how *th*e latter can be avoyded. That what ||, or spake in this kinde you did Ignorantly[,] I willingly beleive[,] [2][23] but as I said to you in my last, Ignorance is one thing, Innocency [another. If] the storke be taken flying & roosting with *th*e Cranes she suffereth as [they do.][24] you "Answer: is this i[ust] as well an Ignorance of Negation, as of Priv[ation?]|| let "it be Privative, am I (say you) to be condemned in a Co*u*rt & cens[ured for] "sedition? Had they bene goeing on in a way of Adultery & Murder || the same "Doctrine occasionally given *the*m Incouragem*en*t (or rather || & the Magis- "trate had therevpon condemned me for an Adult[erer] || had their ce[nsu]re "& execution, thereof bene just?[25]

Reply 1. I cannot say *tha*t yo*u*r Ignorance was of meere N[egation] || heard something you owne? || yo*u*r sister Hutchinsons s|| sanctification. you knew also how Mr Coxall in *th*e || New-creature to be as a New-nothing & you kn|| & Censorious Practices || yo*u*r owne heart could || Civill Justice looketh more at the Bulke of the [action than at the intention] of the worker: they attend more to Finis operis [than to finis operantis;[26] not] onely they of the Fact[ion] nor onely the Magi[strates]|| them but all *tha*t heard or read yo*u*r sermon with || Application as strongly [illegible word] *th*e one party as || the other. yo*u*r "selfe confesse *tha*t you could be noe m|| If it had bene made to certaine Indi- "viduall person[s]|| but yet (you thinke) those vehem*en*t expressions were || [(to "your appre]hension) to the sort or kinde of such as you turned || are not Ignorant *tha*t men of God doe not speake in || Bent of their Application ag*ains*t Individua vaga[27] but (as || observe the state of the people to whome they speake), they || therevnto in the scope & drift of their Applications. Now as the|| of Persons, stoode ~~with~~ ^amongst^ vs, yo*u*r Application[28] (be not offended || of trueth & faithfullnesse was an Aberration from *th*e true estate of *th*||

Reply 2. Let us consider the comparison you alledge: suppose *tha*t || in a congregation had committed Adultery & to their Adultery had || of their Husbands & were suspected thereof by sundry of the Countrey || should come in and Preach amongst *the*m & vtter some wholesome Doct[rine]|| Duetyes of Husbands to their wives, should Apply my Doctrine to || all wives to expect such & such Duetyes from their husbands, but || faile thereof then to handle Such wicked men as enemyes to Conjugall || as Philistines & Aegypt[ian] whome Moses slew & hid in the sand[29] as He || & Pilates Scribes & Phari[se]es & Antichrist, & so leave it: might not all that k|| the estate of the Congregation justly Judge mee as an Abeto*u*r of the Adulter[y]|| & [one illegible word] com*m*itted amongst *the*m. The Lord helpe vs to lay aside selfe-lov[e] & to Judge [?with righte]ous Judgm*en*t: without Præiudice or Partiality to o*u*r selves or others.

" But say you, I may nott confesse ^my selfe justly^ p*ro*ceeded ag*ains*t for all "*th*e world. the tyme of mine Application I may not altogether condemne lest "I should || the spirit of Grace by whom I am fully pers[w]aded I did speake "|| much weakenesse of mine owne.

Reply [3?.] I tooke ||[v]pon me to Judge yo*u*r spirit by w*hi*ch you || [2v] || the faithfullnesse of vnfeigned brotherly love give me leave ^(in *th*e name of Christ)^ [30] to discerne || of (with yo*u*r helpe) [31] by the scriptures *th*e trueth. The Doctrinall part [of] yo*u*r sermon, I doe beleive was spoken by [the] spirit of Grace, as holding [fo]rth words of Trueth & spirituall wisedome in the sence you meant it, as [I co]nceive; But the latter part of yo*u*r sermon (*th*e Application [32] to yo*u*r hearers) ||[p]lainely appeare not to have bene guided (beare with my Plainenesse) || of Discerning of *th*e true estate of yo*u*r Hearers, not by *tha*t wise[dome]|| from above: but (as yo*u*r selfe doe freely & Chri*sti*anly acknow[ledge]|| of yo*u*r l*ett*er) by a spirit of P*re*iudice, this being too highly of such ||[as d]id stand for free grace & too hardly of such as did oppose || Application accordingly, as likewise yo*u*r cariage towards them. || (as indeede you did) occasionally encourage corrupt hearts || were found for w*hi*ch [al]so you p*ro*fesse you desire to be ||[in the] sight of god & man.

||r (good Brother) you know very well, the spirit of grace || wisedome & of spirituall Discerning as well as a God of Trueth. || by Him. He guideth vs to speake more p*er*tinently to *th*e || then many times [t]o[g]ether did know & vnderstand. If || Appeare that by Præiudice or misprision, or misinformation || some Doctrine to the estate of o*u*r Hearers, wee cannot ||od, *tha*t in such Application we spake by *th*e spirit of Grace, ||wne spirit w*hi*ch though it be also a spirit of Grace yet it is ||aned aside through præjudice & Ignorance.

" || I had sufficient Grounds to suspect *tha*t there might be such || [among?] "the Hearers vpon whome my Application might justly fall; but || [who?] they "were, I left to *th*e Lord, & mens owne consciences.

[Re]ply 4. I conceive you thought you had sufficient Grounds so to suspect: but if it [ha]d bene so indeede, time would have declared it: whereas the events of things in ||te *th*e co*u*rse of yo*u*r Hearers hath plainely declared it since, that *th*e Doctrine [of fr]ee grace had noe greater enemyes amongst yo*u*r Hearers then they *tha*t seemed [most?] forward & bold in *th*e holding forth of free Grace, & yet have, most cun*n*ingly & [wi]ckedly subverted the trueth & life of free Grace.

[Rep]ly I feare you had more sufficient & evident grounds to suspect *th*e subversion of free Grace by Mrs Hutchinson & Mr Coxall having heard the expressions of them both. You had also sufficient grounds to suspect that if such Ringleaders were of *tha*t corrupt Judgm*en*t many moe were likely to be leavened & corrupted by them. And oh how seasonable had it bene if the T[ex]t of yo*u*r Application had bene bent ag*ains*t them through whom not onely yo*u*r l[a]bo*u*r & mine but *th*e saving Trueth of the Gospell hath so deepely suffered.

" But it may seeme (say you) one ground of my Censure was my Doctrine "seeing Samuel Hutchinson & Mr Knolles [33] were reje[cte]d vpon *th*e [same "ground?].

Reply you are misinformed about both. For though I have now forgotten the [groun]ds in Co*u*rt of Samuel Hutchinson, yet when I heard of *th*em by such as were p[resen]t, I was troubled at them for his sake, as knowing they were justly offensive. F[or] besides his Pragm[a]ticallnesse & verbosity at the synod & eager Defence of [his] sister, He justified some Persons & Passages of the Island [34] who ought [not to] have bene approved. And as for Mr Knolles himselfe told me He [3] was not enjoyned to depart, but permitted to stay, till they had further tryall of Him. But having a call offered him to Pascatoq*ua* [35] by some of *tha*t people, He tooke the opportunity to [de]part & was loth to stay to give tryall of himselfe to *th*em here. That w*hi*ch bred in some of the Magistrates a jealousie of his vnsoundnesse in Judgem*en*t was, *tha*t being demaunded by the Deputy-Governo*u*r [w]hether God Justifie an vn[g]odly vnbeleiver He affirmed it, yet added it was not Applyed but by faith: w*hi*ch made *th*em feare, *tha*t he omitted vocation, & held forth Justification applye[d] on Gods part without & before Faith & so before vnion.

" But againe (say you) God forbid *tha*t I should Justifie mine Adversaries: "till I dye will I not remoove mine Integrity from me. My righteousnesse I "hold fast & will not lett it goe. &c.

Reply. you allude to *th*e words of Job [36] & if you applyed them to *th*e same end with Job I would consent to you. He applyed *th*em to the Justification of the sincerity of his heart before god & man, ag*ains*t all the Imputations of Hypocrisy Bribery & Atheisme cast vpon him by his Adversary-freinds. If he had applyed the same to *th*e maintenance of all his Passionate & vnreverent & Impatient expressions He must have revoked his words as himselfe acknowledgeth before Elihu by his silence & before || his Repentance i, tu quoq*ue,* & fac fimi? [illegible word] [37] & expect the like spi[rit]|| found.

To proceede to some [re]maining Passages of yo*u*r l*ett*er: yo*u*r Refusing "the Counsell of voluntary Secession you say you doe not take it to be a lean- "ing to yo*u*r owne counsell, though therein you refused both the counsell & "motion of the Magistrates & of my selfe also.[38] Yo*u*r Reason is, because Pauls "example may be some ground [of y]o*u*r Practise, Acts. 16. 37.[39] Sure I am (say "you) Secession in this case would have [argued] Guilt &c.

Reply. Consider (Deare Brother) whether some Temptation doe not darken yo[ur] true Discerning of yo*u*r owne case & co*u*rse in this buisinesse. For the Ap*ost*les example doeth evidently appeare to me to hold forth a contrary Practise vnto yo*u*rs. Let vs paralell yo*u*r case & his, as farre as it will goe. The Magistrates at Philippi caused Paul to be beaten for teaching customes contrary to the Law: o*u*r Magistrates condemned y[ou] for sedition & contempt of Authority. The Magistrates of Philippi having thus beaten Pa[ul] cast him into P[ris]on & o*u*r Magistrates cast you vnder Com*m*aund to Attend the Co*u*rt when you should be called for. The Magistrates of Philippi sent word to Paul, privily to be gone the next day: but he refused because they had punished him openly & would send him away privily. But o*u*r Magistrates did not send to you privily at all to be gone nor did you refuse to goe vpon their private motion. Afterwards when the Magistrates came openly in Person & persuaded Paul to goe then away, he went. O*u*r Magistrates spake openly to you in publique Co*u*rt Advising & p*er*suading you to Depart: but you vtterly refused it directly contrary to the Ap*ost*les example. Had they sent to you privily to the Mount to be gone[40] after they had openly condemned you you might have refused it vpon Pauls Example. But when in Publique Co*u*rt they openly in their owne Persons offer and advise yo*u*r Departure, how could you then still Refuse the motion, w*hi*ch the Ap*ost*le did not, though the com*m*ing of the Magistr[ates] to him was not in so publique & Judiciall a maner vpon the Bench as the motio[n] of o*u*r Magistrates came to you?

" But surely (say you) such a Departure would have Argued guil[t] in me.

[3v] Ans*wer.* doubtlesse; noe more, then Pauls Departure in the like case argued Guilt in him: yea yo*u*r Departure vpon their Publique motion in open Co*u*rt, would rather have bene a strong Argum*en*t of yo*u*r Innocency to all *th*e world. For when they had in open Co*u*rt condemned you of Sedition & Contempt of Authority if instead of punishing you according to the nature of such offences, they did openly offer you a Departure in peace surely in case you had accepted their offer All *tha*t should have heard of the matter would have thought you guiltlesse of such crimes, at least in any dangerous measure. Whereas you by Putting *the*m vpon Actuall censure of you, have as much as in you lyeth rejected the Testimony of yo*u*r Innocency (either a toto or a tanto),[41] w*hi*ch they had putt into yo*u*r hand.

" But you are afraid, lest by vnwarrantable confession you should shut "a Doore of Repentance to some who must come in thereat, before God "Accept.

Reply: True, if you should make an vnwarrantable confession: but God forbid *tha*t I should Advise or persuade you to any vnwarrantable Act, for any end, though never so good; the Lord needeth not to direct vs to doe any vnwarrantable Acts to bring to passe either his owne glory or a Good. But I cannot see *tha*t such a confession is vnwarrantable, but just & lawfull, "To acknowledge[42] *tha*t you did overvalue the ||rtly an hæretical & seditious "Faction *tha*t you did vnder value their || that you did not (according to *th*e "Rule of Brotherly faithfullnesse) observ|| s[u]spect the speaches *tha*t savoured "ranckly of hæreticall Pravity w*hi*ch in yo*u*r hearing fell f[r]om the mouthes "of some of *the*m that *th*e Application of yo*u*r sermon was framed according "to yo*u*r p*re*conceyved p*re*judice of overmuch good in the erroneous Party, & "of overmuch evill [in] their opposers that you have cause to || that thereby (though vnawares) you strengthened *th*e hands of corrupt m[en]|| made the hearts of *the*m sad who were more sound. That you were in y[our] carriage toward the Magistrates & Elders lesse studious of Peace then the rule requireth w*hi*ch calleth v[s] to seeke Peace & pursue it. Psal. 34. 14:[43] yea, & as much as [in] vs lyeth & as is possible to have peace with all men. Rom. 12: 18:[44] That you were not enough cautious & distinct in yo*u*r Expressions "in the Synod ab[out] vnion. That whereinsoever any further light from *th*e "word shall be brought to you to convince you of any further failing, you will "be ready according to God to give further satisfaction. But still you beleive "& as you beleive you cannot but speake *tha*t the Doctrine delivered by you "in yo[ur] sermons rightly vnderstoode not according to *th*e misconstruction "of some Phrases but according to yo*u*r true [mea]ning is truely agreeable to "the Doctrine of the Gos[pe]ll.

Beloved Brother I speake the trueth in Christ || not I doe verely beleive such a [co]nfession were not onely warrantable, but an Acceptable Sacrifice to o*u*r Lord Jesus Christ, & to *th*e hearts of all *tha*t truely beleive in *th*e grace of Christ throughout both Englands. yea those *tha*t rose vp ag*ains*t you & yet shall observe any Failings in their owne proceedings shall thereby the sooner by yo*u*r Example be brought to Judge themselves for Judging you more deepely tainted with the spirit of o*u*r erroneous brethren [t]hen they now finde y[ou]. And o*u*r poore Brethren who have suffered deepely for their inordinate zeale to yo*u*r Innocency may by this meanes the sooner be brought to give such satisfaction to o*u*r Magistrates, as may restore *the*m to former libertyes both in church, & com*m*on-wealth.[45] Now the lord open o*u*r hearts with *th*e rest of Christs [4] Elders (the living members of his holy visible Church) to cast downe o*u*r crownes before him *tha*t sitteth vpon the Throne & before the Lambe, whose name is onely to be exalted (whatsoever become of vs:) Rev: 4. 10.[46]

Concerning yo*u*r Doctrine & the Doctrine of the Elders you acknowledge "rightly in your le*tte*r That if you had called the Elders Hæreticks, that were "a greivous sinne & required deepe humiliation; but *tha*t (you say) you may "not owne.

Reply. Wee thinke the spirit of Peace beateth in the Pulses of yo*ur* heart; onely to helpe yo*ur* memory & right perception of things in this Case I pray you call to minde *tha*t w*hi*ch fell from yo*ur* penne in one of yo*ur* short writings to *the* Elders That you tell *the*m the Difference is great betweene them & you, the Doctrine of the one is the Doctrine of æternall life, the other, of ever lasting damnation. The writing I have not at hand & so may ^mis^Expresse yo*ur* words: but the thing I remember too well & so do many of *the*m with much greife. The other Passage of yo*urs* in yo*ur* l[ette]r to Mr. Keayne[47] had neede of some explication to cleare it selfe & being rightly cleared, It may “be, *the* Elders will not dissent with you about it. That sanctification (say you) “is the Prime evidence I have, & must beare wittnesse ag*ains*t it [as] a wicked & “pernitious Hæresie ag*ains*t all legall Professo*urs*. Wherein if yo*ur* meaning be as you Expres[s]e yo*ur*se[l]fe in yo*ur* last l*ette*r to me, The Elders (I conceive[)] “will sub[mit] to you. For [one word mutilated] [(]say you) To make Qualifi- “cations the ground of that fai[th]|| none is Justified or beleiveth himselfe “to be Justified, I still looke at [it as a] Doctrine tending to damnatio[n.][48]

If in yo*ur* sence by Qualifications you meane sanctification, the Elders will freely tell you they looke at sanctification [as] the fruite of faith & therefore it cannot be the ground or c[au]se of faith by w*hi*ch we are Justif[ie]d. If you meane by any qualifications f[a]ith (as they doe in this ||[) they] will tell you though Faith be not *the* ground of *tha*t Faith by [which we are] Justified, yet it is it selfe an Instrumentall Cause of o*ur* Justifica[tion]|| doe not many of o*ur* best Divines consent with *the*m therein? And ||[as] {Faith} may be accounted some kinde of cause of o*ur* Justification witho[ut charge] of Hæresy, may not *the* sight of Faith be some cause of *the* sight ||{of Justifi}cation without staine of Hæresy? If Christ vpon sight {o}f Faith [say]|| of the Palsey sonne, thy sinnes be forgiven thee (& so witness || Him both his Adoption & Justification) Mar 2.5:[49] what Præiudi[c]e is {this to free} Grace seeing it is *the* proper worke & office of Faith to Discl{aim all confi}dence in workes yea, & ||{all} worth in it selfe? If you [one word faded] yet ||{must} be a former evidence from the free Promise of gr[ace] (calling me || Revealed & Effectually Applyed to my soule even to *the* begetting of Faith, befor[e] I can have any true or lively Faith begotten in me. The Elders will graunt you every whit as much. Yo*ur* neighbo*ur* Compton, who hath bene lately freed from his censure at Rocksbury, will tell you *tha*t the Elders of Rocksbury did accept his confession of *tha*t Point in those Termes.[50] Quicknesse of spirit[51] on both sides hath bene noe small Præiudice not onely to the right vnderstanding of one anothers mindes, but even to *the* Trueth it selfe & to Publique Peace. The Lord pardon all faylings on all hands, for his holy names sake in Jesus Christ.

The onely way w*hi*ch you propound for p*ro*cur[i]ng peace according to

God [I] willingly acknowledge & Embrace It fully, to wit: that all offend-"o*u*r[s] [4v] should make acknowledgm*en*t & satisfaction to the full. If Re-"pentance be called for on the one hand & not on the other what is this but "Partiality, w*hi*ch the Lord vehemently forbiddeth 1. Tim. 5.21.[52]

I wholly consent with you herein & therefor conceyving *tha*t some (& a considerable part of o*u*r Church) had offended in their Proceedings ag*ains*t you, & some others of o*u*r members, I verely Purposed, seeing we could not Proceede ag*ains*t *the*m according to Rule in a Church way (by Reason of the Prævalency of the contrary Party both in o*u*r owne Church & in other Churches abroade, who would have bene called in to Judge betweene vs) I say I verely Purposed openly to have protested ag*ains*t all such proceedings as I took to be injurious & offensive & to have Departed into some other Parts of this Countrey. Sundry others of o*u*r Brethren both in Towne & countrey were of like minde with mee. But all this was before we cert[ainly][53] Discerned the Hæreticall & seditious & contemptuous spirit & co*u*rse of o*u*r ?ous Brethren: as also before I had found by Conference with *th*e Governo*u*r & Deputy-Governo*u*r; that *th*e Ground of these Proceedings ag*ains*t o*u*r Brethren was not for Point of Doctrine about v[ni]on or [e]videncing of vnion or[54] for their censorious & seditious & contemp[tuous] [carr]yage [in th]e maintenance of their grosse Erro*u*rs. Both w*hi*ch things when I saw (w*hi*ch || the subtilty of o*u*r Brethren were hid from me) I then [s]aw noe just cau[se of] Remoovall—noe nor any Just cause of Proceeding ag*ains*t such of o*u*r || way as had proceeded ag*ains*t *the*m in a way of civill Justice || I saw cause to blame my selfe & others of my minde, who were asleepe whilest the enemy came [and] sowed Tares.[55] I could not but ||[56] In [illegible word] sprea[d] so farre & grow so high in *th*e sight || countrey & I {(with some few others)} *th*e onely strangers in || see not these things! But so the Lord hath taught mee what || who so blinde as my servant?[57] Vnlesse the Lord himselfe || was to his People in his tyme) eyes to *th*e blinde & feete {to the} lame[58] (or what wee are[)]. But thus the wisedome of Christ {our Lord}|| Bl[es]s[ed]nesse & his Power in o*u*r weakenesse Blessed for ||ame & let all his saints say Amen, Amen.

|| soe, if you can make it appeare to me, wherein any of o*u*r Brethren || side have offended, I trust the Lord Jesus (who is o*u*r strength) will help me to call vpon them as I now doe vpon you for serious Repentance before the Lord, & due satisfaction before his People.:

Fear not to [acce]pt this labo*u*r of love in good Part & beare with my Tædiousnesse w*hi*ch the variety & weight of the matters in hand hath forced me vnto. The Lord Helpe vs to see & Doe with Acceptable will in all o*u*r wayes, & Pardon all o*u*r Ignorances & Infirmityes in Christ Jesus & keepe vs from the Pathes of the pr*es*?[e]dent[59] & Præsumptuous for his holy names sake. In him [I] salute you[60] & yo*u*rs & desiring continuance of mutuall Prayers [I] doe rest

Yo*u*r loveing brother in him,
John Cott{on}

Bos{to}n this 18 of 2d
1640.

1. For the full text of this sermon, see Hall, *Antinomian Controversy,* 152–172.

2. The Cotton Papers in the Thomas Prince Library include this note in Prince's hand: "1640/I have seen Part of a letter à *th*e R. Mr. Wheelwright to *th*e R. Mr. Cotton of Boston Dated East Hampton 2d 8m. 1640." BPL, Ms. Am. 1506, pt. 2, no. 17b.

3. Two rather different letters from Wheelwright to Winthrop, dated Sept. 10, 1643, and Mar. 1, 1643/4, are included in Winthrop, *Journal,* 505–507. Cotton noted his role in the process of Wheelwright's repatriation in his *Way of Congregational Churches Cleared* when he parenthetically observed that Wheelwright, "upon further conference and consideration," had "retracted" offensive "passages" from his sermon. Cotton in the same work reported that Wheelwright "hath since confessed, that being but new come into the Countrey, having but little acquaintance but with his kindred, and their friends, (who were many of them levened this way) he spake some things, which if he had before discerned their Familisme, he would not have expressed himself as he did." Both of these remarks are clearly made with Cotton's 1640 correspondence with Wheelwright in mind, while also pointing to Wheelwright's 1643 exchange with Winthrop. *The Way of Congregational Churches Cleared* . . . (London, 1648), 40, 60; reprinted in Hall, *Antinomian Controversy,* 400, 422.

4. See Hall, *Antinomian Controversy,* 165, 166.

5. Winthrop, *Journal,* 505.

6. The first five-eighths of the transcription have been lost.

7. Right edge of paper is worn away.

8. Hole in paper.

9. Henry Vane, Anne Hutchinson, and John Coggeshall.

10. Though the paper at this point is badly mutilated, the passage clearly makes a point which Wheelwright liked to phrase in this way. In *The Way of Congregational Churches Cleared,* Cotton, trying to separate Wheelwright from the profounder errors of the Hutchinsonians, wrote that the exiles in Rhode Island wrote to Wheelwright in Exeter "and urged him much to come to them, to a far richer soyle, and richer company then where hee lived: yet hee constantly refused, and upon that very ground, because of the corruption of their judgments: 'Professing often, whilst they pleaded for the Covenant of Grace, they took away the Grace of the Covenant.'" In Hall, *Antinomian Controversy,* 423.

11. Possibly Hugh Peter.

12. The synod, held in August and September 1637, drew up a list of eighty-two "errours" that were discovered in the Antinomian group. The list is appended to Winthrop's *Short Story of the Rise, Reign, and Ruin of the Antinomians, Familists, and Libertines* . . . (London, 1644). Error 17 reads: "True poverty of spirit doth kill and take away the sight of grace," and Error 35 is: "The efficacy of Christs death is to kill all activity of graces in his members, that he might act all in all." See Hall, *Antinomian Controversy,* 223, 228.

13. Cotton later recalled that the elders gathered certain of his supposed opinions "to inquire in a brotherly conference with mee, how far I would own them, or how I did understand them, that so the true state of the questions in difference might appeare; and withal, if there were any aguish distemper, or disaffection growen in any of our spirits amongst our selves, it might be healed in a private brotherly way, and mutuall satisfaction given and taken on all hands. Accordingly we had such a meeting in private; wherein five questions were propounded unto mee, with desire of my plaine and explicite answer to the same: which also upon their demand, I gave suddenly." The first of these questions was: "Whether our Union with Christ be compleat before and without Faith?" *The Way of Congregational Churches Cleared,* in Hall, *Antinomian Controversy,* 400–401; Ziff, *Cotton on the Churches,* 226–227.

14. This refers to the "Catalogue . . . of erroneous opinions," or errors, discussed at the synod. See Hall, ed., *Antinomian Controversy,* 219–243.

15. The word y^m^ is squeezed between the preceding and succeeding words in Cotton's hand and ink.

16. William Aspinwall (d. 1662?) had come to the colony in 1630 and became a magistrate in 1636. During the trial of John Wheelwright, in March 1637, Aspinwall drew up a petition declaring Wheelwright's innocence that was signed by some sixty people. He was disarmed, disfranchised, and banished. He was among the founders of Portsmouth, Rhode Island, in March 1637/8. Readmitted to the Massachusetts Bay Colony and to the Boston church in 1642, he finally returned to England in 1652, where he became a Fifth Monarchist (see his *Brief Description of the Fifth Monarchy* . . . [London, 1653]). On Aspinwall, see Savage, *Genealogical Dictionary,* I, 70–71; Battis, *Saints and Sectaries,* 304, 330; B. S. Capp, *The Fifth Monarchy Men: A Study in Seventeenth-Century English Millenarianism* (London, 1972), 240–241; Anderson, *Great Migration,* 55–60.

17. In *The Way of Congregational Churches Cleared,* Cotton repeated this account of this event, again using the trope of the fathering of "Bastardly Opinions" on the Boston church; see Hall, *Antinomian Controversy,* 408.

18. Cotton.

19. Cotton refers to John Wilson's speech to the General Court in December 1636, which Winthrop described as "a very sad speech of the condition of our churches, and the inevitable danger of separation, if these differences and alienations among brethren were not speedily remedied." Wilson's speech "was taken very ill by Mr. Cotton and others of the same church." See Winthrop, *Journal,* 203–206; Stoever, *"A Faire and Easie Way to Heaven,"* 27–28.

20. Mildewed.

21. "The Mount" is Mount Wollaston (now Braintree), where Wheelwright was preaching, though a church had not yet been formally organized there. A movement, supported by then-Governor Henry Vane, was afoot in late 1636 to make it an independent town, with its own church and residences, thus "an House-towne." Such an idea so early in the settlement of Boston was viewed by the opposition as an act of secession, a threat to the unity of the colony. See Winthrop, *Journal,* 187; Rutman, *Winthrop's Boston,* 95–96, 250–251.

22. Hole and mildew.

23. The entire right edge of the second sheet of the MS, pages 3 and 4 of the letter, is torn off. The loss is irregular, up to a maximum width from the edge of the paper of 2 ¼ inches. The portion of the sheet that remains, amounting to perhaps three-fifths of the original sheet, is badly mildewed and water-stained even after recent restoration.

24. This is a reference to one of Aesop's fables, "The Farmer and the Stork," in which "A

Farmer placed nets on his newly-sown plowlands and caught a number of Cranes, which came to pick up his seed. With them he trapped a Stork that . . . was earnestly beseeching the Farmer to spare his life. 'Pray save me, Master,' he said, 'and let me go free this once. . . . I am no Crane, I am a Stork, a bird of excellent character. . . .' The Farmer laughed aloud and said, 'It may be all as you say, I only know this: I have taken you with these robbers, the Cranes, and you must die in their company.' Birds of a feather flock together." *Aesop's Fables,* based on the translation of George Fyler Townsend (New York, 1968), 51.

25. Though the broken paper here makes full clarity elusive, Wheelwright seems to be arguing that it does not make sense—is not "just"—that the wrongs committed by others are also charged against him. He asks, Suppose, hypothetically, the people had heard encouragement in his message to commit adultery or murder (rather than heresy or sedition). Would it then be sensible for the court to find *him* guilty of the crimes they committed?

26. finis operis: the end, or purpose, of the deed; finis operantis: the end, or purpose, of the doer.

27. individua vaga: undefined (or indefinite) individuals.

28. Cotton changed the initial A from lowercase to capital.

29. See Exod. 2:11–15 and Acts 7:24–25.

30. This inserted phrase in parentheses is in Cotton's hand.

31. Cotton himself added the parentheses around this phrase.

32. Cotton changed the initial A from lowercase to capital.

33. Samuel Hutchinson (1590–1667) and Hanserd (also Hansard) Knollys (1598–1691) came to New England during the height of the Antinomian controversy, in July 1637, and were not permitted to remain in the Massachusetts Bay Colony for, as Winthrop wrote of Knollys, "holding some of Mrs. Hutchinson's opinions" (*Journal,* 285). Samuel Hutchinson was Anne Hutchinson's brother-in-law, and Knollys was a Puritan minister recently fled from Lincolnshire who stayed in the colonies about six years, ministering at Dover (1638–1640) near Wheelwright's Exeter location, before returning to England, where he became a leading Baptist. While Cotton was working to bring Wheelwright to a frame of mind that would allow his repatriation in Massachusetts Bay, Hugh Peter was doing the same with Hanserd Knollys (see Raymond Phineas Stearns, *The Strenuous Puritan: Hugh Peter, 1598–1660* [Urbana, Ill., 1954], 146). The colony's refusal to welcome these men caught the attention of colleagues in England, who questioned the New Englanders on the matter in subsequent controversial transatlantic exchanges. On Knollys, see Brook, *Lives of the Puritans,* III, 491–500; Venn, *Alumni Cantabrigienses,* III, 31; *DNB.* On Samuel Hutchinson, see Savage, *Genealogical Dictionary,* II, 512; Battis, *Saints and Sectaries,* 157, 314.

34. Aquidneck.

35. A colonial jurisdiction comprising several communities, including Dover, Exeter, Hampton, and Portsmouth, in what is now New Hampshire, outside the legal jurisdiction of the Massachusetts Bay Colony.

36. Job 27:5, where Job says, God forbid that I should justify you: till I die I will not remove mine integrity from me.

37. The broken paper combined with illegibility at this point leaves too little Latin text to be coherent.

38. In the court trial of Wheelwright, which found him guilty of sedition and contempt of authority, the magistrates delayed sentencing for several months in the hope and perhaps expectation that Wheelwright would voluntarily take himself beyond the jurisdiction of the colony. When he did not do so, his sentence of banishment was pronounced in early November 1637.

39. The number 3 is written over 1, correcting verse 17 to 37. Acts 16:36–37, describing the magistrates' release of Paul and Silas from prison at Philippi: And the keeper of the prison told this saying to Paul, The magistrates have sent to let you go: now therefore depart, and go in peace. But Paul said unto them, They have beaten us openly uncondemned, being Romans, and have cast us into prison; and now do they thrust us out privily? nay verily; but let them come themselves and fetch us out.

40. The fragmentary Massachusetts Historical Society transcription of this letter begins at this point. Details taken from that transcription that are no longer present or discernible in the MS are enclosed in braces.

41. a toto or a tanto: of the whole [charge] or of so great [a charge].

42. Here Cotton begins his summary of the eight points he believes Wheelwright ought to fold into a "confession" of his errors in the Antinomian controversy. Cotton is suggesting that, if Wheelwright can bring himself to make such a confession, it will be "an Acceptable Sacrifice," that is, enable a reconciliation with the Massachusetts magistrates and clergy and a lifting of his banishment.

43. Ps. 34:14: Depart from evil, and do good; seek peace, and pursue it.

44. Rom. 12:18: If it be possible, as much as lieth in you, live peaceably with all men.

45. More than sixty signers of a petition defending Wheelwright at the time of his court trial had been forced to surrender their guns and, in many cases, were disfranchised (*Records of Massachusetts Bay,* I, 207; Winthrop, *Journal,* 239–242). Battis identifies individuals and punishments by name (*Saints and Sectaries,* 304–307, 312–316, 322–328).

46. Rev. 4:9–11: And when those [four] beasts give glory and honour and thanks to him that sat on the throne, who liveth for ever and ever, The four and twenty elders fall down before him that sat on the throne, and worship him that liveth for ever and ever, and cast their crowns before the throne, saying, Thou art worthy, O Lord, to receive glory and honour and power: for thou hast created all things, and for thy pleasure they are and were created.

47. Robert Keayne, a Boston merchant.

48. The Antinomian party had claimed that the New Englanders typically used the outward signs of faith—evidence of sanctification—as a basis for ("ground of") faith. But Cotton says that they will agree with Wheelwright that this is wrong. The outward signs are an effect, not a cause, of faith.

49. Mark 2:5: And when Jesus saw their faith, he said unto the sick of the palsy, Son, thy sins be forgiven thee.

50. John Compton of Roxbury (a laborer, property owner, church member, and freeman) had been disarmed on November 30, 1637, for his connection with the Wheelwright faction and had subsequently moved with Wheelwright to Exeter. The exact date of his reinstatement in the Roxbury church is not recorded, but in September 1642 he transferred his membership to the Boston church. See Charles H. Bell, *History of the Town of Exeter, New Hampshire* (Exeter, N.H., 1888), 21–22; Battis, *Saints and Sectaries,* 304; Savage, *Genealogical Dictionary,* I, 439.

51. That is, shortness of temper, emotional volatility.

52. 1 Tim. 5:21: I charge thee before God, and the Lord Jesus, and the elect angels, that thou observe these things without preferring one before another, doing nothing by partiality.

53. Mildew.

54. or: Cotton or his scribe probably meant to write but.

55. Matt. 13:24, 25: Another parable put he forth unto them, saying, The kingdom of heaven

is likened unto a man which sowed good seed in his field: But while men slept, his enemy came and sowed tares among the wheat, and went his way.

Cotton used this parable when he spoke publicly about his deception by church members. Cotton Mather tells of Cotton's emotional self-accusations: "When he perceived the advantage, which erroneous and heretical persons in his church, had from his abused charity, taken to spread their dangerous opinions, before he was *aware* of them, he did publickly sometimes with *tears* bewail it, *That the enemy had sown so many tares whilst he had been asleep.*" Mather, *Magnalia,* I, 245.

56. Here about two inches of the left side of the page are either entirely worn away or especially badly stained, mildewed, and mutilated, affecting parts of some thirteen lines in the manuscript.

57. He paraphrases Isa. 42:19a: Who is blind, but my servant? or deaf, as my messenger that I sent?

58. He quotes Job 29:15: I was eyes to the blind, and feet was I to the lame.

59. That is, precedent?

60. Here Cotton wrote you you.

John Wheelwright to John Cotton

June 3, 1640

ALS. MS: BPL, Ms. Am. 1506, pt. 2, no. 19

Wheelwright's reply to Cotton selectively takes up certain of Cotton's points, arguing about what he did and did not say in his notorious Fast Day sermon on January 19, 1637, with particular attention to the question whether the General Court convicted him for his "doctrine" or for his "application." He contends that his application, or "use," was relatively harmless and that he was (improperly) expelled for his doctrine, that is, his beliefs. Here he summarizes what he believes was the essential message of his application(s) in the sermon preached three and a half years earlier. He preached four applications, or uses, in that sermon. The longest, a "use of exhortation," is subdivided into two separate exhortations. His letter sometimes quotes the uses almost verbatim, but condenses a very long sequence, some of it certainly inflammatory, into just a few brief sentences.[1]

The letter is written on two sides of a single sheet. Two inches of the top of the page are mostly torn away. The page is also water-stained, frayed at the bottom (affecting the text only on the recto), and part of the left edge is worn away (affecting the text only on the right edge of the verso). The following reading starts on the third line, near the right margin.

The Boston Public Library's microfilm copy of the letter includes an address block in Wheelwright's hand on a separate slip of paper, probably clipped from what had been the envelope sheet:

To the Reverend his very louing
brother Mr Cotton Teacher
of the church of Boston
these Del*iver.*

[i]n my last, Ignoranc[e]|| a stor[k]|| flying, & roosting w*i*th the Cr[anes]|| Thoug[h ignorance] be one thing & innocency [another]||[a]n ignorant man be [inno]cent in some case.[2] If I had done || any evell, then ignorance would onel[y] excuse a tanto:[3] but ||s to be proued. Seeing I neither spake, nor did any thing w*hi*ch was not [o]f ||[T]he substance good, mine ignorance of their purpose to abuse it to Con[tempt of] Authority or seditio*n*[4] (if there was any such thing) sufficiently cleares me. ||[Com]parison of the storke & Crane (to my best app^re^hension) holds not. This flying & roosting ~~roosting~~ w*i*th them, must be a joyning w*i*th them in some vnlawfull action, w*hi*ch I did not.[5] If they did run in such a course as y*o*w speake of, then (blessed be the name of the Lord) I neither walked in their counsell nor stood in their way, nor sate in their seate.[6] Howsoever (say y*o*w) ciuil justice lookes more at the bulke of the action, then at the intentio*n* of the worker: they attend more to finis operis, then fini[s] operantis.[7] Repl[y]: This will easily be graunted: but it makes not against me. Let the bulke of the actio*n* be viewed, for w*hi*ch (y*o*w say) I am condemned & censure[d]: let the worke it selfe be duely examined: & if ciuil justice can finde any con[tempt] of Authority or seditio*n,* therein, or aymed at, I am much deceiued. The substance of mine applicatio*n*[8] (w*hi*ch y*o*w now of late account hæreticall, & seditious) is this; yee who hold forth the doctrine of free grace, especially such as I haue described, contend earnestly for the same in a spirituall man*n*er against all such as doe, or shall oppose ^it^ ~~the same~~, though y*o*w meete w*i*th as grieuous enemys to the trueth as were the Scribes, Pharisees, Herod, Pontius Pilate &c. And be sure [t]hat y*o*w so cary y*ou*r selves, as y*o*w giue no just occasion to any to suspect that y*o*w are Antinomians, & Libertines.[9] & w*i*thall take heed of all tumultuous, or seditious practises; but rather goe on in a way of suffering even v*n*to death: & be willing (being called therev*n*to) to be killed like sheepe, imitating the holy martyrs who loued not their liues v*n*to death. Rev: 12.11.[10] That this is the substance, (if not in expresse tearmes, yet in equivalent) may plainely be seene in my sermon. If here be any intrinsecall force, or efficacy to produce, beget[,] fome*n*t, heresy, [con]tempt of Authority or seditio*n,* let mine enemys judge. The examples of Paule & Job I doe not yet apprehend to be imp*er*tinently alledged, & alluded v*n*to. Paule saw no grounds why he in his case should depart w*i*thout an honourable Testimony of his in*n*ocency, & their injury: no more did I as the case stood w*i*th me. Indeed he obtained more at the magistrates hands, then I did. That was my misery, not my sin. Job being vnjustly

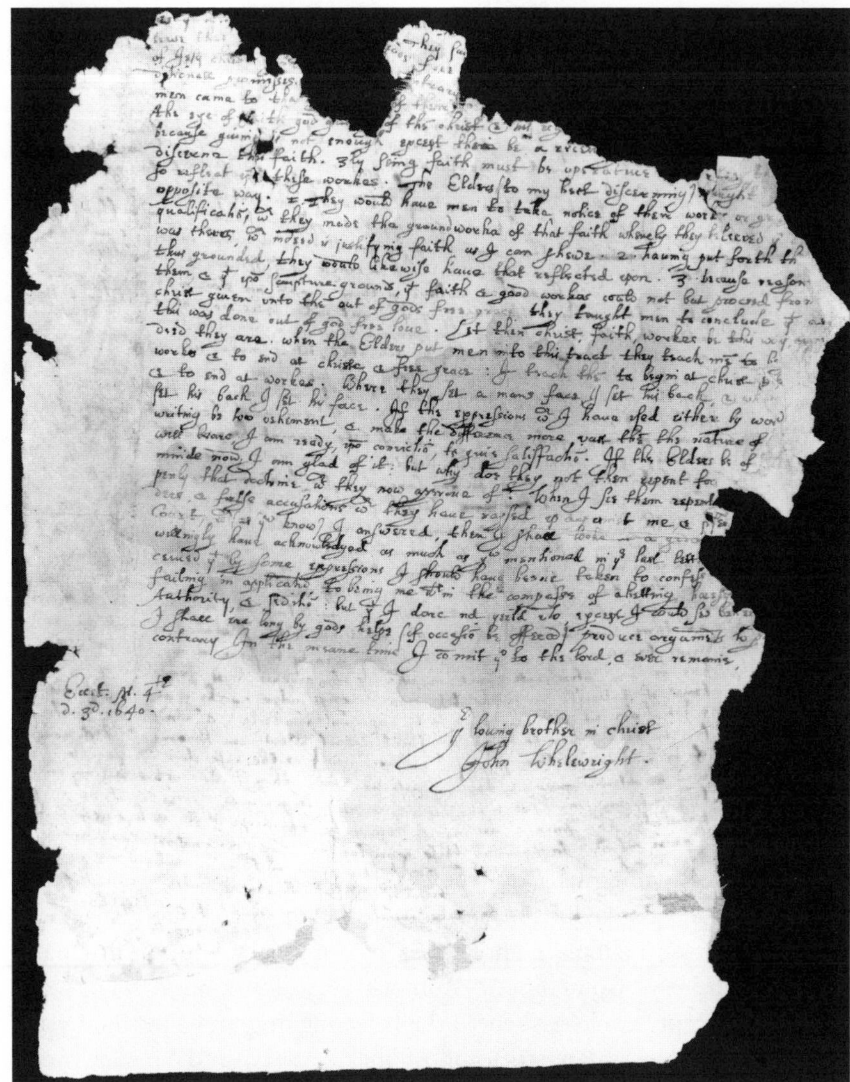

PLATE 13. John Wheelwright to Cotton, June 3, 1640, verso. *Boston Public Library, Ms. Am. 1506, pt. 2, no. 19. Courtesy of the Trustees of the Boston Public Library*

accused of grieuous crimes would not acknowledge the same: no more shall I by the helpe of god, as long as I liue[.] I never intended to parallel these examples in every circumstance (as yow con[ceive] the matter[)]. It is enough for me *tha*t they agree in that w*hi*ch makes to my pur[pose.] The carriage of the magistrates towards Mr Knolls, & my brother Samuel H[utch]inso[n][11] seemes yet to me to make my doct[r]ines the ground of my banishment[.] But [e]xcept we [had?] spake, face to face, I [know] n[ot] how things can be well cleared || should I [men]tion ~~why~~ as ju[dg]me*n*ts her||[m]a[g]istrates refusing to condemne me in Court befor[e] the Elders ||[conde]mned my doctrine. & to ||[ba]nishme*n*t || the Syn[od]|| with me about doctrin|| w*hi*ch y*o*w ||[12]

[iv]|| because giuing [i]s not enough except there[13] be a recei[uing]|| discerne this faith. 3ly seing faith must be operatiue || so reflect vp[on] these workes. The Elders (to my best discerning) taught [the] opposite way. 1. They would haue men to take notice of their works or gra[cious?] qualificatio*n*s, w*hi*ch they made the groundworke of that faith whereby they beleeved *tha*t [faith?] was theres, w*hi*ch indeed is justifying faith as I can shewe. 2. hauing put forth th|| thus grounded, they would likewise haue that reflected vpon. 3. be[c]ause reason || them, & *tha*t vpo*n* scripture grounds, *tha*t faith & good workes could not but proceed from christ giuen vnto the*m* out of gods free grace they taught men to conclude *tha*t a[ll] this was done out of god free loue. Let then christ, faith, workes be this way, as [in]deed they are. When the Elders put men into this tract they teach me*n* to beg[in at] workes & to end at christ & free grace: I teach the*m* to begin at christ & f[aith] & to end at workes. Where they set a mans face, I set his back, & whe[re they] set his back I set his face. If the expressions w*hi*ch I haue vsed either by word [or by] writing be too vehement, & make the difference more vast the*n* the nature of [the case] will beare, I am ready, vpo*n* convictio*n,* to giue satisfactio*n.* If the Elders be of || minde now, I am glad of it: but why doe they not then repent for||penly that doctrine w*hi*ch they now approue of? When I see them repent [of the slan]ders, & false accusations w*hi*ch they haue raysed vp against me & p*re*sen[ted to the] Court, which (as y*o*w know) I answered, then I shall looke at a grea|| willingly haue acknowledged as much as y*o*w mentioned in y*ou*r last lett[er]|| [con]cerned *tha*t by some expressions I should haue beene taken to confesse || failing in applicatio*n,* to bring me w*i*thin the compasse of abetting hæresy[, Contempt of] Authority, & seditio*n:* but *tha*t I dare not yeild v*n*to, except I could see bene|| I shall ere long by gods helpe (if occasio*n* be offered) produce argume*n*ts to pr[ove the] contrary. In the meane time I com*m*it y*o*w to the Lord, & ever remaine,

Y*ou*r louing brother in christ
John Whelewright.

Eccet.[14] M. 4th
d. 3d 1640.

1. The text of the sermon is in Hall, *Antinomian Controversy;* for the "application" section, see 156–172, esp. 157–169. The sermon was not published until the nineteenth century, but was preserved in manuscript copies, two of which survive to the present day in the Massachusetts Historical Society and the Massachusetts State Archives.

2. See Cotton to [Wheelwright], Apr. 18, 1640, n. 25.

3. a tanto: from so great [a charge], that is, reduce the severity of the offense.

4. The offenses of which Wheelwright had been accused and convicted. For a partial account of his trial, see [John Winthrop], *A Short Story of the Rise, Reign, and Ruin of the Antinomians, Familists, and Libertines . . .* (London, 1644), in Hall, *Antinomian Controversy,* 248–261, 282–300.

5. Here Wheelwright again uses the analogy to Aesop's fable, "The Farmer and the Stork." See Cotton to [Wheelwright], Apr. 18, 1640, n. 24.

6. Wheelwright is adapting Ps. 1:1: Blessed is the man that walketh not in the counsel of the ungodly, nor standeth in the way of sinners, nor sitteth in the seat of the scornful.

7. finis operis: the end (or purpose) of the deed; finis operantis: the end (or purpose) of the doer.

8. The "application," or "use," of his Fast Day sermon.

9. This point appears in his sermon (Hall, *Antinomian Controversy,* 168–169).

10. Rev. 12:11: And they overcame him by the blood of the Lamb, and by the word of their testimony; and they loved not their lives unto death.

See Wheelwright's sermon, which he is quoting (Hall, *Antinomian Controversy,* 166).

11. Samuel Hutchinson was the brother of Wheelwright's wife, Mary Hutchinson Wheelwright, and thus his brother-in-law. See Cotton to [Wheelwright], Apr. 18, 1640, n. 33.

12. The bottom two lines of the recto are here badly faded and mutilated, and the top of the verso is torn away. This text resumes, therefore, with the seventh line on the verso. The breaks in the text from here on are all caused by mutilation of the entire right edge of the verso.

13. Wheelwright first wrote their, then wrote re over the ir.

14. Exeter.

John Cotton to Francis Hutchinson

August 12, [1640]

ALS. MS: MSA, CCXL, Hutchinson Papers, I, fols. 35, 35a

Published: *Hutchinson Papers,* MHS, *Colls.,* 2d Ser., X (1823), 184–186

In L. Thompson, "Letters of John Cotton," 148–151

Francis Hutchinson was the sixth of Anne and William Hutchinson's fourteen children. When the Boston church, on March 15, 1638, voted to excommunicate his mother, Francis, then seventeen years old, loyally refused to join the rest of the church in their action.[1] In 1640 he remained with his parents in their exile at Aquidneck, though still a member of the Boston church. His letter of July 9, 1640, requesting dismissal, partially quoted at the beginning of Cotton's reply, appears to have been diplomatically phrased, if not scripturally compelling to the recipients. The church's refusal to grant his request, however, must have rankled. When he and his brother-in-law, William Collins, returned to Boston in the summer of 1641, they were jailed and fined.[2] On July 18, 1641, Francis was "Excommunicated out of the Church for sundry Errors," which included "giveing Revyling speeches against this our Church of Boston—Calling it a Whore, a Strympett."[3] So, although his attempt to cancel his membership began peaceably enough, it ended with more bad blood between the church and the Hutchinsons.

Robert Keayne, the Boston merchant and inveterate note-taker at church services and meetings, recorded the essential features of the discussion of Hutchinson's request for dismissal at the close of the service of July 20, 1640.[4] That discussion led directly to Cotton's reply to Hutchinson, which follows.

The manuscript is in Cotton's own hand and is nearly intact, excepting only the loss of small fragments of paper in the lower right margin of the recto. The missing letters are supplied within braces from the version printed from the Hutchinson Papers, except as otherwise noted.

Boston, this 12. of 6. /

To o*ur* beloved brother Frauncis Hutchinson at Acquethnick.

Beloved brother in o*ur* Lord Jesus,

Yo*ur* l*ett*ers of *th*e 9th of *th*e 5th: were read to *th*e Church the 19th of *th*e "same: In w*hi*ch you Desired to be Recom*m*ended to *th*e word of Gods Grace, "according to Acts. 20.32;[5] & so to be Dismissed from yo*ur* Coven*an*t w*it*h "vs, because you being forced to Attend vpon yo*ur* Parents there where you "live, you could not Attend vpon *th*e Duetyes of *th*e Covenant. But though wee finde the Church willing to gratify you in any lawfull motion, because they heare a good Report of yo*ur* Constancy in *th*e Trueth, & Faith of *th*e Gospell: yet ˆinˆ this motion they neyther can, nor dare Assent vnto you, as wanting warrant from Scripture-light. The Place w*hi*ch you quote doeth not suite w*it*h your Case. For in Acts 20.32: when Paul Com*m*ended the Elders of Ephesus to *th*e word of Gods Grace, It was not a Recom*m*endation or Dismission from One Church to another (much lesse from a Church to noe-Church, w*hi*ch is yo*ur* case:) but they being Elders of a Christian Church at Ephesus, Paul Com*m*ended theim to *th*e study of *th*e scriptures, & to *th*e Preaching of *th*e word of Grace, w*hi*ch was fitt (by *th*e Blessing of Christ) to build vp *th*em, & their Hearers, to Salvation. Were you gifted of God to Preach *th*e word to his People, or if there were Elders *tha*t could Preach *th*e same to you in a Church-estate (as they did at Ephesus) wee should readily Recom*m*end you vnto theim, & to *th*e word of Grace dispensed by *th*em. But wee ˆdareˆ not Recom*m*end you from a Church to noe Church. For the Covenant of *th*e Church is a perpetuall & everlasting Covenant Jer.50.5.[6] And therefore though wee may recom*m*end you from one Church to another, & {so} from one Covenant to another: yet wee cannot Recom*m*end you to noe Church, nor Dismisse you from o*ur* Covenant, till *th*e Lord Dismisse you. Doe not thinke *th*e Lord dismisseth you by yo*ur* Parents Authority, who call you to serve *th*em in a place so farre distant, *tha*t *th*e Duetyes of Church-

Covenant cannot be performed betweene vs & you. For first, yo*u*r Pare*nt*{s} deale sinfully, & bring vpon *the*mselves the guilt of yo*u*r Breach of Covenant, if they detayne you there needelesly: seeing the Covenant w*hi*ch you entred into w*i*th *th*e Church, was vndertaken w*i*th their Consent & D{esire} & therefore now it will stand in force before *th*e Lord both ag*ains*t *the*m {&} you, if you doe breake yo*u*r Coven*an*t, Num*bers* 30.4.[7] Secondly Distance of Place, though it hinder some Duetyes of Church-Fellowship, yet not all: wee may still be helpefull One to another, in Prayers, & Counsells, & o{thers.} And when Gods hand calleth to such Distance, He accepteth such Due{tyes} [IV] as wee can performe: & exacteth not such Duetyes, as wee cannot p*er*forme. Wee reade of some Proselytes & members of *th*e Church of *th*e Jewes at Hierusalem, who were scattered in a farre greater Distance, then you are from vs. For some dwelt in Parthia, some in Mesopotamia, some in Pontus & Asia, some in Phrygia, & Pamphylia, & others in many other Regions, Acts: 2.8, to ii.[8] And yet they still kept Coven*an*t & Com*m*union w*i*th *th*e Church of Israel.[9] As did also *th*e Eunuch of Aethyopia, who came when he could (though He could come very seldome) vp to Hierusalem for to worship, Acts. 8.27.[10] And Solomons Mariners *tha*t made a three-years voyage for Gold (i. kings. io.22.)[11] they were not dismissed from their Church-Covenant, by their farre Distance, & long Absence: but still continued as before: & wee doubt not, the Prayers of *th*e Church were not in vaine to make their voyages safe & prosperous.

But *tha*t w*hi*ch is *th*e sum*m*e of yo*u*r Request, so farre as ^it^ is lawfull, wee would be loath to neglect. Wee are Desirous to Recom*m*end you to *th*e Guidance & keeping of *th*e Grace of Christ in all o*u*r solemne Assemblyes: & if God will be pleased to give yo*u*r Father to hearken to o*u*r Counsell, to Remoove to any Orthodoxe, & Orderly Church, wee shall at yo*u*r Request, be willing to Recom*m*end you to *the*m: but further to goe, the Lord doeth not allow vs.

One thing wee thought good further to Acquaint you w*i*th, That o*u*r Teacher being thought by some to say, that you forbore sitting at Table w*i*th yo*u*r mother, though others deny it, & others remember it not, nor he himself: yet to be sure, *tha*t noe mistake might follow of it, He publiquely p*ro*fessed before *th*e face of *th*e Church, That if he so spake, it was his forgettfullness, but verely thinketh it was ^either his owne misplacing of his Intentions & words, or^ a mistake in *th*e Hearers, who a{pp}lyed what He spake in generall, to your particular Case. For in *th*e generall he said indeede, *tha*t w*i*th excom*m*unicate p*er*sons noe Religious Com*m*union is to be held, nor any civill familiar Com*m*union, as sitting at Table. But yet He did putt a Difference betweene other Brethren in Church-fellowship, & such as were ioyned in naturall, or civill neere Relations, as Parents & Children, Husband

& wife &c. God did allow *th*em *tha*t liberty, w*hi*ch He denyed others. Vpon his speach, the Offence *tha*t was conceyved by some was remooved: & wee hope, neyther doeth any Offence rest vpon you therefrom. To yo*u*r Father & self, & others of o*u*r brethren wee have written at large, to satisfy such Doubts, as wee vnderstand by o*u*r Messengers[12] have troubled *th*em.

The Lord watch over you all for good, & keepe you spotlesse, & blamelesse, faithfull & fruitfull to him to his heavenly kingdome in Christ Jesus. In whom wee rest, yo*u*r loving Brethren,

J. Cotton, with *th*e rest of *th*e Elders in *th*e Name of *th*e Church.

1. George E. Ellis, *Life of Anne Hutchinson,* in Jared Sparks, ed., *The Library of American Biography,* 2d Ser., VI (Boston, 1852), 345–346.

2. See Winthrop, *Journal,* 362.

3. *Records of the First Church,* 34.

4. Robert Keayne's notes, MS, MHS. Although he does not mention Francis Hutchinson's request, Larzer Ziff discusses other entries in Keayne's notebook that reflect the church's consistent thinking on the importance of maintaining one's covenant with the church. A request from Robert Harding for dismissal to Rhode Island just two months earlier was very similar to Hutchinson's and had also been denied. See Ziff, "The Social Bond of Church Covenant," *American Quarterly,* X (1958), 454–462.

5. Acts 20:32: And now brethren, I commend you to God, and to the word of his grace, which is able to build you up, and to give you an inheritance among all them which are sanctified.

Keayne's summary indicates Hutchinson's careful incorporation of the language of this verse into his request: "Francis Hutchison . . . desired, by a letter to the church *tha*t we would dismiss him to God & to the word of his Grace, seeing he knew of no church thear to be dismissed to" (Keayne's notes, MS, MHS). Ellis, *Life of Anne Hutchinson,* 338–340, includes a lengthy quotation from this section of Keayne's notebook.

6. Jer. 50:5: They shall ask the way to Zion with their faces thitherward, saying, Come, and let us join ourselves to the Lord in a perpetual covenant that shall not be forgotten.

7. Num. 30:3–4: If a woman also vow a vow unto the Lord, and bind herself by a bond, being in her father's house in her youth; And her father hear her vow, and her bond wherewith she hath bound her soul, and her father shall hold his peace at her: then all her vows shall stand, and every bond wherewith she hath bound her soul shall stand.

8. Acts 2:8–11: And how hear we every man in our tongue, wherein we were born? Parthians, and Medes, and Elamites, and the dwellers in Mesopotamia, and in Judæa, and Cappadocia, in Pontus, and Asia, Phrygia, and Pamphylia, in Egypt, and in the parts of Libya about Cyrene, and strangers of Rome, Jews and proselytes, Cretes and Arabians, we do hear them speak in our tongues the wonderful works of God.

9. The Hutchinson Papers transcription reads this word as Jews.

10. Acts 8:27: And he arose and went: and, behold, a man of Ethiopia, an eunuch of great authority under Candace queen of the Ethiopians, who had the charge of all her treasure, and had come to Jerusalem for to worship.

11. 1 Kings 10:22: For the king had at sea a navy of Tharshish with the navy of Hiram: once in three years came the navy of Tharshish, bringing gold, and silver, ivory, and apes, and peacocks.

12. In February 1640 the Boston church had sent Edward Gibbons, William Hibbins, and John Oliver to Rhode Island to talk with and counsel their fellow members there and also to talk with Mistress Hutchinson. Keayne's notes record the essential outlines of the messengers' report to the congregation on March 16, 1639/40. See Hall, *Antinomian Controversy,* 389–395.

John Cotton to [John] Elmeston

August 26, 1640

Copy. MS: BPL, Ms Am. 1506, pt. 2, no. 22

In L. Thompson, "Letters of John Cotton," 154–158

The parish registers of St. Dunstan's Church in Cranbrook, Kent, record the christenings of four children of a Mr. John Elmston, schoolmaster, between March 13, 1614, and April 11, 1619. On July 24, 1661, is recorded the burial of "John ELMESTONE of Cranbrook, Schoolmaster, s. of Thomas, Gent:"[1] This would appear to be Cotton's correspondent, for in the letter that follows, after addressing him as "Reverend & deare S*i*r" and comparing him to a church building stone that has been "layed asside" when other "sandy and vnstable stones" are being used to build the church, Cotton indicates that his correspondent has been forced to choose "Consenescere in pueris instituendis"—to grow old in teaching boys. Elmeston might have been or hoped to be a minister when Cotton was in England, but had to be content with a role as schoolteacher because of differences with church authorities. His association with Puritan activities in the Kentish weald is confirmed in a letter to Sir Edward Dering written on December 1, 1640, just four months after this letter to Cotton.[2] Cotton clearly sees Elmeston's enforced "silence" as yet another evidence of the corruption of the church under Charles I and Archbishop Laud.

Elmeston seems to have been aware of the issues that Cotton and others had been grappling with in New England in the late 1630s, judging from Cotton's reply to Elmeston's own expression of his opinions on the matter of the sequence of faith, justification, and evidences of them. Cotton seems gratified by his perception that he and Elmeston are in essential agreement on central points in this matter and expresses his delight in such discourse with his ancient friend, whom he now realizes he will not see again. Speaking of key issues in the recent controversy in New England—the relationship between faith, justification, and assurance of faith—he is comfortable again with making clear statements that tend to diminish differences between people who agree on the key issues. "Good divines," he says, can express minor differences in their understandings while still agreeing on the larger matter of the process of grace.[3] He has regained confidence in his ability to pronounce truth, and he does so more clearly here than in some of his earlier replies to his colleagues' questions.

The manuscript, although water-stained, is almost perfectly preserved. At the head of the page the address block is written in Cotton's own hand. The letter itself is in another hand; the scribe was the same one who copied out Cotton's letters of January 16 and August 7, 1641, to Peter Bulkeley and the letter of March 9, 1641/2 to Stephen Bachiler as well as other manuscripts of Cotton's from the same period.[4]

To Mr Elmeston of Crenbrooke in Kent: to be left in London
at *th*e House of Mr Joshua Foote[5] at *th*e signe of *th*e Cock in Gracious[6] street.
Reverend & deare S*ir*,

Yo*u*r old neighbo*u*r John Compton was restored to Fellowship with *th*e Church, before yo*u*r letter came into the Countrey. yet because you left it to my discretion, whether to deliver it to *th*e Elders of Rockesbury, or noe, I thought it best, it should be delivered to them: as tending to confirme their Act in Restoring him.[7]

For yo*u*r l*ette*re to me, It did much refresh me to reade *th*e Fellowship of yo*u*r love, & Prayers, & freedome of spirit in com*m*unicating yo*u*r Thoughts in so weighty a matter. In *th*e Substance of yo*u*r disco*u*rse, I see there is noe varyance between yo*u*r Thoughts & mine: & theref[ore] I will not spende time with any large disquisition about *th*e Particulars. For though you make "Faith *th*e First Evidence of a Justifyed estate, & give *th*e second Evidence to "*th*e Spirit: yet you Explaine yo*u*r selfe, you meane not *th*e spirit in *th*e first Gift "& worke thereof: but in some after-worke vpon the Receiving of *th*e Gos- "pell by Faith. And so you acknowledge two workes, & as it were sealings of "the spirit: one in Nature before Faith, sealing to o*u*r hearts *th*e Trueth of *th*e "Promise, & Gods good will to vs in it, *tha*t wee might beleive. The 2d, after "Faith to seale vs vp for Justifyed persones, & to confirme to vs an assurance "of o*u*r gratious estate. This doctrine I willingly embrace as sound, & Ortho- doxall: onely in this sense there are not two sealings, but many, three at least, the spirit of Adoption, the water of Sanctification, *th*e bloud of Attonement. "But when you demaund how *th*e spirit could be putt in his first worke for an "Evidence of a Justifyed estate, when as it goeth before the same, & serveth "to prepare vs for it? you may please to remember, There may be as Evident a demonstration of a thing from *th*e Cause a Priori, as an Evident Proofe of a thing from *th*e Effect a Posteriori.[8] And you know there be good Divines *tha*t speake of Faith as an Instrumentall Cause of o*u*r Justification, though others take it as a way & means of Justification: but both agree, It goeth be- fore Justification in order of Nature. And yet yo*u*r self graunt it to be a first

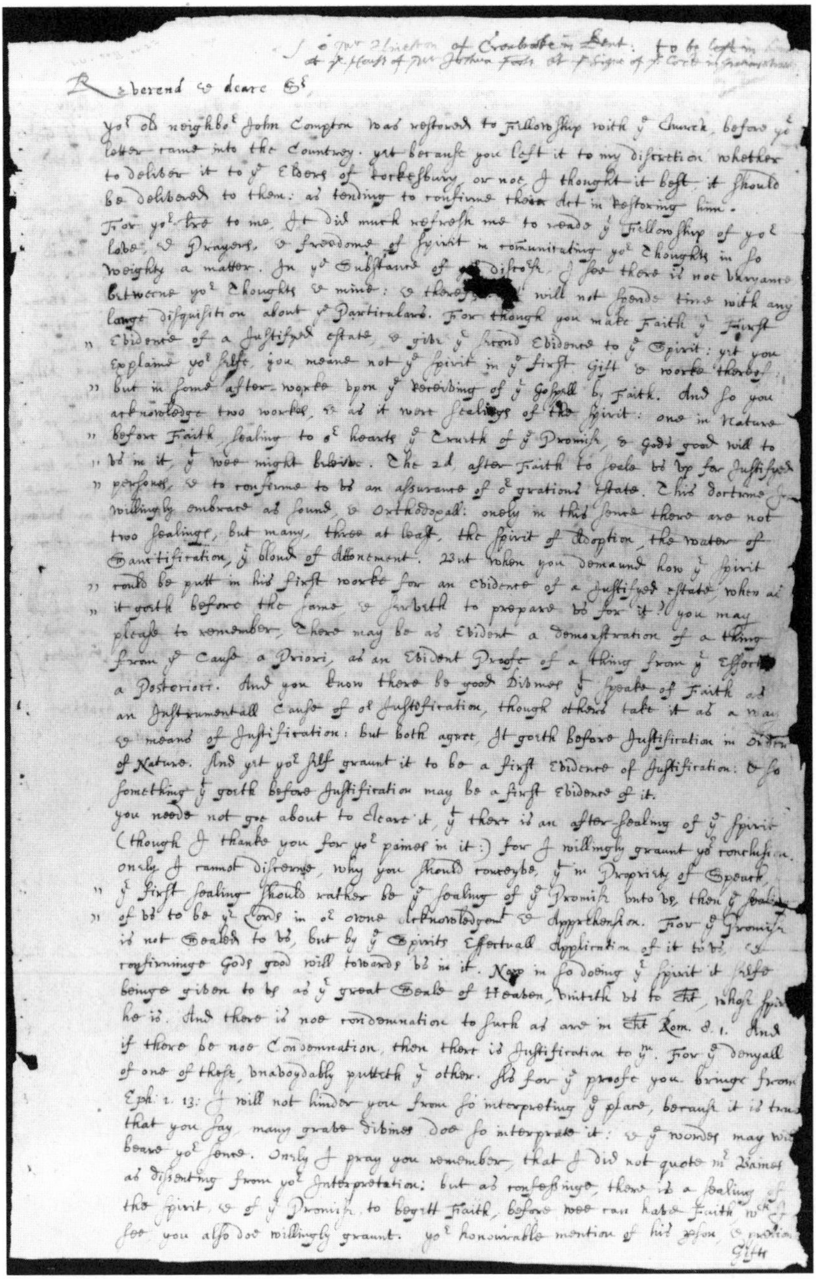

PLATE 14. Cotton to John Elmeston, August 26, 1640, recto only. This is a copy made by an amanuensis for Cotton's letter book. The same hand copied several letters and other documents for Cotton in the late 1630s and early 1640s. The address heading, however, is in Cotton's hand. *Boston Public Library Ms. Am. 1506, pt. 2, no. 22. Courtesy of the Trustees of the Boston Public Library*

Evidence of Justification: & so something *tha*t goeth before Justification may be a first Evidence of it.

you neede not goe about to cleare it, *tha*t there is an after-sealing of *th*e spirit (though I thanke you for yo*u*r paines in it:) for I willingly graunt yo*u*r "conclusion. onley I cannot discerne, why you should conceyve, *tha*t in Pro- "priety of Speach, *th*e first sealing should rather be *th*e sealing of *th*e Promise "vnto vs, then *th*e sealing of vs to be *th*e Lords in o*u*r owne Acknowledgem*en*t "& Apprehension. For *th*e Promise is not Sealed to vs, but by *th*e Spirits Effectuall Application of it to vs, & confirminge Gods good will towards vs in it. Now in so doeing *th*e spirit it selfe beinge given to vs as *th*e great Seale of Heaven, vniteth vs to Ch*ris*t, whose spir[it] he is. And there is noe condemnation to such as are in Ch*ris*t Rom. 8.1.[9] And if there be noe Condemnation, then there is Justification to *th*em. For *th*e denyall of one of these, vnavoydably putteth *th*e other. As for *th*e proofe you bringe from Eph: i.13:[10] I will not hinder you from so interpreting *th*e place, because it is true that you say, many grave divines doe so interprete[11] it: & *th*e wordes may wel[l] beare yo*u*r sence. Onely I pray you remember, that I did not quote Mr Baines[12] as dissenting from yo*u*r Interpretation: but as confessinge, there is a sealing of the spirit, & of *th*e Promise, to begett Faith, before wee can have Faith, w*hi*ch I see, you also doe willingly graunt.[13] Yo*u*r honourable mention of his p*er*son, & pretiou[s] [iv] Gifts, I reade with much delight: as one who doe willingly & deservedly sett *th*e same seale to yo*u*r Testimony, w*hi*ch you give of him. yea *th*e spirit of God himself hath sett his seale to him & his fruitfull conferences whilest he lived, & to his godly & iudicious labo*u*rs after his death.[14]

I could right heartily spend much time with you in this kinde of conference by l*ett*ere, since I see it is not *th*e good Pleasure of God to allow me yo*u*r sight & Conference face to face. It doeth much afflict me *tha*t such as you should be layed asside (as a Refus[ed] stone) by *th*e M*aste*r Builders, whilest many sandy & vnstable stones are th[rust i]nto *th*e Building of *th*e Churches of Ch*ris*t, & vpheld in them with all authority in Church & Com*m*on Wealth. But thus it was with *th*e choise Corner stone, the Head of *th*e Corner: wee loose nothing by conformity to him either in Grace, or sufferings. It is more acceptable to the Lord to teach Children with a Conscience voyde of offence, then to teach men, w*i*th Prostituting *th*e Conscience to vnwarrantable inventions of *th*e Sonnes of men. And yet even yo*u*r silence from teaching men in a way of publique ministery, Cryeth with a loude voyce, That there be such Corruptions in publique Administrations, as a tender Conscience would rather choose Consenescere in pueris instituendis,[15] & meane while suffer the Arke to shake & fall, then seeke to Support it by an vnlawfull hand. The Lord supporte yo*u*r spirit in all yo*u*r Employm*en*ts, & p*ro*sper them to *th*e best furtherance of yo*u*r Reckoning in Ch*ris*t Jesus.

It did refresh me to reade Mr Wilsons Name in yo*u*r l*ette*re, to whom I am so much beholding for his loving & Ch*ris*tian Intertaynm*ent*.[16] I knew not where he was, but now perceyving you may convey a l*ette*re to him, I purpose to send him one inclosed. Forgett me not (deare brethren) in yo*u*r earnest Prayers before *th*e Lord: wee cannot forgett you. So takeing leave, I rest

yo*u*r vnworthy, yet very loving freind & brother

John Cotton./

Boston. this 26. of 6. 1640./

1. For these facts I am indebted to Gerald Cousins of Cranbrook, Kent, the unofficial historian of Cranbrook, who generously shared relevant details of his research in county archives with me. Nicholas Tyacke also notes relevant details, including Elmeston's being licensed to teach at Cranbrook in 1612: *The Fortunes of English Puritanism, 1603–1640,* Friends of Dr. Williams's Library Lecture Series (London, 1989), 10–11.

2. E. Melling, ed., *Kent and the Civil War* . . . (Maidstone, 1960), 3–4. I am grateful to Gerald Cousins for calling this letter to my attention.

3. On the orthodox Protestant tenet that faith precedes justification, and different views on how to make use of this truth, see Stoever, *"A Faire and Easie Way to Heaven,"* chap. 7, esp. 130.

4. See "Provenance," above, esp. note 8.

5. Joshua Foote's address is elsewhere recorded as "at the Cocke in Grace church streete." Edward Everett Hale, ed. and trans., *Note-Book Kept by Thomas Lechford, Esq., Lawyer, in Boston, Massachusetts Bay, from June 27, 1638, to July 29, 1641,* American Antiquarian Society, *Transactions,* VII (1885), 437.

6. Cotton seems to have begun to write Grat, then corrected it to Gracious.

7. On Compton, see Cotton to [John Wheelwright], Apr. 18, 1640, n. 50.

8. a priori: from what precedes; a posteriori: from what follows after.

9. Rom. 8:1: There is therefore now no condemnation to them which are in Christ Jesus, who walk not after the flesh, but after the Spirit.

10. Eph. 1:13: In whom ye also trusted, after that ye heard the word of truth, the gospel of your salvation: in whom also after that ye believed, ye were sealed with that holy Spirit of promise.

11. In the same ink with which he wrote the address at the top of the recto, Cotton corrected interprate to interprete by overwriting the a.

12. Paul Baynes (d. 1617), a graduate and fellow of Christ's College, Cambridge (bachelor of arts, 1593/4; master's, 1597), was a prominent Puritan divine who became the successor to William Perkins in the lectureship at Great St. Andrews in Cambridge, until silenced for nonconformity. His thought was influential on many leading Puritans, and he is credited with converting Richard Sibbes, whose preaching in turn made a Puritan of Cotton. Ziff notes that "it was in this tradition"—that of Baynes and Sibbes—"rather than in that of William Perkins that [Cotton] taught" (*Career of John Cotton,* 41). Baynes had "frequently preached at Cranbrook," where his sister was married to Harman Sheafe (C. C. R. Pile, *Dissenting Congregations in Cranbrook,* Cranbrook and District Local History Society, Cranbrook Notes and Record no. 5 [n.p., 1953], 4), one of whose relatives, Jacob Sheafe, had emigrated from Cranbrook to Boston in the 1630s. I am grateful to Gerald Cousins for the reference to Jacob Sheafe; for more on the Sheafe-Baynes connection, see Patrick Collinson, "Cranbrook and the Fletchers: Popular and

Unpopular Religion in the Kentish Weald," in Collinson, *Godly People: Essays on English Protestantism and Puritanism* (London, 1983), 412. Cotton Mather credits Baynes with recommending Cotton's first wife, Elizabeth Horrocks, to him "to become his consort in a *married estate*" (*Magnalia,* I, 237). On Baynes / Baines, see also Samuel Clarke, *The Lives of Thirty-two English Divines,* 3d ed. (London, 1677), 22–24; Brook, *Lives of the Puritans,* II, 261–264; Venn, *Alumni Cantabrigienses,* I, 113; Tyacke, *The Fortunes of English Puritanism,* 8–12.

13. Cotton's argument throughout this paragraph turns on the importance of Christ's centrality to the believer's faith; Christ is always the object of one's faith and is at the heart of his covenant theology. He makes the point more directly in *The New Covenant* . . . (London, 1654): "Take heed you doe not close with promises before we have Jesus Christ in them: especially take heed you make not use of a promise to a gracious qualification, to give you your part in Christ" (103). On the importance of this idea to Cotton's covenant theology, see John S. Coolidge, *The Pauline Renaissance in England: Puritanism and the Bible* (Oxford, 1970), 131–138.

14. Baynes's published works appeared posthumously.

15. Consenescere in pueris instituendis: to grow old in teaching boys. Cotton appears to have corrected the scribe's insticuerdis to instituendis.

16. Probably Thomas Wilson (1601–1653), rector of Otham, Kent, from 1631 to 1634, then suspended by Laud and restored in 1640. See Venn, *Alumni Cantabrigienses,* IV, 432, and G. S[winnock], *The Life and Death of Mr. Tho. Wilson* (n.p., 1672). He is also mentioned in a letter of December 1, 1640, from Elmeston to Sir Edward Dering, published in Melling, ed., *Kent and the Civil War,* 3–4. The "Intertainment" which Wilson afforded Cotton is matter for speculation, but it is possible that it was provided just before Cotton sailed from the Downs in the *Griffin* in early July 1633. Traveling from London to reach the seacoast on the Downs (between Dover and Folkestone on the Strait of Dover) one might well pass through Otham, which is adjacent to Maidstone, the county town.

Thomas Lechford to the Elders of the Boston Church

[September 9, 1640]

Published: Thomas Lechford, *Plain Dealing; or, Newes from New-England* . . . (London, 1642), 55; reissued as *New-Englands Advice to Old-England* . . . ([London], 1644), 55; MHS, *Colls.,* 3d Ser., III (1833), 107; Lechford, *Plain Dealing; or, News from New England,* ed. J. Hammond Trumbull (Boston, 1867), 128 (rpt. New York, 1970, with preface by Everett H. Emerson)

Thomas Lechford (d. 1642), a London lawyer, migrated to New England in June 1638, where he managed to put himself at odds with both church and civil officials fairly quickly. He was temporarily prevented from practicing law in New England in the fall of 1639 and also denied admission to the church of Boston. He returned to

England in 1641 and died the next year. As to the church's denial of membership to Lechford, Cotton later wrote in *The Way of Congregational Churches Cleared:*

> The book is unfitly called Plain dealing, which (in respect of many passages in it) might rather be called false and fraudulent. I forbear to speak of the man himself, because soon after the publishing of that book, himself was called away out of the world to give account of his book and whole life before the highest judge. He was indeed himself not received into the fellowship of the church, for his professed errors: as 1. that the Antichrist described in the Revelation was not yet come, nor any part of that prophecy yet fulfilled from the 4. chapter to the end.
>
> 2. That the apostolic function was not yet ceased: but that there still ought to be such, who should by their transcendent authority govern all churches.[1]

Lechford printed his letter only as a series of three questions, without including a salutation or signature block. The reply is likewise stripped of all but the direct answers to the questions, if it ever contained more. They are included here because, as Lechford's description of the deliveries indicates, they were clearly treated as personal communications. The text is that of the first edition.

Questions to the Elders of Boston, *delivered* 9. *Septemb.* 1640.

1. Whether a people may gather themselves into a Church, without a Minister *sent* of God?

2. Whether any People, or Congregation, may *ordaine* their owne Officers?

3. Whether the Ordination, by the hands of such as are *not Ministers,* be good?

1. Cotton, *The Way of Congregational Churches Cleared* (1648), in Ziff, *Cotton on the Churches,* 264–265. Lechford wrote of some of his disagreements with the churches in the Bay in his shorthand notebook; see Edward Everett Hale, ed. and trans., *Note-Book Kept by Thomas Lechford, Esq., Lawyer, in Boston, Massachusetts Bay, from June 27, 1638, to July 29, 1641,* American Antiquarian Society, *Transactions,* VII (1885), 274–278. This notebook contains copies of all the legal documents Lechford wrote while in New England, noting fees received, including a letter of attorney for John Cotton dated October 30, 1638.

[John Cotton and John Wilson] to Thomas Lechford

September 9, 1640

Published: Thomas Lechford, *Plain Dealing; or, Newes from New-England* . . . (London, 1642), 55–56; reissued as *New-Englands Advice to Old-England* . . . ([London], 1644), 55–56; MHS, *Colls.,* 3d Ser., III (1833), 107–108; Lechford, *Plain Dealing; or, News from New England,* ed. J. Hammond Trumbull (Boston, 1867), 128 (rpt. New York, 1970, with preface by Everett H. Emerson)

Lechford introduces the reply to his questions: *To the which I received an Answer the same day.*

To the first, the Answer is affirmative; for though the people in this Countrey are not wont to gather themselves into a Church, but (as you would have it) with the presence and advice of sundry Ministers; yet it were lawfull for them to gather into a Church without them. For if it be the priviledge of every Church to choose their owne Ministers, then there may be a Church, before they have Ministers of their owne; for Ministers of another Church have no power but in their owne Church.

To the second and third; The second and third *Questions* are coincident, and one Answer may serve for both: The Children of *Israel* did impose hands upon the *Levites, Num.* 8. 10.[1] and if the people have power to elect their owne officers, they have power also to ordaine them; for Ordination is but an Installment of a man into that office, whereto election giveth him right, neverthelesse such a Church as hath a *Presbyterie,* ought to ordain their Officers by a *Presbyterie,* according to I *Tim.* 4.14.[2]

This Answer was brought me by Master Oliver, *one of the Elders, and Master* Pierce, *a Brother of* Boston.[3]

1. Num. 8:10: And thou shalt bring the Levites before the Lord: and the children of Israel shall put their hands upon the Levites.

2. 1 Tim. 4:14: Neglect not the gift that is in thee, which was given thee by prophecy, with the laying on of the hands of the presbytery.

3. Thomas Oliver was the ruling elder of the Boston congregation; Master Pierce was probably William Pierce, who had arrived on the *Griffin* with Cotton in 1633 and had been a freeman since 1634 (Savage, *Genealogical Dictionary,* III, 432; Anderson, *Great Migration,* 1472–1478). It seems most likely that a letter addressed "to the Elders of Boston" was answered by Wilson

and Cotton alone. Oliver, a layman, doubtless knew of the contents and might have signed the letter, but would have deferred to his ministers, the teaching elders, to answer Lechford's questions.

John Cotton to Members of the Boston Church Living at Aquidneck

September [20–26], 1640

MS. MHS, Robert Keayne's Sermon Notes (September 26, 1640)

Robert Keayne, a successful merchant and member of the Boston church, for many years took careful notes summarizing Cotton's sermons.[1] He also recorded discussions at occasional meetings of the congregation following the worship service. His notes for September 26, 1640, duly record in six pages the major points of Cotton's afternoon sermon on the ninth chapter of Luke, and then in four more pages report discussion of the ongoing issue of the members of the congregation who had left to establish the colony at Aquidneck (Rhode Island). Immediately following the sermon, Keayne recorded a speech by the pastor, John Wilson, that set the context for his congregation on that day:

> Yow haue herd this day what the estate of euery man by Nature is to wander & goe astray from the fold of ch*rist* & to be caried away w*i*th euery p*r*ufe of vayne doctrine, but such is the mercy of god to set vp officers to send out desiples to seek them vp agayne. & ch*rist* him selfe were a-fishing for soules w*hi*ch puts vs not owt of hope. for yow know bretheren, we haue some stray soules. these are gone from vs, some owt of Ignorance, others owt of pride & Arrogance. & haue forsaken the fold of ch*rist* & haue stoped thear eares agaynst the Counsell of ch*rist,* to the greife of thear Bretheren: for the church hath sent messengers to them & souch messages as might haue wonn & perswaded them. but they haue stoped thear eares, & hardened thear neckes. & some made one exscuse & some another to hinder thear returne to vs. Yow know thear hath bine much patience & lenitie vsed towards them, some vnder our censure & some vnder another, but because we know not what god may doe, or who may ^be^ called from them, god hath put it agayne into the hart of owr Teacher to giue an Answ*e*r to such scruples & obiections as thay haue made the Causes of thear hindrances from returninge to vs. That the whole church may be witnises of owr cares, & indeuors to gayne them & call them backe, or if thay shall obstinetly harden thear neckes, then to proceed to such farther Censures, as the church shalbe guided to, the writinge is directed to them all, *tha*t are not vnder the censure of the church.

This is then followed by Wilson's reading from the letter itself. At the end of his reading, Wilson remarked, "If these letters be such as yo*u*r harts goe always w*i*th & if the church consent we should send the Name of the Name of the church[2] for the recallinge of some of them; if yow be silent we shall take yo*u*r silence for consent. if yow consent not yow haue Libertie to express your selues."

John Wilson begins with a sentence that appears to paraphrase Cotton's summary of the departed members' "first objection," then proceeds to a reading of the letter. The irregularities of spelling and punctuation are, of course, Keayne's, who, transcribing the speaker's words in haste, often wrote a period where a comma was needed and often omitted periods altogether. His ambiguous marks are interpreted here as the sense requires. Missing periods are provided in brackets.

The first obiection w*hi*ch kepes them from vs, is thear scruple abowt church-couenant, & abowt owr breach of couenant w*i*th them.

Answ*er*. Thear is 2 Couenants. the Couenant of grace, & church Couenant,
Esa.56.7.6.[4] made w*i*th Moses, & renued in the playnes of Moab[.][3] is it possible
*tha*t yow cane beleue the church Couenant w*i*th the Jewes was a p*ar*t of
the Couenant of grace & yet the church-Couenant of the Gentiles is no
p*ar*t of the Couenant of Grace. it is manifest the church vnder the Gospell is called a spowse, a Bride, as well as the church vnder the Law. &
thear cane be no marriage w*i*thout a Couenant[.] when one Acan sined,
Esa.62.5[5] it was accounted the sine of the whole congregation becaus thay wear
in Couenant together.[6] therfor we hope that none of yow are entred
soe far into famelesme[7] as to thinke thear is no church-Couenant but
ch*rist*[.] but church Couenant is sacred & inviolable. it is a p*er*petuall
& euerlastinge Couenant not to be dissolued by any mans power: it is
a p*ar*t of the Couenant of grace.

obiect i church Couenant bindes one no farder than while I stay in the church.

Answ i Christians must not be nonresidents. euniches and prosolites, kept
1 King 10.22[8] couenants w*i*th the church & Sollimans marriners, though absent by
residence, & necessary absence as marriners, & once a year thay came
to Jerusalem to worship. the ch*urch* prayd for them, & kept comunion.

obiect 2[9] But distance of habitation hinders ~~man~~ all offices of church fellowship & watchinge ouer one another[.]

Answ*er* It doth hinder some offices of ouersight but not all for captiues & ~~chu~~ marriners may kepe church Couenant as Israell did[.] thear wear captiues in Babilon the church cane pray for them, & send to them though presence wear mor desirable or to requier a lawfull dismission ~~if~~ to some other church, if thear be a necessitie of absence. & not to rend your selues from the church[.]

obiect.3 Our parents & wiues are cast owt of thear church & thear necessetie requiers owr presence to supply to thear wants.

Answer The Couenant of ch*rist* & the church is to be prefered before owr Couenant w*i*th owr wiues or Parents. Therfor if Parents haue giuen vp[10] thear children to the church how cane thay rend them away from the Couenant of the church, an Euer-lastinge Couenant canot be rent assunder by Temporall power, for owr Couenant is in Heauen.

obiect 4 But the Cowrt hath Censured vs & droue vs owt of the Country. & Mr Winthrop aduised vs to dep*ar*t.

Answ. Mr Winthrop affirmes, his aduice was not as Gouernor nor as the mowth of the Cowrt, but only in christian Loue to dep*ar*t for a time till thay could giue the ~~church~~ Cowrt satisfaction.

2 He Answers he did not aduise all to depart: for he perswaded Mr Coddington earnestly to stay, & to vndertake to make his peace w*i*th the Cowrt, nayther did the Cowrt banish or driue any away, but 2 Mr Aspinall & Mrs Huchison. Some wear vnder no offence at all w*i*th the Cowrt as owr brother Hazard[.][11]

obiect 5 persicution dissipateth the church. & soe it hath done vs.

Answ Persecution doth not allwayes dissipat & dissolue churches, but scatters them[.] then the Couenant can not be dissolued. but the church in Boston is not dissipated. Therfor yow are not loosed from the Couenant of the church[.]

obiect.6. All the sts[12] in the world make but one church: & therfor thear is but one couenant[.]

Answer All the sts doe make vp mor than one vissible p*ar*ticular church, if all sts made but one church than the officers of one church had power ouer another & than how cane the church meete all together in one place as the Apostell speakes[?]

obiect 7 Sayth one I am freed, from the Couenant of the church because of the churches breach of Couenant first in that some of the church had a hand in owr Brother Whelewrights Censure & Banishment, & the church hath not delt w*i*th those members for it[.]

Answ 1 If the church should breake Couenant w*i*th yow, yet that doth not loose the Couenant betweene the church and yow.

2 Though some of the members of the church had a hand in his Censure & Banishment yet it followes not that the church should deale w*i*th them when he suffred justly for his errors, & his misplyinge of his doctrine, to rayse vp much trouble & Comotion to the greate distraction, both of church & Comonwealth. therfor We canot yet see that the church hath violated thear Couenant w*i*th yow: or dissolued yo*ur* Couenant w*i*th ~~them~~ vs: therfor Bretheren, doe not walke like lambes

in a large place but returne *tha*t we may watch ouer you. for we seeke not yo*u*rs, but yow: & your good & peace[.]

I am grateful to Michael P. Winship for calling this letter to my attention.

1. Some of these have been transcribed in Helle M. Alpert, "Robert Keayne: Notes of Sermons by John Cotton and Proceedings of the First Church of Boston from 23 November 1639 to 1 June 1640" (Ph.D. diss., Tufts University, 1974).

2. Here Keayne inadvertently repeats "the Name of."

3. See Deut. 2:1–3, 29:1.

4. Isa. 56:6, 7: Also, the sons of the stranger, that join themselves to the Lord, to serve him, and to love the name of the Lord, to be his servants, every one that keepeth the sabbath from polluting it, and taketh hold of my covenant; Even them will I bring to my holy mountain, and make them joyful in my house of prayer: their burnt offerings and their sacrifices shall be accepted upon mine altar; for mine house shall be called an house of prayer for all people.

5. Isa. 62:5: For as a young man marrieth a virgin, so shall thy sons marry thee: and as the bridegroom rejoiceth over the bride, so shall thy God rejoice over thee.

6. For the story of Achan's sin, see Josh. 7.

7. That is, Familism.

8. 1 Kings 10:22: For the king had at sea a navy of Tharshish with the navy of Hiram: once in three years came the navy of Tharshish, bringing gold, and silver, ivory, and apes, and peacocks.

9. Keayne mistakenly wrote obiect i.

10. Keayne inadvertently left a semicolon in the middle of the phrase: "giuen; vp."

11. Thomas Hazard, a ship's carpenter, had arrived in Massachusetts Bay in 1636 and became enfranchised and joined the church in 1636. Battis, *Saints and Sectaries,* 319, 324, 336.

12. That is, saints.

Peter Bulkeley to John Cotton

December 17, 1640

MS. BPL, Ms. Am. 1506, pt. 2, no. 23

This letter is closely related to the two that follow, Bulkeley's letter of January 4, 1640/1, and Cotton's reply of January 16, 1640/1. These three letters and at least one other to which Cotton refers ("I have now received a 3[d] l*ette*re from [you]") deal with a common topic, the Covenants of Works and Grace. As earlier letters have shown, this topic was at the heart of the Antinomian controversy. That episode had piqued Bulkeley's deeper interest in the subject. He preached on the covenants at some length, finally producing his only book, the major treatise from his generation of New Englanders on the subject, *The Gospel-Covenant; or, The Covenant of Grace Opened* . . . (London, 1646; 2d ed., 1651). In his epistle "To the Christian Reader," Bulkeley gives an account of the slow germination of the book's manuscript. He remarks: "It is now some five or six yeares since I first began to handle this doctrine now published, a time then full of trouble in these American Churches. . . . The disputes about the two Covenants did then exceedingly trouble the minds of many, amongst whom there was little speech but about the covenant of grace and of workes" (1646, sig. A4v). When he wrote to Cotton in December and January of 1640/1, Bulkeley had probably already begun his sermon series on the Covenant of Grace,[1] but it is clear that he was still thinking through the ideas that would figure in his treatise. In these letters, he puts difficult questions on the subject to Cotton, hoping to benefit from the "light" "which god hath imp*ar*ted vnto yow."

This entire letter occupies one side of a single small sheet. Thomas Prince has written across the top of the sheet: "to the Rev. M[r] Joh[n] Cotton of Boston." The paper is torn and badly water-damaged in the upper left quadrant. Although it was written without paragraphing, Bulkeley left extra blank space between sentences where a paragraph break would have come. He seems to have been trying to squeeze the message onto one side of the sheet. The transcription has been aided and supplemented by reference to the microfilm copy made by the Boston Public Library and to the earlier negative photostat in the Massachusetts Historical Society. Further deterioration of the paper occurred between the creation of those photographic copies and the recent restoration of the manuscript. There are places in those copies, therefore, especially the Massachusetts Historical Society photostat, where material is legible that has subsequently crumbled away from the manuscript. In the following text, the passages supplied by these sources are in braces. Square brackets, as elsewhere, indicate editorial additions. Since there was already considerable damage to the paper before the photostat was made, however, there are still interruptions in the text due to holes in the paper.

Decemb. 17, 1640.
Reverend and beloved in *th*e L. Jesus.

[I] thanke you for yo*u*r last letter of newes fro*m th*e natiue cou[ntre]y || what was then wanting by ~~rea~~ reason of the interrup[tion] ||en hindred yow. Le{tt m}e alsoe {att} the [next o]pportunitye || the light from you {conc[ernin]g *th*e [time]} when g[o]d made the co[vent of wor]kes w*i*th Adam. Whether in his creati[on] or aft[erwar]ds. {I}f on[ely afterwar]des there is some difficultye. If we say it was made w*i*th him [in] creation, he being {sealed} vnder that couent (as {some speake}) {th[en] the} making of *tha*t couent must be referred rather to [the] worke of crea{tio}n then of prouid[ence] as it is distinguished ag*ains*t creation. but it is vsually referred to pr{oviden}ce{.} *er*go[2] {[n]ott} in creation. againe if it were in creation [th]en ther[e] could be noe [deleted word] act of Adams will in accepting the couenant{,} or in entr{ing in[to a] c]ouent} w*i*th god, w*hi*ch act seemes necessary to the being of that {couent.}

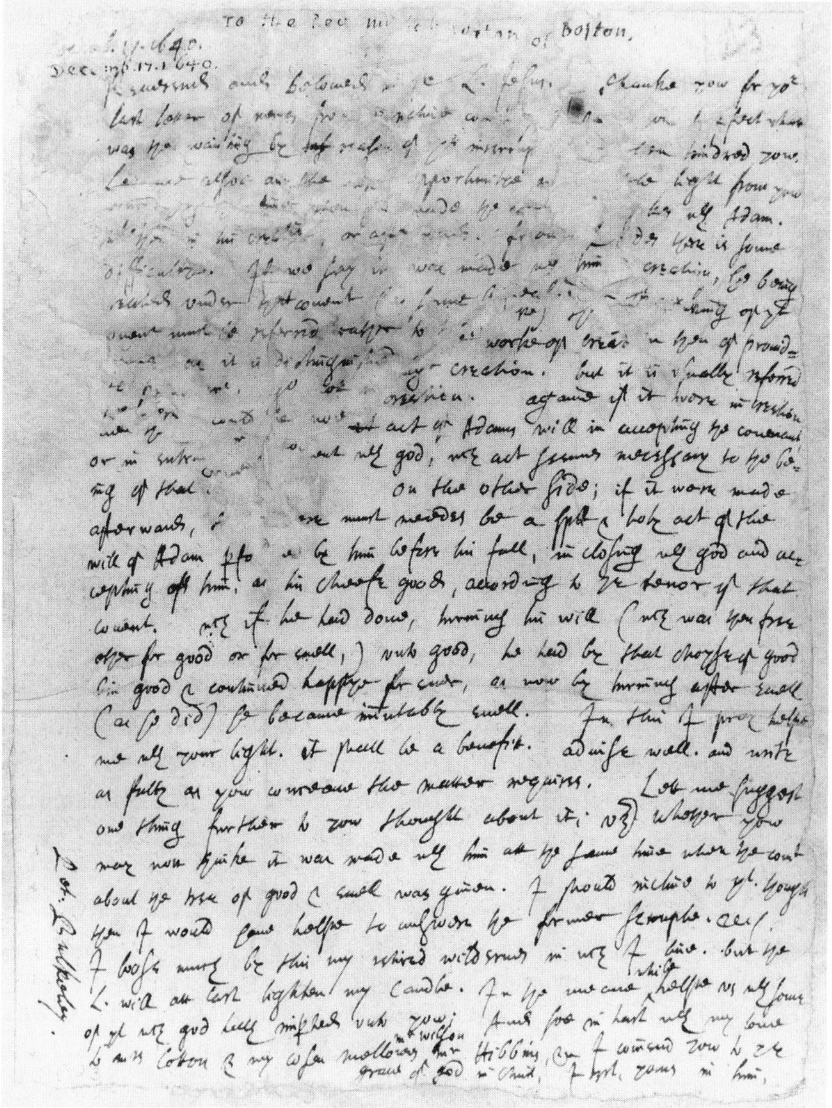

PLATE 15. Peter Bulkeley to Cotton, December 17, 1640. Characteristically for Bulkeley, the letter is squeezed onto a relatively small sheet of paper (7¾″ x 6″) so that it could be folded and addressed on the verso. Bulkeley seems to have been particularly conscious of paper conservation. The blurred script in the upper left hand quadrant is due to water damage. *Boston Public Library, Ms. Am. 1506, pt. 2, no. 23. Courtesy of the Trustees of the Boston Public Library*

On the other side; if it were made afterwards, t[hen th]ere must needes be a sp*iritua*l & holy act of the will of Adam p*er*fo[r]med by him before his fall, in closing w*i*th god and accepting of him, as his cheefe good, according to the tenor of that couent. w*hi*ch if he had done, turning his will (w*hi*ch was then free ether for good or for euell,) vnto good, he had by that choyse of good bin good & continued happye for euer, as now by turning after euell (as he did) he became im*m*utably euell. In this I pray helpe me w*i*th your light. it shall be a benefitt. aduise well. and write as fully as yow conceaue the matter requires.

Lett me suggest one thing further to yow thought about it; viz. whether yow may nott thinke it was made w*i*th him att the same time when the com*mandmen*t about the tree of good & euell was giuen. I should incline to *tha*t. though then I would haue helpe to answer the former scruple. &c/.

I loose much by this my retired wildernes in w*hi*ch I liue. but the L*ord* will att last lighten my Candle. In the meane ^while^ helpe vs w*i*th some of *tha*t w*hi*ch god hath imp*ar*ted vnto yow; And soe in hast w*i*th my loue to Mrs Cotton & my cosen Mellowes[3] ^Mr Wilson^[4] Mr Hibbins,[5] & I com*m*end yow to the grace of god in Christ, I rest, yours in him,

Pet: Bulkeley.[6]

1. As Michael McGiffert notes, Bulkeley's comments on chronology place the beginning of these sermons "near the close of the first decade of Puritan settlement in the Massachusetts Bay Colony," that is, the late 1630s. See McGiffert, "The Problem of the Covenant in Puritan Thought: Peter Bulkeley's *Gospel-Covenant,*" *NEHGR,* CXXX (1976), 107.

2. Bulkeley frequently wrote g° to abbreviate ergo, the Latin word for therefore.

3. Edward Mellowes (1610–1650), the second son of Abraham Mellowes and Martha Bulkeley Mellowes, Peter Bulkeley's sister. Abraham and his older son, Oliver, had died in New England in 1639 and 1638, respectively. Edward Mellowes was thus actually Bulkeley's nephew, but the term "cosen" was used generally for various relations. In a later letter, Bulkeley addressed Edward's widow, Hannah, and her two surviving children as his "Loving cosens." Donald Lines Jacobus, *The Bulkeley Genealogy* . . . (New Haven, Conn., 1933), 24–27.

4. The Reverend John Wilson, Cotton's colleague at the Boston church.

5. William Hibbins, who had arrived in Boston just two years earlier, in late 1638, became a selectman in December 1639 and a freeman in May 1640. He later served as a justice of the peace (1643–1649).

6. Signed along the lower left margin for lack of space at the bottom of the sheet.

Peter Bulkeley to John Cotton

January 4, 1640/1

ALS. BPL, Ms. Am. 1506, pt. 3, no. 1

The manuscript of this letter is severely mutilated. Two large holes and several smaller ones remove significant amounts of text, and the paper is water-damaged and stained throughout. Bulkeley's ink is relatively light in color, adding to the problem. Yet the gist of the letter's further queries to Cotton on the matter of the covenants is discernible. The braces indicate material that is legible on the microfilm copy but no longer present in the manuscript.

The letter occupies the right-hand half of the recto. The opposite half of the recto contains Bulkeley's address block:

> To the revere[nd]||[ve]ry [lov]ing/
> frend M^r C[otton, Tea]cher of/
> *th*e Church in [Boston,] giue/
> these.

Most of Bulkeley's seal remains on the address sheet.

Reverend & [beloved in the] Lord Jesus, I wrote to yow about a month agoe, concerni[ng the] time of god making the couent of [works] w*i*th Ada*m*. desiring your th[ou]ghts about *tha*t poynt.[1] I hope you haue now read that. soe as I will spare ˆnowˆ to wri[te] whatt I then [pro]pounded. onely I shall adde a word of my bed-thoughts w*hi*ch I [ha]d about it this morning, before it was day. viz. *tha*t whereas I p[ro]pounded then this (as to me most probable) namely that that couen[t] || he then made when the com*mandmen*t was giuen concerning the ~~making~~ ˆnottˆ [eating?]|| of the forbidden tree; [deleted word] the reason seemes probable he co||t. namely, that the couent was then made up, when the seale[s of the cou]ent were appoynted. but then were *th*e seales of the couent appo||ed in those two trees, g[ood &] evill as || *th*e couent of grace made [wi]th [deleted word][2] Abraha*m* when *th*e com*mandment*[?] was broken then was the seale of coven[t] appoyn[t]ed also. soe it seemes probable || in this alsoe.

T*hen* || are some doubts w*hi*ch yow expressed. one I propounded in || other now fro*m* my morning thoughts this morn*ing*[.]/ Th|| now naturall when[?] all the sonns of Adam may see[m]e to r||{that} w*hi*ch is from the verye beg|| as contracted w*i*th him ˆand soe is a morall to||ˆ but it is || all the sonns of

Adam to looke for righteousnes & life by work||{all to} co[ue]nt of works was na[t]urall[?] to Adam w|| created ||[3] {againe} the same a[s] my last, & fr|| if yow haue both, I pray lett me || (as by the next[?] occasion) yett noe sooner then till you haue || write as y[ow] desire. And soe in hast I com*m*end || your beloued & [lit]tle ones to the blessing of *th*e almightye,

Yours ever in {him,}
Pet. Bulkeley

Jan 4, 1640
Rem*em*ber
me to me to [M^r^] ~~Wilson~~
Mr Wilson,
Mr Hibbens

Besides; the law w*hi*ch is the sum*m*e of the couent of workes, was || in his creation. *er*go it may seeme the couent was then made ||[4]

1. Bulkeley to Cotton, Dec. 17, 1640.

2. Possibly: ~~Adam~~.

3. Six lines here are too severely mutilated to read.

4. This postscript is written in two lines along the left margin; about the final one-third of each line is lost.

John Cotton to Peter Bulkeley

January 16, 1640/1

Copy. MS: BPL, Ms. Am. 1506, pt. 3, no. 1a

In L. Thompson, "Letters of John Cotton," 159–161

Written in two columns on either side of a central fold on the verso of Bulkeley's letter of January 4, the ink in this manuscript is much darker than Bulkeley's, and it is generally more legible. It is written neatly but not in Cotton's hand, though it was read and corrected in minor details by Cotton, who also added a marginal footnote, all in his own hand and with a different ink—now a lighter brown. The scribe was the amanuensis of several other letters and documents from this period.[1] It is thus a copy made for Cotton's records, not the one sent to Bulkeley. The text is stained and frequently interrupted by holes in the paper, two of which are large. Though much of the text is thus lost, it is partially reclaimable because of copies and transcriptions preserved at various points in the troubled history of the manuscript but also because of Cotton's meticulous scholarly practice of giving a full citation for an extended Latin quotation. The latter quotation falls in a part of the page particularly mangled by holes, but the beginning reference to what he is quoting is fully preserved, enabling complete reconstruction of the missing quotation from the edition of the work he used. Also helpful for reclaiming smaller details, however, are the photostatic copy owned by the Massachusetts Historical Society and the somewhat later microfilm copy made by the Boston Public Library. Subsequently, small amounts of damage resulted in further loss of text that can now be reclaimed through the use of the earlier photographs. The following text is derived by treating the various versions of the manuscript as a kind of palimpsest. The gaps in the text are still substantial and thus frustrating to the reader, but this text represents the most complete version that exists. Details added from the photographic copies are included within braces. Square brackets indicate editorial additions, with one exception (see note 6).

Reverend & deare brother in ||s,

[I] have now received a 3d l*ett*ere from [you] whereto for want of a Bearer, I could returne noe A[n]swer till now. Now hearing || one G. Chaund[le]r[2] *tha*t one of Concord will call on him fro[m] Braintree on *th*e 2d day: I steale time from Sabbaths P*re*parations to p*re*pare an Answer ag*ains*t his com*m*ing.

I am g[lad that] God inclineth yo*u*r spirit to take paines in *tha*t noble & ||ll Com*m*on-place of *th*e Coven*an*ts: w*hi*ch *th*e more wee study [the] more[3] wee shall feare him: & *th*e more wee feare him[, the] more wee shall vnderstand his seacret Counsell in them.[4] Psal: [2]5:14.[5] Touching yo*u*r Quæstion, I am wholly of their {mind} *tha*t conceive *th*e Coven*an*t [of] workes God made with Ada[m] {cre}ating *th*e Imag of Go[d] in him. My Reason is, when God {gave} him *th*e Tables of *th*e Coven*an*t, then he made *th*e Coven*an*t || him. [By *th*e Tables of *th*e Coven*an*t I meane metonymical*ly* *th*e Articles of *th*e Coven*an*t writt in Tables.][6] But *th*e Tables of *th*e Coven*an*t he gave him, when he wrote *th*e Law of Holynesse & Righteousne[ss]e in his heart. whence also it is as you rightly note, *tha*t al[l] {his p}oste{rity} are borne vnder *th*e Co[v]en*an*t, it being ||ed. || Law {is} [wr]itten in their hearts, even {whe}n *th*e soul {is} || to their B[o]dyes ||

" The 1. ob*jection* y[o]u putt, Then *th*e Doctri{ne of the Couent} belonge[s] to "Creation, not to Providence: w|| {sundry Divines} referr{e}|| it to Providence;

It Receiveth this Answer, The {E}xplicite Re{newall of *th*e} Coven*an*t of workes, belongeth to P*ro*[v]idence, but not *th*e {first} striking of it. If it be said, Then *th*e Coven*an*t of workes {is} more auntient then *th*e Cov[enant] of Grace. I Answer it {foll}[ow]eth not: For *th*e p*ro*mise of æternal life was given before [the wo]rld begann*e*, Tit.1.2.[7] And t{here}fore *th*e Coven*an*t [o]f Grace [by w]*hi*{ch *tha*t} p*ro*mise [wa]s made was s{trucke} betweene God {the} Fath[er] [2] & *th*e Lord Jesus Ch*ris*t (the mediato*u*r of *tha*t Coven*an*t) before *th*e world began*ne*.[8] The Coven*an*t of workes came after to Præpare *th*e way for *th*e manifestation of *th*e Coven*an*t of Grace, by *th*e Trans||sion of *th*e Coven*an*t of workes, Gen: 3.15.[9]

" Yo*ur* 2d ob*jection* That *the*n noe Act of Adams will passed in *th*e Acceptance "of this Coven*ant*, w*hi*ch Act seemeth necessary to *th*e be{ing o}f it:

It Admitteth this Answer from Junius in his [Thes]es Theologicæ Thesi 25, de Fœderib*us* Di{vin}is sect. 4.[10] Fœdus (saith [Junius) s]ive Partu*m* dicimus, non p*ro*pr[ia] illâ sig[ni]ficatione qu[a pro] mu[tu]o [contractu] & duarum Patriu*m* disposit[ion]e semitur:[11] [(Nam eiusmodi foedu]s in[ter] partes, personarum, & juris æquali[tatem quandam] p*rae*supponit,[12] q[uae] inter Deu*m* et Creaturam nunquam [esse] potest[). Sed] eo sensû vsurp[am]us quo vnius tantùm partis Dis[positi]o denot[atur:] vt cum Bello vict[is] indicuntur Leges a victorib||.[13] The Reason he giveth is not pungent nor vrgent: but his Jud[gment][14] of *th*e point is sound & Orthodoxe. The Reasons yo*ur* self alledge are more weighty, If Adam had putt forth an explicite Act of his will ~~will~~ to choose to strike *tha*t Coven*an*t w*i*th God, [h]e had turned[15] himself to *th*e Im*m*utable good God, & had thereby become im*m*utably good.

Againe yo*ur* other Reason is of like weig{ht *tha*t} w*hi*ch is connaturall to all *th*e s{on}nes of Adam is noe le{ss to your} self.

" Yo*ur* 3[d] obiection, That *th*e Cove[nant] [wa]s [made] when *th*e seales of *th*e "covent were given, it is[16] iustly {de}||{d}. {God} struck a Coven*an*t of Grace with *th*e heart of Abraham, Gen: 12. 1, 2, 3:[17] {in} his effectuall calling, & Added a farther Revelation of his Justification to him, Gen. 15; 5, 6.[18] And both these by *th*e Coven*an*t of Grace. And yet *th*e Seale of *th*e Coven*an*t was not given, till Gen. 17[19] ++ If you concurre with me in Judgem*en*t, let me knowe: if not lend me yo*ur* Reasons in opposition.

In much hast I com*m*end m[ine] hearty love to you & yo*ur*s: br: Johnes[20] & his, with yo*ur* children & friend with you. The Lord dwell with you all in *th*e faithfulnesse of his gratious Coven*an*t in Ch*ris*t Jesus. In whom I rest

Yo*urs* heartily in him

Boston this 16 of 11. 1640. / J[ohn Co]tton. /

++For we may not thinke, *tha*t vocation or justification were eyther of *the*m given, but the Covenant of Grace.[21]

1. Other letters in the same hand: Cotton to Elmeston, Aug. 26, 1640; Cotton to Bulkeley, Aug. 7, 1641, [February 1641/2]; Cotton to Bachiler, Mar. 9, 1641/2.

2. Possibly William Chandler, who had settled in Roxbury in 1637 with his wife Annis and their four small children. I find no record of a G. Chandler in the colony at this time. Cotton's phrasing, "one G. Chaundler," suggests he did not know the man. There was also a John Chandler, a freeman of Concord at this time, but the context suggests that the man in question

lived closer to Cotton than to Bulkeley. In addition, there is a record of an Edmund Chandler and a Roger Chandler in Duxbury from as early as 1633. See George Chandler, *The Chandler Family* . . . (Boston, 1872), 1–3; Savage, *Genealogical Dictionary,* I, 357–359; Anderson, *Great Migration,* 326–332.

3. In restoration, small scraps of paper had to be reassembled. The *mo* and the *re,* which are on different scraps of paper, were separated as if they were parts of different words.

4. them is written over it in Cotton's hand.

5. Loss of paper has removed the 2 in 25; the passage cited is Ps. 25:14: The secret of the Lord is with them that fear him: and he will shew them his covenant.

6. The brackets around this sentence are Cotton's brackets. All other brackets in the letter are editorial.

7. Titus 1:2: In hope of eternal life, which God, that cannot lie, promised before the world began.

8. Bulkeley presents a similar argument and wording in his *Gospel-Covenant:* "The Covenant and promises of grace are built upon the unchangeable purpose of God, which is a foundation remaining sure, and cannot be shaken, 2 *Tim.* 2.19 and for this cause it is, that in *Tit.* 1.2. the Lord is said to have promised eternall life, before the world began; not that any promise could then be made to us in person; but because, first, God then purposed it in himselfe." *The Gospel-Covenant; or, The Covenant of Grace Opened . . . ,* 2d. ed. (London, 1651), 407–408.

9. Gen. 3:15: And I will put enmity between thee and the woman, and between thy seed and her seed; it shall bruise thy head, and thou shalt bruise his heel.

10. The following quotation falls in a badly mutilated section of the paper. The bracketed portions of the passage are supplied from the text that Cotton quotes: Franciscus Junius, *Opera theologica* (Geneva, 1613), cols. 2048–2049.

11. Cotton must have intended to write sumitur, as in Junius's text.

12. The n in p*rae*supponit was written as an r and subsequently written over with the n in a lighter ink. The comma following the word was also added in the same ink.

13. In his *Theses theologicae,* Junius's twenty-fifth thesis is entitled "De foederibvs et testamentis diuinis" ("On Divine Covenants and Testaments"). All his paragraphs are numbered. Cotton quotes most of paragraph 4 ("sect. 4"), which can be translated:

> We use "covenant" or "treaty" not in its proper sense, by which it is applied to a mutual contract and disposition of two parties (for such a covenant between parties presupposes a certain equality of persons and rights, which can never obtain between God and his creation), but in the sense by which is denoted the disposition of a single party, as when in war laws are imposed on the vanquished.

14. The Jud is written in a lighter ink. The rest of the word, which is lost, was probably part of this same correction.

15. The d in turned was added in a lighter ink.

16. The phrase it is is written over the word as in a lighter ink.

17. Gen. 12:1–3: Now the Lord had said unto Abram, Get thee out of thy country, and from thy kindred, and from thy father's house, unto a land that I will shew thee: And I will make of thee a great nation, and I will bless thee, and make thy name great; and thou shalt be a blessing: And I will bless them that bless thee, and curse him that curseth thee: and in thee shall all families of the earth be blessed.

18. Gen. 15:5–6: And he brought him forth abroad, and said, Look now toward heaven, and

tell the stars, if thou be able to number them: and he said unto him, So shall thy seed be. And he believed in the Lord; and he counted it to him for righteousness.

19. It is in Genesis 17 that God promises the ninety-year-old Abraham that he will give him a son by his wife Sarah. Gen. 17:4: As for me, behold, my covenant is with thee, and thou shalt be a father of many nations. Gen. 17:21: But my covenant will I establish with Isaac, which Sarah shall bear unto thee at this set time in the next year.

20. John Jones, Bulkeley's ministerial colleague at the Concord church.

21. Cotton's note, written vertically along the bottom two inches of left margin of page 2.

John Cotton to a "Dear Sister"

February 19, 1640/1

Tr. MS: MH, Ms. Am. 1165: Josiah Cotton, [Account of the Cotton Family], 26–29

Josiah Cotton (1680–1756), son of John Cotton, Jr., created a miscellaneous journal of Cotton family matters. The document was first written in 1727 and thereafter supplemented annually. In introducing the following letter he writes, "I shall finish this Part of my Narrative With some strokes of a Letter from my Grand-Father Cotton to one whom he calls Dear Sister that desired his Opinion about Childrens asking a Blessing of their Parents ^&c The Letter is dated from Bost*o*n 19. of 12: 1640.^" "Sister" designates a woman who is a fellow believer, probably a church member.

i. I doubt not (saith he) God hath given Power to Parents to bless Obedient Children for in Deuteron. 5:16.[1] the original Text Runs thus Hon*ou*r thy Father & Mother &c. that they may prolong thy Days, as if *th*e Lord were pleased to make Parents his stewards to Dispense a Blessing of long & many ~~&~~ and good Days to such Children as Hon*ou*r them, & without Controversy *th*e Less is blessed of *th*e Greater. Heb. 7. 7.[2]
.2 Neither do I doubt but as Parents may give a Blessing so Children may ask it—as Jacob & Esau asked Blessing of Isaac Gen: 27. 19, 30, 31, 34.[3]—& Joseph came with his two sons unto Jacob for *tha*t End. Gen: 48[4]—
[p. 27] 3. I find that Parents have Blessed their Children not only when themselves have been ready to leave the World, but when their Children have had some Journey or weighty Enterprize in hand & so were for a time to leave their Parents, as Jacob being to take a Journey & seek a Wife his Father sent him away with a Blessing Gen: 28. 1, 2, 3, 4.[5]
4. It may easily be believed that Godly Parents did daily Pray to God for a Blessing upon *thei*r Children, both in their Closet & Family Duties, though We never read *tha*t Children did daily Crave *th*e same at their Hands—
5. I dare not press it upon Children to ask Blessing of their Parents (Mornings

& Evenings) but only at such solemn times when either the Parents are about to leave their Children or Children about to leave their Parents, Whether by Death or Journeys; For hereof We find Patterns in scripture, & not of daily Practice. Nevertheless I think it comely that Children when they see their Parents [p. 28] first in a Morning, & last at Evening, they should then Express a more lowly Reverence to them (though in silence) then all *th*e Rest of *th*e Day as being times of more solemn salutation, & so I have seen it practised in the Family of *th*e Countess of Lincolne—

6. When Children do ask Blessing of their Parents at their Departure (whether by Death or Journeys) I would not advise Children to ask it upon their Knees —For—

1. I find no Pattern for that in scripture

2^{ly}. Kneeling to ask a Spiritual & Heavenly Blessing is not a Civil but a Religious Worship, and therefore Peter forbad it to Cornelius (Acts. 10. 25, 26).[6] As *tha*t w*hi*ch doth imply *tha*t Parents or other Super*iou*rs had a Power in their own hands to bestow such a Blessing, and that they who recieve it so prostrate stand & fall thereby at their Pleasure—But say you, subjects are wont to ask Favours & Pardons at Prince's hands upon their Bended Knees & no man scrupleth it. True, But that is in such a Case but Civil [p. 29] Worship, because they ask but Outward and Civil Fav*ou*rs and so I doubt not, a Child may ask (upon Commission of some great Faults) Pardon upon his Knees or some such like outward Fav*ou*r at his Parents Hands; But spiritual Blessings are not to be asked or Reciev*ed* at *th*e Hands of Men upon the Knee: which also maketh Kneeling to Recieve *th*e sacrament at *th*e Hands of the Minist*er* (as in Other Respects so in this) utterly unseasonable—

. . . .[7]

I do not think it unlawfull ~~upon any~~ (saith He)[8] upon any Weighty Occasion to Preach *th*e Word, but yet I cannot say it is as ~~well~~ well Expedient as lawfull &c—

1. Deut. 5:16: Honour thy father and thy mother, as the Lord thy God hath commanded thee; that thy days may be prolonged, and that it may go well with thee, in the land which the Lord thy God giveth thee.

2. Heb. 7:7: And without all contradiction the less is blessed of the better.

3. Gen. 27:19, 30, 31, 34 (Josiah first wrote 19, 31, 32, 34, then corrected 31 to 30 and 32 to 31 by writing over the second digit in each case): And Jacob said unto his father, I am Esau thy firstborn; I have done according as thou badest me: arise, I pray thee, sit and eat of my venison, that my soul may bless me.

And it came to pass, as soon as Isaac had made an end of blessing Jacob, and Jacob was yet scarce gone out from the presence of Isaac his father, that Esau his brother came in from his hunting. And he also had made savoury meat, and brought it unto his father, and said unto his father, Let my father arise, and eat of his son's venison, that thy soul may bless me.

And when Esau heard the words of his father, he cried with a great and exceding bitter cry, and said unto his father, Bless me, even me also, O my father.

4. Gen. 48 tells of Joseph's visit to Jacob and of Jacob's blessing on Joseph's sons.

5. Gen. 28:1–4: And Isaac called Jacob, and blessed him, and charged him, and said unto him, Thou shalt not take a wife of the daughters of Canaan. Arise, go to Padanarum, to the house of Bethuel thy mother's father; and take thee a wife from thence of the daughters of Laban thy mother's brother. And God Almighty bless thee, that thou mayest be a multitude of people: and give thee the blessing of Abraham, to thee, and to thy seed with thee; that thou mayest inherit the land wherein thou art a stranger, which God gave unto Abraham.

6. Acts 10:25, 26: And as Peter was coming in, Cornelius met him, and fell down at his feet, and worshipped him. But Peter took him up, saying, Stand up; I myself also am a man.

7. Josiah Cotton introduces the final sentence that he copied from this letter by saying: "In *th*e same Letter he answers another Question touching sermons at Marriages & Funerals."

8. saith He is written over upon any.

William Coddington to John Cotton

[March–April 1641]

Tr. MS: YBei, Ezra Stiles Papers, "Itineraries," fols. 6–8

Published: Dexter, *Extracts,* 370–372

William Coddington was among the most prominent of the Boston colonists banished in 1638. He went first to Portsmouth, then to Newport in 1639. His changing relationship with Cotton dated back to their friendship in England.[1] On March 23, 1640, the Boston church heard from the three messengers they had sent to the two settlements on the island of Aquidneck. Their mission was to talk with members of the Boston church "to understand their judgments in divers points of religion, formerly maintained by all, or divers of them, and to require them to give account to the church of their unwarrantable practice in communicating with excommunicated persons, etc." But "they refused to hear them as messengers of our church, or to receive the church's letters."[2] Two weeks later, on further consideration of the Boston church's relationship with its members at Newport, Pastor John Wilson said to the Boston congregation (as recorded by Robert Keayne): "Some have given Satisfaction in part to the church and doe hould them Selves still as members of the church, and doe yet harken to us and Seeke to give Satisfaction, and others thear be that doe renownce the power of the church, and doe refuse to hear the church, as mr Coddington mr Dyar and mr Cogshell." Possibly referring to letters from Cotton or others, he adds:

> The 2 first have bine qwestioned in the church and delt with and are under Admonition, and have bine Soe Longe, yet this act of the church hath bine Soe farr from doinge them any good, that thay are rather growen worse under the Same, for mr Coddington beinge delt with all abowt hearinge of excomuni-

> cat persons Prophecy, he was Sensable of an Evell in it, and Sayd he had not before Soe well Considerd of it. Yet Since he hath not only heard Such by accident as befor, but both him Selfe and owr brother Diar, and mr Cogshell have gathered them Selves into church fellowship, not regardinge the Covenant that thay have made with this church, nayther have taken owr advise and Consent herin, nayther have thay regarded it, but thay have Joyned them Selves in fellowship with Some that are excomunicated.

Wilson believed their case looked hopeless, and in such a case "the Rule of Christ is playne" in "Cuttinge them of from us," yet he advised delay: "It is thought meete to forbare owr proseeding yet a little Longer agaynst them, and patientlye to wayte a while to See if yet thay will indeaver to give Satisfaction, if not we shall take a Seasonable time to proceed with them."[3]

A year later, when Coddington wrote to Cotton, these same issues remained unresolved. The letter is undated, but Stiles's chronological arrangement of his collection of documents places Coddington's letter to Cotton after reference to "Another entry Feb. 6" and before reference to a letter dated April 26, 1641. This sequence, together with the reference to William Baulston as "Left. Baulston," a rank acquired in March 1641, helps to date this letter in March or April 1641.

Stiles transcribed what he described as "Extracts from an antient MSS. in the Office of the Town-Clerk in Newport: w*hich* MS. consists of a Number of Letters of the first Gov. W*illia*m Coddington, in his own hand-Writing." Dexter's note suggests that "the manuscript was undoubtedly destroyed when Newport was taken by the British in 1776."[4] Happily, Stiles and Dexter retained Coddington's unique orthography, though Dexter did not include Coddington's deletions, as Stiles had. Coddington, unlike most of his contemporaries, used a period after virtually every contraction or abbreviation (thus, "togeather wth. yor. owne Judgment as in yor. Let^{r}. to M^{r}. Skelton. . . ."). Here the periods are dropped where contractions are expanded, but included where the abbreviation is retained, as in proper names.

To M^{r} Jo. Cotton of Boston

Worthy S*ir* I have received tow Let*te*rs from yow one by Lef^{t} Balston[5] the other by Mr Lamberton[6] w*ith* w*hi*ch Let*te*r I recaived 20^{s} & Mr Gould[7] hath ordered to be paid in the Baye other 20^{s} so that I have recaived the 2£ sent you for my Debt from Tho. Holder[8] for yo*u*r paynes & care ther in I returne yow thankes.

Toutching such matters w*hi*ch conserne the Churche yow forbeare as being informed yow should write in vayne. I say no more to it but this *tha*t I doe belive both yow & wee of one hand & other are informed more then is trew so that wee need to inquier if these Things be so before that wee recaive them. for the Let*te*r sent by the Ch~~urch~~ to the Brethren of Portesmouth I have had it some tyme beinge desirous to have it copyed out that I might at Lassuer consider of the Grounds of it w*hi*ch I have never ~~doun~~ donn but not had tyme serously to peruse it sence. Its a poynt I perceive much controverted amongest those that are godly amongest yo*u*rselves & in England. Mr Barnard hath written & Mr Bawle printed as I am informed A book called Observations agaienst Sep*ar*ation,[9] togeather w*i*th yo*u*r owne Judgment as in yo*u*r Let*te*r to Mr Skelton w*hi*ch remaynes w*i*th me is to be sene to the contrary* makes me to desire that yow would not be urgent in the pressing of the Consequence of yo*u*r Brethren[.] I could wish that more tyme wos spent in those mayne & fundamentall trewths that some tymes the lord did carey yow out to hould forth most clerely viz. *tha*t the l J C is the first sought for the first given the first revealed the first in every action. w*hi*ch is the substance of w*ha*t I yet belive unto this daye. & I hope is mentayned for teaching by yo*u*rselfe untill this daye, tho myselfe & wife[10] have w*i*th sad & greef of heart thought of *tha*t place in Esa. 28. 11. 12. 13.[11] when it hath ~~been~~ bene reported to us that Mr Cotton Now houlds forth things so darkely *tha*t if we had not knowne w*ha*t he had houlden forth before we knew not how to understand him. yow must shortly lay downe that earthly tabernacle & Com*m*end yo*u*r flock to god & the word of his Grace. Therefore the desire of yo*u*r pore neclected reiected frend is *tha*t yow meet do it w*i*th Joye & not w*i*th sorowe, the Spirit be as fyre in yo*u*r bonne, *tha*t yow could not ~~with~~ w*i*thhould *tha*t yow meet shyne as the sonne to the perfect day. So yo*u*r last dayes might be yo*u*r best. but I must not vexte an Elder but exhort as a faither w*hi*ch I desire maye be so imbr d[12] w*i*th love & tendernes as its intended by mee[.] Optunety of speech is now bared & let*te*r some tymes unseasonably devolayed & the sence wrested *tha*t for my owne p*ar*te I am resolved to be silent but thus far have I written to yow At this tyme to yo and w*ha*t I intended when I set pen to pap*er* thus w*i*th the remembrance of my owne & Wife love, & endeared affection to yow & yo*u*rs & all *tha*t remember us I rest yo*u*r neclected reiected afflicted frind

Wm Coddington.

*then Mr Skelton did not well not to recaive to lords Sup*per* & o*u*r children to Baptizme, seeing we had recaived the holy ghost[13] then my recaiveing to p*ar*take of the Ordenances ~~never *the* lesse~~ was well donn by onely makeing A p*ro*feshon of my fayth ~~w*hi*ch was all was required of me~~ (as I Pet 3. 21.)[14] & by that p*ro*feshon I did p*ar*take of the Ordenances At Boston & Now by yo*u*r Consent & others I am removed, wher I doe p*ar*take of all the Ordenances of God. (if yow have any thing againest me yow may be pleased to informe the Ch wherof I stand a member.)[15]

1. On Coddington, see Cotton to Pelham, Oct. 3, 1630, n. 4.

2. Winthrop, *Journal,* 321.

3. Helle M. Alpert, "Robert Keayne: Notes of Sermons by John Cotton and Proceedings of the First Church of Boston from 23 November 1639 to 1 June 1640" (Ph.D. diss., Tufts University, 1974), 277–279. See also Winthrop, *Journal,* 321, where another part of the report is quoted.

4. Dexter, *Extracts,* 368.

5. William Baulston had been licensed to keep a "house of intertainment" and to sell beer, wine, and food in Boston, but in the Antinomian episode was disfranchised, barred from office, and fined. He went to Aquidneck in 1638, as did Coddington. He became a sergeant and, in the election of March 16 and 17, 1641, was made a "Lieftenant" and was elected a magistrate and treasurer of Aquidneck. *Records of the Court of Assistants of the Colony of the Massachusetts Bay, 1630–1692* (Boston, 1904–1908), II, 68; Howard M. Chapin, *Documentary History of Rhode Island* (Providence, R.I., 1916–1919), II, 79, 107, 123.

6. George Lamberton was a prominent inhabitant of New Haven occasionally commissioned to conduct some business for the Massachusetts Bay Colony; see Winthrop, *Journal,* 479–480.

7. Probably Jeremiah Gould, who was in Rhode Island by 1638 and who was admitted as freeman at Aquidneck August 6, 1640. Chapin, *Documentary History,* II, 103.

8. In the years between 1640 and 1650 one Mr. Holder served "at the head" of a small group who separated from the church attended by Coddington to engage in worship practices that Ezra Stiles recognized as the beginnings of Quakerism in Rhode Island. Dexter, *Extracts,* 162.

9. Richard Bernard, *Christian Advertisements and Counsels of Peace, Also Disswasions from the Separatists Schisme, Commonly Called Brownisme* . . . (London, 1608); Bernard, *Plaine Evidences: The Church of England Is Apostolicall, the Seperation Schismaticall* . . . (London, 1610); John Ball, *A Friendly Triall of the Grounds Tending to Separation* . . . (London, 1640).

10. His second wife, Mary Moseley Coddington.

11. Isa. 28:11–13: For with stammering lips and another tongue will he speak to this people. To whom he said, This is the rest wherewith ye may cause the weary to rest; and this is the refreshing: yet they would not hear. But the word of the Lord was unto them precept upon precept, precept upon precept; line upon line, line upon line; here a little, and there a little; that they might go, and fall backward, and be broken, and snared, and taken.

12. Stiles wrote the text this way, probably reflecting the loss of a portion of the word in the manuscript he was transcribing. A possible reading: imbr[ace]d.

13. A reference to the refusal of Samuel Skelton to baptize the Coddingtons' baby in Salem in 1630. See Cotton to Skelton, Oct. 2, 1630.

14. 1 Pet. 3:21: The like figure whereunto even baptism doth also now save us (not the putting away of the filth of the flesh, but the answer of a good conscience toward God,) by the resurrection of Jesus Christ.

15. In Coddington's note, Stiles underlined "I am removed . . . of God." and "to informe . . . a member" and added his own note: "N.B. This shews that there was a Chh in Newport AD 1641 in which M[r] Coddington then partook of all the Ordinances of God."

John Cotton to Peter Bulkeley

August 7, 1641

Copy. MS: BPL, Ms. Am. 1506, pt. 3, no. 3

In L. Thompson, "Letters of John Cotton," 173–174

As with the exchange between the two in the preceding December and January, Bulkeley has again asked for Cotton's opinions on some questions relating to the process of grace. Here his interest is in the relationship between the nature of Christ's dual divinity and humanity and the process of grace for sinful believers. These are issues in which Bulkeley was increasingly interested as he prepared to write his book on the Covenant of Grace.[1]

Cotton suddenly stops his discussion of this matter, however, saying he is "knocked off" from his writing, meaning called away or otherwise prevented from continuing his work.[2] Here the high seriousness of Cotton's scholarly dedication meets the reality of a busy life. Whether the interruption is due to professional or to domestic duties he does not say. His familiarity with Bulkeley and his questions over the years have probably made it easier for Cotton to cut short his answer, which is, however brief, a highly efficient statement.

The letter is written on both sides of a half-sheet. The paper contains staining from water damage but is fully intact and legible. The heading, which replaces the usual salutation, is in Cotton's hand; the rest of the letter is not.

To Mr Bulkeley.

Touching yo*u*r Quæstion, I willingly goe along w*i*th *th*e Streame of o*u*r divines, who conceive both Active & Passive Righteousnesse of Ch*ris*t imputed to o*u*r Justification. This Reason leadeth me, That w*hi*ch is Pretium Redemptionis[3] is materia Justificationis:[4] [For pay a Ransome to Satisfy for o*u*r guilt, & to sett vs in a state of liberty, & wee are Justifyed & Absolved.][5]

But Ch*ris*t himself (whole Ch*ris*t, living & dying) is Pretium Redemptionis. [The *Δικαίωμα*[6] of *th*e Law is not Satisfyed, nor discharged, vnlesse perfect obedience be performed answerable to *th*e law, aswell as a perfect sacrifice offered.][7]

Therefore *th*e whole Righteousnesse of Ch*ris*t (his life & death) is materia Justificationis.

To *th*e Obiection you propound, *th*e Answer your self give is Sufficient: That as in *th*e infirmityes, w*hi*ch he tooke vpon him, he tooke those *tha*t are com*m*on & naturall, not personall, & yet by bearing *the*m he removed all: So in *th*e duetyes of Obedience required in *th*e law, though he performed not *th*e duetyes of all men in their personall relation, yet he performed *th*e ˆcom*m*onˆ duetyes of all, & so performed perfect obedience for all.

Besides it may be added (for ought I see) That as in performing *th*e duety of a [childe / servant / subject] he discharged all the Relations of Inferiority, either actually, or p*ro*portionally: So in discharge of *th*e three Offices of [Prophet, / Preist, / King] he discharged therein either actually or p*ro*portionally all Relations of Superiority.

[IV] But I am knocked off & may not enlarge my self. The lord enlarge himself in all aboundant goodnesse to yo*u*r self, wif & children, w*i*th o*u*r brother Johnes[8] & his with other freinds. So taking leave I rest,

yo*u*rs in him

Boston. this 7: of 6. 1641./

J.C.

1. In *The Gospel-Covenant; or, The Covenant of Grace Opened* . . . , 2d ed. (London, 1651), Bulkeley deals with the imputation of Christ's sacrifice to the believer (361–372) but does not use the language of "Active Righteousness" or "Passive Righteousness."

2. The *OED*'s second and third definitions of "knock off" give this meaning. A 1651 work of Gataker is quoted there, indicating a usage very close to Cotton's: "He returned . . . to his study, where he sat, unless suitors or some other affairs knocked him off."

3. Pretium Redemptionis: the price of redemption.

4. materia Justificationis: the material or stuff of justification.

5. Cotton's brackets.

6. *Δικαίωμα*: among its several possible meanings, this Greek word can be translated ordinance or decree, probably the intended meaning here. Cotton may be implying a reference to Rom. 2:26, where this Greek word is used in the same way: *τὰ δικαιώματα τοῦ νόμου*.

7. Cotton's brackets.

8. The Reverend John Jones, Bulkeley's colleague in the Concord church.

William Coddington to John Cotton

August 27, [1641]

Tr. MS: YBei, Ezra Stiles Papers, "Itineraries," fols. 11, 12

Published: Dexter, *Extracts,* 374

Following this letter, Ezra Stiles described his source:

The Collection of Letters from whence I have made these Extracts, consists of twenty pages folio. This of Aug. 27 to M[r] Cotton is so near the End that there are not a doz*en* Lines after it, i.e. it is the last but one, w*hich* however is of the same Date. The period of this Collection or the Time in w*hich* they were written is from June 30 1640 to Aug*us*t 27. 1641.

Extracted from the Original MS in Gov. Coddingtons Hand, Oct. 15 1774
By Ezra Stiles

The manuscript is among Newport Town Records.

To Mr Cotton. Worthy S*i*r & my aunchant & deare frind yo*u*rs of the 23 of the 6 I recaived for w*hi*ch I kindly thanke yow &c. &c.[1]

—for the last clause in yo*u*r let*te*r as its p*ro*fessed out of aunchant Love soe I doe accept of it, & as Sol.[2] sayth in the moultetude of Counsellers ther is saftye.[3] & the mercey I did inioye ther in from yo*u*rselfe I blesse the lord for it & acknowledge the instrument by w*hi*ch it was convayed, & I hope as speedely as yow may will descover to me what those wayes of heresy be that are to be avoyded, & my desire is that the Daye springe from a hye would visit yow & us to guide o*u*r feete into the wayes of peace & trewth[4] & in whome I rest, com*m*ending my love & respect to yow & yo*u*rs. Mr Leveret[5] & his &c. yo*u*r old & uselesse frind

W.C. Dat. Aug. 27.

1. Here Stiles inserted a note in the text of the letter, indicating that he omitted a portion of the letter from his transcription: "(On secular Business. This however shews the Continuance of their Friendship.)."

2. Solomon.

3. Prov. 24:6: For by wise counsel thou shalt make thy war: and in multitude of counsellors there is safety.

4. Coddington is paraphrasing Luke 1:78, 79: Through the tender mercy of our God; whereby the dayspring from on high hath visited us, To give light to them that sit in darkness and in the shadow of death, to guide our feet into the way of peace.

5. Thomas Leverett (1585?–1650) was chosen a ruling elder of the Boston church at the same time Cotton was chosen as teacher. He had previously been an alderman and key supporter of Cotton in Boston, Lincolnshire. See Rutman, *Winthrop's Boston,* 65; Ziff, *Career of John Cotton,* 49, 83–84.

Peter Bulkeley to John Cotton

February 1641/2

ALS. MS: BPL, Ms. Am. 1506, pt. 3, no. 4

In L. Thompson, "Letters of John Cotton," 167–170

This letter is badly mutilated and mildewed in the lower left quadrant of the single sheet on which it is written. In that portion of the sheet, paper has been lost in an area about two inches long along the left margin and extending progressively inward down to about one inch from the bottom of the page. The result is a triangular hole removing part of the text on some sixteen lines, with deterioration in legibility from water damage in additional lines around the lost paper. The text on the verso extends down only about two-thirds of the sheet, so that the damage to the paper interferes with very little of the text on that side of the paper.

The address block is written along the left edge of the recto:

To his reverend & deare freind m^r^
Cotton Teacher of the Church
att Boston giue these./

Reuerend and beloued,

q.1. I desire your opinion in these few cases following. First whether a sister taking offence against a brother[1] hath nott the same libertye as a brother hath, to deale w*i*th *th*e offending brother for his offence. It may seeme then, because in Christ Jesus there is nether male nor female, &c.[2] and yett on the other side, this doubt ariseth. *tha*t seeing the calling of a brother in question is an act of power, it may seeme nott sutable to that sexe, w*hi*ch may nott take autoritye ouer *th*e man.

2 Whether women in a church being charged w*i*th some obliquitye in their carriage, wherein they conceaue themselues to be cleare & innocent, may not [ope]nly defend themselues before the congregation if they be publickely blamed. It may seeme probable they may. from numb: 5:18.[3] concerning the womans head w*hi*ch was to be vncouered, being called in question by her husband. Att other times whiles shee and her husband stand as one p*ar*tye, shee is to haue her couering on her head, as the token of her husbands pow*e*r, but now when her husband and shee stand as partye and partye, one to accuse, the other to defend, now the woman was to stand w*i*th her head vncouered, for laying downe the signe [of] her husbands pow*e*r. After the same propor-

tion, and vpon the same grounds, it may seeme *tha*t women in the church being accused, may haue the same libertye.

3] Suppose a company of a church (as 8 or 10 familyes both men & women) [b]e [m]eete together for their mutuall edification, by answering some [que]s-tion propounded by some one, as they vse to doe in their courses, || may it be expedient (when the men haue spoken and finish[ed]||tended,) for one of the women to propound a question or || p*r*esence of the men, or whether it ˆbeˆ more expedient || by some ˆotherˆ in her behalfe? In i cor: 14.34[4] It is wr[itten]|| aske in the Church, but we see the company of believers in one familye ||ch. *er*go many familyes may be called a Church much more.[5]

4] || but of another nature. concerning the im*m*anent acts of || say, are ipsa dei voluntas,[6] and ~~by~~ by consequence, ipsiss||isse Deus. my question is, whether these kinds of ||ds? for if they be, then his decree is his essen: and if his dec[ree]|| s||e then it could not be otherwise then it is. and soe he c[ould] nott [h]aue decreed to saue Judas, or nott to sau[e] Peter. and soe the [d]ecree of such an ones saluation, must flow out of the necessitye of gods nature, & nott out of the ~~necess~~ libertye of his will. hîc hac eo.[7]

[5] [W]hatt thinke yow of Dr Twisse his way, making god to decree our saluation [IV] to be giuen vnto vs per modu*m* præmij.[8] for the manifestation of his mercye cum Justitia temperatæ;[9] w*hi*ch yow may finde in his defence of Mr Perk*ins* ag*ains*t Armin*ius* in fol*io,* lib: 1. digress: pag: 36. and pag: 45. and 46. and p: 70.b.[10] he hath some things to the same purpose & whence he calls gods mercye, misericordia*m* præmiatam, vel remuneratiuua*m,*[11] p: 45.a. and, eligimur ˆsayth heˆ ad salute*m* adipiscendam per Christu*m,* ita tamen vt sit etîam pêr modu*m* præmij.[12] p: 45.b. and, *tha*t, saluatio est actus dei remuneratiuus,[13] p: 46.a. versus fine*m*[14] and, pag: 70.b. he hath these words. gloria conferetur hominib*us* non modo ex ~~hominibus~~ ˆmisericordiaˆ s[ed] et ex iustitia remuneratiua.[15] and vpon this ground he builds di[sp]aritye of glory in the life to come. pag: 72.a.

6. Touching w*hi*ch alsoe (that in the disparitye of glory to be giuen to the S*ain*ts) I desire to know whatt you thinke. whether there shall be an equalitye of all, or any disparitye. Camero inclines to equalitye tom: 2: p: 325.[16] and soe doth Peter Martyr in his com*mon* places.[17] If yow || will p*er*mit, I should desire an answ*er* by our brother || If nott, keepe my letter by yow, till a fitter season. And so w*i*th my loue rem*em*bred to Mrs Cotton, & yourselfe, I com*m*end y[ou] to the grace of god, resting,

Yours euer ||,

Febr: 1641. Pet. [Bulkeley]

Concerning the 3 first cases, I could desire a sp[eedy reply.?]

1. Bulkeley is using "sister" and "brother" in the sense of female and male members of the church.

2. "There is neither male nor female" is a partial quotation from Gal. 3:28.

3. Numbers 5 offers the Lord's description to Moses of the way a jealous husband should present his wife before the priest for a trial of jealousy. Num. 5:18: And the priest shall set the woman before the Lord, and uncover the woman's head, and put the offering of memorial in her hands, which is the jealousy offering. . . .

4. 1 Cor. 14:34: Let your women keep silence in the churches: for it is not permitted unto them to speak; but they are commanded to be under obedience, as also saith the law.

5. The final sentence of this paragraph ("In i cor . . . much more.") is closely written on three lines, obviously inserted after the surrounding text had already been written.

6. ipsa dei voluntas: the very will of God.

7. hîc hac eo: here I go in this way (or: these are my thoughts in this matter).

8. per modum præmij: in the manner of a reward.

9. cum Justitia temperatæ: tempered with justice.

10. Bulkeley is here citing William Twisse, *Vindiciae gratiae, potestatis, ac providentiae Dei* . . . (Amsterdam, 1632). His quotations of Twisse's Latin are not exact, but the page references are accurate, as verified in the copy in the Houghton Library, which was Samuel Sewall's copy.

11. misericordia*m* præmiatam, vel remuneratiuua*m:* mercy given as a reward, or remunerative. Bulkeley probably meant to write the ending of the last word -tiua*m.*

12. eligimur . . . ad salutem adipiscendam per Christum ita tamen ut sit etîam pêr modum præmij: we are elected by Christ to achieve salvation, but in such a way that it is also in the way of a reward.

13. saluatio est actus dei remunerativus: salvation is a remunerative act of God.

14. versus fine*m:* toward the end.

15. gloria conferetur hominibus non modo ex misericordia sed et ex iustitia remunerativa: Glory is given to men not just out of mercy but also out of remunerative justice.

16. Bulkeley is citing John Cameron (1579–1625), *Praelectiones in selectiora quaedam loca Novi Testamenti* . . . , 3 vols. (Saumur, 1626–1628), II, 325, where Cameron outlines the stages of an argument that he will pursue for several pages, looking at the question "andentur varij in vitâ æternâ gloriæ gradus," whether different degrees of glory are given in the eternal life. As Bulkeley says, he will decide in favor of the negative.

17. [Pietro Martire Vermigli] (1499–1562), *The Common Places of the Most Famous . . . Divine Doctor Peter Martyr,* trans. Anthonie Marten (London, 1583), pt. 3, 389: "That all mens glorie in heauen shall be alike." This proposition is discussed, 389–393.

[John Cotton] to [Peter Bulkeley]

[February 1641/2]

Copy. MS: BPL, Ms. Am. 1506, pt. 3, no. 5

In L. Thompson, "Letters of John Cotton," 171–172

Cotton's reply to Bulkeley's letter of February 1641/2 was written either the evening of the day on which it was received or early the next morning, as he indicates in his concluding sentence. This copy is a contemporary transcription made by someone other than Cotton himself. The handwriting is the same as that of Cotton to Bulkeley, January 16, August 7, 1641, to [John] Elmeston, August 26, 1640, and to Stephen Bachiler, March 9, 1641/2. In the absence of a salutation and a signature block, neither person's name appears anywhere in the letter. The content, however, unambiguously indicates that it is a reply to Bulkeley's February letter. This letter was obviously stored with Bulkeley's letter when the water damage occurred, because the damage here is virtually identical to that on the former—a triangular-shaped area in the lower left quadrant of the page, with total loss of paper affecting about one and a half inches along the left margin, extending into the page about two inches at its extreme point. Portions of some ten lines of text are missing, and the surrounding area suffers from mildew and staining. The context in this letter together with Bulkeley's questions makes reconstruction of certain missing details possible. The text on the verso is written only on the upper one-third of the page, well above the hole, and thus suffers no loss of text.

Reverende & deare brother,

Yo*u*r 1. Quæstion I would Answer affirmatively vpon *th*e same Reason w*hi*ch yo*u*r self give; A sister hath *th*e like Power of dealing with an offending brother, as a brother hath to deale w*i*th a brother, primâ vice.[1] but if *th*e offender doe not heare the sister, & she therevpon take one or two more to deale w*i*th him, it were meeter those one or two, were brethren rather then sisters; & *tha*t if he heare not *th*em, they should p*re*sent *th*e matter before *th*e church, & not she.

Neither doeth she vsurpe Authority over *th*e brother, whom she dealeth with in way of private Admonition for his offfence, for though such an Admonition be an Act of Power yet it is not power vsurped by hir, but is putt vpon hir as by *th*e offendo*u*r, so by God. If a man borrow money of a rich woman, you know Solomons Proverbe (Chapt. 22.7:)[2] *th*e borrower (or debter) is Servant to *th*e lender, now a Trespasser is a debter.

To yo*u*r 2[d] Quæstion my Answer would be Affirmative also. Women publickly charged with offence before *th*e church ought to give Satisfaction before *th*e church, p*re*supposing the church require [an] Answer of *the*m by *th*e mouth of one of their Elders. It is [not superi?]ority, but subiection, to Give Account, to such as [require an?] Account of their Actions.

[To your 3d?] I would choose a negative Answer, In *th*e meetings || familyes If a woma*n* desire any further satisfactio*n* let hir ||[pro]pound hir doubt by hir husband or some other D|| neighbo*ur* at least. It neither suiteth well w*i*th w[omanly?] {m}odesty nor will superfluity & vnseasonablnesse of sp*irit*|| be easily avoyded if a woman shall p*ro*pound and argue Cases before a gret company of men. [IV] It is scarse fitt at Table much lesse in a p*ro*fessed Religious exercise & Assembly of men.

Yo*ur* 3. latter Quæstions as you give me leave ~~as you give me leave~~ to respit mine Answer to them, so I willingly accept it: for though I might soone tell you my p*re*sent Thoughts about them, yet I had rather keepe silence altogether, as p*re*ferring Sobriety of ædification before Curiosity of Speculation, especially now, when yo*ur* neighbo*ur* giveing me yo*ur* letter at Sunsett, or after, ˆ&ˆ requireth an Answer ˆan houreˆ after Sunrise.

1. primâ vice: in the first instance.

2. Prov. 22:7: The rich ruleth over the poor, and the borrower is servant to the lender.

John Cotton to Stephen Bachiler

March 9, 1641/2

Copy. MS: BPL, Ms. Am. 1506, pt. 3, no. 2

In L. Thompson, "Letters of John Cotton," 162–166

John Winthrop records the arrival on June 5, 1632, of "olde mr Batcheleer (beinge aged 71:)," a seasoned Puritan who had been ejected as vicar at Wherwell, Hampshire, in 1605, and in 1632 was still considered "a notorious inconformist."[1] He immediately went to Lynn, which was then still called Saugus, where he began to conduct worship services, even though no church had been formally established. Just four months later, on October 3, 1632, the General Court ordered that Stephen Bachiler "forbear exercising his Guifts as a pastor or teacher publiquely . . . for his contempt of authority & till some scandles be removed." Five months later he was cleared to resume his calling.[2] But by March 1635, dissension was evident as some members of the congregation found fault with Bachiler's ministry and separated from the congregation, meanwhile questioning whether the church was a duly organized one at all. A delegation of ministers arbitrated the problem, temporarily restoring peace, but in January 1636 he was dismissed. His subsequent travels took him to Ipswich in 1636 and to Newbury in 1638, when he received permission from the Massachusetts Bay authorities to settle Hampton (now New Hampshire). A church was constituted there in 1639, with Bachiler as pastor and Timothy Dalton as teacher. Differences between the two surfaced quickly, with Bachiler's supporters being outnumbered by Dalton's. Adding to those problems, in 1641, Bachiler, as Winthrop tells it, "did solicit the chastity of his neighbor's wife, who acquainted her husband therewith." Bachiler "stiffly denied it," but is said subsequently to have "confess[ed] the attempt."[3] He was excommunicated, and then resorted to the advice and counsel of Governor Winthrop and fellow clergymen, including John Cotton and John Wilson. In 1643 he was restored to membership, but not to his pastorate. Severe divisions between the Dalton and Bachiler factions in Hampton remained, exacerbated by the two ministers' personalities. Winthrop says that both men were "very passionate, and wanting discretion and moderation."[4] In the course of these troubles, which also included the burning down of his house and loss of his books and other possessions in 1641, Bachiler was corresponding with Cotton and others whose opinions he apparently valued, including both John and Margaret Winthrop.[5]

Despite these problems, two congregations, one at Casco, which Cotton mistakenly identifies as Saco, in Maine, and the other at Exeter, sought his services in 1644. When neither materialized for him, he moved to Strawberry Banke (Portsmouth), where he lived until he returned to England in the early 1650s, having by then been widowed, remarried, endured his young wife Mary's adultery, and sought a divorce.[6] The veracity of the charge by Mary that he remarried bigamously in England in his nineties has not been proven. Indeed, the charge against him of attempted adultery was never prosecuted, and he continued to protest his innocence and to lament the absence of legal proceedings that would enable him to clear his name (Bachiler to Winthrop, Cotton, and Wilson, Feb. 26, 1643/4). The comment by a nineteenth-century historian seems an apt summary of the long life (1561–1661) of Stephen Bachiler: "His sojourn here was one of trials."[7]

Though this manuscript is water-stained, it is wholly intact. The letter is written on both sides of a single sheet. The handwriting is not Cotton's except for one interlinear insertion and the "Mr Bachelo*u*r" written at the top of the recto in a somewhat darker ink than was used for the text of the letter otherwise. Thomas Prince inserted a few underlinings throughout the text.

As regards the date of the letter, Prince wrote "April 1641" just under Cotton's numerical version of the date. His reading is understandable but incorrect. Cotton's amanuensis wrote "Boston. this 9. of i. i641./" but without dotting either i in the date. Those two digits—and especially the first—look very much like the number 2. However, the number 2 appears in the third line and again midway through the manuscript, each time looking decidedly different from these numbers. It was a common practice, especially in the date lines of letters of the period, to use the lower case i in place of a 1, which is what was done here. Because reading i instead of 2 puts the letter in early March instead of April, as Prince believed, the 1641 must be read as an Old Style date, or March 1641/2, eleven months later than Prince supposed.

Mr Bachel*our*

Reverend & beloved brother,

For so I must still call you, not to Gainesay *th*e Censure of *th*e church, but to fullfill *th*e Com*mandmen*t of *th*e Apo*st*le, Not to Account a man vnder church-Censure, as an Enemy, but to Admonish him as a brother, 2 Thess. 3.15.[8]

You have long since (even 20 yeares before I was borne) well vnderstood, that a Sparrow falleth not to *th*e ground, much lesse an officer & Father in *th*e church falleth into open Scandall, & into church-Censure, w*i*thout *th*e hand of o*ur* heavenly Father.[9] And therefore I would thinke it a speciall part of yo*ur* wisedome, & piety, first to looke vp to his hand, who in very Faithfullnesse Correcteth you, & *the*n to those Corruptions in yo*ur* owne heart (w*hi*ch even old disciples are still subiect to) whereby you have p*ro*voked *th*e Lord both to leave you to secret Ebullitions of lust, & to bring secret Sinnes to light in *th*e sight of this sunne, as he did those of David. And *th*e Lord helpe you to looke at Davids Exemplary Carriage after Gods Chastening hand was gone out ag*ainst* him in this kinde. He neither Cryeth out vpon *th*e vnnaturall Iniquity of Absoloms Conspiracy, nor vpon *th*e vniust revilings of Shimei, but is so wholly taken vp with *th*e deepe desert of his owne wickednesse, & *th*e iust hand of God vpon him for it, *tha*t he cannot cast his eye vpon *th*e vnworthy dealings of his sonne or subiects.[10] Doe you so likewise (deare brother:) let *th*e plaister lye vpon *th*e sore quiately, *tha*t there may be a perfect healing.[11]

Had I lived neere you, I should have dissuaded you from p*ro*secuting an offence against yo*ur* Teacher, till yo*ur* owne offence had bene wholly removed. A mote in o*ur* brothers eye may lye (for vs) till wee have plucked *th*e mote ˆor beame,ˆ [12] out of o*ur* owne Eye.[13] It is true, Blasphemy is not a mote, but every Comparison of a finite thinge with an infinite, is not blasphemy: Seeing *th*e Comparison is not intended in the equall quantity, but in *th*e like Quality. As when John calleth vs to be righteous, as he is righteous (1.John. 3.7:)[14] & Peter calleth vs to be holy, as he is holy (1. Pet. 1.16)[15] neither of them intendeth æquality of measure but likenesse of quality. If o*ur* Colleague should say, This or *tha*t is false, yea as false, as God is true, If he meant æquality of measure, It were indeede Blasphemy: but when the speach may be as well taken to hold forth resemblance, brotherly love is bound to take a doubtfull speach in the better ~~sense~~ part: especially seeing if he were asked I p*re*sume he would abhorre to make Comparison of æqualls betweene a Creature, & *th*e infinite Creato*ur*. He durst not owne it, *tha*t Satan is æqually as false, as God is true, seeing God [i]s infinitely true, & Satan false in a finite measure. Indeede if *th*e speach should proove (as you say it will) a very Trueth, when yet o*u*r brother yo*u*r Teacher[16] said, it was as false, as God is true, *th*e speach can by noe means be Excused from great Rashnesse, & Falshood, yea & Blasphemy too, though I dare not think, he durst have said it, if he had thought it to be such.

I doe not heare, *tha*t any Appeale (as you call it) of yo*u*rs, or any l*ette*res from *th*e Church are come to *th*e Elders hereabout touching yo*u*r Case. It may well be, they sent noe further then to Rowly, & Ipswich, & *th*e churches adioyning. An Appeale (you know) lyeth not from one church to another, every church having Received *th*e Power of *th*e keyes within it self. Onely if you or they required any Advice from other Elders, this liberty wee mutually take & give to one another: & all of vs doe owe *th*e Right hand of Fellowship Each to other. But if the church did send abroade for advice, & should meanewhile finde out some Cleare light f[r]om amongst themselves for speedy p*ro*ceedings without Advice, either some vrgent necessity must force them to it, or else it should seeme like Sauls Act, [iv] to call for *th*e Ephod to enquire of God, & then vpon *th*e Increase of a Noyse in *th*e Host, to Call againe to *th*e Preist to withdraw his hand 1 Sam. 14. 18, 19.[17] But I dare not Judge of a churches Act but vpon Cleare Evidence of variety of witnesses: but would rather fall vnder the churches feete, according to Isay 49: 23:[18] & by humble Acknowledgem*en*t seeke to Remoove *th*e stumbling block of offence, w*hi*ch I had layed before them, were my soule in yo*u*r soules stead.

Doe not feare an Impossibility of giving Satisfaction, vnlesse it be w*i*th Acknowledgem*en*t of *th*e churches Infallibility. Noe Reason, any church should require an offendo*u*r to Acknowledge their absolute Innocency in the Carryage of any church-Administration; noe, it will be enough, If you Acknowledge you gave them by your sinne iust Occasion of offence, & Greife, & *th*e more in regard of *th*e Eminency of yo*u*r person & Calling. you cannot but Remember Omne animi vitium tantò conspectius in se Crimen habet, quantò major qui peccat habetur.[19] If you can also finde *tha*t yo*u*r Confession of yo*u*r sinne before them was not so open, & full & Contrite, as might give full & cleare Testimony of yo*u*r Repentance at *tha*t time, but *tha*t both God & *th*e church might still thinke it needefull to call you to further humiliation, surely I should hope, *th*e church might & ought freely to forgive you, & restore you both to Com*m*union with them, & Administration amongst them. Or if otherwise, they might honourably dismisse you to *tha*t other employm*en*t you spake of to Sacoe, or elsewhere, if they shall see Gods hand calling you from *the*m. Whereas otherwise were my soule in yo*u*r Case, I should be loth to vndertake a publick Calling abroade, till I had first remooved offences at home, & such Censure, as might withdraw a blessing from me.[20]

What I said or did, soe long agoe at Saugust, I doe not remember: sure I am, I came thither, & (whilest I was there) walked amongst o*u*r brethren w*i*thout partiality or p*re*iudice either to you or to *th*e brethren of *th*e church. If any thing passed then from me doubtfull to you, I shall endeavour meekely to give you Account of it, either by giving you iust Reason for mine Action or humble Acknowledge*me*nt of my fayling. I am cleare in this, I did noething of mine owne head, w*i*thout Consent of fellow Elders: & it is as cleare, neither they, nor I could take vpon vs to heare or discerne of yo*u*r Cause, or *th*e Churches, w*i*thout *th*e free Consent of you both. As for com*m*ing or sending to you, or to *th*e church, It is not meete, *tha*t any of o*u*r Elders or churches should neglect any service of brotherly love w*hi*ch they & yo*u*r self shall call for, especially such as live neerest to you. But you know vnlesse o*u*r Advice be called for, we cannot im*m*ittere falcem in ali[e]nam segetem[21] lest wee be thought to be ἀλλοτριοεπίσκοποι[22] But [the] Lord delight to Croune yo*u*r hoary head with this hono*u*r, to rest yo*u*r Croune at *th*e feete of *th*e Lord Jesus, as all *th*e Elders did, Rev. 4.10.[23]

I feele yo*u*r distresse of inner & outward man at my heart & shall not Cease (God helping) to mourne with you in secret, till I heare this Calamity be overpast. Com*m*end my deare love to yo*u*r good wife, *th*e Companion of yo*u*r Labo*u*rs, & Traveyles, & Sorrowes:[24] & *th*e Lord enlarge hir heart to holy helpefullnesse to you vnder this heavy burden. W*i*th like respect, & love to yo*u*r self I rest

Sensible of yo*u*r burden, yo*u*r
loving poore brother
John Cotton./

Boston, this 9. of
i. 1641. /

1. Winthrop, *Journal,* 69; Samuel Maverick, *A Brief Description of New England* (1660), quoted in Frederick Clifton Pierce, *Batchelder, Batcheller Genealogy: Descendants of Rev. Stephen Bachiler* . . . (Chicago, 1898), 27. Among various spellings, that used by Bachiler himself is adopted here.

2. Pierce, *Batchelder, Batcheller Genealogy,* 29.

3. Winthrop, *Journal,* 368–369.

4. Ibid., 519.

5. See Bachiler to John Winthrop, Oct. 9, 1638, May 18 or 19, 1644, to Margaret Winthrop, Oct. 17 or 18, 1638, *Winthrop Papers,* IV, 69–70, 144–145, 457–459, in addition to Bachiler to Winthrop, Cotton, and Wilson, Feb. 26, 1643/4, below.

A small fragment of a letter dated "Hampton. *th*e 22. Septem. 1643" in Bachiler's hand has been preserved among the Cotton Papers at the Boston Public Library. Prince's note at the end of this fragment says, "This letter contains complaints of Mr Dalton," though not enough of the letter remains to verify this. Prince apparently saw the letter when it was still more or less whole. His marginal note identifies a reference to "yo*u*r colleague" as indicating Cotton, thus identifying the letter's recipient as John Wilson.

6. These troubles led to further correspondence with Winthrop, Cotton, and Wilson. Though these later letters to and from Cotton do not survive, a letter from Bachiler to Winthrop on May 3, 1647, asks him "to read (as your important busynesses may permit) this inclosed letter to my two beloued and Reuerend brethren your Elders and in them, as you and they shall see cause (on whose judgments and wisedom I much depend) to the whole Synode wherin you shall fully knowe my distressed case and condicion: and so (as you shall se cause) to joyne with them in counsayle, what best to do for my releefe." *Winthrop Papers,* V, 153.

7. Joseph B. Felt, *The Ecclesiastical History of New England* . . . (Boston, 1855–1862), I, 453. A descendant, Charles E. Batchelder, published a lengthy account in *NEHGR,* XLVI (1892), 58–64, 157–161, 246–251, 345–350. While most accounts, including Winthrop and Cotton here, seem to assume Bachiler's guilt in the charge of attempted adultery, another descendant concludes that the charges are "utterly unworthy of belief" (Pierce, *Batchelder, Batcheller Genealogy,* 25–39, esp. 34). Bringing comprehensive research and present-day objectivity to these matters is Anderson (*Great Migration,* 61–69), who points to the "careful and accurate" account in V. C. Sanborn, *Genealogy of the Family of Samborne or Sanborn in England and America, 1194–1898* ([Concord, N.H.], 1899), 59–66. See also Sanborn's "Stephen Bachiler: An Unforgiven Puritan," New Hampshire Historical Society, *Proceedings,* V (Concord, N.H., 1917), 172–205. For an argument suggesting the relevance of Bachiler's case to Nathaniel Hawthorne's creation of a fictional story with striking similarities, see Frederick Newberry, "A Red-Hot *A* and a Lusting Divine: Sources for *The Scarlet Letter,*" *NEQ,* LX (1987), 256–264.

8. 2 Thess. 3:15: Yet count him not as an enemy, but admonish him as a brother.

9. Matt. 10:29: Are not two sparrows sold for a farthing? and one of them shall not fall on the ground without your Father.

10. See 2 Sam. 15–19.

11. Reference to Isa. 38:21 may be intended: For Isaiah said, Let them take a lump of figs, and lay it for a plaster upon the boil, and he shall recover.

12. This interlinear insertion is in Cotton's hand.

13. Cotton here alludes to Matt. 7:3–5 and Luke 6:41–42.

14. 1 John 3:7: Little children, let no man deceive you: he that doeth righteousness is righteous, even as he is righteous.

15. 1 Pet. 1:16: Because it is written, Be ye holy; for I am holy.

16. Timothy Dalton (c. 1588–1661), the teacher at the Hampton church from its establishment in 1639 until his death.

17. 1 Sam. 14:18, 19: And Saul said unto Ahiah, Bring hither the ark of God. For the ark of God was at that time with the children of Israel. And it came to pass, while Saul talked unto the priest, that the noise that was in the host of the Philistines went on and increased: and Saul said unto the priest, Withdraw thine hand.

Verse 3, preceding this passage, states that Ahiah was "wearing an ephod."

18. Isa. 49:23: And kings shall be thy nursing fathers, and their queens thy nursing mothers: they shall bow down to thee with their face toward the earth, and lick up the dust of thy feet; and thou shalt know that I am the Lord: for they shall not be ashamed that wait for me.

19. Omne . . . habetur: The greater the repute of the sinner, the more conspicuous the reproach of every fault of the soul.

20. For evidence that Bachiler took this advice to heart, see Bachiler to Winthrop, Cotton, and Wilson, Feb. 26, 1643/4, below: "I see not how I can dep*ar*te hence, till I haue . . . cleered & vindicated the cause & wronges I haue suffered of the church I liue yet in."

21. Immittere . . . segetem: thrust our scythe into another's field.

22. ἀλλοτριοεπίσκοποι: overseers of others' business; busybodies. The word occurs in the Greek original of 1 Pet. 4:15, which it is possible Cotton had in mind: But let none of you suffer as a murderer, or as a thief, or as an evildoer, or as a busybody in other men's matters.

23. Rev. 4:10: The four and twenty elders fall down before him that sat on the throne, and worship him that liveth for ever and ever, and cast their crowns before the throne. . . .

24. Bachiler's second wife, Helen, to whom he was already married when he left England in 1632. She is described by Winthrop as "a lusty comely woman." Winthrop, *Journal,* 368.

Members of Parliament to John Cotton, Thomas Hooker, and John Davenport

Summer 1642

Published: Hutchinson, *History,* I, 116

A major consequence of the political events of the late 1630s and very early 1640s, especially the abolition of the episcopacy, was the convening of the Westminster Assembly of Divines to debate and settle the contested issues of church liturgy, theology, and polity. As Robert S. Paul has put it, "Under the terms of the Solemn League and Covenant with the Scots, the Assembly was charged with formulating and establishing a new form of church government on the basis of the scriptural evidence alone: the authority of the Bible was invoked over the claims of either church tradition or royal prerogative."[1] It was an opportunity to formalize the eminence of Presbyterian polity and doctrine in England, contra the traditional episcopate. Independents who remained in England, though a decided minority in the assembly, were prepared to represent their congregationalist opinions on church polity as strenuously as possible.[2] Accordingly, they looked to New England for assistance, both through the hoped-for attendance of eminent divines there and through writings about the New England Way that came forth from the London press in abundance in the 1640s. In several cases, these works were prepared and published with the assembly as the intended audience.[3] Cotton's *Keyes of the Kingdom of Heaven* was mentioned in the assembly's debates and, like other works on New England's practice, drew written responses.[4]

Hutchinson says, "In the year 1642 letters came to Mr. Cotton of Boston, Mr. Hooker of Hartford, and Mr. Davenport of New-Haven, signed by several of the nobility, divers members of the house of commons, and some ministers, to call them or some of them, if all could not come, to assist in the assembly of divines at Westminster." In a footnote he adds: "I have the original papers which accompanied these letters. The following is an exact copy."[5] Though he refers to more than one such letter, the only one surviving is that which he included in his published volume, all the manuscripts having been lost.

None of the three attended the assembly, declining the invitation for different reasons, according to Hutchinson. "Mr. Hooker did not like the business, and thought it was not a sufficient call to go a thousand leagues to confer about matters of church government. Mr. Davenport thought otherwise, but his church having but one minister would not spare him. Mr. Cotton thought it a clear call and would have undertaken the voyage if others would have gone with him. Soon after, other letters were received which diverted them from any thoughts of proceeding."[6]

The expression of the desires of those honorable and worthy personages of both houses of parlament who call and wish the presence of Mr. Cotton, Mr. Hooker and Mr. Davenport to come ovar with all possible speed, all or any of them, if all cannot. The condityon whearein the state of things in this kingdom doth now stand wee suppose you have from the relations of others, wheareby you cannot but understand how greate need there is of the healp of prayer and improvement of all good meanes from all parts for the seatlinge and composeing the affaires of the church. Wee therefore present unto you our earnest desires of you all. To shewe whearein or howe many wayes you may be useful would easely bee done by us and fownd by you weare you present with us. In all likelyhood you will finde opportunity enough to draw forth all that healpefullness that God shall affoard by you. And wee doubt not these advantages will be sutch as will fully answer all inconveniencies your sealves, churches or plantations may sustaine in this your voyage and short absence from them. Onely the sooner you come the bettar.

Warwick[7]

W. Say & Seale
Mandeville
Rob. Brooke

Ph. Wharton

Nath. Fiennes
Gilb[t] Gerrard
Tho: Barrington
Richard Browne
Henry Martin
Oliver Cromwell
A. Haselrig

Wm. Stricland
Henry Darley
Valentine Walton
Will[m] Cawleys
John Gurdon
John Blakiston
Godfrey Rossevile

Tho: Hoyle
Cor: Holland
Anth. Stapley
Humfrey Salway
William Hay
J. Wastill

Wm. Masham
Mart. Lumley
Nath. Barnardiston
Ar. Goodwin

H. Ruthin
Ro. Cooke
Sam. Lake
John Francklyn

Gilbert Pickering
Ol. St. John
Isaac Pennington
Miles Corbett

Alex. Bence
Wm. Spurstowe

1. The formal call of the assembly was issued in the summer of 1643; the assembly concluded in 1648. See Robert S. Paul, *The Assembly of the Lord: Politics and Religion in the Westminster Assembly and the "Grand Debate"* (Edinburgh, 1985), 9, chaps. 2, 16; Benjamin B. Warfield, *The Westminster Assembly and Its Work* (New York, 1931), chap. 1.

2. There were five at the outset: Jeremiah Burroughes, Thomas Goodwin, Philip Nye, Sydrach Simpson, and William Bridge.

3. Among the works on polity published at this time were Cotton's *Way of the Churches of Christ in New-England* (London, 1645) and *The Keyes of the Kingdom of Heaven* (six editions in 1644) and Thomas Hooker's *Survey of the Summe of Church-Discipline* (London, 1648), which was written first in about 1644 but had to be rewritten when the vessel taking it to England sank. I have argued that other books by Hooker—*A Briefe Exposition of the Lords Prayer, Heavens Treasury Opened,* and *An Exposition of the Principles of Religion,* all published in 1645—were sent for publication with an intention of influencing the assembly's deliberations on its catechisms and confession of faith; see Sargent Bush, Jr., "Thomas Hooker and the Westminster Assembly," *WMQ,* 3d Ser., XXIX (1972), 291–300.

4. See, for instance, Paul, *The Assembly of the Lord,* 435, 442.

5. Hutchinson, *History,* I, 115.

6. Ibid., I, 116.

7. Unless otherwise indicated, these brief identifications are drawn from one or more of the following: *DNB;* D. Brunton and D. H. Pennington, *Members of the Long Parliament* (London, 1954; rpt. 1968), appendixes 5 and 6, 200–245; W. M. Hetherington, *History of the Westminster Assembly of Divines,* ed. Robert Williamson, 4th ed. (Edinburgh, 1878), 103–106. M.P. indicates a member of Parliament's House of Commons; M.P. (Lords) indicates a member of Parliament's House of Lords. W.A. indicates a delegate to the Westminster Assembly. Several of these men had other important roles as members of key committees, military posts, visitors to the Scottish Commons, judges in the king's trial, and relatives of Cromwell or of each other, and so forth. No attempt is made here to list such details.

Warwick: Sir Philip Warwick (1609–1683), M.P. for Radnor.

W. Say & Seale: William Fiennes, first Viscount Saye and Sele (1582–1562), M.P. (Lords); W.A.

Ph. Wharton: Philip Wharton, fourth Baron Wharton (1613–1696), M.P. (Lords); W.A.

Mandeville: Edward Montague, Viscount Mandeville, later second earl of Manchester (1602–1671), M.P. (Lords); W.A.

Rob. Brooke: Robert Greville, second Baron Brooke (1608–1643), speaker, House of Lords, 1642.

Nath. Fiennes: Nathaniel Fiennes (1608?–1669), M.P. for Banbury.

Gilb[t] Gerrard: Sir Gilbert Gerard, M.P. for Middlesex; W.A.

Tho: Barrington: Sir Thomas Barrington, M.P. for Colchester.

Richard Browne: either Richard Browne (d. 1669), M.P. for New Romney, or Richard Browne, M.P. for Chipping Wycomb.

Henry Martin: Henry Marten (1602–1680), M.P. for Berkshire.

Oliver Cromwell (1599–1658), M.P. for Cambridge.

A. Haselrig: Sir Arthur Haselrig or Heselrige (d. 1661), M.P. for Leicestershire; W.A.

Wm. Stricland: Sir William Stickland, M.P. for Hedon.

Henry Darley, M.P. for Northallerton.

Valentine Walton (d. 1661?): M.P. for Huntingdonshire.

Will[m] Cawleys: William Cawley (1602–1667), M.P. for Midhurst.

John Gurdon (1595?–1579), M.P. for Ipswich.

John Blakiston (1603–1649), M.P. for Newcastle-on-Tyne.

Godfrey Rossevile: not identified.

Tho: Hoyle: Thomas Hoyle, M.P. for York.

Cor: Holland: Cornelius Holland, M.P. for New Windsor.

Anth. Stapley: Anthony Stapley (1590–1655), M.P. for Sussex.

Humfrey Salway: Humphrey Salwey (1575?–1652), M.P. for Worcestershire; W.A.

William Hay, M.P. for Rye.

J. Wastill: John Wastell (d. 1660), M.P. for Northallerton.

Wm. Masham: Sir William Masham or Massam, M.P. for Shrewsbury; W.A.

Mart. Lumley: Sir Martin Lumley, M.P. for Essex.

Nath. Barnardiston: Sir Nathaniel Barnardiston (1588–1653), M.P. for Suffolk.

Ar. Goodwin: Arthur Goodwin (1593?–1643), M.P. for Buckinghamshire.

H. Ruthin: Henry L. Grey, lord of Ruthyn, ninth earl of Kent (1594–1651), M.P. for Leicestershire, M.P. (Lords) after November 1643.

Ro. Cooke: Sir Robert Cooke, M.P. for Tewksbury.

Sam. Lake: Sir Samuel Luke (d. 1670), M.P. for Bedford.

John Francklyn: either Sir John Francklyn, M.P. for Middlesex, or John Francklyn, M.P. for Marlborough.

Gilbert Pickering: Sir Gilbert Pickering (1613–1668), M.P. for Northamptonshire.

Ol. St. John: Oliver St. John (1598?–1673), M.P. for Totnes; W.A.

Isaac Pennington (1587?–1660), M.P. for City of London (and lord mayor of London, 1642, 1643).

Miles Corbett: Miles Corbet (d. 1662), M.P. for Great Yarmouth.

Alex. Bence: Alexander Bence, M.P. for Aldeburgh.

Wm. Spurstowe: William Spurstowe (1605?–1666), Puritan divine (one of five who wrote in 1641 as "Smectymnuus"); W.A.

Peter Bulkeley to John Cotton

September 26, 1642

ALS. MS: MSA, CCXL, Hutchinson Papers, I, fol. 42

Published: Lemuel Shattuck, *A History of the Town of Concord . . .* (Boston, 1835), 155

In L. Thompson, "Letters of John Cotton," 175

Nearly a decade after his departure from Lincolnshire, Cotton's communication with his friends there continued, as this letter confirms. Bulkeley addressed the letter on a separate envelope sheet:

> To his reuerend and louing
> frend M[r] Cotton Teacher

of the Church att
Boston these

A piece of Bulkeley's imprinted sealing wax remains on the paper. The verso of this sheet contains Cotton's draft of a letter to another correspondent (Cotton to [Unknown], after Sept. 26, 1642).

Reuerend in *th*e L. these are to desire yow to conuey this letter inclosed in one of your owne to Boston. I doe the rather send it to yow, because I suppose those yow com*m*itt your letters to, will be carefu[l] [1] of the deliuerye, and this letter concernes matters of some moment, in regard whereof I desire yow to take the more notice of it, and conuey it by a safe hand.

If the busines concerning Virginia be finished, I desire to know how it stands. or if nott finished, whatt is intended or thought vpon.[2]

My wife hath bin ill euer since our com*m*ing home. but now I thanke the Lord, begins to recouer. This day shee began to goe downe into the house. Rem*em*b*e*r ˆherˆ in your prayers, and vs all. And soe w*i*th both our loues to yourselfe and M[rs] Cotton, I leaue yow w*i*th all yours to *th*e Lords rich goodnes & grace, resting

Yours euer in him,

Sept 26. 1642.

Pet: Bulkeley

1. Bulkeley inadvertently omitted the l in this word.

2. Winthrop tells of the arrival in September 1642 of "one Mr. Bennet, a gentleman of Virginia, with letters from many well disposed people" who, "bewailing their sad condition for want of the means of salvation," requested "a supply of faithful ministers, whom, upon experience of their gifts and godliness, they might call to office." Winthrop reports that the New England elders met and picked George Phillips of Watertown, William Tompson of Braintree, and John Miller of Rowley, "for these churches had each of them two" ministers. Of these, only Tompson agreed to go, but he was joined by John Knolles, Phillips's colleague at Watertown, and Thomas James of New Haven. They departed on October 7 (Winthrop, *Journal,* 405, 426). The return of Knolles and his report on the missionary success in Virginia is recorded by Winthrop the following June (427). See also Philip Alexander Bruce, *Institutional History of Virginia in the Seventeenth Century* (New York, 1910), I, 252–255.

John Cotton to [Unknown]

[After September 26, 1642]

ADf. MS: MSA, CCXL, Hutchinson Papers, I, fol. 43

In L. Thompson, "Letters of John Cotton," 176–177

This is an unsigned draft in Cotton's hand of a letter to an unidentified correspondent, apparently in England, written on the verso of the envelope sheet in which Peter Bulkeley's letter of September 26, 1642, arrived. Since Bulkeley's letter enclosed a letter of his own to someone in Boston, Lincolnshire, asking Cotton to include it in his own next correspondence with Boston, it may be that Cotton took the occasion of that request to write this letter to someone there. If so, he would then have copied this draft out in fair copy for transmission with the letter from Bulkeley.

The letter again addresses questions about the opinions of certain members of the Antinomian faction in his congregation. (Cotton's feelings of betrayal by that group had been more fully expressed in his letter to John Wheelwright, Apr. 18, 1640.)

I doe Acknowledge that such an Answer as this, was written by me. But I desire *th*e Reader, either not to Reade it at all, or if He doe, let him know, That It was written at such a time, when some members of o*u*r Church did ˆsecretlyˆ nourish some grosse Erro*u*rs ~~secretly~~ [several more words deleted] & let fall in conference abroade sundry corrupt speaches to *th*e Offence of many Godly mindes.: but yet openly so carryed it to me, as if they had held forth noething, but according to *th*e Doctrine publickly taught by me ˆtouching o*u*r vnion w*i*th Christ, & evidencing of it to *th*e soule,ˆ whence It came to passe, *tha*t in this Answer, I Conceyving well of *th*e men, endeavoured to make the ˆfayrest &ˆ best construction of their speaches, ˆso farre asˆ [deleted word] their Words would well beare, ˆ[deleted word] & *th*e rather because I perceyved, others who opposed *th*em did not ˆthereinˆ walke w*i*th a right foote according to *th*e Trueth of *th*e Gospell T|| Agitations whereofˆ [1] hath taken vp ˆ& filledˆ sundry Passages in this Disco*u*rse. But since that I have Discerned by their open venting of theimselves ˆafterwards,ˆ what their Ambiguous, & suspicious speaches ˆof *th*e Brethren of o*u*r Churchˆ aymed at, I have thought my time ~~not~~ ill bestowed, in making a better Construction of their words then now I perceive *th*emselves intended. And therefore as I thinke mine owne time & labo*u*r lost in clearing their mindes, so I would not wish ˆanyˆ others to loose their owne time & labo*u*r in perusing *th*e same. But rather if any be Inquisitive into points of this nature, let *th*em Peruse other writings of my self & others, where *th*e naked Trueth of those Poynts is ~~declared~~ more plainely & fully declared, & ^much^ more vsefully vnto ædification.

1. This long interlinear insertion ("[deleted word] . . . whereof")is written in three lines along the left margin of the letter, keyed to this point in the text by Cotton's mark: +.

Thomas Allen to John Cotton

November 21, 1642

ALS. MS: MSA, CCXL, Hutchinson Papers, I, fols. 44, 44a

Thomas Allen (1608–1673) was educated at Caius College, Cambridge (bachelor of arts, 1627/8; master's, 1631); his Cambridge training in Ramist logic, with its organizational dependence on dualistic reasoning, is everywhere evident in this letter. From Cambridge, he had returned to minister at St. Edmund's Church in his native Norwich, Norfolk, in 1633. Silenced by Bishop Matthew Wren for refusing to read the so-called Book of Sports, he emigrated soon thereafter, arriving in New England in 1638. He became the minister at Charlestown, a post he held until he decided to return to Norwich in 1651. Thereafter, he was instrumental in seeing several of Cotton's works into print.[1]

Allen is responding to an invitation by Cotton to react to ideas he was propounding in sermons and perhaps in writing as well, to which Allen poses queries on ten major issues. His opening remarks make it clear that Cotton was working on the subjects with an eye to publication. This eventually occurred, chiefly in *The Way of the Churches of Christ in New England* (London, 1645), which addressed points 3–5 and 7–10. The first issue Allen raised, the power of the magistrates in church matters, was taken up in Cotton's posthumous *Certain Queries Tending to Accommodation and Communion of Presbyterian and Congregationall Churches* (London, 1654).

The manuscript is neatly written in a minute hand on both sides of a single folio sheet. The paper is intact throughout, but some obliteration of letters has resulted from the ink's bleeding through the paper.

The transcription in the Massachusetts Historical Society records an address that is no longer present on the manuscript itself:

To the Reverend & His much esteemed
Friend M[r] Cotton Teacher of the
Church of Christ in Boston
These
p*re*sent./

Reverend S*ir*

Yow were pleased to express yo*u*r willingness and desire to haue any scruples ˆpropoundedˆ *tha*t might be made about *th*e great Buisyness w*hi*ch the L*ord* hath bin pleased to direct yow to speake off (w*hi*ch I hope may through His Blessing be very vsefull to the churches & people of Christ both here & elswhere) And therefore I am *th*e more bold to p*re*sent vnto yow, these few things following.

1. About *th*e Power of Magistrates in Reb*us* Ecclesiasticis,[2] It being a Com*m*on Position *tha*t they are Custodes vtriusq*ue* Tabulae,[3] & as walls & Hedges to the Churches; &c.

Quær. whether they be
- only to p*re*serve and defend the churches from Injuries & disturbances:
- both to p*re*serue, & also to Constraine them to walke according to the word.

If so, then either according to
- the Express Letter of *th*e word: w*hi*ch p*er*aduent. is not alwaies ˆ~~safe~~ˆ to be followed.
- their Expositions & app*re*hensions of *th*e meaning. But how dangerous *tha*t may proue we haue seene by exper. in Engl. where authority fro*m* Rom. 13.1. & 1. Cor. 14.40.[4] haue laid such burdens as *th*e churches were not able to beare.

2. About the Power of *th*e Church in Matters Ceremoniall in *th*e worshipp of God.

- All such things are to be ordered only by *th*e word? If so then how may Churches vary in diuerse things w*i*thout sin: Ex. gr.[5] In
  - The Time of Administrat. of *th*e L. Supp*er;* we here doeing it in *th*e morning; as suppose others should doe it in the Euening according to *th*e 1st Institution, & *th*e primitiue practise. 1. Cor. 11, 21.[6]
  - Sprinckling in Bapt. Others Dipping.
  - The Time of Church-Assemblings, for
    - Beginning
    - Continuance.

Qu. whether

Some things be arbitrary to the churches to doe them or not, or to doe them thus or otherwise;

Then

What those things are? & if some things, why not more?

Wherein are the churches of England to be blamed in taking such Liberty?

3. About Gathering of Churches.

Qu. whether

Any Rule or Examp. ^be^ in the N.T. for such solemne Manner of Gathering churches, & by Fasting, as w*i*th vs? we read indeed of *th*e people being conu*er*ted & bapt. & Continueing together &c were therevppon accounted a church. but no such Manner of Gathering *them* as w*i*th vs.

Any Chri*sti*ans ^in a Towne^ haueing bin bapt. are not to be accounted of *th*e church, till such time as they breake out into some scandall ^for w*hi*ch they are to be censured.^? There was one w*i*th vs this very day Expressing ^*tha*t^ himselfe & many others in this Country were of this Judgm*en*t.

Chri*sti*ans may not gather into church-fellowshipp In consulto (if not also renuente) magistratu,[7] fro*m* Act. 4.19.[8] & *th*e Practise of *th*e Apostolick times? If so, then Quær. How safe or warrantable it may be for *th*e Court Order ~~to *tha*t purpose~~ to stand w*hi*ch seems Contrary, especially for any nu*m*ber of yeares?

4. About Ordination. Qu: whether Imposition of Hands be a Necessary Ordinance, or Arbitrary (as *th*e Scotsh hold) . If it be Necess. then why not also to be still vsed vppon *th*e sick? [deleted word]

5. About Giueing *th*e Right-Hand-of-Fellowshipp.

Qu. whether That place in Gal. 2.9.[9] holds forth *th*e outw. Ceremony of giueing *th*e right Hand, or Only a Manifestation or Expression of Consent & mutuall Agreem*en*t?

It be to be vsed as an Ordinance (fro*m* *th*e pl. Gal. 2.9.) at

Gathering of Churches,
Ordination of Officers, &c.

6. About Ministers Pronounceing a Blessing vppon *th*e People after *th*e Preaching of *th*e word.

Qu. whether It be a ministeriall duty now vnder *th*e Gospell, seeing

There is no express mention in *th*e N.T. *tha*t Christ or *th*e Apostles did vse it.

The Preists vnder *th*e Law might doe it as Types of Christ who should Come & bless His people Indeed.
Priuate Chri*st*ians may also pronounce them Blessed *tha*t heare *th*e word & keep it. & wh[e]rein is *th*e Euill, of

a priuate Brothers pronounceing a Blessing after he hath prophesyed?
peoples departure before *th*e Blessing, If it be not an Ordinance?

7. About Administration of *th*e Seales of *th*e Coven*an*t.

Quær. whether
Officers of One Church may not administer *th*e Sacram*en*ts in another from 1 Cor. 3.22,23?[10]
[deleted word] Bread or wine being brought ^newly^ in to *th*e Church after *th*e prayer for a Blessing vppon *th*e former, It be not as necessary to pray de nouo for a Blessing vppon it, as for *th*e Minister to Break such Bread?
In want of wine or Bread

*th*e Sacrament is to be deferred?
other Elem*en*ts may not be vsed? or suppose One cannot endure to drinke wine what is to be done in *tha*t case?

8. About Admission or Recejveing of members into the Church.

Qu: whether
It be necessary to make both

A Declaration of *th*e Chri*st*ian Faith? for though possibly they might doe it in *th*e Apostles times being Pagans before, yet there is not *th*e same reason now for these to doe it that are professed chri*st*ians before.
A narration of *th*e worke of grace in them; seeing ther's no express examp. for it in scr.

What measure of *th*e work of grace must be held forth to *th*e Church, w*hi*ch if one fall short off he is not to be admitted, when as we neuer read of any *tha*t were refused by *th*e Apostles *tha*t did offer theselues.
~~What~~ The Body of *th*e church hath Liberty & Power to refuse *th*e admittance of any when *th*e Officers & some memb[ers] doe testify their approbation. & so Contr. w*ha*t power to recejue where *th*e Officers approue not?

9. About Offences & Censures.

One member may w*i*thdraw fro*m* another for an offence after ~~selling~~ ^dealing w*i*th^ Him & no satisfaction; yea when the church doth neglect to proceed? fro*m* 1. Cor. 5.9,10,11.[11]

Qu. whether

~~How farre~~ tis lawfull to haue Com*m*union w*i*th an Excom*m*unicate p*er*son, or how farr?

If such be only as an Heathen, then tis

lawfull to eat & drinke, pray, & conuerse & deale ordinarily w*i*th *them.*

vnlawf. only to haue Com*m*un. w*i*th *them* at *th*e L. Table, &c.

10. About Baptizeing of childr. of Chri*sti*an Parents not yet joyned in Cove*nan*t to any p*ar*tic. church, for some reason p*er*haps *tha*t is warrantable; as suppose thay are vncertaine of abiding in *th*e place where they are, or p*er*haps *th*e wife being godly would joyne but *th*e Husband will not suffer her, or *th*e like.

1. Whether childr. of such may not be Baptized? Argum*en*t pro Affirm.[12]

not to speake of *th*e

practise of other churches generally ~~ag~~ contrary vnto o*u*rs

great offence taken at o*u*r Practise herein, both

abroad

here.

many murmurring *tha*t we come to make Heathens rather then conv*er*t Heathens to Chri*sti*ans.

1. From 1. Cor. 3.22,23. All are yo*u*rs [both Ministers & Ordinances][13] w*hi*ch seemes to be spoken of people quà Christians not ~~by~~ ^quà^ members of any p*ar*tic. church; bec. of *tha*t Reas. added, [for yow are Christs][14]

2. Circu*m*cis. was administred to all Professed Jewes & their children, & *tha*t vppon paine of Cutting off:

Theref.

why not Bapt. to *th*e childr. of all professing christianity?

whether may not *th*e danger of Omission lye vppon *th*e churches that refuse it.

3. From *th*e Com*man*dm*en*t In Math. 28.19.[15] where the Apost. & so all Ministers are Com*m*anded to bapt. *the*m *tha*t are taught & made Disciples (their childr. also being included w*i*th them) where there is no restriction of Bapt. only to them *tha*t should be first brought into church estate, for men are made Disciples by being Conuerts & Chri*sti*ans though as yet of no partic. church.

4. we find no Examples of refusing to bapt. such childr. either in *th*e [Apostles time
churches succeeding *th*e Apost.

But Contr. we haue th*e* Apost. Example of Bapt. p*er*sons into no partic. Church. Act. [8.
16.[16]

Indeed the Apost. were Extraordinary Persons (viz: in being Officers in all churches, & be[ing]||[one or two words lost] of *th*e H. Ghost &c) yet this hinders not but *tha*t their Practise in ^the manner of^ dispensing Ordinan[ces] be Exemplary & a Rule for vs to imitate (except we heare some worde to *th*e Contrary) If not, then

[when, & wherein, & how farr, only Is their practise Exemplary & a Rule for vs?
what reason is there why they are to be exemplary to vs in some practises & not in all?

Quær.

5. From *th*e Inualidity of *th*e Reason vsually alledged to the Contrary, viz: [A ministers haueing no power ouer such &c.][17] ^for^ neither haue a minister power ouer members of other churches vnto whom He doth sometimes administer *th*e L. Supper. yea why may not a Minister as well bapt. such childr. being desired, as well as (vppon request) preach, & Ordaine an Officer, & administer both Sacram*en*ts to another church (ou*er* w*hi*ch he hath no Power) by warrant of 1. Cor. 3.22,23?

Here Quær.

[Whether Administrat. of *th*e Sacram*en*ts be an Act of Iurisdiction? & If it be, then whether may not one exercise An Act of some Power towards *them tha*t neuer did actually yield *the*ms. vnto Him, supposing *tha*t Christ hath giuen it? as for one Chri*sti*an to admonish & reproue another whom He neuer saw before.
How farr or to how many descents Bapt. is to be ~~dispens~~ administred?
What if ^Power yelded^ so farr, as till Parents seeme to renounce Chri*sti*anity by [Apostacy
Scandalous sins. 1. Cor. 5.11. Eph. 5.11.[18]

2. Whether childr. borne before the Conuersion & admission of their Parents to church-fellowshipp are to be accounted mem-

bers also w*it*h their Parents? yea, what if growne to some yeares but expressing no Truth of grace, what is *th*e Church to doe in such a Case?

3. When one is Conuerted & joyned to a church haueing childr. of some yeares, whether are all such childr. to be baptized as well as Infants? If not, then at what yeares are they to be refused?

Sir, these are some things *tha*t I haue thought off (for I haue thoughts of some other, but am loath to be too burdensome) I beseech yow be pleased to pardon my boldness & beare w*it*h my rudeness & weakness. Thus tendring my humble respect to yo*u*rself & yo*u*rs, & craueing *th*e help of yo*u*r Prayers to *th*e L. for me for *tha*t Reuealation of Himselfe & Truth whereby I may be *th*e more enabled for His Service w*hi*ch through His grace He hath called me vnto *th*e most vnfitt & unworthy of all His servants, I doe take my leaue, resting

Yo*u*rs in any Chri*sti*an Service
Tho: Allen./

Charles-Towne 21th of Nov. 1642./

1. On the voyage he carried an early draft version of Cotton's *Certain Queries,* which he published, supplementing Cotton's eleven queries with a twelfth of his own. Allen arranged for the printing of *The New Covenant* . . . (London, 1654), "corrected by [Cotton's] own hand," and wrote epistles "To the Reader" for this volume and for Cotton's *Covenant of Grace* . . . (London, 1655). Later, he "fitted for the Press" a larger edition of the latter, published as *A Treatise of the Covenant of Grace* . . . (London, 1659). These details are contained in front matter in the books themselves and summarized by Julius H. Tuttle in "Writings of Rev. John Cotton," in *Bibliographical Essays: A Tribute to Wilberforce Eames* (Cambridge, Mass., 1924), 377–379.

2. in Reb*us* Ecclesiasticis: in church affairs.

3. Custodes vtriusq*ue* Tabulae: guardians of both tablets, that is, of civil and ecclesiastical law.

4. Rom. 13:1: Let every soul be subject unto the higher powers. For there is no power but of God: the powers that be are ordained of God.

1 Cor. 14:40: Let all things be done decently and in order.

5. ex[empli] gr[atia]: for example.

6. 1 Cor. 11:21: Ye cannot drink the cup of the Lord, and the cup of devils: ye cannot be partakers of the Lord's table, and of the table of devils.

7. In consulto (if not also renuente) magistratu: literally, the magistrate not having been consulted (if not also forbidding). The sense intended is: [at least] without the permission—if not also against the express decree—of a magistrate.

8. Acts 4:19: But Peter and John answered and said unto them, Whether it be right in the sight of God to hearken unto you more than unto God, judge ye.

9. Gal. 2:9: And when James, Cephas, and John, who seemed to be pillars, perceived the

grace that was given unto me, they gave to me and Barnabas the right hands of fellowship; that we should go unto the heathen, and they unto the uncircumcision.

10. 1 Cor. 3:22, 23: Whether Paul, or Apollos, or Cephas, or the world, or life, or death, or things present, or things to come; all are yours; And ye are Christ's; and Christ is God's.

11. 1 Cor. 5:9–11: I wrote unto you in an epistle not to company with fornicators: Yet not altogether with the fornicators of this world, or with the covetous, or extortioners, or with idolaters; for then must ye needs go out of the world. But now I have written unto you not to keep company, if any man that is called a brother be a fornicator, or covetous, or an idolater, or a railer, or a drunkard, or an extortioner; with such an one no not to eat.

12. Argumenta pro Affirmatione: arguments in favor.

13. These brackets are Allen's.

14. These brackets are Allen's.

15. Matt. 28:19: Go ye therefore, and teach all nations, baptizing them in the name of the Father, and of the Son, and of the Holy Ghost.

16. Acts 8 tells of Philip's baptism of many Samarians, including Simon the sorcerer, and also of the Ethiopian eunuch. Acts 16 tells of Paul's baptism of Lydia "and her household" in Macedonia and of the jailer at Philippi "and all his."

17. These brackets are Allen's.

18. Eph. 5:11: And have no fellowship with the unfruitful works of darkness, but rather reprove them.

Stephen Bachiler to John Winthrop, John Cotton, and John Wilson

February 26, 1643/4

ALS. MS: MHS, Winthrop Papers

Published: MHS, *Colls.,* 4th Ser., VII (1865), 100–105; *Winthrop Papers,* IV, 446–449

Here Bachiler is still agonizing over the charges brought against him some three years earlier in the Hampton church (see Cotton to Bachiler, Mar. 9, 1641/2). The absence of either church or town records for Hampton in this period makes precise reconstruction of the events impossible, but by this time Bachiler's excommunication had presumably been revoked. He had not been restored to his ministerial position, however, nor would he be. The fact that the settlers at Casco were trying to hire him and that the residents at Exeter, planning to form a new church, would soon enter the competition for his services suggests that perhaps the adultery charge had been satisfactorily answered or dropped, though Winthrop's account is silent on this point.[1] His reputation for womanizing did not die, however, for three years later he complained to Winthrop and apparently to Cotton and Wilson as well that, after his wife died and before he remarried, gossip was rife.[2]

The manuscript is written on both sides of a single well-preserved sheet, which contains some staining and on which the ink in some places has bled through. Although the letter is very neatly written, Bachiler's punctuation is somewhat erratic, as he treats dashes and commas interchangeably and occasionally leaves parentheses uncompleted. The text in the *Winthrop Papers* silently corrects these instances; the present edition does not. The paragraph indentation is added at points where Bachiler left extra space between his sentences.

Grace, mercy, & peace in our L. Jes. Ch*ris*t

Right Worship*fu*ll & Reuerend Brethren,

Myne humble duty & service in Christ remembred. I had no sooner written and ended this inclosed letter to my brother Cotton,[3] for some satisfaction to certaine cases, waiting for a convenient messenger, but, Casco-messenger came w*i*th yo*u*r Christian & carefull letter of my good & Gods glory (I should haue first said), was deliuerd to me, W*hi*ch inclosed letter (tho p*ro*perly belonging to my brother Cotton; yet because it may concerne you all, in respect of a reason or motiue, (w*hi*ch after will appeare in the sequell of this letter) for my furtherance to *tha*t work and place, wherto yo*u*r advice & p*er*swasion seemeth to ayme) I thought good to inclose it & send it to you all (vpon my second thoughts[)][4] as before I intended it to my brother Cotton alone. & this I desire you all to vnderstand to be the true Cause of com*m*unicating it vnto you all. Now, as Touching the maine thing it selfe of my calleing to Casco, The reasons & motiues w*hi*ch you vse to further me, were all presented vnto me, & were runing dayly in my Consideration of *th*e said calling, In so much, as it caused me to remember a passage of a Sermon of my brother Cottons (speaking long since vpon thos words in *th*e Acts of christ being made the Cornerstone, he vttered words to this effect (& I do think he will remember & owne the very words themselues) That all the p*ro*ceedings of the Scribes & Pharisies & all their adherents together—that by them all, they did but thrust & shoue at Ch*ris*t, till they had thrust him into that very place (vidzt, of being the Corner stone of the fathers building for *th*e strength & p*er*fecting of the same) to w*hi*ch the father had appoynted him. so, said I to my wife, considering what a calling I had, some .14.[5] yeres agon, (by *tha*t Company of the ploughe)[6] there to sit downe w*i*th them (not as a Planter only, but as a Pastor also) & considering how the Lord (thinking to haue rested at New Towne (then so called) vpon that disaster w*hi*ch happened to the goods of the Company by the false dealing of thos entrusted by vs w*i*th the ploughe ship, & our goods therin) I say, how the Lord shou'd me thence by an other calling to Sagust.[7] then, from Sagust to Newbury; then from Newbury, to Hampton: & now—seemes to do the like from Hampton to the very place it selfe[8]—(all the former shoveings & remoueings being still directly towards *tha*t place. w*hi*ch, I thought in my minde might haue some resemblance to the Pharisies dealing w*i*th my Lord & M*aste*r.) / Howbeit, I thought w*i*thall, I could not certainely conclude, any such secret counsayle of the Lorde, seeing the intervenient callings were also of God. & *th*e last to Hampton, not least certaine to me to be of God. As (also) *tha*t the two last remouealls (N. from Sagust to Newbury, & from Newbury to our Hampton—not being so p*ro*per from god, as from Satan & some vnjust instrum*en*ts—& this now from Hampton to Casco to be (after a sort) forced by ˆlikeˆ vnjust p*ro*ceedings,[9] as well (or as much) as by an honorable calling from Casco, & like honorable advice from you &c I was & am the more doubtfull in my selfe & is to my speciall frends, whose harts I haue cause to satisfye—why I should remoue ag*ains*t so many reasons objected ag*ains*t me. but (I feare) I am too tedious & large, takeing vp too much of yo*u*r tyme from imploym*en*ts of greater moment. I will therfore come to *th*e very poynt. and to the maine stick of all—w*hi*ch is this—I see not how I can dep*ar*te hence, till I haue (or (I meane) God for me) cleered & vindicated the cause & wronges I haue suffered of the church I liue yet in—that is—from the Teacher[10] (indeed), who hath don all & ben the cause of all the dishonour *tha*t hath accrew'd to god shame to my selfe, & griefe to all Gods people, by his irregular p*ro*ceedings, & abuse of the power of the church in his hand by the maior p*ar*te cleaveing to him—being his Countrymen & acquaintance in old Engl.—whiles my cause (tho looked sleitly into by diverse Elders & brethren) could neuer come to a judiciall searching forth of things, & an imp*ar*tiall tryall of my allegations & his defence secundum allegata et p*ro*bata.[11] w*hi*ch, if (yet) they might, I am confident in God (vpon certaine knowledge & due proufe before yo*u*r Selues whose hands are subscribed to this letter or calling of advice) the Teachers act of his excomunicateing me, (such as I am (to say no more of my selfe), would proue the foulest matter (both for the cause alleged, of *tha*t excom. & the impulsiue cause (even wroth & revenge) & also the manner of his p*ro*ceeding thorough out to *th*e very ende: & lastly—his keeping me still vnder bonds, & much more then here I may mention for—[IV] diverse causes—(Christes wrongs & sufferings excepted) that euer was committed ag*ains*t any member of a church. W*hi*ch (to beare on my shoulder in going hence) is so vncomfortable: tho I can refer it to Gods revenging hand, & wait vpon him (Eccles*iastes* 4. 1.2. & 5.7. w*i*th Psal. 10. 13.14 v*er*ses.)[12] yet (then) I am taught againe, that such sinnes, endangering the very state of church & com*m*onwealth for neglecting of the complaintes of the afflicted in such a state, as wherin, both Magistrates, Elders & brethren—all are, in the sincerest manner set, to finde out Sin, &

(*w*ith Levie) to search into the complaintes of *th*e poore not knowing father nor mother—church, or Elder—In such a state (I say) In such a wine Seller to finde such a cock-atrice,[13] & not to kill him—to haue such monstrous & fearfull p*ro*ceedings passed ouer *w*ithout due justice in p*ro*ceeding—&c this againe stirs vp my spirit to seek for, and labour to obteine a writ ad melius inquirendu*m*.[14] Towards w*hi*ch the inclosed letter tendeth (as you may perceaue.) Yet (notw*i*thstanding all *tha*t I haue said of my burthen & temtations, if yo*u*r wisedomes shall think it & judg it more safe & reasonable to refer all my wronges (conceaued) to Gods owne judgm*en*t, I blesse the Lord for his grace (if I know myne owne hart herein) I can submit my selfe to be over ruled by you.

And (here) I give you all more thankes then my pen can expresse, for that aboundant vndeserued care, you plainly ~~exp~~ shew forthe, in this yo*u*r letter of advise. Whervpon, I presume, that in case the Lord shall so prevayle *w*ith me & vpon me, as (~~vpon~~ ˆinˆ yo*u*r w*orshi*ps short postscript—you suppose I will not engage my selfe so fully & sodainly, till I ˆshallˆ haue had good experience, both of place & persons) you will ever haue me in yo*u*r memories (as occasion shalbe offered) for my gloryfying of God there, & to be ayding & assisting to *tha*t whole Province—because I am there, by yo*u*r encouradgm*en*t? that I may still depend vpon you, for yo*u*r Christian Loue and faithfullnes to me & mine.

The truth is, I haue sent them of Casco—this answer, brieflye. 1. that their necessityes, hunger & thirst after Ch. their so free choyse of my selfe (so vnworthy), their offers of Reverence, Credence, & subjection to Christes ordinances administred (according vnto God) &c. I purpose (God willing) to come & confer *w*ith them about the last week of the next monthe (our first) & *tha*t, the will of God shall over rule me ag*ains*t all the difficulties of this case (w*hi*ch are many) if that will, or as that will shall cleerlye appeare vnto ˆmeˆ: ag*ains*t w*hi*ch I shall not willfully or hypocritically shut myne eyes. This I haue p*ro*mised, & so far I haue engaged my selfe & no further. And (indeed) the being of *tha*t (my deare brother Jenner) and m^r^. Wheelwright stablished in thos p*ar*tes—is not a weak motiue to drive, or a cord to drawe me that waye.[15]

And (now) to conclude) if the Apostles words should be objected—that this is thankes worthy, if a man (for Conscience sake towards god,) shall endure griefe, suffering wrongfully—that (therfore) I ought (in this afforesaid cause of mine, to endure the greefe therof, in what soeuer I suffer wrongfully, *w*ithout seeking for any redresse or justice ag*ains*t the offender) I confesse it was more absolutly necessary so to suffer when the church had no civill power to seek vnto, then (as affore is said) in such a land of righteousnes as our new England is? But, I ende, & commending you all to God, w*i*th my poore selfe & cause—I rest

Hampton. Yo*u*r worships at com*m*aund in the Lorde, his
this 26. of *thi*s last M. moste vnworthy Servant
1643./ Stephen Bachiler

1. Bachiler's letter to Winthrop, dated May "18 or 19," 1644, discusses in some detail his decision to accept the call at Exeter, not the one at Casco. See *Winthrop Papers,* IV, 457–459. Just ten days after that letter, the General Court of Massachusetts took action to prevent Exeter's calling anyone for the time being, citing recent "divisions and contentions" there and probably feeling that a minister with Bachiler's record might not be the one to restore order. *Records of Massachusetts Bay,* II, 67–68.

2. After mentioning the death of "my deare helper and yoke fellowe," he complains that "wheras by approbation of the whole planta[tion] of Strabury Banke they haue assigned an honest neighbour (a widowe) to haue some eye and care towards my family, for washing, baking and other such common services, it is a world of woes to think what rumors detracting spirits raise vp, that I am marryed to her, or certainly shalbe, and cast on her such aspertions without ground or proufe, as that I see not how possibly I shall subsist in the place to do them that service, from which (otherwise) they cannot endure to hear, I shall departe" (Bachiler to Winthrop, May 3, 1647, *Winthrop Papers,* V, 153). In this letter Bachiler mentions "an inclosed letter to my two beloued and Reuerend brethren your elders" on the same subject.

3. Not preserved. Thanks are due to Jennifer Tolpa, Reference Librarian at the Massachusetts Historical Society, for helping to confirm the absence of this enclosure from the Winthrop Papers manuscripts.

4. The word thoughts extends to the edge of the paper; the parenthesis in this instance might have been lost to wear or trimming of the edge.

5. The 4 has been written over another number, probably a 3.

6. A company of colonists, organized in England in 1630, was known as the Company of the Plough, named after the ship that carried some of them to New England, sometimes also called the Company of Husbandmen. On June 26, 1630, they were awarded the Plough Patent, forty square miles of land between Cape Porpoise (now near Kennebunkport) and Cape Elizabeth (now southeast of Portland), which was first named Lygonia. The Saco River reaches the sea in that coastal area. On seeing the land in early July 1631, however, the colonists headed south for Massachusetts Bay, never settling the Plough Patent. The rights to the Saco area were contested by others who eventually prevailed. The Plough investors, of whom Bachiler was one, lost their money when the company ended in bankruptcy. Winthrop paints them with a broad brush, claiming that "most of them proved famylistes, & vanished away" (*Journal,* 53–54), though he did not intend to include Bachiler in this description. See Henry S. Burrage, *The Beginnings of Colonial Maine, 1602–1658* (Portland, Maine, 1914), 204–206; Wilbur D. Spencer, *Pioneers on Maine Rivers, with Lists to 1651* (Portland, Maine, 1930), 174, 245, 267–268; Philip F. Gura, *A Glimpse of Sion's Glory: Puritan Radicalism in New England, 1620–1660* (Middletown, Conn., 1984), 3–4.

7. Saugus.

8. That is, Saco, the coastal community that was his company's intended destination in

1630–1631, about fifteen miles south of what was then Casco. Both locations were north of the boundary of the Massachusetts Bay Colony in what is now Maine.

9. Bachiler was dismissed at Saugus after complaints about him, first in 1632 and again in 1635, and had recently been charged with attempted adultery in Hampton.

10. Timothy Dalton, teacher of the church at Hampton. On accepting the church's call, Dalton had brought with him additional members, who outnumbered those few who had followed Bachiler to Hampton. Winthrop notes: "Dalton's party being the most of the church, and so freemen, had great advantage of the other, though a considerable party, and some of them of the church also, whereby they carried all affairs both in church and town according to their own minds, and not with that respect to their brethren and neighbors which had been fit" (*Journal,* 519). In the Cotton Papers portion of the Thomas Prince Library at the BPL, a tiny fragment of a letter survives that was written by Bachiler on September 22, 1643 (Ms. Am. 1506, pt. 3, no. 6). The addressee's name does not survive, but Prince saw the letter when it was more fully intact and in the margin next to Bachiler's phrase "your colleague," Prince wrote "Cotton," indicating thereby that the letter was written to John Wilson. At the lower left corner of the fragment, Prince wrote, "This letter contain[s] complaints of Mr Dalton."

11. secundum allegata et probata: according to what was alleged and proved.

12. Eccles. 4:1, 2, 5–7: So I returned, and considered all the oppressions that are done under the sun: and behold the tears of such as were oppressed, and they had no comforter; and on the side of their oppressors there was power; but they had no comforter. Wherefore I praised the dead more than the living which are yet alive.

The fool foldeth his hands together, and eateth his own flesh. Better is an handful with quietness, than both hands full with travail and vexation of spirit. Then I returned, and I saw vanity under the sun.

Ps. 10:13–14: Wherefore doth the wicked contemn God? he hath said in his heart, Thou wilt not require it. Thou hast seen it; for thou beholdest mischief and spite, to requite it with thy hand: the poor committeth himself unto thee; thou art the helper of the fatherless.

13. Cockatrice: a serpent, fabulously said to kill by its glance (*OED*). A gloss for "cockatrice" at Isa. 59:5 in the Geneva Bible says, "Whatsoeuer cometh from the*m,* is poyson and bringeth death." For similar use of the word, see also Isa. 11:8, 14:29, and Jer. 8:17.

14. ad melius inquirendum: for the better investigation.

15. Thomas Jenner had been minister at Saco from 1640, and John Wheelwright had been at Wells since the spring of 1643, both to the south of Casco Bay, on what is now the southern coast of Maine. Spencer, *Pioneers of Maine Rivers,* 180; Edmund M. Wheelwright, "A Frontier Family," CSM, *Publs.,* I, *Trans.* (1892–1894), 276.

John Cotton to Master R. M.

Late 1644

Published: "Epistle to the Reader," by N. H. and I. H. in J[ohn] Cotton, *The Way of the Churches of Christ in New-England* . . . (London, 1645), sig. [A3]

N. H. and I. H., the authors of the "Epistle to the Reader" in Cotton's *Way of the Churches of Christ in New-England,*[1] introduce this fragment with the observation:

> *Least any should imagine, that every thing in the* Keyes *doth not fit all the* wards *in this Treatise to an haire, wee will here insert Mr.* Cottons *own words, in his Letter coming from him in* New-England *to our hands in the very nick of time, whiles this Epistle lay under the Presse.*[2]

Immediately after Cotton's words comes the sentence: *"So Mr.* Cotton *in his Letter to Mr.* R. M." Master R. M. has not been definitely identified.[3]

If you think the Draught of CHURCH-DISCIPLINE, which was sent over in your Ship, varieth from that of the POVVER OF THE KEYES,[4] sent over the yeare after;[5] you may have some occasion so to conceive from some difference of expression in LOGICALL TERMES, but not a jote in any DOCTRINE OF DIVINITIE, *or* CHURCH-PRACTISE.

1. That N. H. is Nathanael Holmes can be concluded from the fact that he wrote and signed with his full name an "Epistle Pacificatory" in Cotton's *Way of Congregational Churches Cleared* . . . (London, 1648), where he mentions that Cotton had sent him that book and a letter asking *"That I would assist the Press."* He sought out the same printer, Matthew Simmons, for that book as he had for *The Way of the Churches of Christ in New-England.* The identity of J. H. is not known.

2. *The Way of the Churches of Christ in New-England* was entered in the Stationers' Register February 27, 1644/5, and probably "lay under the Presse" soon after (*A Transcript of the Worshipful Company of Stationers: From 1640–1708 A.D.,* 3 vols. [London, 1913–1914], I, 151). Allowing time for the ocean journey, it seems safe to assume Cotton wrote his letter to R. M. in very late 1644.

3. R. M. was probably one Richard More (1614 to 1694–1696?), who as a boy was in the original *Mayflower* group that settled Plymouth Colony in 1620 but was later a freeman in Salem. He is described in colonial records as "Capt. More" and, more commonly, a "mariner." Cotton refers to R. M.'s ship, suggesting, it would seem, that he is the ship's master. There is some confusion in the identity in that more than one Richard More was in the Salem area at this time. One of them, in fact, was married in England in October 1645. Cotton's correspondent clearly sailed to England in the course of his business. See Anderson, *Great Migration,* 1283–1287, and

George Ernest Bowman, "The Only Mayflower Gravestone," *Mayflower Descendant,* III (1901), 193–201.

4. The text here mistakenly prints KEKES; the reference is to Cotton's *Keyes of the Kingdom of Heaven* . . . (London, 1644).

5. This indication that Cotton's *Way of the Churches of Christ in New-England,* published in 1645, was written and sent to England before *The Keyes of the Kingdom of Heaven,* which was published in 1644, is borne out in John Owen's *Defence of John Cotton* . . . (Oxford, 1658), where Owen claims *The Way* was written several years earlier than *The Keyes;* see Julius H. Tuttle, "The Writings of Rev. John Cotton," in *Bibliographical Essays: A Tribute to Wilberforce Eames* (Cambridge, Mass., 1924), 371–372.

John Cotton to [Robert Harding?]

[About 1638–1644]

Tr. MS: MHS, Mather Papers: Cotton Mather, "Biblia Americana," II

Cotton Mather's "Biblia Americana," a six-volume collection of miscellaneous documents arranged as a biblical commentary, in the section on Numbers 35, contains a quotation from a Cotton letter.[1] Mather introduces the excerpt:

> It happened that in the dayes of ~~old~~ Mr *Cotton,* a gentleman belonging to his church here in ~~Boston~~ the *American Boston,* left the church, and went and lived in ˆaˆ plantation, which did not maintain *th*e Institutions of o*u*r glorious Lord. This gentleman, by some unhappy sort of *chance-medley,* did happen to kill an *Indian.* On that occasion the venerable old man wrote unto him a Letter full of wise and grave Admonitions, which I happen at this Instant to be entertained withal. In one of his Admonitions, I find an *Illustration,* which indeed I thought worth Transcribing and præserving. It runs in these Terms.

Cotton's correspondent may be Robert Harding, a Boston merchant who had gone to Newport, Rhode Island, when his wife was admonished as a supporter of Anne Hutchinson in 1638. Harding himself was disarmed November 20, 1637, for supporting Hutchinson and John Wheelwright. He returned to the Boston church on June 2, 1644, when, according to Robert Keayne's notes, he addressed the congregation after the morning sermon, noting as one of the mercies he had experienced John Winthrop's writing to a Narragansett sachem and saving his life after Harding had killed an Indian.[2]

In the *Law,* it was appointed, that he who *slew a man unawares,* should fly to a *City of Refuge,* (which was a *city of priests,*) and there abide. Num. 35.25 to 28.[3]

Which did argue (tho' it were a *Judicial Law*) that such a man as had been left of God to *manslaughter* (though unawares) had not walked so close with God, and with his ordinances, as was meet, and therefore God left him to do such a mischief, and now (upon peril of his life) required him to live among the *priests* all his dayes, that he might grow more spiritual, by living among them. We know, the *Law* is abrogated; yett surely the *Equity* still continueth, both in the *cause* of the mischief, & in the *cure*. We beleeve, this evil fell upon you, and by you upon the poor pagan, because your Heart sate loose from the Ordinances of *the* Lord. And now, we beleeve, that if God give you to clear yourself from Guilt of Innocent Blood, the Lord then calleth you with a strong Hand, to Live in the Fellowship of His ordinances, and not to wander still like a Lamb *in a large place,* or like a *sheep without a shepherd*.[4]

1. I am grateful to Michael P. Winship for calling this letter to my attention.

2. MHS, MS, Robert Keayne's Sermon Notes for "Mo 4 2, 1644," that is, June 2, 1644. Michael P. Winship also called this entry in Keayne's notes to my attention. The date of the murder is unknown. On Harding, see Anderson, *Great Migration,* 855–858; Winthrop, *Journal,* 248–249, 364 n. 89.

3. Num. 35:25–28: And the congregation shall deliver the slayer out of the hand of the revenger of blood, and the congregation shall restore him to the city of his refuge, whither he was fled: and he shall abide in it unto the death of the high priest, which was anointed with the holy oil. But if the slayer shall at any time come without the border of the city of his refuge, whither he was fled; And the revenger of blood find him without the borders of the city of his refuge, and the revenger of blood kill the slayer; he shall not be guilty of blood: Because he should have remained in the city of his refuge until the death of the high priest: but after the death of the high priest the slayer shall return into the land of his possession.

4. This sounds like Cotton's urging Harding to return to Boston to resume church fellowship there, suggesting that the letter might have been written toward the end of the Hardings' six-year absence—closer to 1644 than to 1638.

Following his transcription of Cotton's letter, Mather adds: "Thus, my grandfather."

John Tombes to John Wilson, John Cotton, and Other New England Ministers

May 25, 1645

ALS. MS: AAS, Henry Jessey Papers

Published: John Tombes, *An Apology; or, Plea for the Two Treatises . . .* (London, 1646), 13–14; Thomas Crosby, *The History of the English Baptists, from the Reformation to the Beginning of the Reign of King George I,* I (London, 1738), 121–122; Isaac Backus, *A History of New England with Particular Reference to the . . . Baptists* (1777–1796), 2d ed., with notes by David Weston (1871; rpt. New York, 1969), I, 147; Philip J. Anderson, "Letters of Henry Jessey and John Tombes to the Churches of New England, 1645," *Baptist Quarterly,* XXVIII (1979), 37–38

John Tombes (1603?–1676) was an English minister who "was by the late 1640s, according to Richard Baxter, 'reputed the most Learned and able Anabaptist in England.'"[1] The letter, which is addressed to various New England ministers but specifically identifies John Cotton and John Wilson as intended recipients, is preserved in the midst of a copy of a letter from Henry Jessey, another Baptist, "To all the Officers of the Churches of Christ in New England. The Elders & Deacons there." Jessey's much longer letter occupies pages numbered 2–12 but is not included in the present collection because it contains no specific address to Cotton, being more like an open letter intended to be widely circulated and perhaps even published. Tombes's letter is in a different hand—presumably his own—and is written on the top two-thirds of page 11, as if it had been written there first and was later surrounded by the final portion of Jessey's copy of his letter.

The New Englanders assigned the task of answering Tombes's treatise to Thomas Cobbett, as Cotton's (unpreserved) reply to Tombes informed him.[2]

To all the Elders of the Churches of Chr*is*t in New=England, and to Each in particular, By name to the Pastor and Teacher of the Church of God at Boston there, These p*re*sent

Reverend Bretheren,

Vnderstanding that there is some disquiet in yo*ur* Churches about Pædobaptisme, and being moved by some (that honour you much in the lord Jesus, and desire yo*ur* comfortable account at the day of Christ), that I would yeild that a copy of my Examen of Mr Marshall his sermon of infants Baptisme might bee transcribed to bee sent to you,[3] I have consented thereto, and doe commend it to yo*u*r examinac*i*on in like manner, as you may perceive by the reading of it, as I did to Mr Marshals, not doubting, but you wil as in gods presence, and accountable to Chr*is*t Jesus weigh the thing, remembring that of o*u*r Lord Chr*is*t. Jo: 7.24. Judge not according to the appearance, but judge righteous iudgement.[4] To the blessing of him, who is yo*u*r god and o*u*r god, yo*u*r Judge, and o*u*r Judge, I leave you, and the flocke of God over which the holy Ghost hath made you overseers, and rest

from my study
at the Temple
in London.
May. 25 1645,

Yo*u*r Brother, and fellow-
servant in the worke of
Christ.
John Tombes.

1. Anderson, "Letters of Jessey and Tombes," *Baptist Quarterly,* XXVIII (1979), 30. See Anderson's essay for more detailed comment on Tombes and his letter.

2. Backus's *History of New England Baptists,* I, 150, notes: "Mr. Tombes says Mr. Cotton wrote to him, that the piece he sent them was delivered to Mr. Cobbet [to] answer."

3. Stephen Marshall, a prominent figure in the Westminster Assembly and frequent preacher to Parliament, had delivered and then published *A Sermon of the Baptizing of Infants, Preached in the Abbey-Church at Westminster* (London, 1644). After he wrote this letter, Tombes's reply was published with the title *An Examen of the Sermon of Mr. Stephen Marshall, about Infant-Baptisme . . .* (London, 1645). The handwritten transcription of the latter is also preserved in the American Antiquarian Society's Baptist Papers.

4. This sentence transcribes exactly John 7:24.

Robert Jordan to John Cotton

July 3, 1645

ALS. MS: BPL, Ms. Am. 1506, pt. 3, no. 7

Published: *Maine Historical and Genealogical Register,* III (1886), 79–81

Robert Jordan here writes from Richmond Island, about a half-mile off the coast just south of Cape Elizabeth near present-day Portland, Maine, where he had arrived from England in May 1641. Raised in the city of Worcester in the English West Country and educated at Balliol College, Oxford (bachelor of arts, 1634), he was decidedly non-Puritan in his church practice and Royalist in his politics. Opponents in Maine represented him to the Massachusetts authorities as radically unorthodox. George Cleeve wrote to John Winthrop from Casco Bay identifying Jordan as "one unworthily called a minister of Christ" and even "a ministar of antichrist."[1] It was doubtless with such charges ringing in his ears that Winthrop had written admonishingly to Jordan, as Jordan announces in his first sentence.

Jordan's letter echoes the kinds of inquiry Cotton had received from younger ministers twenty years earlier in England, though Jordan's adoption of the guise of the "humble supplicant," stressing his own "Imbecillity" in contrast to Cotton's "not doubted ability," sounds less genuine than the deference in the earlier letters from Cotton's students and peers, coming as it does from one already identified as an adversary of the New England congregationalists. But, like Cotton's earlier correspondents, Jordan has heard "the Generall report of your Clement disposition" and so presumes to present to him a "rude tract" he has written, asking Cotton to identify and comment on its shortcomings. With Cotton on the verge of turning sixty, his reputation as a wise and willing epistolary commentator on prickly issues remains very much intact. The manuscript that Jordan enclosed was apparently a partial rejoinder to Cotton's recently published work on church polity, *The Keyes of the Kingdom of Heaven* (1644). The enclosure does not survive, nor does any response to it by Cotton. The manuscript of this letter, however, which was the copy Jordan actually sent to Cotton, remains in excellent condition.

Despite his reputation for unorthodoxy, Jordan spent a long life on Richmond Island and the neighboring mainland, well outside the jurisdiction of the Massachusetts Bay orthodoxy, ultimately acquiring several thousand acres of land and considerable influence in the province. This letter was written after Jordan had married Sarah Winter and become well known locally, though his and the region's prosperity still lay ahead.[2]

The letter is written on a single sheet, folded once, making four pages. Jordan filled two pages on the recto and the left one on the verso. The address block is written on the right-hand side of the verso:

> To the Reuerend & Judicious
> Mr John Cotton. Elder of the Church at
> Bostonne present thees./

Honoured In *Chris*t Jesus

Your seruant hauing formerly receaued a letter of Godly councell, Intermixed with deep Intimations of an irregular Judgment, blamable practice and Dangerous Consequenc, from the hand of that Eminent father of this Country Mr John Winthrope, though the particular grounds are still to mee latent. Ther sinc coming to my sight, (by a Diuine permission) a certaine book Intituled The Keyes;[3] owning your name. ~~and~~ Reached out vnto me by the hand of Mr John Holland,[4] a man not to you vnfaithfull and to me christianly frendly: At sight wherof I was suddenly Jelouse of mine owne suspected misguidance. And as time would permitt I drew=forth an Imperfect

Coppy therof that by hit I might try my former thoughts and by all meanes possible Indeauour a submission of mind to all the wayes of verity and peace. Amongst other contents to me as yet very dubious, I applyed my mean & vnapt faculties, to the due examination of the ~~text~~ 2 first texts of scripture alleaged to proue the firt act of the breatherens liberty,[5] whervnto they did call me you will perceaue by the ill dresed & illiterat discource Being vnable In my self to reduce my thoughts from theyr former current. The Generall report of your Clement disposition, togeather with the Resolued ex^pec^tancy of your not doubted ability, raysed In mee (although not so Intended at my first onsett) a resolution of presenting [2] presenting thees vnto your Fatherly Construction. My hopes are; that you will forgiue the trespas; and acquitt me from the lest Inclinations willingly to offend. Lett mee speak (In proportion) it is a blessing I wreastle for, Truth I am sedulous after: my haltings and shame shall bee my Glory; so that, I may obtaine what I persue. As a humble supplicant therfore I begg your patienc if I haue In any thing mistaken your Intentions; lay it to the account of humane frailty, If ought vnsauory hath dropped from my penn; Imput it to ill nurtriture, for it neuer flowed from a crossing temper, nor disrespecting breast: That you will not apprehend this attempt as an act of ostentation, the consciousnes of myn Imbecillity hath already assured mee. Did I not præsume the same moderation to bee In you, as In Paule. Phil: 3.15.16.[6] I should not haue so highly attempted. My Request to you is; as your leisure shall permitt; (euen for the cause of him, who hath bought a peculiar[7] to him self) with a correcting pen to note what you find herin dissonant from the Truth; and Candidly afford som farther light, That my error being euinced; my practise may find (by Gods blessing) a seuere Repentanc[,] Ready Relinquishment and a sincere Retractation: till when I shall soarly mistrust my self like thoes 2. disciples, going to Emaus, talking with and of Christ, but theyr Eies were holden that they could not see him.[8] Good S*ir* let mee see the [3] the deceauablnes of my reason: and I shall with an earnest violation take hold on your skirt; and say, I will goe with you; for I haue found that God is with you Zac. 8[.][9]

Thus expecting your peculiar suruaigh of this rude tract, and considing that you will to mee remitt it togeather with your better Instructions (A fauour though vnmannerly demanded, yet not Ingloriously performed) I comend you to *th*e bosom of him, who is able to direct and crouned the endeauours of his. I rest

Yours In all christian seruice though
by face vnknowne
Robert Jordan,

From Richmonds Island.
July the 3^{d} 1645./

1. George Cleeve and Others to the Governor, Deputy Governor, and Assistants of Massachusetts, Feb. 18, 1645/6, *Winthrop Papers,* V, 60; George Cleeve to John Winthrop, Jan. 27, 1643/4, *Winthrop Papers,* IV, 434.

2. For further information on Jordan, see Henry S. Burrage, *The Beginnings of Colonial Maine, 1602–1658* (Portland, Maine, 1914), 305–306, 342–355, 380–382; *Alumni Oxonienses,* II, 834.

3. Cotton, *The Keyes of the Kingdom of Heaven* . . . (London, 1644).

4. The *Records of Massachusetts Bay* first mentions John Holland on August 4, 1635, in connection with a complaint against one Thomas Wonnarton for striking him and calling him names (I, 152). At this time Holland was said to be "att the eastward," which probably places him in Maine. A month later on September 3, 1635, Holland was authorized to operate a ferry "betwixte the Capt. Poynt att Dorchest[r], & Mr Newberryes Creeke" (I, 159). He is subsequently mentioned as a jury member on more than one occasion.

5. In chapter 2 of Cotton's *Keyes,* there is a discussion of Church "liberty" based on Gal. 5:13 ("Brethren, you have been called unto Liberty, onely use not your liberty as an occasion to the flesh, but by love serve one another"). Jordan may, however, be referring more specifically to Cotton's chapter 4, which is headed *"Of the subject to whom the key of Church* priviledge, power, *or* Liberty *is given,"* which begins by observing, "This key is given to the Brethren of the Church: for so saith the Apostle, in *Gal.* 5. 13 . . . *Brethren, you have been called to liberty.*" He then goes on to list and discuss the various powers, or liberties, possessed by "the Brethren," the first of which is the *"liberty* to choose their Officers," in support of which he cites Acts 1, which describes the selection of an apostle from among 120 people, as well as Acts 14:23, where *"They ordained them Elders, chosen by lifting up of hands"* (*Keyes,* 12, 13). We have too little context from Jordan's letter to be sure any of these are the biblical passages in Cotton's text that Jordan was interested in, but "the breatherens liberty" is a central theme of Cotton's book.

6. Phil. 3:15, 16: Let us therefore, as many as be perfect, be thus minded: and if in any thing ye be otherwise minded, God shall reveal even this unto you. Nevertheless, whereto we have already attained, let us walk by the same rule, let us mind the same thing.

7. Jordan probably meant to write a people peculiar.

8. Luke 24:13–53 tells of Jesus and the two disciples on the road to Emmaus. Verse 16: But their eyes were holden that they should not know him.

9. Zech. 8:8: And I will bring them, and they shall dwell in the midst of Jerusalem: and they shall be my people, and I will be their God, in truth and in righteousness.

John Cotton to Thomas Shepard

[April 3, 1646]

ALS. MS: MSA, CCXL, Hutchinson Papers, I, fols. 103, 104

In L. Thompson, "Letters of John Cotton," 178–181

In 1646, Thomas Shepard was at work on his lengthy treatise on the Sabbath, *Theses Sabbaticae; or, The Doctrine of the Sabbath* (London, 1649), which would be published at just about the time of his death.[1] He apparently made an attempt from 1646 to 1648 to glean the wisdom of several of his New England colleagues as he put down his own thoughts, for we know he wrote to and received answers on the subject from Thomas Hooker, John Allen, Richard Mather, and Thomas Cobbett. All of their replies survive, along with this letter from Cotton, in the Hutchinson Papers.[2]

The Puritans' interest in Sabbatarianism had been a matter of public discourse for a half-century, ever since Nicholas Bownde published *The Doctrine of the Sabbath* in 1595. Interest in the subject grew as Puritan acceptance of Sabbatarianism spread, leading up to the English church's challenge in the issuing of "The Book of Sports" in 1618. The issue became one that helped to define the Puritans in the public's consciousness. As early as 1610, John Cotton had addressed his "Christian freindes and beloved Brethren" at Emmanuel College on the subject of "the time when the Lordes day beginneth whether at the Eveninge or in the morninge." In his opening remarks, he noted that he had prepared this "shorte discourse" "upon your renewed requestes."[3] In soliciting Cotton's answers to his specific questions, then, Shepard was calling on someone who had long thought seriously about what Scripture had to say on the subject. The issue of what time of day the Sabbath begins is the third of four major subjects taken up in Shepard's *Theses Sabbaticae.* The other three major sections of the book deal with "The Morality of the Sabbath," "The Change of the Sabbath" (from the seventh to the first day of the week), and "The Sanctification of the Sabbath." These latter three subjects are all touched upon in Cotton's brief replies in this letter to Shepard's questions to him; the former—the subject of Cotton's discourse at Emmanuel—is not, though it is the subject of the following partial letter (see Cotton to [Unknown], [1646–1648?]).[4]

The manuscript in Cotton's hand is well preserved, having suffered only the loss of a small piece from the upper right-hand corner of the recto and the date line at the bottom left-hand corner of the verso. Fortunately, the latter line was recorded in the Massachusetts Historical Society's nineteenth-century transcription, enabling us to recapture the precise dating of the letter. Water stains cover the entire right half of the recto and have caused fading of the ink in the first four lines and the top half of the right margin of the recto. The letter is addressed on an additional sheet that served as the envelope:

> To my reverend & deare brother
> Mr Thomas Shepard, Pastor
> of *th*e Church at Cambridge
> Del*iver* these w*i*th speede./

Shepard wrote his own cryptic, crabbed, and now partially illegible notes in four lines at right angles to this address block.

Deare brother,

To yo*u*r former Quæstion, I would Answer in these Theses:

[1. not onely some sett statum Tempus Cultus:[5]
2. nor onely, *th*e 7th Part of Time:

[1] The morality of *the* 4th Com*mandmen*t, is
3. nor onely such a 7th Part of time, as reserveth sex co{ntinuos} dies,[6] for labo*u*r: but
4. That 7th Part of time (reserving sex continuos Dies fo{r} labo*u*r) w*hi*ch God himself (*th*e Author of all Holynesse) {App}ointeth: w*hi*ch was
1. before Christ, *th*e last Day of *th*e 7, sixe working dayes goeing before:
2. since Christ, *th*e First of *th*e 7; 6 working dayes following after.

2. The 7th day of Holy Rest given to Adam, as a monum*en*t of *th*e Creation, {&} of Gods Rest from *th*e work of it, was morall, & had noething vmbratile[7] or Ceremoniall in it, before *th*e Fall.

3. After *th*e Fall, when wee in Adam had lost o*u*r Holynesse, The Holy Day was then Invested w*i*th a Ceremoniall σχεσις,[8] a Typicall signification, that *th*e Lord o*u*r God did, & would sanctify vs. Exod. 3i. i3.[9]

And seeing, after o*u*r Fallen estate, sanctification is an Effect of o*u*r Redemption, The Sabbath being now given for a signe of o*u*r sanctification by God, It Argued, That it had now a Typicall vse putt vpon it of o*u*r Redemption, & so of o*u*r sanctification by Christ. If it be asked, wherein stoode *th*e Resemblance of that Type? As *th*e mysticall Body of Christ (*th*e Church of Israel) Rested on *th*e 7th Day from labo*u*r: so *th*e naturall Body of Christ Rested in *th*e Grave, *th*e whole 7th Day, night & Day, from[10] all Actions of Humane life: & by *tha*t Rest Procured o*u*r Rest from sinne vnto himself in Peace, as being *th*e Accomplishm*en*t of his Death & Humiliation. Here *th*e Sabbath (even *th*e weekely Sabbath) is fitly called by *th*e Ap*ost*le, a shadow of Christ, & *th*e Body, Christ (to wit, his Body Resting in *th*e Grave) Coloss. 2. i6, i7.[11] [This I learned from Brightman (whose le*tt*ere I send you to peruse) & finde it also avouched by Broughton.][12]

4. Now because this shadowy vse of *th*e Sabbath (for a type of o*u*r Redemption & sanctification) was vnto man fallen, of farre greater Consideration, then *th*e first morall vse of it (as it was a monum*en*t of *th*e Creation:) Therefore *th*e Body of this shadow being come, It was meete, *th*e shadow of *th*e Sabbath of *th*e 7th Day, should be Abolished. And yet because *th*e morall vse of it (as a monum*en*t of the Creation) was still to be p*re*served, Therefore Christ Appointed [iv] {*th*e First} day of *th*e weeke, to be kept in *th*e stead of it, w*hi*ch was *th*e First {Day of} *th*e Breaking forth both of o*u*r Redemption, & Creation,

The Obiection in yo*u*r syllogisme, to Proove *tha*t *th*e 7th Day sabbath was onely p*re*sent in *th*e Com*mandmen*t, because the Blessing was given onely to it, will not hold, For I would Deny the Minor. God in Blessing *th*e Day of Rest, w*hi*ch He then sanctifyed, did virtually & Analogically Blesse *tha*t other

Sabbath of *th*e First Day of *th*e weeke, w*hi*ch He intended to substitute, in fulnesse of time, in *th*e roome of this. Moses in Blessing *th*e Tribe of Levi (Deut. 33. 7, to ii:)[13] blessed all *th*e Ministers of *th*e Gospell, though wee then had not Actuall Being, & though *th*e Jewes were not then bound to Attend to vs, till *th*e Leviticall Ministery was Remooved, & o*u*rs substituted. w*hi*ch may satisfy yo*u*r 2. Reasons brought to Back yo*u*r Minor.

Ob*jection*. If vi Analogiæ, then not vi mandati 4ti.[14]

Ans*wer*. It followeth not. A man whose Dog worryeth a man, after warning, is justly Putt to Death vi Analogiæ of *tha*t Com*mandmen*t, w*hi*ch Adiudgeth him to Death, whose Oxe, after warning goreth sonne, or Daughter.

To Q. 2

As for Reference of *th*e Jewish Feasts, to *th*e 4th Com*mandmen*t, though my weake Judgem*en*t goeth not along w*i*th it, yet if any man would have it so, I will not contend. Vrsine,[15] & divers others, doe so referre *th*emselves fruatur quisq*ue* Judicio suo.[16]

But *th*e Reason, why I conceyve, *th*e Jewish Festivalls did rather pertayne to *th*e 2d Com*mandmen*t, is not, because in *th*em the Time was Taken vp for *th*e Duetyes sake: but because both *th*e Time, & Place, & Duetyes were Cultus Institutus,[17] w*hi*ch (you know) is *th*e p*ro*per subiect of *th*e 2d Com*mandmen*t: Whereas *th*e Sabbath eandem planè vim et rationem habet cum ijs quæ ex naturâ suâ sunt moralis, & naturalis Juris. Ames*ius*. Medull. L. 2. c. 15. s. 6.[18]

As you Desired a speedy Answer, so I have (as I could in these straits) returned it, & kept *th*e children (yours & mine owne) to take it w*i*th *th*em: w*i*th *th*em I send also Mr Brightmans l*ett*ere of *th*e Sabbath, though it be accompanyed w*i*th other scripts, as Mr Ames l*ett*ere of Cards & Dice iustifying his sermon (w*hi*ch I heard him Preach at Cambridge) about *th*em,[19] & *th*e enterco*u*rse betweene Mr Wotten & Dr Overall[20] about Ceremonyes, & Another l*ett*ere of Padri Paulo to an Abbott in Fraunce about Direction in studyes of Divinity.[21] When you have made what vse you please of *th*e Booke, I pray you, Returne it againe by a safe hand. The Lord carry along yo*u*r labo*u*rs, & your wifes Burden to a gratious & blessed Issue.[22] W*i*th hearty love & thanks to you & hir, for my boy, I rest,

Yo*u*rs as his owne,

{Boston, this 3. of 2. 1646} Joh*n* Cotton./

1. The book was registered with the Stationers' Company in London on May 28, 1649; Shepard must have completed his work by early April at the latest. He died at Cambridge, Massachusetts, on August 25. *A Transcript of the Register of the Worshipful Company of Stationers: From 1640–1708 A.D.* (London, 1913–1914), I, 318; Thomas Werge, *Thomas Shepard* (Boston, 1987), [vi].

2. MSA, CCXL, Hutchinson Papers, I, fols. 100, 107, 129, 160.

3. Winton U. Solberg, "John Cotton's Treatise on the Duration of the Lord's Day," in Fred-

erick S. Allis, Jr., and Philip Chadwick Foster Smith, eds., *Sibley's Heir: A Volume in Memory of Clifford Kenyon Shipton,* CSM, *Publs.,* LIX, *Colls.* (1982), 509. Solberg's valuable edition of this manuscript owned by the Emmanuel College Library made available the full text of this previously unpublished lecture. On Cotton's 1610 discourse and on Shepard's *Theses Sabbaticae,* see Solberg, *Redeem the Time: The Puritan Sabbath in Early America* (Cambridge, Mass., 1977), 111–112, 153–157. For a helpful summary of the late-sixteenth-century context, see also Patrick Collinson, "The Beginnings of English Sabbatarianism," *Studies in Church History,* I (1964), 207–221.

4. The relationship of the present letter to this undated fragmentary Cotton manuscript in the Hutchinson Papers is unclear. Both treat questions related to the Sabbath, but the fragment is not, as Lawrance Thompson supposed ("Letters of John Cotton," 181), a part of this letter.

5. statum Tempus Cultus: a set time for worship.

6. sex continuos dies: six days in a row.

7. The *OED* gives as sense 2c (obsolete) for umbratile: "serving as a token or type," with an example dated 1663.

8. σχεσις: quality.

9. Exod. 31:13: Speak thou also unto the children of Israel, saying, Verily my sabbaths ye shall keep: for it is a sign between me and you throughout your generations; that ye may know that I am the Lord that doth sanctify you.

10. Here Cotton inadvertently wrote "from from all Actions," repeating the word "from" at the end of one line and the beginning of the next.

11. Col. 2:16, 17: Let no man therefore judge you in meat, or in drink, or in respect of an holyday, or of the new moon, or of the sabbath days: Which are but a shadow of things to come; but the body is of Christ.

12. The brackets around this sentence are Cotton's.

Thomas Brightman (1562–1607), graduate of Queen's College, Cambridge (bachelor of arts, 1580/1; master's, 1584); Hugh Broughton (1549–1612), graduate of Magdalen College, Cambridge (bachelor of arts, 1569/70; master's, 1573), fellow of St. John's and then of Christ's College, famous divine, learned Hebraist, and prolific author. On Brightman's millennialism and its influence on Cotton, see Theodore Dwight Bozeman, *To Live Ancient Lives: The Primitivist Dimension in Puritanism* (Chapel Hill, N.C., 1988), 198–216. Shepard's *Theses Sabbaticae* expresses strong disagreement with Cotton and his sources, Brightman and Broughton, on this typological interpretation: "If the question be, What type is affixed and annexed to the Sabbath? I think it difficult to find out, although man's wanton wit can easily allegorize and readily frame imaginations enough in this point. Some think it typified Christ's rest in the grave; but I fear this will not hold, no more than many other Popish conjectures, wherein their allegorizing postilers abound. . . . Some scruples I see not yet through, about this text, enforce me herein to be silent, and therefore to leave it to such as think they may defend it, as one ground of some affixed type unto the Jewish Sabbath." *Theses Sabbaticae,* in *The Works of Thomas Shepard* (1853; rpt. New York, 1967), III, 196–197.

13. Deut. 33:7–11: And this is the blessing of Judah: and he said, Hear, Lord, the voice of Judah, and bring him unto his people: let his hands be sufficient for him; and be thou an help to him from his enemies.

And of Levi he said, Let thy Thummim and thy Urim be with thy holy one, whom thou didst prove at Massah, and with whom thou didst strive at the waters of Meribah; Who said unto his father and to his mother, I have not seen him; neither did he acknowledge his brethren, nor knew his own children: for they have observed thy word, and kept thy covenant. They shall teach Jacob thy judgments, and Israel thy law: they shall put incense before thee, and whole burnt sacrifice upon thine altar. Bless, Lord, his substance, and accept the work of his hands: smite through the loins of them that rise against him, and of them that hate him, that they rise not again.

14. vi Analogiæ: by force of analogy; vi mandati 4ti: by force of the fourth commandment.

15. Zacharias Ursinus (1534–1583), a Calvinist from Breslau and chief author of the Heidelberg Catechism (1563) who helped to spread Calvinism in Europe.

16. fruatur quisq*ue* Judicio suo: let each enjoy his own judgment.

17. cultus institutus: an established form of worship.

18. The Latin passage is an exact quotation from William Ames, *Medulla SS. Theologiae,* 4th ed. [London, 1630], book 2, chap. 15 ("De Tempore Cultus"), section (or paragraph) 6, 348–349. A translation of this book was published as *The Marrow of Sacred Divinity* (London, 1642); the Latin passage is translated there: "it hath the very same force and reason with those [laws] that are of morall and naturall right" (323).

19. William Ames (1576–1633), whose *Medulla* Cotton has just quoted, was a graduate and fellow of Christ's College, Cambridge, when on December 21, 1609, he preached a sermon at St. Mary's Church in which he opposed playing cards and dice, which was generally condoned in the colleges during the Christmas season. Otherwise known as a radical Nonconformist, Ames was suspended from his ecclesiastical duties one month later and chose to leave Cambridge immediately. Soon afterward, having been denied a lectureship at Colchester by the bishop of London, he went to Holland, where he remained until his death. For Cotton's own views on card playing, see his exchange of letters with Ralph Levett in March 1626, above. On Ames's sermon, see Sprunger, *William Ames,* 22–26.

20. Anthony Wotton (1561?–1626), graduate and fellow of King's College, Cambridge, and John Overall (1561–1619), fellow of Trinity College, had both stood for the vacant Regius professorship of divinity at Cambridge in 1596. As Thomas Fuller puts it, noting their equal capacity, "Wotton was not rejected, though Overall was preferred to the chair" (*The History of the University of Cambridge, from the Conquest to the Year 1634* [Cambridge, 1840], 288). Cotton apparently refers to an unpublished exchange between them.

21. Paul Sarpi (1552–1623), author of the influential *History of the Council of Trent* and noted for his efforts to propagate Calvinism from his base in Venice, was widely known as Father Paul or Padri Paolo. The letter to which Cotton refers may be letter 122 in *The Letters of the Renowned Father Paul . . . Written to . . . Monsieur Gillot, and Others . . . ,* trans. Edward Brown (London, 1693), 411–415. That letter (which does suggest good educational practice), the English translator tells us, "went about in divers Copies in more Countries than one. Arch-Bishop *Usher* got a Copy of it; and Dr. *Parr* printed it amongst the Additional Letters in the end of the Arch-Bishop's Life and Letters."

22. Cotton did not yet know that on the previous day, April 2, 1646, Joanna Shepard had given birth to their son, John, who would survive only four months. Joanna herself would soon die, "after three weeks lying in." Thomas Shepard, *The Autobiography,* in Michael McGiffert, ed., *God's Plot: Puritan Spirituality in Thomas Shepard's Cambridge,* rev. ed. (Amherst, Mass., 1994), 72.

Benjamin Keayne to John Cotton

March 12, 1646/7

Copy. MS: transcription, September 29, 1647, Court House, Suffolk County, Massachusetts

Published: W. B. Trask, ed., *Suffolk Deeds,* I (Boston, 1880), 84

Benjamin Keayne (c. 1619–1662), a Boston merchant, married Sarah Dudley (1620–1659), the younger sister of the poet Anne Dudley Bradstreet, in 1638. Keayne was in England in 1646, where he had gone with his wife, probably for business. By this time she had already committed the sexual profligacy of which her husband accuses her here, and he had sent her back to Massachusetts Bay. In the summer of 1647 the couple was divorced, apparently through the assistance of her father, Thomas Dudley, who was then deputy governor of the colony. The scandal was surely a serious concern to him and his family. After the divorce, Sarah Dudley Keayne was excommunicated from the Boston church in October 1647 for "Irregular prophecying" and for "odious, lewd, and scandalous uncleane behaviour with . . . an Excommunicate person."[1]

This letter survives in a partial transcription, copied into a book of deeds just six months after it was written. The transcription was made on "29 (7) *1647,*" that is, September 29, 1647. Though it is not a deed at all, nor directly related to property ownership, the letter's author might have been building a case to disinherit his estranged wife, whose infidelity the letter alleges.[2] On March 15, three days after his letter to Cotton, Keayne wrote on the same subject to Cotton's colleague, John Wilson. He avers there, "I haue spent my estate to maintaine my strength to content, & hazarded my health & life, to satisfy the vnsatiable desire & lust of a wife that in requitall impoysoned my body w*i*th such a running of the reines that would, if not (through mercie) cured, haue turned vnto the French Pox & so indangered my life."[3] A third letter, dated March 18, also from London, is addressed to Keayne's father-in-law, Thomas Dudley, who had apparently asked Keayne to clarify his intention with regard to Sarah, for Keayne wrote, "Therefore as you desire, I doe plainely declare my resolution, never againe to liue w*i*th her as a husband."[4] These letters thus cumulatively and purposefully establish, on the grounds of adultery, the absent Keayne's basis for a divorce, a result which was soon to follow.[5]

The transcription is preceded by the following headnote:

> 29(7)*1647* A part of a l*ett*re written from Benjamin Keaine vnto Mr John Cotton. Dat. London. March. 12th 1646.

For belieue it S*ir*: had not a divine hand supported I should haue sunck vnder so greate a burden, of vnworthines from her, to whom (as in the relation of a husband) I haue a quiet conscience not accuseing of any intentionall faileinge: & also a conscience as fully & compleatly satisfyed of her breach of the Conjugall ~~yoke~~[6] knott, as I know, my finger being cutt of by another, that his knife acted by the strength of his hand hath done it: for it is a cleare & vnfallible case that no poyson can be receiued from the bodie of a woman, but what shee first has receiued from the infected body of some other: but yo*u*r doubt may be whether I might not receiue this p*re*juidice from the bodye[7] of another woman? To w*hi*ch I answer w*i*thout any attestations, for the clearnes[8] of my conscience needs[9] them not. That I never gaue the due benevolence of a wife to any woman in the world liueing or dead, saue only, to her that has not deserved the name of my wife. And this one thing (imprinted w*i*th so deepe a Caracter on my body) besides many others that I haue my selfe seene, & more that my Godly frends daily heare & speake of to mee, w*hi*ch I shall omitt, as not desireing to insist vppon those things w*hi*ch come from others, I say this one thing is that w*hi*ch to mee Wittnesses inough in foro Conscientiæ,[10] though it may not be accepted of as so full a testimonie in the Court of Mans Justice, & therefore I impart it to yo*u*r selfe, as a thing not publicke.

1. *Records of the First Church,* 49.

2. This suggestion was offered by the Register of Deeds in 1993, Paul R. Tierney, whose opinion is cited in a letter to the editor from Elizabeth C. Bouvier, Head of Archives, Supreme Judicial Court, Boston, Massachusetts, Feb. 26, 1993. This suggestion implicitly agrees with Elizabeth Wade White, *Anne Bradstreet: "The Tenth Muse"* (New York, 1971), 175. Thanks for assistance in locating and interpreting the provenance of this item are due to Mr. Paul R. Tierney, by whose permission it is here published, Elizabeth Bouvier, Head of Archives, Supreme Judicial Court, Boston, Massachusetts, and Martha Clark, Special Assistant to the Archivist of the Commonwealth of Massachusetts.

3. Trask, ed., *Suffolk Deeds,* I, 84. He adds that the disease left him in "december last," that is, 1646.

4. Ibid., I, 83. This letter is also in *Winthrop Papers,* V, 144, but I quote here from the manuscript transcription for *Suffolk Deeds,* with numerous differences in spelling as a result.

5. See the astute discussion of this matter in White, *Anne Bradstreet,* 174–177, and in Laurel Thatcher Ulrich, *Good Wives: Image and Reality in the Lives of Women in Northern New England, 1650–1750* (New York, 1982), 110–113.

6. Trask, ed., *Suffolk Deeds* (SD), omits this deletion.

7. bodye] SD: body.

8. clearnes] SD: cleames.

9. Here the transcription reads: needs needs them not. The repetition was probably the transcriber's error.

10. in foro Conscientiæ: in the court of [my own] conscience.

[Unknown] to John Cotton

[After July 7, 1647]

Published: Cotton Mather, "Piscator Evangelicus; or, The Life of Thomas Hooker, the Renowned, Pastor of Hartford-Church, and Pillar of Connecticut-Colony, in New England," in *Johannes in Eremo* . . . (Boston, 1695), 42

Cotton Mather's biography of Thomas Hooker, published first in 1695, then incorporated into *Magnalia Christi Americana* . . . (London, 1702), gives details of Hooker's death in Hartford, reported in a letter to Cotton from "a worthy spectator." Mather quotes only one sentence.

Truly Syr, the sight of his Death, will make me have more pleasant Thoughts of Death, than ever I yet had in my Life!

Nathanael Norcross to John Cotton

July 1647

ALS. MS: BPL, Ms. Am. 1506, pt. 3, no. 8

In L. Thompson, "Letters of John Cotton," 186–187

Nathanael Norcross was educated at Catharine Hall, now St. Catharine's College, Cambridge, where he matriculated in 1633, the year of Cotton's departure for New England. He received his bachelor of arts degree in 1636/7 and went to New England in 1638, still a very young man. He stayed in New England for more than a decade, hoping to become the minister at different locations, but never realizing this hope. He settled first at Salem, then moved to Watertown in 1642 and then to Nashaway, which later became Lancaster. By 1644 the plan to organize that community had failed. He apparently went next to Exeter and was there when the town was seeking a replacement for John Wheelwright, who had left in 1644. A call to the church was issued to Norcross in the spring of 1646, with the added inducement that the Wheelwright house was purchased by the town for Norcross's use as minister. But he declined the call, perhaps because of "the divisions which still continued among the people."[1] The letter below suggests this may be so, as Norcross appears to have felt some rivalry for preeminence among would-be church leaders in the town, which no doubt included himself. But the issue raised in Norcross's final question regarding the relative likelihood of finding a spouse in a given location might well have been an overriding issue, despite Cotton's reply on that point. In any case, as this letter shows, he was still in Exeter a year later. He never did find a place to minister in New England, though he did find a wife (Mary, daughter of John Gilbert of Dorchester, Dorset, and Taunton, Massachusetts). He returned to England in 1650, becoming the vicar of churches in Norfolk and Kent during the 1650s. He died in 1662.[2]

The letter is written on two sides of a single sheet folded once vertically. The text appears on the right-hand half of the recto and the left-hand half of the verso. Norcross wrote the address block on the left-hand half of the recto, where sealing wax is still present. The address, written in eight short lines, reads:

> To The Reverent/ his much honoured/ friend Mr John/ Cotton Tea-/ cher of the/ Churche in/ Boston,/ these:

Cotton wrote the notes for his reply on the right-hand half of the verso.

Reverent sir,

I am much engaged to your selfe for your readinesse to advise in difficulte cases,

Suffer mee I beseeche you to propounde

---

1. Qværitur,[3] whither an offense, suppose it uncleannesse in words, and gestures onely com*m*itted 2, or 3 yeares since, newly talked of, party offendinge privately satisfyinge parties offended, yet *th*e Grandjury man heares of it, pleades conscience, I must present his party, yet parties offended, and party offendinge satisfied, whither this suffice not without presentment[.]

2ly Qværitur, whither if a private man merely carnall openly sin one a sabb*ath* day and smite his neighbour cruelly, *th*e lawe is satisfied, but *th*e carnall man sees hee sinned openly, desires to confesse his sin openly, one a sabb*ath* day, whither it bee convenient for a carnall man soe to doe[.]

3ly A private person takes offense at one *tha*t dispenseth *th*e word, if hee bee justly offended, yet may hee refuse to heare *tha*t man preache[.]

[IV] Wee suppose *th*e offense to bee but betweene man, and man; If a minister suppose a man is hereticall, *tha*t supposeth himselfe orthodox, may a private person hereupon refuse to heare such a minister, or if hee doe, may hee refuse to come into *th*e place of meeteinge?

Againe, whither a private person gifted is to bee esteemed eqvall with one called and fitted, and accepted, and learned, yet not in office. Now in such a mans absence a brother is called to exercise, Is hee all one with another called, and deputed for *the* office, but not ordained, and whither *that* is not a Brownisticall[4] Tenent.

Againe whither churche worke desired may bee deferred in case of marriage, if probality of matcheinge bee not likely in such a place *that* one lives in, yet to gather into a churche at peradventure, whither *that* bee soe convenient, in case there is not a cleare way for materialls of a chur*ch*.

If you please to give satisfaction herein I shall humbly Rest sir youres
much engaged
Exiter 5th Nathanael Norcrosse
month 1647/

This bearer may bringe answeare
if you please.

If this bearer require not an answeare, if you please to sende to Christopher Lawsons house, his wife can sende by a boate /[5]

1. Charles H. Bell, *History of the Town of Exeter, New Hampshire* (1888; rpt. Bowie, Md., 1979), 157.

2. Except where otherwise indicated, biographical details are from Venn, *Alumni Cantabrigienses,* III, 263.

3. Qværitur: It is asked.

4. Separatist. Robert Browne, a young Norfolk minister, had in the 1580s set forth the principle that the truly godly should separate themselves "from the vnbeleevers and heathen of the land" and form distinct churches. Thereafter, "Brownism" was synonymous with Separatism. See Perry Miller, *Orthodoxy in Massachusetts, 1630–1650: A Genetic Study* (Cambridge, Mass., 1933), chap. 3, esp. 56.

5. This note was written along the left margin. Christopher Lawson, "a cooper by trade, and a trader by nature," "vibrated for some years between Exeter and Boston." He owned a house on the water in Boston and had been authorized to build a wharf in front of it, thus making him and his wife a ready conduit for communication between Boston and Exeter. He appears to have been trusted by his fellow townsmen to execute various official duties in Exeter in the mid-forties, including carrying the call in 1648 to the next ministerial candidate, William Tompson (who also declined). Bell, *History of Exeter,* 28, 47, 133, 158, 447; Samuel G. Drake, *The History and Antiquities of Boston . . . from Its First Settlement in 1630, to the Year 1770* (Boston, 1856), 302.

John Cotton to [Nathanael Norcross]

[July 1647]

ADf. MS: BPL, Ms. Am. 1506, pt. 3, no. 8

In L. Thompson, "Letters of John Cotton," 188–189

Cotton wrote this copy of his reply to Norcross in a very small hand, on the right-hand half of the verso of Norcross's letter. There is no salutation or signature; Cotton doubtless copied these comments onto a clean page for transmission to Norcross.

i. The Grandjury man is not bound to p*r*esent s[uc]h an offence so circumstanced. His Oath excepts private cases. Nor are such sinnes (though vncleane before *th*e Lord) much liable to civill Justice, especially com*m*itted so long agoe, & satisfaction given.

2. If a carnall man would doe so, I would not hinder him. Conscience (though natvrall) may vrge him to it, & *th*e Action in it self is good.

3. A private man hath not just Reason to forbear to hear a Minister for any private Offence to himself: vnlesse *th*e Offence be heynous, & *th*e Minister have bene convinced & Admonished of it in a way of God, & yet persisteth in his Offence ag*ains*t light. The Pharisees thought Christ a seducer, & Blasphemer, & so spake openly of Him: ~~(a~~ & yet Christ calleth to Heare *th*em. An Hæretick is noe greater Reproach[.]

4: A Private brother though well Gifted is not æquall in *th*e esteeme of *th*e Church to a brother Gifted (it may be better) as being learned, & in proximâ potentiâ[1] to Office. The nearer & fitter to Office, is to [be] p*re*ferred before *th*e more remote & lesse fitt.

5: To *th*e last I am ^loth^ ~~loth~~ to speake, as having spoken of it to you before. I think noe Place in *th*e Countrey, but may finde way for Marryage. Materialls & *th*em fitted wee must P*r*esuppose: or else God Denyeth effectum,[2] where He giveth not matter. /

1. in proximâ potentiâ: literally, in nearest power, that is, with power or authority close to that possessed by one in office.

2. effectum: effect, successful outcome.

John Cotton to John Winthrop

[Late March or April 1648]

AL. MS: MHS, Winthrop Papers

Published: MHS, *Colls.,* 5th Ser., I (1871), 356–358; *Winthrop Papers,* V, 192–193

In L. Thompson, "Letters of John Cotton," 190–192

The Massachusetts Bay Colony's General Court began to consider the need to formulate a body of laws for the colony at least as early as 1634. John Cotton's opinions were sought very early in the process. On May 6, 1635, the court appointed a committee of four elected officials "to make a draught of such lawes as they shall iudge needefull for the well ordering of this plantc*i*on, & to p*re*sent the same to the Court."[1] Nothing came of this, and on May 26, 1636, the court constituted a new committee, this time adding three ministers (Cotton, Hugh Peter, and Thomas Shepard) "to make a draught of lawes agreeable to the word of God, w*hi*ch may be the Fundamentalls of this com*m*onwealth."[2] Winthrop reported that later that year, October 25, 1636, "Mr. Cotton . . . did this court, present a copy of Moses his judicials, compiled in an exact method, which were taken into further consideration till the next general court."[3]

But no action was ever taken on Cotton's draft. In March 1638, the court tried to move the process along, inviting the freemen of every town to meet and consider what laws were needed for the colony. In November of that year, several magistrates, including Governor Winthrop and Deputy Governor Dudley, were asked to "pervse all those modells, w*hi*ch have bene, or shalbee further p*re*sented to this Court, or themselues."[4] But Winthrop finally says, "At last it was referred to Mr. Cotton and Mr. Nathaniel Warde, etc., and each of them framed a model, which were presented to this general court, and by them committed to the governour and deputy and some others to consider of."[5] In the end, Cotton's draft—"Moses His Judicials"—was set aside while the *Body of Liberties* by Ward (a former barrister in London) was accepted as the colony's working document.

This result is obscured by the fact that in 1641 a book by John Cotton called *An Abstract of the Laws of New England, as They Are Now Established* was published in London. A prominent student of early laws in America, John D. Cushing, noted: "All accounts agree that the work prepared by Cotton at the behest of the General Court in 1639 was the same 'Moses his Judicials' which he had originally submitted in 1636. If that assumption is valid, then it is not unreasonable to suppose that a copy might have found its way to one of Cotton's numerous English correspondents during the intervening years."[6] It was doubtless accepted by many in England as an authoritative copy of New England's laws (though there were *no* laws governing all of New England). This misunderstanding was compounded when William Aspinwall published an expanded version of Cotton's *Abstract* in London in 1655, perhaps intending it to instruct Cromwell's Commonwealth in the way to make Scripture fundamental to a nation's legal code, as Aspinwall's subtitle suggests: *Wherein as in a Mirrour May Be Seen the Wisdome and Perfection of the Government of Christs Kingdome.* Aspinwall acknowledged in his introduction that Cotton's laws had not been accepted in New England.

Ward's *Body of Liberties* became the working document for the colony from the late 1630s on, but it was not published. By the mid-1640s, it was becoming evident that publication of the laws then in effect was desirable, to enable wider distribution. The occasion was taken for revision of the laws, and, ultimately, a new draft document emerged. How Cotton became involved in the process this time is not known, but the following letter clearly indicates that Winthrop must have asked him for reactions at least to the preface, which in the printed version of 1648 extends to two folio pages. Cotton offers suggested revisions to the opening and closing paragraphs of the preface, or "Præamble," as he calls it, hoping to clarify how and to what extent the colony's statutes are based in scriptural precedent. If we compare the passages in quotation marks in the following letter with the relevant passages that finally appeared in the published *Book of the General Lawes and Libertyes concerning the Inhabitants of the Massachusets* (Cambridge, Mass., 1648), it is clear that the two published passages (included here in the endnotes) do contain much of the wording in Cotton's letter, but in each case omit his most detailed attempts to bring scriptural exegesis fully into play.

There is the remaining question, however, whether Cotton's wording was entirely new or whether he took the wording that was already in the text, modifying only parts of it. We cannot know this certainly, but in one instance it appears Cotton's wording was accepted but improved before printing. He suggests a simile at the end of his revision of the first paragraph: "a Common-wealth w*i*thout Fundamentall Lawes, & statutes clearely deducted from *the*m . . . is as a ship, w*i*thout Rigging, or sterne." The General Court's final version reads "is like a Ship without rigging and steeradge," a much more sensible analogy; a ship without steerage (steering mechanism, or rudder) is a ship adrift and thus an appropriate analogue for a lawless country, whereas a ship without a stern, as Cotton would have it, is simply a doomed vessel. If this detail is representative, it appears the court accepted much of his wording but improved it, as in this example, or shortened it by omitting passages that became, in the first paragraph, too exegetically detailed for the general audience intended and, in the final paragraph, too insistent on the divine origin of power for those administering the law.

The date of the letter is provided by John Winthrop, who endorsed Cotton's letter, "Mr Cotton about the preface to the Lawes, 1648." Since Winthrop would have written 1647 for any time up until March 25, 1648, Cotton's letter probably was written between that date and early May at the latest. On November 11, 1647, the records of the General Court say, "The laws now being in a manner agreed upon . . ." Then in March 1648, the court ordered the clerk, Mr. Rawson, and Mr. Hill to "compare the amendments of the book of laws passed, and make them as one."[7] By May 10, the court record could refer to clear progress: "the copy now in the press," a state of affairs still in effect on October 27, 1648: "the book of laws, now at the press."[8] Thus, late March or April of 1648 seems a likely date for this letter, particularly as the preparation of a preface would probably have been the last step in preparing the materials for publication.

As it was unsigned, but clearly the delivered copy, as is indicated by the sealing wax and by Winthrop's endorsement, Cotton might have delivered it to Winthrop himself. The letter is addressed in Cotton's hand:

> For o*u*r honoured
> Governo*u*r. /

The signet in the sealing wax is intact: It represents a standing bird with wings spread, with tail extended downward to the right.

Honoured & Deare S*ir*,

Two things onely I could wish Considered w*i*th some Caution: One in *th*e Præamble: the other in *th*e Conclusion.

In *th*e Præamble, I Doubt, whether any of *th*e Succeeding Governo*u*rs did d[raw] forth out of Moses his Fundamentall Principles, any other Lawes: save onely, That, in their Definitive Sentences, They made such Deductions from Moses Lawes, as were Explications, & Applications of those Primitive Lawes, & either[9] by Necessary Consequence, or by just Proportion. And those Deductions, if rightly & evidently gathered, were taken for statutes & ordinances in Israel. One speciall Example hereof wee Reade of, i. Sam*uel*. 30. 24, 25:[10] where David made it a statute in Israel, That as his Part is *tha*t goeth to *th*e Battell: so shall his Part be, that tarryeth by *th*e stuffe. W*hi*ch was an Evident Deduction, & Application of *th*e Law, or P[r]æcedent, w*hi*ch Moses gave in a like Case, Num 31. 27.[11] And yet I doe not Remember, That wee Reade of any more Definitive sentences Ordeyned to be statutes in Israel, save *tha*t onely. But neverthelesse, *tha*t one may serve for a Patterne in like Cases.

It is true, Judah is Called a Lawgiver, (& *tha*t, not onely in Reference to Christ, but to *th*e Princes before Him) Gen. 49. 10.[12] Psal*m* 60.7.[13] But *th*e word doeth indifferently signify such, qui jus Populo dicunt[14] (as *th*e Judges in England doe:) as qui jura Populo dant,[15] as their Parliam*en*t doe. And so *th*e same word is vsed for those qui jus Populo dicunt, Judg*es* 5. 14.[16] For *th*e Machirites were of *th*e Tribe of Menasseh, not of Judah.[17] Therefore, you may Please to Consider, whether the words may not runne to such like effect, as this:

" These were breife & Fundamentall Principles: & yet w*i*th all so full & "comprehensive, That out of *the*m *th*e Succeeding Governo*u*rs were to draw "out ^cleare^ Deductions to all Particular Cases, in all their Definitive Sen-"tences, w*hi*ch had in *the*m the Force of Lawes, & Ordinances in Israel. As "David did, in i. Sam*uel*. 30. 24, 25: out of *th*e Law in Moses, Num*bers*. 3i. For a "Com*m*on-wealth wthout Fundamentall Lawes, & statutes clearely deducted "from *the*m (as Rules of Publick Judicature, & of Private Converse amongst "men) is as a ship, w*i*thout Rigging, or sterne.[18]

[IV] In *th*e Conclusion, you may Please to Consider, whether it may not Runne more free from Scruple, to some such like Purpose as this.

" [Th]at Distinction w*hi*ch is Putt betweene *th*e Lawes of God, & *th*e Lawes "of men, becom*m*eth a snare to many, as it is misapplyed in *th*e Ordering of "their Obedience to Civill Authority. For when *th*e Authority is of God, (& "*tha*t in way of an Ordinance, Rom*ans*. i3. i:)[19] And when *th*e Administration "of it is according to Deductions & Rules gathered from *th*e word of God, "& *th*e cleare Light of Nature in Civill Nations; surely there is noe Humane "Law *tha*t tendeth to *th*e Com*m*on Good, according to those Principles, but "*th*e same is mediately a Law of God. & *th*e Administ[ra]ti[on of] Justice, & "all Lawfull Acts of Power according thereto, is of God also: & *tha*t in way "of an Ordinance, w*hi*ch all are to submitt vnto, even for Conscience sake, "Rom*ans*. i3. 5.[20] /[21]

1. *Records of Massachusetts Bay,* I, 147. Before these *Records* were published, F. C. Gray drew on them to provide a narrative account of the emergence of New England's laws: "Remarks on the Early Laws of Massachusetts Bay; with the Code Adopted in 1641, and Called 'The Body of Liberties,' Now First Printed," in MHS, *Colls.,* 3d Ser., VIII (1843), 191–237.

2. *Records of Massachusetts Bay,* I, 174.

3. Winthrop, *Journal,* 195.

4. *Records of Massachusetts Bay,* I, 279.

5. Winthrop, *Journal,* 314.

6. John D. Cushing, introduction, *The Laws and Liberties of Massachusetts, 1641–1691: A Facsimile Edition, Containing also Council Orders and Executive Proclamations* (Wilmington, Del., 1976), I, xvii.

7. William H. Whitmore, *A Bibliographical Sketch of the Laws of the Massachusetts Colony from 1630 to 1686* (Boston, 1890), 77.

8. Ibid., 79.

9. The e of either is written over the &.

10. 1 Sam. 30:24, 25: For who will hearken unto you in this matter? but as his part is that goeth down to the battle, so shall his part be that tarrieth by the stuff: they shall part alike. And it was so from that day forward, that he made it a statute and an ordinance for Israel unto this day.

11. Num. 31:27: And divide the prey into two parts; between them that took the war upon them, who went out to battle, and between all the congregation.

12. Gen. 49:10: The sceptre shall not depart from Judah, nor a lawgiver from between his feet, until Shiloh come; and unto him shall the gathering of the people be.

13. Ps. 60:7: Gilead is mine, and Manasseh is mine; Ephraim also is the strength of mine head; Judah is my lawgiver.

14. qui jus Populo dicunt: who administer the law to the people.

15. qui jura Populo dant: who give laws to the people. The distinction being made here is between the singular *jus,* which indicates law in the abstract—a system of laws or justice—and the plural, *jura,* which means individual laws.

16. Judg. 5:14: Out of Ephraim was there a root of them against Amalek; after thee, Benjamin, among thy people; out of Machii came down governors, and out of Zebulon they that handle the pen of the writer.

17. This is a subtle point, based on Cotton's familiarity with the Hebrew texts of the Old Testament books he cites. "The word" to which he refers is the Hebrew word for lawgiver (see the texts he cites in Genesis and Psalms). He suggests that such a word can have shadings of meaning that are significant. The tribe of Judah were "lawgivers" who *made* the laws, but the Machirites, of the tribe of Menasseh, were *not.* They (the Machirites and their modern-day antitypes, including the New Englanders) should accept the laws established by God (Jehovah is the original judge and lawgiver) and handed down to them and administer them as best they can, without seeking to usurp the role of the people of Judah, the lawgivers. On "lawgiver" in the Bible, see J. D. Douglas, ed., *The New Bible Dictionary* (Grand Rapids, Mich., 1962), 723; James Hastings, ed., *Dictionary of the Bible* (New York, 1948), 537.

18. The passage as published later in 1648 reads: "These were breif and fundamental principles, yet withall so full and comprehensive as out of them clear deductions were to be drawne to all particular cases in future times. For a Common-wealth without lawes is like a Ship without rigging and steeradge."

19. Rom. 13:1: Let every soul be subject unto higher powers. For there is no power but of God: the powers that be are ordained of God.

20. Rom. 13:5: Wherefore ye must needs be subject not only for wrath, but also for conscience sake.

21. The passage as adopted and published is virtually identical to this, with minor changes in punctuation and spelling, except for the telling omission of the following clauses in Cotton's version: "& the Administ[ra]ti[on of] Justice, & all Lawfull Acts of Power according thereto, is of God also."

John Cotton to [Lydia Gaunt]

September 14, 1648

Copy. MS: BPL, Ms. Am. 1506, pt. 3, no. 9

In L. Thompson, "Letters of John Cotton," 193–194

Lydia Gaunt is probably the wife of Peter Gaunt, who had moved from Lynn in 1637 to Sandwich, Massachusetts, where they had five children between 1640 and

1646. Peter Gaunt had become identified with the Quakers by at least early 1658, and Lydia's will, dated 1691, included the "Friends, Called quakers," among her beneficiaries. Peter was associated with a group of Anabaptists in Sandwich in 1651, when "Peeter Gaunt & his wife" were fined "for not frequenting the publick worship of God, contrary to order." Such an association would help to account for Lydia's writing to Cotton about baptism. Cotton's recently published *Grounds and Ends of the Baptisme of the Children of the Faithfull*... (London, 1647) might have helped motivate her to write to him.[1] Cotton's reference to "New [Apos]tles" suggests the relevance to Lydia Gaunt's dilemma of her probable contact with still other radical departures from Massachusetts orthodoxy (note 6, below), sectarian ideas with which Cotton already seems at least nominally acquainted.

This somewhat laboriously written copy of Cotton's letter is essentially printed, seemingly by a literate but somewhat immature writer. Cotton's amanuensis in this case was his oldest son, Seaborn, who was just fifteen when this was written. Comparison with Seaborn's Latin letter to his father, probably written a couple of years later, reveals identical traits in a number of particulars, the differences perhaps attributable to the maturation of the writer's script in the later example.

This item is badly mutilated, soiled, and water-damaged, with the loss of paper at the bottom of the first sheet resulting in the absence of nearly all the text of several lines. The addressee is nowhere definitively identified by Cotton, though the name Lydia does appear at the end of a fragmented parenthetical remark of direct address to her near the end of the first verso. Thomas Prince noted at the top of the first recto, "Ans. to Mrs Lydia Grant's Let^{r}." Prince might have had her letter to Cotton in his possession, but it is not now a part of the Prince Collection at the Boston Public Library. Since Prince writes the surname as "Grant," it is possible that Cotton did too, though his spelling of the verb "to grant" was always "graunt."

Loving Freind

If my letter to you l^a^y long in the hand of the bearer, It was Against my minde: and since you have received it I thanke god, *tha*t you take it in good part, as indeed I wrote it out of vnfeigned goodwill and love to you.

Y[ou] say, you see plainly, the way wherin you formerly walked, not to be according to the word, from Acts. 2. where Beleevers onely are to be baptized.[2]

But bee not deceived though the place speaketh of Beleevers Baptized: yet it doth not speake, that beleevers onely are to be baptized. For Peter telleth them, the p[ro]mise is made not onely to them (to beleevers) but also to theire children. v. 39. And therefore the children of beleivers, have right to the promise, & so to the [two or three deleted words] seale of the promise, as well as there fathere. And certaine it is, the children of the Jewes were pertakers of the covenant, and of the [s]eale of the covenant, whilest they

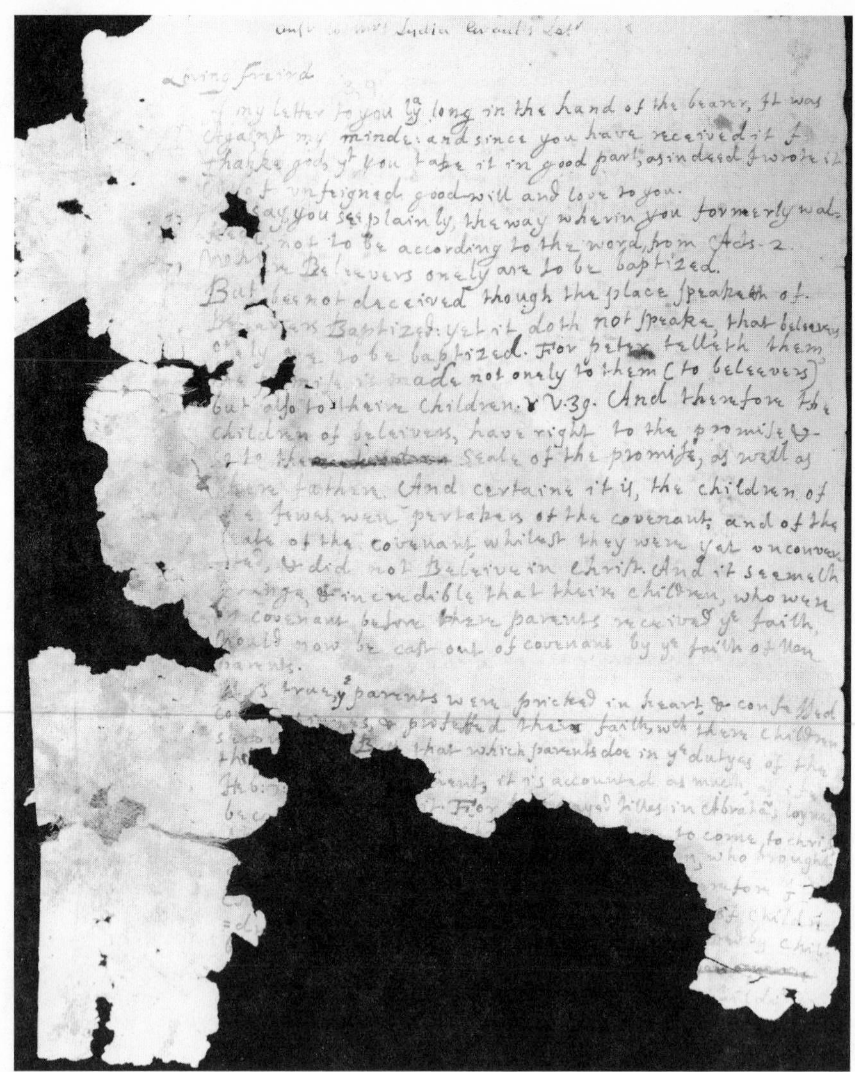

Loving Friend

my letter to you lay long in the hand of the bearer, It was
Against my minde: and since you have received it I
thanke god yt you take it in good part, as indeed I wrote it
out of unfeigned goodwill and love to you.
[illegible] say you see plainly, the way wherein you formerly wal-
[illegible] not to be according to the word, from Acts 2
[illegible] Beleevers onely are to be baptized.
But bee not deceived though the place speaketh of
[illegible] Baptized: yet it doth not speake that beleevers
only are to be baptized. For peter telleth them
[illegible] made not onely to them (to beleevers)
but also to theire children. v 39. And therefore the
children of beleevers, have right to the promise &
[illegible] seale of the promise, as well as
theire fathers. And certaine it is, the children of
the Jewes were partakers of the covenant, and of the
seale of the covenant whilest they were yet vnconverted, & did not Beleive in Christ. And it seemeth
strange, & incredible that theire children, who were
in covenant before there parents received ye faith,
should now be cast out of covenant by ye faith of there
parents.
It is true ye parents were pricked in heart & confessed
[illegible] & professed there faith, wch there children
[illegible] But that which parents doe in ye dutyes of the
[illegible] it is accounted as much, as [illegible]
[illegible]

PLATE 16. Cotton to [Lydia Gaunt], September 14, 1648, first page. The holograph is a copy made by Cotton's oldest child, Seaborn, who was then fifteen years old. *Boston Public Library Ms. Am. 1506, pt. 3, no. 9. Courtesy of the Trustees of the Boston Public Library*

were yet vnconverted, & did not Beleive in Christ. And it seemeth strange, & incredible that theire children, who were in covenant before there parents received *th*e faith, should now be cast out of covenant by *th*e faith of there parents.

It is true, *th*e parents were pricked in heart, & confessed [their] sinnes & professed their faith, w*hi*ch there children co|| But that which parents doe in *th*e dutyes of the secon[d comman]dement, it is accounted as much, as if the [child had done?] it. For [Levi pa]yed tithes in Abraha*m*s loynes Heb: 7: [9–10][3] ||

[iv] We despise the wayes of christ & we hinder the free passage of his light and truth to us. plaine it is, Christ Commaundeth Desciples to be baptized, Math. 28: 19.[4] goe mak[e] desciples (as the word signifyeth), & baptiz[e] *them.* And Peter calleth the children of Beleevers, Discip[les,] Acts. 15: 10.[5] For Peter there blameth *th*e false teachers, who would put a yoke vpon the neckes of the Disciples: & that yoke was circumsision, which t[h]ey would have put vpon Beleevers, & theire seede, whome He by one name [deleted word] calleth disciples.

What your Judgement is of New [Apos]tles [I do]e not kno[w.] I speake of them to you onely by hearesay. If you expect none such, you will be the "lesse deceived.[6] It is true, Much hay and stubble hath been built vpon stone "fou*n*da[tions,] which the lord will consume and doth consu[m]e dayly. But the covenant of grace, & the subiect of *th*e covena[nt,] which is beleivers, and theire seede, hath beene, & will be one and the same, for ever, Rom. 11: 26:[7] Isay. 65: 20–23?[8]

" It is true, which you say, christs dove is one, that is[, the] vniversall church is one; though *tha*t place of sc[ripture] which so calleth it (Canticles. 6:9.)[9] speaketh of || particular churches, more vndefiled, then [Solomon's] Queenes, & foure score concubines. But || it is in the new Testament, *tha*t Christ hath ||ted particular churches of particular congregat[ions to] which he hath given pastors, and teachers, || perfected.

Eph. 4: 11. 12 .13.[10] D|| not the|| Lydia) withdraw your selfe f[rom? the] congre[gation] || its people: [called] Apos[tles]||[11]

[2] The Lord guide and blesse you, leading you in to all his holy truth fitt for you to know, and saving you from paths that swerve from the wayes of everlasting peace, for his names sake in christ. In whome I com*m*end my hearty love to your selfe, & husband, & rest.

Your very loving freind & brother
Joh*n* Cotton.

Boston, this 14 of 7:
1648.

1. Maclean W. McLean, "Peter Gaunt (*ca.* 1615–*ca.* 1678) of Sandwich, Mass.," *National Genealogical Society Quarterly,* LXII (1974), 247–254. John Osborne Austin, *The Genealogical Dictionary of Rhode Island: Comprising Three Generations of Settlers Who Came before 1690* (1887; Baltimore, 1982), 31–32, 294, includes information about both Lydia and Mehitable, two of Peter and Lydia Gaunt's children and both residents of Rhode Island in their adulthood. Her will is printed in George Ernest Bowman, "Abstracts of Barnstable County, Mass., Probate Records," *Mayflower Descendant,* XV (1913), 76–77.

2. The reference is to Acts 2:37–39: Now when they heard this [Peter's sermon], they were

pricked in their heart, and said unto Peter and to the rest of the apostles, Men and brethren, what shall we do? Then Peter said unto them, Repent, and be baptized every one of you in the name of Jesus Christ for the remission of sins, and ye shall receive the gift of the Holy Ghost. For the promise is unto you, and to all your children, and to all that are afar off, even as many as the Lord our God shall call.

3. Heb. 7:9–10: And as I may so say, Levi also, who receiveth tithes, payed tithes in Abraham. For he was yet in the loins of his father, when Melchisedec met him.

At this point, six lines are almost entirely lost to mutilation of the paper.

4. Matt. 28:19: Go ye therefore, and teach all nations, baptizing them in the name of the Father, and of the Son, and of the Holy Ghost.

5. Acts 15:10: Now therefore why tempt ye God, to put a yoke upon the neck of the disciples, which neither our fathers nor we were able to bear?

6. William Hubbard, writing soon after midcentury, made reference to the "New Apostles" in connection with his discussion of Roger Williams's expulsion from Salem and his radical views on baptism, the issue on which Cotton is also addressing Lydia Gaunt. Hubbard writes that Williams and his followers "had not long been [in Providence] together, but from rigid Separation they fell to Anabaptistry, renouncing the baptism which they had received in their infancy, and taking up another baptism, began a church in that way. But Mr. Williams stopped not there long, for after some time, he told the people that had followed him, and joined with him in a new baptism, either from his own unstable mind, or from the suggestion of some other, that he was out of the way himself, and had misled them, for he did not find that there was any upon earth that could administer baptism, and therefore their last baptism was a nullity, as well as their first, and therefore *they must lay down all, and wait for the coming of new Apostles.* And so they dissolved themselves and turned Seekers." *A General History of New England from the Discovery to MDCLXXX* (1815), 2d ed., ed. William Thaddeus Harris, MHS, *Colls.,* 2d Ser., V–VI (Boston, 1848), 207–208 (italics added).

7. Rom. 11:26: And so all Israel shall be saved: as it is written, There shall come out of Sion the Deliverer, and shall turn away ungodliness from Jacob.

8. Isa. 65:20–23: There shall be no more thence an infant of days, nor an old man that hath not filled his days: for the child shall die an hundred years old; but the sinner being an hundred years old shall be accursed. And they shall build houses, and inhabit them; and they shall plant vineyards, and eat the fruit of them. They shall not build, and another inhabit; they shall not plant, and another eat: for as the days of a tree are the days of my people, and mine elect shall long enjoy the work of their hands. They shall not labor in vain, nor bring forth for trouble; for they are the seed of the blessed of the Lord, and their offspring with them.

9. Song of Sol. 6:9: My dove, my undefiled is but one; she is the only one of her mother, she is the choice one of her that bare her. The daughters saw her, and blessed her; yea, the queens and the concubines, and they praised her.

10. Eph. 4:11–13: And he gave some, apostles; and some, prophets; and some, evangelists; and some, pastors and teachers; For the perfecting of the saints, for the work of the ministry, for the edifying of the body of Christ: Till we all come in the unity of the faith, and of the knowledge of the son of God, unto a perfect man, unto the measure of the stature of the fulness of Christ.

11. The mutilation at the bottom of the sheet has removed most of the last eight lines.

John Cotton to [Unknown]

[1646–1648?]

AD. MS: MSA, CCXL, Hutchinson Papers, I, fols. 105–106a

In L. Thompson, "Letters of John Cotton," 181–185

This partial manuscript in Cotton's hand is undated. The supposition that it is from the period 1646–1648 is based upon two kinds of evidence. First, this was the period in which questions about Sabbatarianism were most intensely an interest of the Massachusetts clergy, aroused in particular by Thomas Shepard's inquiries directed to several of them as he prepared his *Theses Sabbaticae*. Second, the handwriting and the paper resemble very closely those of the Cotton letter to Shepard of April 3, 1646, which addresses Shepard's questions on the Sabbath. The paper is the same size in each case, although there is no watermark on the paper used for this undated letter, while the letter to Shepard is on paper watermarked with a fleur-de-lis. Nevertheless, they are contemporaneous. Since the subject matter here complements that in Cotton's April 3, 1646, letter, this may also be to Shepard, replying to a different letter from him.

The fragment is missing its first sheet. It starts in midsentence on a page numbered 3 by Cotton (fol. 105). The verso of folio 105 has no page number, but folio 106 has Cotton's number 5 in the upper right corner; there is no number on 106v. At the bottom of the last page, 106v, where the signature would normally be, is written in another hand: "Mr Jno Cotton's Lett^{er}." Yet another writer turned the sheet upside down and wrote, next to the previous endorsement, "Cottons answer on to Sabbath."

*th*e first Day. By this Reckoning Mr Chauncy convinced B*ish*op Laud, that *th*e Lords Day began w*i*th *th*e Evening.

5. I finde noe place in scripture, *tha*t argueth, the Jewes began their Dayes in *th*e morning. Beare w*i*th me, if I wave yo*u*r Instances. In Exod. 10. 4,13: God threatneth to send locusts into their Coasts: & He did so in *th*e morning following.[1] Gods word had bene truely fulfilled, if He had not sent *th*em till afternoone: & yet *tha*t would not argue, *tha*t *th*e morrow began at noone. That w*hi*ch is done on any part of *th*e morrow (whether night, or morning, or after noone) is done on *th*e morrow. Exod. 12. 6,12,22.[2] It is true, they were to kill *th*e Passeover on *th*e 14th Day, & they might Eate it, or continue eating *th*e night following. But *tha*t night following was part of *th*e 15th day, not of *th*e 14. For at Midnight there was great Cry in Aegypt for *th*e Death of their First borne, v. 30, 31.[3] And by night Pharaoh calleth for Moses & Aaron to carry forth *th*e People in hast, v. 33.[4] And *tha*t night they went from Rame-

ses to Succoth, v. 37: w*i*th 42.[5] And *tha*t night is called (or at least, *tha*t time) *the* i5. day of *the* i[st] moneth, *the* morrow after *the* Passeover. Num*bers* ^33.3.^[6] It is noe Inconvenience they should kill the Passeover one Day, & continue eating of it part of *the* Day following. There is noe Rule (*tha*t I know of) broken in *tha*t. Though they were to have none of it till the morning, It will not argue, *tha*t *tha*t night was part of *the* Day before: but *tha*t if they tarryed till morning, they should not have liberty to feede on it then being to be thrust out in hast *tha*t night. And God would teach his People to feede on whole Christ, before they sleepe.

The Cause of sanctifying *the* Day was existent, though the Angells Passing over their houses followed after. For the Cause of sanctifying a Day is not, a worke of God done for vs on *the* Day (for then let vs keepe Christmasse, good Fryday, Holy Thursday:)[7] but [105v] a word of Institution, w*hi*ch they had before *the* i4[th] Day. Nor doe I know, whether the i4[th] Day was counted Holy, though *the* Lambe was slayen in *the* last part of it: If *the* one & twentith day was one of *the* 7 Days ^of *the* Holy Feast,^ then *the* i4[th] Day was none, Exod. i2.i5,i6,i8.[8]

^Of *the* ἐναντιόφαμος?, see *the* Postscript.^[9]

In Levit. 7.i5: w*i*th 22.29,30:[10] I finde, *the* Flesh of *the* Peace-offrings was to be eaten *the* same Day, & noething left of it till *the* morning. But this will not argue *tha*t it might be eaten *tha*t night, or *tha*t *the* night following was part of *the* Day before. Neither would I think, *tha*t if *the* Peace Offerings were offered in *the* morning, but *tha*t it might be lawfull to eate it not onely at Dinner, but at supper also: & though supper might last an houre or two w*i*thin evening, yet still the Peace Offerings might be said to be eaten *the* same Day they were killed, because they were eaten in the meales belonging to *tha*t Day, though the latter meale might continue an houre of *the* night following, or lesse or more. The Synecdoche is easy.

In Sam. 24.i5,i3:[11] be it graunted, *tha*t David was to suffer 3 dayes Pestilence, & *tha*t *the* first Day of *the* Pestilence began in *the* morning: yet *tha*t will onely Argue, *tha*t if they were complete 3 dayes, then *the* Pestilence ended in *the* morning after 3 dayes expired: & so it might, for ought is ^expresly^ Recorded. But I rather conceive, *tha*t *the* Angell broke off before *the* 3[d] Day was expired, because when He was goeing on to stretch forth his hand vpon Hierusalem, (w*hi*ch it is not likely He would offer to Doe beyond his Com*m*ission) the Lord com*m*aunded him to stay his hand, 2. Sam. 24.i6.[12] And then 3 Dayes must necessarily be vnderstoode by a synecdoche for part of 3 Dayes.

In Mat. 26.34: w*i*th Mark. i4.30:[13] the Text holdeth forth, That Peter should Deny Christ *tha*t night, even [5/106] that night wherein having eaten *the* Passeover, & afterwards the Lords Supper, they went forth. And Night it was when Judas went forth, Joh. 13.30.[14] And Christ spake of Peters Denyall after Judas was gone, v. 38.[15] And *th*e same Night Christ was Taken, & Peter Denyed Him. But there is noe title in *th*e Text ^sounding *tha*t way,^ *tha*t that Night was part of *th*e Day goeing before.

In Mark. 15.42.[16] the even before *th*e sabbath is said to be *th*e P*r*eparation to *th*e sabbath: but not *th*e latter even, ^I meane, *th*e even after sunsett.^ There is noe Ground in *th*e Text, to Conceive *tha*t *th*e Body of Christ was taken downe after sunsett, (w*hi*ch is *th*e latter even) when as *th*e Bodyes of both *th*e Theives were taken downe before sunsett, & Christs Body before *th*em.

As for *th*e Place in Gen. 1: I referre you to a larger clearing of it in *th*e other Script to *th*e Brethren of Oxfordshyre.[17] Yet let me give you a word or two to yo*ur* Advertisem*en*ts thereof. To yo*ur* 1st, I cannot goe along w*i*th you, to thinke it evident, that not *th*e totall Darknesse was called Night. For during *tha*t totall Darknesse, God made *th*e highest Heaven, the Earth, & *th*e waters. And these all being made w*i*thin *th*e sixe Dayes, & yet made during *the* time of *tha*t totall Darknesse, that totall Darknesse must either be accounted the first Day, or *th*e first night. The first Day it was not (I meane, artificiall Day:) Night therefore it must neede be. It is true *tha*t Night was *th*e divided Darknesse. For God having made light in *th*e morning divided *tha*t light from *tha*t Darknes[se] by placing light in this hemisphere, *tha*t Darknesse in *th*e other.

[106v] To y*our* 2d. It is a Mistake, *tha*t evening in Scripture is never putt for *th*e whole Night. Reade *th*e Originall word, Job. 7.4. Deut. 28.67.[18]

To 3d, There is as much Reason to Judge *th*e time of *th*e totall Darknesse to be *th*e space of a whole night (12, houres) as to count *th*e time of *th*e light following to be a Day of 12, houres. For in *th*e time of *tha*t totall Darknesse God made both *th*e Highest Heavens (& likely enough, *th*e Angells therein) as also two whole elem*en*ts of earth & water. Whereas in *th*e time of *th*e Day, there was noething made, but *th*e light, ^*tha*t is *th*e elem*en*t of Fire.^ And in *th*e whole 2d Day, noething ^was^ made, but the Elem*en*t of Aire. Why should either of those two elem*en*ts take vp *th*e space of 12 houres a piece for *th*e making of *th*em, & those two heavy elem*en*ts of earth & water, together w*i*th *th*e highest Heaven, be all made together in an houre or two of twilight?

It is an Holy labo*ur* to search out *th*e season of Holy Rest: *tha*t in *th*e Holy Keeping of it, wee may enter into His Rest, who is gone before vs, *th*e Lord o*ur* Redeemer.

His Name be Blessed./

1. Exod. 10:4, 13: Else, if thou refuse to let my people go, behold, to morrow will I bring the locusts into thy coast. . . . And Moses stretched forth his rod over the land of Egypt, and the Lord brought an east wind upon all the land that day, and all that night; and when it was morning, the east wind brought the locusts.

2. Exod. 12:6, 12, 22: And ye shall keep it up until the fourteenth day of the same month: and the whole assembly of the congregation of Israel shall kill it in the evening. . . . For I will pass through the land of Egypt this night, and will smite all the firstborn in the land of Egypt, both man and beast; and against all the gods of Egypt I will execute judgment: I am the Lord. . . . And ye shall take a bunch of hyssop, and dip it in the blood that is in the bason, and strike the lintel and the two side posts with the blood that is in the bason; and none of you shall go out at the door of his house until the morning.

3. Exod. 12:30, 31: And Pharaoh rose up in the night, he, and all his servants, and all the Egyptians; and there was a great cry in Egypt: for there was not a house where there was not one dead. And he called for Moses and Aaron by night, and said, Rise up, and get you forth from among my people, both ye and the children of Israel; and go, serve the Lord, as ye have said.

4. Exod. 12:33: And the Egyptians were urgent upon the people, that they might send them out of the land in haste; for they said, we be all dead men.

5. Exod. 12:37: And the children of Israel journeyed from Rameses to Succoth, about six hundred thousand on foot that were men, beside children. Exod. 12:42: It is a night to be much observed unto the Lord for bringing them out from the land of Egypt: this is that night of the Lord to be observed of all the children of Israel in their generations.

6. This Scripture reference was added after the surrounding text was written. "Num." fills all the space between the end of the previous sentence and the right-hand edge of the sheet, and "33:3:" is inserted between the lines at the left margin. Num. 33:3: And they departed from Rameses in the first month, on the fifteenth day of the first month; on the morrow after the passover the children of Israel went out with an high hand in the sight of all the Egyptians.

7. The Puritans did not celebrate these days as holidays. As Bruce C. Daniels has said: "Puritans attacked regularly scheduled religious holidays. . . . The logic behind their vigorous affirmation of Sabbatarianism had as a corollary an equally vigorous denunciation of all other holy days celebrated by the Catholic church" (*Puritans at Play: Leisure and Recreation in Colonial New England* [New York, 1995], 88, 89–91). In 1647 the Puritan-dominated Parliament abolished Christmas, Easter, and other traditional festival days; see Christopher Durston, "Puritan Rule and the Failure of Cultural Revolution, 1645–1660," in Durston and Jacqueline Eales, eds., *The Culture of English Puritanism, 1560–1700* (London, 1996), 210–214. On New England practice, see Charles E. Hambrick-Stowe, *The Practice of Piety: Puritan Devotional Disciplines in Seventeenth-Century New England* (Chapel Hill, N.C., 1982), 96–103.

8. Exod. 12:15, 16, 18: Seven days shall ye eat unleavened bread; even the first day ye shall put away leaven out of your houses: for whosoever eateth leavened bread from the first day until the seventh day, that soul shall be cut off from Israel. And in the first day there shall be an holy convocation to you; no manner of work shall be done in them, save that which every man must eat, that only may be done of you. . . . In the first month, on the fourteenth day of the month at even, ye shall eat unleavened bread, until the one and twentieth day of the month at even.

9. This line is crowded between paragraphs and appears to have been inserted after the following text was written.

The ending of this Greek word is somewhat blurred. As transcribed here, the word means contradicting or, in its nominal form, contradiction. Here, as elsewhere, I am grateful to George Goebel for his assistance with translation, and to Jeffrey Wills.

10. Lev. 7:15, 22, 29, 30: And the flesh of the sacrifice of his peace offerings for thanksgiving shall be eaten the same day that it is offered; he shall not leave any of it until the morning. . . . And the Lord spake unto Moses, saying, . . . Speak unto the children of Israel, saying, He that

offereth the sacrifice of his peace offerings unto the Lord shall bring his oblation unto the Lord of the sacrifice of his peace offerings. His own hands shall bring the offerings of the Lord made by fire, the fat with the breast, it shall he bring, that the breast may be waved for a wave offering before the Lord.

11. 2 Sam. 24:15, 13: So the Lord sent a pestilence upon Israel from the morning even to the time appointed: and there died of the people from Dan even to Beersheba seventy thousand men.

So Gad came to David, and told him, and said unto him, Shall seven years of famine come unto thee in thy land? or wilt thou flee three months before thine enemies, while they pursue thee? or that there be three days' pestilence in thy land? now advise and see what answer I shall return to him that sent me.

12. 2 Sam. 24:16: And when the angel stretched out his hand upon Jerusalem to destroy it, the Lord repented him of the evil, and said to the angel that destroyed the people, It is enough: stay now thine hand. And the angel of the Lord was by the threshingplace of Araunah the Jebusite.

13. Matt. 26:34: Jesus said unto him, Verily I say unto thee, That this night, before the cock crow, thou shalt deny me thrice.

Mark 14:30: And Jesus saith unto him, Verily I say unto thee, That this day, even in this night, before the cock crow twice, thou shalt deny me thrice.

14. John 13:30: He then having received the sop went immediately out: and it was night.

15. John 13:38: Jesus answered him, Wilt thou lay down thy life for my sake? Verily, verily, I say unto thee, The cock shall not crow, till thou hast denyed me thrice.

16. Mark 15:42: And now when the even was come, because it was the preparation, that is, the day before the sabbath.

17. Apparently a manuscript enclosure.

18. Job 7:4: When I lie down, I say, When shall I arise, and the night be gone? and I am full of tossings to and fro unto the dawning of the day.

Deut. 28:67: In the morning thou shalt say, Would God it were even! and at even thou shalt say, Would God it were morning! for the fear of thine heart wherewith thou shalt fear, and for the sight of thine eyes which thou shalt see.

John Cotton to a Friend in England

January 8, 1648/9

Published: I. Mather, *First Principles,* 5

Increase Mather introduces this passage from a letter by his father-in-law by describing its context as a "large and Judicious Letter of Mr. *Cottons* written with his own hand to a Friend of his in *England* touching accommodation and Communion between those of the Presbyterian and Congregational perswasion. The Letter bears the date 8. 11. *moneth* 1648, and therein Mr. *Cotton* delivers his judgement in twelve propositions, which are too large here to be inserted, only the eighth of these Propositions being directly to our purpose, we shall here transcribe it, The words of it are these."

If the godly members of a Congregation formerly Subject to Episcopacy, repenting of their sinful subordination thereto shall be studious of Reformation, and shall solemnly Covenant to endeavour the same, and shall choose their former godly Ministers, into the Pastors & Teachers office, it is not necessary they should take the ignorant or Carnal members of the Parish into the fellowship of this renewed Election of their Ministers, and yet it is not improbable, but the Ministers may perform some Ministerial acts to them, as not only to preach the word to them, but (happily) also to baptize their Children. For such members are like the Church members, with us baptized in their Infancy, yet not received to the Lords Supper, when they come to Age, nor admitted to fellowship of voting in Admissions, Elections, Censures, till they come to profess their faith, and repentence, and lay hold of the Covenant of their Parents before the Church. And yet they being not cast out of the Church, nor the Covenant thereof, their Children may be capable of the first Seal of the Covenant, so in this Case, till the Parents themselves grow Scandalous, and thereby cast off, out of the Covenant of the Church.

Richard Bellingham, John Cotton, John Clark, and John Wilson to John Winthrop, Jr.

March 26, 1649

ALS. MS: MHS, Winthrop Papers

Published: Robert C. Winthrop, *Life and Letters of John Winthrop . . .*, 2d ed. (Boston, 1869), II, 395; *Winthrop Papers,* V, 325.

When John Winthrop died of a fever and sickness of more than a month's duration,[1] his son, John, Jr., was living at Pequot (soon to become New London) in Connecticut, where this letter reached him. It was written on the day Winthrop died and is in the handwriting of John Wilson but was individually signed by the four men.

A separate small slip of paper, now attached to the verso of the letter, contains the address block:

To o*u*r deare & honoured
friend John Winthrope
Esqr: at Pequod
these del.

On the same paper, in John Winthrop, Jr.'s hand:

m^r^ Bellingha*m* m^r^ Cotton &
m^r^ Wilson & m^r^ Clarke
about my fathers funerall.
1649

Deare S*i*r

It having pleased God, to take Home vnto his blessed Rest ˆ&ˆ Glory his most deare servant our Governor, (of whom we haue bene so vnworthie), Ther was here soone after his decease, a Consultation (among the principall of o*u*r Towne) how to order his Funeralls for the time, & otherwise. It being the desire of All that in that solempnity it may appeare of what precious account & desert he hath ben, & how blessed his memoriall. & the time agreed vpon is this 3^d^ day come 7 night, (w*hi*ch is now the 26. of march) w*hi*ch will be the 3^d^ day of the next moneth that is April. & to the end *tha*t yo*u*rself might haue opportunity to be pr*e*sent (as one aboue others Interested in him) if God shall giue you leaue, they haue sent Nahawton, whom they did esteeme a Trustie & Swift messenger, to giue you notice hereof.[2] Our deepe sorrow, is not a little allayed by the Consideration of gods m*e*rciefull dealing w*i*th him in his sicknesse, & the man*n*er of it. as well in regard of his soule & body, besides all the Assurance we haue otherwise of his deare Indearement to o*u*r God in Christ Jesus. w*hi*ch we desire may be yo*u*r Comfort also, & so do rest,

26. of the this
First mon. cald
March. 1649.
Boston
From yo*u*r Fathers
parlor./

Your most loving
brethren & Freinds
in the Lord
Ri: Bellingham[3]

Joh*n* Cotton./
John Wilson.

your loving frind John Clark[4]

1. As Richard Dunn notes, "Winthrop became bedridden in early Feb., and by 14 Mar. he was too weak to write." Introduction to Winthrop, *Journal,* xxvii n. 40.

2. R. A. Douglas-Lithgow, *Dictionary of American-Indian Place and Proper Names in New England* (Salem, Mass., 1909), identifies *Nahanton* as "an Indian sachem and 'wise-man,' " and *Nahaton* as "William, a Christian Indian of Massachusetts, same as Ahaton?" (328, 329). See also the *Records of Massachusetts Bay,* II, 26, 27. On the various spellings, see Richard W. Cogley, *John Eliot's Mission to the Indians before King Philip's War* (Cambridge, Mass., 1999), 253.

The younger Winthrop "contrived, by water and by horse, to reach Boston in time for the funeral on April 3 and walked with the casket in solemn procession amid the thud of the minute guns." Robert C. Black III, *The Younger John Winthrop* (New York, 1966), 151.

3. Richard Bellingham (c. 1592–1672), a native of Boston, Lincolnshire, had been a member of Parliament for Boston. He emigrated to New England in 1634, became deputy governor the next year, and served as magistrate, deputy governor, and governor at various times thereafter, sometimes being at odds with Winthrop. When this letter was written, he was a magistrate. *DAB.*

4. There is some confusion about the John Clarks who appear in early records for Cambridge, Hartford, and Saybrook, among other places. Savage believed John Clark had removed from Boston with John Winthrop, Jr., to help found the town of Ipswich. Anderson says this man was actually William Clark. The John Clark who went to Hartford is known to have owned land in Saybrook and is probably the person in question here, who signs himself John Winthrop, Jr.'s "loving frind." He was a man of consequence in Connecticut and might have been visiting Boston because of the seriousness of Governor Winthrop's illness, though this is not known. Savage, *Genealogical Dictionary,* I, 394–395; Anderson, *Great Migration,* 371–372.

Peter Bulkeley to [John Cotton]

April 30, 1649

AL. MS: BPL, Ms. Am. 1506, pt. 3, no. 12

A strip of paper some two inches high, this item is a fragmentary remnant of what was the top of a sheet that had been folded vertically in Bulkeley's usual fashion. It contained Bulkeley's letter on the right-hand half of the recto and part of the left-hand half of the verso. Cotton's reply (Cotton to [Bulkeley], May 1649), in his son Seaborn's handwriting, began at the bottom of Bulkeley's second page and continued at the top of the right-hand half of the verso. Thus, the tops of three pages, two from Bulkeley's letter and one from Cotton's copy of his reply, are all that remain. The only evidence that Bulkeley's letter was in fact written to Cotton, and that the reply is from Cotton, is the fact that the reply is in his son's handwriting.

In the upper right of the first page appears "Rev. Peter Bulkley" in an unidentified hand. The following is all in Bulkeley's own hand.

April 30, 1649

Reuerend and honoured in the Lord, I suppose yow are not ignorant of the state our church hath bin in of these later times by reason of some disagreem*en*t betwixt our Elder & my selfe, concerning w*hi*ch I will (for the present) nether blame him, nor excuse myselfe, ~~he~~ nether ˆheˆ being ~~prest~~ present to answere for hims*elf* nor I to proue the things I might write. My intent is onely to desire ~~to~~ your iudgm*en*t concerning a place of scripture I haue propounded to consideration, w*hi*ch is the 1 Corinth*ians* 6: about the apostles aduice to sett vp some in the church to end controuersyes amongst them.

The occasion was this. I seeing the different apprehensions w*hi*ch || and are in t|| in my s|| and especially ||[1]

[IV] This morning, Mr Eliot[2] being w*i*th me, a little conference w*i*th him, gives me occasion of raising another doubt. w*hi*ch is concerning the endeauour of some w*i*th vs, to bring matters to the church, w*i*thout the Elders. Now interpreting that place in math*ew* 18. Tell the church, of the whole fraternitye, w*hi*ch as they say, is to be done next to taking one or two:[3] The doubt is, how yow will auoyd this their practice, if yow follow that interpretation of the place forenamed. There being noe mention there of bringing it to the Elders, before yow tell the Church. People are apt to take hould of the vtmost of their libera[lity]e, but not soe easye to admitt restraynt, vnless it be || grounds. T|| require the ||

1. In the upper left corner of this first page, written down the margin are four partial lines in Bulkeley's hand, mostly illegible because of the combination of his crabbed small script there and badly water-stained paper.

2. John Eliot, teacher of the Roxbury church.

3. Matt. 18:15–17: Moreover if thy brother shall trespass against thee, go and tell him his fault between thee and him alone: if he shall hear thee, thou hast gained thy brother. But if he will not hear thee, then take with thee one or two more, that in the mouth of two or three witnesses every word may be established. And if he shall neglect to hear them, tell it unto the church: but if he neglect to hear the church, let him be unto thee as an heathen man and a publican.

[John Cotton] to [Peter Bulkeley]

May 1649

Copy. MS: BPL, Ms. Am. 1506, pt. 3, no. 12a

This letter is in the hand of Seaborn Cotton and is a reply to Bulkeley to Cotton, April 30, 1649. A portion of the manuscript is missing, so this text begins in medias res and is cut off by the fragmented paper before its ending.

(whereof the Apostle speaketh.) I would not presse the Point of *th*e Reason so farre. for in civill differences, the church may Improove *th*e civill prudence, and civill Justice of theire Members to wayve civill suite. But In matters spirituall No means will atteyne spirituall ends But spiritual means, *tha*t is, such means as the spirit in the word hath appointed. But for *tha*t end w*hi*ch you propound, for preparing things for the churches Cognisance & Judgement (In case the select men cannot amongst your selves compose them) I am Clearely of your Minde.

But if the church it selfe be divided In Judgement about your differences you know the rules calleth the church to call ~~from~~ counsel from other churches. Acts 15.2.[1] whether it be by sending your case to [them] (as in the Acts 15:) or in sending for the ||ers & on||

1. Acts 15:2: When therefore Paul and Barnabas had no small dissension and disputation with them, they determined that Paul and Barnabas, and certain other of them, should go up to Jerusalem unto the apostles and elders about this question.

A New England Minister to John Cotton

June 4, 1649

Published: I. Mather, *First Principles,* 5

Increase Mather identifies this author as "a Reverend person yet surviving in this Country, who in a Letter bearing date, 4. 4 *Moneth* 1649. propounded this Question, *A Father that was in the Iudgement of Charity,*" after which he quotes the following excerpt.

one that feared the Lord, but no Church member, dies and gives his Little Infant to a Church member and Brother of ours, which brother having no Child of his own gladly accepts it, the question is whether such an adopted Child, may by the will *of Christ be baptized or not.*

John Cotton to a New England Minister

[After June 4, 1649]

Published: I. Mather, *First Principles,* 5–6

Increase Mather, following his quotation of the fragment from A New England Minister to Cotton, June 4, 1649, simply states, "Mr. *Cottons* Answer was in these words."

your Case of baptizing of the Child, of one fearing God, and in his death giving his Child to a Church member, *&c.* I propounded to some of our fellow Elders, Mr. *Wilson.* Mr. *Eliot.* and I think Mr. *Mather.*[1] and as I remember, they all inclined to the Affirmative, their ground was the Text in *Gen. 17. 12, 13.*[2] for mine own part I lean to the Affirmative; as you put the Case, the Parent of this Child was not an Indian or Pagan, but a Christian, and baptized himself, and so confederate with such a Church as we renounce not, and I do not disswade the ministring of the Seal of the Covenant, where the Covenant it self is not wanting, *&c.*

1. John Wilson, pastor at Boston, John Eliot, of Roxbury, and Richard Mather, of Dorchester.

2. Gen. 17:12, 13: And he that is eight days old shall be circumcised among you, every man child in your generations, he that is born in the house, or bought with money of any stranger, which is not of thy seed. He that is born in thy house, and he that is bought with thy money, must needs be circumcised: and my covenant shall be in your flesh for an everlasting covenant.

John Cotton to Richard Saltonstall, Jr.

[1649]

ADf. MS: BPL Ms. Am. 1506, pt. 3, app. no. 5

Richard Saltonstall (1610–1694), the son of Sir Richard Saltonstall, entered Emmanuel College, Cambridge, in 1627, but left to sail to New England in 1630. He settled first in Watertown, but moved to Ipswich in 1635, staying there and serving as deputy and assistant until his return to England in 1649. The following letter explains that this return was motivated by the illness of his wife, Muriel, who seems to have preceded him to England. Saltonstall's own departure must have occurred in or shortly before October 1649: Nathaniel B. Shurtleff notes that on October 17, 1649, at a session of court in Boston, two other men were put in charge of an estate, "being M[r] Saltonstall cannot attend it in regard of his voyadge to England."[1] Although this draft letter has never been published, early historians were aware of its existence; Thomas Hutchinson, for one, probably had it in hand as he wrote his *History of the Colony and Province of Massachusetts-Bay* (see Lawrence Shaw Mayo, ed. [Cambridge, Mass., 1936], 83n).

This manuscript, which lacks a signature, is Cotton's own draft, with deletions and interlinear revisions. Certain passages are underlined, but these markings were probably not Cotton's, though the evidence is somewhat less definitive than in most other instances of this. The difference in the color of the ink between the letter and the underlinings is not conspicuous here; in the other cases in which Thomas Prince clearly did the underlining, he also made notes on the sheets, but no such notes are present on the two pages of this manuscript. The underlined passages, which are identified in the footnotes, relate to the addressee's location (at Ipswich) and other matters of chronology or historical circumstance in the colony, the kinds of details in which Prince was interested.

To Richard Saltonstall Esquire./

Honoured ~~& deare Sir~~ S*i*r,

The case you putt is of such Importance, as *tha*t I had ^much rather^ ~~rather~~ ^heare^ *th*e Judgem*en*t of others about it, *tha*n give ^you^ mine owne. But because you Desire to heare my Judgem*en*t amongst others, I will not Refuse to cast in my mite amongst *the*m. The lord make your way plaine before his face, by his wisedome & goodnesse in Christ Jesus.

In *th*e times of *th*e vnsetled Hvrryes of many mens spirits to Returne for England,[2] you to ^settle^ ~~establish~~ yo*u*r owne Thoughts, made a vow to god not to leave *th*e Countrey, whilest *th*e Ordinances of god continued ^here^ in Purity. Since w*hi*ch time, your wifes Infirmityes of Body finding noe Cure nor release her[e], caused hir to seeke Helpe in England;[3] w*hi*ch having found (through mercy) in so^me^ measure, ~~that~~ Perceyving by Counsell of Physicians, that hir Returne hither would cause a Relapse into hir wonted Infirmity, she is thereby necessitated (according to *th*e Advice of freinds) to continue there. Your Q. therefore ^(I take it)^ is, whether notw*i*thstanding your vow of continuance here, you may lawfully ~~goe for~~ Remoove your Family to England to Cohabite there w*i*th your wife.

The sum*m*e of my Thoughts [deleted word] amount to this Answer, reserving to others a more full Discovery of gods minde to you.

i. I conceive, god calleth you to a due & serious Humiliation of yourself for your vow of Continuance here ^vpon *th*e condition alone.^ For though it was made vpon a weighty Occasion, & for a pious Inte*n*t: yet a [deleted word] Christian man may be Called of God (vpon sundry just Grounds) to Remoove from one countrey to another, even whilest *th*e Ordinances of God remaine in Purity. And therefore It was vnlawfull & vnsafe, to Restrayne (as by this vow you did) either [IV] Gods Soveraigne ^Right^ ~~Decision~~ in Disposing of you, or yo*u*r owne Chri*sti*an liberty, by confining yo*u*r self to dwell in this countrey, reserving noe other Condition, but *th*e Continuance of *th*e Gospell, you ought further to have pleded[4] a Reservation of liberty ^Alwayes^ to Follow gods call, wheresoever his hand should necessarily call you.

2. I conceive, your Removall hence will ^be noe small^ ~~be a great~~ weakning not onely to *th*e Towne & Church where you ^now live^ but (in regard of yo*u*r Publick Place) to *th*e whole Countrey.[5]

3. Considering how vncertaine the state of matters in England now stand,[6] I thinke it vns[a]fe to hazard *th*e safety of yo*u*r p*er*son & Family in a p*r*esent Remoovall, w*i*thout further Intelligence.

4. Notw*i*thstanding all this ~~this~~, I ^Believe^ ~~suppose~~, the vnsafe vow w*hi*ch you made of continuance here vpon *tha*t [deleted word] condition alone (being duely Repented of) ^It^ ought to give Place to *tha*t solemne vow w*hi*ch you made to ^God w*i*th^ yo*u*r wife (in marryage) of Cohabitation w*i*th

hir ^& cherishing & nourishing hir [h]ealth, & comfort, as your owne Flesh.^ Or else *th*e vow of man might Dispense w*i*th the ^morall^ com*mandmen*t of God.

5. Because vowes though somewhat vnsafely & vnwarrantably conditioned, yet are to be kept so farre as they are lawfull, I should therefore thinke it your Duety, If either your wife should so farre Recover, as to ^be fitt to^ enjoy hir Health in this Countrey, or if God should Call hir out of this world, That then you should Returne againe to fullfill your vow here, vnlesse *th*e Hand of God should Dispense w*i*th yo*u*r vow by some other necessary Deteynem*en*t there.

The lord Dispose of all yo*u*r Times & Talents to his best Advantage in Christ Jesus./

1. *Records of Massachusetts Bay,* III, 171. On Saltonstall, see the biography by Robert E. Moody in *The Saltonstall Papers,* I, 25–41; see also Joseph B. Felt, *History of Ipswich, Essex, and Hamilton* (1834; rpt. Bowtel, Md., 1991), 77–78; *DAB.*

2. Underlined: "In the times . . . for England."

3. Underlined: "Since which time . . . in England." Saltonstall's wife was Muriel Gurdon, daughter of Brampton Gurdon, Esq., of Assington, county Suffolk, and Letton, county Norfolk. They were married July 4, 1633. *NEHGR,* XXXIII (1879), 228.

4. pleded is written over another word.

5. Underlined phrases: "your Removall hence"; "weakning not onely"; "Towne & Church"; "Publick Place"; "whole Countrey."

Cotton refers here to Saltonstall's long tenure (1635–1649) as a magistrate for Ipswich on the General Court. See Felt, *History of Ipswich, Essex, and Hamilton,* 77.

6. Underlined: "how vncertaine . . . now stand."

John Cotton to the Congregation and Church at Boston, Lincolnshire

[1650]

Published: John Cotton, *Of the Holinesse of Church-Members* (London, 1650), sig. A2–[A2v]

Though printed as a brief preface to a book, this epistle is a genuine letter to a particular group of people in a particular place, his friends in St. Botolph's Church, Boston, Lincolnshire. It is unusually personal, in fact, in the amount of autobiographical detail included in it. That it is not the first such letter Cotton had written to his former congregation is indicated in a remark he had made in *The Way of Congregational Churches Cleared* (1648), where he mentions "a letter to some friends in Boston" and goes on to quote the letter of October 5, 1635, to Anthony Tuckney.[1]

The printer set this prefatory epistle in italics, except for proper names, biblical references, and the salutation and signature block, which are set in roman type. These typographical conventions are eliminated here, since they were clearly not of Cotton's creation.

To my honored, worshipfull, and worthy Friends, the Major, and Justices, the Aldermen and Common Councell, together with the whole Congregation and Church at Boston: Mercy, Peace, and Truth be multiplyed in Christ Jesus.

Honoured and dear Friends,

In that twenty yeers Service, (or thereabouts) wherein according to the call of God and you, I fed his flock amongst you, and his, and your lambs (as Jacob did Labans for the like space, Gen. 31. 38.)[2] I do with thankfulnesse acknowledge to God, and you, you have not dealt with me (as Laban with him) grudgingly, and deceitfully: but rather (as the Macedonians dealt with Paul) you gave up your own selves, first to the Lord, and then to your Ministers by the will of God: 2 Cor. 8. 5.[3] And ye became followers of us, and of the Lord, and shewed your selves ensamples, in some first-fruits of Reformation, unto many neighbour Congregations about you: 1 Thes. 1. 6, 7.[4] And though you saw that any small measure of Reformation (which then was offensive to the State, and suffered under the name of Non-conformity) would expose your selves to some suffering, unlesse you deserted me; yet I bear you record, you chose rather to expose your selves to charge and hazard for many yeers together, then to expose my Ministery to silence. And though at the last, in that houre and power of darknesse, when the late High Commission began to stretch forth their malignant Arm against us, I was forced (as Jacob did from Laban) to depart secretly from you, (from some of you I say) howbeit not without the privity and consent of the chief:)[5] yet sundry of you yeelded up your selves (as Ittai to David)[6] to follow the Lord whithersoever he should call, and to go along with me, whether to life or death, in this (late) howling wildernesse; And though after my departure you were somewhat carried aside, with the torrent of the times, yet I beleeve, not without some apprehension of the light of the word going before you, in your judgements, to the satisfaction of your own consciences. And even since that time wherein the strong hand of the Lord, and the malignancy of the times, had set this vast distance of place, and great gulf of Seas between us: yet still you claimed an interest in me, and have yeerly ministred, some reall testimony of your love: and at last when the Lord (of his rich grace) had dispelled the storme of malignant Church-government, you invited me again and again, to return to the place and work wherein I had walked, before the Lord and you in former times. But the estate of those of you, who came along with me, (and who thereby had most interest in me) could not bear that: nor would my relation to the Church here suffer it: Nor would my Age now stricken in yeers, nor infirm body ill brooking the Seas be able to undergo it, without extreame perill of becoming utterly unserviceable, either to your selves or others. Besides, the estate of our Church, admitting more then professed Saints to the fellowship of the seals, and the government of your Church subjected to an extrinsecall Ecclesiasticall power would have been a perpetuall scruple and torment to my conscience, which knowing the terrors of the Lord, and the conviction of my own judgement, I durst not venture upon. Not that I mis-judge others, who can satisfie their consciences in a larger latitude: but because every man is to be fully perswaded in his own minde, and I must live by my own faith. Rom. 14. 5. 23.[7]

Neverthelesse touching the former of these (the true estate of Church members, and what is the holinesse required of them) that you may see I am not pinched with groundlesse scruples about it; I have for the satisfaction of your selves, and of sundry others, who have written to me about the same, penned this ensuing Treatise, Of the Holinesse of Church-members; wherein if the Lord should be pleased to reach forth, any satisfaction to your selves, I hope it would tend much, if not towards union, yet towards a mutuall communion between your own Church, and the other Congregationall Church which (I hear) the Lord Jesus hath planted amongst you. For if both of you could consent in that qualification of your Church-members which this Treatise pleadeth for, the other scruple which concerneth the subjection of your Church to an extrinsecall Church power might haply be well eased, if not wholly removed, in such a way as this. The Elders of your neighbour Churches (who were wont to be favourable to the Church at Boston) as they would accept your Elders into fellowship of publick consultation with them about Church affairs: so they might give your Elders counsell in matters that concern your own Church, & the members thereof: but leave the transaction and execution therof to your own Elders, in the presence and with the consent of your own Church. And who can tell how much and how far the Lord might stretch forth the blessing of such a peaceable condescendency, to more generall acceptance, and accommodation?[8] Surely the Lord hath done great things for you in your late marvellous deliverances, when an Army of Malignants passed and returned by you, and might easily have swallowed you up quick, if the Lord himself had not encamped about you.[9] The pondering of Gods goodnes to you herein, brought to my minde, the former like dealing of God with his people, Zach. 9. 8.[10] And wherefore hath the Lord thus saved you (as a firebrand out of the burning)[11] but that you might live to the advancement of his kingdom, in exemplary Truth and Peace. The same good hand of the Lord still protect and direct you, in all your holy and civill administrations, in Christ Jesus. In whom saluting you all, and all your relations, I take leave and rest,

Once your unworthy Pastor, ever your faithfull
Servant in Christ, John Cotton.

1. *The Way of Congregational Churches Cleared* (1648), in Ziff, *Cotton on the Churches,* 209. Cotton added there, "I do remember such a letter I wrote; whether to one or more in Boston I remember not: some say it is printed, but I know not, nor have I seen it" (210). *The Way of Congregational Churches Cleared* was an answer to Robert Baillie's *Dissuasive from the Errours of the Time* . . . (London, 1645), Samuel Rutherford's *Due Right of Presbyteries* . . . (London, 1644), and Daniel Cawdry's *Vindiciae Clavium* . . . (London, 1645), so was written in the period 1646–1647. Everett Emerson suggests 1647 (*Cotton,* 141).

2. Gen. 31:38: This twenty years have I been with thee; thy ewes and thy she goats have not cast their young, and the rams of thy flock have I not eaten.

3. 2 Cor. 8:5: And this they did, not as we hoped, but first gave their own selves to the Lord, and unto us by the will of God.

4. 1 Thess. 1:6, 7: And ye became followers of us, and of the Lord, having received the word in much affliction, with joy of the Holy Ghost: So that ye were ensamples to all that believe in Macedonia and Achaia.

5. This closing parenthesis has no opening parenthesis in the printed text.

6. Ittai was a Philistine in David's army when he fled from Jerusalem in Absalom's rebellion. See 2 Sam. 15:19, 22.

7. Rom. 14:5, 23: One man esteemeth one day above another: another esteemeth every day alike. Let every man be fully persuaded in his own mind. . . . And he that doubteth is damned if he eat, because he eateth not of faith: for whatsoever is not of faith is sin.

Cotton might have intended to write Romans 14:5–23. In his letter to Bishop Williams, May 7, 1633, Cotton had also cited Rom. 14:5 and had drawn the same personal conclusion from it: "I must . . . live by mine own fayth."

8. Here Cotton has in mind not only the repair of traditional Puritan differences with the Church of England but also the recent struggles for ascendancy in the Puritan movement between Independent and Presbyterian factions. He makes reference to this issue and even to this letter to his former congregation in his 1651 "Sermon upon A Day of Publique thanksgiving": "As for presbitterie & Independency it was Noe greate Difficulty, to provide for toleration of both: for present, it is certaine the Body of the Nation of England, is not Capable of Fellowship in Independent churches: there will be A Necessity therefore of giving way to the other way of goverment; for those that are fitt for to become materialls for churches Acording to god, if they allso be Alowed it might put an end to much Difference, But for more perticuler Acomodation of Both waies, it is more Distinckly though Briefly in A short epistle prefaccing to the holyness of church members." Francis J. Bremer, "In Defense of Regicide: John Cotton on the Execution of Charles I," *WMQ,* 3d Ser., XXXVII (1980), 122.

9. Cotton's repeated usage of "Malignants" in this letter has a particular historical connotation, as the *OED* explains: "Used by opponents as a designation for a member of the party which supported Charles I against the Parliament; a Royalist, Cavalier. Also, in a religious sense, applied by Puritans and Covenanters to their ecclesiastical adversaries. (The two applications are often coincident.)"

Cotton's Boston correspondents had obviously sent him word of the renewed military activity in the area in mid-1648 during the Second Civil War. In late June and early July a Royalist force under the command of Sir Philip Monckton, thinking that Boston would fall easily, marched into Lincoln, where they routed a small parliamentary force, and planned to continue on to Boston, "understanding that Boston would be delivered to them, and that they would be joined by 'divers thousands' from Lincolnshire, Norfolk, Leicestershire, Derbyshire, and Rutland" (E. W. Hensman, "The East Midlands and the Second Civil War, May to July, 1648," Royal Historical Society, *Transactions,* 4th Ser., VI [1923], 144). Such reinforcements did not appear, however, and Boston escaped further strife. Cotton might well have known more about the details of troop movements than modern historians now do. See Clive Holmes, *Seventeenth-Century Lincolnshire* (Lincoln, Lincs., 1980), 200–201; J. W. F. Hill, *Tudor and Stuart Lincoln* (Cambridge, 1956), 161–162.

10. Zech. 9:8: And I will encamp about mine house because of the army, because of him that passeth by, and because of him that returneth: and no oppressor shall pass through them any more: for now have I seen with mine eyes.

11. See Amos 4:11.

Samuel Whiting to John Cotton

[Late January–Early February 1649/50]

ALS. BPL: Ms. Am. 1506, pt. 2, no. 8

Thomas Prince's annotation at the top of the single sheet on which this undated letter is written mistakenly surmises, "This seems to be wrote in *th*e time of *th*e synod, w*hich* Began on Aug. 30. 1637." The letter's references to "afflictions" that Cotton and his wife ("my Deare Cousin") were suffering when the letter was written caused Prince to assume they related to Cotton's embroilment in the Antinomian troubles. Another kind of suffering, however, experienced more than a decade later, is indicated. The attempts at consolation in phrases like "the resurrection of *th*e just" and "drops of compassion" together with the hope that Cotton can put off his "mourning weed" clearly indicate personal loss through death. The context is the sudden death of two of the Cottons' children in a smallpox outbreak. Their oldest daughter and her mother's namesake, Sarah, died at age fourteen on January 20, 1649/50, and their sixth and youngest child, six-year-old Rowland, died nine days later on January 29.[1] We do not have Cotton's reply to Whiting's letter, if he wrote one, but Cotton Mather preserved Cotton's poetic effort at self-consolation from "a spare leaf of his *Alamanack*" where "he wrote in *Greek* letters these *English verses*":

In Saram.

Farewel, dear Daughter *Sara,* Now Thou'rt gone,
(Whither thou much desiredst) to thine Home:

Pray, my Dear Father, Let me now go Home!
Were the last Words thou spak'st to me alone.
   Go then, sweet *Sara,* take thy *Sabbeth Rest,*
   With thy Great Lord, and all in Heaven Blest.

In Rolandum.

Our Eldest *Daughter,* and our Youngest *Son,*
Within Nine Days, both have their full Race run.
On th' *Twentieth* of th' *Eleventh,* Died She,
And on the *Twenty Ninth* Day Died He.
Both in their *Lives* were *Lovely* and *United.*
And in their *Deaths* they were not much *Divided.*
Christ gave them *Both,* and *He* takes both again
To live with Him; *Blest* be His Holy *Name.*

In Utrumque.[2]

Suffer, Saith Christ, *Your Little Ones,*
   To Come forth, Me unto,
For of such Ones my Kingdom is,
   Of Grace and Glory too.
We do not only *Suffer* them,
   But *Offer* them to Thee,
Now, Blessed Lord, Let us Believe,
   Accepted, that they be:
That Thou hast *Took* them, in Thine Arms,
   And on them *Put thine Hand,*
And *Blessed* them with *Sight of Thee,*
   Wherein our *Blessings* Stand.[3]

The letter's address block written on the recto reads:

To my Reuerend & Deare
Cousin Mr John Cotton
Teacher of *th*e Church
at Boston p*re*sent
these.

A portion of Whiting's sealing wax remains on the paper.

Other notes are written along the left margin of the letter and at the bottom in a hand that appears both less mature and of a later date than the document itself.[4]

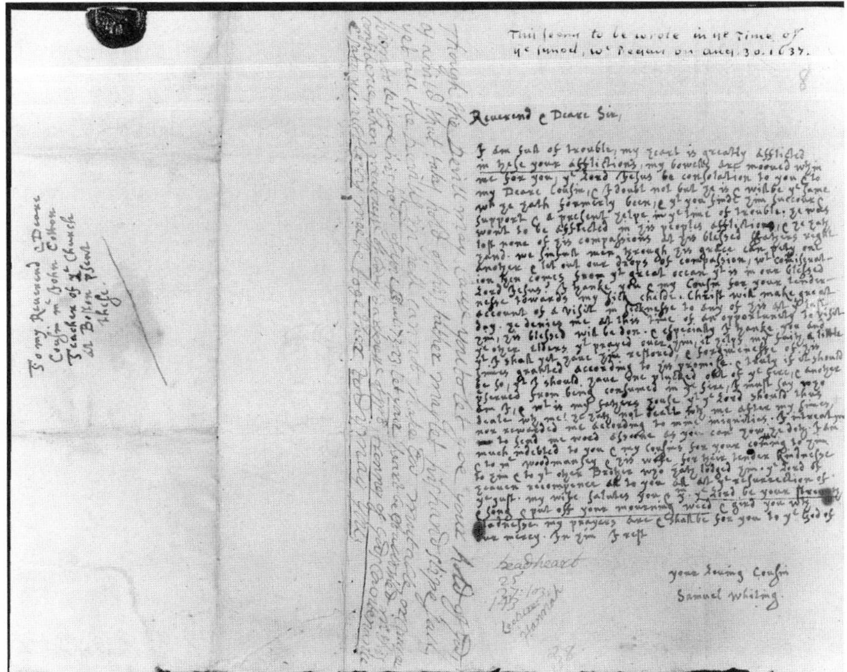

PLATE 17. Samuel Whiting to Cotton, [Late January / Early February 1649/50]. This letter, in vague terms but clear enough for the correspondents to understand each other, offers sympathy to the Cottons on the occasion of the recent deaths of two of their children in a smallpox epidemic. The marginalia are from a later period, including Thomas Prince's hand just above Whiting's letter. *Boston Public Library Ms. Am. 1506, pt. 2, no. 8. Courtesy of the Trustees of the Boston Public Library*

Reuerend & Deare Sir,

I am full of trouble, my heart is greatly afflicted in these your afflictions,[5] my bowells are mooued w*i*thin me for you,[6] *th*e Lord Jesus be consolation to you & to my Deare Cousin,[7] & I doubt not but he is & will be *th*e same w*hic*h he hath formerly been, & *tha*t you finde him succour & support & a present helpe in *th*e time of trouble. he was wont to be afflicted in his peoples afflictions, & he hath lost none of his compassions at his blessed Fathers right hand. We sinfull men through his grace can pity one another & let out our drops of compassion, w*ha*t com*m*iseration then comes from *tha*t great ocean *tha*t is in our blessed Lord Jesus? I thanke you and my Cousin for your tendernesse towards my sick childe. Christ will make great account of a visit in sicknesse to any of his at *th*e last day. he denies me at this time of an opportunity to visit him,[8] his blessed will be don. & especially I thanke you and *th*e other elders *tha*t prayed ouer him, it helps my faith a little *tha*t I shall yet haue him restored, & forgiuenesse of his sinnes granted according to his promise.

& truly if it should be so, *tha*t I should haue one plucked out of *the* fire, & another[9] p*r*eserued from being consumed in *th*e fire, I must say who am I, & w*ha*t is my fathers house *tha*t *th*e Lord should thus deale w*i*th me![10] he hath not dealt w*i*th me after my sinnes, nor rewarded me according to mine iniquities.[11] I intreat you [deleted word] to send me word assoone as you can how he doth. I am much indebted to you & my Cousins for your com*m*ing to him & to Mr Woodmansey and his wife[12] for their tender kindnesse to him & to *tha*t other Brother who hath lodged him. *Th*e Lord of heauen recompence all to you all at *th*e resurrection of *th*e just.[13] my wife salutes you & *th*em. *th*e Lord be your stre[ng]th & Song & put off your mourning weed & gird you w*i*th [g]ladnesse.[14] my prayers are & shall be for you to *th*e God of [o]ur mercy. In him I rest

Your louing Cousin
Samuel Whiting.

1. Savage, *Genealogical Dictionary,* I, 462; Anderson, *Great Migration,* 486–487.

2. In Utrumque: on both.

3. Mather, *Magnalia Christi Americana* . . . (London, 1702), book III, 31.

4. "Though the Devill may cause you to let goe your hold of god, as a child that takes hold of his father may let his hand slipe fall, yet all the Devills in hell cannot make God mutable, or cause him to let goe his hold of you, Psal. 73:23: let your heart be established in this confidence, when weaknesse of body, darknesse of sp*iri*t fronnes of Gods countenance & Satans subtlety meete together to dismay you." In the same hand at the bottom of the letter is scribbled on six lines: "headheart/ 25/ 27.103/ 143/ Lecture/ Hannah."

5. The phrase "in these your afflictions" is underlined, probably by Prince.

6. The bowels were traditionally considered the seat of tenderness, compassion, or pity.

7. Sarah Cotton, Sr.

8. We know of three male children in the Whiting family, Samuel (b. 1633), John (b. 1637), and Joseph (b. 1641). The son in question here may be Samuel, who graduated from Harvard College in 1653, so might have been living at this time in the Boston area.

9. It is not clear whether this reference is also to a son. Whiting had a daughter, Dorothy, by his first wife; she was born before 1633 and married Thomas Weld in 1650. Whiting and his second wife had a second daughter, Elizabeth.

10. Whiting quotes selectively from either 2 Sam. 7:18 or 1 Chron. 17:16, both of which give David's response to God's promise to establish him and his seed in God's "house," forever. The former verse reads: Then went King David in, and sat before the Lord, and he said, who am I, O Lord God? and what is my house, that thou hast brought me hitherto?

Whiting might also have in mind the similar 1 Sam. 18:18: And David said unto Saul, Who am I? and what is my life, or my father's family in Israel, that I should be son-in-law to the king?

11. Whiting is quoting from Ps. 103:10: He hath not dealt with us after our sins: nor rewarded us according to our iniquities.

12. Robert and Margaret Woodmansy. He was the schoolmaster in Boston. An entry in the Boston town records about a month after this letter was written says, "M^r. Woodmansey, the Schoolmaster, shall have fiftye pounds per annum for his teachinge the schollers, and his pro-

portion to be made up by ratte" (Boston, Record Commissioners, *Second Report of the Record Commissioners of the City of Boston, Containing the Boston Records, 1634–1660, and the Book of Possessions,* 2d ed. [Boston, 1881], 99).

13. See Luke 14:14: And thou shalt be blessed; for they cannot recompense thee: for thou shalt be recompensed at the resurrection of the just.

14. See Ps. 30:11: Thou hast turned for me my mourning into dancing: Thou hast put off my sackcloth, and girded me with gladness.

"Lord be your stre[ng]th & Song & put off your mourning weed" is underlined, probably by Prince.

Peter Bulkeley to John Cotton

April 4, 1650

ALS. MS: NEHGS, Spec. Coll. 11.S. 1–41 Sewall-Shattuck Collection 11-S-1 I/C/7/1

Published: Lemuel Shattuck, *A History of the Town of Concord . . .* (Boston, 1835), 155–157 (partial transcription)

This letter contains intriguing references by Bulkeley to two situations, neither of which has been identified in any particular detail. In the first paragraph Bulkeley refers to a previous reply from Cotton regarding a woman's making a public complaint against a man in Bulkeley's congregation. Unfortunately, the church records from Concord in this period no longer exist.

Bulkeley also refers to reports both of Cotton's thriving ministry in Boston and of attacks on or complaints against Cotton. His lament about the loss of virtue in New England, contrasting it unfavorably with the conditions that used to exist "in old Boston," is familiar from earlier letters of Bulkeley. He seems in the course of his fifteen years in Concord to have retained a disgruntled sense that his contemporaries were wanting in both virtue and collegiality—always excepting Cotton, whom he continues to approach for the answers to vexing cases of conscience.

The letter is on a single sheet, which Bulkeley folded once. It begins on the right-hand half of the recto and continues on to the left-hand half of the verso. On the left-hand half of the recto is the address block, in Bulkeley's hand, which reads:

> To the Reuerend his honoured
> frend M[r] Cotton Teacher
> to the church att Boston
> giue these

The letter retains the sealing wax, imprinted with the Bulkeley crest. The preservation of the letter by Cotton's descendants is indicated in two notes in different hands on the same portion of the recto as the address block: "From m[r] Bulkley to my Grandfather

April. 4. 1650.—" and "To my Great, great, ~~great~~ Grandfather the first Minister of Boston M Cotton."

Reuerend in the Lord,

I am glad to see your concurrence concerning that place in Job. As touching the other case about the wife dealing w*i*th her husband, I think we shall ˆrestˆ in your aduice; onely the reason w*hi*ch yow giue ag*ains*t it, (sc: because an admonition hath aliquid potestatiu*m,*)[1] I know nott how farre that will sway, considering whatt I once heard from yow, vpon a question propounded to yow, the first time yow were here att Concord, att w*hi*ch time one asked yow concerning a sister being offended by a brother, whether shee might nott take libertye to deale w*i*th him, by way of admonition. to w*hi*ch (as I remember) your answere was, *tha*t shee might, adding this reason, bec*ause* the sin of a brother makes him a debter, and soe in that respect, putts him into a degree of inferioritye, & [deleted letter] makes the other his superiour. which reason did then beare sway w*i*th vs. and the like seemes to be the case here. for though the husband (as an husband) is sup*er*iour to the wife, yett being alsoe a brother, and an offending brother, whether the like case may nott be taken ~~be taken~~ betwixt them, may yett seeme doubtfull. If *th*e Lord offer any further thoughts to yow about this, I could willingly vnderstand, otherwise, I shall rest in whatt yow haue written.

Some other things I am full of, but will nott write w*i*th paper & ink; onely in a word; I blesse god for whatt I heare, how the L. doth fill your ministry w*i*th abundance of grace, life, and pow*er*, to the exceeding ioy of those *tha*t are true hearted towards *th*e Lord. Butt w*i*thall I stand amazed and wonder att gods forbearance, considering whatt I heare in another kind. w*hi*ch I doe also beleeue to be true in some p*ar*te; true I meane, as done and spoken by some, though vntrue in respect of any cause giuen on your p*ar*te. Truly S*i*r, it is to me a wonder *tha*t *th*e earth swallowes nott vp such wretches, or *tha*t fire comes nott downe from heauen to consume them. The L. hath a number of holy and humble ones here amongst vs, for whose sakes he doth spare, and will spare long. but were it nott for such a remnant, we should see the L. would make quick work amongst vs. Shall I tell yow whatt I think to be the ground of all this insolencye w*hi*ch discouers itselfe in the sp*iri*ts of men? Truly I cannott ascribe it soe much to any outward thing, as to the putting of too much libertye and pow*er* into the hands of *th*e multitude, w*hi*ch they are too weak to manage, many growing conceited, proud, arrogant, selfe sufficient, as wanting nothing. And I am p*er*swaded that except there be some meanes vsed to change *th*e course of things in this poynt, our churches will grow more corrupt day by day; and tumults will arise, hardly to be stilled. Rem*em*ber the former dayes w*hi*ch yow had in old Boston. where though (through *th*e L*ord*s blessing vpon your labour) there was an increase dayly added to *th*e church, yett the number of professours is farre more here, then it was there. Butt answere me, which place was better gouerned? Whether matters were swayed there by your wisdome & counsell, matters went on w*i*th strength & power for good. Butt here where the headye, or headles multitude [IV] haue gotten the power into their hands, there is insolencye and confusion. And I know nott how it can be auoyded in this way, vnlesse we should make the dores of the church narrower, then we haue warrant for, fro*m* *th*e word. w*hi*ch course if it should be taken, would bring its inconueniences also in an other kind. Butt of these things noe more. Onely I pray the L. to heale the euells of ˆtheˆ places & times we liue in, and remoue that wofull contempt of his gospell, w*hi*ch doth abound. Oh whatt mischeefe doth one proud, lofty sp*iri*t *tha*t is in reputation for vnderstanding, among a number of others ˆ*tha*t are weak.ˆ and some of both sorts there are in euery place. Butt our comfort is, gods end, and work shall goe forward. Some shall be conuerted, some hardened. The god of mercye carrye on ~~our~~ his work in our hearts & hands, to the glorifying of his rich grace in Christ Jesus. I pray rem*em*ber my heartye loue to good M[rs] Cotton, thanking her for her louing rem*em*brance of my little ones.[2] I pray god giue vs both to see his grace increasing in those *tha*t he hath continued towards vs. Farewell dearely beloued & honoured in the Lord. Comfort yourselfe in him, whoe is most readye to be found in a time of neede. In him I rest,

Apr*il* 4. 1650.

Yours euer

Pet: Bulkeley.

I could wish you would write to M[r] Goodwin[3] to deale w*i*th those *tha*t are in place of autoritye in England to take care *tha*t *th*e scripture may be printed more truly. I haue a bible printed 1648, w*hi*ch hath (little & great) about an 100 faults in the printing of it. and I haue an old bible printed ~~16~~ 1581. w*hi*ch hath but one or two and those very small ones. I intend to write to my Nephew St John[4] about it. a word from yours*elf* to M[r] Goodwin, whoe is a man of soe much respect there, would doe much good.

1. aliquid potestatium: literally, something of powers, that is, a measure of authority.

2. Bulkeley's four children by his second wife, Grace Chetwood, were Gershom (b. 1636), Eleazer (b. 1638), Dorothy (b. 1640), and Peter (b. 1643). Only four of his ten children by his first wife, Jane Allen, were living in 1650, all then adults. Donald Lines Jacobus, *The Bulkeley Genealogy* . . . (New Haven, Conn., 1933), 111; Anderson, *Great Migration,* 459–465.

3. Thomas Goodwin (1600–1680) had been one of the five Independents at the Westminster Assembly and was a correspondent and editor of prominent clergymen in New England, including Cotton and Thomas Hooker. In 1647 Cotton had invited Goodwin to emigrate to New England. As chaplain to the lord protector, he was at this time a member of Cromwell's

inner circle and on January 8, 1650, he had just become master of Magdalen College, Oxford. See Brook, *Lives of the Puritans,* III, 156; *DNB;* Christopher Hill, *The Experience of Defeat: Milton and Some Contemporaries* (New York, 1984), 179–184.

4. Oliver St. John (c. 1598–1673), a lawyer who on October 12, 1648, had become chief justice of the Common Pleas and was a prominent member of the Westminster Assembly. Peter Bulkeley's sister, Sarah Bulkeley St. John, was Chief Justice Oliver St. John's mother. Jacobus, *Bulkeley Genealogy,* 30–31; on Oliver St. John, see also *DNB.*

John Cotton to Peter Bulkeley

[After April 4, 1650]

ADf. MS: NEHGS, Spec. Coll. 11.S. 1–41 Sewall-Shattuck Collection 11-S-1 I/C/7/1

Cotton's notes for a reply to Bulkeley's letter of April 4, 1650, are written in nine lines on the blank right-hand half-sheet of the verso of Bulkeley to Cotton, April 4, 1650.

The liberty w*hi*ch I gave to a sister to Deale w*i*th an Offending brother doeth not (as I conceive) allow *th*e like liberty to a wife, to Deale in a Church-way ag*ains*t an Offending Husband, in case of any Personall Injury done by him to hir self, but such as might concerne, either hir life, or his Conjugall Fidelity: w*hi*ch might give just Occasion of Separation, & Divorce from Him. For in other Cases, & Offences ag*ains*t Other Man[1] ^or woman,^ though ^a^ Man[2] looseth his Church-Power, yet an[3] ^Husband offending his wife^ looseth not his Husbandly Authority, but onely in those 2 Cases, of Daunger of Life, or ^breach of^ Conjugall Fidelity.

1. ag*ains*t Other is written over of another. Man is written over an illegible word.
2. Man is written over He.
3. an is written over He.

John Cotton to [Nathaniell White]

April 29, 1650

ALS. MS: BPL, Ms. Am. 1506, pt. 3, no. 15

In L. Thompson, "Letters of John Cotton," 195–198

This manuscript, written in Cotton's own hand on both sides of a single sheet, is very badly mutilated by water damage and loss of paper in the upper right corner and in two places in the center of the sheet. Only about five lines are uninterrupted by the loss of paper. Lawrance Thompson says of this letter, "to see it is to know why it has never been printed" ("Letters of John Cotton," 198). The breaks in the text are frustrating, but enough remains to indicate its essential message, which concerns the plight of Nathaniell White's congregation in the Caribbean. White's name appears nowhere in the letter, but Cotton's remarks identify the recipient as "a Pastor to that Flock of Christ." It appears that White and Cotton had corresponded previously—at least as early as 1647.[1]

Nathaniell White began his ecclesiastical career in England as an adamant supporter of the church's enforcement of conformity, but later in Bermuda formally separated from the English Church and covenanted with other ministers and members of his congregation in an Independent church. For a while in Bermuda he was a member of the controlling political faction but eventually lost this power and was imprisoned before leaving Bermuda for the island of Eleuthera in the Bahamas. He eventually returned to Bermuda and lived until 1668, apparently becoming a conformist once again in his later years.

An unusual amount of information supplementing and corroborating the details in this letter is available from other sources. As the letter itself explains, churches in the Bay Colony had collected money to send to Eleuthera for the relief of the people there in a time of dire need. Cotton Mather might have had the letter in hand as he explained the situation that motivated the charity of the Massachusetts churches:

> A little church, whereof the worthy Mr. *White* was pastor, being by the strange and strong malice of their prevailing adversaries, forced of[f] *Barmudas* in much misery, into a desart of *America,* the report of their distresses came to their fellow-sufferers, though not alike sufferers, at *New-England.* Mr. *Cotton* immediately applied himself to obtain a collection, for the relief of those *distressed saints;* and a collection of about 700*l.* was immediately obtained, whereof two hundred was gathered in that one church of *Boston,* where there was no man who did exceed, and but one man who did equal, this *deviser of liberal things,* in that contribution. But behold the wonderful providence of God! This *contribution* arrived unto the poor people on the *very day,* after they had been brought into a personal division of the little *meal* then left in the barrel; upon the spending whereof, they could foresee nothing but a lingring death; and on that *very day,* when their pastor had preached unto them, upon that most suitable text, *Psal.* xxiii. 1, *The Lord is my shepherd, I shall not want.*[2]

The essential details of the letter appear also in two nearly contemporary accounts, a letter written on September 7, 1650, from Captain Josias Forster from Bermuda to the Company of Adventurers for the Summer Islands in London, and in Edward Johnson's *Wonder-Working Providence of Sion's Saviour in New England* (1654), written in the period 1650–1651. Forster's letter tells of White's company going to a "little Island" which "is a most barren Rock, shallow Earth, not hopeful to produce food for the Inhabitants, which hath stirred up the hearts of their Christian friends in *New England,* to manifest their exceeding Bounty towards them, by a charitable Contribution of at least six or seven hundred Pounds sterling." Johnson mentions that "six or eight" New England churches contributed "about 800 £ to supply their necessity."[3]

The relevant entry in the *Records of the First Church* was made by the messenger himself:

> Our Brother James Penn was chosen by the Church with a unanimus Consent to be a Messenger to goe and Distribut the Churches Contributions (to the poore Church of Christ that was banished from Bermudos for the Gospells sake to Segoton)[4] And he was sent out to sea on the 13th day of the 3d moneth. And on the 17th day of the 4th moneth 1650 we arived at Segotea. where I found the people in wants. who when I had Given the Churches letters and Declared the end of my coming they thanked god and the churches.[5]

Cotton's letter was thus written two weeks before the ship's departure on May 13, 1650.

[Rever]end & deare brother in o*ur* Lord Jes[us Christ:]

I blesse *th*e Lord w*it*h you, who hath delivered you || Tumults of those malignant Spirits at Bermu[da]|| to Cygotea. It was *th*e Thankfull Acknowledge[ment]|| David (*th*e Lord Jesus) Thou hast Delivered me f[rom the strivings of the people]|| Psal. 18. 43.[6] The Oyntm*en*t of Salvation, w*hi*ch was po[ured]|| Head, *th*e Lord Jesus, wee see by experience in all his || downe to *th*e skirts of his Garm*en*ts.[7] His Name be blessed || It was *th*e good hand of God *tha*t guided ^you^ to write such a || & Proce[edin]gs of *tha*t Tumult ag*ains*t you, & of yo*u*r Deliverance o|| therefore thought ^it meete^ to Publish it (on *th*e Lords day soone after) ||[congre]gation, who were so much affected therew*it*h *tha*t fearing many || sort of Church members & others (who went along w*it*h *the*m) might be in some straites (being hurryed out so sodainely into [a] D[e]sert) they willingly Offered to Contrib[ute] f[o]r their Releife, & accord[in]gly did indeede P[rese]nt to *th*e Lord, & to his p[oo]r servants w*it*h [y]o[u] about *th*e sum*m*e of 240[£]|| [The which] our neighbo*u*r Chur[ches] hearing of, ^ha[ve se]verally^ augmented *th*e || I doe not k[now] how much. But ||[se]nd it more particularly by o*ur* belo[ved] & faithfull Broth[er James Pen]ne,[8] who was chosen by o*ur* Church to Carry this grace || vnto you, for those end[s], w*hi*ch they beleived, Gods ha[nd]||end to Christly to Releive [the] Necessityes of *th*e Chur[ch]|| yo*u*r Advice He|| see to stand in Neede of || som[e other?] Churches have || also o*ur* brother Penne to be || *th*e conveyance, & [D]ispos[er of] their Contribution. It || some other Brother may || by some other church to Ac[c]ompany Him, & to Joyne in *th*e Disposall o[f the] Gift. The Lord goe forth w*i*th *the*m & bring *the*m safe to you, & make their service acceptable to himself, & to his Saints [w]*i*th you.

Yo*u*r gove[r]no*u*r & *the* Councell wrote to some of o*u*r Me[mbers?] to send o[ver] to *the*m some Provisions in way of Merchandise. What they [will s]end & Doe in *tha*t kinde, I doe not know as yet: or whether, they t[hinke i]t meete to Respite *tha*t to another time. But you will be certefyed of all more particul[arly] by this Bearer, o*u*r brother Penne.

And now (deare brother) since *the* Lord hath Called you to be a Pasto*u*r to *tha*t Flock of Christ, I neede not Putt you in minde (who are taught of God to be faithfull to Him, & *the*m) how much it concerneth you to see, *tha*t *the* Place where *the* Church setteth downe, may (through Gods Ble[ssing] ˆvpon their Industry)ˆ [b]e fitt to yeild *the*m safety, & subsistence: & *tha*t the Civill Governm*en*t (as [e]ver they looke to Prosper, in a way of G[od]) may be so moulded by yo*u*r wise Advise, as *tha*t neither *the* Church, [nor] Posterity [IV] || straitned. The Seedes of Corruption, & Desolation || *the* first Plantation & Constitution of Church, & Com*m*onweal[th]||, That *the* Lord Jesus himself layeth *the* Foundations of his owne ||t vp Jerusalem w*i*th his owne hands, & hath founded the || world, so as may best conduce to his Churches good. To *the* ||[h]is vnsearchable wisedome, & rich grace I com*m*end you, w*i*th || to yo*u*r wife, & sonne, Mr Reyner,[9] & *the* whole Church of Christ || And so w*i*th Desire of continuance of mutuall Prayers, I rest,

Yo*u*rs in brotherly love,

Joh*n* Cotton. /

Boston in NE.
29. of 2. i650.

1. An elderly ministerial colleague of White's in Bermuda, Patrick Copeland, wrote to John Winthrop on July 31, 1647, mentioning that he supposed "brother White hath more at large writen of our Troubles to your Teacher Mr. Cotton or to your Pastor, Mr. Wilson" (*Winthrop Papers,* V, 183). J. H. Lefroy, *Memorials of the Discovery and Early Settlement of the Bermudas, or Somers Islands, 1515–1685* (London, 1877), I, 700.

2. Mather, *Magnalia,* I, 254.

3. [Edward Johnson], *Wonder-Working Providence of Sion's Saviour in New England,* ed. J. Franklin Jameson (1910; rpt. New York, 1967), 267; Lefroy, *Memorials of the Discovery,* II, 9.

4. Segoton: the island of Eleuthera in the Bahamas, variously called Segotea, Segatto, or (as Cotton spells it in letter) Cygotea.

5. *Records of the First Church,* 50–51.

6. Ps. 18:43: Thou hast delivered me from the strivings of the people; and thou hast made me the head of the heathen: a people whom I have not known shall serve me (KJV). The Geneva Bible reads: Thou hast delivered me from the contentions of the people. . . .

7. The allusion is to Ps. 133:1–2: Behold, how good and how pleasant it is for brethren to dwell together in unity! It is like the precious ointment upon the head, that ran down upon the beard, even Aaron's beard: that went down to the skirts of his garments.

8. James Penn (c. 1601–1671) and his wife Katherine had settled in Boston in 1630 and were admitted to the new church there in the autumn of 1630. See Anderson, *Great Migration,* 1423–1426.

9. William Reyner, the sheriff in Bermuda from at least as early as 1642 (Lefroy, *Memorials of the Discovery,* I, 571). A letter from Reyner to John Winthrop in 1646 had detailed the problems the Bermuda colony was having and had explained that the Independents, led by White, were hoping "to discouer some considerable Iland for us to settle upon; hopeing there to enioye Christe, in the puritye of his ordinances, without this Bermudian Imbitterment" (*Winthrop Papers,* V, 72).

John Davenport to John Cotton

May 6, 1650

ALS. MS: NHCHS, MS #125, The Whitney Library

Published: A. Benedict Davenport, *A History and Genealogy of the Davenport Family* . . . (New York, 1851), 343–346; Isabel MacBeath Calder, ed., *Letters of John Davenport: Puritan Divine* (New Haven, Conn., 1937), 83–86

In L. Thompson, "Letters of John Cotton," 199–203

Beyond the personal friendship established many years before this letter, Davenport (and the New Haven Colony generally) looked to John Cotton as a voice of authority on matters of colonial government. Cotton's code of laws, known in the Bay as "Moses His Judicials," had been adopted as the foundation of the New Haven Colony's legal system.[1] This may help explain why Davenport seems so anxious to have Cotton's prompt ruling on the issue he raises near the end of this letter regarding the legality of evidence produced by sole witnesses against accused individuals. In Davenport's mind, Cotton's word on such questions was as good as law.

The letter is addressed on the verso, in Davenport's hand:

> To the Reverend and his
> worthily much honoured freind
> & brother Mr John Cotton
> Teacher to *th*e church in
> Boston these present

Reverend & worthy Sir,

Yours dated *th*e 22th of *th*e i^st^ m. 1649[2] was not brought to my hand till this 2^d^ day of the 3^d^ month 1650 whereby I understand that Brother Pierce[3] hath delivered unto you a Copie of some sermons preached by me, in our weekely lecture, wherein my intendm*ent* was to stablish the hearers in assurance that Jesus *th*e sonne of *th*e Virgin Mary is the onely true Messiah.[4] The Forenamed brother dilligently wrote, as his manner was, but finding that his head and pen could not carry away some materiall expressions, he earnestly desired me to lett him have my notes, to perfect his owne by them, which I promised him in *th*e winter was twelve moneths. Having other hinderances, he called not for them, when he was here, but being in *th*e Bay, & unresolved about his stay there, or passage ~~hith~~ for England, or returne hither, he wrote for those notes, clayming my promise, w*hi*ch accordingly I sent to him by brother Livermore,[5] with a double charge, 1, *tha*t when he had transcribed them, he would returne my copie againe, by a safe land=messenger, not by sea; remembring that I lost my autographs of all *th*e sermons I preached out of the epistle of christ to the church of philadelphia Rev. 3. concerning *th*e houre of Temptac*i*on,[6] & sundry others about christs shaking heaven & earth to establish his kingdom, in Heb: 12.[7] w*hi*ch I gave Mr Gregson,[8] at his request, to carry with him when he went hence for England. My 2d charge was, that when he had transcribed them, he would shew them unto you, and make no other use of them then privatly for himselfe, but by your advise. This I added, because I feared *tha*t he had a purpose for *th*e presse, from some words that I observed now and then to fall from him. Now, I am glad that you have them with you to peruse, where I pray, keepe them, till you have sifted them thoroughly. I thanck you for your faithfull advise about *th*e Interpretac*i*on of Phill. 2: 6. 7. 8, which I did afterwards handle at large, unto v*ers.* 12, in sundry sermons, according to *th*e method I had propounded, for handling the grounds of religion. In those sermons I did interpret that scripture in *th*e largest & most comprehensive sense, and particularly, as holding forth christs personall Godh[9] humbling himselfe to Assume our humane Nature. Nor can I tell what other or ~~streight &~~ narrower Interpretac*i*on I adhæred unto, in the notes under your hand: but, well knowing *tha*t *th*e one may & *th*e other will suite the scope of that discourse, I leave it wholly to your wisdom, to add, or alter, as you find expedient, & analogous with other scriptures, that allegac*i*on with its interpretac*i*on. I shall further pray you to cast your eye upon *tha*t type ~~of~~, the rocke in *th*e wildernes, to see, whether I have safely expressed the rockes following *th*em, w*hi*ch, I conceive, was that *th*e water flowing from *th*e rock followed *th*em all *th*e way in *th*e wildernes, meaning it of *tha*t 2d rock in Rephidim & kept by *th*em here & there in wells digged Numb. 20. 18.[10] which also Tertullian (lib. de patient.)[11] seemeth to intend by his petræ aquatilem sequelam.[12] Such have bene my thoughts, but whether I did there so wright *th*em downe, I doe not remember. others have other apprehensions of it. If you meet with any thing, in *tha*t, or any thing else, *tha*t you doe not approve, deleatur.[13] I thought it better to lett him have myne owne noates, to rectifye his by them, then to lett him print greate mistakes for [IV] want of that helpe. I wish the wrong *that* is done Reipub. literariæ[14] by imp*er*fect copies may warne you to improve *the* present season for *the* perfecting of as many Tractates & Com*m*entaryes, as you have for *the* publick good. one thing more give me leave to propound, and, as earnestly as my modesty will p*er*mit, to importune, that you would take into your serious thaughts the question about single testimony of severall p*er*sons, who speake fully to[15] *the* things, & with concurrence therein, though not joyntly in *the* circu*m*stances of time & place, and to answer that Logicall querk w*hi*ch Mr Prudden[16] told you of, and what other Argum*en*ts you find in *tha*t postscript of M*r* Cheivers[17] his answer to *the* Church or which you have elsewhere mett with. you will much oblige me, if you will hasten a copie of yo*u*r labours upon that subject. If you list not to appeare in the controversie, you shall be wholly concealed by me. For [deleted word] *the* manadging of my ˆspeech or silenceˆ your letter of advise shall have the force of a law with me. onely be intreated to dispatch it unto me, by the 1st opportunity, whether by land or sea. Bis dat qui cito dat.[18] The reason of this my earnestnes for a speedy returne I will give, at your demand, by the next; which, I beleive, you will judge to be weighty. I had rather ease then add to your burdens, but that we are, in a speciall manner, called to a serious considera*ci*on & determina*ci*on concerning this point. The Lord Jesus dwell with you in peace, and preserve your life & health, & comforts, & crowne your holy labours with a plentifull ꝑ blessing! In whom I rest

Newhaven *the* 6th d. of the 3d m. 1650.

Your obliged freind & brother
John Davenporte

I am told that this vessell will speedily returne againe. I hope *er*go[19] that you will returne an answer by him, if no other passenger come sooner, w*i*th speed, w*hi*ch I earnestly desire.

1. See Isabel M. Calder, "John Cotton and the New Haven Colony," *NEQ,* III (1930), 82–94. Cotton's "Moses His Judicials" had found less welcome in his own colony; see Cotton to John Winthrop, late March–early April 1648, headnote.

2. That is, March 22, 1649/50.

3. Calder notes: "Probably Mark Pierce, who had offered to teach writing and arithmetic to the children of New Haven in 1645. "Cotton and the New Haven Colony," *NEQ,* III (1930), 83 n. 2, citing Charles J. Hoadly, ed., *Records of the Colony and Plantation of New Haven, from 1638 to 1649* (Hartford, 1857), 156.

4. Davenport refers to the manuscript of *The Knowledge of Christ . . . ; or, Demonstrative Proofs from Scripture, That Crucified Jesus Is the Christ* (London, 1653). His epistle "To the Christian Reader," written "From my study in New-haven, this 13th of the 9th moneth, MDCLII," echoes the fear of losing the manuscript at sea that this letter to Cotton expresses, but professes, "I have yeilded

to the persuasions of some Brethren (ayming at the common good) to publish that which some yeers since was preached in my weekly Lecture."

5. One John Livermore had arrived in New Haven by late 1640. See Isabel McBeath Calder, *The New Haven Colony* (New Haven, Conn., 1934), 67–68; Calder, ed., *Letters of John Davenport,* 84 n. 3.

6. In Rev. 3:10 St. John the Divine says to "the angel of the church in Philadelphia" (verse 7): Because thou hast kept the word of my patience, I also will keep thee from the hour of temptation, which shall come upon all the world, to try them that dwell upon the earth.

7. See esp. Heb. 12:25, 26.

8. Thomas Gregson of New Haven had sailed aboard the now legendary "phantom ship" in 1646, which had disappeared without a trace. It had carried manuscripts by Thomas Hooker as well as Davenport. Calder, *New Haven Colony,* 160.

9. Calder: Godh[ead].

10. The reference is incorrect; Davenport might have meant to write Num. 20:8, though verses 8–11 are all relevant. Rephidim is not mentioned here, however, but in Exodus 17 is described as a campsite and battle scene near Horeb, where Moses, following God's instructions, smote a rock to obtain water for his people.

11. Tertullian's *De patientia.*

12. petræ aquatilem sequelam: the water that followed and flowed from the rock. See ibid., 5.24.

13. deleatur: let it be deleted.

14. Reipub. literariæ: to the republic of letters.

15. The t in to is written over &.

16. Peter Prudden helped Davenport and others settle New Haven in 1637. He became the first minister at Milford, then in the colony of New Haven, in 1639, serving there until his death in 1656. Venn, *Alumni Cantabrigienses,* III, 404; Calder, *New Haven Colony,* 86.

17. Ezekiel Cheever (1615–1708), school teacher in New Haven from 1637 to 1649, had been censured by the New Haven church on May 20, 1649, for refusing to vote with a majority to absolve the elders, Davenport and William Hooke, of the imputation of "partiality" in the exercise of their authority and for holding out stiffly in his refusal. In the course of those formal proceedings against him, he raised the "Logicall querk" to which Davenport refers—the claim that single witnesses of isolated offenses, regardless of how many such single witnesses reported similar offenses, were not sufficient to convict an accused person, since the law requires more than one witness of any single offense. The record of his church trial is in the Connecticut Historical Society, *Collections,* I (1860), 22–51; see 46–51 for the "postscript." In late 1650, Cheever moved to Ipswich in the Bay Colony, where his school achieved considerable fame. Later a teacher at Charlestown (1661–1670) and finally at the Boston Latin School (1670–1708), he became New England's most famous schoolmaster. Venn, *Alumni Cantabrigienses,* I, 328; *DAB;* Calder, *New Haven Colony,* 93–94.

18. Bis dat qui cito dat: He gives double who gives quickly. Isabel Calder cites Publius Syrus *Sententiae* 235, "inopi beneficium bis dat, qui dat celeriter": He gives aid to the needy twice, who gives quickly. Calder, ed., *Letters of John Davenport,* 85 n. 10.

19. ergo: therefore.

John Cotton to John Davenport

[May 1650]

ADf. MS: NHCHS, MS #125, The Whitney Library

Published: Isabel MacBeath Calder, ed., *Letters of John Davenport: Puritan Divine* (New Haven, Conn., 1937), 86

In L. Thompson, "Letters of John Cotton," 204–205

Cotton's draft for a reply is written on the verso of Davenport to Cotton, May 6, 1650, on the right-hand half of the sheet, opposite the concluding section of Davenport's text. The recto of this part of the sheet contains Davenport's address block directing the letter to Cotton. The editorial brackets indicate slight loss of paper along a fold at the start of the third paragraph and along a few lines at each margin. There is no salutation or signature.

Mr Pierce [1] tooke from me both his owne, & yo*u*r Copy long before *th*e Receipt of this.

The Rock is safely Putt for *th*e water gushing out of *th*e Rock, by a metonymy. And *tha*t water followed *the*m: ˆIt was not vnius Diei Beneficium.ˆ [2] But not all *th*e way to Chanaan. For He should not have needed to have struck another Rock, Num. 20. ii.[3] nor should *th*e People have murmured againe for want of water.

The wells digged N[um. 2]i. i6, i7, i8.[4] were [not] to Receive *th*e waters of *th*e River *tha*t followed *the*m, but to open a fresh spring[.] Had the water of *th*e River bene Received into those wells, the water had Descended:[5] but the Text calleth it to Ascend. The water of *th*e Rock in Rephidim might well follow [the]m, till they spake scornfully of *th*e Holyland, Psal. [1]06. 24.[6] w*hi*ch was done chiefly: Num. i6. i3, i4. w*hi*ch was [n]oe lesse then Blasphemy ag*ains*t *th*e H. Ghost.[7]

So *tha*t *th*e Rock may very well still goe for a Type of Christ, *tha*t giveth vs Drink, & followeth vs all *th*e way of o*u*r Pilgrimage in this world, till wee sinne ag*ains*t *th*e H. Ghost. And then we marvell, if *th*e water of *th*e Rock left *th*e Israelites, & Christ leave malicious Apostates: when they first leave, & Reject Him.

1. See Davenport to Cotton, May 6, 1650, n. 3.

2. vnius Diei Benficium: a gift for one day. (Calder reads this as "Omen Diei . . ." and translates it: an assurance of daily benefactions.)

3. Num. 20:11: And Moses lifted up his hand, and with his rod he smote the rock twice: and the water came out abundantly, and the congregation drank, and their beasts also.

4. Num. 21:16–18: And from thence they went to Beer: that is the well whereof the Lord spake unto Moses, Gather the people together, and I will give them water. Then Israel sang this song, Spring up, O well; sing ye unto it: The princes digged the well, the nobles of the people digged it, by the direction of the lawgiver, with their staves. And from the wilderness they went to Mattanah.

5. The capital D is written over a capital A.

6. Ps. 106:24: Yea, they despised the pleasant land, they believed not his word.

Some loss of paper at this point apparently caused Isabel Calder to misread this reference as Deut. 6:24.

7. In Num. 16:13, 14, Dathan and Abiram say to Moses: Is it a small thing that thou hast brought us up out of a land that floweth with milk and honey, to kill us in the wilderness, except thou make thyself altogether a prince over us? Moreover thou hast not brought us into a land that floweth with milk and honey, or given us inheritance of fields and vineyards: wilt thou put out the eyes of these men? we will not come up.

John Cotton, John Wilson, and Thomas Oliver to [James Fitch] and "Beloved Brethren" of the Saybrook Church

July 23, 1650

ALS. MS: MHS, Winthrop Papers

Published: MHS, *Procs.,* 2d Ser., III (1886–1887), 200; *Winthrop Papers,* VI, 52–53

This letter from the two ministers and the ruling elder of the Boston church enacts a standard transaction in recommending the transfer of membership from one church to another. A church had not yet been established at Pequot (later New London, Connecticut), so that Saybrook, about twenty miles west on Long Island Sound, was the nearest church. John Winthrop, Jr., the principal founder of Pequot, would become the governor of the colony of Connecticut in 1657.[1]

It is in John Wilson's hand but is signed personally by each of the three elders of Boston's church. Wilson addressed the letter on a separate sheet, now cut down to a small slip and pasted to the verso: "To the Church of Christ, at Seabrooke fort." Occasional differences from the text in the *Winthrop Papers* (WP) are indicated in the notes.

To the R. pastor,[2] & Bel. Brethren in the Church of Christ at Seabrooke Grace & peace in our Lord Jesus.

It having[3] pleased the Lord by his All wise providence to remove the honored brother of our church m^r^ John Winthrop, *wi*th our Beloved sister his wife m[ris] Elizabeth Winthorp, & together w*i*th them our beloved s^isters^ Eliz. the wife of Samuel Lothorp, & Johan*n*a the wife of Izhak Willy, vnto the new plantation at Pekott, there to dwell & abide[4] (where before now they well hoped as we did also, that the Good ordinances of Christ may be Established, according to his owne Institution, & still we doe hope for the same Good blessing, w*hi*ch they pursue after:[5] but in the meanewhile) the Lord so disposing that they be destitute thereof, neyther can enioy at such a distance their wonted com*m*union w*i*th vs, & therfore haue desired our Recom*m*endation vnto your church, to the end *tha*t as God doth Giue them opportunity, they or any of them may partake[6] of the holy things of God amonge you, & the Comfort~~ab~~[7] of yo*u*r holy Fellowship therin—wee[8] do therfore Recom*m*end them ~~them~~ & each one of them vnto you for the same end, Beseeching ^you^ accordingly to receive them in the Lord as becom*m*eth Saints: vnto whose Abundant Grace wee Com*m*ende you All, as by yo*u*r selves we desire to ^be^ com*m*ended. Through Christ Jesus

This 23. of the 5th. 50.
Boston

your very Loving brethren the Eld*e*rs[9] of the Church of Christ at Boston

Joh*n* Cotton.
John Wilson.
Tho. Oliver

In the Behalfe, & vpon the deliberate & exprest Consent of *th*e whole Ch. here.[10]

1. Robert C. Black III, *The Younger John Winthrop* (New York, 1966), 152, 387 n. 24.

2. James Fitch (1622–1702) had become the first minister of the church at Saybrook when it was formally organized in 1646 and held the post until 1660. See *The First Church of Christ, (Congregational) Old Saybrook, Conn.* (Middletown, Conn., 1896), xiii, 7–9.

3. having] WP: haveing.

4. These three families were already living at Pequot. John Winthrop, Jr., Stephen Lothrop, and Isaac Willey were among the first six men to be assigned lots in the town, and they were among the five men entrusted by the other settlers in February 1647/8, "to act in all Town affaires." The town records include a reference to Isaac Willey's mowing a meadow or marsh there as early as the summer of 1645. Frances Manwaring Caulkins, *History of New London, Connecticut, from the First Survey of the Coast in 1612, to 1852* (New London, Conn., 1852), 44, 57, 59–60.

5. For some four years Winthrop had tried unsuccessfully to find a minister to come to Pequot, having offered invitations to at least three individuals, Thomas Peter, John Jones, and Marmaduke Matthews. Late in 1650, however, Richard Blinman, the minister at Gloucester, accepted the opportunity. See Black, *Younger John Winthrop,* 147–148.

6. partake] WP: partaake.

7. The last two letters were blotted out while the ink was still wet.

8. wee] WP: we.

9. Eld*e*rs] WP: Eldrs.

10. here] WP: there.

Samuel Stone to John Cotton

September 16, 1650

ALS. MS: BPL, Ms. Am. 1506, pt. 3, no. 16

The New Haven church's excommunication of Ezekiel Cheever (mentioned in John Davenport to Cotton, May 6, 1650) became the subject of consultation among various ministers in both the Connecticut River valley and the Bay. This letter from Stone, the minister at Hartford, indicates that he had earlier solicited Cotton's opinions on the issues in this case and that Cotton had replied. Here Stone responds to ten points in Cotton's letter (not found). Moreover, Stone relates that the New Haven elders had circulated the particulars of the case to other ministers for their reactions and that, on his own initiative, he was also consulting ministers in Connecticut. Cheever might have been in Hartford at this time, given Stone's statements in his point 3 that he hopes "to conuince Mr Cheevers of the iust cause of his excommunication" and of "his great miscarriages since that time."[1]

The manuscript consists of two sheets, which show a little damage on the edges resulting in occasional loss of portions of words, supplied here in brackets. Stone wrote the address on the verso of the second sheet:

To the Reuerend
his dearest friend,
Mr John Cotton Teacher
to the Ch. of *Chris*t at
Boston.

Reuerend, & worthie Sir,

I receiued your louing l*ette*re, for w*hi*ch I am much indebted to you. I shall answer in a few words what my present thoughts are, concerning mr Cheeuers his matters, as represented in your l*ette*re.

1 we dislike his way, & his spirit ^so farre,^ as it appears in ^his^ sinfull expressions.

2 The cause seemed to be stated by com*m*on consent of both partyes; w*hi*ch may appeare, if you consider these passages:

1 The first writing of the Reuerend Elders of N. Ha. w*hi*ch they deliuered to mr Cheeuers, contained the grounds of his excom*m*unication. 2 Their seco[nd] writing is the Churches reply to mr Ch. his answ[er] to his charges. 3 They say they are confident, *tha*t the Elders (hauing receiued those papers) will conuince him of the euills for w*hi*ch he is censured. 4 They affirme *tha*t

the case was a iust cause of excom*m*unication, & sufficiently p*ro*ued against him; therefore the censure is dispensed according to the mind of Christ; wherein they imply, *tha*t in their papers, they haue giuen to the elders (to who*m* they are sent), a sufficient demonstration, *tha*t his excom*munication* was dispensed according to the mind of Christ. 5 They except nothing but onely a disanulling, or ratifying iudgme[nt], w*hi*ch is not in the power of all Churches. 6 They affirme, *tha*t the Ch*urch* would rest in that w*hi*ch was written, though much more might be added, & *tha*t they would not be troubled w*i*th farther rep[l]y[s.]

3 we are so farre fro*m* bearing witnesse against those Reuerend & worthie Elders & that much honoured, & beloued Ch, (the cause not being stated) *tha*t we doe not beare witnesse against them, the cause being stated. we doe not ~~the~~ determine the case, but aske counsell of those, who are able to counsell vs: being resolued to conclude nothing without your aduice, & help: we haue p*ro*fessed, *tha*t we were willing to [deleted word] receiue light, not onely [IV] fro*m* those Elders, to who*m* the papers had been sent but also fro*m* any others: because in the multitude of counsellers there is safety.[2] we haue fairly p*ro*pounded the grounds of our present apprehensions.

4 You conceiue *tha*t his calumniation of the Ch*urch* & Elders confessed by himselfe was no lesse then λοιδορία:[3] 1 Cor 5, 1[1][4] To w*hi*ch I can swer, *tha*t 3 things here would be exceeding vsefull, for the clearing of this cause: 1 Let that sinne be exactly described, & the description applyed to mr Cheeuers his fact, & that fact be found answerable.

2ly Let it appeare *tha*t Mr Chee. was conuinced of this sinne, as deseruing that censure, & *tha*t he was charged as guilty of it, before his excom*m*unication. 3 Let it appeare *tha*t mr Ch. is λοίδορος[5] 1 Cor 5. 11 a wicked, vnregenerate man, who shall not inherit the kingdome of heauen i Cor 6. 10.[6] If these things were cleared, I should haue matter to conuince ~~him~~ mr Cheevers of the iust cause of his excom*m*unication & it would not be difficult to conuince him of his great miscarriages since that time.

5. I am not cleare *tha*t Miriam deserued excom*m*unication for the acknowledgement of her owne administrations. neither doth it yett appeare to me, that she was excom*m*unicated, & cast out of that Ch to Satan.[7] If you haue any cogent argume[nt] for it, I pray help me with it.

6 I know not *tha*t we haue testified *tha*t Mr Cheevers gaue satisfaction to the Ch*urch*. A man may acknowledge his failing in a conference, w*hi*ch may be sufficient to satisfy, in respect of the place, where the offence was com*m*itted, & in respect of persons there present where the offence was giuen (& I thinke the Church takes notice of his acknowledgment of some miscarriages in the end of that meeting) *tha*t the offence ~~sho~~ [2] should not be brought to the

Ch*urch* & yet it may be the Ch is not satisfyed, when those offences are presented to it.

7 We hope, *tha*t the testimony of our present apprehensions may rather be a means to soften m^{r} Cheeuers, because it tends of its owne nature tow[a]rds conuiction. The refusing to answer his papers seemeth rather to harden him. If a booke of errours be extant, & not answerd, the Author will be in danger of being hardened. As for our papers, let those be blamed that made them known to h[im].[8]

8 We hope that our lrs to your selues about this case, will not trouble our Reuerend, & Beloued Brethren at N.H. all things being duly considered.

9 We see not but it may be safe for the Elde[rs] in one Country, to p*ro*pound their apprehensions to the Elders in another Country (w*i*thout the concurrence of Churches) about a Ch act. They may confer one w*i*th another about it.

10 We see not that Churches are a superiour Judicatory ouer a Ch.

I haue scribled these few lines in hast, w*hi*ch I pray accept, & send me, what you would direct me to doe in this buisinesse; I hope I shall be guided by you in all things according to God. God hath lately giuen vs another daughter, whose name is Abigail, my wife is but weake, but I hope shee will doe well. We remember our due respec[t] & seruice to your selfe, & Mrs Cotton, & rest,

Your seruant in *Chris*t.
S Stone.

Hartf. 7ber 16, 1650.

1. For the New Haven Church's account of Cheever's "Offences" and his "Answers" to the charges, see "The Trial of Ezekiel Cheever before New Haven Church, 1649," Connecticut Historical Society, *Collections,* I (1860), 22–51.

2. Prov. 11:14: Where no counsel is, the people fall: but in the multitude of counsellors there is safety. See also Prov. 24:6.

3. *λοιδορία*: railing; scurrilous abuse.

4. 1 Cor. 5:11: But now I have written unto you not to keep company, if any man that is called a brother be a fornicator, or covetous, or an idolater, or a railer, or a drunkard, or an extortioner; with such an one no not to eat.

5. *λοίδορος*: a railer.

6. 1 Cor. 6:10: Nor thieves, nor covetous, nor drunkards, nor revilers, nor extortioners, shall inherit the kingdom of God.

7. In Num. 12:1–16, Miriam claimed to be equal with Moses in being God's spokesperson, a presumptuous claim that earned the wrath of God. In the church trial of Cheever, two people reported that Cheever had said, "we are all Clerks now," that is, we all have churchly authority, with the elders. This was interpreted as "a slander against the Ch: and against the Elders" and was believed to be "a partaking in that sin of Miriam, for which the Lord would have her cast out

of the camp, Numb., 12: 2." In his "Answer" to the church's charges against him, Cheever said, "For that slander, or grossness in it to be equal to Miriam's sin, or to deserve such a censure, I cannot yet see it." "The Trial of Ezekiel Cheever," Conn. Hist. Soc., *Colls.,* I (1860), 29–30, 47.

8. This last sentence was squeezed in on two half-lines after the following text had been written.

John Eliot to [John Cotton]

June 6, 1651

ALS. MS: MSA, CCXLI, Hutchinson Papers, II, fol. 190

On the verso of this letter is written "Eliot to Hooker about Pastors & Teachers." Hooker's name was later deleted and a comment added below his name: "(Hooker was dead before 1651)." So he was, and since the reply is in Cotton's handwriting, it is clear Eliot's letter was written to him.

The occasion for the letter was, as Eliot says, his receipt from "Mr Williams" of a brand-new book entitled *A Sober Word to a Serious People* that sets out to defend the Seekers from charges by "several men, in several books" who "under that term of *Seekers,* comprehend all those which differ from themselves touching the present exercise of Visible Administrations."[1] The author of this sixty-two-page octavo volume is not named on the title page, but it is attributed to one John Jackson. The book focuses on the nature and functions of the ministry, agreeing with the Seeker point of view that the present-day ministry is corrupt but also asserting the reclaimability of that ministry.

What is more to the point in the present context is the fact that Eliot received the volume from Roger Williams. At this point, Williams was on his way to becoming a Seeker, so was doubtless influenced by *A Sober Word,* though the book is more moderate in its Seekerism than Williams would be.[2] It seems unlikely that Williams thought he could make a Seeker of Eliot. A more probable motivation for his giving Eliot this book is that the two men shared an interest in the condition of New England's native American population. Though Williams played an important role as a peacemaker between the white colonists and the native people on various occasions, he was not involved in efforts to convert them, believing that they must first be made more civilized. In fact, in 1654, he defended the right of the Indians to retain their own religions.[3] Jackson argues that one of the things standing between the present condition of the church and its reclamation under a purified ministry and practice is the need to convert the many nations who have not heard of Christianity. About two-thirds of the way through the small volume, he comes to a point that might well have made Williams think of Eliot: "How is the end for which Christ ascended, and for which he gave gifts to men, accomplished, *if the work of the Ministery* be not again restored unto its pristine and primitive Constitution? as well to respect the Nations which are *without,* viz., *the out-casts of Israel,* together with those worshipers of the Sun and Moon, the Moors and Indians, and the people that know not God, nor have ever heard the sound of him, nor of the salvation which through Christ Jesus he holds forth to Mankinde." He further insists: "It were to be desired that the Lord would stir up the hearts of his people to cry mightily to him, and give him no rest, till he accomplish the work of gathering together his number out of all Nations, Kindreds, Tongues, and Peoples." "It must be done to fulfill the Word of the Lord."[4] Here is the admonition that Eliot, already acquiring his reputation as Apostle to the Indians, would have found heartening. While Jackson is urging patience in expectation of the needed arrival of newly appointed Apostles,[5] it seems unlikely that Williams was hinting that Eliot was such a person. But he surely knew of Eliot's work for the past five years to establish a community of Indians at Natick.[6]

Rev*er*end S*ir*

Mr Williams[7] sent me this booke to read, sent him fro*m* England. the auth*o*r is (I judg) holy, able, & a pure seeker. it is well worth the Labour to answ*e*r, & needfull, & not much of the booke needeth answ*e*r, but is ~~to~~ worthy acknowledgm*en*t, as it seems to me, only what p*er*teines to *tha*t poynt of the seekers. I am bold to send it to your selfe, & not bring it because I am goeing forth into the Country,[8] & not to returne vntill the com*m*encm*en*t,[9] & I was loath to let it ly by so long if the Lord should put it into your heart to vndertake it. I doe hope your labour would be both very acceptable, & much blessed; I beg your prayers to be continued for me, for now now[10] my work increaseth, & calleth for more wisdo*m,* & attendance, thus com*m*ending your holy labours & all yours vnto the L*o*rd, I rest

Roxbury this 4^t^. 6. 51. your vnw*o*rthy [deleted word] ^fellow laborer^
in christ his vinyard
John Eliot

1. [John Jackson], *A Sober Word to a Serious People* . . . (London, 1651), [sig. A2v].

2. Whereas, as Philip Gura says, Williams "denied the validity of all outward church ordinances," the author of *A Sober Word* insists that Seekers, including himself, "are not alike unsatisfied concerning the practise of all Ordinances," approving in particular scripture reading, prayer, and even "coming together some place on the First-dayes, and at other times" (2) (Gura, *A Glimpse of Sion's Glory: Puritan Radicalism in New England, 1620–1660* [Middletown, Conn., 1984], 190). The discovery of Williams's familiarity with John Jackson's anonymous *Sober Word* and his putting it in the hands of others like Eliot may well serve to answer Edmund S. Morgan's doubts that Williams ever truly was a Seeker: "Nowhere in Williams' own writings have I found the word [Seeker] used or any evidence that Williams knew or corresponded with English Seekers" (Morgan, *Roger Williams: The Church and the State* [New York, 1967], 152 n. 56).

3. See Roger Williams to the General Court of Massachusetts Bay, Oct. 5, 1654, in Wil-

liams, *Correspondence,* 409. Glenn LaFantasie reminds us that, although Williams claimed he *could have* converted thousands of Indians, "he never took credit for having saved any Indian souls" (*Correspondence,* 11 n. 8). See also LaFantasie's headnote, "Expectations of Indian Conversions, 1637/8," 141–144, and 301 n. 6.

4. [Jackson], *A Sober Word,* 38, 40, 41.

5. See esp. ibid., 41, where Jackson says that those who will perform the missionary role of converting all the "Nations of the World" will be "such Messengers which shall be endued with like power of Evidence and Demonstration, both of Tongues and Gifts, as the first Messengers or Apostles had, to preach to the Nations in their proper Language." The abilities of both Williams and Eliot to relate effectively to the Indians was based on their learning and documenting their language.

6. In a book written about this time, Williams expresssed skepticism about Eliot's effectiveness based upon his belief that Eliot did not have a sufficient command of the Indians' language, even though Eliot was "the ablest amongst them in the *Indian speech*" (Roger Williams, *The Bloody Tenent Yet More Bloody* . . . [London, 1652], 370–374). I appreciate Richard W. Cogley's directing my attention to this passage.

7. Roger Williams. As Philip F. Gura has observed, "Williams was instrumental in bringing to wide public attention the tenets of this loosely organized sect," the Seekers (*A Glimpse of Sion's Glory,* 74). Though he does not mention the book that Eliot asked Cotton to comment on in this exchange of letters, Gura's brief discussion of the Seekers and Williams is relevant; see 74–76.

8. That is, to pursue his missionary work with the native Americans. The summer would be productive for him. On August, 6, 1651, the inhabitants at the "praying town" of Natick would choose their civic rulers, and on September 24 they would adopt a civic covenant. See Ola Elizabeth Winslow, *John Eliot: "Apostle to the Indians"* (Boston, 1968), 127–129; Jean M. O'Brien, *Dispossession by Degrees: Indian Land and Identity in Natick, Massachusetts, 1650–1790* (Cambridge, Mass., 1997), 27–36; Richard W. Cogley, *John Eliot's Mission to the Indians before King Philip's War* (Cambridge, Mass., 1999), 111–113.

Eliot had been consulting with Cotton about these matters, and Cotton had given Eliot some wording for the covenant the Indians signed on September, 24, 1651. See the letter from Eliot to the New England Company in London [c. October–November 1651], in Henry Whitfield, *Strength out of Weaknesse* (London, 1652), rpt. in MHS, *Colls.,* 3d Ser., IV (1834), 173. Further comments on Eliot's consultations with Cotton on Indian matters appear in Eliot's letter to Edward Winslow in England, Oct.21, 1650, printed in Henry Whitfield, *The Light Appearing More and More towards the Perfect Day; or, A Farther Discovery of the Present State of the Indians in New-England* . . . (London, 1651), rpt. in MHS, *Colls.,* 3d Ser., IV (1834), 127, 137–138, 140. I am grateful to Richard Cogley for his assistance in clarifying the context of the Eliot-Cotton exchange.

9. Cotton and Eliot had both been members of Harvard College's Board of Overseers since 1642 and would thus normally have attended commencement, which in 1651 occurred on August 12. (For this date I am grateful to Brian A. Sullivan, Archival Associate for Reference at the Harvard University Archives.) The twenty-one members of the first Board of Overseers (1642) are listed in Samuel Eliot Morison, *The Founding of Harvard College* (Cambridge, Mass., 1935), 327–328.

10. Eliot repeated the word now.

John Cotton to John Eliot

[June 1651]

AL. MS: MSA, CCXLI, Hutchinson Papers, II, fols. 186–189v

Cotton's reply gives Eliot some of the response he sought, but in looking into Jackson's book he limits himself to places where the Seekers' interest in the nature and authority of the ministry and of church worship are immediately relevant. After starting off with a sweeping indictment of the book, he actually ends up suggesting it is not such an extreme argument after all. At least, Cotton is able to agree with half the points he singles out for discussion, though he then goes on forcefully to assert the validity of the present ministry, with abundant reference to Scripture proof texts. It may be that in his initial comments, where he vehemently attacks the Seekers' negation of the present-day ministry, he was thinking more of Roger Williams—with whom his *Bloody Tenent* debate was still active in 1651 and whom he knew to hold some of these critical opinions—than of the anonymous author of the book Eliot had shown him. In the end, his reply is not a full-scale analysis of Jackson's book, but is limited to comment on roughly the first one-third of the text. Whether he intended to write more about it, we cannot now know.

Reverend & dear Brother Eliot,

It is not long since, you sent me a Booke, entituled A sober word to a serious People.[1] The Intent of *th*e Booke is to Take off the People of God from Attending to Church-Com*m*union, & ˆtoˆ [deleted word] the Ministery of *th*e word, [deleted word] as ˆThey & *th*eˆ Times now stand, since *th*e Apostacy of Antichrist. The Intent of Him *tha*t sent the Booke to you[2] ˆ(though not *th*e Author) [two deleted words]ˆ [deleted words] ˆIf it wereˆ to Take you off ˆ(for want of an Apostolick Office)ˆ from Attending *th*e Holy, & Honourable work of *th*e Conversion of *th*e Indians, w*hi*ch Christ, & his Churches, & the Bent of yo*u*r owne spirit ˆ(& the Blessing of *th*e spirit of Grace)ˆ hath encouraged you vnto[3] ˆthe Lord lay it not vnto his Charge, But if it were for some other end,ˆ [deleted line] ˆas to search into the grounds of o*u*r callings & standing, I hope, theˆ [deleted line] ˆLord will Improve it, to *th*e clearing & establishing of his owne wayes.ˆ

And because you have againe & againe earnestly Desired my Thoughts about it: & for *tha*t I see, such Bookes as take off *th*e People from *th*e Ordinances of Christ doe Take ~~Hold~~ not onely w*i*th vnstable ˆmindesˆ [deleted word], but even w*i*th some Honest Heartes, I thought it meete to follow the

Holy Example of Paul, who when his Calling to *th*e Ap*ost*leship was Quæstioned, He seri[ously?] Addressed himself to cleare it both in his Epistles [to] *th*e Corinthyans, & to *th*e Galatians also. And so [186v/2] much *th*e rather, because He was sollicitous to maintaine his owne Personall Calling to his Office; but now the Office of all Past*ou*rs & Teachers is Quæstioned, yea & the standing of all Christian Churches, & *th*e pr*e*sent Administration of all of *th*e ^Publick Gospell^ Ordinances of *th*e Lord Jesus.[4] ~~& his holy spirit~~ It hath bene of late the wise ^& gratious^ Counsell of Christ & *th*e mighty Power of his Hand, to Cast out all *th*e Inventions of Man out of his Church.[5] And now Satan feeling his Head bruised, hath bestirred himself ^mightily^ w*i*th all subtilty of Deceivablenesse to Roote out all *th*e Institutions of Christ also: *tha*t so at once He might both Rob *th*e soules of Gods People of all the meanes of Conversion & Aedification: & w*i*thall Rob God ^Himself^ of all *tha*t Glory due to his great Name, & that Aboundant Thankfullnesse due from his People for Restoring vnto *the*m the Light, & Liberty & Purity, of his owne Ordinaunces,.[6] But the Lord Rebuke Satan, & keepe *th*e Feete of his Saints, & Helpe his servants to Beare witnesse to his Trueth, as it is in Jesus.

[187/3] Chapt*er* i. Of *th*e Title.

The words of *th*e Booke (w*hi*ch you sent to me) are indede (according to *th*e Title) Sober Words, as Sobriety is opposed to Intemprate Rayling: but not, as Sobriety is opposite to Curiosity, as w*i*th Paul, *τὸ σωφρονεῖν*[7] is opposed *τῷ ὑπερφρονεῖν*.[8] Rom. 12.3.[9] I cannot say, That *th*e words of *th*e Booke are all of *the*m sober words in this sence. Paul fully cleared himself from *tha*t vice, when He said before Festus, I speake *th*e words of Trueth & sobernesse, Acts. 26.25.[10] In *th*e sober words of this Booke, I readily Discerne & Acknowledge sundry holy Truethes: but not w*i*thout mixture of sundry Err*ou*rs, w*hi*ch breath forth a wisedome above *tha*t w*hi*ch is written: w*hi*ch is not to be wise according to Sobriety.

Chapt*er* 2. Opening *th*e state
of *th*e Quæstion.

Four Poynts there be, whereinto *th*e Author maketh Inqu[iry][11] the better to cleare his way for *th*e supplanting of *th*e pr*e*sent Churches, & Ministery.[12]

i. "Whether Christ did not Com*m*itt *th*e Preaching of *th*e w[ord] & Administra-"tion of Baptisme, to a Ministery. [187v/4]

2. "What *th*e Nature & End of *th*e Ministery was, w*hi*ch *th*e Lord Jesus Appointed "to succeede Him:

3. "Whether there be any Patterne of any visible Congregated Church vnder *th*e "Gospell, w*i*thout, or before a Ministery for Baptisme?

4. "Whether *th*e Pr*e*sent Ministery, & pr*e*sent Churches may be Acknowledged "the Ministery, & Churches of Christ, according to *th*e first Patterne:

To *th*e i[st] of these He Answereth in words of Trueth & sobernesse, & Confirmeth his Answer w*i*th Demonstration of Orthodoxall Soundnesse.[13]

" To *th*e 2[d], The Sum*m*e of his Answer is, That *th*e Nature & End of *th*e Min-
"istery appointed by Christ, was for a 2fold End: i. for *th*e Breeding of *th*e
"Saints: & 2. for *th*e Feeding of *th*em.[14] W*h*ich He Prooveth from Ephes*ians*
"4.ii,i2,i3 [15]: where He maketh *th*e Apostles, Prophets, & Evangelists to be a
"Breeding Ministery: And *th*e Pasto*u*rs, & Teachers to be given for a Feeding
"Ministery: & both to Endure alike till all *th*e Saints be Gathered, & all of
theim Perfected.

[188/5] In this expression of his Judgem*en*t touching *th*e three latter Propositions, wee Agree w*i*th Him in 2, things: & Dissent w*i*th Him in [the] [16] other two.

i. Wee Agree w*i*th Him, That *th*e Nature & End of *th*e Ministery is for *th*e Breeding, & Feeding of *th*e saints: to wit, for Conversion, & Aedification.

2. Wee Agree also, That both these Ministeryes, Apostles, Prophets, & Evangelists, as well as Pasto*u*rs, & Teachers, shall all of *th*em continue in *th*e Church (though not in *th*e same way) till *th*e whole Body of *th*e Church be Growen vp vnto a Perfect Man in Christ Jesus.

But in these things wee Dissent:

i. That He Confineth the Breeding Ministery, Onely to *th*e Apostles, Prophets, & Evangelists: & Reserveth Feeding only, to *th*e Pasto*u*rs, & Teachers. Whereas wee Beleive both sorts of *th*em, are both a Breeding, & a Feeding Ministery.[17]

2. That He maketh the Ap*os*tles, Prophets, & Evangelists to Continue in *th*e Church in *th*e same way, & sort, as doe *th*e Pasto*u*rs, & Teachers: either both of *th*em to Continue in *th*e Personall succession of men alike Qualifyed in *th*e same Calling: or if *th*e One Cease[,] then *th*e other to Cease also.

[188v/6] Whereas wee doe hold, That P[asto*u*]rs, & Teachers doe indeede Continue in *th*e Personall succession in men alike Gifted (more, or [les]s[e]) in *th*e same Calling. But as for Ap*os*tles, Prophets, & Evangelists, They still Continue in *th*e Power & Perfection of their writings, w*h*ich by *th*e Inspiration of *th*e Holy Ghost, they Drew vp in their Life time, to hold forth the Sum*m*e of their Ministery, for the vse of all *th*e Churches till Christs second Com*m*ing.

And this Continuance of their Ministery in the Churches by their writings, doeth farre exceede *th*e Ministery of Pasto*u*rs, & Teachers in a 4fold Pr*e*heminence.

i. All the words of *th*e Ministery of *th*e Ap*os*tles, Prophets, & Evangelists are given by Divine Inspiration, so as they are all Authenticall, & Infallible: so *tha*t there is noething erroneous, or perverse in *th*em. 2. Tim. 3.i6. Psal. i2.6. Prov. 30.5. & 8.7,8.[18]

But *th*e Ministery of Pasto*u*rs & Teachers is subiect to Humane Frailty of Erro*u*rs, & Ignorance, Defects, & Redundancyes, misapprehensions & Misapplications.

[189/7] Wee know in Part, & Prophecy in Part, i. Cor. i3.9. w*hi*ch so farre as *th*e Apo*st*les spake it of *th*eimselves, hath respect onely to a ˆmore perfectˆ ~~greater~~ measure of knowledge in Heavenly Glory: but it concerneth vs, in respect of o*u*r wants of *tha*t knowledge, w*hi*ch wee ought to Atteyne here for *th*e Guidance of o*u*rselves, & of *th*e Church of Christ. Jobs Freinds spake many Holy Truths, but not Right, Job. 42.7.[19]

2. The Ministery of *th*e Apo*st*les, Prophets, & Evangelists is *th*e standard, & Rule of o*u*r Ministery, Isay. 8.20. Psal. ii9.io5. 2 Tim. 3.i7.[20]

The Ministery of Pasto*u*rs & Teachers is so farre to be Receyved, as it is Agreeable to their scriptures: else to be avoyded. Rom*ans* i6.i7.[21]

3. The Preaching of *th*e word, though it be *th*e Ordinary Instrum*en*t sanctifyed of God for *th*e Begetting of Faith, (Rom*ans* io.i7:)[22] & *tha*t by *th*e Ministery of Pasto*u*rs, & Teachers, as well as of Apostles, & Prophets, Eph. 4.ii,i2: i. Cor. i.2i:)[23] yet the word written by *th*e Apostles & Prophets, is *th*e onely Foundation & Groundwork of all *th*e Faith of Gods Elect, & of al[l] *th*e Churches of Christ. Hence Christ Prayeth onely f[or] such as shall Beleive on Him, through their word[s] Joh. i7.20.[24] Their word, whether Preached by [189v] theimselves in their life time, or opened & Applyed by Pasto*u*rs, & Teachers after their Departure. A Chr*ist*ian shall have little Comfort of his Faith in sad Houres of Temptation, if it be Built onely vpon *th*e word of *th*e Minister, & not vpon some word or other of some Prophet, & Apostle, Opened, & Applyed by *th*e Minister.

4. The Ministery of *th*e Apo*st*les, Prophets, & Evangelists, is not subiect to mans Judgem*en*t i. Cor. 4.3. Gal. i.8,9.[25]

But *th*e Ministery of Pasto*u*rs & Teachers is subiect ˆvntoˆ mans Judgem*en*t, & Censure, i. Cor. i4.32.[26]

In all these 4. Respect, the Ministery of *th*e Apo*st*les, Prophets, & Evangelists, doeth still continue, & *tha*t in a more eminent measure, then doeth *th*e Ministery of Pasto*u*rs, & Teachers.

1. [John Jackson], *A Sober Word to a Serious People* . . . (London, 1651).

2. Roger Williams.

3. Here two lines are deleted, and the remaining text in the paragraph is written in three lines of smaller writing, to squeeze it into the space above, between, and below the deleted lines.

4. "Those other Ordinances, wherein they do not see sufficient ground for their Practice, may be comprehended in these two: The present Churches, and the present Ministery." [Jackson], *A Sober Word,* 4.

5. A reference to the reforms of the English Church in the late 1630s when the bishopry was abolished by the parliamentary reformers.

6. The MS has both a comma and a period, the latter written more darkly, as if meant to be a revision.

7. *τὸ σωφρονεῖν*: sobriety, moderation.

8. *τῷ ὑπερφρονεῖν*: to pride, arrogance. But Cotton, perhaps misled by the etymology, apparently interprets it to mean "to over-curiosity." He apparently reads Paul's injunction in Rom. 12:3 to mean that one should not be overly curious, inquiring into inappropriate subjects.

9. Rom. 12:3: For I say, through the grace given unto me, to every man that is among you, not to think of himself more highly than he ought to think: but to think soberly, according as God hath dealt to every man the measure of faith.

10. Acts 26:25: But he said, I am not mad, most noble Festus; but speak forth the words of truth and soberness.

11. Paper is lost at the right margin.

12. The four points which follow here are a quotation from [Jackson], *A Sober Word,* 6–7.

13. Ibid.

14. Ibid.

15. Eph. 4:11–13: And he gave some, apostles; and some, prophets; and some, evangelists; and some, pastors and teachers; For the perfecting of the saints, for the work of the ministry, for the edifying of the body of Christ: Till we all come in the unity of the faith, and of the knowledge of the Son of God, unto a perfect man, unto the measure of the stature of the fulness of Christ.

16. Hole in paper

17. See [Jackson], *A Sober Word,* 12.

18. 2 Tim. 3:16: All scripture is given by inspiration of God, and is profitable for doctrine, for reproof, for correction, for instruction in righteousness.

Ps. 12:6: The words of the Lord are pure words: as silver tried in a furnace of earth, purified seven times.

Prov. 30:5: Every word of God is pure: he is a shield unto them that put their trust in him.

Prov. 8:7, 8: For my mouth shall speak truth; and wickedness is an abomination to my lips. All the words of my mouth are in righteousness; there is nothing froward or perverse in them.

19. Job 42:7: And it was so, that after the Lord had spoken these words unto Job, the Lord said to Eliphaz the Temanite, My wrath is kindled against thee, and against thy two friends: for ye have not spoken of me the thing that is right, as my servant Job hath.

20. Isa. 8:20: To the law and to the testimony: if they speak not according to this word, it is because there is no light in them.

Ps. 119:105: Thy word is a lamp unto my feet, and a light unto my path.

2 Tim. 3:17: That the man of God may be perfect, throughly furnished unto all good works.

21. Rom. 16:17: Now I beseech you, brethren, mark them which cause divisions and offences contrary to the doctrine which ye have learned; and avoid them.

22. Rom. 10:17: So then faith cometh by hearing, and hearing by the word of God.

23. 1 Cor. 1:21: For after that in the wisdom of God the world by wisdom knew not God, it pleased God by the foolishness of preaching to save them that believe.

24. John 17:20: Neither pray I for these alone, but for them also which shall believe on me through their word.

25. 1 Cor. 4:3: But with me it is a very small thing that I should be judged of you, or of man's judgment: yea, I judge not mine own self.

Gal. 1:8, 9: But though we, or an angel from heaven, preach any other gospel unto you than that which we have preached unto you, let him be accursed. As we said before, so say I now again, If any man preach any other gospel unto you than that ye have received, let him be accursed.

26. 1 Cor. 14:32: And the spirits of the prophets are subject to the prophets.

John Cotton, Richard Mather, Zechariah Symmes, John Wilson, and William Thompson to Ministers in England

[Summer 1651]

Published: John Norton, *A Discussion of that Great Point in Divinity, the Sufferings of Christ* . . . (London, 1653), unpag. app.; Henry M. Burt, *The First Century of the History of Springfield: The Official Records from 1636 to 1736* (Springfield, Mass., 1898–1899), I, 122–123

The occasion of the following letter from five Massachusetts ministers was a letter from clerical colleagues in England defending the orthodoxy of William Pynchon's book, *The Meritorious Price of Our Redemption, Justification, etc.* . . . (London, 1650).[1] The Massachusetts General Court's condemnation of the book—it ordered a public burning of the work—and the court's admonition of Pynchon had made the defense seem necessary to the English ministers. The issues involved were at the heart of New England's understanding of the theology of grace. As Michael Winship has suggested, what was at issue was who and what was "orthodox." The lengthy title page described the book's main points: *The Meritorious Price of Our Redemption, Iustification, etc. Cleering It from Some Common Errors; and Proving, Part I. 1. That Christ Did Not Suffer for Us Those Unutterable Torments of Gods Wrath, That Commonly Are Called Hell-torments, to Redeem Our Soules from Them. 2. That Christ Did Not Bear Our Sins by Gods Imputation, and Therefore He Did Not Bear the Curse of the Law for Them. Part II. 3. That Christ Hath Redeemed Us from the Curse of the Law (Not by Suffering the Said Curse for Us, But) by a Satisfactory Price of Attonement; Viz. by Paying or Performing unto His Father That Invaluable Precious Thing of His Mediatoriall Obedience, Wherof His Mediatoriall Sacrifice of Attonement Was the Master-piece. 4. A Sinners Righteousness or Justification Is Explained, and Cleered from Some Common Errors.*

Through the act of publishing such a work, Pynchon declared himself confident of his command of central theological matters—a layman prepared, like the magisterial colleagues noticed in this letter, to deal with "Dogmaticall and Controversall points of Divinity." His unwillingness to compromise further with the New England authorities on these opinions was no doubt a large factor in his decision to walk away from the controversy and return permanently to England.[2]

The Copy of a Letter written from New England, *in Answer to a Letter which they had received from some Brethren in* Old England, *in the behalf of* Mr Pinchin.

Reverend and Beloved Brethren in our Lord Jesus,

We see by your Letters you have thought it meet to address your selves to us (the Elders of these Churches) in behalf of Mr *Pinchin* and his Book,[3] to incline us to a favourable construction of the Tenets held forth in it as Disputable, and (and to some of note) probable; and for himself to move us to intercede with our Magistrates to deal favourably with him as a Gentleman pious and well deserving. In both which we shall give you a just account of our Proceedings.

When Mr *Pinchin's* Book came over to us, it was the time of the sitting of our Generall Court,[4] wherein both the Magistrates and Deputies of every Town in the Country, do assemble to consider and determine of the chiefest affairs which concern this Colony: At the same time a Ship in the Harbour was ready to set sayl for *England.* Now the Court (both parts of them, the Magistrates and Deputies) perceiving by the Title Page that the Contents of the Book were unsound, and Derogatory, both to the Justice of God and the Grace of Christ, which being published in *England* might adde to the heap of many Errours and Heresies already too much abounding, and this Book being published under the name of a *New English* Gentleman,[5] might occasion many to think, that *New England* also concurred in the allowance of such Exorbitant Aberrations: They therefore judged it meet, not to stay till the Elders could be gathered together;[6] but whilst the Ship yet stayed, to declare their own Judgement against the Book, and to send a Copy of their Declaration to *England* by the Ship, then ready to depart: Had the Tenets therein seemed to them to be matters, either of doubtfull disputation, or of small moment, we doubt not, they would either not at all have declared themselves against the Book, or if they had; they would have stayed for some opportunity of previous consultation with the Elders; but some of the Tenets seemed to them so directly to shake the Fundamentals of Religion, and to wound the vitals of Christianity, that they being many of them well versed both in Dogmaticall and Controversall points of Divinity, thought it their duty to profess their Orthodox faith against all destructive Paradoxes, and dangerous Innovations vented from amongst our selves;[7] for according as they beleeve, they do also profess (as our selves likewise do) That the Obedience of Christ to the whole Law (which is the Law of Righteousness) is the matter of our Justification; and the Imputation of our sins to Christ (and thereupon his suffering the sense of the wrath of God upon him for our sin) and the Imputation of his obedience and sufferings are the formall cause of our Justification, and that they that do deny this, do now take away both these, both the matter and the form of our Justification (as this Book doth) and take away also our Justification, which is the Life of our souls and of our Religion, and therefore called Justification of life, *Rom.* 5.18.[8] As for the Notion which you conceive he declineth, of Infinite wrath, we readily conceive with you, that though Gods wrath be (as himself is infinite, yet no creature can bear infinite wrath) but be swallowed up of it; and therefore the wicked are put to suffer finite wrath in an infinite time; yet this suffering in an infinite time is accidentall, in regard of the finitenesse of the creature, but Christ being infinite God, as well as finite man, his manhood suffering, though in a finite measure, the sense of Gods wrath both in soul and body, the infiniteness of his Godhead (whereto his manhood was united in one person) made his finite suffering, in a finite time, to become of infinite value and efficacy, for the satisfaction of Gods Justice, and transaction of our Redemption. (Thus much for the Book.)

Now for the Author of the Book; before your Letter came to our hands the Court dealt favourably with him, according to your desire: Before they knew your desire, they appointed three of our fellow Elders and Brethren, all of them his friends and acquaintance (such as himself chose) to conferre with him,[9] and finding him yielding in some main point (which he expressed willingly under his own hand) the Court readily accepted the same, as a fruit of his ingenuity, and a pledge of more full satisfaction;[10] withall they gave him a Book, penned (at their appointment by our Reverend Brother M[r] *Norton*) in way of Answer to all his grounds,[11] which he thankfully accepted, and promised upon due perusal & consideration thereof, to return further Answer: All which, though it pleased God to have done, before your Letter came to our hands; yet we acquainted our Magistrates with the contents of your Letter, whereto they returned this Answer; They doubted, either you had not read the Book throughout, or that having seriously weighed it (as the matter required) you would find some Fundamentall Errours in it, meet to be duly witnessed against: For our selves we thankfully accept of your labour of love in advertising us of what you think behooffull; wherein though we differ, and (as we beleeve) justly differ from you, yet if we did not lovingly accept advertisements from our Reverend Brethren sometimes when there is less need, we might discourage ourselves and other Brethren from sending us due advertisements when there is more need. Now the Lord Jesus Christ, the God of Truth and Peace, lead you by his Spirit of Truth into all Truth; and support you with a Spirit of faithfulness and holy zeal, to stand in the gap against the Inundation of all the Errors and Heresies of this present Age; and by his Spirit of Peace, guide and blesse your Studies and holy Labours, to the advancement and establishment of Peace with Truth throughout the Nation; So desiring the Fellowship of your Prayers, we take leave and rest,

Your loving Brethren in the Lord Jesus
and in the Fellowship of his Gospel,

John Cotton,	*John Wilson,*
Rich. Mather,	
Zech. Symmes,	*Will. Thompson.*

1. William Pynchon (1590–1662), one of the founding patentees of the Massachusetts Bay Colony, had sailed from England with the Winthrop fleet in 1630, settled briefly at Dorchester, and soon moved to Roxbury, where he was one of the founders of the church in 1631. In 1636, with seven other men, he settled Springfield, Massachusetts, on the Connecticut River, where he pursued his business interests—already begun in Roxbury—in the fur trade. He became a respected figure there and served as a magistrate until, shortly after the incidents described in the letter, he returned to England sometime in 1652, where he lived for the rest of his life.

For Pynchon's biography, see Ezra Hoyt Byington, "William Pynchon," Connecticut Valley Historical Society, *Proceedings,* II (1904), 20–40; Samuel Eliot Morison, "William Pynchon, the Founder of Springfield," MHS, *Procs.,* LXIV (1932), 67–111, rpt. in *Builders of the Bay Colony,* 2d ed. (Boston, 1964), 337–375; Ruth A. McIntyre, *William Pynchon: Merchant and Colonizer, 1590–1662* (Springfield, Mass., 1961); Anderson, *Great Migration,* 1536–1538.

2. Pynchon's independence of mind is further illustrated by the fact that he took back to England with him yet another book in manuscript reflecting differences with standard New England practice that he would soon publish, *The Jewes Synagogue* . . . (London, 1652). There, as Michael P. Winship points out, Pynchon argued for a church order that was "a *via media* between that espoused by rigid Congregationalists, on the one hand, and rigid Presbyterians, on the other" ("William Pynchon's *The Jewes Synagogue,*" *NEQ,* LXXI [1998], 295). Winship also suggests Pynchon's ideas on church polity "took root" later in New England with Solomon Stoddard.

3. Pynchon's *Meritorious Price of Our Redemption* . . . (London, 1650). This work and its place in current controversy is discussed in Philip F. Gura, " 'The Contagion of Corrupt Opinions' in Puritan Massachusetts: The Case of William Pynchon," *WMQ,* 3d Ser., XXXIX (1982), 469–491; Gura, *A Glimpse of Sion's Glory: Puritan Radicalism in New England, 1620–1660* (Middletown, Conn., 1984), 304–322; Michael W. Vella, "Heresy and *The Meritorious Price of Our Redemption* (1650)," in *The Meritorious Price of Our Redemption by William Pynchon (1590–1662),* in Worcester Polytechnic Institute, *Studies in Science, Technology, and Culture,* X, a facsimile edition with introduction and editorial apparatus by Michael W. Vella, Lance Schachterle, and Louis Mackey (New York, 1992), xix–xxx; Michael P. Winship, "Contesting Control of Orthodoxy among the Godly: William Pynchon Reexamined," *WMQ,* 3d Ser., LIV (1997), 795–822.

4. October 1650.

5. The title page identifies the author as "*William Pinchin,* Gentleman, in New-England."

6. That is, without taking the time required to solicit advice from the ministers.

7. On October 19, 1650, the court formally stated a "declaration & p*ro*testation," proclaiming that "we detest & abhorre many of the opinions & assertions therein as false, eronyous, & hereticall . . . & for proffe & euidence of o*ur* sincere & playne meaninge therein, we doe

hereby condemne the s*ai*d booke to be burned in the market place, at Boston, by the common executiono*u*r." *Records of Massachusetts Bay,* III, 215.

8. Rom. 5:18: Therefore as by the offence of one judgment came upon all men to condemnation; even so by the righteousness of one the free gift came upon all men unto justification of life.

9. In his statement at the next General Court in May 1651, Pynchon identified the three ministers as John Cotton, John Norton, and Edward Norris.

10. On May 22, 1651, Pynchon made the following "retractation": "Accordinge to the Courts advise, I haue conferred w*i*th the Reuerend Mr Cotton, Mr Norrice, & Mr Norton about some poynts of the greatest consequence in my booke, & I hope I haue so explayned my meaninge to them as to take off the worst construction; & it hath pleased God to let me see that I haue not spoken in my booke so fully of the price & merrit of Christ suffrings as I should haue done, for in my booke I call them but trialls of his obedience, yet intendinge thereby to amplyfy & exalt the mediatoriall obedyence of Christ as the only meritorious price of mans redemption; but now at p*re*sent I am much inclined to thinke that his sufferinges were appoynted by God for a further end, namely, as the due punishment of o*u*r sins by way of satisfactio*n* to diuine justice for mans redemption." At this, the court found him "in a hopefull way to giue good satisfaction" and released him to return home with Norton's newly written book "to consider thereof," requiring him to return to the next session of the court, in October 1651, to "giue all due satisfaction." He did not appear then, but the court chose to exercise patience, enjoining him without fail to report at the next General Court (May 1652), "vnder the pœnalty of one hundred pounds" if he failed to come. Since there is no mention of him at all in the records for that General Court session, he apparently left for England before that time. *Records of Massachusetts Bay,* III, 229–230, 257.

11. This was presumably a manuscript of Norton's *Discussion of That Great Point in Divinity, the Sufferings of Christ* . . . (London, 1653).

John Cotton to Oliver Cromwell

July 28, 1651

Tr. Belknap Papers, MHS

Published: Hutchinson, *Collection,* 233–235 (rpt., with occasional changes in spelling and punctuation, in *Hutchinson Papers,* Prince Society, Publications [Albany, N.Y., 1865], I, 262–265); abridged printing in Joseph S. Clark, "John Cotton," *Congregational Quarterly,* III (April 1861), 144–145

In L. Thompson, "Letters of John Cotton," 206–210

This letter to the Lord General Oliver Cromwell and the reply are a singular exchange in which Cotton's maintenance of his links with England is thoroughly evident. Though this is clearly the first—but possibly not the only—letter Cotton wrote to Cromwell, it demonstrates, despite its display of modesty and claim of "native bashfullnesse," not only Cotton's interest in the military and political developments in England during the interregnum but also his assumption that he is still known and well regarded in the Puritan camp in his native country.[1] He apparently suspects Cromwell can use some pastoral counseling at a time when he is being charged with various wrongs against state and law by his enemies in England and Scotland, so Cotton undertakes to reassure Cromwell of the merit and justice of his cause and therefore his actions. He brings to bear his recent thinking on covenants, together with some poignant biblical passages, to accomplish this. Cromwell's gracious reply must have given Cotton full assurance that his act was taken in the spirit in which it was intended.[2] Unlike Cromwell's reply, Cotton's letter has attracted little attention.

As Francis J. Bremer has shown, at about the same time as this letter was written, a day of thanksgiving was declared in the Massachusetts Bay Colony, to commemorate the triumph of reformation of church and state in England. Cotton preached a sermon on that occasion that survives in manuscript. Cotton's sermon and letter to Cromwell cover some of the same territory, though the letter is necessarily much briefer.[3]

In the following text, the earlier published version is preferred, as taken by Hutchinson from a manuscript copy that was more legible at the time of its transcription than the version seen by the transcriber of the manuscript copy now in the Belknap Papers at the Massachusetts Historical Society. The latter leaves blank spaces where words were illegible to the transcriber, but which are included in the version in Hutchinson's *Collection*. At two points, however, the Hutchinson transcription is clearly faulty. In each instance the Belknap Papers (BP) transcription is preferred. Braces indicate departure from the 1769 Hutchinson version (H), with a textual note describing the options. Only the BP version includes Cotton's address block:

To his Highness Oliver Cromwell Lord Protector of England

Right Honourable,

For so I must acknowledge you, not only for the eminency of place and command which the God of power and honour hath called you unto; but also for that the Lord hath sat you forth as a vessell of honour to his name, in working many and great deliverances for his people, and for his truth, by you; and yet helping you to reserve all the honour to him, who is the God of salvation, and the Lord of hoasts, mighty in battell.[4] I am not ignorant that you suffer no small dishonour in the tongues of many, not only as a sectary, but as out of your calling, being sat on worke (as is pretended) by an usurped power, and yourselfe (with the army) exercising a power destructive in some cases to the priviledges of parliament, and the liberty and safety of the kingdome. But 3 or 4 principles there be, upon which it seemeth to me your proceedings have been grounded and carryed on, and whe{re}in[5] my judgment ({weak as} it is)[6] hath been fully satisfyed: 1. That the concessions of the late king never came up to such a posture as whereon to lay a firme foundation of a safe peace, either to church or commonwealth.[7] 2. That when the Parliament was full, and assisted with the commissioners of Scotland (in the treaty at Uxbridge or Newport, or elsewhere)[8] they agreed together that the king could not be restored to his former state upon such termes.[9] And therefore (unles his concessions afterwards in the Isle of Wight were more safe and satisfactory)[10] if the Parliament of England voted the contrary afterwards, in a mighty consultation, it was not an act of Parliament, but a prævarication of a former just and lawfull act.[11] And therefore, when the army discerned, not only their owne safetyes, but the safety of religion and state, and their cause and victoryes given in defence thereof, all of them given away in that prævarication, I know not how they could have approved their faithfullnesse better to the state and cause, then by purging the Parliament of such corrupt humours, and presenting the king to publique tryall.[12] 3. That the army, though they be inferiour and subordinate to the state that giveth them commission and pay; yet neither their consciences nor services are mercenary, though they doe receive wages for their support in the service; though soldiers may take oathes of fidelity to the state, in undertaking an expedition, yet they, regarding the cause as well as the persons that set them on worke, doe performe their fidelity, if they attend to the cause for which they fight, rather than to the private ends or lusts of such as send them forth. Joab (the generall of Davids hoast) though he went beyond his commission in putting Absalom to death, yet not beyond his fidelity.[13] 4. That when covenants are plighted, which consist of many articles (some principall and fundamentall, others subordinate and accessary) if it so fall out that all the articles cannot be performed without breach of some or other, there may be just cause of repenting the undertaking of such covenants; but yet, if some articles cannot be performed without breach of others, the covenanters must chiefely attend to the performance of the principall articles, though (with griefe) they be put to it to violate the subordinate.[14] These things are so cleare to mine owne apprehension, that I am fully satisfyed, that you have all this while fought the Lords battells, and the Lord hath owned you, and honoured himselfe in you, in all your expeditions, which maketh my poor prayers the more serious and faithfull and affectionate (as God helpeth) in your behalfe. In like frame (as I conceive) are the spirits of our brethren (the elders and churches of these parts) carried forth, and the Lord accept us, and help you in Christ.

If you aske upon what structure I have made thus bold to addresse myselfe in these rude lynes to your Lordship, I must acknowledge it is abhorrent from my native bashfullnesse to run into the presence of great men: But I received the other day a letter from my reverend brother Mr. [Hooke] of Newhaven,[15] who certifyeth me that your Lordship made speciall mention of me in your late letters to him, with tender of loving and more respectfull salutations than I could expect; withall he moved me to write to your Lordship, as believing you would accept the same in good part. This is my excuse, such as it is.

The Scots, whom God delivered into your hands at Dunbarre,[16] and whereof sundry were sent hither, we have been desirous (as we could) to make their yoke easy. Such as were sick of the scurvy or other diseases have not wanted physick and chyrurgery. They have not been sold for slaves to perpetuall servitude, but for 6 or 7 or 8 yeares, as we do our owne; and he that bought the most of them (I heare) buildeth houses for them, for every 4 an house, layeth some acres of ground thereto, which he giveth them as their owne, requiring 3 dayes in the weeke to worke for him (by turnes) and 4 dayes for themselves, and promiseth, assoone as they can repay him the money he layed out for them, he will set them at liberty.

As for the aspersion of factious men, I hear, by Mr. Desboroughs[17] letter last night, that you have well vindicated yourselfe therefrom by cashiering sundry corrupt spirits out of the army. And truly, Sir, better a few and faithfull, than many and unsound. The army on Christs side (which he maketh victorious) are called chosen and faithfull, Rev. 17. 14. a verse worthy your Lordships frequent and deepe meditation.[18] Go on therefore (good Sir) to overcome yourselfe (Prov. 16. 32.)[19] to overcome your army, (Deut. 29. 9, with v. 14.)[20] and to vindicate your orthodoxe integrity to the world.

Pardon, I beseech you, my boldnesse and rudenesse, which not arrogancy but due respect and observancy to your Lordship hath put upon me.

The Lord Jesus who is your righteousnesse goe before you, and the glory of the Lord be still your rearward, Isai. 58. 8.[21] Thus humbly taking leave, I remain,

desirous of the accomplishment of the Lords worke
in your hands,
John Cotton.

Boston in N.E.
28. of 5th, 1651.

1. In 1784 Samuel Mather claimed that his collection of family papers had included "several . . . original Letters, written by the renowned Oliver Cromwell, to my great Grandfather, Mr. John Cotton" but that he had lent them to Thomas Hutchinson "and, as I suppose, they are irrecoverably lost and gone" (Dr. Samuel Mather to Samuel Mather [his son], June 9, 1784, quoted by Samuel G. Drake in *The History of King Philip's War, by the Rev. Increase Mather, D.D.; Also, A History of the Same War, by the Rev. Cotton Mather, D.D.* [Boston, 1862], xv). If Mather's memory is accurate here, the correspondence must have continued to the end of Cotton's life and, perhaps on Cromwell's part, slightly beyond. Secondhand corroboration of this possibility appears forty-five years later in Samuel Sewall's diary, where, on November 11, 1696, Sewall records a visit to the Reverend John Higginson in Salem, who "tells me that the protector, Oliver Cromwell, when Gen[l], wrot to Mr. Hook of Newhaven, and therein sent comenda-

tions to Mr. Cotton; upon which Mr. Cotton was writt to by Mr. Hook and desir'd to write to the Gen[l], which He did, and advis'd him that to take from the Spaniards in America would be to dry up Euphrates; which was one thing put Him upon his Expedition to Hispaniola, and Mr. Higginson and 3 more were to have gone to Hispaniola if the Place had been taken. O. Cromwell would have had Capt. Leverett to have gone thether Gov[r], told him twas drying up Euphrates, and He intended not to desist till He came to the Gates of Rome. This Mr. Cook [Sewall's companion on the trip to Salem] said He had heard his father Leverett tell many a time" (*The Diary of Samuel Sewall, 1674–1729,* ed. M. Halsey Thomas [New York, 1973], I, 359). (Rev. 16:12 says that the sixth vial was poured into the Euphrates "and the water thereof was dried up, that the way of the kings of the east might be prepared." Cotton apparently meant to suggest to Cromwell that adding Hispaniola to his conquests would further confirm the Lord's triumph over the Antichrist through Cromwell's victories.) Since the one surviving exchange between Cotton and Cromwell makes no mention of the Spanish island of Hispaniola, Higginson's report to Sewall recalls another, later exchange of letters between the two. It also suggests that Cotton's advice influenced Cromwell's plans in the Caribbean, where in 1655 his expedition was defeated at Hispaniola.

2. In fact, Cromwell had quickly seized on the victory at Dunbar as a sign of God's continued blessing on his people. See discussion of this in J. S. A. Admason, "Oliver Cromwell and the Long Parliament," and Johann Sommerville, "Oliver Cromwell and English Political Thought," both in John Morrill, ed., *Oliver Cromwell and the English Revolution* (London, 1990), 86, 249–250.

3. See Francis J. Bremer, "In Defense of Regicide: John Cotton on the Execution of Charles I," *WMQ,* 3d Ser., XXXVII (1980), 103–124; Bremer presents the complete sermon on 110–124.

4. Ps. 24:8–10: Who is this King of glory? The Lord strong and mighty, the Lord mighty in battle. . . . Who is this King of glory? The Lord of hosts, he is the King of glory.

5. BP: wherein; H: whein.

6. BP: (weak as it is); H: (reasonable it is).

7. Cotton's "Sermon upon A Day of Publique thanksgiving" makes the same point: "Both Comissioners of England & Scottland agree in this that the kings Concessions was not Safe to Center upon & to Settle A firme peace," in Bremer, "In Defense of Regicide," *WMQ,* 3d Ser., XXXVII (1980), 120.

8. In the autumn of 1648, Parliament had conducted negotiations with the king at Newport, a process that Cromwell "detested" because "it had betrayed the political and religious objectives for which, in Cromwell's view, the war had been fought." Adamson, "Oliver Cromwell and the Long Parliament," in Morrill, ed., *Oliver Cromwell and the English Revolution,* 80.

9. These points are also discussed in Cotton's Thanksgiving Day sermon, in Bremer, "In Defense of Regicide," *WMQ,* 3d Ser., XXXVII (1980), 119–120.

10. Cromwell had secretly visited Charles on the Isle of Wight in early 1648 to try to dissuade him from a Scottish alliance, but the mission failed. Later, Parliament's Newport Treaty negotiations, about which Cromwell was skeptical, occurred on the Isle of Wight. See Adamson, "Oliver Cromwell and the Long Parliament," in Morrill, ed., *Oliver Cromwell and the English Revolution,* 78; Peter Gaunt, *Oliver Cromwell* (Oxford, 1996), 99.

11. In 1648, sixteen new members favorable to making concessions with the king were elected to Parliament and achieved a majority wishing to overturn the previous act (the Vote of No Addresses) prohibiting further discussions with the king. As Cotton said in his sermon,

"If the former Act was An act of parlament then the other was A prevarication of that Act." Bremer, "In Defense of Regicide," *WMQ,* 3d Ser., XXXVII (1980), 121.

12. The reference is to Pride's Purge, the exclusion from Westminster of members of Parliament who were favorably inclined to negotiation with Charles in December 1648, by Colonel Thomas Pride. See David Underdown, *Pride's Purge: Politics in the Puritan Revolution* (Oxford, 1971). Cotton refers to this controversial action approvingly in his Thanksgiving Day sermon; see Bremer, "In Defense of Regicide," *WMQ,* 3d Ser., XXXVII (1980), 121.

13. Absalom had conspired against his father, King David, and was slain by David's commander, Joab, against the orders of David. See 2 Sam. 15–18.

14. In his Thanksgiving Day sermon Cotton also discusses the priority of elements of covenants—both the Solemn League and Covenant between Scotland and the English Parliament in 1643 and Old Testament precedents—affirming there also: "If this be an article in the third place, then the two former must have the prosedency & preehemenence, & if the king Cannot be Restored But with prejudish to the purity of Religion, & Restoring of prelacy [or] inclination to popery or if he Canot be Restored without prejudice of the Liberty & Safety of the people: they must Now of Necessity Be excused, from maintaining the third article which Comes But in the third place, & presoposeth the other two to Be Maintained & preserved." See Bremer, "In Defense of Regicide," *WMQ,* 3d Ser., XXXVII (1980), 119–120.

15. BP: M[r] Hook of Newnham; H: M[r] Hooker of Newhaven. Neither reading seems correct. The letter must have read M[r] Hooke [or Hook] of Newhaven, unless Cotton himself slipped in writing Hooker, who had been pastor at Hartford, not New Haven, and in any case had died in 1647. William Hooke (1601–1678), a graduate of Trinity College, Oxford (bachelor of arts, 1620; master's, 1623), after seven years at Taunton in the Bay Colony became teacher of the New Haven church, joining the pastor, John Davenport, in 1644. Hooke's wife, Jane, was the sister of the regicide Edward Whalley and Cromwell's cousin. When he returned to England in 1656, he became one of Cromwell's chaplains at Whitehall. Cromwell's "late letters" to Hooke have not been preserved, but references to correspondence between the two appear elsewhere. The fullest account of his life is Charles Ray Palmer, "Rev. William Hooke, 1601–1678," New Haven Colony Historical Society, *Papers,* VIII (1914), 56–81. See also *DNB;* William Hooke to John Winthrop, Jr., Apr. 13, 1657, in *Hutchinson Papers,* MHS, *Colls.,* 3d Ser., I (Boston, 1825), 181–185; Isabel MacBeath Calder, *The New Haven Colony* (New Haven, Conn., 1934), 85; Wilbur Cortez Abbott, ed., *The Writings and Speeches of Oliver Cromwell* (Cambridge, Mass., 1937–1947), III, 185, IV, 475.

16. Cotton possessed a detailed awareness of the battle on September 3, 1650, at Dunbar at which the outnumbered English army defeated the Scottish forces. See his Thanksgiving Day sermon, ed. Bremer, "In Defense of Regicide," *WMQ,* 3d Ser., XXXVII (1980), 122, where he includes details of weather and military tactics. For a detailed description of the battle at Dunbar, see John D. Grainger, *Cromwell against the Scots: The Last Anglo-Scottish War, 1650–1652* (East Linton, East Lothian, Scot., 1997), 37–50. Brief accounts appear in C. V. Wedgwood, *Oliver Cromwell,* rev. ed. (London, 1973), 72–73, Pauline Gregg, *Oliver Cromwell* (London, 1988), 195–197; Gaunt, *Oliver Cromwell,* 127–128.

In September 1650, the month of the battle, a decision was made to transport many of the Scottish prisoners. The ship *Unity* sailed for New England from London on November 11 with 150 prisoners, arriving in the Bay in late December. Sixty of them were sent to work at the Saugus ironworks, and the rest were dispersed to a variety of masters and locations for their periods of indenture. Charles Edward Banks, "Scotch Prisoners Deported to New England by

Cromwell, 1651–52," MHS, *Procs.,* LXI (1927–1928), 4–29, esp. 8–15; see also Grainger, *Cromwell against the Scots,* 55–58.

17. John Desborough (1608–1680), Cromwell's brother-in-law, husband of Cromwell's sister, Jane. He was Cromwell's quartermaster and captain of a troop early in the war and ultimately rose to major general. He was a trusted officer and later member of Cromwell's Council of State and of Parliament. Cotton's reference to him as a correspondent suggests that perhaps he was the source of the political and military details that Cotton reveals in this letter and in his Thanksgiving Day sermon in the same year. See Gregg, *Oliver Cromwell,* 35, 72, 79, 242, 293.

18. Rev. 17:14: These shall make war with the Lamb, and the Lamb shall overcome them: for he is Lord of lords, and King of kings: and they that are with him are called, and chosen, and faithful.

19. Prov. 16:32: He that is slow to anger is better than the mighty; and he that ruleth his spirit than he that taketh a city.

20. Deut. 29:9, 14: Keep therefore the words of this covenant, and do them, that ye may prosper in all that ye do. . . . Neither with you only do I make this covenant and this oath.

21. Isa. 58:8: Then shall thy light break forth as the morning, and thine health shall spring forth speedily: and thy righteousness shall go before thee: the glory of the Lord shall be thy rereward.

Richard Mather to John Cotton

September 15, 1651

ALS. MS: AAS: Mather Family Papers, octavo vol. I, item d

A synod to discuss issues of faith and polity was begun in Cambridge in 1646, resumed the following year when it was cut short by an epidemic, and finally completed in August 1648.[1] By then the work of the Westminster Assembly in London had been completed; consequently, the New England ministers unanimously approved and accepted for the use of their churches the assembly's *Confession of Faith.* In the matter of church polity, however, they still differed with their English brethren and so constructed their own document, the Cambridge *Platform of Church Discipline.*[2] This had been drafted by Richard Mather, probably with the help of Cotton. There was from the time of the 1646 synod strong but minority opposition from Cotton's own Boston church, the new document being perceived by some laymen as vesting too much church authority in the ministers and the General Court. The court sought the reactions of "the seuerall churches w*i*thin this jurisdicc*i*on" before taking final action.[3] Individuals who still had some problems with the version published in 1649—"some younge heades in the Countrye," according to Winthrop[4]—prepared formal objections to it. As Mather's letter indicates, he and Cotton were engaged in organizing answers to those objections that could be presented to the General Court for some resolution of the lingering doubts about the form of the New England Way to be adopted. The Mather Family Papers include a manuscript of twenty-eight leaves entitled "An Answere of the Elders to certayne doubts and objecc*i*ons ag*ains*t sundry passages in the Platfourme of discipline agreed vpon by the late synod, sent from some churches and p*ar*ticular brethren to the much Honoured Gen*er*all Court, or the Secretary, and by order of the Court com*m*ended to the Elders for Answer." Mather refers to this document in his letter to Cotton, where he suggests the detailed orchestration the leading ministers conducted in getting their version of church polity accepted, a polity that would be the standard for many years to come. Finally, in October 1651, the General Court approved the document as representing "that wee have practised and doe believe."[5]

The letter is written on both sides of a single sheet. The page is worn away all down the right margin and for about an inch in the middle of the left margin. Mather's hand is careless, giving every indication of rapid composition. He has a peculiar habit of omitting the syllable -er- or -re-, sometimes inserting but often omitting a diacritical mark to indicate an abbreviation. Where he has included such a mark, the omitted letters are provided here in italics; where he neglects to mark his omission, the missing letters are inserted in brackets, though his copy is so rough that certainty whether or not such a mark is present is not always possible. Although this looks like too rough a draft to be the one Mather sent to Cotton, nevertheless Mather addressed the letter on the verso:

> To the Rev*er*end
> his much respected
> in *th*e Lord M[r] John
> Cotton teacher to
> [th]e ch*urch* at boston
> these./

Mather was reusing a sheet of paper from an earlier letter to him. Written in the same area of the verso as the above address block:

> To my louing
> much respected friend
> mr Rich Mather
> pastor of the church
> at Dorchester
> in new England
> these

Rev*er*end S*i*r, M[r] Allin[6] & I haue had sundry meetings to draw-vp || [answers?] to the excepc*i*ons ag*ains*t *th*e book of *th*e Synod, out of those heads or hu[?]|| w*hi*ch w*er*e com*m*unicated by yo*u*r selfe & *th*e oth*er* Elders at Camb[ridge.][7] W*ha*t we haue done I haue now transcribed and here ||[enclose?]

desyring that yo*u*r selfe as you see meet would revise || adding, w*i*thdrawing, or oth*er*wise altering as the[re] may be ca[use?]|| that as was intended it may ^[deleted words]^ be sent to o*u*r brethren ~~of~~ ^in th||^ of the Countrey, that ^they^ may do the like, and that afore the || [court?] there might be another meeting ^of *the*m & the Elders in these p*ar*ts togeath[er]||^ that so w*he*n *the* court sh[all?]|| co*m*e it might be given ^in^ as agreed vpo*n* w*i*th as full co[mmon?]|| consent of the Elders as may be. W[he]n Mr Allin & I || to looke ov*er* w*ha*t we rec*eive*d, at Cambridge, [8]we [1]found [2]that ||[in] *the* excepc*i*ons [4]th*ere* was [3]in his notes [5]no answ*ere* at all, to ||[any of?] the excepc*i*ons ~~at all~~ ^in the^ pap*er*s, & to these we haue ^aduentured^ || such ~~as~~ Answ*ere*s as the Lord helped vs w*i*thall; but I s|| may be some A[n]s[wer]s w*hi*ch ^we^ ~~might~~ haue not obs*er*ved, and || may remayne w*i*thout Answ*ere*, in w*hi*ch regard the[re] ~~may be~~ ^is the mo[re need?]||^ of diligent p*er*vsall of the pap*er*s afore *the* Ans*were* be giuen ||[so that?] noth*ing* pr*o*per of moment may be left ~~of~~ vnspoken to. We haue || abridged & contracted the objecc*i*ons, & excepc*i*ons, but this ^also^ had n[ext?]|| to be revised ^& co*m*pared w*i*th the papers^ lest any of their str: be not set downe. So*m*e th[ings?]|| we haue enlarged further then we rec*eive*d at Cambridge, || that point of the Elders p*re*paring matters in private; ~~w*hi*ch~~ || ~~you~~ to be seene p. 29, &c.[9] but this may either stand or be res|| out as yo*u*r selfe and o*u*r brethren shall judge best. we haue also added a short p*re*face, ^the[re]in^ giving notise of the way & man*ner* || [of] *the* 9th Answ*ere* & ^of^ o*u*r calling th*ere*to. We find in the pap*er*s of Ed[ward] breck[10] tow*ard*s the lat*ter* end th*ere*of, something about the [deleted word] ^non-^ reason of A*nswer*s in these dayes; but ~~we [illegible word] passe ^past^ the ? 6th ch*apter* of || the booke to w*hi*ch these excepc*i*ons of his haue ref*er*ence, afore we met w*i*th ^them^ these in the afore we met ^them^ ? these excepc*i*ons of the~~ we *were* the[re]of the 6th ch*apter* of the booke to w*hi*ch ~~they~~ ^these excepc*i*ons^ haue ref*er*ence ^as we [illegible word]^ and so nothing is yet said thereto. ~~Lastly~~ And yesterday I vnd*er*stood f[rom] Mr Rawson the Secretary,[11] that the[re] are more excepc*i*ons co*m*e in w[hic]h a[ll] the Elders haue not seene, ~~In regard of all ^these^ w*hi*ch things ^I [illegible word]^ the|| need of~~ all w*hi*ch things consid*er*ed the[re] will be much need ^[illegible phrase]^|| of anoth[er] meeting afore the court, & *tha*t as soone as might be, lest *the* court be p? [IV] be ready and need also ~~after~~ ^that^ o*u*r brethren would peruse and || revise w*ha*t is here ^thus farre^ done. [deleted word] ^I propound here these things I sought until ||^ ~~which things I~~ whereto to yo*u*r || [judgment?] that if you thinke ~~meet you might certify of bot~~ ^good o*u*r brethren in the other p*ar*t^ of the || might ~~be~~ by you be certified the[re]of: desyring also that w*hi*ch ||se oppertunity [deleted word] you would convey these pap*er*s to *them,* w*hi*ch herew*i*th || [I send] you ^no more &c.^ ~~no more~~ at [illegible word]. I p*ro*pound also to consid*er*ac*i*on whether ^[it is] not meet^ ~~not be well~~ in the end ^of^ *the* answer*e* to the excepc*i*ons to annex || motiues to ~~*the*~~ ^p*er*suade *th*e^ court to giue th[ei]r testimony & approbac*i*on to [this b]ooke; I conceiue the[re][12] are many of *them* inclinable so to do, but this ||nceiue ^[illegible word]^ might be of vse to rely on the ^same^. ~~thing~~ These things & more, at p*re*sent, but w*i*th Remembrance of my best rep*ect*s to yo*u*r ||[sel]fe, Mrs Cotton & all yo*u*rs, I rest

Yo*u*rs in *th*e Lord Jesus

[Dorcheste]r 7^m^ 15°. 51. R: M:

1. On the synod, see Winthrop, *Journal,* 628, 634–638, 688, 714–715; Perry Miller, *Orthodoxy in Massachusetts, 1630–1650: A Genetic Study* (Cambridge, Mass., 1933), chap. 6, "The New England Way"; Frederick L. Fagley, "The Narrative of the Cambridge Synod," in Henry Wilder Foote, ed., *The Cambridge Platform of 1648: Tercentenary Commemoration at Cambridge, Massachusetts, October 27, 1948* (Boston, 1949), 1–28; Ziff, *Career of John Cotton,* 222–228; Rutman, *Winthrop's Boston,* 262–268; Hall, *Faithful Shepherd,* chap. 5, "To the Cambridge Platform"; Harry S. Stout, *The New England Soul: Preaching and Religious Culture in Colonial New England* (New York, 1986), 52–53; Theodore Dwight Bozeman, *To Live Ancient Lives: The Primitivist Dimension in Puritanism* (Chapel Hill, N.C., 1988), 125–130; Foster, *Long Argument,* 170–172.

2. [Westminster Assembly of Divines], *The Humble Advice of the Assembly of Divines . . . concerning a Confession of Faith . . .* (London, 1648); [Cambridge Synod], *A Platform of Church Discipline Gathered out of the Word of God: and Agreed upon by the Elders: and Messengers of the Churches Assembled in the Synod at Cambridge in New England to Be Presented to the Churches and Generall Court for Their Consideration and Acceptance* (Cambridge, Mass., 1649). This latter publication includes a preface by Cotton and is reprinted in Williston Walker, *The Creeds and Platforms of Congregationalism* (1893; rpt. Boston, 1960), 194–237, with Walker's cross-references to various contemporary publications on church polity by New England divines. Cotton Mather in book V of the *Magnalia* omits the preface but otherwise includes the full text of the platform.

3. Henry Martyn Dexter, *The Congregationalism of the Last Three Hundred Years as Seen in Its Literature* (1880; rpt. New York, 1970), I, 447, quoting from the *Records of Massachusetts Bay,* III, 178.

4. Winthrop, *Journal,* 715.

5. Dexter, *Congregationalism,* I, 448, quoting *Records of Massachusetts Bay,* IV, 57, 58.

6. John Allin (1596–1671), minister at Dedham. Winthrop records the fact that at the convening of the 1648 synod on August 15, "mr Allen of dedham preached out of Actes 15: a very godly, learned & particular handlinge of neer all the Doctrines & applications concerninge that subiecte, with a cleare discovery & refutation of suche errors, obiections, & scruples as had been raysed about it, by some younge heades in the Countrye" (*Journal,* 715). On Allin, see *DNB;* Venn, *Alumni Cantabrigienses,* I, 18.

7. A manuscript in Cotton's hand in the Boston Public Library's Cotton Papers is headed "Exceptions ag*ains*t some things in *th*e synod at Cambr*idge.* 1649." It contains fifteen points, each referring to a particular point in the *Cambridge Platform* to which someone has objected. See Appendix, below, for the full text of this previously unpublished document.

8. The five italic superscript numbers were over the various phrases they precede in this sentence; they were written in by Mather to indicate a reordering of the sentence, which he presumably accomplished in making a fair copy of the letter.

9. In the middle of p. 29 of the MS in the Mather Papers entitled "An Answere of the Elders"

appears a paragraph beginning: "This matter of the Elders p*re*paring things in private we haue now 3 or 4 seue*r*all tymes met w*i*th expressions ag*ains*t it in these papers. . . ."

10. Edward Breck (d. 1662) was a resident of Dorchester at this time. He is mentioned several times in the manuscript "An Answere of the Elders . . ." (4, 6, 12, 13, 14, 10, 39). Brief biographical details are in Charles Henry Pope, *The Pioneers of Massachusetts: A Descriptive List Drawn from Records of the Colonies, Towns, and Churches, and Other Contemporaneous Documents* (1900; Baltimore, 1977), 66.

11. Edward Rawson was the longtime secretary of the Massachusetts Bay Colony.

12. Here Mather wrote the but more likely meant to write there.

Oliver Cromwell to John Cotton

October 2, 1651

ALS. MS: NYPL, Personal Misc. Tr: BL, MHS (by different hands, both probably from eighteenth century)

Published: Hutchinson, *Collection,* 236–237; William Harris, *An Historical and Critical Account of the Life of Oliver Cromwell . . . to Which Is Added an Appendix of Original Papers,* 2d ed. (London, 1772), 539–540, rpt. in Harris, *An Historical and Critical Account of the Lives and Writings of James I. and Charles I. and of the Lives of Oliver Cromwell and Charles II . . .* (London, 1814), III, 518–519; Brook, *Lives of the Puritans,* III, 158–159; Thomas Carlyle, *Oliver Cromwell's Letters and Speeches: With Elucidations* (London, 1845), 161–162; *Hutchinson Papers,* Prince Society, Publications (Albany, N.Y., 1865), I, 266–267; Arthur B. Ellis, *History of the First Church in Boston, 1630–1880* (Boston, 1881), 38–39; Dexter, *Extracts,* 261–262; Wilbur Cortez Abbott, ed., *The Writings and Speeches of Oliver Cromwell* (Cambridge, Mass., 1937–1947), II, 482–483

In L. Thompson, "Letters of John Cotton," 211–212

After Cotton had written his letter to Cromwell, the general had met Charles II's forces in a decisive battle at Worcester. Both armies had marched south from Scotland. Unlike the battle at Dunbar, where the Scottish forces had been about double those of Cromwell, here Cromwell's army had twenty-eight thousand men to the king's fourteen thousand. One year exactly after the Battle of Dunbar, on September 3, 1651, the Cromwellian forces won an overwhelming victory. Charles was able to escape through the countryside, but he was now forced to seek exile in France. It was the final battle of the English Civil War.[1]

The letter is written on two sheets, using both sides of the first and the recto of the second for the message. Loss of paper at the right edge of the second sheet causes partial loss of text in five lines. The text supplied in braces at these points is from Hutchinson, the earliest printed version, though every publication of the letter includes the missing portions without giving any indication of an interruption. The same is true of the two eighteenth-century transcriptions. On the verso of the second sheet, Cromwell addressed the letter:

> For my esteemed frend
> Mr Cotton Pastor
> to the church at Boston
> in New England.
> theise

Worthye S*i*r, and my Christian freind/

I receaued yours a few dayes sithence, it was welcom to mee, because signed by you, whome I loue and Honour in the Lord. but more to see ^some of^ the same grounds of ^our^ actions[2] stirringe in you, that doe[3] in vs to quiet vs to our worke, and support vs therein, w*hi*ch hath had greatest difficultye in our engagement in Scotland, by reason wee haue had to doe w*i*th some, whoe were (I verily thinke) Godly, but thorough weaknesse, and the subtiltye of Sathan, inuolued in intersts, against the Lord, and his people. w*i*th what tendernesse wee haue proceeded w*i*th such, and that in synceritye, our papers w*hi*ch (I suppose you haue seen) will in part manifest, and I giue you some comfortable assurance off. The Lord hath maruelously appeared euen [1v] against them and now againe when all the power was deuolued into the Scottish Kinge[4] and the malignant partie, they inuadeinge England, the Lord [deleted word] rayned vpon them such snares as the enclosed will shew, ~~howeuer~~ only the narratiue is short in this, that of their whole armie when the Narrative was framed not fiue of their whole Armie were returned.[5] Surely S*i*r the Lord is greatly to bee feared, as to bee praised. wee need y*ou*r [deleted word] prayers in this as much as euer, how shall wee behaue our selues after such mercyes? what is the Lord a doeinge? what prophesies are now fullfillinge? whoe is a God like our's? [2r] To knowe his will, to doe his will are both of him.

I tooke this libertye from businesse to salute you thus in a word, truly I am readye to serue you, and the rest of our brethren and the churches w*i*th you. I am a poore weake creature, and not worthye the name of a worme{,} yett accepted to ser{ue the Lord} and his people, indeed {my deare} freind betweene you {and me,} you knowe not mee, {my weak}nesses, my ^inordinate^ passions, my {unskill}fullnesse, and euery way vnfittnesse to my worke, yett, yett, the Lord whoe will haue mercye on whome Hee will, does as you see. pray for mee, salute all christian frendes though vnknowen, I rest

your affectionate frend,

~~Sept. 29th~~ to serue you

October 2d. 1651 O Cromwell

1. On the battle at Worcester and its significance, see John D. Grainger, *Cromwell against the Scots: The Last Anglo-Scottish War, 1650–1652* (East Linton, East Lothian, Scot., 1997), 128–146; Pauline Gregg, *Oliver Cromwell* (London, 1988), 209–215; Maurice Ashley, *The English Civil War* (New York, 1990), 186–189; Peter Gaunt, *Oliver Cromwell* (Oxford, 1996), 132–134.

2. Cromwell wrote actinge, then wrote -ons over the -nge.

3. doe is written over haue.

4. Charles, son of Charles I, and later to become Charles II of England, had been crowned king of Scotland and had raised an army of Scots with which he invaded England.

5. The enclosed "Narrative" was probably, as Thomas Carlyle suggested, the Parliament's Narrative of Worcester Battle, published in September 1651 together with "the Act appointing a Day of Thanksgiving; 26th September, 1651" (Carlyle, *Oliver Cromwell's Letters and Speeches,* 162). It was reprinted in *The Parliamentary or Constitutional History of England . . . from the Earliest Times to the Restoration of King Charles II,* XX, (London, 1757), 58–65.

John Cotton to Mr. [John] Elmeston

October 18, 1651

Published: [John Elmeston], *A Censure of That Reverend and Learned Man of God Mr. John Cotton, Lately of New-England, upon the Way of Mr. Henden of Bennenden in Kent, Expressed in Some Animadversions of His upon a Letter of Mr. Henden's, Sometimes Sent to Mr. Elmeston* (London, 1656), 47

John Elmeston, the schoolmaster in Cranbrook, Kent, to whom Cotton had written in 1640, retired from his position at the town's grammar school in 1650, after thirty-eight years of service.[1] His activities thereafter included writing introductions (including his own Latin poem) to two medical books by his Cranbrook friend Robert Pemell.[2] In a somewhat larger literary product of Elmeston's retirement, he included among other documents two more letters to him from Cotton. Elmeston had become concerned at reports that one Simon Henden in nearby Bennenden was heretically promulgating notions about the church's misuse of its power. So he had written to Henden to ask him to clarify his views, whereupon Henden wrote back on January 2, 1649/50, confidently asserting his new insight that "the breathing of the Spirit in these both Officers and Ordinances in the Primitive Age, the life and soul of both, was since restrained, being as a carcasse without a soul," citing Scripture proofs liberally.[3] The church, in short, had become degenerate, and separation from it was the appropriate action for those who trusted in Christ's eventual return. Henden invited Elmeston to come to see him and discuss the issues. Elmeston chose instead to go public to expose Henden's sectarianism, which he did by publishing his own letters, Henden's response, and his own lengthy rejoinder to Henden, in a book called *An Essay for the Discovery and Discouraging of the New Sprung Schism, Raised and Maintained by Mr Simon Henden of Bennenden in Kent* (London, 1652). Elmeston wanted to do more, however, so he looked abroad for an authoritative opinion. He told Henden in a letter dated December 20, 1651, "Such was my desire to be satisfied about your new Way and Principles, and to inform your self and followers about them, that I sent your Letter wrote to me to Mr. *Cotton* to *New-England,* and by Letter requested his judgements thereupon." Elmeston reports that Cotton in return "condescended to me, and sent me in writing his censure upon your Letter; which I received but the last Saturday." It may be, he says, "that truth commended to you from a place so remote, and from so learned and godly a man, will sooner be embraced than coming from a neighbour and ordinary friend."[4]

When he published these exchanges in 1656, Elmeston included, in a little over six quarto pages, Cotton's reply to the document he had received. Henden's relatively brief letter (printed in three quarto pages) had presented his interpretations of certain Scripture passages having to do with the organization, practice, and authority of churches, particularly passages in Revelation interpreting the dragon and the beast, the seven angels, and the pouring out of the angels' vials, all familiar material to Cotton, whose earlier books on church discipline and on *The Powring out of the Seven Vials* (1642, 1645) probably helped motivate Elmeston to write to Cotton for help. Cotton's answer to Henden, in a separate document that accompanied his letter to Elmeston, has never been reprinted and is never included in bibliographies of Cotton's works; it is included here in the Appendix.

The letter is printed in italics, with occasional words or phrases left in roman type; here that publishing convention is reversed, though, given Cotton's usual practice, it is unlikely that he underlined any passages.

Reverend and dear Sir,

It is indeed a busie season with me to return due answer to sundry Friends, who expect the same by this vessell. But because your Letter is not onely yours, but a voice from the Lord Jesus, in which he calleth me to beare witnesse to the truth (for which end he came himself into the world, *John 18.37.*[5] and sent his servants) I durst not omit this first opportunity of returning answer to the scruples which your Letter enclosed. If when you have perused the same, your judgement concur therein, you may please to communicate them to your Christian friend: If otherwise, reserve them by your selfe. Be intreated to accept the labour of my love from your fellow-servant, and cease not to pray for me, whose businesses are more than my dayes. The Lord Jesus be still the staff of your age, and perfect his work in your heart and head, till he translate you to his heavenly Kingdome in Christ Jesus:[6] In whom with hearty salutes to you and Mrs. *Denly,* I take leave, and rest,

Boston the *18.* of the eighth moneth. *1651.*

Yours in Brotherly love unfeigned,

JOHN COTTON.

1. I am grateful to Mr. Gerald Cousins of Cranbrook, Kent, for this information and to Mr. Peter Allen, Deputy Headmaster and Archivist of Cranbrook School. Mr. Allen, consulting the historical notes of the late Mr. Anthony Congreve, also of Cranbrook School, confirmed details (and lacunae) on Elmeston's career. Elmeston's position at the school is also mentioned by William Tarbutt in *Annals of Cranbrook Church* (Cranbrook, 1870), 34.

2. His Latin poem appears in R[obert] P[emell], *De Morbis Capitis; or, Of the Chief Internall Diseases of the Head . . .* (London, 1650). Much earlier, he had written introductions, including Latin verse, in posthumous publications of Paul Baynes. See his "Epistle Dedicatory" and elegiac poem in Baynes's *The Mirrour; or, Miracle of Gods Love unto the World of his Elect . . .* (London, 1619).

3. Henden to Elmeston, Jan. 2, 1649/50, in John Elmeston, *An Essay for the Discovery and Discouraging of the New Sprung Schism . . .* (London, 1652), 4. Brief comment on Simon Henden appears in Francis Haslewood, *The Parish of Benenden, Kent: Its Monuments, Vicars, and Persons of Note* (Ipswich, 1889), 179–180.

4. [Elmeston], *A Censure,* 48.

5. John 18:37: Pilate therefore said unto him, Art thou a king then? Jesus answered, Thou sayest that I am a king. To this end was I born, and for this cause came I into the world, that I should bear witness unto the truth. Every one that is of the truth heareth my voice.

6. This gentle reference to Elmeston's age is particularly appropriate if this John Elmeston is the same as the "Elmestone, John, of Kent," who matriculated at Lincoln College, Oxford, in 1579 at the age of twenty-two (bachelor of arts, 1581/2; master's, 1585) (*Alumni Oxonienses,* II, 460). He would have been 93 years old in 1651 and 103 when he died in 1661. He remarks on his age himself in "A Postscript" to *An Essay* in complaining that Mr. Henden had sent him an answer that was "so closely written, so often interlined, and much blotted, that in such places mine eyes thorow age being dim, I cannot make out his full sense and meaning" (42).

S[eaborn] C[otton] to [John Cotton]

[About 1648–1651]

ALI. MS: Seaborn Cotton's Commonplace Book, NEHGS, Mss Cb 1031, 87–88

Published: Samuel Eliot Morison, "The Reverend Seaborn Cotton's Commonplace Book," CSM, *Publs.,* XXXII, *Trans.* (1933–1937), 338

Translation by George Goebel

The contents of this undated Latin letter, copied by Seaborn Cotton (1633–1686) into his commonplace book, clearly establish that it is written to his father. Copied somewhat carelessly in a tiny hand, the manuscript poses a few intractable textual problems. Its previous editor, Samuel Eliot Morison, believed the letter was "certainly not original" with Seaborn, but a kind of form letter from a grateful son to a father / benefactor that Seaborn copied out for his father. The letter does, indeed, seem extravagant and stilted in its expressions of gratitude, but Morison gives as the main reason for his surmise the impression that "the mistakes in Latin are of the sort that creep into a text recopied several times."[1] One might as easily assume, however, that the errors are scribal errors the author made in his own writing, or in copying the original into his commonplace book (writing auscutare for auscultare, for instance, or intio for initio). Some of the errors are grammatical and thus probably Seaborn's own rather than those of an authoritative text from which he was copying. Other problem spots occurred where Morison misread the manuscript. It is possible, however, that Morison was correct in guessing that the text is at least somehow related to Seaborn's work at Harvard. One can imagine an assignment to create such a letter of gratitude to one's parent as a rhetorical exercise. Alternatively, it seems possible that the letter was the young Seaborn's attempt to demonstrate the benefits of his father's early instruction of him in Latin by writing such a letter. His gratitude for his father's desire to make him a "learned man" would be consistent with such an effort. Moreover, his passing mention of Greek myths in his references to Homer's Achilles and to Pandora may simply be a bit of showing off by one now trained in the reading of Greek literature. If the reader simply assumes that the letter, one way or another, is a sincere expression from the son to the father, however, it sheds interesting light on Cotton's earlier relationship with his eldest child.

The manuscript is the source text. This edition improves somewhat upon Morison's reading; variants are noted. Morison's careful study of handwriting in the commonplace book led him to conclude that this letter is in what he calls Seaborn Cotton's earliest hand. (It is not as early, of course, as the youthful script in Seaborn's copy of Cotton's letter to Lydia Gaunt three years earlier.) The inclusive dates for the letter indicated above follow Morison's suggestion, placing it during the young man's years at Harvard College; he graduated in 1651 at the age of eighteen.

P. R. H. et Ch.[2]

Quum ab Ingratitudine non secus ab=Horream[3] quam Achilles ille Homericus a Mendacio, et mecum Perpenderem quam esset Immensu*m* quod tuæ debeam Benignitati ut Meritum omne, omne quoq*ue* officium exsvperet meum, credidi te Accepturu*m* si tibi Literariâ strenulâ, aut flosculo quopiam e Musarum Hortulis dece^r^pto animu*m* Memorem et Gratum utcunq*ue* testarer. Oh vtinam tua in Me Perpetuò collata (multò plùs meritò) Beneficia vnquam solvendo esse queam. Grates persolvere Dignas, Hoc opus ~~est~~, Hic[4] Labor est.

Pro tuo Mei summo amore,[5] et in me Jam sæpè collocatâ Benignitate, et gratias quas habeo Maximas animo perquam Libentissimo rependo, et Omnia Mea deinceps in Posteru*m* officia paratissimâ voluntate[6] offero et addico. Non latent tuæ solicitudines anxiæ, nec Anxetates[7] quotidianæ Mei Boni gratiâ tibi emergentes. patent Molestiæ, patent angores tui, patent deniq*ue* omnes Curæ tuæ, mei Com*m*odi Gratiâ. Novi quantu*m* Olei operæq*ue*[8] sumpsisti ut doctus evadam, Novi (et melius mihi esset si melius Nossem)[9] quot consilia quot svasoria verba ^mihi dixisti^ quotis[10] me Monitu*m* voluisti ut Probus existam. quoties svasisti quoties Incitasti ne[11] tibi dedecori[12] et aliis scandalo fierem. Deus novit, quam tua tunc Concilia posthabui, et non secundu*m* ea vitam degi: nunc vero Me meæ Negligentiæ pedet[13] nunc Me parvi earu*m* æstimationis tædet pœnitetq*ue*[14] sed, ah Me videre est Me potius propter omnia tua beneficia tibi pandoram esse potius quam illis grates[15] referentem vel saltem [88] juxta eorum merita memet[16] gerentem.

Spero[17] tamen Me Hinc inde Melius Conciliis tuis auscutare,[18] monitis tuis obedire ^pro virili^[19] conatu*m* fore. Et quanta in Me posita est vis Me filium patris Jussa præstare gaudentem præbiturum esse, et memet non patris svasiones vili æstimantem esse exhibiturum. quid tibi, quid inquam pollicear? num[20] meipsum quantars[?][21] sim dedam? et exiguum est Me illi dedere,[22] qui nisi fuisset Ipse non essem, tibi[23] deniq*ue* quod possum et quod non possum[24] debeo, et ut solvam quæ debeo, te Humillime obtestor ut in propiisimis ad thronum gratiæ accessibus deum obnixe petas, ut cor novum mihi det, et lapidem in Carneum Mutet,[25] et quod[26] in postero vitæ Meæ cursu, m^a^gis ad illius Honorem et gratiæ suæ gloriam vitam degam, quam in intio[27] ætatis meæ adhuc vixi[28] et ut Deus ille Misericors Omnipotens, peccata Mea sanguine Christi abluat, ut quum vivos et Mortuos Judicat Ego inter Oves apud Dextra*m* suam integer et Immaculatus appaream.

Hæc [deleted word] supliciter petens acquiesco.

O. F.[29]

S. C.

To my most reverend, honored, and dear father:

Since I no less abhor ingratitude than Homer's Achilles[30] a falsehood, and as I was considering to myself how immeasurable was my debt to your kindness, so that it exceeds all my merit and indeed all my service, I thought it would be acceptable to you if I bore witness, as best I could, to a mindful and grateful spirit with a little gift of letters or a little flower plucked from the garden of the Muses. Oh, that I might ever be in a position to repay the benefactions that you have continually, and far beyond my merits, conferred on me! To give adequate thanks—"there's the task, there the painful toil."

In return for your great love for me, and the kindness you have often shown toward me, I not only return most gladly the great thanks that I feel, but also offer and dedicate with a most ready will all my future duties. The anxious cares, the daily anxieties that you suffered for my benefit have not gone unnoticed. Your troubles, your griefs—in short, all your cares for my advantage—are clear. I know how much oil and toil[31] you have spent that I might become a learned man; I know (and better would it have been for me had I known better) how many counsels, how many words of advice you spoke to me, how often you wanted to warn me, that I might become an upright man. How often you advised me, how often you urged me, that I might not become a disgrace to you and a scandal to others! God knows how I then slighted your counsels and did not lead my life according to them; now, however, I am ashamed of my negligence, now I am sick and sorry for my low valuation of them. But ah me! one can see that because of all your benefactions to me I am a Pandora[32] to you, rather than returning thanks for them or even conducting myself according to their merits.

I hope, however, that from now on I will better heed your counsels; that it will be my endeavor to obey your warnings to the best of my ability; that with all the power that is in me I will show myself a son who rejoices to do his father's biddings; and that I will demonstrate that I do not hold my father's persuasions worthless. What, what, I say, should I promise to you? Am I to dedicate myself, such as I am, to you? But it is a meager thing to dedicate myself to him who, had he not existed, I would not exist, and indeed I owe you all that I can do—and what I cannot do. And that I may pay what I owe, I most humbly beg that in your very close approaches to the throne of divine grace you strenuously pray God that he give me a new heart, and change stone to flesh, and that as for the remaining course of my life I may lead my life more for his honor and the glory of his grace than I have hitherto lived in the first part of it, and that merciful and omnipotent God wash off my sins with the blood of Christ, so that when he judges the living and dead I may appear whole and stainless among the sheep at his right hand.

Begging this suppliantly I take comfort

Your most obedient son,

S. C.

1. Morison, "The Reverend Seaborn Cotton's Commonplace Book," CSM, *Publs.,* XXXII, *Trans.* (1933–1937), 338.

2. Morison reports that Edward Kennard Rand, in transcribing the Latin text for the 1937 printing, suggested these initials be expanded to: Patri Reverendissimo Honorabilissimo et Charissimo. George Goebel, whose translation follows, gave invaluable assistance in transcribing the Latin text for the present edition.

3. End-line hyphenation: ab=Horream. Morison and Rand read: abhorream.

4. Morison and Rand: His. The phrase is a much-quoted phrase from Vergil *Aeneid* 6.129.

5. The number 2 is written above the word summo, and the number 1 above the word amore, apparently indicating that the writer wanted the word order reversed.

6. The number 2 is written above paratissimâ, and the number i is written above voluntate, suggesting the author's desire to reverse the word order.

7. Anxietates was intended.

8. Morison and Rand transcribe the word operaci and say: *"Operaeque* is called for." In fact, the manuscript says operæq*ue.*

9. Morison and Rand: possem.

10. Morison and Rand: quoties; quoties was probably intended.

11. Morison and Rand: neu.

12. Cotton first wrote idededori, then wrote a c over the third d.

13. Morison and Rand transcribe the word pendet and say: "should be *poenitet.*" It would seem, however, that pudet was intended.

14. Morison and Rand: poenitet e[ ].

15. Morison and Rand: illas gratias.

16. Morison and Rand: merent.

17. Morison and Rand: Ipero [*sic*], adding the footnote: *"Juro* is called for."

18. auscultare was intended.

19. pro virili parte was probably intended.

20. Morison and Rand: nam.

21. Morison and Rand transcribe this word "quantæ [?]"; quantus might have been intended.

22. Morison and Rand: dedendum. It appears, however, that Seaborn wrote dedede and then deleted the third d and inserted an r.

23. Morison and Rand: essem. Tibi.

24. Morison and Rand: possim.

25. Morison and Rand: Mutat.

26. Morison and Rand: ut quid.

27. initio was intended.

28. Morison and Rand: vixerim [?]. In fact, the final i in vixi is written over an e. Seaborn Cotton might have begun to write vixerim, but altered it to vixi.

29. Morison and Rand suggest this expansion: *"Obedientissimus Filius?"*

30. A reference to the central hero in *The Iliad,* which depicts the consequences of Achilles' wrath against Agamemnon.

31. The phrase is an idiom serving the same use as the English "time and trouble."

32. In Greek myth, Pandora's box contained all the troubles that have beset humanity since she opened it and released them.

John Cotton to a Minister

[1651–1652?]

ADf. MS: BPL, Ms. Am. 1506, pt. 3, app. 4

This letter, engaging in abstract logic chopping about the nature of certain kinds of violation of moral law, with continual use of Latin and Greek phrasing, returns Cotton—reluctantly—to the skills he had developed as a young man at Cambridge and practiced in numerous letters earlier in his life. As his letters repeatedly show, he had always been known for his ability to break down knotty problems, whether theological, ecclesiastical, or simply rational, to reach a balanced conclusion about what he held to be truth. Yet here his opening comments indicate that he is losing his relish for such discourse. He attributes this change to his sense of physical aging, a factor that he would mention again in correspondence of this late period. His "old Head" now prefers "Popular & familiar Disc*o*urse" to "subtile," "scholasticall Quæstions."

Something of this feeling may be reflected in the many deletions, revisions, and blottings on these pages. In this case the holograph is a rough draft. The paper is of inferior quality, with the result that Cotton's ink bled through from each side. The pen frequently cut through, leaving the paper riddled with holes where individual words once were, though occasionally the outlines of the letters remain decipherable. In addition, water damage, especially at the top of the sheet, blurs and sometimes obscures the already crabbed script.

The draft is unsigned and undated. Cotton's complaint of old age is characteristic only of his final year or two, so that Darrett Rutman's suggestion that the letter is from "after 1650" seems accurate.[1] Braces enclose details added from the MHS transcription.

Reverend & deare brother in o*u*r Lord Jesus,

Such scholasticall Quæstions as you p*ro*pound to me, are too subtile for my ˆoldˆ Head ˆ[several illegible words]||edˆ [deleted word] w*i*th Age & wont ˆnot to curious Disputes, butˆ to Popular ~~Disco*u*rse~~ & familiar Disco*u*rse.

But because you Desire a word ^hereof^ from me, [illegibile word] If I might moderate betweene you, & yo*ur* antagonist I should Divide *th*e Trueth [equa]lly betweene you, || Adiudging the Trueth {to} you {in your} 2d Question, {&} to Him in *th*e First. For ^I dare not^ [deleted word] ~~I would say,~~ [five more deleted words] say as He doeth in *th*e 2d Question, *tha*t sinne is a meere Privation i John? 3.[2]

For i. There be some sinnes *tha*t are opposite to Duety, not onely Privative (as He saith) not only [illegible word] (as you iustly alledge) but ^also^ contradictorie. A sinne of Omission is rather ^*th*e^ Absentia Of a Duety, then *th*e Privatio of it.[3]

2. If a sinne of Omission {be}[4] a Privation, is a sin of Com*m*ission a ^me[er]e^ Privation [deleted word] also? Doeth it ^not^ Prove something over & above Omission?

3. Suppose God gave a Com*mandmen*t (as He did) to Moses, spea[ke] noe more to me of this matter, (Deut. 3. 26:)[5] & Putt *th*e Case, Moses had spoken againe of *tha*t matter to God (as humane frailty in a saint of god might have done:) here, the very positive speach of Moses touching this matter had bene a sinne: over & above whatsoever privative Defect might be found in his other speaches.

But He obiecteth, If it be not a meere Privation, then It is Ens,[6] & Omne Ens [est] bonum,[7] & a D[eo] *er*go.[8]

i. T[hou]gh it were a meere Privative, yet still it is Ens, though Ens Privativum:[9] ^Ens privativum is not absoluta non Ens.^[10] As Tenebræ is not non ens, nor ^is^ cæcitas, non ens; they both are bonu*m* ||.[11]

2. Since being Ens is bonum in genere Entis[12] ^though^ not in genere moris:[13] *tha*t is, It is Bonum Metaphysicum, not morale.[14] It is bonum metaphysicum, because ^though it breake a morall Rule yet by a Supernaturall & transcendent Power^ it tendeth to ^supernaturally [deleted word] good ends, to^ Abase *th*e cr[eatu]re, & to glorify god [either his Justice, in Punishing: or his Mercy, in Pardoning.

If it be said, If sinne be a Deo,[15] then God is Author Peccatè:[16] It followeth not. For Author is Causa per se:[17] but sinne is of God, not per se, but per Accidens.[18] And whatsoever is of God any way, is bonum in genere Entis, though not moris.

[IV] But in yo*ur* former Quæstion, I cannot so freely ^goe along w*i*th you:^ [three or four deleted words] which It may be is my owne Dullnesse. ^I doe not Discerne that there is^ || very positive goodnesse ^{in the creature}^ w*i*thout Respect to *th*e {end}.

^For i,^ As Ens & bonum Convertuntur,[19] soe finis & bonum convertuntur:[20] As ||sum Bonum, & finis supre[mus?]|| convertuntur, so also || & Finis supradictus[21] are convertable also.

2. If there might be any posit{ive} goodnesse in *th*e creature {w*i*tho}ut respect, to *th*e end, then god might make a [c]rea[ture] to noe End & yet make it good. But to make a Creature to noe end, is {such a vanitye} as is not possible to be compatible to Divine wisdome & goodnesse. All things *tha*t be, are at least ˆfrom Himself.ˆ

3. This light of Nature shineth forth in com*m*on sp[ea]ch amongst Men: If a man say, This, or *tha*t thing is Good: Another might streight way Aske, Good, for what? for what, implyeth *οὗ ἕνεκα*,[22] *th*e End. If good for nothing, it is not good at all. The Homonymy w*hi*ch you suspect in *th*e Forma Physica, & Forma Logica,[23] I [deleted word] doe not Discerne; for whatsoever *th*e Forme be (Physica, or Logica) the good of it, is || for a proportionable End; Logica forma for a Logicall End, & Physica Forma for a Physicall End.

" The Inference w*hi*ch you ˆObiectˆ||, I doubt will not hold, If finis habet "formam,[24] & forma be alwayes p*ro*pter finem,[25] & be good onely p*ro*pter finem, then God must be good onely for something w*hi*ch is beyond himself &c.

Yo*u*r Antagonist will Answer, the Quæstion is of Positive Good in Creatures ˆw*hi*ch have their {Causes} distinct from *the*ms[elve]sˆ not || *th*e Creato*u*r, T|| hath neither efficient, matter, forme, or end, but ˆin [him]self all h[is]ˆ || ˆcauses toˆ himself. || As He is from Himself, of himself, by himself, so is He also for Himself; w*hi*ch is not compatible to a Created Being.

1. Rutman, *Winthrop's Boston,* 271 n. 57.

2. The final word of this sentence is nearly obscured in the manuscript. The third chapter of 1 John is a strong statement on the seriousness of sin. Verse 4: Whosoever committeth sin transgresseth also the law: for sin is the transgression of the law. Verse 8: He that committeth sin is of the devil. Verse 9: Whosoever is born of God doth not commit sin.

3. Absentia: absence. Privatio: privation or negation.

4. The word be is written over the word were.

5. Deut. 3:26: But the Lord was wroth with me for your sakes, and would not hear me: and the Lord said unto me, Let it suffice thee; speak no more unto me of the matter.

6. Ens: an entity; something that exists.

7. Omne Ens [est] bonum: every entity is good.

8. a Deo *ergo*: from God therefore.

9. Ens privativum: a privative entity.

10. absoluta non ens: an absolute non-entity.

11. As Tenebrae . . . bonu*m:* As darkness is not a nonentity nor is blindness a nonentity; they both are good.

12. bonum in genere Entis: good in respect to existence.

13. in genere moris: in respect to morality.

14. Bonum . . . morale: a metaphysical, not a moral good.

15. a Deo: from God.

16. Author Peccatè: author of sin.

17. Causa per se: cause by itself; essential cause.

18. per Accidens: accidental; contingent.

19. Ens & bonum convertuntur: [The terms] entity and good are convertible (that is, interchangeable).

20. finis & bonum convertuntur: end & good are convertible / interchangeable.

21. Finis supradictus: the aforesaid end.

22. *οὗ ἕνεκα*: wherefore.

23. Forma Physica, & Forma Logica: physical form and logical form.

24. finis habet formam: the end / purpose has a form.

25. propter finem: because of an end / purpose.

John Cotton to [Edward?] Naylor

[1651–1652]

ALS. MS: BPL, Ms. Am. 1506, pt. 3, app. 3

This letter in Cotton's own hand is the most severely mutilated of any of the surviving manuscript letters. It consists of four large sheets, all of which have a large irregular circular hole in the center, apparently created when the twice-folded sheets suffered water damage and then harsh abrasion at one corner. The hole measures 9″ × 5″ at its largest points on the fourth sheet. The question for the editor is whether it is worth trying to present the remaining text at all. The conclusion has been to salvage what can be reclaimed. Though now extremely fragmentary, it is an important letter for its scholarly treatment of the precedents justifying a congregational church polity, and the broken text yields enough substance to give us some idea of Cotton's late thinking on this subject while also adding to our knowledge of Cotton's ongoing dialogue with the church at old Boston.

Cotton addressed the letter "To Mr Naylor of Boston./" at the head of the first page. The historian of the old Boston tells us, "The Corporation Records state, that Mr. *Edward* Naylor was appointed on the 6th August, 1648, to perform the ordinance of baptism within the borough for one year; this was continued in 1650, when Mr. *Edward* Naylor was also appointed to preach within the borough every 3rd Sunday of the year." A footnote to this passage, however, adds: "Mr. *John* Naylor was appointed *'Lecturer* or *Preacher'* in 1645. There is probably a mistake in the name."[1] As Venn indicates, a number of Lincolnshire Naylors matriculated at Cambridge colleges in the first half of the seventeenth century, tending to be Emmanuel, Christ's, and Corpus Christi graduates. An Edward and a John were both ministering in Lincolnshire at the time. Both entries quoted by Thompson could, in fact, be correct, though Cotton's addressee was probably Edward, given his official standing in the Boston church in 1650.

What is clear is that Naylor had written to Cotton in response to his book, *Of the Holinesse of Church-Members* (1650), which, although largely an answer to the two Scottish Presbyterians, Robert Baillie and Samuel Rutherford, had also been intended to benefit Cotton's old friends in Boston (see Cotton to the Boston Congregation, c. 1649–1650). Despite his recurrent complaints of the symptoms of old age, Cotton here roused himself to an energetic and lengthy reply. The letter, when whole, would have provided an interesting supplement to his book.

To Mr Naylor of Boston./

Reverend S*ir*

Yo*ur* Conference ˆw*i*th me,ˆ about the Church estate ˆof Boston,ˆ I willingly & lovingly Accept, both out of my love to Boston (w*hi*ch is engraven in my Heart) & out of my love to the Trueth, w*hi*ch is to be searched after more then hidden Treasur[.]

Two Defects I touched in their Church-estate: i. Their Admission of mor[e] then Prof[essors]|| vnto *th*e Fellowship of *th*e seales. 2. Their Church-governm*en*t ||cted to an entrinsecall Ecclesiasticall Power.
To this latter || first.

You tell me, || the Church w*hi*ch is w*i*thout it, But your ˆway ||ˆ eas|| th*e* Church ˆ||y be said 2 wayes, i. *that*ˆ w*hi*ch pertayneth to noe Chur[ch]|| be w*i*thout *th*e Church, 2. Cor. 5 || ˆthatˆ Particular church, but to || [ἀ]λλοτριοεπισκόπος,[2] if He || who are noe members of his Church ||[bro]therly love. Tertullians [t]estimon[y]||[two or three deleted words] (*that th*e Customs || chu[rc]hes are not extra || chur[ches] are ||

* *[3]

||pose their Custome vpon *th*em *tha*t vsed ||

The Antiqu[ity] of || may be prooven from Scripture, though it seeme Di|| yet I see *tha*t by *th*e Light of his Trueth hath cleared to you || Antiquity of Episcopacy, will in time cleare vp also *th*e Antiquity of *tha*t || w*hi*ch was oppressed by it.

" The Testimony of *th*e Magdeburgenses (in Centur*ians* 2. c*hap*t*er* 7:).[4] you "suppose in it I might easily know, They speake not in o*ur* sence of single "Church[es]|| neither the auntient Churches mentioned by *th*em ˆwereˆ Con-"gregationall || Churches in Germany.

But you must beare w*i*th me, though I doe not know what you think || know. For though I know *tha*t *th*e [chu]rch of Ro[me], & *tha*t of Alexandria did soone goe [deleted word] vltra[5] ||[ch]urches did soone learne to Invade *th*e ||, & o||et I came ||[C]ongregatio[n] [1v] know, or learne by diligent search, but *tha*t some Churches both in *th*e 2d, & 3d century p*re*served, & practiced their Congregationall Power, The Magdeburgenses speaking of *th*e Form of *th*e Governm*en*t of those Churches in *th*e 2d century like vnto a Democ-"racy, doe expresly speake of such singulæ ecclesiæ,[6] w*hi*ch had *th*e same

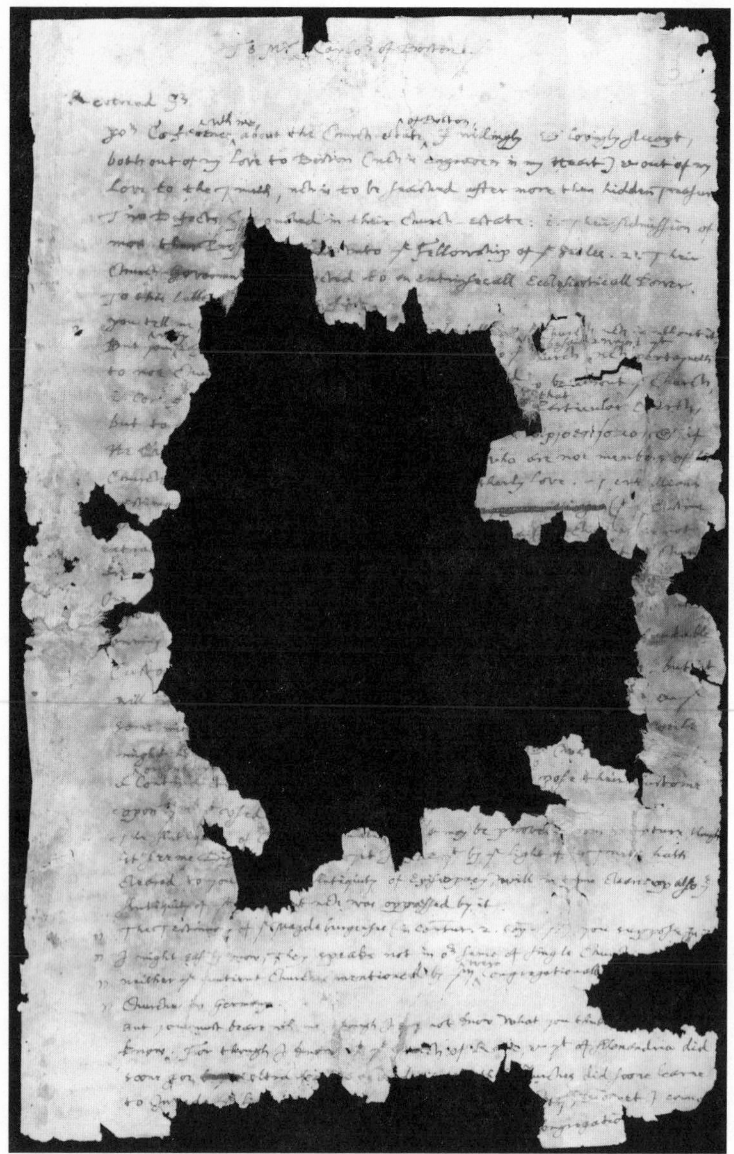

PLATE 18. Cotton to "Mr. Naylor," [1651–1652], first sheet. Written to a minister at Boston, Lincolnshire, Cotton's old parish, in this letter Cotton complains of his weakened eyesight, but wrote the letter neatly with no evidence of physical weakness. This is an extreme example of the severe mutilation suffered by items in Thomas Prince's Library while it was stored in the belfry of Boston's Old South Church following Prince's death. Such a picture indicates the reason for the many frustrating breaks in the printed text of this and other letters in the collection. *Boston Public Library, Ms. Am. 1506, pt. 3, app. 3. Courtesy of the Trustees of the Boston Public Library*

"æquall Power of Preaching *th*e word purely, o[f] Administring sacram*en*ts, of "excom*m*unicating Hæreticks, & notorious offe[nders]|| of choosing, calling, "ordayning & (for iust cause) deposing Ministers, & || of synods &c: w*hi*ch are *th*e Acts [of?] ˆCongregational Churches.ˆ He speaketh therefore of such single churc[hes]|| *th*e word is preached, & sacraments Administred: w*hi*ch ˆAdministrations doe ||ˆ ||[con]gregationall Churches.

And though ||in point of governm*en*t neerly congrega[tional]|| of their superintendents are Modera||hes w*hi*ch *th*e Centurists speake of ||[congrega]tionall Churches. It was enough to||nt Churches from *th*e supremacy of || Churches ||then in Germany, Fraunce || to the [fe]llowship of *th*e Con[gr]egat[ionall]|| go[ve]rnment

* *[7]

"||[C]arthage was a || & you declare ||self to ||tion to be a better witnesse || then "any of former, or latter times || whom *th*|| so mu[ch] as I doe in *tha*t section, "& Practise.

I doe not know wherein I vary from Cyp[rian]|| Practise of Church Discipline, or in this section. If your self vary noe [more from] Him, then I doe, wee shall not vary one from another in this Point; & ˆthe [church at?]ˆ B[osto]n will ˆsoone come toˆ Resemble the church at Carthage. For though the City of Carthage durst sometime emulate Rome, yet I doe not finde, *tha*t *th*e Church of Carthage was as large as *th*e city. I am [no]t afrayd to say (though you think, I will not say it) that the Church [at] Carthage, whereof Cyprian was Bishop, was in his time, a Congregationall [C]hurch.[8] All his Addresses to *th*e Elders & Brethren of *th*e Church in his Epistles, will not fitly be applicable to any Classicall; or Provinciall Church. W[ha]t though He had a great Influence into the Ordering of many Ch[urches] in Numid[ia][9]|| yet *tha*t was not [2] by way of Dominion, but of Brotherly Counsell. It being *th*e maner of the Churches in *tha*t Age, & formerly, to seeke, & give, & take Counsell, one from & to another, not out of subordination, or stated combination, but out of Respect of *th*e Eminent Gifts of Wisedome & Grace, w*hi*ch shined forth in some Churches, above others. Casaubons Testimony of Cyprian[10] is iust ||ingly Accept what you speake of it.

What I spake ||tisfaction [in?] *th*e Presbyterian stating of *th*e Controversy[11] || *th*e sam[e as y]o*ur* dissatisfaction of both *th*e One s[id]e, & other, B[eca]us[e] you || of my vnsatisfaction in their [s]tating of it || their severall Propositions about || their words seeming so much ||ing to || for I||to could ˆnotˆ gather vp their failed judgem*en*t in *th*e P|| though ||hat I meane: &c then I see not why you should ||

* *[12]

What Defects your Elihu[13] findeth in *th*e first Conclusion I am s[orry?] I cannot Discerne. The Decay of my sight, & *th*e sm[allness of?] yo*ur* hand,

& sometimes *the* Abbreviation of yo*u*r words || so hard to it, *tha*t ^(I tell you true)^ I cannot spell [deleted word] what yo|| [It is] w*i*th old men, as w*i*th child[r]en, where they can[no]t ||[they] must skip over it ||

* *[14]

[2v] The latter Part of *the* i. Conclusion, That such Professed Chr*isti*ans ^& such onely^ as doe not scandalize their Profession w*i*th an vnchri*sti*an conversation, are lawfully Receyved members in to *the* visible Church,[15] if this doe not satisfy your Elihu, let him consider, *tha*t scandalous Chri*sti*ans, are *the* p*r*op*er* subjects of excom*m*unication, & therefore not [fit?] materialls for Church Com*m*union.

What I Allege^d^ from P|| doeth ^ [not justify the?] [1]st Conclusion, but *the* 2[d]. It ||

* *[16]

doeth ^not^ Inferre, that *the* Persons gathered were only members of *the* Catholick Church, not of any Particular: [four or five deleted words] For a [g]athering of members may be ^as well^ out of many Particular (though corrupt) [Ch]urches, into One ^more^ Reformed: as out of *the* Catholick.

[Th]e Difference ^betweene^ Confirming members, & gathering of ^a^ Church, doeth not [(for o]ught I see) quite [a]lter *the* [sta]te of *the* Quæstion (as you say, it ||f members into a Church, is || the Confirming || [3] of Members is "spoken to in the 2[d]. And both ^sorts of members^ Agree in this That they doe "Professe before *the* Lord & his People, their Repent[an]ce & Faith in Christ, "& subiection to his Ordinances: & neither of *the*m doe scandalize their Pro- "fession w*i*th an vnchristian Conversation. ^But, say you^ ~~Because you say~~, "Elihu observeth, *tha*t though I state *the* Quæstion of Holynesse required || "Admission, yet some of my strongest Proofes speake of Holyn[esse]|| Ad- "mitted, & *tha*t some [deleted word] time after, w*hi*ch is noe ||all w||rying. As "from i. Cor. i. 2:[17] w*hi*ch is *the* Title of Church-members[18] of some g[r]ounds "^&^ more pl|| where Paul expresseth his go[o]d Thoughts of *the*m a[ll?] beca|| "Partaking of his grace not onely in Beleiving [i]n Christ, || for Him: Now "to Argue from *the* Ap*ost*les Judgem*ent* || after || Tryall by sufferings to what "his Thoughts were of *the*m || is vnsound. And yet much of yo*u*r Argueing "p*ro*ceedeth [on thes]e grounds.

Ans. i If some of my strongest Pr[oofs (as you] call *the*m) speake of H[oly-nesse]||

* *[19]

And when Paul & || (v. 40:) It is said, they comfort || with *the* Brethren of *tha*t Church were then partners of Pa[ul]|| suffering, & had Neede to be Comforted.

Ans. 3. What virtues are re[q]uired in members Ecclesiæ con[stituendæ] some are requisite to be found in Members Ecclesiæ [constitutæ][20]|| sure in *the* first Primitive Church [s]ome were Recey[ved]|| such as gladly Receyved || of Repen|| of Christ, & of saving *th*em || 4i. Neither did *th*e || [3v] Onely if there be any Difference of Holynesse to be Attended betweene members Ecclesiæ constituendæ, & constitutæ, It is more Required (I mean magis, not major)[21] in members of a Church to be constituted, then in some members of a Church constituted. For *th*e Infants of a Church constituted are Accepted as members by a Relati[v]e Holynesse, nor are they cast out of *th*e Church ~~for a single Ignorant~~ || (though they be Absented from *th*e lords supper) for living [in?] Ig[no]rance, till their Ignorance breake forth into open scandall. Th[e] Act [of] *th*e Honourable Parliam*en*t of o||[I]gnorant & scandalous P[er]sons from *th*e Lord[s] Table, wa||me good Advancem*en*t vnto combination betweene *th*e || It were to be wished (besides *th*e ||asing of the || Church by *th*e Elders of another) is That such members of *th*e P|| [who are] not onely Ignorant, but scandalous, might be sequestered fro[m]||ch (as well as from *th*e Lords Table), if they Remaine impœnite[nt]|| such members as ||

* *[22]

Neither doeth it Appeare *tha*t ||m to be of *th*e Tri[be] of Benjamin: or *th*e || that all Benjaminites would b[e] wolves perpetually: ||ally since they did know Isay's Prophecy || as Jacobs, T[h]at *th*e wolf (in *th*e Dayes of *th*e Messiah) should [lie down] w*i*th *th*e Lambe, Jer. 7.ii.[23] Howsoever, that Text is expresse || the church ||ayed of Saul, because they Beleive || not || was a Dis|| non-Disciple is not a wolf. And || *tha*t *th*e Churches Feare we noe || will ||ken, & looking [4] Vpon *th*e Text, He could ˆnot butˆ Discerne [that?] the cause of their F|| was ˆonelyˆ their Doubt[e]s of his Discipleship.

The text in Rom. i4. 1,2,3 with 15.7:[24] was Alledged to Proove, That who|| hath Receyved to Fellowship w*i*th Christ, the Church may Receyve ||w*i*th hirself. || therefore neither doe wee Deny to Accept su[ch] into o*u*r Church-Fellowship, though Presbyteriall || see God hath Re[ceyved them] to [h]is grace in Christ || just Allowance to Receive ignorant Ca[rnall]|| nor will it give ||os just ev||

a Church, where ˆIgnorantˆ Carnall world ||

In sect. i2, the Type of Hewing || Solomons Temple,[25] was Applyed to || to "Christ & equaræ? to their Bret|| Church Fellowship: you say this T|| *th*e Peace "of *th*e Church (soe[?] from || *the*n by the gentiles. ||

* *[26]

In sect [i3]||

"*th*e Te|| Jerome Inte|| keepe || w*hi*ch ||

what then? || yet many class|| by Examination might || vncleane Persons: so || In sect. i4:[27] something is s|| Rev. 2i. 27. & 22. i5[28] || Reade, till I be better || I shall never be || so dim||[4v] [j]udicious Interpreters who take it otherwise. I cannot easily beleive Satan hath bene bound vp these i000 yeares last past, whilst Antichrist, & *th*e Turk & so many malignant Christian Princes have both raged ag*ains*t *th*e Church w*i*th Persecution, & Deceived the Church w*i*th so much Hæresy in Doctrine, Idolatry & Supersti*ti*on [in] worship, & Tyranny in Church-governm*en*t. Faith can beleive ag*ains*t Car[nall?] Grace. but not ag*ains*t ||ight.

|| have not: if you p[lease t]o send me one, I shall give || whiting, to Repay you *th*e price. The Interpretation || I gathered ||ly out of Calvin's, || am I Indulgent to my Fa|| but yeilding to my || by the Civill || I neither finde || nor Old. The People of Christ were || the Rod of his Power: but *th*e Rod was || word. What if they be a willing People in || were not therefore His People in church.

||sling or before the s|| hi[s] People. ||

* *[29]

|| In those || onely) Paul speaketh || Entrance. For *th*e P|| sect. || in Beleiving, & in suffer||retheren ||[Pa]ul calleth *th*e Saints at ||m. For example, || at *th*e first Preaching of || would gratify ||eth expresse Testi|| Enough of Jus|| *th*e Jo|| Alledged from || meanewhile,

* *[30]

|| way of Interpretation of *th*|| Desire, to communicate yo*u*r minde to || Draw vp yo*u*r Thoughts vpon what || Forme of a spirituall Temple is held forth || Church, as Cerebus to Corinth: || of vs engaged to meet in all || you || through his rich

||brotherly love,
||[Co]tton/

1. P. Thompson, *History of Boston,* 164–165.

2. [ἀ]λλοτριοεπισκόπους: busybody. Literally, an overseer of other people's business. See the only scriptural use of the word in 1 Pet. 4:15.

3. Here seven lines contain only one or two complete words each, the rest being lost to the middle of a huge hole in the paper. More text is present nearer the bottom of the page.

4. The so-called Centuriators of Magdeburg, chief of whom was the Lutheran Matthias Flacius, who wrote a thirteen-volume history of the Christian church from its beginnings to 1400, devoting one volume to each century. Published as *Historia Ecclesia Christi* (Basel, 1559–1574), it became known among English scholars as the Magdeburg Centuries.

5. vltra: beyond

6. singulæ ecclesiæ: single, or individual, churches.

7. Five extremely fragmented lines here are omitted.

8. Cotton had long since established in his own mind that Cyprian's example in the very early Christian church justified a congregational church polity. He had mentioned it at length, for instance, in his letter to Samuel Skelton, Oct. 2, 1630, as well as in published works such as *The Keyes of the Kingdom of Heaven* . . . (London, 1644) and *The Way of Congregational Churches Cleared* . . . (London, 1648). His sometime adversary in Scotland, Robert Baillie, would ask, "Why does M. *Cotton* so much labour to make *Cyprian* an Independent, and his rule congre-

gational?" *The Disswasive from the Errors of the Time, Vindicated from the Exceptions of Mr. Cotton and Mr. Tombes* (London, 1655), 50.

9. Numidia was a province of North Africa in the Roman Empire, to the west of Carthage.

10. Isaac Casaubon (1559–1614), a learned Continental scholar who spent his final years in England, studied and wrote about the Church Fathers, though he never wrote a separate volume on Cyprian.

11. Cotton's *Of the Holinesse of Church-Members* (London, 1650) frequently replies to passages in Robert Baillie's *Dissuasive from the Errours of the Time* (London, 1645); and Samuel Rutherford's *Due Right of Presbyteries . . .* (London, 1644).

12. Four lines here are too badly mutilated to be coherent, followed by thirteen lines of text deleted by Cotton. The text resumes for seven lines at the bottom of the page, each interrupted by some paper loss in the lower right corner and in the entire final line.

13. Elihu was apparently used by Naylor as a mask for a person in the St. Botolph's congregation who had criticized some of Cotton's opinions. The allusion is to Job 32–37, where Elihu, a younger friend of Job, reproves Job and the three friends who had not been helpful to Job. Elihu declares his sense of God's justice and wisdom.

14. The remainder of the final two lines on the recto are gone.

15. He is quoting here from *Of the Holinesse,* 19.

16. Here about nineteen lines in the middle of the sheet are badly mutilated, though many words and phrases are legible. Eight lines at the bottom are more coherent.

17. 1 Cor. 1:2: Unto the church of God which is at Corinth, to them that are sanctified in Christ Jesus, called to be saints, with all that in every place call upon the name of Jesus Christ our Lord, both theirs and ours.

18. See Cotton, *Of the Holinesse,* 46.

19. At least nine lines are almost totally gone here.

20. Cotton translates these two phrases himself, just below. Ecclesiæ constituendæ: "of a church to be constituted." Ecclesiæ constitutæ: "of a church constituted."

21. magis = more; major = greater. Cotton means to emphasize the idea that holiness is not necessarily *greater* in a church "to be constituted," only *more needed.*

22. About nine lines here are mostly lost to a hole approximately 6″ wide and 3″ long.

23. Although Cotton clearly cites Jer. 7:11, he appears to be alluding to Isaiah 11, which prophesies the coming of the Messiah. Verse 6: The wolf also shall dwell with the lamb . . . and a little child shall lead them.

24. Here he returns to his discussion in *Of the Holinesse,* 54–55.

Rom. 14:1–3: Him that is weak in the faith receive ye, but not to doubtful disputations. For one believeth that he may eat all things: another, who is weak, eateth herbs. Let not him that eateth despise him that eateth not; and let not him which eateth not judge him that eateth: for God hath received him.

Rom. 15:7: Wherefore receive ye one another, as Christ also received us to the glory of God.

25. See Cotton, *Of the Holinesse,* 80–88.

26. Here some seven lines are either totally lost or suffer so badly from broken paper that very few words can be reconstructed. From 2″ to 4″ is lost from the right edge of the recto here.

27. See Cotton, *Of the Holinesse,* 93–95.

28. Rev. 21:27: And there shall in no wise enter in to it any thing that defileth, neither whatsoever worketh abomination, or maketh a lie: but they which are written in the Lamb's book of life.

Rev. 22:15: For without are dogs, and sorcerers, and whoremongers, and murderers, and idolaters, and whatsoever loveth and maketh a lie.

29. Entire line is lost.

30. Here, again, for some five lines, practically nothing is legible.

A "Scrupler" to John Cotton

[1647–1652]

Published: I. Mather, *First Principles,* 6

Increase Mather introduces this fragment by a "Scrupler" with "And to one who complained of being in the dark about the truth asserted in Mr. *Cottons* printed book concerning the Baptisme of Infants,[1] and that amongst other made this Objection."

when (said that Scrupler)[2] a child comes to know that his Parents are no visible Saints, but appear to be contrary both in Life and Doctrine, and the children had only words and water poured on them, how come these persons to have right to it, the Parents having no visible faith to act in that Ordinance, and their children likewise being uncapable, to hold forth the acts of faith before men.

1. John Cotton, *The Grounds and Ends of the Baptisme of the Children of the Faithfull* . . . (London, 1647).

2. The parenthetical remark is Mather's.

John Cotton to a "Scrupler"

[1647–1652]

Published: I. Mather, *First Principles,* 6

Ieroboam and his wife were neither of them visible Saints, in your Sense, but appeared to be contrary both in *Life* and *Doctrine,* yet the *Circumcision* of their *Son* was not in vain to him, *1 Kings 14. 13.*[1] In this *Case* when the faith of the Parents is wanting, and yet they still live within the *Pale* of the *Church,* though the *Church* be *Corrupt,* and the *Parents* also, yet here the *Speech* of the *Apostle* takes place, what though some believed not, *shall their unbelief make the faith of God of none effect, God forbid,* Rom. 3. 3,4.[2] now the *Faithfulness* of *God* who *keepeth Covenant and mercy to thousands,* supplies the defect of the *Faith* of the *next Parents,* and *maketh good his Covenant* to the *Children* in respect of the *Faith* of their *former Ancestors* in *Elder Ages.*

1. 1 Kings 14:13: And all Israel shall mourn for him, and bury him: for he only of Jeroboam shall come to the grave, because in him there is found some good thing toward the Lord God of Israel in the house of Jeroboam.

2. Rom. 3:3, 4: For what if some did not believe? shall their unbelief make the faith of God without effect? God forbid: yea, let God be true, but every man a liar; as it is written, That thou mightest be justified in thy sayings, and mightest overcome when thou art judged.

John Cotton to [Unknown]

[1647–1652?]

Published: I. Mather, *First Principles,* 6

In the context of his discussion of early New England views on baptism, Increase Mather, paraphrasing a question from a Cotton correspondent, says, "Likewise, in another letter, which is extant, under Mr. *Cottons* own hand writing, to one who thus objected, Carnal children are not fit to renew their Covenant, whilst they are unfit to partake in the Seal of the Covenant, &c. He replies in these words."

Though they be not fit to make such profession of visible faith, as to admit them to the Lords Table, yet they may make profession full enough to receive them to Baptisme, or to the same estate *Ishmael* stood in after Circumcission.[1]

1. Ishmael, born to Abram and the servant woman, Haggai, was circumcised at age thirteen but remained outside God's and Abram and Sarah's full blessing, which was reserved for the child of God's promise, Isaac; see Gen. 16, 17. Cotton is aware of Paul's interpretation of this story in Gal. 4:22–31.

Robert and Mary Burle to "Ministers of Jesus Christ in N England"

[1649–1652?]

Copy. MS: BPL, Ms. Am. 1506, pt. 3, app. 1

The published catalog *The Prince Library* (Boston, 1870) identifies this letter as written by Robert and Mary Burkes. The letter-writers in this case are, rather, Robert and Mary Burle, a relatively obscure couple who when they wrote this letter were living in Providence in the colony of Maryland. This determination is aided by labeling on the verso of the second sheet in the same handwriting as the letter itself, identifying a Mr. Durand as the source of ideas that had become troubling to the Burles.[1] William Durand, an Oxford-educated man (matriculated at Christ Church in 1611 at age eighteen), had written to John Davenport in 1642 indicating that he had been influenced by Davenport's preaching while they were both still in England. He had been in Lower Norfolk County in Virginia, where he was apparently serving as ruling elder and sometime preacher until May 1648, when he and his minister, Thomas Harrison, were expelled from the colony by Governor William Berkeley for refusing to use the Book of Common Prayer. As principled Puritans living in a colony that was mainly loyal to the king and the traditional English church establishment, they were apparently distant victims of the strife of the English Civil Wars.[2] Durand went to the town of Providence in Maryland, but Harrison was in Boston by October 1648. He married a niece of John Winthrop there and remained about two years before returning to England. Meanwhile, in 1649, Robert and Mary Burle were among a group of perhaps as many as three hundred Puritans from Virginia who moved to Providence, Maryland. This letter, therefore, cannot be earlier than 1649 and, given the detail with which it relates the state of religious belief there, was probably written after at least several months' residence there. Robert Burle's will was probated in Maryland in 1672; the records indicate that Mary had died earlier.[3]

There is no mention of Cotton or even of Boston anywhere in this letter. There is no particular reason, therefore, to think it was specifically intended for Cotton, though Durand's membership in the Boston church in 1644 confirms that Cotton would have known him, a fact that could have encouraged the Burles to check with his former teacher. The presence of the letter in the Cotton Papers within the Prince Library clearly associates it with Cotton's correspondence, but is not in itself proof that Cotton received the letter or answered it. Since it is a contemporary copy of the Burles' letter, and not the original, it appears that someone made this copy to make sure it reached the very broad group of "Ministers of Jesus Christ in N England" to whom the authors addressed it. If it was written before 1653, Cotton was surely included in that group, though it is possible that it was written after Cotton's death in December 1652. Its contents are thoroughly consistent with the kind of questions Cotton was repeatedly asked by his correspondents to address, though in this case they are much more uniformly based on radical sectarian departures from accepted Puritan belief and practice than the usual queries.

Many of the ideas described in this letter would have been anathema to the New England ministers, being directly opposed to the norms of Puritan piety. Indeed, they smack primarily of antinomianism, starting quite blatantly with the first one listed in the letter: "That god seeth no sinne in his people," a doctrine which was the "central teaching" of John Eaton, one of the six leading antinomians in England who had constituted "a substantial first wave of Antinomian opinion."[4] Likewise, the claims that the Burles report being preached to their congregation include the ideas that it is unnecessary to pray for forgiveness of sin, given that Christ's sacrifice has already achieved that forgiveness for the elect, and that striving to perform duties that are in keeping with a redeemed life is unnecessary. These claims, like the one that "wee must not stri[v]e to beeleiue" are versions of the Antinomian objections made in New England in the previous decade that the majority of church members and ministers there were under a Covenant of Works. Moreover, the blatant opposition to public "ordina[n]ces" strikes at the very core of Puritan identity, since it was the desire to purify the practice of church ordinances that drove them to become Nonconformists in England and ultimately to emigrate. Such criticism of formal worship and churches was typical of the Seekers as well as the early Quakers. The latter sect became strong in Maryland in the 1650s and counted William Durand among its converts, even while he was playing a prominent role in the colony's government in the period 1654–1658. We do not know whether Durand was the one chiefly responsible for promulgating the ideas listed by the Burles, but some of the tenets could well be evidence of his incipient Quakerism.[5] Indeed, although the Burles end their letter wishing to believe "many of these to be truthes," the New England clerics whom they addressed would not have found them so.

Occasional underlining in the letter appears to be by Prince and is eliminated.

Concerning the differences in Judgment amongst vs here at Prouidence truly
so it is that wee are in a very sadd condition: thereby, beeing a Company
(most of vs) very weake & darke in the things of god, many things haue
been held forth in publike and affirmed to bee the teachings of god, but
being nott cleare to vs by scripture wee dare not so receue them, least wee
deceue o*u*r owne soules, some few of them I shall here sett downe as the
1. Lord shall strengthen my weakend memory; one is That god seeth no sinne in
his people: & takes no notice of sinne in his people, maintained from the 16.
Eeckel where the L*or*d setts forth the wickednes of his people there, especialy
in the 48: & 60 verses (ˆthe L*or*d saithˆ notwithstanding their wickednes
w*hi*ch was greater then the sinn of Samaria & Sodome) yet neuertheles I will
remmember my Couenant[6] & in Jer: 31:37.[7]

2 Annother thing is, that Christ & the soule haue vnion & Comunion
together, as well when the soule is in the ~~act~~ act of sinne as at any other tyme:[8]
yea more as a father when his child is dangerously sicke hee will bestir ˆhimˆ
~~it~~ selfe most to do it good.

3 That gods people haue no cause of feare, although they should be ou*er*-
come w*i*th great sinnes. as murther, adultrey &c p*ro*ued out 49 psa 5.[9]

4 Annother is that wee must not striue to beeleue, but *tha*t wee mayst sitt
still in sillence & *tha*t wee must not rest vppon p*ro*mises. for the people of
the old world might hang vppon the outsides of the Arke, but the tempest
washed them all away, none were saued but those *tha*t got into the arke so

none shalbe saued but those *tha*t are in *Chris*t & Christ real*l*y in them, & exept they & *Chris*t be one as *Chris*t & the father is one [this is truth but many poore soules cannot experie*n*c this vnion with *Chris*t therfore the p*ro*phet ~~Haggie~~ ˆEsay:ˆ saith if their bee any in darknes & seeth no light let him stay himselfe vpon his god.][10] and when the L*or*d doth not experience this vnion w*i*th *Chris*t the Lord (I hope hath taught me to wait vpon his mercy psal 147: 10: 11[11]

5 Annother thing is that wee must not pray for pardon of sinne, if euer the Lord hath made it out to vs, that all our sinns are done away in the blood of *Chris*t (for *Chris*t hath ˆonceˆ offered him selfe a full & sufficient sacrifice for all o*u*r sinnes past p*re*sent & to come, if therfore a *Chris*tian falling into any sinne, do pray for forgiuenes, it argues *tha*t he doth not beeleue, that *Chris*t did offer such a sufficient sacrifice, that therfore god may say to such a one what would you haue, would you haue me giue my sonne againe to die for you (further) that for a *Chris*tian to aske pardon for sinne after god hath made it out to him that all his sinnes are done away in *Chris*t, it is as if a poore man begging an almes of a Rich man & haueing receaued it, shall still cry I pray sir bestow somthing vpon me[.]

6 Annother thing is that all a mans praiers & Performance of dutyes, if they bee not the pure breathings of the spiritt, they are but our owne actings & ~~the~~ ˆbutˆ the words and the crying of the creature for things contrary to the will of god, if a mans praiers be the pure breathings of the spiritt, then a man in duties is carried forth in power, aboue & beyond himselfe: if a man in duties be not so acted & carried forth in such a powerfull manner, theˆnˆ his duties are but his owne actings, & but from a principle of the old adam & but from flesh & the acting of the creature, a mans striueing to saue himselfe, & if therfor wee must cease from such our owne actings, because our owne actings do hinder & p*re*uent gods acctings in vs [[12]and vpon this ground family duties a[re] neglegted by very many amongst vs, yea the crauing of a blessing vpon god[s] creatures before the are eaten & Returning thanks for them after they are receiued, is also neglegted, & some *tha*t haue done so beeing asked the Reson [IV] why they did neglegt the~~ir~~ duty they haue answered because the were not moued by the spirit, so to do, it is accompted but a formall thing to do it, or to pray euening & morning, I was tould by one of the bretheren that one beeing bidden to eat (beeing from home) hee lifted vp his eyes to heuen & in his thoughts, sought god for a blessing on *tha*t he went about to receue, & was reproued by annother that stood by, so brother you cannot leaue your formes yett.

7 Singing of psalmes is also left of as a ceremony, a forme, a dead ordince[13] & it is affirmed *tha*t now *Chris*t is comming to destroy all formes of worshipp & that he will haue a glorious church vpon earth without spott; a people of

pure language, beeing altogether accted by the spiritt, & *tha*t they shall haue such a fulnes & p*re*sence of *Chris*t in spiritt that they shall desire no more of the spiritt, that all their workes are done by *Chris*t for them ~~heb: 4: 10~~ so *tha*t now a saint hath nothing to do nor act for it is done for them heb: 4: 10 [14]

8 Oridinaces (in the publike) are held forth to be ^but^ loss & dung & to be our Idolls & if god do not take *the*m away & giue vs Christ, their is nothing but perishing. And continualy ordinances are hinted at & spoken against, w*hi*ch is much trouble to vs to heere, they beeing gods owne appointments. the Lord hauing holpen vs through mercy (when wee inioyed them) to find & feele his p*er*sonne in them, & further I hope the Lord hath taught vs not to esteeme of them ^further^ *tha*n hee is pleased to ~~p~~ appere in them & to comunicate him selfe in them, for true it is they are empty things ~~without~~ without his presence in them, but the soule, that hath found gods p*er*sonne in them, hath good gronds wee thinke to wait vpon God in them as the lame & impotent man at the poole of Bethesday for the spirtts moueing of the watter,[15]

9 Annother thing held forth is *tha*t all the p*ro*mises in scripture are made vnto Christ the second Adam, & not vnto vs therfore if wee rest vpon p*ro*m-ises & lay hold ^vp^on them wee doe but as one *tha*t may gett the deeds of an heiresse lands into his hands w*hi*ch will doe him no good exept hee be mar-ried to the heiresse, for they shalbe all fetched out of his hands againe. So exept a soule bee married to *Chris*t, to whome all the p*ro*mises are made & bee in vnion w*i*th *Chris*t those p*ro*mises will do him no good & stand him in no stead [but many poore soules may not experience marriadge to & vnion w*i*th *Chris*t & then hath nothing to do with p*ro*mises][16] that god the father should say to Christ, man will sinne & fall & destroy himselfe, exept thou who art a mighty p*er*son wilt vndertake for him: I will saith *Chris*t. if they ow thee any thing put *tha*t to my acct & vppon *tha*t condition *tha*t *Chris*t would lay downe his life for man. all the p*ro*mises were made to him Philemon verse 18[17]

10 Annother is that wee must not stri[v]e to beeleiue, for that is but the act-ing of the creature to saue it selfe & is from the Antichrist within vs; that in so doeing man is sett to worke from the same principle, as if he should goe about to keepe the law to bee saued, therfore wee must sitt still in silence till god worke faith in vs, for man to endeuor to beleue, is butt gadding about to chainge his way Jer 2:36.[18] that god will make all his ashamed of their acct-ings to beleue & striueing to beeleue, as well as their striueing to obey the lawe as there in Jer 2:36, god would make his people ashamed of Egipt as they were of Assiria, that a man striueing to beleeue ~~doth but~~ doth but seeke to find his life in his owne hand, therfore he shalbe wearied in the greatnes of his way Isay 57: 10: 12:[19] & therfore the L*or*d saith I will declare thy Righ-teosnes & thy workes for they shall not p*ro*fitt thee. [but I suppose that there

the Lord meanes as [2] A rightiousnes & workes, w*hi*ch they sought, that was contrary to his word, & not for practising any thing that he commanded][20] the seeming acting of the creature is but from the first Adam & the more wee do the farther wee are from *Chris*t the more in the mire,

11 That place In the 33 Esay 21[21] hath bee thus opend, the Lord shalbe vnto all his a place of broad rivers ~~with~~ & streames wherin shall goe no galley w*i*th oares that is their shalbe no need of tugging of the creature in duties, neither shal gallant shipp pas ^there^ by, *tha*t is their shall not need any sailes or topsailes w*i*th flags & streamers no highe & loftiy actings of man or creatures; but the Lord shalbe all to & doe all for his people [deleted letter] this is applied to be the condition of all *tha*t are in *Chris*t, *tha*t inioy *Chris*t in spirit *tha*t are in a full inioyment of god./

Wee ~~be~~ doe suppose many of these to be truthes, but do apr*e*hend them to bee held forth darkley, & do apr*e*hend some of them to be held forth contrary to the current of scriptures, & not according to the mouing of the holy Ghost, the Lord in mery[22] teach vs by his spiritt in his word, wee know not what to doe but desire to haue our eyes towards him, I pray God if it bee his will to send vs our Pastour & his ordinces againe[23] (although that some amongst vs looke vpon both pastour & Ordinaces ~~to be~~ ^as our^ Idols) in the meane time while the Lord is pleased to exercisse vs without them to suply our wants by the p*re*sence of his spiritt, & concerning these things wherin wee are vnsatisfied our desires is to haue ^the^ Judgment of some of the ministeres of Jesus *Chris*t in N England;

your poore weake brother & sister in Christ
Robert & Mary Burle

1. "Mr Burles & his wife/ Their l*ett*er desiring solution/ in some doctrines d*elivere*d among/ them; by Mr Durand,/ which they question the truth/ of ~~them~~ & intreat some/ ministers of *Chris*t in N England/ to deliver their Judgment/ in them."

2. For this perspective and further detail on Harrison, Durand, and the context as well as consequences of their removal from Virginia, see James Horn, *Adapting to a New World: English Society in the Seventeenth-Century Chesapeake* (Chapel Hill, N.C., 1994), 388–394.

3. On Durand and the settlement of Providence, see Edward D. Neill, *The Founders of Maryland* . . . (Albany, N.Y., 1876), 116 n. 1; *Alumni Oxonienses,* I, 434; John Fiske, *Old Virginia and Her Neighbors* (Boston, 1902), 365; Babette M. Levy, "Early Puritanism in the Southern and Island Colonies," in American Antiquarian Society, *Proceedings,* LXX (1960), 130, 237. Robert and Mary Burle were transported to Maryland, with "three sons and three other persons," including the wife of Robert, Jr., suggesting that the Burles were at least middle-aged. See Gust Skordas, ed., *The Early Settlers of Maryland* (Baltimore, 1968), 72; see also Jane Baldwin, comp., *The Maryland Calendar of Wills,* I (Baltimore, 1901), 184.

The most authoritative source on Thomas Harrison is Francis Burton Harrison, "Commentaries upon the Ancestry of Benjamin Harrison IV: The Reverend Thomas Harrison, Berkeley's 'Chaplain,'" *Virginia Magazine of History and Biography,* LIII (1945), 302–311. For relevant primary documents and further discussion, see also Edward D. Neill, *Virginia Carolorum: The Colony under the Rule of Charles the First and Second, A.D. 1625–A.D. 1685, Based upon Manuscripts and Documents of the Period* (Albany, N.Y., 1886), 195–207, 250–251, 418–419.

4. T. D. Bozeman, "The Glory of the 'Third Time': John Eaton as Contra-Puritan," *Journal of Ecclesiastical History,* XLVII (1996), 640, 645n.

5. On Durand and the Quakers, see Kenneth L. Carroll, "Elizabeth Harris, the Founder of American Quakerism," *Quaker History,* LVII (1968), 100–101.

6. Ezek. 16:48: As I live, saith the Lord God, Sodom thy sister hath not done, she nor her daughters, as thou hast done, thou and thy daughters. Ezek. 16:60: Nevertheless I will remember my covenant with thee in the days of thy youth, and I will establish unto thee an everlasting covenant.

7. Jer. 31:37: Thus saith the Lord; If heaven above can be measured, and the foundations of the earth searched out beneath, I will also cast off all the seed of Israel for all that they have done, saith the Lord.

8. An anonymous publication in London in 1644, *A Declaration against the Antinomians and Their Doctrine of Liberty,* had listed seven basic "Antinomian Conclusions." The fourth was "That only such as are elected, are at all times beloved of God, in what condition soever they be, be they never so great sinners, yea in the very act of sinne itself." Quoted in Gertrude Huehns, *Antinomianism in English History, with Special Reference to the Period 1640–1660* (London, 1951), 8.

9. Ps. 49:5: Wherefore should I fear in the days of evil, when the iniquity of my heels shall compass me about?

This doctrine appears to be a compressed version of three of "The Antinomian Conclusions" listed in 1644: "(1) That God doth never inflict punishment upon the Elect for his sins. (2) That God is never angry with his children. (3) That God sees no sin in those that are his." Quoted in Huehns, *Antinomianism in English History,* 8.

10. These are the letter-writers' brackets.

11. Ps. 147:10–11: He delighteth not in the strength of the horse: he taketh not pleasure in the legs of a man. The Lord taketh pleasure in them that fear him, in those that hope in his mercy.

12. This bracket was inserted by the letter-writers; either they or the copyist neglected to put in a closing bracket.

13. Contrast this view with Cotton's "Doctrine of Truth": "That singing of Psalmes with a lively voyce is an holy Duty of Gods Worship," in his *Singing of Psalmes a Gospel-Ordinance . . .* (London, 1647), 2.

14. Heb. 4:10: For he that is entered into his rest, he also hath ceased from his own works, as God did from his.

15. See John 5:1–9.

16. These are the letter-writers' brackets.

17. Philem. 18: If he hath wronged thee, or oweth thee ought, put that on mine account.

18. Jer. 2:36: Why gaddest thou about so much to change thy way? thou also shalt be ashamed of Egypt, as thou wast ashamed of Assyria.

19. Isa. 57:10, 12: Thou art wearied in the greatness of thy way; yet saidst thou not, There is no hope: thou hast found the life of thine hand; therefore thou wast not grieved. . . . I will declare thy righteousness, and thy works; for they shall not profit thee.

20. These are the letter writers' brackets.

21. Isa. 33:21: But there the glorious Lord will be unto us a place of broad rivers and streams; wherein shall go no galley with oars, neither shall gallant ship pass thereby.

22. That is, mercy.

23. Thomas Harrison, who had been the congregation's pastor at Nansemond, Virginia, before its expulsion by Governor Berkeley, was at this time either in New England or England, depending on when the letter was written. His stay in Boston was from at least October 1648 until sometime in 1650, and perhaps longer. He never returned to Maryland, instead becoming minister of St. Dunstan's in London, where he occasionally preached before Oliver Cromwell. By 1657 Harrison was in Dublin, serving as chaplain to Cromwell's son, Henry, the lord lieutenant of Ireland.

Sir Richard Saltonstall to John Cotton and John Wilson

[Late 1651–Early 1652]

Published: Hutchinson, *Collection,* 401–402; MHS, *Colls.,* 2d Ser., IV (1846), 171–172; [Leverett Saltonstall], *Ancestry and Descendants of Sir Richard Saltonstall, First Associate of the Massachusetts Bay Colony and Patentee of Connecticut* (Boston, 1897), 67–68; *Saltonstall Papers,* I, 148–150; John Adair, *Founding Fathers: The Puritans in England and America* (London, 1982), 240–241; Myra Jehlen and Michael Warner, eds., *The English Literatures of America, 1500–1800* (New York, 1997), 457–458 (misattributed to Sir Richard's son). Abridged versions, often with no indication of elisions: Isaac Backus, *A History of New England, with Particular Reference to the . . . Baptists,* I (Boston, 1777), 245–246, and 2d ed., with notes by David Weston (1871; rpt. New York, 1969), I, 199–200; "The Fathers of New England," *Edinburgh Review,* CII (1855), 564; Joseph B. Felt, *Ecclesiastical History of New England . . .* (Boston, 1855–1862), II, 60–61; Richard Hildreth, *The History of the United States of America,* rev. ed. (New York, 1877), I, 382–383; Augustine Jones, *The Life and Work of Thomas Dudley, the Second Governor of Massachusetts* (Boston, 1900), 241

In L. Thompson, "Letters of John Cotton," 213–215

Sir Richard Saltonstall (1586–1661) was one of the founders of the Massachusetts Bay Colony and was a signer of the original charter. A widower, he migrated with five of his six children to New England with the Winthrop company and settled at Watertown in 1630, where he was immediately selected as magistrate and justice of the peace. He stayed in the colony less than a year, however, embarking for England with three of his children on April 1, 1631. He remained interested in the colony for several years but never returned. The following letter is his last known contact with the colony of Massachusetts Bay.[1] Saltonstall forcefully raises an issue that had surfaced frequently among New England's friends and foes alike in the old country during the previous decade: their apparent unwillingness to tolerate religious difference. The reply from Cotton and Wilson is usually cited for its harshness, which is then taken as typically Puritan. Usually ignored in such constructions—which are of course not entirely inaccurate—is the assertion in the New Englanders' reply that there *is* in fact room in New England for a range of practices and beliefs: "wee have tolerated in our church some Anabaptists, some Antinomians, and some Seekers, and do so still at this day." Though Cotton begins his reply to Sir Richard sternly, pointing out that the sectaries of whom Saltonstall speaks had arrived uninvited and that there is nothing unlawful in compelling people to honor the Sabbath, he follows that attitude with a mid-seventeenth-century Massachusetts view of what had been accomplished so far by way of establishing a working community. The majority do not insist on unanimity, he says, and they do not claim infallibility. They have learned over time the lesson of "unity in the foundation of religion and of church order." They have learned and now practice, Cotton says, "unity of the spirit." He does not add, but might have added, that it was the extent of their enthusiasm for their views that determined the level of tolerance (or intolerance) that sectarian newcomers were afforded. He did say, by way of balance, that "wee are loth to be blowne up and downe (like chaff) by every wind of new notions."[2] The exchange is important for demonstrating the differing views on the two sides of the ocean of New England's position on toleration. Cotton warns Sir Richard against making a simplistic accusation from a much too-distant point of view.

Hutchinson's note says that this letter and Cotton's reply "are without date. . . . These Letters must have been wrote between 1645 and 1653." Since the trial and punishment of the three Baptists mentioned in both letters occurred on July 31, 1651, however, Saltonstall's letter could not have been written before autumn of 1651, and the reply from Cotton was probably written in early 1652. Hutchinson, in a footnote to his printing of the letter, says that it "was sent me by the Rev. Mr. Mather."[3] The address block is printed by Hutchinson at the end of the letter:

> For my reverend and worthyly much
> esteemed friends Mr. Cotton and
> Mr. Wilson, preachers to the church
> which is at Boston in New-England,
> give this.

Reverend and deare friends, whom I unfaynedly love and respect,

It doth not a little grieve my spirit to heare what sadd things are reported dayly of your tyranny and persecutions in New-England, as that you fyne, whip and imprison men for their consciences.[4] First, you compell such to come into your assemblyes as you know will not joyne with you in your worship, and when they shew their dislike thereof or witnes against it, then you styrre up your magistrates to punish them for such (as you conceyve) their publicke affronts. Truely, friends, this your practice of compelling any in matters of worship to doe that whereof they are not fully persuaded, is to make them sin, for soe the apostle (Rom. 14 and 23.) tells us,[5] and many are made hypocrites thereby, conforming in their outward man for feare of punishment. We pray for you and wish you prosperitie every way, hoped the Lord would have given you so much light and love there, that you might have been eyes to God's people here, and not to practice those courses in a wildernes, which you went so farre to prevent. These rigid wayes have layed you very lowe in the hearts of the saynts. I doe assure you I have heard them pray in the publique assemblies that the Lord would give you meeke and humble spirits, not to stryve soe much for uniformity as to keepe the unity of the spirit in the bond of peace.

When I was in Holland about the beginning of our warres,[6] I remember some christians there that then had serious thoughts of planting in New-England, desired me to write to the governor thereof to know if those that differ from you in opinion, yet houlding the same foundation in religion, as Anabaptists, Seekers, Antinomians, and the like, might be permitted to live among you, to which I received this short answer from your then governour Mr. Dudley,[7] God forbid (said he) our love for the truth should be growne soe could that we should tolerate errours, and when (for satisfaction of myself and others) I desired to know your grounds, he referred me to the books written here between the Presbyterians and Independents, which if that had been sufficient, I needed not have sent soe farre to understand the reasons of your practice, I hope you doe not assume to yourselves infallibilitie of judgment, when the most learned of the Apostles confesseth he knew but in parte and sawe but darkely as through a glass,[8] for God is light, and no further than he doth illuminate us can we see, be our partes and learning never soe great. Oh that all those who are brethren, though yet they cannot thinke and speake the same things might be of one accord in the Lord. Now the God of patience and consolation grant you to be thus mynded towards one another, after the example of Jesus Christ our blessed Savyor, in whose everlasting armes of protection hee leaves you who will never leave to be

Your truly and much affectionate
friend in the nearest union,
Ric. Saltonstall

1. See the biography of Sir Richard Saltonstall by Robert E. Moody in *Saltonstall Papers,* I, 3–24.

2. Cotton had expressed these views in print previously. See his *Reply to Mr. Williams, His Examination . . . ,* in *The Complete Writings of Roger Williams* (New York, 1963), II, 28, and *The Bloudy Tenent, Washed, and Made White . . .* (London, 1647), 27. Timothy L. Hall comments briefly on these passages in *Separating Church and State: Roger Williams and Religious Liberty* (Urbana, Ill., 1998), 61–62.

3. Hutchinson, *Collection,* 401, 407. He refers here to Samuel Mather.

4. Sir Richard had in mind the recent experiences of three Rhode Island Baptists who in 1651 had gone to Lynn, where they were apprehended and jailed on July 31 for speaking against infant baptism. John Crandall was fined five pounds but released on bail. John Clarke was fined twenty pounds, which someone paid for him, gaining his release. Obadiah Holmes was deemed the greatest offender and was fined thirty pounds, which he refused to pay. He was accordingly taken to the whipping post, where alternative punishment, thirty lashes with a three-corded whip, was inflicted. By the time Saltonstall wrote this letter, John Clarke was back in England, where he published an attack on the Massachusetts Bay Colony called *Ill Newes from New-England; or, A Narrative of New-Englands Persecution . . .* (London, 1652). Whether Saltonstall knew about this affair from Clarke's book or Clarke himself, or perhaps from a meeting with Roger Williams, who was in England in late 1651, is not known. The case became notorious in early Baptist historiography; see, for instance, Backus, *A History of New England* (1777), I, 207–266, which includes a first-person narrative by Obadiah Holmes himself. Ultimately, it was ranked as "one of the most celebrated cases of American Baptist martyrology." William G. McLoughlin, *Soul Liberty: The Baptists' Struggle in New England, 1630–1833* (Hanover, N.H., 1991), 30. Sydney V. James also provides a brief narration of the incident in *John Clarke and His Legacies: Religion and Law in Colonial Rhode Island, 1638–1750,* ed. Theodore Dwight Bozeman (University Park, Pa., 1999), 45–48.

5. Rom. 14:23: And he that doubteth is damned if he eat, because he eateth not of faith: for whatsoever is not of faith is sin.

6. Sir Richard was in Holland in 1640, 1643, and 1644 (*Saltonstall Papers,* I, 150 n. 3). The English Civil Wars began in late 1642.

7. Thomas Dudley was governor of Massachusetts Bay in 1634, 1640, 1645, and 1650. Saltonstall's letter was probably written in 1644, arriving in New England early in Dudley's 1645 term as governor.

8. Paul, "the most learned of the Apostles," wrote in 1 Cor. 13:12: For now we see through a glass, darkly; but then face to face: now I know in part; but then shall I know even as also I am known.

John Cotton [and John Wilson(?)] to Sir Richard Saltonstall

[1652]

Published: Hutchinson, *Collection,* I, 403–407; abridged version: Isaac Backus, *A History of New England, with Particular Reference to the . . . Baptists,* I (Boston, 1777), 246–249, and 2d ed., with notes by David Weston (1871; rpt. New York, 1969), I, 199–200; Myra Jehlen and Michael Warner, eds., *The English Literatures of America, 1500–1800* (New York, 1997), 458–460 (misidentifies the recipient as Sir Richard's son)

In L. Thompson, "Letters of John Cotton," 216–221

Hutchinson does not print a signature line, so it is not clear whether this letter was signed by both Cotton and Wilson, or just Cotton. The use throughout of first person plural pronouns suggests dual authorship, although Hutchinson's heading reads: "Copy of Mr. Cotton's Answer to a Letter from Sir Richard Saltonstall."

Honoured and deare Sir,

My brother Wilson and selfe doe both of us acknowledge your love, as otherwise formerly, so now in the late lines wee received from you, that you grieve in spirit to heare dayly complaints against us, it springeth from your compassion of our afflictions therein, wherein wee see just cause to desire you may never suffer like injury yourselfe, but may finde others to compassionate and condole with you. For when the complaints you hear of are against our tyranny and persecutions in fining, whipping and imprisoning men for their consciences, be pleased to understand wee looke at such complaints as altogether injurious in respect of ourselves, who had noe hand or tongue at all to promote either the coming of the persons you ayme at into our assemblyes, or their punishment for their carriage there. Righteous judgment will not take up reports, much lesse reproaches, against the innocent. The cry of the sinnes of Sodome was great and loude, and reached up to heaven; yet the righteous God (giving us an example what to doe in the like case) he would first goe downe to see whether their crime were altogether according to the cry, before he would proceede to judgement, Gen. 18. 20, 21.[1] and when he did finde the truth of the cry, he did not wrap up all alike promiscuously in the judgement, but spared such as he found innocent; wee are amongst those whom (if you knew us better) you would account of (as the matron of

Abel spake of herselfe) peaceable in Israel, 2 Sam. 20. 19.[2] Yet neither are wee so vast in our indulgence or toleration as to thinke the men you speake of suffered an unjust censure. For one of them (Obadiah Holmes)[3] being an excommunicate person himselfe, out of a church in Plymouth patent, came into this jurisdiction and took upon him to baptize, which I thinke himselfe will not say he was compelled here to performe. And he was not ignorant that the rebaptizing of an elder person, and that by a private person out of office and under excommunication, are all of them manifest contestations against the order and government of our churches established (wee know) by Gods law, and (he knoweth) by the lawes of the country. And wee conceive wee may safely appeale to the ingenuity of your owne judgement, whether it would be tolerated in any civill state, for a stranger to come and practise contrary to the knowne principles of their church estate? As for his whipping, it was more voluntarily chosen by him than inflicted on him. His censure by the court was to have payed (as I know) 30 pounds or else to be whipt, his fine was offered to be payed by friends for him freely; but he chose rather to be whipt; in which case, if his suffering of stripes was any worship of God at all, surely it could be accounted no better than will-worship. The other (Mr. Clarke)[4] was wiser in that point and his offence was lesse, so was his fine lesse, and himselfe (as I heare) was contented to have it payed for him, whereupon he was released. The imprisonment of either of them was noe detriment. I believe they fared neither of them better at home, and I am sure Holmes had not been so well clad of many yeares before.[5]

But be pleased to consider this point a little further. You thinke to compell men in matter of worship is to make men sinne, according to Rom. 14. 23.[6] If the worship be lawfull in itselfe, the magistrate compelling him to come to it compelleth him not to sinne, but the sinne is in his will that needs to be compelled to a christian duty. Josiah compelled all Israel, or (which is all one) made to serve the Lord their God, 2 Chron. 34. 33.[7] yet his act herein was not blamed but recorded amongst his virtuous actions. For a governour to suffer any within his gates to prophane the sabbath, is a sinne aginst the 4th commandment, both in the private householder and in the magistrate; and if he requires them to present themselves before the Lord, the magistrate sinneth not, nor doth the subject sinne so great a sinne as if he did refraine to come. If the magistrate connive at his absenting himselfe from sabbath duties the sinne will be greater in the magistrate than can be in the others passive comeing. Naamans passive goeing into the house of Rimmon did not violate the peace of his conscience, 2 Kings 5. 18, 19.[8] Bodily presence in a stewes,[9] forced to behold the leudnesse of whoredomes there committed, is noe whoredome at all. Noe more is it spirituall whoredome to be compelled by force to goe to masse.

But (say you) it doth but make men hypocrites, to compell men to conforme the outward man for feare of punishment. If it did so, yet better to be hypocrites than prophane persons. Hypocrites give God part of his due, the outward man, but the prophane person giveth God neither outward nor inward man.

Your prayers for us wee thankfully acccept, and wee hope God hath given us so much light and love (which you thinke wee want) that if our native country were more zealous against horrid blasphemies and heresies than wee be, wee believe the Lord would looke at it as a better improvement of all the great salvations he hath wrought for them than to sett open a wide doore to all abominations in religion. Doe you thinke the Lord hath crowned the state with so many victoryes that they should suffer so many miscreants to pluck the crown of soveraignty from Christs head? Some to deny his godhead, some his manhood; some to acknowledge noe Christ, nor heaven, nor hell, but what is in a mans selfe? Some to deny all churches and ordinances, and so to leave Christ noe visible kingdome upon earth? And thus Christ by easing England of the yoke of a kingdome shall forfeit his owne kingdome among the people of England. Now God forbid, God from heaven forbid, that the people and state of England should so ill requite the Lord Jesus. You know not, if you thinke wee came into this wildernesse to practise those courses here which wee fled from in England. Wee believe there is a vast difference betweene mens inventions and God's institutions; wee fled from mens inventions, to which wee else should have beene compelled; wee compell none to mens inventions.

If our wayes (rigid wayes as you call them) have layd us low in the hearts of God's people, yea and of the saints (as you stile them) wee doe not believe it is any part of their saintship. Michal had a low esteeme of Davids zeale, but he was never a whit lower in the sight of God, nor the higher.[10]

What you wrote out of Holland to our then governor Mr. Dudley, in behalfe of Anabaptists, Antinomians, Seekers, and the like, it seemeth, mett with a short answer from him, but zealous; for zeal will not beare such mixtures as coldnesse or lukewarmenesse will, Revel. 2. 2. 14. 15. 20.[11] Neverthelesse, I tell you the truth, wee have tolerated in our church some Anabaptists, some Antinomians, and some Seekers, and do so still at this day; though Seekers of all others have least reason to desire toleration in church fellowship. For they that deny all churches and church ordinances since the apostacy of Antichrist, they cannot continue in church fellowship but against their owne judgment and conscience; and therefore 4 or 5 of them who openly renounced the church fellowship which they had long enjoyed, the church said amen to their act, and (after serious debate with them till they had nothing to answer) they were removed from their fellowship.[12] Others carry their dissent more privately and inoffensively, and so are borne withall in much meekenesse. Wee are farr from arrogating infallibility of judgement to ourselves or affecting uniformity; uniformity God never required, infallibility he never granted us. Wee content ourselves with unity in the foundation of religion and of church order: Superstructures wee suffer to varie; wee have here presbyterian churches as well as congregationall, and have learned (through grace) to keepe the unity of the spirit in the bond of peace; onely wee are loth to be blowne up and downe (like chaff) by every winde of new notions.

You see how desirous wee are to give you what satisfaction wee may to your loveing expostulation, which wee pray you to accept with the same spirit of love wherewith it is endited. The Lord Jesus guide and keepe your heart for ever in the wayes of his trueth and peace. So humbly commending our due respect and hearty affection to your worship, wee take leave and rest.

1. Gen. 18:20–21: And the Lord said, Because the cry of Sodom and Gomorrah is great, and because their sin is very grievous; I will go down now, and see whether they have done altogether according to the cry of it, which is come unto me; and if not, I will know.

2. 2 Sam. 20:19: I am one of them that are peaceable and faithful in Israel: thou seekest to destroy a city and a mother in Israel: why wilt thou swallow up the inheritance of the Lord?

3. Obadiah Holmes: see Saltonstall to Cotton and Wilson, late 1651–early 1652, n. 3.

4. Dr. John Clarke: see ibid., n. 4.

5. According to John Spur, a member of the Boston church who witnessed Holmes's whipping, Cotton had been less temperate on the subject of punishment of the Baptists in a sermon preached just before their sentencing. John Clarke wrote: "Mr. *Cotton* (saith [Spur]) in his Sermon immediatly before the Court gave their Sentence against M. *Clark, Obediah Holmes,* and *Iohn Crandall,* affirmed, that denying Infants Baptism would overthrow all; & this was a capitall offence; and therefore they were soul-murtherers; when therefore the Governor M. *Iohn Indicot* came into the Court to pass Sentence against them, he said thus, you deserve to dy, but this we agreed upon, that Mr. *Clarke* shall pay 20 li. Fine, and *Obediah Holmes* 30 li. Fine, and *Jo. Crandall* 5 li. Fine, and to remain in prison untill their Fines be either payed or security given for them or else they are all of them to be well whipped." *Ill Newes from New-England; or, A Narration of New-Englands Persecution* . . . (London, 1652), 26–27.

6. Rom. 14:23: And he that doubteth is damned if he eat, because he eateth not of faith: for whatsoever is not of faith is sin.

7. 2 Chron. 34:33: And Josiah took away all the abominations, out of all the countries that pertained to the children of Israel, and made all that were present in Israel to serve, even to serve the Lord their God. And all his days they departed not from following the Lord, the God of their fathers.

8. 2 Kings 5:18, 19: In this thing the Lord pardon thy servant, that when my master goeth into the house of Rimmon to worship there, and he leaneth on my hand, and I bow myself in the house of Rimmon: when I bow down myself in the house of Rimmon, the Lord pardon thy servant in this thing. And he said unto him, Go in peace. So he departed from them a little way.

9. a stewes: a brothel or a quarter of a city occupied by houses of ill repute. See *OED,* "stew," 4a, b.

10. After David became king of Israel, he danced before the Ark of the Lord, and his wife, Michal, a daughter of Saul, disapproved; see 2 Sam. 6:12–23.

11. Rev. 2:2, 14, 15, 20: I know thy works, and thy labour, and thy patience, and how thou canst not bear them which are evil; and thou hast tried them which say they are apostles, and are not, and hast found them liars: . . .

But I have a few things against thee, because thou hast there them that hold the doctrine of Balaam, who taught Balac to cast a stumblingblock before the children of Israel, to eat things sacrificed unto idols, and to commit fornication. So hast thou also them that hold the doctrine of the Nicolaitanes, which thing I hate. . . .

Notwithstanding I have a few things against thee, because thou sufferest that woman Jezebel, which calleth herself a prophetess, to teach and to seduce my servants to commit fornication, and to eat things sacrificed unto idols.

12. The Seekers denied that there were any true churches. Cotton could have had in mind various radicals who had been expelled by churches in the Bay, including Roger Williams and Samuel Gorton, though Williams's identification with the Seekers dates from after his expulsion from Massachusetts. Even Francis Hutchinson (see Cotton to Hutchinson, Aug. 12, [1640]) might have struck Cotton as having views tending to those of the Seekers, as his brother-in-law, William Collins, did more pronouncedly. See Philip Gura, *A Glimpse of Sion's Glory: Puritan Radicalism in New England, 1620–1660* (Middletown, Conn., 1984), 73–76. See also Stephen Foster, "New England and the Challenge of Heresy, 1630–1660: The Puritan Crisis in Transatlantic Perspective," *WMQ*, 3d Ser., XXXVIII (1981), 624–660. Edmund Morgan, *Roger Williams: The Church and the State* (1967; rpt. New York, 1987), 52–53, 152 n. 56, denies the claim that Williams was a Seeker. William G. McLoughlin, *New England Dissent, 1630–1833: The Baptists and the Separation of Church and State* (Cambridge, Mass., 1971), observes: "The spectrum of the seventeenth century pietistic movement . . . went from Presbyterianism on the right to Quakerism and Seekerism on the left. Roger Williams ran the spectrum from right to left" (I, 6). See also John Eliot to Cotton, June 6, 1651, and Cotton to Eliot, [June 1651].

John Cotton to John Elmeston

October 12, 1652

Published: [John Elmeston], *A Censure of That Reverend and Learned Man of God Mr. John Cotton, Lately of New-England, upon the Way of Mr. Henden of Bennenden in Kent, Expresssed in Some Animadversions of His upon a Letter of Mr. Henden's, Sometimes Sent to Mr. Elmeston* (London, 1656), 55–56

This is the last surviving letter from Cotton, written after he had contracted his final illness, which he mentions here as preventing his attendance at the ceremony organized and conducted by John Eliot at Natick, one of the "praying towns" of native Americans established by Eliot according to scriptural example. On the Day of Humiliation, the Indians' confessions would be heard in the first attempt to bring them into formal membership of a church at Natick. His enforced absence from this occasion surely caused Cotton deeper regret than he signals in this letter to the distant and therefore uninvolved Elmeston. Eliot had had "weekly communicate counsels" with Cotton, whom Cotton Mather later described as Eliot's "loved and blessed patron."[1]

Author of the first published biography of Cotton and his successor as teacher at the Boston church, John Norton wrote in detail of Cotton's last illness. He notes that, going to preach "at a Neighbor-Church, he took wet in his passage over the Ferry, and not many hours after he felt the effect, being seised with an extreme illness in the Sermon." Then "after a short time he complained of an inflammation of the lungs, and thereupon found himself Asthmatical afterwards Scorbutical (which both meeting in a complicated disease ended his days)." Norton adds that Cotton preached his last lecture on November 18, 1652, and on "the Lords Day following, he preached his last Sermon upon *John* 1. 14."[2]

His final illness, therefore, had already begun before October 12, so it lasted more than two and a half months. By early December his death was expected.[3] His death on December 23 was marked, according to the quickly developing folklore, by a comet in the sky. Joshua Scottow remembered it this way: "The Venerable *Cotton,* our *New-Englands* . . . brightest and most shining Star in our Firmament; so i[n] his Sickness and Death he was wonderfully remarkable by a *Satelles* to the *Pleiades,* or an attendant to the seven Stars, which continued visible all that while, and until his buryal, which was six days after his death, and then disappeared." John Hull recorded a similar observation in his diary.[4]

Elmeston's headnote reads: "Mr. *Cottons* Letter to Mr. *Elmeston,* upon his writing back to thank him for his labour of love in imparting unto me his judgment upon Mr. *Hendens* Letter, and my signifying the slight account that Mr. *Henden* made thereof." The letter is printed in italics, with occasional words or phrases in roman type. Here, those typographical conventions are reversed, though the emphasis implied by this convention was not Cotton's practice and was probably introduced by Hutchinson.

Deare Sir,

I thank you for your last Letter, of *March 5. 1651.*[5] whereunto I would have returned you a large Answer, but that God having lately afflicted me with an *Asthma,* I finde, stooping to write somewhat painfull to me; which distemper, though (I thank the Lord) it doth not yet silence me from publick Ministry, yet it keepeth me within the town, that I cannot go to neighbour towns to hear, else I had gone abroad to have joyned this day with the *Indians* at *Natick* (about *20* miles from us) in a day of Humiliation, wherein they intend to give themselves to the Lord, and to the worship of Christ in a Church-way.[6] It is a wise dispensation of the Lord that when many Christians with you, and with us too, fall off from Christs Institution and Ordinances, that now God should stir up poor Pagans to seek after the same. But so it was in the dayes of old, *Acts 13. 46, 47, 48. and 28. 28.*[7] As for your Neighbour, I do not expect the Word should convince him, till the Spirit convert him more from himself, and perswade him. I do not easily believe his saying, that he had met before with all the things presented to him, but self is self-full. I should spend time in vaine to run over the particulars of his notions, unlesse all his grounds were laid open in them. To cut off some sprigs when other lye hid: The best help for such is the prayer of faith, to him that toucheth hearts as well as judgements. If God returne him not, I feare he will fall to more and greater exorbitances, till he be filled with his owne way, and have enough of himself. But the Lord Jesus redeem him. I commend my affectionate love to you, and you to the riches of his grace, in whom I rest, desirous of your prayers, and yours in brotherly love,

John Cotton.

Boston *this 12. of the 8.*
1652.

1. See "John Eliot's Description of New England in 1650," in MHS, *Procs.,* 2d Ser., II (1885), 50; Mather, *Magnalia,* I, 487. For discussion of these references and of the Cotton-Eliot relationship, see Theodore Dwight Bozeman, *To Live Ancient Lives: The Primitivist Dimension in Puritanism* (Chapel Hill, 1988), 264–280, esp. nn. 8, 9.

2. Norton, *Abel Being Dead yet Speaketh* . . . (London, 1658), 42–43. Norton and Samuel Whiting both wrote brief biographies of Cotton soon after his death. Of the two, only Norton published his work.

3. Writing to John Winthrop, Jr., on December 2, Amos Richardson noted: "Mr. Cotton is very ill and it is much feared will not escape this sickness to live. He hath great swellings in his Leggs and body, as I heare." *Winthrop Papers,* VI, 235.

4. [Joshua Scottow], *Old Mens Tears for Their Own Declensions* . . . (Boston, 1691), 16. Scottow recorded similar observations on this "Cælestial Flambeau in the Starry Region" in his *Narrative of the Planting of the Massachusetts Colony* . . . (Boston, 1694), rpt. in MHS, *Colls.,* 4th Ser., IV (1858), 283–284. See also *Diaries of John Hull, Mint-master and Treasurer of the Colony of Massachusetts Bay* (Boston, 1857), 173 n. 2. Some thirty years later Increase Mather's *Kometographia; or, A Discourse concerning Comets* . . . (Boston, 1683), 111, dates the appearance of the comet on December 10, 1652, and says it continued for twenty-one days. On Puritan reactions to comets, including this one, see Peter Lockwood Rumsey, *Acts of God and the People, 1620–1730* (Ann Arbor, Mich., 1986), 99–115. Larzer Ziff briefly discusses the mythology surrounding Cotton's death in *Career of John Cotton,* 253–254. Nathaniel Hawthorne's adaptation of the legend two centuries later in *The Scarlet Letter* has been observed by various readers; see especially Charles Ryskamp, "The New England Sources of *The Scarlet Letter,*" *American Literature,* XXXI (1959), 270–271; and Michael J. Colacurcio, "Footsteps of Ann Hutchinson: The Context of *The Scarlet Letter,*" *ELH,* XXXIX (1972), 465.

5. That is, 1652 N.S.

6. Church-way is an end-line hyphenation in the original printing.

7. Acts 13:46–48: Then Paul and Barnabas waxed bold, and said, It was necessary that the word of God should first have been spoken to you: but seeing ye put it from you, and judge

yourselves unworthy of everlasting life, lo, we turn to the Gentiles. For so hath the Lord commanded us, saying, I have set thee to be a light of the Gentiles, that thou shouldest be for salvation unto the ends of the earth. And when the Gentiles heard this, they were glad, and glorified the word of the Lord: and as many as were ordained to eternal life believed.

Acts 28:28: Be it known therefore unto you, that the salvation of God is sent unto the Gentiles, and that they will hear it.

Samuel Whiting to John Cotton

[?1637–1652]

ALS. MS: BPL, Ms. Am. 1506, pt.2, no. 24

Samuel Whiting (1597–1679) was a native of Boston, Lincolnshire, where his father and two of his brothers were at various times mayor. He was acquainted with Cotton before emigration as well as afterward and became Cotton's first biographer.[1] He addresses him here and in his letter of early 1650 as his "Cousen," probably because he was related to Cotton's second wife, Sarah, and also to Anthony Tuckney. The family relationship, it seems, was not a close one, though the friendship was, as this letter indicates.

Whiting arrived at Emmanuel College in 1613, the year after Cotton had left.[2] He received his bachelor of arts degree in 1616 and his master's in 1620, then served three years as chaplain to Sir Nathanael Bacon and Sir Roger Townsend before assuming a ministerial position at Lynn Regis, Norfolk, until, after another three years, he was cited to the Court of High Commission for nonconformity. He moved to Skirbeck, outside the bishopric of Norwich and very near Boston in Lincolnshire, where he served as minister for nearly ten years until, because of reactions to his nonconformity, he again felt a "feare of trouble" and was "desirous to remo[ve himse]lfe to some other place."[3] He did so in the spring of 1636, taking the same ship as John Wheelwright to New England. A month or so after his arrival there, he moved to Saugus (soon to become Lynn) and in November was installed as the minister.

Whiting's letters to Cotton are undated. No letter in Cotton's correspondence poses as large a problem in dating as this one. Single-mindedly focused on Whiting's personal spiritual condition, its references to his temporal situation are minimal, and then somewhat vague. The references to "my Brother Cobbet" and to "my coming hither" encourage one to think he is writing the letter in New England. This is not entirely certain, however, since Thomas Cobbet, his colleague at Lynn, had been a near neighbor in Lincolnshire, and the "coming hither" could as well refer to his moving to any of his first three positions in England as to Saugus / Lynn. The spiritual uncertainty expressed in the letter suggests that it is relatively early in his career rather than after his successive brushes with ecclesiastical authority in Norfolk and Lincolnshire, but, again, the doubts he here expresses could have come after his emigration.

Two other details lead one to conclude a New England origin. First, Whiting's use of the word "Cousen" would have been appropriate only after Sarah Hawkred Story married Cotton in April 1632, just fifteen months before Cotton emigrated. Second, in the very last phrase, where Whiting commends "you & all yours" to the Lord, the "all yours" would normally mean one's spouse and children; Cotton's children were all born after leaving England.

Though it seems likely that it was written before very late in his period at Lynn, in the absence of definitive evidence to this effect the inclusive dates, cautiously assuming a New England origin, would be 1637 (the year of Cobbet's arrival) and 1652 (the year of Cotton's death). Whenever it was written, however, it is the clearest example of spiritual autobiography in the letters of first-generation New England colonists. Knowing the contents of Whiting's letter suggests personal poignancy in his later report that Cotton "answered many letters that were sent far and near; wherein were handled many difficult cases of conscience, and many doubts by him cleared to the greatest satisfaction."[4]

Thomas Prince underlined several passages, which are identified in the notes. At the bottom of the letter, Prince made the following notes:

1597. Nov. 20 — S[l] Whiting Born at Boston ˆin Lincolnshireˆ in England. Educated at Emanuel in Cambridg

1636. May. 26 — arrived at New England, (suppose at Boston about a month after, remoued to Linn

1637. Summer. — His old Friend *th*e R. Mr Tho. Cobbet, w*ho* h*a*d been a min*iste*r in Lincolnshire came to Boston in NE, with *th*e R. Mr. Dauenport & s*ai*d Whiting ˆsoon afterˆ obt*ain*ing Him for his colleague.

Written on the verso, in a different hand:

A holy Letter
from M[r] Whiting
to M[r] Cotton.

Deare Cousen

I am bold to acquaint you with my sad condition desiring your helpe in *th*e Lord & your aduice & counsell as hauing none w*hic*h would be ˆmoreˆ ~~so~~ faithfull ˆthenˆ ~~as~~ your selfe to my soule. & before I relate *th*e troubles *tha*t are vpon my soule I shall desire to lett you know how God hath formerly dealt w*i*th mee. not long after my Fathers death about *th*e time I was middle Batchelour,[5] hauing stood out ag*ain*st many strong conuictions of *th*e badnesse & vnsafenesse of my condition both from your searching ministery & *th*e ministery of *th*e Lords other seruants, at last God met w*i*th me in M[r] Hookers at Cambridge[6] where he was pressing *th*e necessity of speedy turning from sin to *th*e Lord & shewing *th*e danger of p*ro*crastination w*hic*h did worke sad thoughts & earnest seekings vnto God *tha*t he would giue repentance vnto such a sinner as I was, w*hic*h afterward was followed by another of *th*e Lords seruants by whome *th*e feare of death was p*r*esented to me & *th*e danger of euerlasting damnation: w*hic*h latter was soe strongly set on vpon my heart *tha*t I saw noe way but p*er*ishing eternally except mercy stepped in to helpe me. This forced me w*i*th all speed to hie to *th*e Lord to beg for mercy in his *Chris*t to saue a pore vndon creature & after many earnest prayers put vp to *th*e God of heauen, he manifested hims. to me in *tha*t p*ro*mise first 43 Is. I euen I am he *tha*t blotteth out thy transgressions for my names sake &c[7] & in *th*e || of his na||, 34 exod*us*[8] w*hic*h did fill [my] heart w*i*th such vnspeakeable joy *tha*t for many dayes together I could doe nothing [el]se but admire *th*e Lo[rd's] loue to such an one as I w*hic*h also did soe breake my heart and soe filled [my d]ayes w*i*th [one word lost] *tha*t ||ld [h]aue fed vpon *the*m diuers nights when other scholars were in bed w[hen] I silently musing of *th*e infinite loue of *th*e L[ord t]o mee & in frosty ni[ghts] in Eman*uel* Coll*ege* walkes[9] looke it out with God without feel[ing] any cold or desiring any rest though it were well toward midnight before I returned into m[y] chamber. at w*hic*h time *th*e Lord made me most vile & base in my owne eyes soe *tha*t I thought *th*e [prof]anest *tha*t I met better then my selfe, & soe thankfull *tha*t I often as I was in secret sang *th*e 103 Ps. [&] others, & was neuer well but when I was praising *tha*t God *tha*t had been soe freely gracious [to] me; & durst not aduenture vpon *th*e least sinne but a little mote in *th*e eye was grieuous & *th*e pr[ic]king of a pinne was painfull to my fleshy heart: then did I hide my comforts & did not make *the*m knowen to others, then did my bowells earn after *th*e good of others & *th*e Lord brought me to be very desirous to doe good to those *tha*t I had sometimes been companion w*i*th in euill: especially to one Clough w*hic*h afterward proued a desp*er*ate wretch, yet my prayers were earnest to God for him.[10] At *tha*t time also my heart was filled [w*i*th] ˆ[one or two faded words] ofˆ *th*e Lords gracious com*m*ing, & oh w*ha*t longings had I after ˆeuerlastingˆ m[a]rriage fellowship *tha*t had tasted (as I thought) *th*e comfort of espousall loue: further in *th*e night my dreames & sleepe were sweet to mee & wheras before my dreames were vaine & sometimes vncleane, then they also had an image of holinesse vpon *the*m. & for *th*e Lords people I could haue rid & run & don any thing for *the*m, yea such was my loue to them [tha]t I could not indure *tha*t any should speake ag*ain*st *the*m but was ready to take their part[.] now after all [t]his I was assaulted w*i*th blasphemous thoughts to deny *th*e deity, & to question *th*e trueth of *th*e scrip[t]ures w*hic*h *th*e Lord helped ˆmeeˆ to loath, & to rise vp in indignation of spirit ag*ain*st *the*m, & at last deliuered [me] from *the*m. afterward when I came into the ministery[11] (w*hic*h I much desired *tha*t *th*e Lord might vse me [to] doe some good before I died) I found his [b]lessing vpon m[y] labours more or lesse in all p*ar*tes. || only I found m|| much lost as || lawfull liberties || by || care I not charge [m]y selfe with walking on in any euill way. But now since my [co]ming hi[t]her[12] I haue called all *th*e former worke into question & am in a sad condition [an]d haue been many dayes, & vpon these grounds, 1 bec. I feare *th*e spirit of bondage was not || ynough vpon me, 2 I feare I haue rested too much vpon *th*e first worke & *tha*t has ~~not~~ made me neglect *th*e renewing of my couenant soe heartily, & solemnely with *th*e Lord as I ought, and *tha*t my hopes haue been built vpon *th*e sand ˆratherˆ then *th*e rock: now Deare Sir I intreat you in *th*e bowels of Jesus *Chris*t *tha*t you would be faithfull to my soule, say w*ha*t you will according to God, it shall not discontent mee, for none can thinke worse of mee then I doe my selfe: tell me if *th*e first worke be sandy, or whether it wilt as you conceiue stand ag*ain*st raine & flouds & winde, & instruct ˆmeˆ w*ha*t to doe in a deserted condition, *th*e Lord knowes w*ha*t doubts & disputes I haue in my pore soule about my condition, I intreat you to haue pity vpon mee & to helpe w*i*th your counsell & prayers when *th*e fire [m]ost kindles in your spir[it], & send me some few lines *tha*t may giue me further direction w*ha*t to doe & h[o]w to be taught w*i*th these briars & thornes of *th*e wildernesse *tha*t I may not run in vain & neither liue vncomfortably nor die vnp*re*paredly. Truly Cous. these sad houres haue made mee looke ouer *th*e first worke wistly w*hic*h I did but cursorily before when I was with you and *th*e other Elders.[13] & the God & father of our Lord Jesus *Chris*t w*hic*h is blessed for euermore knoweth *tha*t I lie not in this relation of my condition. I have some helpe from my Brother Cobbet[14] & some creuises of light sometimes breake in in hearing & praying & my heart is more broken w*i*th any intimations of mercy more then euer ex[*c*]ept *tha*t time when *th*e first worke was wrought, yet these are gone againe & soone are lost. *th*e Lord helpe me to wait vpon him till he reuerse himselfe againe to mee in mercy. I am in a great strait, for if I should whol[y] reject *th*e first worke I feare I should sin ag*ain*st *th*e Lord by vnbeliefe, & if I should hold to it, then I feare it will not be well because though I haue been terrified before, yett not ynough. Deare Cousen[15] helpe me out of this maze & saue me if you can from dashing ag*ain*st either of these rocks: & *th*e Lord speake by you to my heart, & requite your loue to my soule herein. I haue written these lines in haste yet not without pondering my condition & earnest prayer to *th*e Lord to be guided herein, *th*e same Lord guide your thoughts & pen & direct a fit answer to my requests herein, [t]o whome I com*m*end you & all yours resting

your Loving Cousen though full of heauinesse

Sa. Whiting

1. [Samuel Whiting], "Concerning the Life of the Famous Mr. Cotton, Teacher to the Church of Christ at Boston, in New-England," in Hutchinson, *Collection,* 242–249; rpt. in Young, *Chronicles of the First Planters,* 419–431. It is generally assumed that this work was written earlier than Norton's biography and that Norton used it in writing *Abel Being Dead yet Speaketh* (1658).

2. Biographical information on Whiting is from Mather, *Magnalia,* I, 452–461; P. Thompson, *History of Boston,* 430–431; Savage, *Genealogical Dictionary,* IV, 520–521; Wesley T. Mott, "Samuel Whiting (1597–1697)," in James A. Levernier and Douglas R. Wilmes, eds., *American Writers before 1800* (Westport, Conn., 1983), III, 1584–1586.

3. Anthony Irby to Bishop John Williams, Dec. 7, 1635, Bishop Williams's Correspondence, MS: COR/B/3, fol. 37, in Lincolnshire Archives.

4. [Whiting], "Concerning the Life of the Famous Mr. Cotton," in Young, *Chronicles of the First Planters,* 425–426.

5. In his second year as an undergraduate student at Emmanuel College, Cambridge, that is, c. 1615.

6. Thomas Hooker was at this time nearing the end of his lengthy stay at Emmanuel College, where he was fellow, catechist, and dean. In this sentence Prince underlined "not long after . . . middle Batchelour," "your searching ministery," "Hookers," and "Cambridge."

7. Isa. 43:25: I, even I, am he that blotteth out thy transgressions for mine own sake, and will not remember thy sins.

8. Perhaps the reference in this mutilated passage is to Exod. 34:5–7: And the Lord descended in the cloud, and stood with him there, and proclaimed the name of the Lord. And the Lord passed by before him, and proclaimed, The Lord, the Lord God, merciful and gracious, longsuffering, and abundant in goodness and truth, Keeping mercy for thousands, forgiving iniquity and transgression and sin. . . .

9. Prince underlined "Eman*uel* Coll*ege* walkes."

10. Alexander Clough (or Clugh) was a student and then fellow at Emmanuel College, dying there in 1621. An inventory of his books at the time of his death is in Cambridge University Archives, Wills, Vice Chancellor's Court Inventories, bundle 9. Prince underlined the name "Clough."

11. Prince underlined "afterward when I came into the ministery."

12. Prince annotates this phrase on the manuscript: "He means at *Skirbeck* near to Boston in England, or at Lyn in NE, seems as certain: tho I am apt to think the latter."

13. In this sentence Prince underlined "Cous." and "when I was . . . Elders."

14. Prince underlined "my Brother Cobbet." Thomas Cobbet (1608–1685) was Whiting's colleague in the church at Lynn from 1637 to 1656, when he succeeded Nathaniel Rogers as pastor at Ipswich. See Alonzo Lewis, *The History of Lynn* (Boston, 1829), 100–105.

15. Prince underlined "Deare Cousen."

APPENDIX

Questions and Reasons Sent by John Hall to John Cotton

[1635]

Published: [Roger Williams], *The Bloudy Tenent, of Persecution, for Cause of Conscience, Discussed* . . . [London], 1644, 1–6; *The Bloudy Tenent* . . . , ed. Edward Bean Underhill (London, 1848), 10–18; *The Bloudy Tenent* . . . , ed. Samuel L. Caldwell, NC, *Publs.*, III (1867), 29–39; John Cotton, *The Controversie concerning Liberty of Conscience in Matters of Religion, Truly Stated, and Distinctly and Plainly Handled* . . . *by Way of Answer to Some Arguments to the Contrary Sent unto Him* . . . (London, 1646), sig. A2–[A4v]

A version of the questions in the following document was originally put to James I by a prisoner in Newgate in a volume titled *A Most Humble Supplication of Many of the King's Majesty's Most Loyal Subjects* . . . (London, 1620), chaps. 6–9 (see John Cotton to [John Hall], late 1634–early 1635). That text was inexactly reprinted in Thomas Crosby, *A History of the English Baptists from the Reformation to the Beginning of the Reign of George I* (London, 1739), II, app., 35–45, and in Edward Bean Underhill, ed., *Tracts on Liberty of Conscience for Persecution, 1614–1661* (London, 1846), 214-225. The source of the following text is Williams's *Bloudy Tenent* (1644).

Scriptures and Reasons written long since by a *Witnesse* of Iesus Christ, close *Prisoner* in *Newgate,* against *Persecution* in cause of *Conscience;* and sent some while since to Mr. *Cotton,* by a Friend who thus wrote:

In the multitude *of* Councellours *there is safety: It is therefore humbly desired to be instructed in this point: viz.*

Whether Persecution *for cause of* Conscience, *be not against the Doctrine of* Iesus Christ *the* King of Kings. *The Scriptures and Reasons are these.*

1 Because *Christ* commandeth that the *Tares* and *Wheat* (which some understand are those that walke in the *Truth,* and those that walke in *Lies*) should be *let alone* in the *World,* and not *plucked* up untill the *Harvest,* which is the end of the *World, Matth.* 13.30.38, &c.

2 The same commandeth *Matth.* 15.14. that they that are *Blinde* (as some interpret, led on in false *Religion,* and are offended with him for teaching true

Religion) should be *let alone,* referring their punishment unto their falling into the *Ditch.*

3 Againe, *Luke* 9.54,55. hee reproved his *Disciples* who would have had *Fire* come down from Heaven and devoure those *Samaritanes* who would not receive Him, in these words: Ye know not of what *Spirit* ye are, the son of Man is not come to destroy *Mens lives,* but to save them.

4 *Paul* the Apostle of our Lord teacheth, 2 *Tim.* [2: 24–26][1] That the servant of the Lord must not *strive,* but must be *gentle* toward *all Men,* suffering the Evill Men, instructing them with *meeknesse* that are contrary minded, proving if *God* at any time will give them *repentance,* that they may acknowledge the Truth, and come to *amendment* out of that snare of the *devill,* &c.

5 According to these blessed *Commandements,* the holy *Prophets* foretold, that when the *Law* of *Moses* (concerning *Worship*) should cease, and *Christs Kingdome* be established, *Esa.* 2.4. *Mic.* 4.3,4. They shall breake their *Swords* into *Mathookes,* and their *Speares* into *Sithes.* And *Esa.* 11.9. Then shall none hurt or destroy in all the *Mountaine* of my Holinesse, &c. And when he came, the same he *taught* and *practised,* as before: so did his *Disciples* after him, for the *Weapons* of his *Warfare* are not *carnall* (saith the Apostle) 2 *Cor.* 10.4.

But he chargeth straitly that his Disciples should be so far from persecuting those that would not bee of their Religion, that when they were *persecuted* they should *pray* (*Matth.* 5.) when they were *cursed* they should *blesse,* &c.

And the Reason seemes to bee, because they who now are *Tares,* may hereafter become *Wheat;* they who are now *blinde,* may hereafter *see;* they that now *resist* him, may hereafter *receive* him; they that are now in the *devils snare,* in *adversenesse* to the *Truth,* may hereafter come to *repentance;* they that are now *blasphemers* and *persecutors* (as *Paul* was) may in time become *faithfull* as he; they that are now *idolators* as the *Corinths* once were (1 *Cor.* 6.9.) may hereafter become *true worshippers* as they; they that are now *no people* of *God,* nor under *mercy* (as the Saints sometimes were, 1 *Pet.* 2.20.) may hereafter become the people of *God,* and obtaine *mercy,* as they.

Some come not till the 11. houre, *Matth.* 20.6. if those that come not till the *last houre* should be *destroyed,* because they come not at the *first,* then should they never come but be prevented.

All which *premises* are in all humility referred to your godly wise *consideration.*

II. Because this *persecution* for cause of *conscience* is against the *profession* and *practise* of *famous Princes.*

First, you may please to consider the speech of *King James,* in his *Majesties Speech* at *Parliament,* 1609. He saith, it is a sure *Rule* in *divinity,* that God never loves to plant his *Church* by *violence* and *bloodshed.*

And in his *Highnesse Apologie,* pag. 4. speaking of such *Papists* that tooke the Oath, thus:

"I gave good proofe that I intended no *persecution* against them for *conscience* "cause, but onely desired to bee secured for *civill obedience,* which for *conscience* "cause they are bound to performe.

And pag. 60. speaking of *Blackwell* (the *Arch-priest*) his *Majesty* saith, "It "was never my intention to lay any thing to the said *Arch-Priests* charge (as I "have never done to any) for *cause of conscience.* And in his *Highnesse Exposition* on *Revel.* 20. printed 1588, and after 1603, his *Majesty* writeth thus: "Sixthly, the "compassing of the *Saints* and the *besieging* of the *beloved City,* declareth unto us "a certaine *note* of a *false Church,* to be *Persecution,* for they come to seeke the "*faithfull,* the *faithfull* are them that are sought: the *wicked* are the *besiegers,* the "*faithfull* are the *besieged.*

Secondly, the saying of *Stephen* King of *Poland:* "I am *King* of *Men,* not of "*Consciences,* a Commander of *Bodies,* not of *Soules.*

Thirdly, the *King* of *Bohemia* hath thus written:

"And notwithstanding the successe of the later times (wherein sundry *opin-*"*ions* have beene hatched about the subject of *Religion*) may make one clearly "discerne with his *eye,* and as it were to touch with his *Finger,* that according to "the veritie of *Holy Scriptures,* and a *Maxime* heretofore told and maintained, "by the ancient Doctors of the *Church;* That *mens consciences* ought in no sort "to bee *violated, urged,* or *constrained;* and whensoever men have attempted any "thing by this *violent course,* whether openly or by secret meanes, the issue hath "beene *pernicious,* and the cause of great and wonderfull *Innovations* in the prin-"cipallest and mightiest *Kingdomes* and *Countries* of all Christendome.

And further his *Majesty* saith: "So that once more we doe professe before "*God* and the *whole World,* that from this time forward wee are firmly resolved "not to *persecute* or *molest,* or suffer to be *persecuted* or *molested,* any person who-"soever for *matter of Religion,* no not they that professe *themselves* to be of the "*Romish Church,* neither to trouble or disturbe them in the exercise of their "*Religion,* so they live conformable to the *Lawes* of the *States,* &c.

And for the practice of this, where is *persecution* for cause of *conscience* except in *England* and where *Popery* reignes, and there neither in all places, as appeareth by *France, Poland,* and other places.

Nay, it is not practised amongst the *Heathen* that acknowledge not the *true God,* as the *Turke, Persian,* and others.

as. Thirdly, because *persecution* for cause of conscience is condemned by the ancient and later *Writers,* yea and *Papists* themselves.

Hilarie against *Auxentius* saith thus: The *Christian Church* doth not *persecute,* but is *persecuted.* And lamentable it is to see the great folly of these times, and to sigh at the foolish opinion of this world, in that men thinke by humane aide to helpe *God,* and with worldly pompe and power to undertake to defend the *Christian Church.* I aske you *Bishops,* what helpe used the *Apostles* in the publishing of the *Gospel?* with the aid of what power did they preach *Christ,* and converted the *Heathen* from their *idolatry* to *God?* When they were in *prisons,* and lay in *chaines,* did they praise and give thankes to God for any *dignities, graces,* and *favours* received from the *Court?* Or do you thinke that *Paul* went about with *Regall Mandates,* or *Kingly authority,* to gather and establish the *Church* of *Christ?* sought he *protection* from *Nero, Vespasian?*

The *Apostles* wrought with their *hands* for their owne *maintenance,* travailing by *land* and *water* from *Towne* to *Citie,* to preach *Christ:* yea the more they were *forbidden,* the more they *taught* and preached *Christ.* But now alas, *humane helpe* must *assist* and *protect* the *Faith,* and give the same countenance to and by vaine and *worldly honours.* Doe men seek to defend the *Church of Christ?* as if hee by his power were unable to performe it.

The same against the *Arrians.*

The *Church* now, which formerly by induring *misery* and *imprisonment* was knowne to be a *true Church,* doth now terrifie others by *imprisonment, banishment,* and *misery,* and boasteth that she is highly esteemed of the *world,* when as the true *Church* cannot but be hated of the same.

Tertull. ad Scapulam: It agreeth both with *humane reason,* and *naturall equity,* that every man *worship* God uncompelled, and beleeve what he will; for it neither hurteth nor profiteth any one another mans *Religion* and *Beleefe:* Neither beseemeth it any *Religion* to compell another to be of their *Religion,* which willingly and freely should be imbraced, and not by constraint: for as much as the *offerings* were required of those that freely and with good will offered, and not from the *contrary.*

Jerom. in proœm. lib. 4. in Jeremiam. Heresie must be cut off with the *Sword* of the *Spirit:* let us strike through with the *Arrowes* of the *Spirit* all *Sonnes* and *Disciples* of mis-led *Heretickes,* that is, with *Testimonies* of holy *Scriptures.* The slaughter of *Heretickes* is by the word of God.

Brentius upon 1 *Cor.* 3. No man hath power to make or give Lawes to *Christians,* whereby to binde their *consciences;* for willingly, freely, and uncompelled, with a ready desire and cheerfull minde, must those that come, run unto *Christ.*

Luther in his Booke of the *Civill Magistrate* saith; The *Lawes* of the *Civill Magistrates* government extends no further then over the *body* or *goods,* and to that which is *externall:* for over the *soule God* will not suffer any man to *rule:* onely he *himselfe* will rule there. Wherefore whosoever doth undertake to give *Lawes* unto the *Soules* and *Consciences* of Men, he usurpeth that *government* himselfe which appertaineth unto *God,* &c.

Therefore upon 1 *Kings* 5. In the building of the *Temple* there was no *sound* of *Iron* heard, to signifie that *Christ* will have in his *Church* a *free* and a *willing* People, not compelled and constrained by *Lawes* and *Statutes.*

Againe he saith upon *Luk.* 22. It is not the true *Catholike Church,* which is defended by the *Secular Arme* or humane Power, but the *false* and *feigned Church,* which although it carries the *Name* of a *Church* yet it denies the power thereof.

And upon *Psal.* 17. he saith: For the true *Church* of *Christ* knoweth not *Brachium sæculare,* which the *Bishops* now adayes, chiefly use.

Againe, in *Postil. Dom. 1. post Epiphan.* he saith: Let not *Christians* be *commanded,* but *exhorted:* for, He that willingly will not doe that, whereunto he is friendly exhorted, he is no *Christian:* wherefore they that doe compell those that are not willing, shew thereby that they are not *Christian Preachers,* but *Worldly Beadles.*

Againe, upon 1 *Pet.* 3. he saith: If the *Civill Magistrate* shall command me to believe thus and thus: I should answer him after this manner: *Lord,* or *Sir,* Looke you to your *Civill* or *Worldly Government.* Your Power extends not so farre as to command any thing in *Gods Kingdome:* Therefore herein I may not heare you. For if you cannot beare it, that any should usurpe *Authoritie* where you have to Command, how doe you thinke that *God* should suffer you to thrust him from his Seat, and to seat your selfe therein?

Lastly, the Papists, the *Inventors of Persecution,* in a wicked Booke of theirs set forth in *K. James* his *Reigne,* thus:

Moreover, the *Meanes* which *Almighty God* appointed his Officers to use in the Conversion of *Kingdomes* and *Nations,* and People, was *Humilitie, Patience, Charitie;* saying, Behold I send you as *Sheepe* in the midst of *Wolves,* Mat. 10.16. He did not say, Behold I send you as *Wolves* among *Sheepe,* to kill, imprison, spoile and devoure those unto whom they were sent.

Againe *vers.* 7. he saith: They to whom I send you, will deliver you up into *Councells,* and in their *Synagogues* they will scourge you; and to *Presidents* and to *Kings* shall you be led for my sake. He doth not say: You whom I send, shall deliver the people (whom you ought to convert) unto *Councells,* and put them in Prisons, and lead them to *Presidents,* and *Tribunall Seates,* and make their *Religion Felony* and *Treason.*

Againe he saith, *vers.* 32. When ye enter into an House, salute it, saying, Peace be unto this House: he doth not say, You shall send *Pursevants* to ransack or spoile his House.

Againe he said, *John* 10. The good *Pastour* giveth his life for his Sheep, the *Thief* commeth not but to steale, kill and destroy. He doth not say, The *Theefe* giveth his life for his Sheep, and the Good *Pastour* commeth not but to steale, kill and destroy.

So that we holding our peace, our *Adversaries* themselves speake for us, or rather for the Truth.

To answer some maine *Objections.*

And first, that it is no *præjudice* to the *Common wealth,* if *Libertie of Conscience* were suffred to such as doe feare *God* indeed, as is or will be manifest in such mens lives and conversations.

Abraham abode among the *Canaanites* a long time, yet contrary to them in *Religion,* Gen. 13.7. & 16.13. Againe he sojourned in *Gerar,* and K. *Abimelech* gave him leave to abide in his Land, *Gen.* 20.21.23.24.

Isaack also dwelt in the same Land, yet contrary in *Religion,* Gen. 26.

Jacob lived 20 yeares in one House with his Unkle *Laban,* yet differed in *Religion,* Gen. 31.

The people of *Israel* were about 430 yeares in that infamous land of *Egypt,* and afterwards 70 yeares in *Babylon,* all which time they differed in *Religion* from the States, *Exod.* 12. & 2 *Chron.* 36.

Come to the time of *Christ,* where *Israel* was under the *Romanes,* where lived divers Sects of *Religion,* as *Herodians, Scribes* and *Pharises, Saduces* and *Libertines, Thudaans* and *Samaritanes,* beside the Common Religion of the *Jewes, Christ* and his *Apostles.* All which differed from the Common *Religion* of the State, which was like the Worship of *Diana,* which almost the whole world then worshipped, *Acts* 19.20.

All these lived under the Government of *Cæsar,* being nothing hurtfull unto the *Common-wealth,* giving unto *Cæsar* that which was his. And for their *Religion* and Consciences towards God, he left them to themselves, as having no Dominion over their *Soules* and *Consciences.* And when the Enemies of the Truth raised up any *Tumults,* the wisedome of the *Magistrate* most wisely appeased them, *Acts* 18.14 & 19.35.

1. Here the 1644 edition prints 2 *Tim.* 24.2, and the 1646 edition has 2 *Tim.* 3.24, neither of which is possible. The subsequent sentence, however, clearly refers to the passage editorially inserted in brackets.

"Certain Proposals made by Lord Say, Lord Brooke, and other Persons of quality, as conditions of their removing to New-England, with the answers thereto"

[1636]

Published: Hutchinson, *History,* I, app. 2, 490–495; Edmund S. Morgan, *Puritan Political Ideas, 1558–1794* (Indianapolis, Ind., 1965), 161–167

This list of "demands" was printed first by Thomas Hutchinson, whose edition is here the copy text. Cotton was designated as New England's respondent to the list (see Cotton to Lord Saye and Sele, 1636). As that letter makes clear, Cotton gathered the opinions of his peers before committing their collective responses to the Saye / Brooke "demands" to paper. Together, this document and Cotton's lengthy accompanying letter firmly resist the notion that power and authority should be hereditary and make the case for the qualification of "godliness" in colonial officials as established by admission to one of the local churches.

DEMAND 1. That the common-wealth should consist of two distinct ranks of men, whereof the one should be for them and their heirs, gentlemen of the country, the other for them and their heirs, freeholders.

ANSWER. Two distinct ranks we willingly acknowledge, from the light of nature and scripture; the one of them called Princes, or Nobles, or Elders (amongst whom gentlemen have their place) the other the people. Hereditary dignity or honours we willingly allow to the former, unless, by the scandalous and base conversation of any of them, they become degenerate. Hereditary liberty, or estate of freemen, we willingly allow to the other, unless they also, by some unworthy and slavish carriage, do disfranchize themselves.

DEM. 2 That in these gentlemen and freeholders, assembled together, the chief power of the commonwealth shall be placed, both for making and repealing laws.

ANS. So it is with us.

DEM. 3. That each of these two ranks should, in all public assemblies, have a negative voice, so as without a mutual consent nothing should be established.

ANS. So it is agreed among us.

DEM. 4. That the first rank, consisting of gentlemen, should have power, for them and their heirs, to come to the parliaments or public assemblies, and there to give their free votes personally; the second rank of freeholders should have the same power for them and their heirs of meeting and voting, but by their deputies.

ANS. Thus far this demand is practised among us. The freemen meet and vote by their deputies; the other rank give their votes personally, only with this difference, there be no more of the gentlemen that give their votes personally but such as are chosen to places of office, either governors, deputy governors, councellors, or assistants. All gentlemen in England have not that honour to meet and vote personally in parliament, much less all their heirs. But of this more fully, in answer to the ninth and tenth demand.

DEM. 5. That for facilitating and dispatch of business, and other reasons, the gentlemen and freeholders should sit and hold their meetings in two distinct houses.

ANS. We willingly approve the motion, only as yet it is not so practised among us, but in time, the variety and discrepancy of sundry occurrences will put them upon a necessity of sitting apart.

DEM. 6. That there shall be set times for these meetings, annually or half yearly, or as shall be thought fit by common consent, which meetings should have a set time for their continuance, but should be adjourned or broken off at the discretion of both houses.

ANS. Public meetings, in general courts, are by charter appointed to be quarterly, which, in this infancy of the colony, wherein many things frequently occur which need settling, hath been of good use, but when things are more fully settled in due order, it is likely that yearly or half yearly meetings will be sufficient. For the continuance or breaking up of these courts, nothing is done but with the joint consent of both branches.

DEM. 7. That it shall be in the power of this parliament, thus constituted and assembled[,] to call the governor and all public officers to account, to create new officers, and to determine them already set up; and, the better to stop the way to insolence and ambition, it may be offered that all offices and fees of office shall, every parliament, determine, unless they be new confirmed the last day of every session.

ANS. This power to call governors and all officers to account, and to create new and determine the old, is settled already in the general court or parliament, only it is not put forth but once in the year, viz. at the great and general court in May, when the governor is chosen.

DEM. 8. That the governor shall ever be chosen out of the rank of gentlemen.

ANS. We never practise otherwise, chusing the governor either out of the assistants, which is our ordinary course, or out of approved known gentlemen, as this year[1] Mr. Vane.

DEM. 9. That, for the present, the Right Honorable the Lord Viscount Say and Seale, the Lord Brooke, who have already been at great disbursements for the public works in New-England, and such other gentlemen of approved sincerity and worth, as they, before their personal remove, shall take into their number, should be admitted, for them and their heirs, gentlemen of the country. But, for the future, none shall be admitted into this rank but by the consent of both houses.

ANS. The great disbursments of these noble personages and worthy gentlemen we thankfully acknowledge, because the safety and presence of our brethren at Connecticut is no small blessing and comfort to us. But, though that charge had never been disbursed, the worth of the honorable persons named is so well known to all, and our need of such supports and guides is so sensible to ourselves, that we do not doubt the country would thankfully accept it, as a singular favor from God and from them, if he should bow their hearts to come into this wilderness and help us. As for accepting them and their heirs into the number of gentlemen of the country, the custom of this country is, and readily would be, to receive and acknowledge, not only all such eminent persons as themselves and the gentlemen they speak of, but others of meaner estate, so be it is of some eminency, to be for them and their heirs, gentlemen of the country. Only, thus standeth our case. Though we receive them with honor and allow them pre-eminence and accommodations according to their condition, yet we do not, ordinarily, call them forth to the power of election, or administration of magistracy, until they be received as members into some of our churches, a privilege, which we doubt not religious gentlemen will willingly desire (as David did in Psal. xxvii.4.) and christian churches will as readily impart to such desirable persons. Hereditary honors both nature and scripture doth acknowledge (Eccles. xix.17.) but hereditary authority and power standeth only by the civil laws of some commonwealths, and yet, even amongst them, the authority and power of the father is no where communicated, together with his honors, unto all his posterity. Where God blesseth any branch of any noble or generous family, with a spirit and gifts fit for government, it would be a taking of God's name in vain to put such a talent under a bushel, and a sin against the honor of magistracy to neglect such in our public elections. But if God should not delight to furnish some of their posterity with gifts fit for magistracy, we should expose them rather to reproach and prejudice, and the commonwealth with them, than exalt them to honor, if we should call them forth, when God doth not, to public authority.

DEM. 10. That the rank of freeholders shall be made up of such, as shall have so much personal estate there, as shall be thought fit for men of that condition, and have contributed, some fit proportion, to the public charge of the country, either by their disbursements or labors.

ANS. We must confess our ordinary practice to be otherwise. For, excepting the old planters, i.e. Mr. Humphry, who himself was admitted an assistant at London, and all of them freemen, before the churches here were established, none are admitted freemen of this commonwealth but such as are first admitted members of some church or other in this country, and, of such, none are excluded from the liberty of freemen. And out of such only, I mean the more eminent sort of such, it is that our magistrates are chosen. Both which points we should willingly persuade our people to change, if we could make it appear to them, that such a change might be made according to God; for, to give you a true account of the grounds of our proceedings herein, it seemeth to them, and also to us, to be a divine ordinance (and moral) that none should be appointed and chosen by the people of God, magistrates over them, but men fearing God (Ex. xviii.21.) chosen out of their brethren (Deut. xvii.15.) saints (1 Cor. vi.1.)[.] Yea, the apostle maketh it a shame to the church, if it be not able to afford wise men from out of themselves, which shall be able to judge all civil matters between their brethren (ver. 5.)[.] And Solomon maketh it the joy of a commonwealth, when the righteous are in authority, and the calamity thereof, when the wicked bear rule. Prov. xxix 2.

OBJ. If it be said, there may be many carnal men whom God hath invested with sundry eminent gifts of wisdom, courage, justice, fit for government.

ANS. Such may be fit to be consulted with and employed by governors, according to the quality and use of their gifts and parts, but yet are men not fit to be trusted with place of standing power or settled authority. Ahitophel's wisdom may be fit to be heard (as an oracle of God) but not fit to be trusted with power of settled magistracy, lest he at last call for 12000 men to lead them forth against David, 2 Sam. xvii. 1,2,3. The best gifts and parts, under a covenant of works (under which all carnal men and hypocrites be) will at length turn aside by crooked ways, to depart from God, and, finally, to fight against God, and are therefore, herein, opposed to good men and upright in heart, Psal. cxxv. 4,5.

OBJ. If it be said again, that then the church estate could not be compatible with any commonwealth under heaven.

ANS. It is one thing for the church, or members of the church, loyally to submit unto any form of government, when it is above their calling to reform it, another thing to chuse a form of government and governors discrepant from the rule. Now, if it be a divine truth, that none are to be trusted with public permanent authority but godly men, who are fit materials for church fellowship, then from the same grounds it will appear, that none are so fit to be trusted with the liberties of the commonwealth as church members. For, the liberties of the freemen of this commonwealth are such, as require men of faithful integrity to God and the state, to preserve the same. Their liberties, among others, are chiefly these. 1. To chuse all magistrates, and to call them to account at their general courts. 2. To chuse such burgesses, every general court, as with the magistrates shall make or repeal all laws. Now, both these liberties are such, as carry along much power with them, either to establish or subvert the commonwealth, and therewith the church, which power, if it be committed to men not according to their godliness, which maketh them fit for church fellowship, but according to their wealth, which, as such, makes them no better than worldly men, then, in case worldly men should prove the major part, as soon they might do, they would as readily set over us magistrates like themselves, such as might hate us according to the curse, Levit. xxvi. 17. and turn the edge of all authority and laws against the church and the members thereof, the maintenance of whose peace is the chief end which God aimed at in the institution of magistracy. 1 Tim. ii. 1,2.

1. 1636. [Hutchinson's note.]

John Eliot's Notes on Cotton to Dudley, March 22, 1638/9, with Cotton's Further Clarifications

AD. MS: BPL, Ms. Am. 1502, pt. 1, no. 9

The first part of this manuscript is not in Eliot's hand, but is apparently a copy made from his notes by someone else. Cotton then added his annotations in his own hand. Eliot's scribe began by transcribing part of the text of Cotton's letter.

When my soule is humbled, the spirit of God, by applying *th*e gospell to me, declareth & wittnesseth *th*e grace & fauour of God to me, in Christ Jesus,[1] & by so doeing worketh at once saving grace in me towards God, & thereby declareth that his wittnesse of *th*e grace of God to me, is not delusion.

And yet because these be two witnesses, the one of Gods loue to me, *th*e other of my faith & loue to God, I giue the first place to *th*e spirits wittnesse of Gods loue to me, *th*e latter to *th*e wittnesse of my faith & loue to God:

The Interpretation of these words, w*hi*ch Mr Cotton maketh, ^not altogether in his owne words, but as o*u*r reverend Teacher Mr Eliott conceyved it.^[2]

when my soule is humbled:	viz: By legall humileation.
The spirit of God by applying the gospell: to me:	viz: Concurring with the ministry of the gospell the minister indeavoring to apply the doctrine of the gospell to me.*
Declareth & wittnesseth to me:	viz: in the ministry, for ministers are witnesses of Christ. Acts, i.8:
the grace & favo*u*r of God in Christ Jesus:	viz: that God is in Christ gratious to all *tha*t beleive in him: & will be so to me if I beleiue:**
and by so doeing worketh at once saving grace in me towards God.	viz: by the ministers preaching & applying the gospell & the free grace of God in Christ, the spirit concuring, doeth worke effectuall vocation, & faith in my heart to beleiue in Jesus Christ:
and thereby declareth that his wittnesse of the grace of God, to me, is noe delusion	viz: by working effectually in my heart, & making me to partake of this grace & fauo*u*r of God, doeth declare that *th*e wittnesse of Gods fauo*u*r in Christ w*hi*ch the minister did beare or hold forth to me was noe delusion:
And because these be two wittnesses I giue *th*e first place to the spirits wittnesse &c.	viz: these are two kinds of witnesses: first the spirit in the ministry by the gospell holds forth Gods loue, wittnesses how gratious he is in Christ: & *tha*t testimony of the spirit in *th*e gospell worketh & begetteth faith in my heart to beleive in Christ; & *tha*t wittnesse of the spirit must be first before I can haue or see any grace in my selfe to wittnesse my good estate: & this I meane by first evidence: & if it should be meant, & interpreted that *th*e spirit wittnesses Gods gratious & Justifying loue to me before I haue faith, & thereby worketh faith in me, it were an

erronious opinion & Justly offensive:***

The former Interpretation Explained, & so Accepted by Mr Cotton.[3]

* Not that I would suspend *th*e Concurence of *th*e Spirit vpon *th*e Ministers Intention, or Endeavo*u*r to Apply the Doctrine of *th*e Gospell to me: but I willingly consent, that the Spirit of God delighteth to Concurre w*i*th such Ministers, as doe Intend & Endeavo*u*r to Apply *th*e Doctrine of *th*e ^Gospell^ to humbled Soules, & to me as such, *tha*t is, to me as one of *th*em.

** And will be so to me, if I believe.][4] Yet so, as *tha*t in my Legall Humiliation, I must not thinke first to bring my Faith to lay hold on *th*e Promise (w*hi*ch I must & shall doe, when I have Faith:) but *tha*t I must come & Attend to *th*e Promise, & waite vpon God in it, that by *th*e Helpe of his spirit Applying it to me, I may come to have Faith, & to Beleive.

*** I willingly Confesse, That God doeth not witnesse Gods Gratious Justifying love to me, before I have Faith, & I doe disclayme it as an Erroneous Opinion, & iustly Offensive, if any so hold it. But 2. things I would say (w*i*th Desire of further Instruction therin:)

1. That *th*e Spirit witnesseth in *th*e Ministery of *th*e Gospell though not Gods Gratious Justifying Love, yet his Gratious Love calling Humbled Sinners to himself, before I have Faith, & thereby worketh Faith in me to Apply Christ, & his Grace vnto my self. As when they said to *th*e Blinde man, Be of good Comfort, Arise, He calleth thee, the Blinde man did Arise, and Came to Christ *tha*t called Him, Mar. 10.49.

2. This I would further say, That when *th*e Ministery of *th*e Gospell preacheth Christs Justifying Love & Grace to Beleivers (as Peter did to *th*e whole Company gathered in *th*e house of Cornelius Acts 10.43: whereof some it is likely did not Beleive before) the Spirit of God concurring therew*i*th to vs (as He did to *th*em V. 44:) He may in Preaching & Declaring Gods Justifying Love to Beleivers, Declare therein Gods [IV] Love Calling *th*em, to Christ, & to Beleive on Him, & thereby worke Faith in *th*em, to their vnion w*i*th Christ, & to their Justification by Christ, at *th*e same time.

1. This phrase, "in Christ Jesus," is not present in Cotton's draft letter, but probably was inserted by him in the letter actually sent. It is the only substantive difference between the draft letter and the portion of it that Eliot transcribed.

2. The opening clause, "The Interpretation . . . maketh," is in Eliot's hand. The superlinear insertion that follows is in Cotton's hand.

3. This line and all that follows is in Cotton's hand. He inserted footnote symbols in Eliot's comments at the points indicated, adding his own refinements of Eliot's glosses.

4. Cotton inserted this bracket.

Cotton's List of "Exceptions against some things in the Synod at Cambridge"

1649

AD. MS: BPL, Ms. Am. 1506, pt. 3, no. 10

This document, written on one sheet, folded once, making four pages, each of which is numbered, is in Cotton's hand. He numbers each of the exceptions, but, starting with the fourth, he begins a second series of numbers in the left margin, so that from #4 on, each of the items has two numbers, the second one typically being placed below the first and next to the second or third line of the text of that "exception." See Richard Mather to Cotton, September 15, 1651.

Exceptions ag*ains*t some things in *th*e Synod at Cambr*idge*. 1649.

1. Wee cannot Assent, & Attest to *tha*t Booke set forth by *th*e Synod in England, as is expressed in *th*e first Page of *th*e Epistle: because wee never saw *th*e same.

2. In chap. 2. pag. 3. sect. 5. They say: The Terme, Independent, wee approve not: to w*hi*ch wee cannot Assent. It being in *tha*t sence it is most vsually taken, proper: because wee doe not Depend on Classes, or Synods, for Determination in Church Censures.

3. In chap. 5. pag. 7. sect. 2: They say, Power of Office is so in *th*e Eldership, *tha*t it cannot Formally be Acted by *th*e church. If *the*y make *th*e whole worke in *th*e House of God, w*hi*ch they vsually performe, as *th*e 6th, & 7th chapters seeme to hold forth, where they tell vs, what is *th*e worke of *th*e Eldership, w*i*thout Distinction, & therefore conclude ag*ains*t *th*e Church Formally Acting in any thing in any of those chapters expressed.

4. Chapt. 7. pag. 8. sect. 1. They make Teaching of *th*e word peculiar to Pasto*ur*,
1 & Teacher. wee think, in case of their Absence, the Ruling Elder, or any other
brother, whom the Church shall Desire, may Attend vpon *th*e same.

5. Chap. 10. pag. 13. sect. 3. The Church is said to be in respect of governm*en*t, a
Monarchy, Democracy, Aristocracy, in *th*e respects, there expressed. w*hi*ch
2. wee judge to be such termes, as few or noe Churches in N.E. doe vnderstand.

[2]

6. Chapt. 10. pag. 3. sect. 6. The Counsell of other Churches to be taken where it
3. may be had, in *th*e Dealing w*i*th an Elder, wee see noe Rule to binde Churches
vnto: but as God hath left *the*m at Liberty, so they should be left: or else they
are not independent indeede.

7. Chap. 10. pag. 14. sect. 8: where it is said, *tha*t men may not speake w*i*thout
4. *th*e Elders leave, nor continue speaking when they require silence, wee judge

not to be alwayes safe; as in case *th*e Elders Offende, then it is in their Power, whether they will be dealt w*i*th, or noe.

Chapt. io. pag. i5. sect. io. It is said, *tha*t what wee doe in *th*e Exercise of
5. Church-Priviledges, is to be done in obedience to, & according to *th*e Direction of o*u*r Ordinary Elders. w*hi*ch wee judge, they cannot clayme, vnlesse
they hold, they cannot Erre.

chapt. io. pag.i5. sect. ii: They say, *tha*t noe Church-Act is consum*m*ated or
perfected w*i*thout *th*e Consent of both, *tha*t is, of Elders & Brethren. w*hi*ch
6. cannot be true, if Churches may deale w*i*th, & cast out their Elders, as in
this Chapter is graunted. Vnlesse it may be supposed, *tha*t men will consent
to their owne Castings out. And wee Desire, *th*e Elders would not strive
to vphold the Negative vote in *th*e Churches, w*hi*ch now is shaking in all
*th*e world.

[3]

chapt. ii. pag. i5. sect. 3. wee think, there is a mistake to say, that Gal. 6.6.
7. doeth Determine what, & how much a man should give to *th*e Ministery.

Chapt. ii. pag. i6. sect. 4: wee doe not thinke, *tha*t *th*e Church ought to take
8 care, *tha*t every man know his p*ro*portion, before He give: w*hi*ch is as much
as to say, That *th*e Church should Rate every man to *th*e maintenance of *th*e
Ministery.

Chapt. i4. pag. 2i. sect. 2. wee know noe Rule for Suspension, especially
9. when *th*e party is willing to leave.

3. Chapt. i5. pag. 25. sect. 4. wee think it noe more Lawfull for *th*e Minister of
one church to Administer in another Church, then for a gifted brother. be-
io. cause he is not a Pastor or Teacher to *tha*t church: but what He doeth there,
he doeth as a Brother, as is often expressed when they Prophesy, & so in
Baptism, w*hi*ch *th*e Place intendeth.

4. Chapt*er* i6. pag. 26. sect. i,4,5. In w*hi*ch they say, A synod is an Ordinance
of God from Acts i5: w*hi*ch Mr Hooker doubteth of, & wee also, & much
ii. more *tha*t they should have Power of Determination, as in sect. 4: or *tha*t
their Determination should be Receyved, for the Power, whereby they are
made, as in sect. 5: And yet noe Place Alledged to Proove their Appointm*ent*
of God, for such an end, but Acts. i5.

[4]

5. Chapt*er* i7. pag. 28. sect. 4. The Place Alledged proove not *th*e thing. And if they may not compell *th*em to one part of Church-worship, to w*hi*ch they are meete, why may they to another?

Enclosure in Cotton to John Elmeston, October 18, 1651

Published: [John Elmeston], *A Censure of That Reverend and Learned Man of God Mr. John Cotton, Lately of New-England, upon the Way of Mr. Henden of Bennenden in Kent, Expressed in Some Animadversions of His upon a Letter of Mr. Henden's, Sometimes Sent to Mr. Elmeston* (London, 1656), 49–54

Certaine Errors noted in the Letter sent to you from a Christian Friend, whereof you desired my judgement.

Error 1. *That the foundation of the Beast consisted in an usurped power of Church-Discipline, footed upon man and his will without the call of God.*

If the Beast be Antichrist, then he is contrary to Christ in all his anoyn[t]-ments, by which he is Christ. Now Christ is the Anoynted, not onely King of his Church, but anoynted Priest, and anoynted Prophet also.

Answ. The Beast is Antichrist, therefore not onely usurping a Kingly power over the Church, in Church-Discipline, but also in usurping the anoynted Priesthood, in suborning to us other propitiatory and meritorious Sacrifices for Sin, and other Mediators of Redemption, as likewise in usurping the office of the anoynted Prophet; in giving us *Apocrypha-rules* of Faith, and advancing himselfe to be Judge of Controversies.

Error 2. *The call of God in our time is onely for Separation and Rewarding, to wit, rewarding evil upon Antichristians.*

Answ. The Scripture acknowledgeth no calling, onely for Separation and rewarding Evil (both which are but detestations of sin) but requireth also the practise of the contrary vertues. *Beloved* (saith John) *follow not that which is evil, but that which is good.* 3 John ver. 11. *Depart from evil* (saith David) *and doe good,* Psal. 34.14. *Cease to doe evil* (saith Isaiah) *and learne to doe well,* Isa. 1.16,17. There is no commandment of God fulfilled submitting to the Negative part only (in forbearing what is forbidden) without performing the Affirmative also, doing what is commanded. The second Commandement is not fulfilled in abandoning or punishing Humane or Antichristian inventions, without establishing and observing Christs own Institutions.

The places of Scripture alledged to prove that all the Calls of God in our times, are for Separation and Rewarding, are misinterpreted, and mis-applied: In *Rev.* 18.46. the very phrase of coming out of *Babel,* implieth not onely a *terminus à quo,* the place from whence they should come, but *Terminus ad quem,* as *Rev.* 12.12. (a time contemporary to the other) come up hither, to wit, into an heavenly and pure estate. That place *Rev.* 15.8. doth not argue that there were no visible Churches, nor Members in them, till all the *seven Vials* were powred forth on the Antichristian state, but the contrary rather. For all the seven Angels, that is, all the Instruments and Ministers of Gods wrath, against the Beast, came out of the Temple, and such a Temple it was, as was opened, that is, was visible, *cap.* 15.5. and therefore there was a visible Church-state, before the powring out of any of the Vials. As for that which is said, *No man was able to enter into the Temple till the seven Plagues of the seven Angels were fulfilled,* It is not understood of Christians (who were in the Temple before) but of Pagan Nations, whose conversion is retarded by the smoke of Gods wrath against Antichristians; which yet, nevertheless, hindereth not the conversion of a Sprinkling of some *Jewes* and *Pagans,* but onely any large or numerous conversion of them. The places in *Rev.* 19.7,8,9. and *Isa.* 62.5. do expresly speak of the conversion of the Jews unto Christ in a Church Estate: And their Espousage or Marriage to Christ doth not argue his divorce from the Gentiles, for the coming of the Jews will not infer a rejection of the Gentiles, but rather their resurrection and provocation to farther zeale, *Rom.* 11.12.15. Much lesse will these places argue, that there is no visible Church-marriage from the *Apostacy,* till this time of the *conversion of the Jewes.* For beside what hath been said of the open and visible estate of these Churches, out of which the seven Angels came, it is evident, that during all the time of Antichrist's reign, the woman and her seed were nourished in the wildernesse, and there persecuted of the Dragon, and his Vicegerent the Beast. *Rev.* 12.14 to 17. Now the Woman is the Church, and the Seed her Members; and their Wildernesse-estate doth not argue them invisible; For the Church of *Israel* in the Wildernesse was visible and goodly, even in the eyes of Pagans, (*Numb.* 23.9 and 24.5) yea so visible were they, that the Dragon and Beast could see them, and persecute them, yea and make war against them. *Rev.* 13.7. The two witnesses are said to be two *Candlesticks. Rev.* 11.4. and *Allegoricall Candlesticks* are ever in St. *Johns* Divinity taken for *visible Churches.* In the *Canticles* before the returne of the *Shulamite* (that is before the co[n]version of the *Jews*) *Cant.* 6.13. there were sixty *Queenes* and eighty *Concubines,* besides one precious *Spouse* above them all, *Cant.* 6.8,9. Now *Queenes* are *Churches* in Marriage-covenant.

The Scriptures alledged for the restraint of the Spirit from breathing on Churches and Ordinances after the Primitive times, doe not argue an Abolition or Cessation of all Churches and Ordinances, but at most a corruption and pollution onely of the most of them, when yet in some Churches the Ordinances were preserved in due purity, that the Saints walked in them as

Virgins, in whom was found no guile nor fault, *Rev.* 14.4,5. The onely Text that seemeth to look a contrary way, *Rev.* 7.1. doth rather beare witnesse to this truth: For the *four Angels* that restrained the *four Winds* from breathing on the Earth, Sea, and Trees, they did not execute that charge untill a stronger Angell than they had sealed all the Servants of God in their foreheads, even twelve times twelve thousand, *ver.* 2. to 8. which argueth, that all the times of the Antichristian Apostacy (though it lasted twelve centuries of years and somewhat upwards, *Rev.* 11.3.) yet there never wanted in any century, at least, twelve thousand that worshipped the Lamb in spirit and truth, by the vertue of the spirit breathing on them in their Church-fellowship, as there wanted not 7000. breathed on by a still, small, soft voyce in the sorest Tyranny of *Jezabel,* and deepest Apostacy of *Israel.* Nor doe the places quoted for the returning of the breathing of the spirit at the brightnesse of Christs coming, speak of Christs future coming, but of the coming past and present, save onely that of *Ezek.* 37.9. which apparently speaketh of the *Jewes,* and the Spirit breathing on them in their future conversion, and not of *Christians.* That of *Isaiah* 32.15. is most fitly accomplished in *Christs* first coming; as likewise that of *Ps.* 97.4. That other place of *Mat.* 24.27,28. sheweth onely that the Gospel shall shine forth from the East to the West, as from Christs time to this it hath ever done; the Gospel still spreading it selfe westward unto this day. In all which time, if any enquire where *Christ* is, he telleth you, *wherever the Eagles* (that is, the clear-sighted, and high-soaring spirited Christians) *are gathered together,* ver. 28.

Error 3: The third Error discovereth in his distinction of Gospel-ordinances, and his explication and application thereof: *We conceive,* saith he, *that Gospel-ordinances are of two sorts; 1. Such as are founded more immediately upon our spirituall Union in the Covenant of Grace, as Ministry, Baptisme, the Lords Supper, Prayer, Profession. 2. Such as are footed upon Church-stating, and appertaine to the officials, as Ordination, Confirmation, Excommunication, Admission, Absolution, &c. The first of these we say the Gates of Hell never prevaile against them, as Teaching, Baptisme, Bread, Wine, Prayer, Profession, &c. But the second sort, to wit, the keyes (deemed essentiall to officials) were not alwayes truly used, &c.*

Answ. This Distinction and the Explication and Application thereof, is not sound nor convenient. 1. Ministry, Baptisme, and the Lords Supper, are essentiall to Officials, and more essentiall too, than Admission, Excommunication, Confirmation, Absolution: For these may all of them be dispensed by an *Homogeneal Church* without *Officers.* But Ministry, Baptisme, and the Lords Supper, cannot be dispensed without Officers. Christ sent forth none to administer Baptisme and the Lords Supper, but such Officers as he sent forth for the Ministry of the Gospel. 2. The Gates of Hell prevailed as much against

Teaching, Baptisme, Bread, and Wine, Prayer, and Profession, as against the power of the Keyes: For as the Keyes were not alwayes truly used, so neither were any of the rest. Teaching was corrupted with many fundamentall Heresies and Errors; Baptisme with many superstitious Ceremonies and undue Power; The Bread transubstantiated into the Body of Christ, and the Wine into the Blood, and both transformed into a propitiatory Sacrifice for the Quick and the Dead; the Wine also taken from the People; Prayer was perverted into the Idolatrous worship of Angels, Saints, Images, and publickly offered in a strange tongue: And profession of Christianity degenerated into the profession and practise of Antichristian Idolatry and Superstition. Greater abuses than these have not prevailed upon the Keyes. True it is that the former sort of these were sooner purged from sundry grosse Pollutions, than the exercise of the Keyes. But two things would be considered:

1. That as all the former Pollutions were not brought into the Church and Ordinances at once, so neither were they purged out at once, but by degrees. And why may we not perceive the Keyes to be at length purged and scoured, as well as all the former?

2. It can never be proved that in the darkest times of the Antichristian Apostacy, the Ordinances of Christ were any of them wholly polluted in all the Churches, no not the power of the Keyes. For the promise of building the Church upon a Rock, against which *the gates of hell should not prevaile,* was given to such a Church, as to whom the power of the Keyes was given expresly, *Mat.* 16.18,19. I know not what place[1] the Author alludeth to, when he saith the name (of the Keyes) was fore-prophecied to be everlasting, yet the hand or keyes, held forth by the hand in the interpreted place, is not so specified, *Isa.* 66.5. but was wholly resolved in the Pope, &c. which is as unsafe as the former. For in that place, *Mat.* 16.19. where the Keyes are promised, the power and efficacy of them is given also. *To thee will I give the keyes of the Kingdome of Heaven* (there is the name) *and whatsoever thou shalt binde on earth shall be bound in heaven; and whatsoever thou shalt loose on earth, shall be loosed in heaven;* there is the power and efficacy of the Keyes; which though the Pope and his Ministers perverted and abused, yea, and exercised another Key, which he received from the bottomlesse pit; yet it is very unsafely said, *That the power of the keyes was wholly resolved in the Pope, and that there was no other face of Officials, but amongst the Papists in* Luthers *time, and that the visible Church, the foundation of these failed, and onely an elect sealed number remained.* For it is evident, and in Story, yea, and in the *Revelation* also, 1. That the sealed number was a visible Church represented to *John* under the resemblance of two *Candlesticks, Rev.* 11.4. discerned and seen not onely by *John* (representing the faithful, *Rev.* 14.1.) but also by the Dragon, and by his Vicegerent the Beast, who persecuted the Woman

and her seed (that is the Church and her Members) *Rev.* 12.13. to 17. and cap. 13.6,7. The *Church* visible to malignant persecutors, was doubtlesse visible in it self, and in its Members one to another. 2. It is evident that in *Luthers* time, and many ages before the *Waldenses* lived, and when *Luther* came, wrote to *Luther* and to *Calvin* also, who not onely kept Church-assemblies amongst themselves, but exercised the power of the keyes among themselves; How then can the Author of the Epistle say, That there was not any face of Officials, but among the Papists in *Luthers* time? What could be spoken more effectually to gratifie the Papists, and to confirme their boasting, that either the Church of *Rome* was the onely visible Church upon the face of the earth, or else Christ had no visible Church upon ea[r]th for above a thousand yeares together? It is a very slender and lean evasion, to excuse the rooting out of Ordinances for having any being upon earth, "to hold they have a beeing in "the Scriptures of truth, and in the mindes and desires of the faithfull. For we might as well say, *Babylon* hath no being upon earth, but is burnt down with fire, and the *New Jerusalem* is come downe from Heaven, because so it is in the Scriptures of truth, and in the mindes and desires of the faithfull. If we doe (as he saith) in this our returne from *Babylon,* carry (as the *Israelites* did of old) the vessels of the Lord along with us, why should we be afraid to officiate in them? "We dare not, saith he, officiate in them, because we are "as yet within the territories of *Babylon,* and so shall be, till we have passed by "the *sixth Viall,* over the River *Euphrates.* Rev. 16.12.

Answ. There might be some colour for this, if the Churches of *Europe,* and of the western *America,* were in Scripture-phrase the *Kings of the East.* For they that are said to passe over the River *Euphrates* in that *sixth Viall,* are expresly styled the *Kings of the East.* But sooner shall a man draw East and West together, than prove *Christian Churches* to be the *Kings of the East,* or that we are still in the territories of *Babylon,* till we have passed by the *sixth Viall* over the River *Euphrates:* yea suppose we were still in the territories of *Babylon,* yet neverthelesse, though the *Jewes* of old did not perform Temple-worship within the territories of *Babylon,* (because that worship was confined to the Temple) yet we in the dayes of the New Testament (where the worship of God is not limited to any place) the true worshippers may worship the Father, even in the midst of *Rome.* And so did the *Waldenses,* and other of our godly forefathers within the Roman territories. The mention of the *sixth Viall* putteth me in minde of an wholsome warning delivered in it by Christ, and that to the Saints of this age in a speciall manner. *Behold I come as a thief* (not to the last Judgement which is no[t] yet, but) *to rob men of their garments of their former profession. Blessed is he that watcheth, and keepeth his garments, lest he walk naked, and men see his shame.* Rev. 16.15. *AMEN.*

1. At this point in the text, John Elmeston inserted within parentheses the following: "there was a mistake in the Letter, quoting *Isa.* 65. for 56. which is the Cause that Mr. *Cotton's* answer is not punctuall to that allegation." Elmeston also noted this problem in his letter to Henden on Dec. 20, 1651: "There was, you see, a mistake in your quotation of *Isa. 65.* for *56.* which I observed not but upon the receit of your last; upon which occasion I could say nothing to it; and Mr. *Cotton* here doth somewhat misse of your meaning." *A Censure,* 48.

Index